THE
Radical Republicans

Lincoln's Vanguard for Racial Justice

THE
Radical
REPUBLICANS

Lincoln's Vanguard for
Racial Justice

Hans L. Trefousse

LOUISIANA STATE
UNIVERSITY PRESS
Baton Rouge

ISBN 0-8071-0169-9 (paper)

Library of Congress Catalog Card Number 68-23937

Copyright © 1968 by Hans L. Trefousse

All rights reserved under International and
Pan-American Copyright Conventions

Manufactured in the United States of America

Louisiana Paperbacks edition, published September, 1975, by
special arrangement with Alfred A. Knopf, Inc.

For Roger

Preface and
Acknowledgments

I N the revolution which has overtaken the writing of American history since 1945, no reversal is more astonishing than the almost complete abandonment of "revisionist" views about the Civil War and Reconstruction. Once again we are told that slavery was a great evil, that the conflict had deep moral causes, and that the generation once called "blundering" was perhaps no more inept than any other. The villains of yesteryear are the heroes of today. Biographies of leading congressional figures have appeared in ever-increasing numbers, and long-dormant statutes are again being enforced by the federal government.

The radical Republicans have benefited greatly by this changed climate of opinion. Once held responsible for the failure of compromise before the war, military blunders during this conflict, and vindictive misrule afterward, they are emerging once more as the great innovators they were: friends of the Negro, protagonists of democracy, agents of reform not necessarily subservient to special interests. Charles Sumner, Thaddeus Stevens, Edwin M. Stanton, Benjamin F. Wade, John P. Hale, George W. Julian, and Benjamin F. Butler have all found sympathetic or unbiased biographers, and doctoral dissertations have been prepared about Hannibal Hamlin, Zachariah Chandler, and many others. That this group of individuals had a great influence upon the history of the United States in the middle of the nineteenth century has never been doubted; exactly what this influence was and how it was applied, however, is still problematic, because no comprehensive study of it has appeared.

This book is designed to fill this void. Who the radicals were, what qualities they had in common, how they differed from one another, and what kind of motives impelled them are questions of importance. It must be determined whether the ultras were really responsible for the failure of compromise prior to the capture of Fort Sumter, whether they can justly be blamed for exacerbating the sectional quarrel, and whether they did in fact hamper the prosecution of the war. What were their strengths? Their weaknesses? Were their policies truly vindictive and were they impelled by mere selfishness and lust for power during the period of Reconstruction? In fact, did they possess any unity other than a common aversion to the slaveholders and their successors? Finally, it is important to ascertain whether they accomplished anything worthwhile, and, if they did, why they disappeared from the stage so quickly and completely after achieving seeming triumphs. The studies of T. Harry Williams, Howard K. Beale, David Donald, and Harold M. Hyman on this subject are indispensable; now it is time to draw together the findings of the last few decades.

———

I am most grateful to the colleagues and friends whose assistance has been of great value. Professors Robert A. East and William Gillette have read the entire manuscript and offered valuable suggestions; Professor Samuel J. Konefsky gave freely of his time and counsel, and Professors Harold M. Hyman, LaWanda Cox, Irwin Unger, and Leonard P. Curry all contributed their advice and gave me the benefit of their knowledge. My research assistant, Mr. Gerald Henig, deserves much credit for his contributions. The generous grants of the Graduate Center of the City University of New York enabled me to undertake a series of research trips, and support from Brooklyn College relieved me of teaching duties. The librarians of Brooklyn College, the Houghton Library at Harvard, the Eleutherian Mills Historical Library, the manuscript division of the Historical Society of Pennsylvania, the Library of Congress, and the Burton Collection of the Detroit Public Library have been especially helpful. I should also like to express my indebtedness to Angus Cameron and Jane Garrett of Alfred A. Knopf, whose encouragement has been most welcome. That my wife, Rashelle F. Trefousse, has my gratitude for her patience and good advice, she knows.

H. L. T.

Contents

Illustrations

following page 208

Early Eastern Radicals in the Senate
Charles Sumner
John P. Hale
William H. Seward

Early Western Radicals in the Senate
Salmon P. Chase
Benjamin F. Wade

Early Radicals in the House
Joshua R. Giddings
George W. Julian

Wartime Radical Leaders in the Senate
Henry Wilson   Zachariah Chandler
Lyman Trumbull   Jacob M. Howard

Wartime Radical Leaders in the House
Schuyler Colfax   James M. Ashley
Henry Winter Davis   John Covode
Owen Lovejoy   William D. Kelley

Postwar Radical Leaders in Congress

Benjamin F. Butler	George H. Williams
Oliver P. Morton	Elihu B. Washburne
Timothy O. Howe	Charles D. Drake

Abraham Lincoln

Andrew Johnson

Prominent Republicans

Hannibal Hamlin	Horace Greeley
Edwin M. Stanton	Carl Schurz
George S. Boutwell	William P. Fessenden

Thaddeus Stevens

Assault on Charles Sumner in the Senate Chamber
(from David A. Harsha, *The Life of Charles Sumner*)

Lincoln Visiting McClellan in the Field
(photograph from the Mathew B. Brady Collection,
Library of Congress)

The Emancipation Proclamation
(painting by Frank Carpenter, U.S. Capitol)

Impeachment of President Johnson:
The High Court of Impeachment
(from J. T. Trowbridge, *A Pictorial History of
the Desolated States and the Work of Restoration*)

The Radical Party on a Heavy Grade
(Currier & Ives, 1868, courtesy of the New York Public Library)

THE
Radical Republicans

Lincoln's Vanguard for Racial Justice

INTRODUCTION

The Concept

THE DATE was January 9, 1865. Congress was in session, and a dark-complexioned senator with jet black, deeply cut eyes and a strong, beardless face held the floor. It was "Bluff" Ben Wade of Ohio, a radical of radicals, who had risen to speak in support of a bill granting freedom to the families of Negroes serving with the Federal forces. "The radical men are the men of principle," he said,

> They are the men who feel what they contend for. They are not your slippery politicians who can jigger this way and that, or construe a thing any way to suit the present occasion. They are the men who go deeply for principle, and having fixed their eyes upon a great principle . . . the liberation of mankind or the welfare of the people, are not to be detached by any of your higgling. The sternness of their purpose has regenerated . . . this whole continent. . . .[1]

Wade's opinions were not shared by the New York *Herald.* Having in 1861 and 1862 accused the radicals of virtually start-

---

[1] *Cong. Globe,* 38th Cong., 2d Sess., 165; William Dean Howells, *Days of My Youth* (New York, 1916), p. 108; L. P. Brockett, *Men of Our Day* (Philadelphia, 1868), p. 253.

ing the war and sacrificing soldiers for their own nefarious purposes, in 1866 the newspaper charged:

> The radicals . . . are the savage and desperate enemies of the government, the country, the Union and order. . . . They assert that their object . . . is to secure the rights of the negro. . . . In truth the negro is a pretext and their philanthropic devotion to his rights a sham.[2]

Although observers since that time have differed widely in attempting to arrive at a proper assessment of the radicals, no one has denied their importance.

Who were the radical Republicans? How did they differ from moderates and conservatives? These are questions difficult to answer, because no firmly organized group calling itself radical existed. But in dealing with the problem of racial adjustment in the nineteenth-century America, a "radical" attitude could be distinguished from a "moderate" and "conservative" one.

Like most reform movements, the American antislavery crusade consisted of different shadings. At one extreme the Garrisonian abolitionists were determined not to compromise, not to yield "a single inch" to the "man stealers," as they termed the Southern planters. At the other, conservative men, often of Whig antecedents, believed in restricting slavery to the area in which it already existed. In between flourished reformers with so many varied ideas that the process of assigning names to the several antislavery factions has led to confusion. Clearly to distinguish one from another is impossible—there never was a strict demarcation line, but after the Republican party had been organized it became customary to refer to one of its components as the radicals. Consisting largely of former Free-Soilers and other determined antislavery politicians who had long been considered radical, before the war they believed in taking an uncompromising stand against the advocates of slavery by asserting the fundamental wrong of the institution and refusing to recede in any way from their insistence that it be kept from spreading. After the start of

2 New York *Herald,* July 23, September 16, 1861; March 25, 31, August 2, 1862; January 17, 1866.

the conflict, they advocated complete emancipation and vigorous prosecution of the war, and during Reconstruction, no restoration of the South until the freedmen had been granted full civil rights. The conservatives, on the other hand, in the 1850's attempted to compromise with slaveholders; in the early sixties, procrastinated about emancipation; and in the late sixties, were willing to maintain the Negro in an inferior position. The moderates, generally sympathizing with many radical objectives but objecting to extreme methods, stood somewhere in between.

The easiest way to identify radicalism is to determine which leaders constituted its core. Although individuals could be moderate at one time and extremist at another, there were a number of statesmen who for extended periods of time were generally considered radical. Before the Civil War, the most conspicuous of these were those members of the Senate who had, for some years, either stood outside any regular organization or had so identified themselves with the antislavery cause that their party affiliation seemed of secondary importance. Foremost among these in the popular imagination was Charles Sumner, not so much because of his real influence, but because of the deliberate way in which he addressed his colleagues, the studied manner in which he prepared his speeches, and the utter honesty of his convictions of racial equality. Tall, handsome, and well built, his determined face shadowed by a wealth of dark locks, he was constantly in the public eye. Born the son of a Massachusetts lawyer who was sheriff of Suffolk County and the descendant of a long line of Yankee forebears, he had studied at Harvard prior to his admission to the bar. After traveling in Europe and America, he practiced his profession and taught law at his alma mater. He had been attracted to antislavery causes early in his career, and his celebrated argument against school segregation in the Roberts case in Massachusetts in 1849 foreshadowed a sociological approach to the problem which was finally successful more than a hundred years later. Disliked because of his aloofness but respected for his cause, Sumner was an orator of distinction. His speeches were widely reprinted and read, and even his opponents conceded his sincerity. "His constituency," wrote James G. Blaine, "was not merely the State of Massachusetts, but the radical and progressive Republicans of the entire country."[3]

Second, there was William H. Seward, who was not really a radical at all, but during the 1850's appeared to be a spokesman for the group. Never a member of the Free-Soil or Liberty parties, Seward had not only long been a leader of the New York Whigs, but was convinced that the major organization opposed to the Democrats must become the main antislavery party. As a successful lawyer in Auburn, New York, he had for many years collaborated with Thurlow Weed in building up his party, had served as governor and senator, and was fond of the everyday deals which constitute practical politics. His slim, sallow face, his overhanging eyebrows, and his small stature seemed to belie his radical utterances, and some antislavery leaders distrusted him from the very beginning. Nevertheless, he occupied a position of great importance. As a close adviser of President Zachary Taylor, he had been blamed by Southerners for Taylor's adamant resistance to the Compromise of 1850, and when he delivered his philippic against the Omnibus bill, Henry Clay's scheme of sectional adjustment, he invoked the concept of "a higher law than the Constitution," an expression which stamped him as a radical. It was not until ten years later that his true moderate if not conservative instincts became clear.[4]

[3] David Donald, *Charles Sumner and the Coming of the War* (New York, 1960); Carl Schurz, *The Reminiscences of Carl Schurz* (New York, 1907), II, 35; George S. Boutwell, *Reminiscences of Sixty Years in Public Affairs* (New York, 1902), II, 215–19; Leonard W. Levy and Harlan B. Phillips, "The *Roberts* Case: Source of the 'Separate but Equal Doctrine,'" *American Historical Review,* LVI (April, 1951), 510–18, esp. 513–14; James G. Blaine, *Twenty Years of Congress* (Norwich, Conn., 1884), I, 317.

[4] Glyndon G. Van Deusen, *William Henry Seward* (New York, 1967), pp. 3–98; Frederick Bancroft, *The Life of William H. Seward* (New York, 1900); Moncure Daniel Conway, *Autobiography* (Boston, 1904), I, 208; Schurz, *Reminiscences,* II, 33; Thomas J. McCormack, ed., *Memoirs of Gustave Koerner, 1809–1896* (Cedar Rapids, 1909), II, 79; Albert Bushnell Hart, ed., *Diary and Correspondence of Salmon*

The third radical leader in the Senate was Salmon P. Chase. A capable lawyer, well educated and cultured, Chase, like many radicals, was born in New England, the son of a New Hampshire farmer. Educated in Ohio and at Dartmouth and greatly influenced by his uncle, an Episcopal bishop, he read law with William Wirt, and, after a brief career as a teacher in Washington, D.C., settled in Cincinnati, where he became a prominent member of the bar. In spite of his Whig antecedents, he gradually came to sympathize with the Democrats. But his first interest in politics was always antislavery, a predilection which led him to take on a variety of fugitive-slave cases. The most famous among these was the defense of John Van Zandt, an Ohio abolitionist who had run afoul of the Fugitive Slave Law of 1793, a statute which required the return of interstate runaways. Chase's intense ambition and pontifical manner precluded his ever achieving great popularity, but he was an astute enough politician to be elected to the United States Senate by a Free-Soil–Democratic coalition after many years of political activity in the antislavery Liberty and Free-Soil parties. Tall and dignified, with a high forehead and handsome face, he looked like a statesman, and although his obvious ambition caused many to doubt his motives, he remained true throughout his life to his faith in human equality under the Constitution.[5]

Benjamin F. Wade was a senator of different caliber. A pugnacious judge from the Western Reserve in Ohio, he too had been born in New England, on a farm near Springfield, Massachusetts. After a difficult young manhood, beset with poverty—once he even worked as a laborer in a construction gang on the Erie Canal—he had settled in Jefferson, Ohio, where he became the law partner of Joshua R. Giddings, later the antislavery apostle of the House of Representatives. For a variety of reasons, however, the

---

P. Chase (*Annual Report of the American Historical Association,* 1902, Vol. II), pp. 206, 224 (hereafter cited as Chase, *Diary and Correspondence*).

[5] J. W. Schuckers, *The Life and Services of Salmon Portland Chase* (New York, 1874), pp. 1–94; Autobiographical Sketch, July 10, 1853, Salmon P. Chase Papers, LC; Chase–J. T. Trowbridge, March 18, 1864, Chase Papers, LC; Charles A. Dana, *Recollections of the Civil War* (New York, 1899), p. 169; Schurz, *Reminiscences,* II, 34, 171.

two men eventually had a falling out, which was aggravated by the fact that Giddings became a Free-Soiler in 1848 when Wade remained loyal to the Whig party. But when in 1850 the unpopular Fugitive Slave Law was passed, Wade, then a state judge, publicly denounced it and declared that he would never enforce it; as a result, he was elected senator by a combination of Whigs and Free-Soilers. His dark complexion, fiery eyes, and scowling mien marked him as a born fighter. He soon became famous for his willingness to meet Southerners on their own grounds in debate, and, if need be, on the dueling ground. "Bluff Ben" seemed the embodiment of the Northern spirit, and never during the eighteen years of his career in Congress would he deviate from the canons of radicalism.[6]

In point of time, the earliest radical antislavery senator was John P. Hale of New Hampshire. Genial, humorous, corpulent, and somewhat lazy, Hale was a former Democrat who broke with his party because of the problem of slavery. According to his biographer, his great days came when he was virtually the only antislavery representative in the upper chamber; later when abler senators joined him, he became less prominent despite a Free Democratic nomination for President in 1852. He finally retired in a welter of corruption charges from which he was never fully able to clear himself. But men remembered his early castigation of slavery in terms so severe that Senator Henry S. Foote of Mississippi had once threatened him with hanging should he venture into the Magnolia State.[7]

After the organization of the Republican party, these five stalwarts were to be joined by several others who soon became identified with radicalism. Zachariah Chandler was a Detroit business-

[6] H. L. Trefousse, *Benjamin Franklin Wade: Radical Republican from Ohio* (New York, 1963); Howells, *Years of My Youth,* p. 108; Brockett, *Men of Our Day,* pp. 253–54.

[7] Richard H. Sewall, *John P. Hale and the Politics of Abolition* (Cambridge, Mass., 1965), esp. pp. 114, 230; Henry S. Foote, *Casket of Reminiscences* (Washington, 1874), pp. 75–7; George W. Julian–Isaac Julian, May 25, 1850, Julian-Giddings Papers, LC: Christian F. Eckloff, Percival G. Melbourne, ed., *Memoirs of a Senate Page, 1855–59* (New York, 1909), pp. 34–5.

man who had long taken part in Whig politics; passionately devoted to the antislavery cause, he had been one of the founders of the party in Michigan, entered the Senate in 1857, and was to become one of the leaders of the extremist wing. Unlike his colleagues, he was not a lawyer, but like many of them, he was born on a New England farm. After his New Hampshire childhood, he moved to Detroit where he amassed a fortune in the drygoods business. Smooth-shaven, he looked grim; his mouth drooped at each corner, and, rarely keeping himself erect, he was in the habit of shuffling along with an ungraceful gait. He was a coarse and determined fighter as well as a shrewd organizer whose political machine survived the fall of radicalism. And although he was closely identified with the stalwarts of the Grant regime—he served the President as Secretary of the Interior—he never abandoned his radical views on the race question.[8]

Henry Wilson, the "Natick Cobbler," was Sumner's colleague. Born in New Hampshire of very poor parents, he was apprenticed at an early age to a shoemaker in Massachusetts, and gradually through his own exertions rose to become a manufacturer. After years of political activity as a Whig, he entered the Republican party and the United States Senate by way of the Know Nothing order. In spite of this nativist interlude, he was not given to bigotry, and throughout his life labored hard for the elevation of the Negro. Beardless, dark-haired, and florid, he was not prepossessing nor a careful speaker, possibly because of a lack of formal education. During the Civil War he gained fame as chairman of the Senate's Committee on Military Affairs. The vice presidency was his reward for services rendered, although he never captured the popular imagination as did the more flamboyant radicals.[9]

[8] Sister Mary Karl George, R. S. M., *Zachariah Chandler: Radical Revisited*, unpublished doctoral dissertation, St. Louis University, 1965; Hamilton Gray Howard, *Civil War Echoes* (Washington, 1907), p. 53; Herbert Mitgang, ed., Noah Brooks, *Washington in Lincoln's Time* (New York, 1958), p. 35; O. E. McCutcheon, "Recollections of Zachariah Chandler," *Michigan History Magazine*, V (January, 1921), 140–9; Blaine, *Twenty Years of Congress*, I, 318–19.

[9] George F. Hoar, *Autobiography of Seventy Years* (New York, 1903), I, 215 ff.; Eckloff, *Memoirs of a Senate Page*, pp. 20–1; How-

From the ranks of the Democrats in Maine came Hannibal Hamlin, an unspectacular but able and determined politician. The son of a Yankee physician, Hamlin studied law and devoted himself to his profession in Hampden in his native state. He became a Democrat in spite of his family's ingrained Whig sympathies, but broke with his party after the passage of the Kansas-Nebraska Act repealing territorial restrictions on slavery, and the nomination of James Buchanan for President. In 1856, he was elected governor by a large Republican majority, and shortly afterward returned to the Senate, where he had represented his state since 1848. Swarthy, dark, and olive-complexioned, with deep-set eyes and stooped shoulders, he resembled Daniel Webster. He enjoyed friendly relations with his colleagues, so that it was not surprising when in 1860 he became Lincoln's running mate. Because of the obscurity of his office, Hamlin did not appear to play an active role during the Civil War, but he always lent his influence to the radicals, and his removal from the ticket in 1864 proved a bitter blow to them. After the war, he re-entered the Senate and remained active in public life long after radicalism as a political movement had disappeared.[1]

Lyman Trumbull, the junior senator from Illinois, in the 1850's and early sixties also tended to collaborate with the radicals. A New England-born scion of an old Connecticut family of professional men, he had been a Democrat until the passage of the Kansas-Nebraska Act, when a coalition of opponents of the measure sent him to Washington. His unprepossessing appearance belied his judicial acumen, and he was as little given to extremism as William H. Seward. But his opposition to slavery was so pronounced that he was often considered a "Jacobin." After performing yeoman service on the Senate Committee on the Judi-

ard, *Civil-War Echoes*, pp. 30–1; Schurz, *Reminiscences*, II, 117; Brooks, *Washington in Lincoln's Time*, pp. 32–3; George W. Julian, *Political Recollections, 1840–1872* (Chicago, 1884), p. 357; Boutwell, *Reminiscences of Sixty Years*, I, 228.

[1] Charles Eugene Hamlin, *The Life and Times of Hannibal Hamlin* (Cambridge, Mass., 1899); Howard, *Civil-War Echoes*, p. 23.

ciary, he lost much of his influence when his essentially moderate tendencies became evident to all.[2]

Other Republican leaders in the Senate—William Pitt Fessenden of Maine, James W. Grimes and James Harlan of Iowa, Jacob Howard of Michigan, Timothy O. Howe of Wisconsin, and James H. Lane and Samuel C. Pomeroy of Kansas—all played important roles in the upper House. But because of various factors, they were either less prominent than their colleagues, entered the Senate later, or were not consistent radicals, although for a time they all collaborated with the extremist faction.

The House of Representatives also contained a number of members whose antislavery stand stamped them as radicals long before the Civil War. Among these one of the best known was Joshua Reed Giddings, who represented a district on the Western Reserve in Ohio. Born in 1795 of New England parents on a Pennsylvania farm, he was taken to Ohio as a child, took part in the War of 1812, and became a lawyer in Jefferson, the county seat of Ashtabula County. After his election to Congress as a Whig in 1838, he became involved almost immediately in the antislavery struggle. Together with William Slade of Vermont, who had delivered his first antislavery speech in the House in 1835, Giddings fought the gag rule requiring instant tabling of abolitionist memorials and became closely associated with John Quincy Adams's efforts to restore the right of petition. Censured in 1842 by his opponents, he resigned his seat, only to be promptly re-elected by his constituents. He always considered himself Adams's heir, although he was much more radical than the former President and in 1848 became a Free-Soiler. Willing to abide by the Constitution but always interpreting it in his own antislavery fashion, Giddings represented a transition between abolitionism and radicalism. Fearless, athletic, tall and broad-shouldered, his importance to the radical movement lay in

[2] Mark M. Krug, *Lyman Trumbull, Conservative Radical* (New York, 1965), esp. p. 190; Horace White, *The Life of Lyman Trumbull* (Boston, 1913), pp. 1–45; Howard, *Civil-War Echoes,* p. 26; Blaine, *Twenty Years in Congress,* I, 319; Julian *Political Recollections,* p. 356.

the role he played in initiating it. Despite his failure in 1858 to win renomination, his example inspired many of his colleagues.[3]

The one representative most influenced by Giddings was George W. Julian, who eventually became his son-in-law. Of Quaker parentage, Julian was born and raised in Indiana, where he practiced law and in 1849 entered Congress as a Free-Soiler with Whig antecedents. Radical in every respect, he was devoted to land reform and opposition to monopolies as well as to human freedom. In 1852, the Free Democrats nominated him as Hale's running mate, and although he did not return to Congress until eight years later, he remained in close contact with the most important antislavery figures in Washington. Giddings always considered him his successor, a role he filled by taking a prominent part in the radical politics of the Civil War and Reconstruction. Fortunately for posterity, he possessed great literary ability, his *Political Recollections* constituting one of the most vivid sources for the study of the movement.[4]

Perhaps the best known and probably the ablest of all the radical congressmen was Thaddeus Stevens. Prominent in the Whig party of Pennsylvania long before he became a radical Republican, Stevens seemed to be the very incarnation of the radical cause. His New England origin, his indomitable will, his singlemindedness of purpose—all added up to qualities of leadership which he was quick to employ to best advantage. Many observers have described his sardonic face with its dark blue and

[3] George W. Julian, *The Life of Joshua R. Giddings* (Chicago, 1892), esp. pp. 11–45, 399; Richard W. Solberg, "Joshua Giddings, Politician and Idealist," unpublished doctoral dissertation, University of Chicago, 1952, pp. 14–15, 20–2, 31, 50, 61–6, 68–9, 117–21, 132, 202, 245–6, 278 ff.; William Slade–Giddings, September 22, 1858, Giddings Papers, Ohio State Museum, Columbus, Ohio; Joshua Reed Giddings, *History of the Rebellion; Its Authors and Causes* (New York, 1864), p. vii; Giddings-Julian, January 30, 1852; Giddings–Mrs. Giddings, January 7, 1852, Julian-Giddings Papers; Giddings-Sumner, September 15, 1853, Sumner Papers, Harvard University; E. L. Pierce–Chase, December 2, 1858, Chase Papers, LC.

[4] Patrick W. Riddleberger, *George Washington Julian, Radical Republican* (Indianapolis, 1966); Julian, *Political Recollections*, pp. 11, 38, 71, 123, 372; Giddings-Julian, December 5, 1858, Julian-Giddings Papers.

dull-looking eyes, overhanging brows, thin stern lips, and an ill-fitting dark-brown wig. Because of a clubfoot, he walked with a limp, but his physical infirmity was belied by the vigor with which he attacked the problems of congressional management. Elected in 1848 to the House of Representatives, he retired after two terms, only to return in 1858, when he was sixty-six years old. His devotion to the cause of the Negro was boundless, and he soon became the most influential radical in the lower House.[5]

James M. Ashley represented the Toledo district. Born in Pennsylvania of Virginia ancestry, the son and grandson of itinerant Campbellite ministers, the Ohio congressman had engaged in journalism, law, and business before he was elected to Congress in 1858. Like Chase, whom he vigorously supported, he had Democratic antecedents. Handsome and courageous, he had a fine physique and a "luxuriant suit of curly brown hair" which, according to Julian, "singled him out among the bald heads of the body as one of its most attractive members." Extreme and emotional in his approach to almost every question, he is remembered chiefly as the prime mover in the impeachment proceedings against President Johnson, but he was an active radical long before the war and persistently held to his views in spite of a certain narrowness of outlook which lessened his effectiveness.[6]

One of the most radical members of Congress was Owen Lovejoy of Illinois. A Congregationalist minister deeply influenced by his Calvinist upbringing in Maine, he had vowed at the bier of his murdered brother Elijah never to forsake the cause for which

[5] Fawn M. Brodie, *Thaddeus Stevens: Scourge of the South* (New York, 1959); Richard N. Current, *Old Thad Stevens, A Story of Ambition* (Madison, Wis., 1942); James Albert Woodburn, *The Life of Thaddeus Stevens* (Indianapolis, 1913); Blaine, *Twenty Years of Congress*, I, 325; Boutwell, *Reminiscences of Sixty Years*, II, 9–10; Julian, *Political Recollections*, p. 361; unsigned memorandum, probably partially written by Edward McPherson, Thaddeus Stevens Papers, LC, XVI, 55295–323.

[6] Margaret Ashley (Paddock), An Ohio Congressman in Reconstruction, unpublished master's essay, Columbia University, 1916, pp. 1–4; Charles S. Ashley, "Governor Ashley's Biography and Messages," *Contributions to the Historical Society of Montana*, VI (1907), 143–289; Julian, *Political Recollections*, p. 364.

the antislavery martyr had died. And he kept his vow. Although he did not look like an agitator—Gustave Koerner recalled him as "a very portly man, with a kind and intellectual face, good eyes, and healthy complexion"—he became an arch-radical. After many years of political activity in the Liberty and Free-Soil parties and a premature attempt in 1854 to establish a Republican organization, in 1856, to the conservatives' dismay, he was elected to Congress, where he soon gained the reputation of being, "next to Giddings, the most aggressive and fully equipped of the anti-slavery orators." Like Giddings, he represented the transition between abolitionism and radical Republicanism.[7]

Galusha Grow of Pennsylvania and Schuyler Colfax of Indiana both served as speakers of the House and were both considered friendly to the radicals. Grow, a jovial lawyer with a gift of looking at the more cheerful aspects of life, was a transplanted Connecticut Yankee who in 1850 was elected to Congress by a coalition of Democrats and Free-Soilers. As a former Democrat and a law partner of David Wilmot, the famous protagonist of freedom in the territories, he carried on the antislavery tradition of his district and in 1861 was elected speaker. Although he is chiefly remembered as the father of the Homestead Law, he was an earnest radical—much more so than his successor, Schuyler Colfax of Indiana.[8] This New York-born newspaper editor had ingratiating manners and wore a genial smile—some observers called him "Smiler"—but he was essentially a politician who rode the crest of a wave and became a radical Republican chiefly when it was useful to be identified with the movement. His involvement in the Crédit Mobilier scandal eventually caused his downfall, and in

[7] Blaine, *Twenty Years of Congress*, I, 329; Koerner, *Memoirs*, II, 181; Benjamin P. Thomas, *Abraham Lincoln* (New York, 1952), p. 152; Isaac N. Phillips–O. G. Lovejoy, December 23, 1895, Lovejoy Papers, University of Michigan; Samuel S. Cox, *Three Decades of Federal Legislation* (Providence, R. I., 1885), p. 75; Edward Magdol, Owen Lovejoy, *Abolitionist in Congress* (New Brunswick, N. J., 1967), esp. p. 24.

[8] James T. DuBois and Gertrude S. Mathews, *Galusha A. Grow, Father of the Homestead Law* (Boston, 1917), pp. 1–46, 173, 181–2; Blaine, *Twenty Years of Congress*, I, 324; Schurz, *Reminiscences*, II, 149.

1873 he retired after serving as Vice President in the first Grant administration.[9]

Many other radicals served in Congress prior to the Civil War. Old Free-Soilers like Edward Wade of Ohio, Charles Durkee and John F. Potter of Wisconsin, Alexander De Witt of Massachusetts, old Whigs like John Covode of Pennsylvania and ex-Democrats like David Wilmot of the same state, to mention but a few, either remained in Congress for too short a time to exert the influence to which their talents might have entitled them, or did not achieve the prominence which would make them leaders. Even an abolitionist like Gerrit Smith was for a brief period a member of the House. These representatives tended to vote together on all measures affecting slavery, so that by the time the war broke out a radical faction had been well established. It had the support of newspapers like Dr. Gamaliel Bailey's Washington *National Era,* Horace Greeley's New York *Tribune,* William Cullen Bryant's New York *Evening Post,* and Samuel Bowles's Springfield *Republican;* it was represented by local leaders like Cassius Marcellus Clay, Kentucky's antislavery firebrand, and at least for a time, the powerful Blair family in Missouri and Maryland seemed to sympathize with it. The men of prominence who afterward emerged in the House—leaders like William Darrah Kelley and Thomas Williams of Pennsylvania, Benjamin F. Butler and George S. Boutwell of Massachusetts, Henry Winter Davis of Maryland and Samuel Shellabarger of Ohio—had no trouble finding able collaborators.

Relations between abolitionists and radicals were very close. Engaged in a similar cause, they associated and corresponded with one another. Sumner enjoyed a life-long personal friendship with Wendell Phillips, Garrison's aristocratic collaborator and later antagonist. He also communicated frequently with such abolitionists as John Jay, Thomas Wentworth Higginson, W. I. Bow-

[9] Willard H. Smith, *Schuyler Colfax: The Changing Fortunes of a Political Idol* (Indianapolis, 1952); Brooks, *Washington in Lincoln's Time,* pp. 29–31; Boutwell, *Reminiscences of Sixty Years,* II, 7.

ditch, Oliver Johnson, Lewis Tappan, and Henry B. Stanton. Gerrit Smith admired him greatly and he reciprocated the compliment.[1] Chase was also on excellent terms with Smith; both Thaddeus Stevens and William H. Seward supported the brilliant former slave Frederick Douglass's outspoken Negro newspaper; prominent abolitionists wrote speeches for John P. Hale, and George W. Julian was friendly with William Lloyd Garrison. The New York *Tribune* consistently printed sympathetic reports of abolitionist meetings, a practice which was hardly surprising since radicals like Henry Wilson, Charles Sumner, and John P. Hale were frequently the featured speakers at such assemblies.[2] But there was a difference between abolitionism and the type of antislavery position which eventually became the radical Republican movement.

The difference was largely a question of means and immediate goals. As Owen Lovejoy said in 1858 at Joliet after receiving the Republican nomination for Congress:

> For myself I hate slavery with deathless, and earnest hatred, and would like to see it exterminated, as some time by some means it must be. But because I thus feel about slavery, it does not follow that I shall seek its extermination in unjustifiable modes. It does not follow that because I am opposed to monarchy that therefore I should be in favor of a naval armament

[1] Donald, *Sumner*, p. 139; Irving H. Bartlett, *Wendell Phillips, Brahmin Radical* (Boston, 1961), pp. 162–3; John Jay–Sumner, September 23, 1853; T. W. Higginson–Sumner, September 6, 1851, August 7, 1853; W. I. Bowditch–Sumner, September 6, 1852; Lewis Tappan–Sumner, September 29, 1855; Oliver Johnson–Sumner, September 11, 1854, November 4, 1854; H. B. Stanton–Sumner, May 31, 1855; Gerrit Smith–Sumner, March 2, 1856, Sumner Papers.

[2] Gerrit Smith–Chase, May 8, 1850, Chase Papers, Historical Society of Pennsylvania, Philadelphia; Chase–E. S. Hamlin, December 31, 1853, Chase Papers, LC; J. Griffith–Stevens, August 10, 1850, Stevens Papers, LC; Douglas-Seward, July 31, 1850, Seward Papers, University of Rochester; Sewall, *Hale*, p. 108; Garrison-Julian, November 10, 1853; Julian-Giddings Papers; New York *Tribune,* January 11, 1851; May 12, September 5, October 5, 1853; May 9, 10, 1855; Samuel May–Hale, December 20, 1850; S. S. Joceleyn–Hale, April 13, 1853, Hale Papers, New Hampshire Historical Society, Concord, N.H. On the combined efforts of varied opponents of slavery, cf. Louis Filler, *The Crusade Against Slavery, 1830–1860* (New York, 1960), pp. 379–80.

to dethrone Queen Victoria. I am content to fight slavery in modes pointed out in the Constitution, and in those modes only.[3]

Salmon P. Chase also insisted upon legal methods. "I am a democrat," he wrote in 1852,

I do not go for the abolition of slavery at all counts and by all means. I never did. I am for protecting freedom by national legislation wherever the general government has exclusive jurisdiction and leaving slavery and the extradition of slaves to the States. This is the formula of a democratic line of action, which will result in the overthrow of slavery. But it is not the formula of those who view the question from the side of Gerrit Smith or of Garrison. . . . The doctrine of the first is Abolition throughout the Union by Congress without compensation—of the second no union with Slaveholders. . . .

One year later, in an autobiographical sketch in which he explained that he had embarked upon his antislavery career after the mob riots in Cincinnati in 1836, he emphasized again:

From this time on, though not technically an abolitionist, I became a decided opponent of Slavery and the Slave Power: and if any chose to call me an abolitionist on that account, I was at no trouble to disclaim the name. I differed from Mr. Garrison and others as to the means by which the Slave Power could be best overthrown & Slavery most safely and fitly abolished under our American Constitution.

Fully understanding his position, admirers wrote to him that they would follow him even though they "would not let their name be associated & confounded with the host of unscrupulous & fanatic Abolitionists who are looked upon almost as Incendiaries."[4]

Many radicals shared a distaste for the more extreme forms of abolitionism, especially of the Garrisonian variety. Their outlook was different. Decades after the war, when George W. Julian

[3] Bureau County *Republican,* Extra, June 30, 1858, Series II, Robert Todd Lincoln Papers, LC (hereafter cited as RTL).

[4] Chase-Cleveland, March 10, 1852, Chase Papers, HSP; Autobiographical Sketch, July 10, 1853, Chase Papers, LC; E. W. Goldsborough –Chase, September 29, 1856, Chase Papers, LC.

and Edward L. Pierce, Sumner's biographer, were exchanging information and reminiscences, Pierce wrote to the aging radical: "I agree with you fully about the Garrisonians. They were distinguished more in writing and speaking than in effective action. Wilson thought them an obstruction after a certain period and so said to me while writing his history." As early as 1857, the "Natick Cobbler" had denounced the extremists in a public letter directed against Garrison's call for disunion, and in a private note to Sumner, he had expressed the wish that "some of them were ever more to keep silent."[5] Giddings, too, denounced the Garrisonians, and Charles Sumner, despite personal acquaintance with many of them, made his disapproval clear. "I have read the Liberator, more or less, since 1835," he wrote. "It was the first paper I ever subscribed for. I did it in the sincerity of my early opposition to slavery. I have never been satisfied with its tone; I have been openly opposed to the doctrines on the Union and the Constitution which it has advocated for several years. It has seemed to me often vindictive, bitter & unchristian." It was this difference which made possible his election to the Senate. As the famous chemist Benjamin Silliman pointed out to him one year later. "By this time, the people who were looking for a Garrison or Wendell Phillips madman in you have learned their blunder. Adherence to your 'peculiar institution' of free soil as a distinct, isolated & independent subject may I am sure not prevent your occupying the position of a wise, enlarged & liberal statesman generally anymore than Calhoun's dogma . . . prevented him from holding the same rank."[6]

Other radicals expressed similar opinions about their differences with the abolitionists. "I have never been, and am not now, an 'abolitionist,' in the strict sense of that word . . .," wrote Cassius M. Clay in 1862. "I proposed always to reach slavery in a con-

---

[5] Pierce-Julian, December 2, 1893, Julian-Giddings Papers; New York *Tribune*, January 16, 17, 1857; Wilson-Sumner, January 19, 1857, Sumner Papers.

[6] New York *Tribune*, January 17, 1857; Sumner–Cornelius C. Fenton, April 9, 1850; Benjamin Silliman–Sumner, March 2, 1852, Sumner Papers.

stitutional way. A State convention—the same omnipotent power which made the slave—I invoked to unmake him; and I always declared in Kentucky that I would defend the master in the possession of the slave against foreign intervention as long as the Constitution remained my protector as well as theirs." William H. Seward, when still considered radical, indignantly turned down Thomas Wentworth Higginson's invitation to a disunion convention. And Benjamin F. Wade was certain that the abolitionists' insistence in 1838 on third-party candidates contributed to the Whigs' defeat in Ohio's state legislature. "No doubt the Whigs lost the State this year through the influence of the Abolitionists," he wrote. "I hope they will learn before it is too late that they have lent themselves to a party who are devoted soul and body to Southern dictation."[7]

That there was a distinction was recognized by the abolitionists themselves. Speaking for himself and Wendell Phillips, the Boston abolitionist W. I. Bowditch wrote to Sumner in 1852, ". . . neither of us, of course, consider your present position a right one for *us* to hold," although he acknowledged the senator's great work for the cause of antislavery. Phillips himself some months later stated emphatically that he could not agree with Sumner's view that all was safe under the Constitution because Congress lacked the power to abolish slavery in the states. And Gerrit Smith, who unlike the Garrisonians, believed in political action, defined the difference between himself and Chase succinctly. "I fully agree with you," he stated, "that the framers . . . of the Constitution did not expect Congress to abolish slavery in the States. They expected the States to abolish it. Nevertheless the words of the Constitution may vest such power in the Congress. But I do not wish Congress to abolish slavery. I wish the Courts to do it. State Courts if they will. If they will not, then Federal Courts." Chase never agreed with this point of view.[8]

[7] New York *Herald,* August 18, 1862; Seward–T. W. Higginson, January 3, 1857, Seward Papers; Wade–Samuel Hendry, December 16, 1838, Joel Blakeselee Papers, Western Reserve Historical Society, Cleveland, Ohio.

[8] W. I. Bowditch–Sumner, April 23, 1852; Phillips-Sumner, March

The radicals, then, were essentially free soilers rather than immediate abolitionists, foes of the expansion of slavery who also favored the extinction of the institution by constitutional means.

The term "radical" applied to antislavery movements had been in use long before the Republican party was founded. In 1848, the Barnburners, who nominated Martin Van Buren for President, were called the "Radical Democracy." Two years later, editor Charles A. Dana referred to the New York *Tribune* as "a radical sheet," and after the passage of the Compromise of 1850, the opponents of the Fugitive Slave Law were often called "radical." "It seems to me," wrote Chase in 1851 to his friend, E. S. Hamlin, "that one true course . . . is to call a convention of Radical Democrats or Jeffersonian Democrats to meet in June. . . . This course will bring Hunkerism to its senses." He also referred to the "Radical Democracy" in connection with Hale's antislavery efforts in New Hampshire. And in reporting a gathering in 1851 of Whigs and coalition Democrats in Iowa, the New York *Tribune* mentioned a "State Convention of Radicals . . . ," in which the "Fugitive Slave Law was strongly condemned, and the most Radical *loco-foco* principles broached." Even the designation "Jacobin," an epithet later employed by John Hay to belittle Lincoln's radical adversaries, was used as early as 1851, when the German refugee Dr. Francis Lieber called "Sumner and his cohorts" "Fifth Monarchy Men and Jacobins." Sometimes the antislavery wing of the Democracy was called "ultra," an expression which was later to be applied to the militant factions of both parties at the time of their fusion into one large group opposed to the Kansas-Nebraska Bill. These were the radicals, and in 1855, Preston King was presented to the voters of the Empire State as "a Democrat of the Radical . . . school," a description which induced the New York *Tribune,* despite its Whig traditions, to endorse him for governor. Unsympathetic papers like the New

7, 1853; Sumner Papers; Smith-Chase, March 1, 1856, Chase Papers, HSP.

York *Herald* picked up the term, and gradually it was used with ever greater frequency.[9]

By 1858, the expression had become fairly common. "I think the radical Republicans are rapidly concentrating on you," wrote Giddings to Chase in February of that year; the New York *Evening Post* endorsed the "Radical Democratic Republican" platform in July, and Martin F. Conway, an antislavery leader in Kansas, reported in November that the " 'radical' or *real* Republicans" of the territory outnumbered all others at least three to one. Carl Schurz, the German immigrant who was to play a large part in the movement, would have preferred to call his associates the "philosophical" rather than the radical wing of the party, but he was not heeded. When the secession crisis came, newspapers and writers all over the country had adopted the appellation.[1]

The use of the term "radical" for the pronounced antislavery faction within the Republican party was not entirely fortuitous. Although the only bond which held the group together was a common attitude toward problems connected with slavery, many of the radical leaders were interested in other reforms as well.

The abolition of capital punishment was one of these. As early as 1850, John P. Hale was singled out to present a petition urging the end of the death penalty; in 1851, William Cullen Bryant, who supported the radical movement during much of his active life, presided over a meeting held for the purpose of ending the

[9] Morgan Dix, compiler, *Memoirs of John Adams Dix* (New York, 1883), I, 233–4; Charles A. Dana–James Pike, May 29, 1850, James S. Pike Papers, Calais Free Library, Calais, Maine; Chase–E. S. Hamlin, February 24, 1851, Chase Papers, LC; Chase-Hale, April 8, 1851, Hale Papers; New York *Tribune*, August 2, 1851; Tyler Dennet, ed., *Lincoln and the Civil War in the Diaries and Letters of John Hay* (New York, 1939), p. 31 (hereafter cited as Hay, *Diaries*); Frank Freidel, *Francis Lieber, Nineteenth Century Liberal* (Baton Rouge, 1947), p. 255; New York *Tribune*, August 25, 1851, June 7, 1854; February 8, 1855; New York *Herald*, October 11, 1855.

[1] Giddings-Chase, February 1, 1858, Chase Papers, HP; New York *Evening Post*, July 10, 1858; Conway-Trumbull, November 24, 1858, Lyman Trumbull Papers, LC; Schurz–Gerrit Smith, September 14, 1858, in Frederick Bancroft, ed., *Speeches, Correspondence and Political Papers of Carl Schurz* (New York, 1913), I, 36; New York *Herald*, March 1, 1861; J. F. Myers–Chase, February 26, 1860, Chase Papers, LC.

supreme penalty in New York; during the 1850's, William D. Kelley, when serving as a judge in Philadelphia, publicly denounced the practice; Charles Sumner wrote against it, and Thaddeus Stevens, refusing to act as a prosecutor in capital cases, made no secret of his aversion to executions. It was therefore not surprising that Salmon P. Chase, when Chief Justice of the United States, wrote to a French correspondent who had sent him material bearing on the cause, "I have not taken personally any part in the controversy concerning the abolition of the death penalty. My sympathies are on the side of abolition; and my convictions are in favor of limiting it to the case of wilful murder." And Hannibal Hamlin, long after his fellow radicals were no longer active in public life, in the winter of 1887 made the abolition of capital punishment the occasion for what proved to be his last appearance before a legislative body.[2]

The opposition of many radicals to the death penalty was part of their general aversion to excessive cruelty. Ever since the 1840's, Charles Sumner had taken a prominent part in prison reform movements; during Reconstruction, Marcus Ward, the radical governor of New Jersey, corresponded with kindred spirits all over the world to effect an amelioration of the criminals' lot; in the 1850's, Salmon P. Chase, denouncing the practice of confining culprits with ball and chain and of making them wear plates marked "thief," opposed unusual and degrading punishments in the armed forces, and John P. Hale was instrumental in securing the abolition of flogging in the navy, a reform which also strongly appealed to Hannibal Hamlin.[3]

[2] Alexander Wilder–Hale, February 11, 1850, Hale Papers; New York Tribune, January 7, 1851; "Political Portraits with Pen and Pencil: William Darrah Kelley," Democratic Review, XXVIII (June, 1851), 558; W. H. Bonee–Sumner, September 16, 1867; M. H. Bruce–Sumner, March 14, 1868, Sumner Papers; Brodie, Stevens, p. 53; Chase–C. Lucas, November 19, 1872, Chase Papers, LC; Hamlin, Hamlin, p. 581.

[3] Donald, Sumner, pp. 120–1; J. A. Lockwood–Marcus Ward, January 22, 1870; Ward–J. W. Wall, November 12, 1868; G. A. Walker–Ward, April 2, 1869, Marcus Ward Papers, New Jersey Historical Society, Newark, N. J.; Cong. Globe, 32d Cong., 1st Sess., 449; J. C. Long–Hale, January 23, 1851, Hale Papers; B. R. Wood–Hamlin, March 11, 1854, Hannibal Hamlin Papers, University of Maine.

Pacifism and antimilitarism also enjoyed the radicals' active support, Sumner especially refusing to be discouraged even after the outbreak of the Civil War. Giddings felt so deeply about restricting the military that in 1858 he wrote to Chase:

> I think the radical Republicans are rapidly concentrating on you. Gov. Seward I regard as your only real competitor. If he carries out what is said to be his intention by making a speech for the increase of the army and votes for it, I do not believe he will present a very strong force to support him for I know of nothing more abhorrent to my own views except the actual *direct* support of slavery.

Charles Durkee, radical congressman and later senator from Wisconsin, was president of his home state's peace society, and Horace Greeley's devotion to the cause also led him to advocate it in the midst of war.[4]

While not many radicals had so exalted a feeling of pacifism, many of them detested the military academy at West Point, which they regarded as a breeding ground for aristocrats. In 1859, when proposing the establishment of land-grant colleges, Benjamin F. Wade complained that the army had its West Point, the navy its Annapolis, but agriculture nothing at all—a mild reference compared to his tirades against the academy during the Civil War. Zachariah Chandler and Benjamin F. Butler were equally hostile to the institution, and as early as 1849 Charles Sumner had expressed his aversion to the military school.[5]

Woman suffrage was another cause which attracted many radicals. In 1848 Lucretia Mott and George W. Julian corresponded about the subject, and to the end of his life the Indiana statesman

---

[4] Sumner-Giddings, June 13, July 11, 1849, Julian-Giddings Papers; Sumner-Giddings, October 8, 1863, Giddings Papers, Ohio State Museum, Columbus; Giddings-Chase, February 1, 1858, Chase Papers, LC; Merle Curti, *The American Peace Crusade, 1815–1860* (Durham, N. C., 1929), pp. 179, 217; Greeley-Sumner, March 16, 1863, Sumner Papers.

[5] *Cong. Globe,* 35th Cong., 2nd Sess., 712–13; 37th Cong., 1st Sess., 89, 189; 3d Sess., 324 ff.; Wilmer C. Harris, *Public Life of Zachariah Chandler, 1851–1875* (Lansing, Mich., 1917), p. 61; Hans Louis Trefousse, *Ben Butler: The South Called Him Beast* (New York, 1957), pp. 20–21; Sumner-Giddings, July 11, 1849, Julian-Giddings Papers.

supported the fighters for women's rights. Horace Greeley endorsed the reform; James M. Ashley and Henry Wilson were sympathetic to it; Samuel C. Pomeroy introduced a constitutional amendment to secure it, while Ben Wade and Ben Butler became its staunch advocates during and after the Civil War. And William H. Seward lent aid to Dorothea Dix's campaign to ameliorate the lot of the insane.[6]

Less dramatic but nevertheless important at the time was the movement to inaugurate a system of cheap postage rates. Advocated for many years by the New England reformer Elihu Burritt, the cause was taken up in the Senate by Sumner, Seward, and Chase, who were instrumental in furthering it. Few indeed were the reform movements which did not interest one radical or the other. Charles Sumner was so well known for his progressive opinions that occasional lapses brought an immediate challenge. "Can such a great libertarian . . . sympathize with . . . reaction," wrote Rabbi David Einhorn, who was perturbed about reports that the senator had given a friendly reply to advocates of an amendment recognizing Christianity in the Constitution. "No! It cannot be. Your mind, your heart, your whole life and its labors deny it."[7] The rabbi had a point, and to the end of his life Sumner remained a friend of liberal causes.

---

[6] Lucretia Mott–Julian, November 14, 1848, Julian-Giddings Papers; Julian–Mrs. Livermore, September 7, 1867, Julian Papers, Indiana Historical Society, Indianapolis; Julian, *Political Recollections,* pp. 324–5; New York *Tribune,* May 9, 1850; Laura Julian–sister, August 21, 1865, Julian Papers; Eleanor Flexner, *Century of Struggle: The Woman's Rights Movement in the United States* (Cambridge, Mass., 1959), pp. 149, 354; Trefousse, *Wade,* pp. 8, 275, 284–5, 320; Victoria Woodhull–B. F. Butler, February 26, 1871; Susan B. Anthony–Butler, December 9, 1872, April 27, 1873, B. F. Butler Papers, LC; Rochester *Evening Express,* February 26, 1874; George Baker, ed., *The Works of William H. Seward* (Boston, 1889), IV, 28–9.

[7] E. Burritt–Sumner, November 7, 1851, January 11, February 13, 1856; David Einhorn–Sumner, February 19, 1864, Sumner Papers; Joshua Leavitt–Chase, May 17, 1848, Chase Papers, HSP. Seward, *Works,* IV, 29. Hamlin was also interested in cheap postage as well as in Dorothea Dix's campaign. Hamlin, *Hamlin,* p. 98; New York *Tribune,* February 23, 1853.

And yet, while generally reform-minded, the radicals differed greatly on the most pressing issues of their day—when these issues were not connected with slavery. That they did not agree on economic questions during the Civil War and Reconstruction is well known; consequently, it is not surprising that they held differing views before. In 1852, in the House of Representatives Thaddeus Stevens delivered a speech favoring a protective tariff, and he never changed his mind about the necessity of safeguarding American industry and labor against foreign competition. Ben Wade in the Senate prior to the Civil War likewise supported measures looking toward protection, as did Zachariah Chandler, who was closely connected with the Michigan industrialist E. B. Ward, a lifelong protagonist of high tariffs. William D. Kelley—"Pig Iron Kelley," as he was known—and Ben Butler became outstanding spokesmen for protectionists afterwards, while in the fifties Julian, Lovejoy, and Chase were considered low-tariff men. Charles Sumner and Henry Wilson, coming from a divided state, remained somewhat noncommittal.[8]

On financial questions also, there was no agreement among radicals. Before the Civil War, no clear lines were drawn on the money question, and the radicals, like other members of Congress, tended to take positions in accordance with their previous party affiliation; during the war, however, they divided on the wisdom of issuing greenbacks. Thaddeus Stevens, Samuel Shellabarger, and John B. Alley, all adherents of the extreme wing of the Republican party, took an inflationary stand when they voted for

[8] Glenn Marston Linden, Congressmen, "Radicalism" and Economic Issues, 1861–1873, unpublished doctoral dissertation, University of Washington, 1963; Stanley Coben, "Northeastern Business and Radical Reconstruction: A Re-examination," *Mississippi Valley Historical Review*, XLVI (June, 1959), 67–90; Woodburn, *Stevens,* pp. 114 ff.; New York *Tribune,* June 12, 1852; *Cong. Globe,* 32nd Cong., 1st Sess., 1302–5; 36th Cong., 2nd Sess., 1065; Trefousse, *Wade,* pp. 54, 68, 79, 99; Detroit *Post and Tribune, Zachariah Chandler, An Outline Sketch of His Life and Public Services* (Detroit, 1880), p. 159; Philadelphia *Public Ledger,* January 10, 1890; Trefousse, *Butler,* pp. 251, 254; Julian, *Political Recollections,* p. 274; Chase–L. D. Campbell, June 2, 1855, Chase Papers, LC; Sumner–Lieber, January 17, 23, 1863, Sumner Papers.

the Legal Tender Bill of 1862; Owen Lovejoy, Charles Sumner, and Justin S. Morrill, equally radical, opposed it. Chandler, Julian, and later Carl Schurz as well as Henry Winter Davis also enjoyed the reputation of financial conservatives.[9]

Even on the advisability of passing a homestead bill, a measure especially dear to many radicals, there was no unanimity. Galusha Grow and Benjamin F. Wade were the chief sponsors of the reform in the House and Senate; George W. Julian considered liberal land policies almost as important as the abolition of slavery, but many Eastern radicals were either lukewarm or hostile. Hannibal Hamlin in 1860 preferred the weak House version to the stronger Senate bill and actually voted against the measure; Thaddeus Stevens attacked the proposal on the grounds that he disliked settling the country with paupers, and Charles Sumner, who sought to woo the West in his own way, in 1852 delivered a three-hour oration in favor not of giving land to the landless, but rather of turning it over to the states in which it was located.[1]

Similar differences divided radicals on questions concerning government relations with industry and business. Stevens, an iron manufacturer himself, had a good understanding of the needs of financial and industrial interests. Sumner sought to the best of his ability to represent the commercial community of Massachusetts, and Chase enjoyed the confidence of Jay Cooke, the famous Philadelphia banker. On the other hand, Julian was a determined foe of monopoly, and business leaders widely distrusted Wade because of his unorthodox views on labor, woman suffrage, and finance. As early as 1852, Seward and Hale favored government subsidies

[9] Woodburn, *Stevens*, pp. 249, 291; J. H. Black–Stevens, July 23, 1868, Stevens Papers; Blaine, *Twenty Years of Congress*, I, 114 ff., 421 ff.; George, *Chandler*, p. 112; Detroit *Post and Tribune, Chandler*, pp. 322–7; Julian, *Political Recollections*, p. 365; Bancroft, *Schurz*, I, 239; Bernard Steiner, *Life of Henry Winter Davis* (Baltimore, 1916), p. 322.

[1] DuBois and Mathews, *Grow*, Ch. XIV; Trefousse, *Wade*, pp. 119–20; 188, 295, 111–13; Julian, MS Diary, August 29, 1869; March 12, 1871, Julian Papers; Brodie, *Stevens*, p. 220; Hamlin–Mrs. Hamlin, May 18, 1860, Hamlin Papers; W. F. Anderson–Trumbull, July 27, 1860, Trumbull Papers, LC; New York *Tribune*, January 30, 1852.

to the privately owned Collins steamship line, while Chase and Wade voted against the proposal.[2]

Sympathy with the problems of labor was not unusual among radicals. In 1852, John P. Hale was the spokesman for the workmen constructing the Capitol and sought relief for them; in 1858, Ben Wade presented petitions praying for higher wages for public employees, and Julian later strongly supported the eight-hour movement. Ebon C. Ingersoll, a radical congressman from Illinois, went even further when he said that eight hours were too much, but Charles Sumner did not always support labor. Chase was not very enlightened about a strike in the New York Customs House, while Chandler's interest in the workingman was merely marginal.[3]

On other issues, the same lack of consensus was evident. Among the advocates of votes for women, Wade, Julian, and later Butler, played a prominent role. Other radicals, however, took no great interest in the feminist movement. Hamlin wrote a sarcastic letter about it to his wife, while George H. Williams, the radical senator from Oregon, actively opposed it.[4] Nor could the radicals

[2] Stevens-McPherson, October 13, 1850; H. W. Watts–Stevens, June 17, 1852; Stevens–S. Stevens, June 23, 1863, Stevens Papers; Brodie, *Stevens,* pp. 29–30, 70–1, 170; J. G. Randall, *Lincoln the President* (New York, 1946–52), III, 102–3; Samuel Hallett–Sumner, May 19, 26, 1863; Edward Atkinson–Sumner, January 5, 1865; February 25, March 4, 1868, Sumner Papers; H. D. Cooke–Chase, October 21, 1864, July 19, 1865, Chase Papers, HSP; Thomas Graham Belden and Marva Robins Belden, *So Fell the Angels* (Boston, 1956), pp. 29–30; Julian, *Political Recollections,* p. 99; Julian, Diary, May 9, 1870, Julian Papers; Trefousse, *Wade,* p. 306; *Cong. Globe,* 32d Cong. 1st Sess., 1483, 1493.

[3] New York *Tribune,* April 15, 1852; *Cong. Globe,* 35th Cong., 1st Sess., 2451; Julian, *Political Recollections,* pp. 274–5; David Montgomery, Labor and the Radical Republicans, 1862–72 unpublished doctoral dissertation, University of Minnesota, 1962, p. 359; David Montgomery, *Beyond Equality: Labor and the Radical Republicans, 1862–1872* (New York, 1967), p. 241; L. U. Reavis–Sumner, October 28, 1868, Sumner Papers; Hiram Barney–Chase, November 27, 1863, Chase Papers, HSP; Detroit *Post and Tribune, Chandler,* pp. 152–3. Sumner opposed the 1868 eight-hour bill, but endorsed the reform in 1872.

[4] Julian–Mrs. Julian, July 7, 1867, Julian Papers; Chase–Nettie Chase, December 12, 1866, Chase Papers, LC; Hamlin–Mrs. Hamlin, June 1, 1860, Hamlin Papers; Flexner, *Century of Struggle,* p. 148.

agree on questions of foreign policy. While generally anti-British, Chandler, Winter Davis, Wade, Butler, and Giddings often going so far as to endanger peaceful relations with the mother country, some also exerted a moderating influence. This was especially true of Charles Sumner, who served for many years as chairman of the Senate Foreign Relations Committee.[5] Individual radicals were extreme on many issues; as a group, however, the extremists possessed no unity on anything except opposition to the defenders of slavery or their successors.

The most obvious example of this lack of agreement was the diversity of approaches to the race question. While all radicals detested slavery and wanted to restrict it, their individual attitudes toward the Negro varied considerably. In mid-century America, belief in racial equality was comparatively rare—at a time when millions were still held in bondage, when scientific evidence was confusing, it would have been surprising to find more than a handful of statesmen so far advanced as to recognize the complete equality of the races. It speaks well for the radicals that some of them did so.

Foremost among these was Charles Sumner. Unshakable in his convictions, he was confident that after emancipation "the profane assumptions of race" would disappear. John P. Hale also believed in equality—an outlook which caused him to ridicule the popular notion of the desirability of colonizing Negroes in the tropics. And Ashley, as early as 1856, said:

> It will be our duty to amend our national constitution and all our state constitutions, so as to secure to every living human soul within our gates, their right to life, liberty and property, and it must also be amended so as to secure to all states, representatives in Congress and in state legislatures—in proportion to the votes cast in each, to the end that all the people, white

[5] George, Chandler, pp. 82–3, 160 f., 229; P. W. Chandler–Sumner, December 24, 1864; Butler-Sumner, June 7, 1869; Sumner-Lieber, December 24, 1861, June 27, 1864; J. B. Alley–Sumner, December 27, 1861, Sumner Papers; Edward L. Pierce, *Memoir and Letters of Charles Sumner* (Boston, 1878), IV, 291; New York *Semi-Weekly Evening Post*, June 11, 1869; Giddings-Julian, n.d., 1863, Julian-Giddings Papers.

and colored shall be fairly represented in state legislative
assemblies and the national Congress.[6]

Similar sentiments were entertained by Hannibal Hamlin, who
thought that if the Negro were treated properly he would develop
into a "useful citizen just as surely as he developed into a good
soldier," a point of view which, at times, was also shared by Salmon P. Chase. Giddings carried his convictions so far as to criticize
severely the exclusion of Negroes from federally donated western
lands.[7]

But there were many radicals who believed in colonization.
That the two races would find it difficult to live together was almost taken for granted, and even such an advanced antislavery
leader as Chase toyed with the idea of sending nonwhites to a
distant part of the world. Writing in 1850 to the famous Negro
abolitionist Frederick Douglass, the Ohio senator queried.

> I should be glad to learn your views as to the probable destiny
> of the Afro-American race in this country. My own opinion has
> been that the Black & White Races, adapted to different lati-
> tudes and countries by the influences of climate and other cir-
> cumstances, operating through many generations, would never
> have been brought together in one community, except under the
> constraint of force, such as that of slavery. I have regarded
> therefore, the coexistence of the two races within . . . the
> United States, as coerced, & therefore, not likely to be perma-
> nent, or to endure for a much longer period, than the coercing
> force, namely slavery. While, therefore, I have been utterly
> opposed to any discrimination in legislation against our colored
> population, and have uniformly maintained the equal rights of
> all men to life, liberty & the pursuit of happiness . . . I have
> always looked forward to the separation of the races. . . . I have
> not thought it unlikely that the islands of the West Indies &
> portions of South America would be peopled from the United

[6] Donald, *Sumner,* p. 235; Levy and Phillips, "The Roberts Case,"
loc. cit., pp. 510–18; Patrick Riddleberger, "The Radicals' Abandonment
of the Negro During Reconstruction," *Journal of Negro History,* XLV
(April, 1960), 88–102, esp. p. 100; Sewall, *Hale,* pp. 210–11; Ashley,
"Governor Ashley's Biography and Messages," loc. cit., pp. 143–289,
esp. p. 152.

[7] Hamlin, *Hamlin,* pp. 528–9; Schuckers, *Chase,* p. 377; New York
Tribune, May 31, 1850.

States by the Black Race,—that, by them, civilization would be carried back into Africa. . . .

Douglass rejoined that he was much more optimistic, that the black man could adapt himself to conditions in the United States, but Chase continued for many years to consider colonization an alternative.[8]

Horace Greeley, though reform-minded, at times entertained similar notions. Taking the Israelite exodus from Egypt as an example, he permitted the columns of the New York *Tribune* to be used for articles suggesting that Negroes be given an opportunity to colonize Africa. Occasionally, the paper still maintained that the races were equal, but when James S. Pike began to write for Greeley, he injected a frankly racist attitude.[9]

Benjamin F. Wade struggled all his life for legal equality for nonwhites. Both privately and publicly, however, he repeatedly urged colonization. Because of the prejudice which existed, he believed the two races could not live side by side, and he advocated sending Negroes to the tropics. "I hope," he said in Congress, "after that is done, to hear no more about Negro equality or anything of that kind. Sir, we shall be as glad to rid ourselves of these people, if we can do it consistently with justice, as anybody else." Even Thaddeus Stevens who finally directed that he be buried in a Negro cemetery, during the Civil War was willing to contribute to colonization funds. Although he disapproved of the unsuccessful project of settling freedmen in Chiriqui on the Isthmus of Panama, he thought that the emancipated slaves of the District of Columbia might well be expatriated to Haiti, Louisiana, or elsewhere. And Samuel C. Pomeroy, radical senator from Kansas, was willing to head the Chiriqui project![1]

[8] Chase-Douglass, May 4, 1850; Douglass-Chase, May 30, 1850, Chase Papers, HSP and LC; Chase-Lincoln, November 12, 1861, RTL.

[9] New York *Tribune*, May 3, 1850; February 3, 1852; Robert F. Durden, *Ambiguities in the Antislavery Crusade of the Republican Party*, in Martin Duberman, ed., *The Antislavery Vanguard: New Essays on the Abolitionists* (Princeton, 1965), pp. 370–80.

[1] William Dennison–Wade, November 30, 1859; February 6, 21, 1860, Wade Papers, LC; *Cong. Globe*, 36th Cong., 1st Sess., Ap., 154–5; Stevens-Chase, August 25, 1862, Chase Papers, HSP; Philadelphia *Press*,

Colonization was often coupled with a racist outlook. Wade was repelled by the Southern atmosphere in Washington. As he wrote to his wife, the food was horrible, all "cooked by Niggers until I can smell and taste the Nigger . . . all over." While he thought the Negroes constituted "the most intelligent part of the population," he could not abide their odor, and his attitude had not changed twenty years later when he wished he could get a white servant instead of a Negro with whom he had had trouble. Lovejoy likewise, in a debate with Southerners, conceded the inferiority of the black race.[2]

That Cassius M. Clay, the Kentucky radical, did not believe in racial equality is hardly surprising. Declaring himself ready to shoulder a musket in order to suppress slave uprisings, he consistently maintained that the black race was inferior to the white. "I have studied the Negro character," he said. "They lack self-reliance—we can make nothing out of them." Senator Trumbull, considered a radical before the war, delivered speeches which were most reassuring to conservative correspondents. As one of them wrote to him, Southerners had "always feared the Republican party favored views countenancing Negro suffrage . . . which of necessity must result in some degree of equality but Sir the noble stand that you & Mr. Fessenden have taken has made a telling effect upon my immediate acquaintances." Even Edward Wade, the senator's more radical brother, believed that Negroes "should neither be 'turned loose' upon the country, nor yet held in slavery." His solution was their employment "in such departments of agricultural or the mechanical arts, as they have been accustomed to." Timothy O. Howe, the radical senator from Wisconsin, regarded "the freedmen, in the main . . . as so much animal life."[3]

September 26, 1862, clipping in RTL; J. G. Randall, ed., *The Diary of Orville Hickman Browning* (Springfield, Ill., 1933), I, 577 (hereafter cited as Browning, *Diary*).

[2] Wade–Mrs. Wade, December 29, 1851; February 1, 1871, Wade Papers; New York *Herald,* April 16, 1860.

[3] David L. Smiley, *Lion of White Hall: The Life of Cassius M. Clay* (Madison, Wis., 1962), p. 56; A. Ballinger–Trumbull, February 16, 1860, Trumbull Papers, LC; Edward Wade–Chase, November 26, 1861,

Frequently, radicals looked upon the Negro question from the point of view of bigoted white labor. William D. Kelley said in 1856, "There is another party in the contest—the Anglo-Saxon, and the whole Caucasian race—working with its own hands. Do you believe the colored race a superior race to that to which we belong? No you don't." This frank appeal to radical prejudice against proslavery Democrats was a potent electioneering device; as Lincoln put it in his Peoria address, "Slave States are places for poor white people to remove from, not to remove to. New free States are the places for poor people to go to, and better their condition. For this use the nation needs these Territories."[4] The radicals were well aware of this attitude.

From all this it does not follow that the agitation against slavery was insincere. Charles Sumner believed so firmly in Negro rights that even his enemies conceded his lack of ulterior motives, although his uncompromising stand did not make him popular, not even in Massachusetts. Ben Wade risked his entire political career by his advocacy of antislavery, and later, pro-Negro measures. Speaking from personal experience, in exhorting the voters to grant colored men the franchise, he said prejudice against Negroes was understandable; citizens were not to blame for it, but they were to blame if they suffered what "they knew to be prejudice to prevail on them to do injustice to anybody." In 1867, because of his commitment to colored suffrage, he was finally beaten, a fate that overtook many other advocates of racial justice. Cassius M. Clay endangered his life frequently to urge his opinions upon his Kentucky neighbors,[5] and Salmon P. Chase might have risen

Chase Papers, HSP; T. O. Howe–Fessenden, August 28, 1864, T. O. Howe Papers, Historical Society of Wisconsin.

[4] Walter Dusinberre, *Civil War Issues in Philadelphia, 1856–1868* (Philadelphia, 1965), p. 34; Roy P. Basler, ed., *The Collected Works of Abraham Lincoln* (New Brunswick, N. J., 1953), II, 268 (hereafter cited as Lincoln, *Works*).

[5] Hugh McCulloch, *Men and Measures of Half a Century* (New York, 1888), pp. 233–4; Boutwell, *Reminiscences of Sixty Years,* II, 215–19; Donald, *Sumner,* p. 169; Cincinnati *Daily Gazette,* August 21, 1867; Thomas Ewing–Thomas Ewing, Jr., October 16, 1867, Thomas Ewing

faster had he not joined the Liberty party. There were few Negro voters prior to the Civil War, and even afterwards; to be known as a radical was rarely an asset, and the politicians who identified themselves with the advanced Republicans did so at their own peril.

Because of the differences between the radicals, it would be difficult to establish a precise sectional pattern for the group as a whole. A great many of the radical leaders were of New England background, and portions of the Northeast continued to elect radical representatives with considerable regularity, as did the Western Reserve and similar areas in the Northwest. But there were many exceptions, and the geographical distribution of radicalism varied.[6]

The radical Republicans, then, were an amorphous group of determined opponents of slavery, who had often held progressive ideas long before the founding of the party. Frequently but not always of New England ancestry, they brought to Washington firmly held ideas of social betterment. Their story is the story of American progress.

Papers, LC; C. M. Clay–Chase, September, 1843; Lexington, Ky., *True American*, August 15, 1845, Chase Papers, HSP; Giddings–Laura Giddings, February 5, 1846, Julian-Giddings Papers.

[6] For efforts to discover sectional patterns, cf. Allen G. Bogue, "Bloc and Party in the United States Senate: 1861–1863," *Civil War History*, XIII (September, 1967), 221–41, esp. 237–8. David Donald, in *The Politics of Reconstruction, 1863–1867* (Baton Rouge, 1965), pp. 11–12, emphasizes the lack of geographical patterns but seeks to establish a correlation between radicalism and the size of Republican majorities in individual districts.

CHAPTER

I

The Beginning

SALMON P. CHASE was annoyed. Having just been elected United States senator from Ohio, he had taken the train to Washington in order to attend the special session of the Senate and the inauguration of the new President, General Zachary Taylor. But his train was delayed, and on the day of the great event, he had only reached Cumberland, Maryland, one hundred and thirty-five miles northwest of the capital. He should have taken the stage, he wrote to his wife; there was no excuse for railroad delays. Ought not the company to fulfill its obligations?

His annoyance was understandable, but it was not so much his failure to witness the inauguration that bothered him as the loss of time to confer with his political friends. Sincerely believing that he was engaged upon a noble crusade, he was nevertheless intensely anxious to play a leading role in it. And he thought he ought to be at the center of political activity on important occasions.[1]

[1] Chase–Mrs. Chase, March 4, 1849, Chase Papers, LC.

The year 1849 had been a milestone in Chase's career. Having long been active in the antislavery Liberty party, in 1848, he had given his all to further the cause of the new Free-Soil organization. This amalgam of antislavery Democrats, antislavery Whigs, and independent adherents of the Liberty party had seemed to him a great step forward because of its programs of containing slavery in a constitutional way. Then, in the winter of 1848–9, the Ohio legislature found itself deadlocked. A dispute had arisen whether a Whig law dividing Hamilton County was constitutional; the Democrats had elected one set of representatives, and the Whigs another. The Free-Soilers held the balance of power. All but two of them, N. S. Townsend and J. F. Morse, were willing to cooperate with the Whigs, but Chase intervened. Having come to Columbus to make a deal, he arranged matters in such a way that the two recusants voted in favor of the Democrats in return for a Democratic pledge to repeal the state's Black Codes. The bargain was carried out; the Democrats were seated, and the laws reducing Negroes to second-class citizenship were repealed. The result was that Chase became the candidate of the Democrats and the Free-Soilers, a coalition which elected him to the United States Senate. The Cincinnati politician had entered upon the national phase of his activities.[2]

When Chase arrived in Washington, he found Dr. Gamaliel Bailey at the depot. The doctor was the editor of the Washington *National Era,* the capital's famous antislavery newspaper, and his house served as a meeting place for sympathetic members of Congress. The arrival of the second avowed foe of the "peculiar institution" to serve in the Senate—Hale had been the only independent representative of antislavery views in the upper House until 1849—was a great event for the editor. Chase must come

[2] Schuckers, *Chase,* pp. 82–8, 96 ff.; Theodore Clarke Smith, *The Liberty and Free Soil Parties in the Northwest* (New York, 1897), pp. 164–75.

with him, he said; it was impossible to get accommodations in Washington, and his house was at the senator's disposal. The Ohioan accepted with pleasure.[3]

Still another newly elected senator arrived in Washington in 1849. William H. Seward had been a successful Whig governor of New York who had made a name for himself by refusing to extradite certain Negroes wanted in Virginia in connection with a fugitive-slave case. Unlike Chase, he had supported Taylor in 1848, and with considerable justification, he expected to exert influence upon the new administration. He was a faithful Whig, but his entry into the Senate greatly strengthened the antislavery forces.[4]

On the Democratic side of the upper House, there was also an adherent of the cause. Hannibal Hamlin had been sent to Washington in 1848 by a combination of Democrats and Free-Soilers. Of course he acted with his party, but when it came to antislavery measures, he was becoming more and more radical every day.[5]

The new Free-Soil senator from Ohio was officially presented to the Senate on March 6, when his colleague, Thomas Corwin, presented his credentials. He took his seat between Sam Houston of Texas and James Shields of Illinois, "two military heroes," as he described them. What was significant, however, was not that Corwin performed the customary service for the junior senator, but that Chase went up to the chamber with John P. Hale. The senator from New Hampshire impressed him as "one of the most pleasing men I ever met with," who seemed "to take great pleasure in introducing his brother Free-Soiler from Ohio." Among his colleagues, Hale presented Chase to Henry S. Foote of Mississippi, Solon Borland of Arkansas, Andrew P. Butler of South Carolina, "and some others of the ultra Southerners." They were

---

[3] Chase–Mrs. Chase, March 6, 1849, Chase Papers, LC; "A Pioneer Editor," *Atlantic Monthly,* XVII (June, 1866), 743–51.
[4] Seward *Works,* I, lxiii–lxvi, xxxiii–iv; Bancroft, *Seward,* I, 211.
[5] Hamlin, *Hamlin,* pp. 176 ff.

civil enough, but, as Chase surmised, "wished in their hearts" that he were "anywhere rather than in that chamber."[6]

Chase had probably gauged his opponents correctly. For years they had watched the antislavery sentiment grow. Incredulous at first, they had become more and more aggressive, and they considered all Northern members who spoke against the "peculiar institution" abolitionists dedicated to the utter ruin of the South.

In their assessment of the Northern antislavery movement in Congress, these Southern representatives were not quite correct. There were no real abolitionists in the national legislature—not if the word meant friends of unconditional, immediate and uncompensated emancipation. Instead of abolitionists, both houses contained several determined antislavery leaders, men who were dedicated to the restriction and eventual abolition of the "peculiar institution" by legal means. These formed the core of the group later constituting the radical Republicans.

The House of Representatives was not in session when Chase took his seat. For some years, however, it had numbered among its members several who were distinctly hostile to human bondage. Joshua Giddings, who had been in Washington since 1838, was a sort of mentor for all his antislavery colleagues. Just before John Quincy Adams died, he had told Giddings of the approaching end. "I must leave you to act upon your own judgment," the former President had said, "which I trust in God you will obey rather than the advice of any other man." Giddings had tried to justify the "Old Man Eloquent's" faith, both before and afterwards. The result was that he achieved a prominence which his predecessor in the antislavery movement, William Slade of Vermont, had never been able to equal.[7]

Various other antislavery members, both Whigs and Democrats, had also distinguished themselves in the House. Among them were Seth Gates of New York, Joseph Root of Ohio, John

[6] Chase–Mrs. Chase, March 6, 7, 1849, Chase Papers, LC.
[7] Giddings–Mrs. Giddings, January 7, 1848, Julian-Giddings Papers; Julian, *Giddings,* pp. 407–8.

Gorham Palfrey of Massachusetts, and Amos Tuck of New Hampshire, Whigs; and Hannibal Hamlin of Maine, David Wilmot of Pennsylvania, and Preston King of New York, Democrats. After John Quincy Adams's death, his seat had been taken over by Horace Mann, the famous Massachusetts educator, who, though diffident about succeeding so great a man, was as faithful as his predecessor to the cause of free soil.[8]

This antislavery contingent was greatly increased in December, 1849, as a result of the elections of the previous year. Thaddeus Stevens entered Congress as a Whig. Already well known among the leaders of his party in his home state, he had harbored some expectations of a Cabinet post under William Henry Harrison—erroneously, as it turned out. Now for the first time he represented the Lancaster district in the House. Destined to achieve great renown as a radical leader, he displayed his parliamentary skill from the first. Nor was there ever any doubt about his devotion to antislavery principles.[9]

Among the new representatives there was also a young man from Indiana, George W. Julian, elected by a coalition of Free-Soilers, Whigs, and Democrats. Thirty-two years old at the time of his arrival in Washington, Julian could not expect to occupy a position at the center of the stage during his first term. But he was observant, worked hard, and, like Stevens, would become an important radical.

The Free-Soil representation resulting from the political upheaval in 1848, when foes of slavery extension in all parties had joined to nominate independent candidates, was remarkable. In addition to Julian, it included Charles Durkee of Wisconsin, William Sprague of Michigan, Charles Allen of Massachusetts, and

[8] William Birney, *James Gillespie Birney and His Times* (New York, 1890), p. 341; Washington *National Era,* August 5, 1847; John Van Buren–Chase, February 23, 1849, Chase Papers, HSP; Chase–A. G. Riddle, December 3, 1849, A. G. Riddle Papers, Western Reserve Historical Society; Allan Nevins, *Ordeal of the Union* (New York, 1947), I, 10–11, 15–16; Mary Peabody Mann, *Life of Horace Mann* (Boston, 1865), p. 259.

[9] Brodie, *Stevens,* pp. 82–83, 105–6, 110; Giddings-Sumner, October 28, 1850, Sumner Papers.

John W. Howe of Pennsylvania. Together with Wilmot, King, Root, and Tuck, Julian called them "the immortal nine."[1]

These radical members of Congress came from different backgrounds, different parties, and different sections of the country. Nevertheless, they shared a common outlook. Seeking to proceed against slavery in a constitutional manner, they consistently interpreted the fundamental law in favor of freedom. Many of the radical leaders of the Civil War and Reconstruction were already hard at work: Chase, Stevens, Julian, Seward, Hamlin, and Giddings in Congress; Sumner, Wilson, and Stanton, outside. Their common detestation of slavery tended to bring them together.

This cooperation was remarkable especially because of the radicals' lack of political unity. Although Chase had voted for Harrison in 1840, he had generally been imbued with Jacksonian notions about banking, internal improvements, and the tariff. After witnessing the persecution of abolitionists by a Cincinnati mob in 1836, he had taken an active interest in the antislavery movement, going so far as to draw up in 1842 a lengthy and succinct address expressing the goals of the Liberty party, with which he was then cooperating. These Democratic and third-party predilections did not keep him from addressing Thaddeus Stevens, a Whig, as early as 1842. "Though personally a stranger to you and perhaps and probably unknown to you even by reputation," he wrote, "I have determined to write you on a subject in which I feel a deep interest, as frankly as I could talk to an old acquaintance. What I hear of your character leads me to believe that you will take what I say in good part." Then he went on to describe the organization of the Liberty party in Ohio. "It had not of course escaped your observation," he continued.

> that a similar party organization has arisen in almost all the non-slave holding States;—and the political sky is not without signs, that the feeling against slavery, which animated the efforts of the Liberty Party, is extending itself into the slave States.

Then he turned to the difficulties with which he had to contend. One of these was the fact that people confounded the Liberty

[1] Julian, *Political Recollections*, pp. 71–73.

party's principles with those of the abolitionists, an error which he was at pains to clear up. As he put it,

> Now the distinction, which we, in Ohio, take is this: Abolition-ism seeks to abolish slavery, everywhere. The means which it employs correspond with the object to be effected. . . . The Liberty Party seeks to abolish slavery wherever it exists within reach of Constitutional action of Congress, to restrict slavery within the slave states, & to deliver the Government from the control of the Slave Power.

What Chase wished to accomplish by this letter was, in his words, "to draw your attention to the movement of the Liberty Party, and to invite an expression of your view, in regard to it. Cannot you take ground with us?"[2]

Stevens was impressed. Chase was evidently a man who had to be taken seriously. As he was informed by his Ohio correspondent, J. Blanchard, "S. P. Chase is esteemed by the lawyers of this city equal if not superior to any other member of the Bar as a jurist." Blanchard thought Stevens ought to help Chase displace James G. Birney as the leader of the Liberty party. And while this suggestion fell on deaf ears, the Pennsylvanian made no secret of his regard for the antislavery leader from Ohio. As he replied to Blanchard, "I admire the address he [Chase] wrote, & proceedings of your convention. The author of that Address possesses a cool head & a deep knowledge of mankind, as well as a right heart, & I beg you to make him my most grateful acknowledgments for the pleasure it has given me."[3] But he never joined the Liberty party. A Whig he was and a Whig he would remain until the demise of the old party.

Another prominent Whig also liked Chase's address. Governor Seward of New York explained that he could not act outside of his own party, but he went so far as to write to the abolitionist Lewis Tappan to express his admiration for the document. Unlike

[2] Autobiographical Sketch, July 10, 1853, Draft Letter, Chase–J. T. Trowbridge, March 18, 1864, Chase Papers, LC; Chase-Stevens, April 8, 1852, Stevens Papers.
[3] J. Blanchard–Stevens, April 9, 1842; Stevens-Blanchard, May 24, 1842, Stevens Papers.

many of his antislavery colleagues, Seward never joined the Free-Soil party. But he cooperated with them wherever he could. Chase, who did not fully trust the governor, nevertheless felt a certain kinship with him. After his own arrival in Washington, he wanted the New Yorker to accompany him to the White House, "as we agree as nearly as a Whig and a Democrat can."[4]

Giddings enjoyed especially close relations with many of the radical leaders. As early as 1842, he corresponded with Chase, who was trying to induce him to join the Liberty party. "It will not do to compromise anymore," the Cincinnati lawyer wrote to the congressman. The government must be divorced from slavery so that the institution would exist only by local sufferance. "I cannot but think that you . . . share these sentiments," he concluded. Why not then act upon them? Giddings remained unconvinced. As he had informed Chase when the year began, "My judgment has been strongly opposed to a distinct political organization of our antislavery friends." He did not change his mind for several years, during which he maintained his friendship with Chase, deserting his party only after the nomination of Zachary Taylor, when he became a Free-Soiler.[5]

Charles Sumner was not in Congress during the 1840's. Nevertheless he was known to many antislavery leaders throughout the country. Famous because of his orations, he conducted a far-flung correspondence. Seward admired him, Hale cooperated with him, and he maintained close contact with Westerners as well. As he wrote in 1845, he had read with "sympathy and delight" Chase's remarks on the presentation of a testimonial from the colored people of Cincinnati, and it gave him "no little pleasure to be remembered . . . by one who [sic] I respect as a powerful champion of truth in the West." Chase reciprocated Sumner's esteem, and the two cooperated in the movement leading to the formation of

[4] Lewis Tappan–Chase, June 7, 1842, Chase Papers, HSP; Chase, *Diary and Correspondence*, p. 224; Chase–Mrs. Chase, January 25, 1850, Chase Papers, LC.
[5] Chase-Giddings, February 14, 1842, Julian-Giddings Papers; Giddings-Chase, January 4, 1842, October 12, 1843, September 18, October 30, 1846, Chase Papers, HSP; Giddings–S. P. Jones, July 5, 1848; Stiles P. Jones Papers, Historical Society of Minnesota.

the Free-Soil party in 1848. With Giddings, too, Sumner enjoyed a cordial relationship. After having read the Boston orator's Phi Beta Kappa address in 1846, Giddings wrote to him that "the blessings of Heaven will reward such efforts," and the two radicals worked together actively in 1848 in planning opposition to Taylor.[6]

Another radical who was not in Congress was Cassius Marcellus Clay. A distant cousin of the Great Compromiser, he was a determined fighter who engaged in bitter feuds with the dominant slaveholders of his home state. In politics, he was a Whig; yet he kept up a steady and friendly correspondence with Chase, whom he tried to convince that the anti-Jackson party was infinitely more promising as a vehicle for antislavery work than its opponent. Although he failed to win Chase to his views, he retained his admiration for him. Giddings, too, was a friend of his, and when the Ohio representative heard of another duel fought by the Kentuckian, he expressed great fear for his life. "Clay's death," he wrote, "will be an affliction to our country and to the world."[7]

Still another politician who would eventually play a major role as a radical was among the early collaborators with the antislavery contingent. Edwin McMasters Stanton was an aspiring young lawyer who lived in Steubenville, Ohio. He was short, stocky, dark-complexioned, with thin black hair, and he was as intense as he was eloquent. His ambition and imperious manner made him many enemies, but his heart was in the cause. As early as 1842, he worked with Chase, and although he refused to forsake the Democratic party, of which he remained a member until 1861, he never broke with the Cincinnati reformer, even after he removed to

[6] Pierce, *Sumner*, III, 32, 63–4; Sewall, *Hale*, p. 86; Sumner-Chase, December 11, 1845, Chase Papers, HSP; Chase, *Diary and Correspondence*, pp. 113–16, 122–7, 128 ff.; Chase-Sumner, April 24, September 22, December 7, 1847; February 19, 1848; Giddings-Sumner, December 13, 1846; Sumner-Giddings, February 1, 1847; Giddings-Sumner, December 4, 1847, Sumner Papers.

[7] Smiley, *Lion of Whitehall*, pp. 6–9, 29, 40; Clay-Chase, December 21, 1841, September, 1843, January 19, 1844, January 28, 1845, Chase Papers, HSP; Clay-Giddings, September 11, 1844; Giddings–Laura Giddings, February 5, 1846, Julian-Giddings Papers.

Pittsburgh, where he soon built up another flourishing law practice.[8]

John P. Hale, genial, well-tempered, and popular, was also on good terms with many radical leaders. He had corresponded with Chase before he was elected to the Senate; then, when the Liberty party nominated him to be its standard-bearer in 1848, he gracefully withdrew at his friends' urging. The Van Buren candidacy promised more success.[9]

George W. Julian found no difficulty in fitting in with his radical colleagues when he arrived in Washington. Giddings, whom he had known before, remained his beau ideal. Living in the same boardinghouse, in an adjoining room, he was with him "nearly all the time." "He is one of the truest men in the nation," Julian wrote. "The whole question of slavery in all its bearings he understands as well as he does his alphabet." Sumner took a great interest in the Indiana congressman's maiden speech, a compliment which the young man cherished greatly, and he sought to become acquainted with Chase before he even left home. He suggested that they travel to the capital together.[1]

The cohesion which had developed among the radicals was strong. But would it withstand the inevitable pressures of ambition and political differences? The antislavery contingent was soon to be put to the test.

Chase's election to the Senate in 1849 constituted one of these strains. At the time of his nomination, the division in the Ohio legislature was such that either a Free-Soil Whig or a Free-Soil

[8] Charles A. Dana, *Recollections of the Civil War* (New York, 1899), p. 157; Brooks, *Washington in Lincoln's Time*, pp. 36–7; Stanton-Chase, August, 1846, November 30, 1846, December 2, 1847, February 16, 1848, September 7, 1851, Chase Papers, HSP; Benjamin P. Thomas and Harold M. Hyman, *Stanton: The Life and Times of Lincoln's Secretary of War* (New York, 1962), pp. 110–11, 30–1.

[9] Hale-Chase, April 13, 1846, June 8, 14, 1848, Chase Papers, HSP; Sewall, *Hale*, p. 104.

[1] Julian–Isaac Julian, January 25, 1850; Charles Sumner–Julian, June 6, 1850, Julian-Giddings Papers; Julian-Sumner, June 11, 1850, Sumner Papers; Julian-Chase, November 6, 1849, Chase Papers, HSP.

Democrat was likely to carry off the prize. Giddings had high hopes of success; for over ten years he had represented his district in the House, where he had made a name for himself as one of the nation's most fearless foes of slavery. A seat in the Senate would have gratified him. But he was a former Whig, and because of Chase's intervention on behalf of the Democrats, the Cincinnati reformer won.

Giddings was annoyed. He had been looking forward to his elevation to the Senate; he thought he had earned it. But he did not allow his good relations with Chase to be disturbed. "As to your election," he wrote to his successful rival, "our friends here are all pleased with it. You was [sic] the next choice of those who desired my election. I need not say to you that I was gratified at your success. I do not pretend that I was indifferent to the office, far from it. I regard it as worthy of the ambition of any man. But as I failed to obtain it, I could not have been as well pleased with the election of any other." Chase wrote in an equally cordial manner, established friendly relations with Giddings in Washington, and expressed his satisfaction "of learning that you take the same view of my election, that I should have taken of yours had you been the successful candidate." As a result, half a year later, Sumner was able to write to his old friend Giddings, "I was glad to see so much of Chase as I did here a month ago. He is a very able senator. I think the friends of Freedom in Ohio will forget old feuds, & old party names. Let us all stick together." The breach was healed, and the radicals had proved that at times they could overcome personal rivalries.[2]

Other pressures also endangered the radicals' unity. The organization in 1848 of the Free-Soil party had disturbed those opponents of slavery who remained loyal to the major political groupings, especially the Whigs. When Congress met in December, 1849, neither Democrats nor Whigs had a majority in the

[2] Giddings-Chase, March 14, 1849, Chase Papers, HSP; Chase-Giddings, March 6, 1849, Giddings Papers; Giddings-Sumner, October 29, 1849, Sumner Papers; Sumner-Giddings, October 19, 1849, Giddings Papers; Chase, *Diary and Correspondence*, pp. 188–9.

house, and weeks of inconclusive balloting for speaker resulted. The Free-Soilers, who held the balance of power, might have elected at any time the more moderate candidate, the Whig Robert C. Winthrop of Massachusetts. But they refused to vote for him. "Our friends are quite certain now that the old organizations must be broken up and new associations formed," wrote Giddings, who placed special hope in those members of the major parties who tended to support Free-Soil ideas. The unwillingness of important Southern Whigs to back Winthrop seemed to him a portent of the end of the Whig party, an organization with which he had already broken. Many of his colleagues concurred, and for seventeen days the deadlock continued.[3]

The result was the election of the extreme Southern Democrat, Howell Cobb, an outcome which caused recrimination among the Whig radicals. "Howell Cobb is Speaker; one of the fiercest . . . proslavery men in all the South," complained Horace Mann. "He loves slavery. . . . And by whom was he allowed to be elevated . . . ? By the Free-Soilers." Admitting that Winthrop was "not unexceptionable," he nevertheless thought that the difference between the Whig candidate and the Georgian was enormous. "With such a committee as Mr. Winthrop would have appointed," he mused some weeks later, "we should have met with no obstacles in getting our measures before the country and the House. Now we shall encounter the most serious of obstacles at every step. . . ."[4]

But the radicals' cohesion did not suffer permanent damage. On the contrary, so close was their cooperation that Chase and Giddings were maturing plans to make it formal. Convinced that the best policy was not to compromise any more, they were hoping for an increase in Free-Soil strength, Giddings being interested in winning over the Whigs, and Chase, the Democrats. Chase carried his determination not to make any further concessions so far as to decide not to go into caucus with the Democrats. Not

---

[3] Nevins, *Ordeal of the Union*, I, 251 ff.; Giddings–Laura Giddings, December 2, 1849, Giddings–J. A. Giddings, December 8, 1849, Giddings Papers; Giddings-Sumner, December 14, 1849, Sumner Papers.

[4] Mann, *Life of Horace Mann*, pp. 283, 285.

that he disliked the party of Andrew Jackson—he was convinced that it was the only political organization which might eventually become the vehicle for antislavery—but he could not see himself compromising with slaveholders. As the Democrats did not even invite him, his resolve was somewhat academic. But he still considered declining to serve on the Committee on Revolutionary Claims to which he was assigned. The whole system of making up committees disgusted him; his own assignment was wholly unsatisfactory to him, and it was only after Hale advised him to do so that he reconsidered and accepted.[5]

The two Free-Soilers' plans were premature. Such radicals as Seward and Hamlin still remained members of the Whig and Democratic parties in good standing, agreed to their committee assignments as a matter of course and caucused with their associates. But their determination to remain loyal to the cause was as firm as their Free-Soil colleagues'. On matters concerning slavery, all radicals continued to collaborate, no matter what their political backgrounds.

The year 1850 afforded proof that the antislavery men's cohesion was firm despite personal or party quarrels. Because of the annexations following the war with Mexico, the problem of slavery extension had become acute. Unless they were permitted to open the newly acquired territories, or at least that portion of them south of 36° 30', to their "peculiar institution," Southerners were threatening to break up the Union. Henry Clay proposed a compromise, and the ensuing debates put the foes of slavery to the test.

They rose to the challenge. Opposing to a man the Omnibus Bill designed to implement Clay's scheme, they delivered forceful speeches against it, supported its foes, and harassed its friends. Radical Democrats and Whigs stood with Free-Soilers to resist

[5] Chase-Riddle, December 3, 1849, Riddle Papers; Chase–E. S. Hamlin, December 15, 17, 1849, January 2, 1850; Chase–Mrs. Chase, January 3, 1850, Chase Papers, LC; Giddings–J. A. Giddings, December 8, 1849, Giddings Papers.

further compromises with the South. Seward and Chase became known as their chief spokesmen, and although they lost the immediate contest, in the long run they scored a success. The enactment of an unpopular fugitive slave law would cause such a furore that their ranks would be materially strengthened by the election to the Senate of Sumner and Wade.

When Henry Clay first set forth his proposals on February 5–6 in a two-day speech, even Chase was impressed by his "grand effort intellectually & oratorically considered." But his pleading for compromise—his advocacy of the admission of California as a free state in return for a fugitive slave law, his plea for the organization of the territories of Utah and New Mexico without reference to slavery, his suggestion that the slave trade but not slavery be abolished in the District of Columbia, and his idea of assuming the Texan debt in order to induce Texas to give up her claim to half of New Mexico—these proposals did not impress Chase at all. "Alas! What a congeries of inconstant beauties & blemishes must the orator exhibit who pleads at the same time the cause of slavery & freedom!" he wrote to his wife. That the measures were unacceptable he had already decided before the speech. "Sentiment for the North—substance for the South," he had called them, and the other radicals agreed.[6]

In their rejection of the compromise, the antislavery leaders were acting upon a very simple premise. According to Chase, the Constitution, having encapsuled slavery in order to contain it, was in essence an antislavery document. Therefore it was the duty of Congress to interpret it as such and to separate the national government as completely as possible from the institution. That California had a perfect right to come in as a free state as she had expressed her desire to do, no radical questioned; the only problem was that any concession to the South on this point would seem to yield a perfectly sound principle. In Utah and New Mexico, the radicals believed the proposed Wilmot Proviso outlawing slavery in territories acquired from Mexico ought to apply; in the District

[6] Chase–Mrs. Chase, February 6, 1850, Chase–E. S. Hamlin, February 2, 1850, Chase Papers, LC.

of Columbia, they were convinced that slavery as well as the slave trade should have been abolished long ago—Giddings had in the previous session introduced a measure for this purpose—and they disputed the right of Texas either to compensation or to territory in New Mexico. As for the fugitive slave law, they had quarreled with the comparatively weak existing one and obviously could not countenance its stronger successor. All these propositions seemed perfectly logical to them; they discounted Southern threats and believed the only course was to stand firm.

On February 20, Thaddeus Stevens set forth the radicals' point of view. Rising for his first important speech in the House, he argued that he was perfectly willing to abide by the compromises of the Constitution. Some of them he greatly disliked; were they now open for consideration, they would never receive his assent. But he found in them the organic law formed in different times and he would not disturb them. Therefore, much as he detested slavery, he would not interfere with it in the states. The territories, however, ought to be free, not merely because Congress possessed power to legislate for them, but because slavery was inimical to free government. "That republic must be feeble," he said, ". . . that has not an intelligent and industrious yeomanry, equally removed from luxury and from poverty. The middling classes who own the soil, and work it with their own hands, are the main support of every free government." And such classes could not flourish where slavery existed.[7]

Stevens's speech was indicative of a philosophy which he was going to uphold until the day of his death. At the time of its delivery, however, it was overshadowed by the debate in the Senate. If the radicals had any hope for support from Daniel Webster, they were to be bitterly disappointed when on March 7 he delivered his famous speech in support of the compromise. "Vae! Vae!" Chase unburdened himself to Sumner. "Massachusetts has spoken, and such a speech! Nothing proposed, nothing apparently thought of but absolute and unconditional surrender."

[7] *Cong. Globe,* 31st Cong., 1st Sess., Ap., 141–3.

Giddings clung to his belief that the address was only one more nail driven into the coffin of the Whig party, but it was the Whig senator from New York, William H. Seward, who four days later pleaded the radicals' cause most eloquently. "I think all legislative compromises radically wrong and essentially vicious," said the New Yorker in an able exposition of the constitutional right of Congress to restrict slavery. And when he went so far as to state that "there is a higher law than the Constitution which regulates our authority over the domain, and devotes it to the same noble purposes [of freedom]," abolitionists like John Jay and Lewis Tappan wrote him congratulatory letters. Overnight, Seward had become an outstanding radical leader, at least in the eyes of many observers throughout the country.[8]

Seward was not the only radical senator whose denunciation of the compromise was widely read. On March 26 and 27, Salmon P. Chase, anxious to set forth his stand, delivered a carefully thought-out oration. Stressing his conviction that the Constitution was an antislavery document, he argued that in respect to slavery, Congress had the power to "prevent its extension, and to prohibit its existence within the sphere of the exclusive jurisdiction of the General Government." Two days earlier, he had written to Sumner that he would limit himself to three propositions: (1) that the original policy of the government was that of slavery restriction, (2) that under the Constitution Congress could not establish or maintain slavery in the territories and (3) that the original policy of the government had been subverted and the Constitution violated for the purpose of extending slavery. He made his points, although he himself was disappointed with both "the matter and the manner" of delivery. But his political supporters were delighted. As B. F. Butler, the New York leader of the Barnburners, the Democratic faction favoring free soil, put it, "If all the opponents of Slavery extension were as careful as you have

[8] Chase-Sumner, March 7, 1850, Chase Papers, LC; Giddings–J. A. Giddings, March 8, 1850, Giddings Papers; *Cong. Globe*, 31st Cong., 1st Sess., Ap., 262–5; John Jay–Sumner, May 15, 1850, Sumner Papers; Lewis Tappan–Seward, March 21, 1850, Seward Papers.

been to avoid extravagances in doctrine . . . we should have less to fear from the influences now at work in the free states."[9]

The fight in the House was less dramatic than that in the Senate, but in addition to Stevens, Julian, Wilmot, and other foes of slavery rarely lost an opportunity to attack the compromise, the Omnibus Bill, and Southern plans for slavery extension. Horace Mann wrote a forty-page letter to his constituents in which he denounced Webster's seventh of March speech, and while Horace Greeley angrily charged Thaddeus Stevens and his Whig colleagues with want of policy, the radicals were nevertheless taking a common stand against Henry Clay's proposals.[1]

In spite of Giddings's hope for the complete break-up of parties and Chase's expectation to win over the Democrats to a Free-Soil position, the Taylor administration's ever more forceful opposition to the compromise and Seward's increasing cordiality with the President pointed the way to entirely different developments. Gradually and grudgingly, the antislavery leaders came to appreciate the old soldier in the White House. They were convinced that Clay's scheme was doomed, and although they had qualms about the President's "Platform of nonaction," they really had little cause for complaint as long as Taylor was in the White House. "Old General Taylor grows upon my good opinion," mused Chase. ". . . I believe him honest and that is much these days." So hopeful did things seem at the beginning of summer that Lewis D. Campbell, an antislavery Ohio politician, suggested that the North draw together and proceed to enact the Wilmot Proviso.[2]

Taylor's death changed all that. Having exposed himself on the Fourth of July to a hot sun, the President had drunk great quantities of iced milk and water, eaten too many cherries, and

[9] *Cong. Globe,* 31st Cong., 1st Sess., Ap., 468–80; Chase-Sumner, March 24, 1850, Sumner Papers; Chase–Mrs. Chase, March 27, 1850, Chase Papers, LC; Butler-Chase, April 29, 1850, Chase Papers, HSP.

[1] *Cong. Globe,* 31st Cong., 1st Sess., Ap., 573–9; New York *Tribune,* May 4, 6, 28, 1850; Greeley-Stevens, May 27, 1850, Stevens Papers.

[2] Bigelow-Sumner, May 20, 1850, Chase-Sumner, April 15, 1850, Sumner Papers; Chase–Mrs. Chase, June 1, 1850, Chase Papers, LC; Campbell-Hale, July 2, 1850, Hale Papers.

fallen ill. "Cholera morbus" set in. On July 9, he died, sincerely mourned by men who had opposed him only a few months before. Bailey, Hale, and other radicals wrote pessimistic letters about the change in administration; Greeley published a fitting eulogy in the New York *Tribune,* and Chase expressed his dread of Vice President Millard Fillmore's accession. Worst hit of all was Seward, whose collaborator Thurlow Weed captured their common mood when on July 10 he wrote: "I woke this morning with a heavy heart to be crushed by the final intelligence. I have your summons, but Washington is no place for me now. I could do no good, and should subject myself to mortifying imputations."[3]

These forebodings were justified. In spite of an initial setback to the Omnibus Bill, by September, because of executive patronage and shrewd management, the entire compromise had been enacted into law. Its authors celebrated by giving mammoth parties at which liquor flowed freely, and for the time being, Chase, Hale, Seward, Hamlin, Stevens, Giddings, Julian, Wilmot, and their allies had been completely defeated. Chase, who had remained in the Senate to the last, even after Seward and Hale had left Washington, unburdened himself to Sumner: "Clouds and darkness are upon us at present," he wrote.

The Slaveholders have succeeded beyond their wildest hopes twelve months ago. True some have demanded even more than they have obtained: but extreme demand was necessary to secure the immense concession which has been made to them. Without it Executive Influence and Bribery would, perhaps, have availed nothing.[4]

Giddings was less pessimistic. "We are beaten, but not conquered," he wrote to Sumner. "Overcome but not dismayed." Believing that slavery might still be kept out of Utah and New

[3] Bailey-Sumner, July 9, 1850, Sumner Papers; Hale–Lucy Hale, July 10, 1850, Hale Papers; A. H. Hood–Stevens, July 10, 1850, Stevens Papers; New York *Tribune,* July 12, 1850; Chase–Eli Tappan, July 22, 1850, Chase Papers, LC; Weed-Seward, July 10, 1850, Seward Papers.

[4] Chase–Mrs. Chase, August 28, 1850, Chase Papers, LC; Chase-Sumner, September 8, 1850, Sumner Papers.

Mexico if proper judicial appointments were made, he took pride in California's consecration to freedom, and thought that the slaveholders had suffered a reverse. How could they benefit by popular sovereignty, the local settlers' right to decide whether the "peculiar institution" was to be permitted? "For while we keep up our motto of no more *Slave States,*" he continued, "they will not risque [sic] Slave property there and freedom will be brought this side of the Rio Grande. I feel we have cause of gratulation and perseverance." Horace Greeley was also not without hope. Even the Fugitive Slave Law would not mean much, editorialized the New York *Tribune.* As the Northern people would not catch slaves, it would remain a dead letter. Their temporary defeat had neither disheartened the radicals nor destroyed their cohesion.[5]

So inequitable a law as the Fugitive Slave Act was bound to cause trouble. Incidents involving the recapture of alleged fugitives would enrage the North, and instead of stilling controversy, the measure would bring home to the free states the most objectionable features of the "peculiar institution." The opponents of slavery would gain friends.

The two areas of the country in which the antislavery spirit was strongest were New England and the Western Reserve in Ohio. By chance, vacancies for the United States Senate occurred that winter in both Massachusetts and the Buckeye State; the fall elections had again placed the Free-Soilers in advantageous positions, and they were able to exert their influence judiciously to elect two radical senators. The unpopularity of the Fugitive Slave Law helped them greatly.

In Ohio, the October elections had given Chase cause for hope that a congenial colleague might join him in the upper House. At times, he even thought Giddings had a chance. Above all, however, he was anxious to have the Free-Soilers—he preferred to call them Free Democrats—cooperate with the Democrats. Any alliance with the Whigs he thought dangerous. Giddings himself

[5] Giddings-Sumner, September 8, 1850, Sumner Papers; New York *Tribune,* September 13, 1850.

would have been glad to succeed where he had failed the year before, but he was not sanguine of success because he was not popular with either of the major parties. Some thought that no election would take place at all. Certainly the conservatives were not hopeful.[6]

At last, however, there was an election. Realizing that they could not elect one of their number, the Free-Soilers finally helped to seat Benjamin F. Wade, presiding judge of the Third Judicial Circuit. The judge had been a loyal Whig, even in 1848. During the fall, however, he had denounced the Fugitive Slave Law "as the most infamous enactment known to the statute books of this country," and he had avowed his intention not to obey it. His election by a combination of Whigs and Free-Soilers constituted a real victory for the radicals.[7]

The triumph of the cause mollified Giddings. Although this second personal disappointment within one year was hard to bear, especially since he had long been at odds with Wade, he nevertheless wrote a laudatory article in the Ashtabula *Sentinel* about his former partner. Horace Greeley used the opportunity to editorialize about the compatibility of Whiggery and Free-Soilism, and William H. Seward learned that the new senator was a decided "Progressman," whom he would find a "staunch and unflinching Ally in all good projects for the elevation of our race and the true permanent interest of our country." Only Chase was peeved. As early as November, he had deprecated the possibility of the election of Wade or any other Whig, and when he heard the news, he complained to Giddings that he was greatly disappointed. Firmly committed to low tariffs and a general philosophy of Jeffersonian laissez-faire ideas usually associated with the Democrats, he ab-

[6] Chase-Giddings, October 22, November 5, 1850, Giddings–J. A. Giddings, December 16, 31, 1850, Giddings Papers; Chase-Sumner, November 18, 1850, Sumner Papers; Chase, *Diary and Correspondence,* pp. 225–7; J. W. Allen–Corwin, December 18, 1850, Thomas Corwin Papers, LC.
[7] Trefousse, *Wade,* pp. 60–71; Conneaut *Reporter,* October 31, 1850; Ashtabula *Sentinel,* November 30, 1850; Columbus *Ohio State Journal,* February 4–March 18, 1851.

horred their opponents' protectionist and largely Hamiltonian outlook which favored internal improvements at government expense. But even he could not deny that the antislavery contingent had been strengthened.[8]

Wade's election was of special significance in the emergence of the radical bloc because it occurred almost at the same time as the even more important triumph of Charles Sumner in Massachusetts. The Boston reformer had been in the forefront of the Free-Soil movement for years, his orations against slavery and racial discrimination had made him known, and he was destined to become one of the most famous radical leaders.

Sumner's chance came in the winter of 1850–1. A coalition of Democrats and Free-Soilers had worked out a scheme which gave the short term United States senatorship and the state offices to the major party and the long-term senatorship to the minor. The Democrats promptly elected George S. Boutwell governor, and even though Sumner had originally been much closer to the Whigs than to the Jacksonians, he became the choice of the coalition for the six-year Senate term. For weeks it seemed likely that a combination of proslavery Democrats and Whigs would prevent the election of the unpopular orator who was considered a dangerous firebrand even though he had announced his full support of the Constitution, but on April 24, 1851, he finally obtained the requisite majority. The Bay State would be represented by one of the country's most eloquent foes of slavery.[9]

Sumner's victory electrified the radicals. "*Laus Deo!*" wrote Chase,

> From the bottom of my heart I congratulate you—no, not you, but all the friends of freedom everywhere upon your election to the Senate. Now I feel as if I had a brother-colleague—one with

[8] Giddings-Chase, April 3, 1851, Chase Papers, HSP; Ashtabula *Sentinel,* March 22, 1851; John Barr—Seward, March 15, 1851, Seward Papers; Chase, *Diary and Correspondence,* pp. 220–22; Chase-Giddings, March 24, 1851, Giddings Papers.

[9] Pierce, *Sumner,* III, 225–7; Donald, *Sumner,* pp. 183–204.

whom I shall sympathize and be able fully to act. Hale, glorious
and noble fellow as he is is yet too much an off-hand man himself to be patient of consultation—while Seward, though meaning to maintain his own position as an antislavery man, means
to maintain it in the Whig party and only in the Whig party.
Wade, who has been elected to be my colleague, is not known
to me personally. I am told he damned Fillmore, Webster & the
Compromise before election. . . . I *think* he will generally go
with Seward. . . . None of them are to me as you are.

The New York journalists John Bigelow and William Cullen
Bryant, the Maine temperance reformer Neal Dow, the abolition-
ist Lewis Tappan, among others, sent enthusiastic letters, and John
P. Hale immediately tried to get a good seat for Sumner in the
Senate. The new senator did not arrive in Washington as an un-
known.[1]

The election to the Senate of Sumner and Wade virtually completed the roster of radicals who were to become outstanding during the Civil War and Reconstruction. As James G. Blaine
commented thirty-four years later, "Mr. Wade entered the Senate
with Mr. Sumner. Their joint coming imparted confidence and
strength to the contest for free soil, and was a powerful reenforce-
ment to Mr. Seward, Mr. Chase, and Mr. Hale, who represented
the distinctively antislavery sentiment in the Senate."[2]

In spite of successes in New England and the West, however, the radicals were still a small and despised minority in Washington. Often outside of regular party organizations and considered
disturbers of the peace, for ordinary companionship, they were
largely dependent on each other. The center of their social life
was Dr. Bailey's house. Here they met every Saturday night, discussed their problems, and made the acquaintance of travelers

[1] Chase-Sumner, April 28, 1851, John Bigelow–Sumner, April 23,
1851, W. C. Bryant–Sumner, April 24, 1851, Neal Dow–Sumner, April
25, 1851, Lewis Tappan–Sumner, April 25, 1851, Hale-Sumner, May 5,
1851, Sumner Papers.
[2] Blaine, *Twenty Years of Congress*, I, 320.

who passed through the capital. "An American salon," one of the participants later called the editor's mansion.[3]

But of course the general trend of events—the constant insistence of leaders of both parties that the slavery problem had been settled and the compromise was a "final" solution—was depressing. "Strange as it may seem," wrote Thaddeus Stevens,

> the cause of Liberty is hard to sustain in this republic. Men with difficulty understand why others than themselves should be free. It seems to be thought that those [who] are weak ignorant, and friendless, are for that reason, unworthy of protection, and are fit subject of oppression. The statesmen of the present day are willing to aid those only who do not need it. Slavery is sustained in the free States by powerful interests. Men who aspire to high places; who have large intellects, and ought to have larger souls, sustain it to purchase Southern support.

Under such circumstances, what kept many of the radicals going was their unquenchable belief in the final triumph of the ideas they considered just. "Let us not despair," Stevens concluded,

> The people will ultimately see that laws which oppress the black man, and deprive him of all safeguards of liberty, will eventually enslave the white man. . . . And why not? What stronger right to freedom has the pale than the dark face? What argument can be used for enslaving the one that does not apply to the other? While we obey the Constitution and the laws let us strive to correct these laws and following the injunctions of Jefferson and Adams and Washington, strive by every lawful means to abolish slavery throughout the land.[4]

And the radicals kept up the fight. No compromise! was their motto in 1850 as later on.

———

Because the antislavery members of Congress were in such a small minority—they even lost Julian's support when in 1850 the Indiana congressman was defeated—they were unable to do

[3] Julian, *Giddings,* pp. 284–5; Grace Greenwood, "An American Salon," *Cosmopolitan,* VIII (February, 1890), 437–47; Giddings-"Sis," February 16, 1851, Julian-Giddings Papers; Milton Ross, *Memoirs of a Reformer, 1832–1890* (Toronto, 1893), p. 5.

[4] Stevens–James Aiken and others, October 25, 1850, Stevens Papers.

much more than to keep alive the opposition to the "peculiar institution." Day in and day out they presented petitions—petitions for the abolition of the interstate slave trade, petitions for the repeal of the Fugitive Slave Law, petitions for the prohibition of slavery in the District of Columbia, and petitions for many other subjects related to slavery.

The debate on the compromise resolutions had hardly got under way when Hale objected to the reception of Southern petitions praying for the dissolution of the Union. Only two senators from the slave states joined in voting against receiving the memorial. Then, to confound his opponents, he presented a similar petition, this time from Northern disunionists. The tables had been turned, and only three Southerners joined him in voting in favor of reception.[5]

The passage of the compromise presented additional opportunities for agitating the free-soil question. Immediately upon the admission of the two new senators from California, Chase emphasized his refusal to abide by the settlement by announcing his intention to press for the abolition of slavery in the territories, and when the bill to prohibit the slave trade in the District of Columbia was under consideration, Seward moved an amendment to abolish slavery as well. Several months before, he had attempted to secure jury trials for fugitive slaves. All these efforts ended in failure, but the radicals had kept their principles inviolate.[6]

As soon as the Fugitive Slave Act was on the books, it became the main target of the foes of slavery, who rarely missed an opportunity to attempt its repeal. The new session of Congress had hardly started when Julian introduced petitions for this purpose in the House, and Hale and Seward did the same in the Senate. "I believe that the law is a reproach on the civilization of the age and a perfect parody on the Constitution," said the New Hampshire radical in support of his petitions, a remark for which he

[5] Chase–Mrs. Chase, February 10, 12, 1850, Chase Papers, LC.
[6] New York *Tribune*, September 11, 12, 1850; *Cong. Globe*, 31st Cong., 1st Sess., 236.

was promptly called to order by his old antagonist Senator Foote of Mississippi, who maintained that it was not in order "thus to characterize the legislation of the country." But on the same day, Seward presented five hundred additional petitions against the law.[7]

Each fugitive-slave case gave the radicals renewed propaganda opportunities. Fillmore's message concerning the case of the Boston runaway Shadrach, who had been rescued by abolitionists, enabled Hale to point out the manifest absurdity of using the military strength of the United States to put down a few thousand Negroes.[8] When the fugitive Thomas Simms was returned from Boston at great expense and trouble, the senator's remarks were given greater validity.

The petitions continued month after month, in the 1852 session as well as that of 1851. On May 26, 1852, Sumner presented a memorial for the repeal of the law; as usual, the Senate decided to table it by a vote of forty to ten, all radicals voting nay. Seward made the attempt again the following day, with virtually the same results.[9]

Sumner now tried a different approach. In August, 1852, he offered an amendment to the pending civil appropriations bill providing that none of the money be spent in enforcing the Fugitive Slave Law. To support his motion, he delivered his first great antislavery oration in the Senate—"Freedom National, Slavery Sectional," he called it—a speech lasting more than four hours, in which he maintained that according to the "true spirit" of the Constitution, the institution of slavery could not claim the protection of the federal government. The Southern labor system was in every respect sectional, never national. Delivered partially to mollify his Free-Soil constituents who had been complaining

[7] New York *Tribune*, January 7, 16, 1851.
[8] New York *Tribune*, January 23, 1851.
[9] New York *Herald*, February 9, 18, 21, 25, 26, 28, 1852; New York *Tribune*, February 12, March 30, May 27, 28, 1852; *Cong. Globe*, 32nd Cong., 1st Sess., 901–2, 1474; Washington *National Intelligencer*, March 30, 1852.

about his silence, Sumner's speech was well constructed. But only four senators—Wade, Hale, Chase, and Sumner—voted for repeal. They constituted the core of the radicals' strength.[1]

The radicals' efforts on behalf of Louis Kossuth were more successful. The famous Hungarian revolutionary, who had been brought to America aboard a federal frigate, arrived at Washington in the winter of 1851, fresh from triumphs in other cities. Exactly how to receive him had given rise to much debate. Southerners had misgivings about his outspoken defense of liberty; Seward introduced resolutions of welcome, and Sumner delivered his first speech on their behalf. Eventually, the opponents of the resolutions lost, and the "Governor," as the Hungarian was called, was widely entertained in the capital. As Giddings had predicted, the Free-Soilers had made "capital out of Kossuth."[2]

No matter how unavailing the radicals' attempts to repeal portions of the compromise, their ceaseless agitation made it very clear that the settlement was by no means final, as its supporters contended. The antislavery members rarely missed an opportunity to say so, and when the *National Era* began to publish installments of *Uncle Tom's Cabin,* a novel which greatly impressed them, no one could fail to see that whatever Congress might do, the subject of slavery could not be laid to rest.[3]

[1] New York *Tribune*, August 27, 1852; *Speech of Hon. Charles Sumner, of Massachusetts, On His Motion to Repeal the Fugitive Slave Bill, in the Senate of the United States, August 26, 1852* (Washington, 1853); J. W. Stone–Sumner, July 17, 1852, Henry Wilson–Sumner, August 3, 1852, Theodore Parker–Sumner, August 4, 1852, Sumner Papers; *Cong. Globe*, 32nd Cong., 1st Sess., 2371.

[2] James Ford Rhodes, *History of the United States from the Compromise of 1850* (new ed., New York, 1936), I, 231–42; New York *Tribune*, December 10, 11, 1851; *Cong. Globe*, 32nd Cong., 1st Sess., 281, 589; Chase–Mrs. Chase, December 10, 11, 1851, Chase Papers, LC; Theodore Sedgwick–Sumner, December 11, 1851, Sumner–S. G. Howe, December 30, 1851, Sumner Papers; Wade–Mrs. Wade, December, 10, 1851, Wade Papers; *National Era*, December 25, 1851; February 26, 1852; Giddings–J. A. Giddings, December 29, 1851, Giddings Papers.

[3] Chase was especially impressed with the novel's religious emphasis. Chase–Mrs. Chase, December 13, 1851, Chase Papers, LC.

The radicals, whose persistent efforts did not make them popular, were often accused of being self-seeking firebrands. Julian remembered many years later that his foes called Giddings and his associates "pestilent fanatics, with whom no normal social or political intercourse was possible." His recollections were not quite accurate, but when Wade was elected to the Senate, the New York *Herald* regretted the fact that New England "abolitionists" had found allies in the West. "Cunning politicians have been laboring to engraft abolitionism on the Whig party to throw the whole country into confusion," wrote the editor, who was unable to detect any but selfish motives animating the foes of slavery. "Abolition fanatics . . . care no more for the slavery in the South than they do for the Kaffirs and Hottentots . . . except to use them for their own purposes." And while these charges were not new in 1851, they have nevertheless been repeated ever since.[4]

To a large degree, however, the accusations were unjustified. The radicals were sincere in their espousal of the cause. Wade not only denounced the Fugitive Slave Act publicly, but privately as well. "I cannot and will not swallow that accursed slave bill," he wrote to his wife, "it is a disgrace to the nation and to the age in which we live." Sumner's sincerity was beyond question; because of his unorthodox notions, Chase had to wait until 1849 to be elected to national office, and Thaddeus Stevens held fast to his antislavery opinions whether they were popular or not, so that he failed of renomination in 1852. The radicals' espousal of detested causes often hindered rather than helped their careers.[5]

By their behavior in Washington the antislavery members showed that they hardly merited the appellation of fanatics. Far from being treated as complete social outcasts, they took part in the major social functions of the capital. On New Year's Day, as

[4] Julian, *Giddings*, pp. 284–5; New York *Herald*, March 25, 1851. Cf. Otto Eisenschiml, *The Celebrated Case of FitzJohn Porter* (New York, 1950), p. 30; J. G. Randall, *Lincoln the Liberal Statesman* (New York, 1947), pp. 69 ff.

[5] Wade–Mrs. Wade, November 5, 1850, Wade Papers; McCulloch, *Men and Measures of Half a Century*, pp. 233–4. Current, *Stevens*, p. 95.

was the custom, they would go and pay their respects to the President. On one such occasion, in 1850, Giddings appeared at the White House in the company of three ladies. After conveying the compliments of the season to General Taylor, he presented his companions, among whom was Mrs. Julian. The President cordially shook them by the hand. Then he turned to the congressman. "Ah Mr. Giddings, you are surely for the Union, let them say what they will about you," he exclaimed in a voice loud enough to be heard in the entire room. The incident afforded great amusement for the onlookers, and Giddings specifically commented on his host's "great dignity and grace."[6]

Chase, too, refused to allow his politics to interfere with his manners. Boarding at the National Hotel, he found himself assigned to a table where all other occupants were Whigs, and many of them Southern Whigs, Henry Clay and Judge John M. Berrien of Georgia among them. Although he would have preferred different company, he made the best of the situation. "I keep on never minding the Judge's peculiarities," he reported, "and endeavor to bring into action only his more estimable qualities." And when Henry Clay took Chase's hat by mistake, the Ohioan told him that the hat had never covered so much eloquence before.[7]

Other members of the group were similarly sociable. Although Julian thought that Calhoun, "sitting in his seat in the Senate," looked "like an old fiend," the Indiana congressman was able to overcome his prejudices against political opponents long enough to sip eggnog with Secretary of State John M. Clayton on New Year's Day and to pay a social visit to Henry Clay, whose eloquence he still admired. Hale's affability was admitted even by Henry S. Foote, who had once threatened him with a hanging; and Wade, much as he disliked such functions, attended dinners given by the President and the Secretary of the Navy. Seward remained on excellent terms with members of all parties and sections until the time of the Civil War—he was incapable of rude-

[6] Giddings–Laura Giddings, January 5, 1850, Giddings Papers.
[7] Chase–Mrs. Chase, January 7, 16, 1850, Chase Papers, LC.

ness; whereas Sumner, later thoroughly unpopular, was at first accorded a certain respect, even by Southerners, because of his eloquence and scholarship. The social ostracism which some old radicals remembered came later; in the early fifties, at least, they were often seen at social events.[8]

The facts showed that the radicals were not unreasonable. Chase was on good enough human terms with opposing counsel in a fugitive-slave case to ask for personal favors. And although he had opposed the Mexican War with all his might, he did not persevere in his hostility once the conflict had begun. "The officers & men in the field were in the service of the country & entitled to the regard & support of the country they served," he explained in 1849.[9]

George W. Julian, too, was as proud of his common sense as he was of his radicalism. "I am as devoted to the Union as any man," he wrote to the Centreville *Democrat* in 1851, "and while I will not belie my profession on the subject of Free Soil, or turn traitor to the friends whose confidence I possess, neither will I, if elected, engage in any idle, unprofitable or dangerous agitation in favor of the repeal of the fugitive law or any other measure." Sumner, who did not think it right "to abjure slave holders socially and politically," was anxious to prove that he was a constructive legislator. Giddings, just before Henry Clay died, visited the old statesman. They spoke of their old friendship, discussed their recent differences about slavery, and agreed that they entertained the kindest feelings toward each other.[1] Wade and Hamlin, despite all provocation, had never even left their respective political organizations.

That the radicals were no wild revolutionaries could be seen

[8] Julian–Isaac Julian, January 25, 1850, Julian-Giddings Papers; Henry S. Foote, *Casket of Reminiscences* (Washington, 1874), p. 76; Wade–Mrs. Wade, January 10, February 11, 1852; Schurz, *Reminiscences,* II, 33; Donald, *Sumner,* p. 209; Greenwood, "An American Salon," loc. cit., p. 444.

[9] Chase, *Diary and Correspondence,* pp. 107, 171–4.

[1] New York *Tribune,* August 13, 1851; Sumner-Chase, September 18, 1849, Chase Papers, LC; Sumner–S. G. Howard, April 5, 1852, Seward-Sumner, May 19, 1853, Sumner Papers; Julian, *Giddings,* p. 299.

also by their continued support of many opposing party positions not connected with slavery. The tariff, internal improvements, homestead legislation, and the regulation of the armed forces tended to enlist them on opposite sides.[2] And despite Chase's hopes, in the quadrennial contest in 1852, they were completely divided about the presidency. The two leading Whig radicals, Seward and Wade, took a prominent part in the nomination of General Winfield Scott; Wade, as a member of the Whig Executive Committee, going so far as to supervise the preparation of a campaign biography and stumping Ohio for the general. Shortly after his arrival in Washington in 1851, he had seen Scott, whom he had told he was the one man who could carry Ohio for the Whigs. Only he must not write any more "South" letters. "Old Fuss and Feathers" as the general was called, had promised to keep his mouth shut. On the other hand Hamlin, a faithful Democrat, was ready to endorse even Stephen A. Douglas, who had been largely responsible for the final success of the compromise. Eventually, he strongly supported Franklin Pierce, a man Wade called "one of the smallest breed of New Hampshire Loco-Focos."[3]

The independents were also split. At first, Chase still entertained hopes of winning the Democratic party for antislavery principles, but Giddings had long been convinced that both political organizations were alike—"awful afraid that the slave question will not rest quiet," and he lent his full support to a separate ticket. Sumner, too, was perturbed. The coalition which had elected him was in trouble. The Whigs, preparing to nominate Scott, were making efforts to break it up, and Henry Wilson wrote that the general seemed to be an acceptable candidate. Sumner, like Chase still hoping for support from the Democrats, cautioned against

---

[2] *Cong. Globe,* 32nd Cong., 1st Sess., 2194, 2267, 2256. Cf. above, pp. 25–6.

[3] Seward-Colfax, July 21, 1852, Seward Papers; Nevins, *Ordeal of the Union,* II, 25–6; Wade–Mrs. Wade, December 10, 1851, February 8, 1852, June 6, 1852, July 2, 1852, Wade Papers; Hamlin–"Dr.," March 28, 1852, Hamlin-Valentine, May 13, 1852, Hamlin Papers; Hamlin, *Hamlin,* pp. 258–9; Wade–Mrs. Wade, June 6, 1852, Wade Papers.

reliance on the Whigs. Under no circumstances would he sacrifice his principles.[4]

When it became clear that both parties would endorse the compromise, Chase, Giddings, Sumner, Hale, Wilson, and Julian, among others, went ahead with plans to revive the Free-Soil party of 1848. In keeping with his Democratic predilections, Chase insisted that it be called "Free Democratic." But many opponents of slavery preferred the election of Scott, no matter how much they might insist on running a separate candidate. For this reason, the Free Democrats nominated John P. Hale rather than the Ohioan for President. Chase had arrived at his Democratic convictions too late, they thought, and Hale would be likely to draw more votes from the old Jacksonian party. As his running mate, they settled upon George W. Julian.

Antislavery Whigs were jubilant about this development. Although the general had been forced to repudiate his remarks against slavery extension, his managers were confident of his success. Obviously, not even the Free Democrats could be accused of fanaticism.[5]

The election results hardly justified the Whigs' optimism. Pierce won by a landslide; Hale not only fell short of Van Buren's vote in 1848, but in December, 1852, also failed of re-election to the Senate. The Whig party was approaching its end, and Thaddeus Stevens would not return to the next Congress. Only the election of a few active foes of slavery—Gerrit Smith in New York, Alexander De Witt in Massachusetts, and Edward Wade in Ohio, among others—partially compensated for these losses.

[4] Chase–E. S. Hamlin, January 9, 1852, Chase Papers, LC; Giddings-Julian, March 2, 1852, Julian-Giddings Papers; Giddings–J. A. Giddings, June 10, 1852, Giddings Papers; Henry Wilson–Sumner, January 5, 1852, Sumner-Wilson, January 10, 1852, Sumner Papers.

[5] Wilson-Sumner, June 23, 1852, July 7, 1852, F. W. Bird–Sumner, June 27, 1852, Sumner–S. G. Howe, July 4, 1852, Sumner Papers; Giddings–J. A. Giddings, June 30, 1852, Wilson-Giddings, August 21, 1852, Giddings Papers; J. W. Gray–Chase, July 12, 1852, Chase Papers, HSP; Chase–E. S. Hamlin, August 3, 1852, August 13, 1852, Chase Papers, LC; Colfax-Seward, August 2, 1852, Seward Papers; Wade–Mrs. Wade, June 6, 1852, Wade Papers.

But failure or success, the foes of the "peculiar institution" could still work together in Congress.

In spite of the rifts which beset the radicals during the presidential excitement, they continued to cooperate in Washington. Dr. Bailey's Saturday night gatherings were as brilliant as ever; petitions to repeal the Fugitive Slave Law and otherwise strike at the "peculiar institution" were still presented in Congress, and radicals of various parties supported Sumner's effort to deny funds for the enforcement of the hated measure. Even after the election, the future seemed bright. "It seems to me that you are the only Whig on his legs," wrote Sumner to Seward. "Now is the time for a new organization. Out of this chaos the party of freedom must arise." In spite of a noncommittal answer, the senator from Massachusetts did not give up. "Sumner is for *agitation,* Seward for lying low," commented Chase after dining with both. He himself was convinced that his friends' position "was never so strong as now." And in Maine, the antislavery Whig William P. Fessenden seemed to substantiate this opinion. "As, since the last election, the Whig party is defunct, we are now all Democrats," he wrote to Hannibal Hamlin.[6] The kernel of a new group was forming.

[6] Greenwood, "An American Salon," loc. cit., p. 444; *National Intelligencer,* March 30, 1852, May 27, August 25, 1852; *Cong. Globe,* 32nd Cong., 1st Sess., 1934, 1950, 2371; Sumner-Seward, November 6, 1852, Seward Papers; Seward-Sumner, November 9, 1852, Sumner Papers; Chase–E. S. Hamlin, December 2, 1852, February 4, 1853, Chase Papers, LC; Fessenden-Hamlin, November 17, 1852, Hamlin Papers.

II

The
Radicals Become
Republicans

"OUR FRIENDS were never in better spirits," wrote Albert G. Browne to John P. Hale in January, 1853. "The skies look bright. ... The Whigs are acting like fools, & every move they make is for our benefit. 'Whom the Gods desire for destruction they first make mad.' "[1] He was referring to the situation in Massachusetts, but he had unwittingly outlined the course of developments in Washington as well.

In 1853, superficial observers might have concluded that the cause of the radicals in general and of the Independent Democrats in particular looked anything but bright. A despised minority in Congress, the antislavery members of both houses had seemingly suffered severe reverses at the polls. Not only had they failed to stop the spread of proslavery measures, but they were denounced as abolitionists and unprincipled agitators. The Presi-

[1] A. G. Browne–Hale, January 28, 1853, Hale Papers.

dent was a close confidant of leading slaveholders; Hale, Stevens, and Julian were no longer members of Congress, and, by January, 1854, Chase was despairing of his chances for reelection. The settlement of 1850 really appeared to have been accepted as a finality.[2]

Appearances, however, were deceiving. The slavery issue could no more be settled by common agreement on outstanding issues than it could be solved by mutual understanding not to discuss it. Sooner or later, some renewed effort to spread the institution would rekindle the enthusiasm of the North. By infuriating the people, such a development would reverse the alleged trends of the time. It would also strengthen the unity of the radical members of Congress.

The Kansas-Nebraska Act was precisely the measure to accomplish this result. Dubious in its genesis and extremely offensive to important segments of Northern opinion because of its repeal of the thirty-four-year-old Missouri Compromise prohibiting slavery in the territories north of 36° 30′, it gave rise to suspicions of a conspiracy. It united the radicals, split the moderates, and shattered the entire American party structure. So profitable was it for the antislavery leaders that they have been blamed for deliberately distorting it for their own purposes ever since. But they did not have to resort to underhanded methods. The impact of the proposal was bound to popularize their cause in any case.

———————

Stephen A. Douglas, the able senator from Illinois who was the author of the Kansas-Nebraska Act, originally sought to sidestep the problem of the Missouri Compromise by omitting any reference to it. Anxious to extend western railroads and settlement and to help his political associates, however, he yielded to Southern pressure. "By God, sir, you are right," he said to Senator

[2] Henry Wilson, *History of the Rise and Fall of the Slave Power in America* (3d ed., Boston, 1876), II, 376–7 (hereafter cited as Wilson, *History*); Chase–E. S. Hamlin, January 22, 1854, Chase Papers, LC. Hale's term expired on March 4, 1853, Stevens's on the same day, and Julian's had ended two years earlier.

Archibald Dixon of Kentucky, who proposed the outright repeal of the prohibition of slavery, "and I will incorporate it [the repeal] in my bill, though I know it will raise a hell of a storm."[3]

His premonitions were justified. When, in January, 1854, he had first made known his intentions of organizing the Nebraska territory without the antislavery restriction of the Missouri Compromise, the radicals immediately made plans to oppose him. That they grasped at once the true impact of the proposal is not certain. "We are under some excitement here on account of Douglas' attempts to spread slavery over Nebraski [sic]," wrote Giddings to his son, "but I think we shall defeat them." Sumner wanted to table the motion instantly, and Hamlin told Douglas that the bill was a wrong which he would oppose. The measure's real importance soon became clear to them, however, and they began to cooperate on a joint manifesto. After Giddings and Chase had drawn it up and others had suggested some final changes, they published the document in the *National Era*. Signed by Sumner, Chase, Giddings, Edward Wade, Gerrit Smith, and Alexander De Witt, it was called an "Appeal of the Independent Democrats."[4]

Like almost everything else connected with the Kansas-Nebraska Act, the Appeal has become a source of controversy among historians. Was the radical manifesto not merely an effort to revive the sagging fortunes of the Free Democratic party? And was not the fact that it was printed in the *National Era* after Douglas had courteously agreed to Chase's request for postponement of debate on the pending bill proof of its authors' underhanded methods? The senator from Illinois immediately answered both of these questions in the affirmative, and some

---

[3] Mrs. Archibald Dixon, *The True History of the Missouri Compromise and Its Repeal* (Cincinnati, 1899), p. 445; Nevins, *Ordeal of the Union*, II, 94–6. For a discussion of the historiographical problems of the Kansas-Nebraska Act, cf. Roy F. Nichols, "The Kansas-Nebraska Act: A Century of Historiography," *Mississippi Valley Historical Review*, XLIII (September, 1956), 187–212.

[4] Giddings–G. R. Giddings, January 15, 1854, Giddings Papers; Sumner–S. G. Howe, January 18, 1854, Sumner Papers; Hamlin, *Hamlin*, pp. 265–6; Julian, *Giddings*, p. 311.

modern writers have agreed. As Avery Craven has stated, "The political shrewdness of the Appeal was matched only by its dishonesty."[5] But these conclusions may be challenged. After all, the Appeal on January 19 constituted the reply to a measure in the main introduced by Douglas, during the first two weeks of the new year, and it was Douglas and his friends who must bear a large share of responsibility for the results which ensued. The independent Democrats were only reacting to a problem presented to them by others.

As soon as it became evident that there was a real chance of the passage of Douglas's plan to repeal the Missouri Compromise, the radicals—both Independent Democrats and members of other parties—consulted on the best way of averting the menace. While Edward Wade and Giddings were discussing Douglas's report in Giddings's quarters, Chase came in and agreed that an address ought to be prepared. Giddings made many suggestions; Chase polished them into a finished report, and Sumner was consulted to help edit the final draft. An original version, signed by Benjamin F. Wade as well, was addressed merely to the voters of Ohio; but the Independent Democrats then decided to issue the document for their party alone, so that Wade's signature was left off.[6]

The Appeal was a stirring manifesto. As senators and representatives, the authors expressed their conviction that it was their duty to warn their constituents "whenever imminent danger" menaced the "freedom of our institutions or the permanency of the Union." The bill for the organization of Nebraska territory seemed to fit this description. "We arraign this bill," they continued,

> as a gross violation of a sacred pledge; as a criminal betrayal of precious rights; as part and parcel of an atrocious plot to exclude from a vast unoccupied region immigrants from the

[5] *Cong. Globe,* 33d Cong., 1st Sess., 275 ff.; Avery Craven, *The Coming of the Civil War* (New York, 1942), pp. 326–7.
[6] Giddings, *History of the Rebellion,* p. 366; New York *Tribune,* January 25, 1854; Schuckers, *Chase,* pp. 140, 160–1; Albert G. Riddle, *The Life of Benjamin Wade* (Cleveland, 1888), p. 226.

Old World and free laborers from our own States, and convert it into a dreary region of despotism inhabited by masters and slaves.

Then they recited the history of antislavery legislation in the United States and forcefully castigated the pending measure as a wanton breach of trust. Imploring "Christians and Christian ministers to interpose," they pledged themselves to resist the bill by "speech and vote." "Even if overcome in the impending struggle," they concluded,

> we shall not submit. We shall go home to our constituents, erect anew the standard of freedom, and call on the people to come to the rescue of the country from the domination of slavery. We will not despair; for the cause of human freedom is the cause of God.[7]

The document created a sensation. Widely reprinted all over the North, it was the opening of a determined campaign against Douglas's proposals and eventually contributed to the complete break-up of the old parties.[8] In fact, however, it contained little that was new. The authors had preached its doctrines for years, and if they saw a nefarious plot where none existed—while friendly with Southerners, the senator from Illinois never lent himself wholeheartedly to their more extreme demands—the accusers were not guilty of malicious invention. Their conviction of Douglas's depravity was deep-seated.[9]

When on January 30, 1854, the Nebraska bill came up for discussion in the Senate, Douglas savagely attacked Chase. His measure was merely the application of the spirit of the Compromise of 1850, he explained, and if there was an uproar because of it, it was the Free-Soilers' fault. "Why should we gratify

[7] *Cong. Globe*, 33d Cong., 1st Sess., 281.

[8] Schuckers, *Chase*, p. 140; Dixon, *The True History of the Missouri Compromise and Its Repeal*, p. 467.

[9] Cf. Wade–Fessenden, April 15, 1856, Fessenden Papers, LC. As late as 1868, General James S. Brisbin still recalled Wade's retort to Douglas when the Illinois senator accused him of entertaining a different code of morals from himself. "Your code of morals!" said Wade. "Your code of morals!! My God, I hope so, sir." Cincinnati *Daily Gazette*, March 11, 1868.

the abolition party in their effort to get up another political tornado of fanaticism and put the country again in peril for the purpose of electing a few agitators to the Congress of the United States?" he asked. Chase, immediately refuting these charges, affirmed that only certain last-minute changes had prevented his colleague from also signing the document which he had already endorsed in an earlier version, an explanation Wade carefully corroborated.[1] Douglas's tactics were driving his enemies more closely together than ever.

In the debates that followed, the radicals emerged as a truly unified force. It was no mere accident that the New York *Herald* referred to Chase, Seward, Sumner, and Wade as members of the Free-Soil party—erroneously, to be sure, since neither Seward nor Wade had yet left the Whig organization—but perceptive of the trend of the time just the same. When on February 3 Chase delivered his well-considered oration against the measure, he established himself as a leader in a grouping which was becoming ever more cohesive. Skillfully rejecting the charge that he and his associates were irresponsible agitators, he pointedly asked,

> Now, sir, who is responsible for this renewal of strife and controversy? Not we, for we have introduced no question of territorial slavery into Congress—not we who are denounced as agitators and factionists. No, sir: the quietists and the finalists have become agitators; they who told us all agitation was quieted and that the resolutions of the political conventions put a final period to the discussion of slavery.

Then he presented a historical review of congressional action involving slavery in the territories and ended on a note of great optimism. So well was the speech received by his admirers that they compared it to Webster's reply to Hayne. "At last the great opportunity of your life has crossed your path," wrote one of them.[2] He was not entirely mistaken.

Three days later, Wade took the floor. Although not a Free

---

[1] *Cong. Globe,* 33d Cong., 1st Sess., 275–80.

[2] New York *Herald,* January 31, 1854; *Cong. Globe,* 33d Cong., 1st Sess., Ap., 133–40; J. W. Taylor–Chase, February 7, 1854, Chase Papers, LC.

Democrat and distrusted by both Chase and Giddings, he took a stand as outspoken as his colleague's. "You may call me an Abolitionist if you will"; he exclaimed, "I care but little for that; for if an undying hatred for slavery and oppression constitutes an Abolitionist, I am that Abolitionist." More significant, perhaps, was his complete endorsement of Chase's position. "I need not refer further to the speech of the Senator from Illinois," he said in reference to Douglas's attack on the authors of the Appeal of the Independent Democrats. "My colleague so entirely pulverized that speech that there is not enough left upon which a man can possibly hang an idea." The Free Democrats appreciated his remarks, and his hometown paper, greatly influenced by Giddings, not only printed a laudatory editorial but circulated the oration together with Chase's previous speech. The occasion constituted the paper's first mention of the senator since 1852, when it had differed sharply with him.[3]

Seward launched his attack on the bill on February 17. Of all the statesmen who cooperated with the radicals, he was perhaps the most circumspect. Careful not to sign the Appeal, he had even entertained hopes of convincing Southern Whigs of its "moderation and dignity." But his denunciation of the measure was all that the most radical Free-Soiler could wish for. "The slavery agitation which you deprecate so much," he pointed out, "is an eternal struggle between conservatism and progress, between truth and error, between right and wrong."

"The greatest of his life," Sumner called Seward's speech. Wade agreed with him.[4]

Sumner, who had held back to give others a chance to speak, finally attacked the Kansas-Nebraska Bill on February 21. Appealing to a Southern sense of honor and pleading the sacred

[3] *Cong. Globe,* 33d Cong., 1st Sess., 337–40; Ashtabula *Sentinel,* February 9, 16, 1854; Giddings–Addison Giddings, February 12, 1854, Julian-Giddings Papers.

[4] *Cong. Globe,* 33d Cong., 1st Sess., Ap., 150 ff.; Seward-Greeley, January 22, 1854, Horace Greeley Papers, New York Public Library; Sumner–Mrs. Seward, February 18, 1854, George E. Baker–F. Seward, February 17, 1854, Seward Papers.

nature of the compact establishing the Missouri Compromise, he argued eloquently for the defeat of Douglas's measure. Aside from a pointed characterization of a "Northern man with Southern principles," his oration was restrained. "The North and the South, Sir," he declaimed,

> as I fondly trust amidst all differences, will ever have hand and heart for each other; and believing in the sure prevalence of Almighty Truth, I confidently look forward to the good time, when both will unite, according to the sentiments of the Fathers and the true spirit of the Constitution, in declaring Freedom, not Slavery NATIONAL....[5]

Even the senator from Massachusetts was aware of the need of not offending moderates at the very moment when they were turning in his direction.

Hannibal Hamlin took little part in the debates. As a Democrat, he was in a difficult position. But he made his point of view clear to Douglas. According to his grandson, he said to the senator from Illinois, "Douglas, your bill is a gross moral wrong. In my judgment it would be a bad party measure. It is vicious in principle, and if enacted, will produce infinite mischief. I shall oppose it." And oppose it he did, despite pressure from the White House and the Attorney General.[6]

The radicals had thus set the tone, but they were by no means alone. That formerly unsympathetic Northerners were beginning to support them became more and more evident. Petitions against the Kansas-Nebraska Bill were drawn up in ever-increasing numbers; protest meetings were held in many parts of the free states, and antislavery candidates were becoming ever more sanguine of success in local elections. A new party was in the making.[7]

For the antislavery stalwarts, the prospect looked promising. Chase, still hopeful of the organization of an antislavery Demo-

---

[5] *The Works of Charles Sumner* (Boston, 1875), III, 277–332 (hereafter cited as Sumner, *Works*).

[6] Hamlin, *Hamlin*, pp. 265–6, 270–1.

[7] New York *Tribune*, February 25, 28, 1854; Wilson, *History*, II, 393.

cratic party, thought the time had come to strike. "There would have, hardly, been a decent resistance here if we Independent Democrats had not been on hand," he wrote to N. S. Townsend, while pleading for support of the Ohio legislature. Although he agreed that independents should cooperate with Whigs and liberal Democrats, he exulted that Wade was "willing to unite in the organization of a New Democratic Party." And he thought that a mere Anti-Nebraska grouping was not enough. "We must adhere to a democratic organization," he insisted, confident that he would be able to induce free-soilers of all antecedents to co-operate.[8]

Other radicals shared his optimism, even if they were not necessarily interested in a Democratic organization. "I feel quite assured that the tide is changing," wrote Seward to Theodore Parker, the famous Boston abolitionist minister, "and that we can all speak henceforth with more boldness and with more effect." By April, he congratulated the clergyman on the "awakening of the spirit of Freedom," adding that he could not see "when or how or by whom it is to be drugged to sleep again." In New England, the novelist Harriet Beecher Stowe reported a grand uprising of the spirit of liberty. So widespread was the indignation about Douglas's proposal that Henry Wilson confided to Sumner, "Whatever the result of the Bill before Congress one good has come of it. The seals are broken and all will now discuss the question of slavery."[9]

If anything was needed to speed the organization of a new party, it was the failure of efforts to prevent passage of the Kansas-Nebraska Bill. In the Senate, where radical members had taken the lead in seeking to stem the tide with amendments and speeches, the final vote came on May 25; in the House, where Giddings and L. D. Campbell of Ohio, ably supported among others, by E. B. Washburne, Israel Washburn, and Richard Yates, had borne the brunt of the struggle, on May 22. But defeat did not spell the

[8] Chase–N. S. Townsend, February 10, 1854, March 9, 1854, Chase Papers, HSP.
[9] Seward-Parker, March 12, April 14, 1854, Seward Papers; Harriet Beecher Stowe–Sumner, February 23, 1854, Wilson-Sumner, February 26, 1854, Sumner Papers.

end of the radicals' efforts. They were more determined than ever to right the wrong—to "expunge the expungers," as Schuyler Colfax put it.[1] And they declared publicly that the Whig party was dead.

It was on the very day of the passage of the Kansas-Nebraska Bill in the Senate that Wade announced his separation from his old political organization. In an embittered speech, he recalled that he had supported it all his life, but now that Southern Whigs had deserted their Northern colleagues, he would do so no more. "I am an Abolitionist at heart while in the slave cursed atmosphere of this capital, whatever I may be at home," he exclaimed. Amid scenes of great excitement, Charles Sumner rose at midnight to offer a protest on behalf of the New England clergy. "The Senator from Ohio, on the other side of the chamber," he said, "has openly declared that Northern Whigs can never again combine with their Southern brethren in support of Slavery. This is a good augury." He called the bill both the worst and the best on which Congress had ever acted, the worst because it constituted a victory for slavery, and the best because it made any future compromise impossible. "Thus it puts Freedom and Slavery face to face, and bids them grapple. Who can doubt the result?" Seward continued to work with the Whig party a little longer, but his zeal for the antislavery cause did not flag.[2]

The passage in May, 1854, of the Kansas-Nebraska Act did not end efforts to defeat proslavery legislation. At a time when large portions of the North were aroused, radical leaders could not be expected to keep quiet. Their task was made easier because of the excitement caused throughout the free states by the rendition of Anthony Burns, a fugitive slave who was recaptured and removed from Boston under heavy guard. Angry crowds surged

[1] Wilson, *History*, II, 396 ff.; New York *Tribune*, May 15, 26, 1854; Isaac N. Arnold, *The History of Abraham Lincoln and the Overthrow of Slavery* (Chicago, 1866), p. 52; Colfax–G. Shryok, May 25, 1854, Schuyler Colfax Papers, Chicago Historical Society.

[2] *Cong. Globe*, 33d Cong., 1st Sess., Ap., 763–5; Sumner, *Works*, III, 337–52; Giddings–Chase, October 16, 1855, Chase Papers, HSP.

through the city's streets, citizens displayed the Stars and Stripes union down, and one of the members of the federal marshal's guard, James Batchelder, was killed. Even conservatives were filled with dismay.[3] Under the circumstances, radicals could do no less than to make the most of the situation.

And they reflected the popular spirit in Congress. Presenting petitions against the Fugitive Slave Act and attacking the repeal of the Missouri Compromise, they made efforts to rescind both laws. In the Senate, Sumner cooperated with Seward in preparing a minority report against the payment of compensation for the murdered Batchelder's widow and delivered impassioned speeches castigating slavery, while Chase introduced a bill for the abolition of the "peculiar institution" in all territories; in the House, Giddings sought to repeal the Kansas-Nebraska Act by offering an appropriate amendment to a general appropriation bill. And although the number of votes radicals could muster against the Fugitive Slave Law was still small, it was beginning to increase. On July 31, ten of forty-five senators present supported Sumner's motion to introduce the subject.[4]

In the meantime, the collapse of the old political organizations throughout the country was becoming ever more evident. The Washington *National Era* hopefully discussed the prospects of a northern "party of freedom." Long-time party organs of radical tendencies, such as William Cullen Bryant's New York *Evening Post* and Horace Greeley's New York *Tribune,* began either to endorse fusion or else open their columns to writers who did; mass meetings of Democrats, Whigs, and Free-Soilers opposed to the Kansas-Nebraska Act were held, and a new organization gradually began to emerge.[5] The Republican party was being born.

[3] Wilson, *History,* II, 435–44; Nevins, *Ordeal of the Union,* II, 150–2; J. B. Alley–Sumner, June 5, 1854, Sumner Papers.

[4] Sumner, *Works,* III, 337, 426–32, 355–67, 368–423, 449 ff.; New York *Tribune,* July 15, 1854, August 1, 1854.

[5] Wilson, *History,* II, 407; *National Era,* April 20, June 1, 8, 1854; New York *Tribune,* June 1, 1854.

In the new party, three elements could eventually be differentiated. In the first place, there were the radicals, distinguished for their extraordinary interest in resisting the spread of slavery and opposed to all compromise with the South. The second group, moderates like Abraham Lincoln, were basically in agreement with many of the radicals' aims, but remained willing to make temporary concessions provided the main objectives of slavery restriction were not abandoned. Finally, there were conservatives like Orville Browning of Illinois, politicians who favored compromise and were often more interested in the economic and social principles of their old parties than in the antislavery commitment of the new. These divisions were not hard and fast, and individuals could and did move from one group into the other. But in some fashion, they persisted until the outbreak of the Civil War, when new issues modified the questions involved.

While the Republican party would in the long run be comprehensive enough to include conservatives and moderates as well as radicals, the extremist wing, whether of Whig, Democratic, or Free-Soil origins, played an important role in its founding. Incessantly working for the cause of fusion, the radicals canvassed the country, gave wavering groups direction, and contributed significantly to the result.

Michigan furnishes an excellent example of the role played by the radicals in the founding of the Republican party. Long a Democratic stronghold because of the popularity of Lewis Cass, Taylor's opponent for the presidency in 1848, the Wolverine State had not offered any great opportunities to either antislavery Whigs or Free-Soilers. Among the former was Zachariah Chandler, already one of the wealthiest merchants in the state, who combined great organizational talents with ultraradical views. Having served in 1851–52 as mayor of Detroit, he had seen his hopes blasted during the presidential election in the general Whig disaster. But the introduction of the Nebraska Bill gave him his chance. He signed the call for a Detroit anti-Nebraska meeting in February, 1854, and, after a brief period of hesitation, became one of the main proponents of fusion. His activities contributed to the success in July of the famous meeting "under the oaks" in Jackson, where the designation "Republican" was formally used for the new organization. And Jacob M. Howard, another later radical, who was to follow Chandler into the United States Senate, wrote the platform which was adopted.[6]

Because of Chandler's efficiency—he soon built up a strong machine in his home state—the radicals' influence in Michigan was especially pronounced. The ultra Detroit *Tribune* lent them its aid, and Kinsley S. Bingham, an inveterate foe of slavery, was elected governor. But in other states, also, they had an important part in the founding of the Republican party. In Ohio, both Chase and Wade cooperated in inducing antislavery members of both parties to coalesce with Free-Soilers. The two senators issued a joint call for a convention and Wade wrote letters to newspapers on the Western Reserve endorsing the movement. Neither was present at a convention held at Columbus in July, but when the new party took shape, their influence was unmistakable.[7] In Indiana, under the leadership of Oliver P. Morton, Schuyler Colfax, and Henry S. Lane, the fusion movement was at first moderate, but Julian, who deplored this trend, never ceased to work for radical principles, while Colfax soon cooperated with the ultras. By 1860, the so-called People's party was to become thoroughly Republican and Julian himself was to return to Congress. In Illinois, Owen Lovejoy, the martyred Elijah's brother, attempted to launch a premature Republican movement which did not quite succeed because of the opposition of moderate Whigs, among whom Abraham Lincoln was then an aspirant for a vacant Senate seat. But as in Indiana, when the party was finally established, it owed much of its philosophy to men like Lovejoy. The

[6] Detroit *Post and Tribune, Chandler,* pp. 80–7, 99 ff.; Harris, *The Public Life of Zachariah Chandler,* pp. 8–11, 14 ff., 21 ff.; Jacob M. Howard, Biographical Sketch by Hamilton Gay Howard, Jacob Howard Papers, Detroit Public Library; Howard, *Civil-War Echoes,* p. 269; *National Era,* July 20, 1854.

[7] Detroit *Post and Tribune, Chandler,* pp. 100–23; Chase–N. S. Townsend, May 30, 1854, Chase Papers, HSP; Ashtabula *Sentinel,* June 8, July 6, August 10, 1854; New York *Tribune,* July 15, 17, 1854.

antislavery leader was sent to Congress; Chase, Giddings, and Cassius Clay lent their aid to the movement, and Lincoln, who was adamantly opposed to the extension of slavery, would stand firm against compromise. In Iowa, James W. Grimes and James Harlan, at that time both friendly to radicalism, became the mainstay of the new grouping, while Wisconsin was from the very beginning under radical leadership. Claiming to be the birthplace of the Republican party, the Badger State elected the determined Charles Durkee to the United States Senate.[8]

What was true of the West was equally true of the East. In New Hampshire, Hale and others ably assisted by Chase, organized the fusion ticket which eventually developed into the Republican party, and Wilson helped in the campaign against the Kansas-Nebraska Bill. In Maine, Israel Washburn, one of three radical brothers who were to distinguish themselves in as many states, took the lead in launching the movement; in New York, where Seward was not ready in 1854 to jettison the Whig party, he nevertheless became the most skillful leader of the new Republican organization before the next presidential election. And in Pennsylvania, Thaddeus Stevens and Thomas Williams, later a radical congressman, were among the earliest organizers of the Republican party.[9]

[8] Francis Curtis, *The Republican Party: A History of its Fifty Years' Existence and a Record of its Measures and Leaders* (New York, 1904), I, 201; *National Era*, July 27, 1854; Kenneth Stampp, *Indiana Politics During the Civil War* (Indianapolis, 1949), pp. 21–9; Julian-Chase, July 22, 1856, Chase Papers, HSP; Colfax–Wheeler, April 5, 1855, Colfax Papers, LC; Thomas, *Lincoln*, p. 152; Lincoln, *Works*, III, 4, 13, 44, II, 471–2; *Illinois State Journal*, November 20, 1856, clipping in David Davis Papers, Chicago Historical Society; Arthur Charles Cole, *The Era of the Civil War, 1848–1870*, Vol. III, *The Centennial History of Illinois* (Springfield, 1919), 128–34; William Salter, *The Life of James W. Grimes* (New York, 1876), pp. 63 ff.; Wilson, *History*, II, 409.

[9] Wilson-Sumner, March 15, 1854, Sumner Papers; *National Era*, September 14, 1854; Sewall, *Hale*, pp. 154–5; Curtis, *The Republican Party*, p. 192; Gordon Kleeberg, *The Formation of the Republican Party As a National Political Organization* (New York, 1911), p. 19; Brodie, *Stevens*, p. 123; Burton Alvey Konkle, *The Life and Speeches of Thomas Williams* (Philadelphia, 1915), I, 293.

The one Eastern state in which the radicals' role was most evident was Massachusetts. Having correctly assessed their opportunity at an early time when the Kansas-Nebraska Bill was still pending, they were prepared to act decisively. As soon as the measure had passed Congress, Sumner addressed a letter to an anti-Nebraska committee in his home state. "As all at the South," he declared, "without distinction of party, unite for Slavery, so all at the North, without distinction of party, forgetting the vain differences of Whig and Democrat, must unite for Freedom." On May 31, the Bay State Free-Soilers met in convention at Boston, where they were addressed by John P. Hale among others and passed resolutions calling for fusion. The rendition of Anthony Burns significantly helped the cause. Old antislavery activists like John B. Alley might deplore the shame that had been visited upon the commonwealth, but they realized that there was another side to the story. "Never since I have engaged in the antislavery cause have I seen occasion for rejoicing as now," Alley confessed to Charles Sumner. "Thank God. The chains that have bound people to their old organizations have been snapped asunder, and they have proved in this case but as pack threads upon the arms of an unshorn Samson." He was full of praise for Henry Wilson, who had delivered a "capital speech at the convention." Seth Webb, Jr., another antislavery stalwart, also recognized the radicals' chance. "Political affairs in Massachusetts are very much at loose ends," he advised in July. "All parties seem to be approaching that happy state of solution & dissolution, for which we have sighed so long."[1]

Sumner took full advantage of this state of affairs. He addressed a Republican state convention at Worcester, made a strong plea for fusion, and professed great hopes for the future. "What a mellowing of the Northern heart towards us heretics seems to have taken place!" he wrote to Mrs. Seward in October. Regretting the

[1] Wilson-Sumner, February 26, 1854, John B. Alley—Sumner, June 5, 1854, Seth Webb, Jr.—Sumner, July 14, 1854, Sumner Papers; Sumner, *Works,* III, 353–54; New York *Tribune,* June 1, 1854.

fact that Massachusetts and New York seemed to lag behind other states in making real radical gains at the polls, he expressed his longing "for *Union* among men who think substantially alike." And although the full organization of the new party was delayed because of the emergence of the Know-Nothing order, when it finally took shape in Massachusetts, it owed much of its success to the efforts of such radicals as Sumner and Wilson. The Natick politician had even used the nativist organization to further the aims of fusion.[2]

The result of these developments was encouraging. As early as February, 1854, the Maine legislature elected William Pitt Fessenden to the Senate. Although basically not extremist, Fessenden entered Congress at a period when Southerners goaded even moderates into radical positions. Because of these circumstances—Fessenden arrived in Washington in time to deliver a spirited oration against the Kansas-Nebraska Bill—he impressed the radicals favorably, cooperated closely with them, and was considered one of their number. Years later, Sumner recalled that the new senator's arrival "had the effect of a reinforcement on the field of battle. . . . One more in our small number was a sensible addition." Wade too was taken with Fessenden, who, he thought, would give strength to "the small band of Northern Whigs in the Senate." When the Republican party was fully organized in Maine, Fessenden naturally became one of its leading members.[3]

The fall elections, too, proved reassuring. Not only were 108

[2] Sumner, *Works,* III, 453–75; Sumner–Mrs. Seward, October 26, 1854, Seward Papers; Wilson, *History,* II, 415, 431 ff.; Theodore Clarke Smith, *Parties and Slavery, 1850–9* (New York, 1906), p. 140; Wilson–Chase, April 16, 1855, Chase Papers, HSP. In Connecticut, radical influence was not marked. Cf. John Niven, *Connecticut for the Union* (New Haven, 1965), p. 20.

[3] New York *Tribune,* February 11, March 7, 1854; Sumner, *Works,* XIII, 189; Francis Fessenden, *Life and Public Services of William Pitt Fessenden* (Boston, 1907), I, 46; Wade–Mrs. Wade, March 4, 1854, Wade Papers; Charles A. Jellison, *Fessenden of Maine: Civil War Senator* (Syracuse, 1962), p. 78.

anti-Nebraska members returned to the House, but many state legislatures reflected the new trend. In Iowa, James W. Grimes won the race for governor, and although fundamentally he was no more extremist than Fessenden, leading radicals considered him one of their own. "The Republican party seems to be going well and is significant of our principles," Cassius M. Clay had written in September. The elections seemed to prove him correct.[4]

Because of the antislavery gains, a number of new senators came to Washington during the year 1855. Massachusetts sent Henry Wilson, a politician who had for years been active in the cause. His collaboration with the Know-Nothings caused some of his supporters misgivings, but he was soon to prove that his commitments to freedom took precedence over his obligations to the order, which he left before the year was out. A radical who could be counted upon to sustain his colleagues no matter what the odds, the Natick cobbler greatly strengthened the movement in the Senate.[5]

From New Hampshire, John P. Hale reappeared as his state's representative. No newcomer to Washington, Hale was not the most effective spokesman for radicalism, and when he was elected in the summer of 1855, the New York *Tribune* expressed the feelings of many when it pointed out that another senator from the Granite State would have been preferable. Nevertheless, his success gave cause for rejoicing. The President had been particularly anxious to defeat him.[6]

Other outspoken foes of slavery expansion also entered the upper House in 1855. In New York, William H. Seward was re-

[4] *National Era,* October 19, September 21, November 23, 1854; T. H. McKee, ed., *The National Conventions and Platforms of All Political Parties, 1789–1905* (Baltimore, 1906), p. 86; Chase-Grimes, November 13, 1854, Chase Papers, HSP; C. M. Clay–Giddings, September 1, 1854, Julian-Giddings Papers.

[5] J. M. Stone–Sumner, January 29, 1855, Sumner Papers; Theodore Parker–Wilson, February 15, 1855, Henry Wilson Papers, LC; Wilson-Chase, November 17, 1855, Chase Papers, HSP; Hoar, *Autobiography of Seventy Years,* I, 215.

[6] New York *Tribune,* June 14, 19, 1855.

elected for a second term. From Illinois came Lyman Trumbull, a former Democrat whose dislike of slavery had caused him to break with Stephen A. Douglas and the regular wing of his party. Not particularly attractive in appearance, Trumbull dressed in black coats not fully buttoned, wore large gold-rimmed glasses, and seldom smiled. But he was an able debater. That he was much less of an ultra than many of his colleagues was not evident as long as he was engaged mainly in warding off the assaults of slaveholders and their allies. In some respects, he resembled Fessenden, with whom he developed a close personal relationship as time went on. Wisconsin sent Charles Durkee, one of the early Free-Soilers in the state, who had served previously in the House and was well known to radical senators. And Iowa chose James Harlan, a young man of outspoken antislavery views who would often collaborate with the extremist wing of the party. The small band of radicals in the upper House was increasing. And the designation Republican was becoming more and more common.[7]

In their success in furthering the fusion movement, the radicals encountered several obstacles which taxed their ingenuity. In the first place, many party workers were still loath to leave their old organizations. Chase, for example, tried desperately to retain the Free Democratic machinery and make it the nucleus of the new party. Congratulating Sumner on his performance at the Republican state convention in Worcester in September, 1854, the Ohioan wrote:

> Your speech was just the thing. I read it with delightful admiration. Only one thing abated my pleasure: The dissolution of the Independent Democracy. I am now without a party: but no matter; I shall soon cease to have any connection with politics.

The statement was an exaggeration, but it was indicative of his mood. Seward likewise disliked disbanding the Whig party, and

---

[7] Seward, *Works*, IV, 35; White, *Trumbull*, pp. 43–5; Howard, *Civil-War Echoes*, p. 26; Krug, *Trumbull*, p. 190; New York *Tribune*, February 5, 1855; Johnson Brigham, *James Harlan* (Iowa City, 1913), p. 89.

Chandler was at first reluctant to give up his former connections.[8] But once they realized the possibilities offered by the new party, the radicals became its most devoted adherents.

A second and more serious problem was the rise of Know-Nothingism. The American party, as its sympathizers called it, was the outgrowth of many years of nativist activity. Directed mainly against foreigners and Catholics, it nevertheless attracted many supporters who had been rendered homeless by the breaking up of the old party structure. How to win these for the antislavery struggle without compromising principle was a major challenge for the antislavery leaders.

Had the radicals been mere self-seeking politicians, they would have found it easy to collaborate with the Know-Nothing order. Almost all of them were Protestants of old American stock who would have encountered no difficulty in joining the nativist organization. But the order's proscriptive tenets were totally incompatible with those ideals of equality which were the hallmark of the radical movement.

It speaks well for the group that, in spite of great temptation, few of its members ever compromised with the Know-Nothings. Anxious to wield all antislavery forces into one large organization, they were willing to accept the nativist party's support and sought to capture sympathetic elements within it. But they generally refused to endorse its intolerant principles.

Among those most immediately affected by the emergence of the bigoted order was Salmon P. Chase, who was anxious to become governor of Ohio. Fundamentally, he loathed the nativists. "I cannot proscribe men on account of their birth. I cannot make religious faith a political test," he declared. However, he was also anxious to obtain as much support from the Know-Nothings as possible. He stood on the Free-Soil platform, he wrote to Julian in January, 1855, but just as he had cooperated with Democrats and Whigs if they were against slavery, he was willing also to work

[8] Chase-Sumner, September 13, 1854, Sumner Papers; Giddings-Chase, October 16, 1855, Chase Papers, HSP; William Livingstone, *Livingstone's History of the Republican Party* (Detroit, 1900), I, 44.

with the nativists if it could be done without "sacrificing principle." The result was that he tried to minimize the issue, a course of action which displeased many of his colleagues. But he made his position clear to the Americans. "It makes me laugh to see how ignorant you Know-Nothings are," he wrote to the nativist congressman Lewis D. Campbell. Pointing out that the proscriptive order was powerless without Republican aid, he emphasized that the anti-slavery forces could not fuse with it "with our convictions and remain honest men." Consequently, the Know-Nothings must subordinate their wishes to the stronger faction. "I don't understand being an Indt. Democrat & a K. N. at the same time," he declared to N. S. Townsend. The result was that Chase was opposed by a nativist as well as by a Democratic candidate, both of whom he defeated in the election of October, 1855. Despite some trimming, he had not seriously sullied himself by endorsing bigotry.[9]

William H. Seward was never even tempted to compromise. Long *persona non grata* to nativists because of his support of aid to parochial schools when governor of New York, he was reelected in 1855 despite bitter Know-Nothing opposition. Even before the returns were in, his putative victory was interpreted as a stunning blow against the power of the order. And his former friend Horace Greeley had for a long time lent his name and newspaper to the cause of antinativism; in 1854, one of his editors, Charles A. Dana, vowed that the Know-Nothings would never again be mentioned in the *Tribune* "except to give 'em a devil of a whale."[1]

In New Hampshire, too, the radicals knew how to make the best of the nativist movement without compromising their principles. "Our whole safety, in my judgment depends upon floating

[9] Chase-Sumner, December 27, 1854, Chase–N. S. Townsend, May 31, 1855, Chase Papers, HSP; Chase-Julian, January 20, 1855, Julian-Giddings Papers; H. Kreisman–Sumner, September 18, December 28, 1855, Sumner Papers; Charles Dummig–Chase, November 4, 1855, Chase–L. D. Campbell, May 29, 1855, Chase Papers, LC; Rhodes, *History of the United States,* II, 49.

[1] New York *Herald,* December 21, 1854, January 6, February 3, 1855; C. A. Dana–Pike, January 24, 1853, November 22, 1854, Pike Papers.

the K. N. movement in a right kind of public current," the anti-slavery politician M. W. Tappan advised Hale, who was re-elected despite the fact that he remained aloof from the order while his friends infiltrated it in order to capture it for the cause. With the rise of the Republican party in the state, nativism declined.[2]

Charles Sumner's relations with the order were also strained. Totally opposed to bigotry, he was nevertheless compelled to take note of the strength of nativism in New England, and at first he refrained from openly antagonizing it. But although he had been advised to be careful and was anxious for re-election, in 1855 he denounced the Know-Nothings and their principles. That German newspapers widely copied his remarks was not surprising. The Massachusetts statesman had lived up to their expectations.[3]

George W. Julian was not in Congress at the time of Know-Nothingism's greatest impact. Nevertheless, considering his vital interest in the formation of a fusion party, his firm antinativist stand was praiseworthy. Calling the movement an "organized scheme of bigotry and proscription, which can only be remembered as the crowning and indelible shame of our politics," he experienced trouble with fellow Republicans who were less radical and less upright than he was. But he himself remained steadfast, and attributed the party's difficulties to "the accursed heresy of nativism which skulked into our camp to divide our friends & break the force of our movement."[4]

Giddings, too, was immovable when it came to Know-Nothingism. "On one thing I am decided," he announced to Chase. "We must have a *Republican* convention known as such and acting without the control of the Know Nothings. . . . You and I owe it to our friends that we stand by our doctrines." And after

[2] M. W. Tappan–Hale, January 30, May 2, 1855, Hale Papers; Sewall, *Hale,* pp. 157–62.
[3] Donald, *Sumner,* pp. 268–70; Hoar, *Autobiography of Seventy Years,* I, 189; Sumner, *Works,* IV, 62–82; H. Kreisman–Sumner, December 28, 1855, Sumner Papers.
[4] Julian, *Political Recollections,* pp. 142–3; Julian–Chase, July 22, 1856, Chase Papers, HSP; Julian–Giddings, January 12, 1855, Giddings Papers.

Governor Henry A. Wise of Virginia in 1855 waged a determined campaign against the nativists, the Ohio radical rejoiced at the victory despite the Southerner's proslavery predelictions. The Know-Nothings must come in on radical terms or not at all, he insisted, satisfied that the defeat in Virginia had shown them that they had reached the end of their road. Bigotry was not part of his makeup.[5]

Giddings's fellow townsman, Benjamin F. Wade, was even more outspoken in his opposition to the restrictive order. In 1854, when the Homestead Bill was under discussion in the Senate, he introduced an amendment making foreigners eligible for its benefits. Explaining that as a descendant of early Puritans and a statesman often at odds with immigrants who supported the Democratic party, he had no particular reason to defend them, he averred that he nevertheless detested bigotry. "These poor men," he said,

> do not deserve the harsh epithets which have been indiscriminately applied to foreigners. Amidst the darkness and barbarism of the middle ages, foreigners and strangers were considered as enemies, and were treated accordingly. . . . But with our glorious Revolution, and with the repeal of the odious alien and sedition law, these illiberal and unjust notions, prejudices and practices passed away, I trust forever. . . . Why, sir, we are all either immigrants or the descendants of immigrants, and it cannot certainly be of much importance at what particular period the emigration took place.

He was perfectly willing for the immigrants to help build up the country. And when Wade was forced to withdraw his amendment in order to facilitate the passage of the bill, Chase immediately moved its reconsideration.[6] In spite of their willingness to be practical, most of the radicals did not easily betray their ideals in order to attract the Know-Nothings.

It cannot be denied that there were exceptions to this fidelity to principle. Henry Wilson and Thaddeus Stevens openly joined

[5] Giddings-Chase, May 1, 1855, Chase Papers, HSP; Giddings-Julian, May 30, 1855, Julian-Giddings Papers.
[6] *Cong. Globe,* 33d Cong., 1st Sess., 1661, 1717.

the organization. Neither of them, however, fully subscribed to its proscriptive tenets. The goal for which both statesmen were working was fusion. Believing that their antislavery convictions would not be compromised, they hoped to strengthen the radical movement by advocating it within the Know-Nothing party.

Henry Wilson benefited greatly from his association with the nativists. His membership in the Know-Nothing order brought about his election to the United States Senate. But it was a phase of his life which he later regretted—he said he would give ten years of his life to wipe out the episode—and it deeply troubled antislavery leaders. "I know you cannot fail to be faithful to this great question of slavery," Theodore Parker cautioned in his letter of congratulations.

> But your connection with the *Know Nothings* makes me fear for other forms of justice. *The Catholics* are even men, the *Foreigners* are men; the North of America is wide . . . enough for them all. I hope you will never give up to *Know Nothings* what was meant for mankind.

Sumner's correspondents also took a dim view of the election of "the authorized national exponent of the Know Nothing creed & party." But Chase assessed the new senator correctly: "Wilson is true as steel on the Slavery question," he wrote, "so are others here. They will break up the order sooner than see it used for the purposes of Slavery." The Massachusetts politician redeemed himself when a few months later he led the antislavery Know-Nothings into the Republican party and never had anything to do with the proscriptive order afterwards.[7]

Thaddeus Stevens also became a member of the nativist party. Fawn Brodie, his latest biographer, has no real explanation for his action, but as she has pointed out, he joined late, deserted early, and made no speeches against Catholics or foreigners. He too was primarily interested in fusion and probably looked upon the order

---

[7] Hoar, *Autobiography of Seventy Years,* I, 189, 215 ff.; Theodore Parker–Wilson, January 29, 1855, Wilson Papers; J. S. Stone–Sumner, January 29, 1855, Sumner Papers; Chase–A. M. Ganzereau, February 14, 1855, Chase Papers, LC; Wilson-Chase, November 17, 1855, Chase Papers, HSP; Wilson, *History,* II, 423, 433.

as the easiest means to attain it. At any rate, he was not in Congress at the time, and when he returned to Washington, it was as a Republican, a leader of a party he had helped found in Pennsylvania.[8]

Although the anti-Nebraska electoral successes in the fall of 1854 would not affect the composition of the House of Representatives until December, 1855, the radicals made the most of their gains in the Senate, and during the short session continued their onslaught against the administration. When Northern Democrats in order to facilitate the execution of the Fugitive Slave Law introduced a bill for the protection of federal officers, Seward, Wade, and other antislavery leaders bitterly attacked it. Sumner moved the repeal of the controversial law as a substitute, but of course the small band of his supporters was still unable to muster more than nine votes in his favor. As the New York *Tribune* pointed out,

> Readers of the debates at a distance may think it all very easy and pleasant on the part of those in the right to maintain their cause here. But when they remember that the Senate and the audience are four fifths on the side of Slavery, as well as the Government, wealth, and fashion of the city, they will more justly appreciate the position of the noble men who *always* stand up to the fight. The speeches yesterday, especially those of Fessenden, Wade and Seward, were encouraging and inspiring, but the vote was small. . . .[9]

While the radicals' position had become easier, they were still far from their goal.

But they were undaunted. Cheered by their election victories, they made plans to carry their organization further and place one of their leading spokesmen into executive office. The obvious candidate for the job was Chase, whose Senate term expired on March 4, 1855. His successor was a Democrat; had the election been held

[8] Brodie, *Stevens,* pp. 121–2. Richard Current, in an earlier biography, attributes Stevens' nativist activities to his penchant for opposition. Current, *Old Thad Stevens,* p. 100.

[9] New York *Tribune,* February 24, 27, 1855.

after the passage of the Kansas-Nebraska Act, Republican papers pointed out, this reverse would never have occurred. But a governor was to be elected in Ohio in the fall, and Eastern papers as well as leading politicians began to work for Chase's nomination.[1]

Among antislavery leaders, the senator from Ohio occupied a position of considerable prestige. Widely known because of his efforts in behalf of the cause, he impressed visitors as "one of the stateliest figures in the Senate." Sumner, Giddings, and Hale were his confidants, and Trumbull regretted the fact that he would not enjoy Chase's company in Congress. Like the Ohioan, the new senator from Illinois still considered himself a Democratic Free-Soiler, and, as he put it, there was in the Senate "scarcely a member whose sympathy and political confidence I can expect fully to possess." Chase's candidacy for governor of Ohio would meet with widespread approval.[2]

At first, the Ohioan was somewhat undecided about the best steps for the future. Ambitious as he was, however, he could be persuaded. "*We must have* such a union of free men as to create a majority power for freedom," a Portland correspondent pointed out to him, and when even former political opponents asked him to run, he found it hard to resist. He met with fellow radicals in New York; the *Tribune* endorsed him, and, after some sparring with the Know-Nothings, he received the nomination in July at a convention in Columbus. "The People's Party," as it was still known, adopted strong anti-Nebraska resolutions, nominated a full ticket, and in effect launched what would soon be called the Republican party on its permanent career. If Joshua Giddings withdrew on the ground that the platform was not radical enough, it was nevertheless so advanced as to upset conservatives elsewhere. And there was a good chance for success.[3]

[1] New York *Tribune,* March 10, May 15, 1855; B. B. Clark–Chase, March 26, 1855; J. M. Ashley–Chase, May 29, 1855, Chase Papers, LC.
[2] Schurz, *Reminiscences,* II, 34; Chase-Hale, January 11, 1856, December 10, 1855, Hale Papers; Giddings-Chase, April 10, 1855, Trumbull-Chase, March 23, 1855, Chase Papers, HSP.
[3] Chase–A. M. Ganzereau, February 14, 1855, B. B. Clark–Chase, March 26, 1855, Chase–L. D. Campbell, May 25, 1855, J. H. Coulter–Chase, May 27, 1855, L. D. Campbell–Chase, May 28, 1855, Chase-

This development was especially pleasing to the radicals because it coincided with John P. Hale's re-election to the Senate. The Ohio campaign would benefit by success in New England, and if Chase's unwillingness to condemn the Know-Nothings in public alienated many Germans, adopted citizens could not really close their eyes to the fact that the nativists refused to endorse him. When the election returns were in, Chase found that he had defeated both of his opponents, Democratic and Whig–Know-Nothing. His triumph was a great victory for radicalism; it marked the progress the antislavery movement had made since the governor-elect first joined the despised Liberty party almost fifteen years earlier.[4]

That summer the radicals cooperated with many foes of slavery expansion to elect friendly candidates to office. In Maine, Wade, Hale, Fessenden, and other political leaders campaigned for the Republican ticket. Nathaniel P. Banks, a moderate Massachusetts Republican, on this occasion went so far as to announce his willingness to let "the Union slide," while Wade remarked that the Whig party was not only dead, but that "it already stinketh." He also offended conservatives by declaring that the Union was virtually gone because of the hatred between North and South. The only way to save it, he advised, was to divorce it completely from any connection with slavery. If the ticket lost, the Republican party had nevertheless been launched on a radical keel. In Pennsylvania, where the organization of the new party had been delayed, the extremists nominated the antislavery leader Passamore Williamson for canal commissioner. Because of conservative pressure, he had to be withdrawn, but the radicals could point out that the ticket lost despite this precaution. They would be firmer

---

Campbell, June 2, 1855, Chase Papers, LC; New York *Tribune,* May 18, 1855; New York *Herald,* May 17, July 17, 1855; John Sherman, *John Sherman's Recollections of Forty Years in the House, Senate and Cabinet* (Chicago, 1895), pp. 76–7.

[4] H. Kreisman–Sumner, September 18, 1855, Chase-Sumner, October 15, 1855, Sumner Papers; New York *Tribune,* October 7, 11, 27, 1855.

next time. And in New York, Seward openly abandoned the Whigs and declared himself a Republican.[5]

These events indicated that the fusion movement, now increasingly called Republican, was more than a temporary expedient. The radicals had finally found a common political home. "I am so happy that you & I are at last on the same platform & in the same political pew," wrote Sumner to Seward. "I feel stronger for it." Even Giddings appreciated the New Yorker's efforts. "Seward has now taken hold of the Republican movement in earnest," he wrote to Chase, and Theodore Parker wholeheartedly agreed. Radical Republicanism was off to a good start. How the extremists would conduct themselves in the new party remained to be seen.[6]

Almost from the beginning, the radicals proved themselves to be the most active Republicans. Their driving force was to spur on the party for years to come, and their political talent would serve it well. Above all, they would always seek to induce it to move forward to ever more advanced positions.

An opportunity for the radicals to show their strength arose very quickly. When the new Congress met, the anti-Nebraska representatives had a plurality. Not all of these were extremists, but those who were were especially anxious to elect a Republican speaker. Giddings, as the oldest member of the House, had ambitions for the position. He was too outspoken, however, and it was evident that it would be impossible to elect him. But a moderate Republican like N. P. Banks might be successful, if only the Re-

[5] Fred Harvey Harrington, *Fighting Politician: Major General N. P. Banks* (Philadelphia, 1948), p. 26; Portland *Advertiser*, August 15, 22, 1855; Fessenden, *Fessenden*, I, 50; Erwin Stanley Bradley, *Simon Cameron: Lincoln's Secretary of War* (Philadelphia, 1956), p. 107; Walter, Dusinberre, *Civil War Issues in Philadelphia, 1856–1868* (Philadelphia, 1965), p. 52; William Birney–Sumner, November 9, 1855, Sumner Papers; Giddings-Chase, October 16, 1855, Chase Papers, HSP.

[6] Sumner-Seward, October 15, 1855, Theodore Parker–Seward, December 23, 1855, Seward Papers; Giddings-Chase, October 15, 1855, Chase Papers, HSP.

publican members could be kept firm.[7] It was the radicals' task to see that this was done.

They did not falter. Bored and tired as Wade was of his work in the capital, he wrote home that he had to keep his "weak brother of the House" steady. Giddings declared publicly that the anti-slavery coalition would support no candidate for speaker who was not pledged "to organize the standing committees of the House by placing on each a majority of the friends of freedom, who are favorable to making reports on all petitions committed to them...." But the difficulty was that the Know-Nothing problem was interfering with the election of a presiding officer. "I am an antislavery Democrat," wrote W. H. Nichols to Chase, "and will not vote for a Know Nothing." And Banks had joined the order.[8]

One of the new members of the House was Schuyler Colfax, politician, newspaperman, and antislavery leader from Indiana. While his radicalism was tempered by his ambition, he was nevertheless able to do much to publicize the cause and did not hesitate to use his newspaper connections to boost his fame. From the very beginning, his winning personality made him popular with his colleagues, friends and opponents alike. Now he exerted his influence to keep the Northern phalanx firm. As he said to William A. Richardson of Illinois and Alexander H. Stephens of Georgia, who predicted that after an all-night session on January 13 there would be no Banks men, "Wait and see." And the Republican lines held.[9]

The protracted balloting had a depressing effect on the country. "And you are still balloting for speaker," wrote Julian to Giddings in January. "What a spectacle! What a pitiful result of the great revolution of 1854!" E. S. Hamlin, the antislavery editor in

[7] McKee, *The National Conventions*, p. 86; Giddings-Bailey, November 11, 1855, Julian-Giddings Papers; M. H. Nichols–Chase, December 11, 1855, Chase Papers, LC; Hale–Theodore Parker, December 16, 1855, Hale Papers.

[8] Wade–Mrs. Wade, January 20, 1856, Wade Papers; New York *Herald*, December 17, 1855; M. H. Nichols–Chase, December 11, 1855, Chase Papers, LC.

[9] Brooks, *Washington in Lincoln's Time*, p. 30; Colfax-Wheeler, December 28, 1855, January 13, 1856, Colfax Papers, LC.

Cincinnati, was equally perturbed. "Our friends in the House are going through a severe ordeal," he wrote to Charles Sumner. "It strikes me that, were I a member of that body, I would go, after a little, for an adjournment *sine die*. The people can go without legislation as long as the Administration can without money." But the voting continued.[1]

By the beginning of February, the speakership controversy was reaching its climax. "All is bustle excitement & confusion in the Hall," reported Giddings. "There is nervousness among the members of this body never witnessed at any former time. This is occasioned by a very general feeling that we are to have an election today or tomorrow." Because he had been accustomed to defeat "for twenty years," he was not at all certain that this feeling was justified. But he was satisfied. Having worked hard to keep waverers in line, he merely hoped for the best, content that the party had been established and "firmly consolidated."[2]

Giddings's pessimism was premature. On the night before the election, a Republican caucus met. Many members were in favor of giving up the struggle. But William A. Howard, a radical representative from Michigan, declared that he was the first man nominated to Congress on a Republican ticket, that his constituents had entrusted him with the Republican banner, and that he would stand by the flag even if he were alone. His address rallied the others, and on February 2, Banks was elected.[3]

Congress recognized the radicals' part in the Republican triumph by giving Joshua Giddings, as the oldest member, the honor of administering the oath to the new speaker, and the veteran antislavery stalwart was so excited that he was unable to sleep at night. "Our victory is most glorious," he reported to his family.

[1] Julian-Giddings, January 12, 1856, Julian-Giddings Papers; Hamlin-Sumner, January 17, 1856, Sumner Papers.

[2] Giddings–L. M. Giddings, February 1, 1856, Julian-Giddings Papers.

[3] Martha Bigelow, "The Political Services of William Alanson Howard," *Michigan History*, XLII (March, 1958), 10; Livingstone, *Livingstone's History of the Republican Party*, I, 63.

I have never witnessed one of such thrilling, such intense interest. At 7 o'clock last evening I administered the oath of office to Mr. Banks in the presence of more than 3,000 people, amid the cheering of men, the flourishing of handkerchiefs and unrivalled demonstrations. Outsiders lost all respect for decorum. They rushed into the hall, shook me and others by the hand, some congratulated us, others unable to speak only gave expression to their feeling by tears & silence. . . . We immediately adjourned, but it required half an hour or more to get out of the hall.[4]

At the very beginning of the party's history, the radicals had played their role of stiffening it well. They would continue to do so for years to come.

The newly organized Republican party still had to prove itself cohesive in the presidential contest which it faced in 1856. Again the radicals took a leading position in the organization's councils. They helped keep it together, steered it reasonably clear of Know-Nothing entanglements, and saw to it that its platform was forthright. And they took a great deal of interest in the nominee.

At first, the ultras thought that they might secure the prize for one of their own. As early as May, 1855, James M. Ashley, the radical politician from Toledo, sought to further Chase's chances for the nomination, and his candidate proved most receptive. Chase's election as governor greatly encouraged his backer. But Ashley cautioned him against possible pitfalls: He must not be mistaken for a fanatic. "I regret that the New York Tribune, in speaking of you should have used the term '*Abolitionist,*'" the Toledo politician wrote.

I am half inclined to think it done purposely and for effect. I hope it was not, but really it does you no good. Our Republican papers ought to call the attention of the Tribune to it, and ask it to make the distinction between an Abolitionist and a Republican.

[4] Giddings–L. M. Giddings, February 3, 1856, Julian-Giddings Papers.

Ashley continued actively to further the Ohioan's prospects.[5]

Other radicals also nursed hopes, but careful observers saw clearly that no outstanding antislavery leader had a chance. "I think neither Seward nor Chase could be elected," commented Schuyler Colfax. "Sumner don't think of such a thing. Senator Wilson has suggested Trumbull of Ills., one of our most doubtful States. . . . Many want Hale on the ticket for Prest. or Vice & then have him stump the Union." He himself thought John C. Frémont, Thomas Hart Benton's son-in-law, the most promising possibility.[6]

Frémont's availability had occurred to others also. Famous throughout the country as the "Pathfinder" of the West, the explorer had come to the radicals' attention because of his firm stand against slavery in California at the time of the Golden State's admission into the Union. Wade considered him perfectly suitable, especially since the Ohio senator was worried about the candidacy of John McLean, the conservative justice of the Supreme Court, who was being groomed for the nomination by political friends. Long before the convention met, many radicals had settled for Frémont as an acceptable alternative to a conservative candidate.[7]

In the meantime, the presidential maneuvering had been overshadowed by events in Kansas. As the acid test of Stephen A. Douglas's idea of popular sovereignty, the territory had attracted wide attention. After both proslavery and free state immigrants had entered the area, a territorial legislature had been elected by proslavery elements helped by border crossers from Missouri,

[5] Ashley-Chase, May 29, 1855, October 21, 22, 1855, January 18, 1856, R. Errett–Chase, November 16, 1855, Chase Papers, LC; Chase–K. S. Bingham, October 19, 1855, Chase Papers, HSP.

[6] Colfax-Wheeler, January 13, 1856, Colfax Papers, LC.

[7] Jessie Frémont's MS Memoirs, Frémont Papers, University of California, Berkeley; Wade–Mrs. Wade, March 30, 1856, Wade Papers; Wade-Fessenden, April 15, 1856, Fessenden Papers; Wade-Chase, May 5, 1856, Chase Papers, HSP; Colfax-Wheeler, April 11, May 8, 1856, Colfax Papers, LC.

while the enemies of the institution organized a free state government at Topeka. The President promptly recognized the territorial government, and the resulting confusion caused bitter debates in Congress. Seward, Wade, Hale, and other radicals scathingly attacked the administration's Kansas policy; Southerners and their supporters heatedly defended it. Any untoward event, any spark, might set off serious trouble in Congress as well as in the territory.[8]

Charles Sumner's speech, "The Crime Against Kansas," provided that spark. Carefully thought out and delivered on May 19–20, 1856, the address was filled with vituperation. Before he had even reached the main part of his oration, Sumner savagely castigated not only Stephen A. Douglas, but also Andrew P. Butler of South Carolina. "The Senator from South Carolina," he said,

> has read many books of chivalry, and believes himself a chivalrous knight, with sentiments of honor and courage. Of course he has chosen a mistress to whom he has made his vows, and who, though ugly to others, is always lovely to him; though polluted in the sight of the world, is chaste in his sight—I mean the harlot, Slavery. For her, his tongue is always profuse in words. . . . The frenzy of Don Quixote, in behalf of his wench, Dulcinea del Toboso, is all surpassed.

Then he launched upon a bitter attack upon the administration's Kansas policy.[9]

The address was not Sumner's best. The personal references were so offensive, and the bad taste with which they were uttered was so evident, that the senator would probably have caused considerable harm to the radical cause had not his opponents made him a martyr. But this they did. Two days after he had spoken, Preston Brooks, the South Carolinian's relative and a member of the House of Representatives, stalked into the Senate chamber,

[8] Nevins, *Ordeal of the Union,* II, 416 ff.; Smith, *Parties and Slavery,* p. 153; Wilson, *History,* II, 462 ff.; New York *Tribune,* April 15, 1856.
[9] *Cong. Globe,* 34th Cong., 1st Sess., Ap., 529–47.

where Sumner was sitting at his desk, and struck him until he sank to the floor.

Public sentiment in the North turned immediately against the assailant. To attack a defenseless man was an outrage; Sumner's injuries kept him away from Congress for a long time so that his empty seat became an effective symbol of his martyrdom. To make matters worse, on the day of the senator's address, proslavery forces in Kansas raided the free-state city of Lawrence. Joshua Giddings, who was in bad health and had recently fainted on the floor of the House, hurriedly returned to Washington to seek Brooks's expulsion; in the Senate, radical members indignantly denounced the attack and became more determined than ever not to yield to the South. When Senator Robert Toombs of Georgia introduced a compromise measure designed to settle the Kansas problem, they attacked it incessantly, and although they were unable to defeat it, they killed it in the House.[1] They were no longer interested in compromise.

The radicals had laid the groundwork carefully for the presidential campaign. In the first place, they took a prominent part in the Republican mass convention which on February 22 assembled at Pittsburgh to effect a permanent organization of the party. Julian, Lovejoy, Chandler, and Durkee served on the committee on national organization; Giddings, Lovejoy, and Julian delivered extremist speeches. As the Indiana politician recalled many years later, "it was the element of uncalculating radicalism which baffled the policy of timidity and hesitation and saved the cause."

Then they grappled with the Know-Nothings. On the day of the Republican meeting, the Americans convened at Philadelphia to nominate Millard Fillmore, only to see a large part of the

[1] Donald, *Sumner*, pp. 289 ff.; New York *Tribune*, May 26, 1856; James Pike, *First Blows of the Civil War* (New York, 1879), p. 343; Giddings–L. A. Giddings, May 8, 28, 1856, Julian-Giddings Papers; B. W. Richmond–Sumner, May 23, 1856, Sumner Papers; New York *Tribune*, July 4, 1856; Nevins, *Ordeal of the Union*, II, 471–72; Rhodes, *History of the United States*, II, 149–51; Sumner, *Works*, IV, 137–256.

Northern delegation, the "North Americans," split off and prepare to join the Republicans. The radicals now bestirred themselves to prevent any truckling to the seceding "North Americans." As astute observers were able to see, in the long run no alliance between the two groups was possible. The Know-Nothings' conservatism would never mix with the Republicans' radicalism, and radical emissaries were at work among the North Americans to keep them on the path of antislavery. The nativists would have to subordinate their tenets to Republican principles.[2]

By the time the Republican convention met on June 17 at Philadelphia, all signs were pointing towards Frémont. That the Pathfinder was not averse to a nomination became obvious on March 17, when he wrote a letter of support to Charles Robinson, the leader of the Free State faction in Kansas. To be sure, many radicals doubted the Californian's reliability, but because of great conservative pressure for a moderate candidate, Frémont's nomination seemed promising. By astute work in the North American convention, the stalwart antislavery men overcame the danger that the nativist seceders might endorse McLean in order to force the Republicans to fall in line, and when the Republicans finally assembled at Philadelphia, Frémont was nominated with the radicals' blessing.[3]

How important the ultras were at Philadelphia was shown by the prominence of their speakers. Lovejoy, Hale, Wilson, and Giddings all addressed the convention, and even though Lovejoy especially had a reputation for extremism, his endorsement of

[2] *Proceedings of the First Three Republican National Conventions, 1856, 1860 and 1864* (Minneapolis, 1893), pp. 7–14; George W. Julian, "The First Republican National Convention," *American Historical Review*, IV (January, 1899), 313–22; *National Era*, March 6, 1856; Wilson, *History*, II, 508–9; Richard Mott–Chase, February 21, 1856, Chase Papers, LC; Dr. John Paul–Chase, February 24, 1856, Chase Papers, HSP.

[3] Jessie Frémont's MS Memoirs, Frémont Papers; Bailey–Chase, February 21, 1856, Chase Papers, LC; C. F. Adams–Sumner, April 1, 1856, E. G. Loring–Sumner, April 9, 1856, Sumner Papers; Colfax-Wheeler, April 11, May 1, 8, 1856, Colfax Papers, LC; Wade-Fessenden, April 15, 1856, Fessenden Papers; Nevins, *Ordeal of the Union*, II, 469; Koerner, *Memoirs*, II, 14.

Frémont was well received. "Many moderate and conservative men were both surprised and delighted with the reasonableness of Mr. Lovejoy's views and position," reported the New York *Tribune* correspondent. "All around us we heard them say, at the close of his speech, if that is Abolitionism, we are Abolitionists." David Wilmot, Thaddeus Stevens, and James M. Ashley also took a significant part in the proceedings, Wilmot particularly distinguishing himself by reporting the platform.

The platform was all that the radicals could desire. After citing the principles of the Declaration of Independence and affirming their devotion to the Constitution and the Union, the Republicans asserted their conviction that Congress possessed the power to outlaw slavery in the territories, a power it ought to use to prohibit "those twin relics of barbarism—Polygamy and Slavery." They called for the immediate admission of Kansas as a free state, denounced the Ostend Manifesto for the acquisition of Cuba, advocated a railroad to the Pacific, and invited men of similar opinions to unite with them. So explicit was the platform that the hostile press averred that "in the event of Frémont's election there will be a power behind the throne composed of Seward, Sumner, Wilson, Hale and Greeley." The radicals had every reason to be content.[4]

Success seemed certain. Sumner, Seward, Wade, Howard, all thought that Frémont would win. And why should they not believe in his victory? The year 1856 had been one of progress for them. Despite the hostility of Know-Nothings and other elements with whom he had refused to compromise, on the last day of February, Ben Wade had been re-elected senator from Ohio. "It is a novel spectacle indeed, and one which five years ago no prophet could have foretold," he wrote to Chase in exultation about the political revolution caused by the Kansas-Nebraska Act, "that B. F. Wade the Abolitionist and disunionist would be elected to the Senate of the United States, and that archagitator and Abolitionist S. P. Chase would be the Gov. of Ohio to certify to his credentials."

[4] *Proceedings of the First Three Republican Conventions*, pp. 15–82; New York *Tribune*, June 20, 1856; New York *Herald*, June 27, 1856.

Then, in July, Owen Lovejoy had been nominated for Congress in Ottawa, Illinois. Much as his candidacy upset the conservatives —even Lincoln, who later supported him, admitted that the news had turned him "blind"—the veteran antislavery fighter won the election, and another staunch radical entered Congress. As for Sumner, after his martyrdom, there could be little doubt about his re-election. The outlook for a Republican victory seemed most favorable.[5]

The first state to go to the polls was Maine, where radical prospects looked especially good because of the energetic campaign waged by Hannibal Hamlin. The senator, who had long cooperated with various antislavery leaders, had until 1856 remained faithful to the Democratic party. Although he had opposed the Kansas-Nebraska Bill and had voted against it, he had continued his lifelong association with the Democrats. But eventually, Pierce's ever more insistent policy in support of slavery had alienated him. The President's message in 1856 seemed disgusting, the attack on Sumner depressing, and Hamlin considered the advisability of resigning his seat. At last, he formally declined a committee assignment as a Democrat, joined the Republican party, and was promptly nominated for the governorship. He won a stunning triumph in September.[6]

The national elections, in spite of all Republican optimism, proved disappointing. Buchanan was elected President and important states favored the Democrats. But the radicals were still hopeful. In spite of temporary setbacks—they had failed to nominate their candidate for governor in Massachusetts—in spite of their chagrin about the Democratic victory, they had made great

[5] Seward-Sumner, October 26, 1856; Sumner-Howe, September 21, 1856, Howard-Sumner, October 26, 1856, Sumner Papers; Wade-Schouler, August 2, 1856, William Schouler Papers, Massachusetts Historical Society; *National Era,* March 6, 1856; Wade-Chase, March 7, 1856, Chase Papers, HSP; I. N. Phillips–O. G. Lovejoy, December 23, 1895; Earle Parker—"General," January 9, 1909, Lovejoy Papers; Lincoln–David Davis, July 7, 1856, David Davis Papers.

[6] Hamlin, *Hamlin,* pp. 281–91, 305–17; Steven Emery–Hamlin, February 1, May 27, June 9, 1856, Hamlin Papers; New York *Tribune,* June 13, 1856.

advances. "We have lost the battle," wrote Chase, "but are stronger than anything except victory could make us. Let us profit by past mistakes. . . ." Colfax was equally optimistic, and Wade agreed. "Our enemies will find," he commented, "that one more such victory will result in their utter annihilation." Even Sumner, who was recuperating from his wounds, was able to say, "Our cause looks grandly. The future at least is ours."[7] Radical Republicanism had become a permanent force in national politics.

[7] Harrington, *Banks*, pp. 38–41; Chase-Sumner, November 8, 1856, Sumner–E. L. Pierce, November 15, 1856, Sumner Papers; Wade-Schouler, November 19, 1856, Schouler Papers; Colfax-Wheeler, November 13, 1856, Colfax Papers, LC.

CHAPTER

III

Keeping
the Party Firm

THE REPUBLICAN PARTY with over one million votes
had made a good showing in 1856, but what was to be its destiny
in the long run? Would it be merely a temporary grouping held
together by nothing more than immediately pressing issues arising
from the repeal of the Missouri Compromise, or was it to be a
permanent organization dedicated to the prevention of the spread
of slavery? This question would be decided in the four years preceding the outbreak of the Civil War, and the radicals were determined to see to it that it was resolved in favor of principle.

The problem of the party's fundamental direction arose immediately after the presidential election. So vast a number of
people had flocked to the Republican banners that the organization's original zeal was bound to be questioned. As Colfax explained to Sumner,

> You have already noticed that the enormous vote for Frémont,
> & the cool, inflexible defiant tone of the Republican Repre-
> sentatives, so unusual after a political defeat, have astounded
> the Proslavery leaders. It has given us peace & quiet here instead
> of insolence and attack. . . . But this truce is only the result of

terror not Principle. Let the reaction come they calculate upon; & it be understood that the Republican party has ceased to be a power in the land, & the tide of Slavery aggression will rise higher & more sweepingly & menacingly than before.

Giddings, too, realized the danger. Pinpointing the problem in a letter to Chase, he wrote:

> In New England and through all the free States the fogies of our own party are studying policy. They believe in outwitting truth, in obtaining a victory by cunning, and have no faith in principle. This party is much smaller than it was . . . , and really our difficulty has always been with this class. I am seeking to elevate the moral feelings of these men.[1]

Chase was also aware of the problem. Replying to Giddings a few days later, he repeated his conviction that either slavery or freedom must perish. "My idea is this," he explained,

> Let those of us who are prepared to do so take the ground of no Slavery outside of Slave States & no favor of the National Government to Slavery anywhere, boldly avowing that we ex-pect as the consequence of such action that Slavery will be abolished everywhere . . . by the State Governments. Let us get rid of that cold indifference to Slavery as a system which some of our prominent men seem anxious to display. . . .

Above all, however, he wanted the party kept true to principle. As he put it in a letter to Sumner, "It always seemed to me that our friends committed an act of positive injustice as well as of impolicy in narrowing their issue during the last campaign to the mere question of freedom or Slavery for Kansas." In considering the challenges to idealism, he might also have mentioned the economic problems which would have to be met, for in spite of the Republicans' failure to agree on such issues as the tariff, home-steads, and internal improvements, these questions could not be avoided. Eventually the party would make a strong appeal to farmers seeking land, industrialists eager for protection, and businessmen interested in aid to private enterprise, although the

[1] Colfax-Sumner, January 2, 1857, Sumner Papers; Giddings-Chase, January 2, 1857, Chase Papers, HSP.

radicals were determined that antislavery must remain the corner-stone of the organization.[2]

In some ways, the Democrats provided their most deter-mined opponents with ammunition in their fight against com-promise. Undaunted by the failure of his administration, the out-going President, Franklin Pierce, took advantage of his last annual message to Congress to denounce the entire Republican party as a cover for abolitionists, subversive and dangerous to the per-manence of the Union. The indictment failed to distinguish be-tween radicals and conservatives, and in a series of able speeches, Fessenden, Wade, and Wilson, among others, turned the tables upon their antagonists. In view of the broad attack upon their party, they found it easy to define Republican principles in terms acceptable to radicals and conservatives alike.[3]

But the Democrats went even further. Two days after the new President, James Buchanan, had taken office, the Supreme Court, in the Dred Scott decision, so completely vindicated John C. Calhoun's doctrines of the legality of Southern institutions in the territories that the Republican principle of slavery restriction itself seemed to fall under judicial ban. And the language used by Chief Justice Roger B. Taney, who asserted that at the time of the adoption of the Constitution Negroes had possessed no rights which a white man was bound to respect, was so offensive that conservative and radical Republicans alike were utterly repelled by it.

Although it has been asserted that the decision was merely the result of the determination of Northern dissenters to bring up the slavery question, there can be little doubt that several of the Southern justices were as anxious as their Northern colleagues to incorporate their favorite notions in the fundamental law of the

---

[2] Chase-Giddings, January 7, 1857, Giddings Papers; Chase-Sumner, May 1, 1857, Sumner Papers. Cf. Andrew Wallace Crandall, *The Early History of the Republican Party* (Boston, 1930), pp. 92–96.

[3] James D. Richardson, ed., *A Compilation of the Messages and Papers of the Presidents,* 1789–97 (Washington, 1896–99), V, 398; New York *Tribune,* December 5, 19, 26, 1856.

land. Moreover, neither Justice Benjamin R. Curtis nor his colleague John McLean, the two dissenters, was radical by any stretch of the imagination. And, an extremist like George W. Julian seems to have been taken completely by surprise. "How shall we meet the issue tendered us in the Scott case?" he queried, expressing his conviction that many Republicans would become more radical as a result—so radical that they would support Gerrit Smith's notions of federal interference with slavery in the states. "The strides of slavery & the timid policy of republican leaders . . . are bringing earnest men into this position," he asserted.[4]

That the case would be useful to them occurred to many radicals. "The decision of the Supreme Court . . . has aroused many to the encroachments of the slave power," wrote Frederick A. Seward, the senator's son. "Light is dawning strong and clear." Chase agreed with this conclusion. Certain that Buchanan's administration thus far had done a great deal for the Republicans, he cited the decision in the Dred Scott case as an example. And John Jay, Sumner's abolitionist friend, informed him that the Supreme Court's verdict was aiding the cause it was intended to subvert.[5]

The radicals' assessment was correct. In the face of so sweeping a proslavery pronouncement, distinctions between radical and conservative Republicans no longer seemed clear. James Rood Doolittle, the new senator from Wisconsin, who was anything but extreme, sounded radical when he first came to Washington. His success was considered a great triumph for the party, and when, in 1858, he wrote to Sumner that the senator's empty seat would inspire Republicans "with a deep sense of atrocious wrong

[4] E. S. Corwin, "The Dred Scott Decision in the Light of Contemporary Legal Doctrine," *American Historical Review*, XVII (October, 1911), 53; George Fort Milton, *The Eve of the Conflict: Stephen A. Douglas and the Needless War* (New York, 1934), pp. 250–1, are among those considering the Northern justices culpable; for the opposite point of view, cf. Allan Nevins, *The Emergence of Lincoln* (New York, 1950), II, 473–7; Julian-Chase, March 24, 1857, Chase Papers, HSP.

[5] F. A. Seward–Sumner, April 23, 1857; Chase-Sumner, May 1, 1857; John Jay–Sumner, April 14, 1857, Sumner Papers.

... and at the same time with ... fixed determination which knows no such word as fail," he expressed the thoughts of many extremists. That Zachariah Chandler, who entered Congress at the same time, was willing to use entirely different methods to gain his ends, including even the risk of force, was not yet evident. And what was true of Doolittle was equally true of Preston King of New York, James Dixon of Connecticut, and others. Fundamentally conservative, during the years before the war these senators sounded almost as unyielding as their radical colleagues. Against the onslaughts of a common opponent, radicals and conservatives had no choice but to stand together.[6]

In spite of this show of unity, there were deep cleavages between the two factions of the party which not even Justice Taney's decision could erase. Whether correctly or not, Sumner, Wilson, Wade, Hale, Seward, Giddings, and Lovejoy were still considered the vanguard of the movement. Such newcomers as John Covode and Zachariah Chandler were not yet well enough known, but before long, they too would rank with the advanced Republicans.[7]

What gave the leading radicals prominence was their intrepid stand in and out of Congress. People remembered Ben Wade's reply to Senator George E. Badger of North Carolina during the Kansas-Nebraska debates. "There was one argument made by the Senator from North Carolina," he had said,

> which struck me as exceedingly singular. He has set forth all the beauties of this patriarchal institution, as he calls it, to show the affectionate relation existing between him and his slaves. ... So wedded was he to the idea that he could not exist anywhere without his old friends, as he called them, and yet he could not take his old "mammy", as he called her, who nursed

[6] New York *Tribune,* January 24, 1857; Doolittle-Sumner, February 2, 1858, Sumner Papers; Bailey-Chase, May 16, 1858, Chase Papers; HSP; *Cong. Globe,* 35th Cong., 1st Sess., 164, 626, 1134.

[7] New York *Herald,* June 22, August 27, 1856; January 20, 1858, November 11, 1859; Cox, *Three Decades of Federal Legislation,* p. 75; Joseph Medill–Lincoln, July 5, 1860, RTL.

him and brought him up to manhood, into that Territory. Why? Because, notwithstanding these intimate relations, he could not take her there, because he could not have the right to sell her when he got there.

Northerners also relished Fessenden's reply to Senator Butler of South Carolina, who, in 1854, had announced that if Fessenden's sentiments were typical of the North, he wanted dissolution of the Union right away. "Do not delay it on my account," was the rejoinder, "do not delay it on account of anybody at the North." And of course Sumner, though absent, still fascinated the public. It seemed like a sign from heaven that both Senator Butler and Representative Brooks died within less than one year after the attack upon Sumner, and in January, 1857, the Massachusetts legislature re-elected him almost unanimously. Other senators and representatives were equally known, their inflexible stand marking them not only as leaders, but as radicals as well.[8]

And the antagonism between the party's radical, moderate, and conservative wings did not disappear. Different in their aims, origin, and methods, these groups might coalesce temporarily, but they were rarely able to forget their differences.

The 1857 gubernatorial race in Massachusetts was a case in point. The moderates favored N. P. Banks, who had distinguished himself as the first Republican speaker of the House, but the radicals, who distrusted him, sought to prevent his nomination. Unreconciled when their efforts failed, they remained petulant. "Mr. Banks and his friends will probably try to consolidate the party on the basis of *great moderation*," wrote Charles Francis Adams to Sumner, "and we, the old set of earnest antislavery men, shall continue to occupy the same position that we have done for many years. Mr. George Lunt calls us the flower pots of the parterre, put out from time to time to add a little ornament to the

[8] *Cong. Globe,* 33rd Cong., 1st Sess., Ap., 313; William W. Williams, *History of Ashtabula County, Ohio, with Illustrations and Biographical Sketches of Its Pioneers and Most Prominent Men* (Philadelphia, 1878), p. 69; Sumner, *Works,* XIII, 190; IV, 408–9, 392; Chase-Sumner, June 20, 1859, Wilson-Sumner, January 20, 1857, Sumner Papers.

more homely parts." But, he concluded, "even flower pots are useful," and the radicals saw to it that in spite of the moderate governor, the Bay State led the nation in antislavery measures.[9]

In Indiana, there was also a sharp conflict among the various wings of the party. Firmly in control of the organization such moderates as Oliver P. Morton and his backers kept to a minimum the influence of the radicals. "We have a very mean scurvy pack of politicians here in our so-called republican party," Julian complained, "doughfaces at heart, whose knavery for the past two years has been greatly facilitated by Know Nothingism; & they have succeeded to a great extent in ostracising me from politics." But in spite of the moderate character of the party, it lost the 1856 elections. "We are the blackest State north by all odds," Julian lamented in the spring of 1857. "Republicanism is an exceedingly diluted article here & Know Nothingism still exists to distract & embarrass our cause."[1] It was not until 1860 that the intrepid radical was returned to Congress.

Similar difficulties existed in other states. While the radicals controlled the governorship of Ohio, they were faced with considerable opposition within the party. In Pennsylvania and New Jersey, the conservatives were so strong that only an occasional stalwart was able to succeed.[2] Internecine fights had wracked the party virtually everywhere else, but the great test of radicalism was the Territory of Kansas. Still torn by perennial violence, the fertile regions west of Missouri had become a battleground between North and South. Regardless of its intrinsic value, Kansas had emerged as a symbol, and the radicals believed that any yield-

[9] Harrington, *Banks,* pp. 42, 45 ff.; Wilson–Covode, July 25, 1857, John Covode Papers, Historical Society of Western Pennsylvania, Pittsburgh; C. F. Adams–Sumner, June 26, 1857, Sumner Papers; William B. Hesseltine, *Lincoln and the War Governors* (New York, 1955), pp. 19–23.

[1] Ibid., pp. 41–3; Julian–Chase, July 22, 1856, March 24, 1857, Chase Papers, HSP.

[2] New York *Tribune,* August 14, 1857; John W. Jones–Wade, September 16, 1858, Wade Papers; Hesseltine, *Lincoln and the War Governors,* pp. 31 ff.; E. D. Gazzam–Chase, February 12, 1858, Chase Papers, LC.

ing on their part would spell the complete defeat of Republican principles. The only question was how to proceed.

———————

Since radicalism was never an organized movement, the problem of what to do about Kansas presented complications. There was no central directory setting policy; some radicals, often of Eastern origin, believed in one set of actions, while others, often closer to the frontier, embraced opposite opinions. Under the circumstances, it is surprising that the group was as successful as it was; but the opposition was so inept and the population so obviously pro-Northern, that even rifts within the radical camp did not prove decisive. What was important was that the stalwarts tended to stiffen the party, no matter what their policy. Eventually, they were completely successful, and Kansas finally came into the Union as a free—and radical—state.

The difficulty confronting the Republicans involved the existence of two governments in the territory—the officially recognized territorial legislature and the rival "free state" organization. Should they pursue a logically defensible but politically inept course of boycotting all elections for the government sponsored by the administration or should they attempt to capture it? That they had not given up their opposition to the territorial organization they showed during the discussion of the Appropriations Bill of 1857, when they sought to block the salaries of its officers. Of course the motion met with overwhelming defeat, but the point had been made. The basic problem remained, however, and the two leading radical newspapers, the Washington *National Era* and the New York *Tribune* took diametrically opposite stands. Viewing participation as the only way to capture Kansas, the *National Era* came out for a full effort to take over the government, but the *Tribune,* reflecting the vagaries of its quixotic editor, Horace Greeley, urged abstention. The former policy was also endorsed by Henry Wilson, who visited the territory in order to give advice to Kansas Free-Soilers. It was eventually adopted, but the senator alienated some local radicals who accused him of playing into the conservatives' hands.[3]

The passage of the Lecompton Constitution by a territorial convention completely dominated by proslavery elements brought matters to a climax. Grossly unfair, the new basic law contained a slave code of utmost severity which was doubly offensive to the settlers because the authors, completely disregarding Stephen A. Douglas's principles of popular sovereignty, failed to make provision for submitting it to the people. Only the slave clauses of the constitution were to be voted upon; if they were approved, Kansas would be ready to come into the Union as a slave state; if they were rejected, slaves already in the territory would still remain in servitude. And the administration decided that it would have to support the Lecompton Constitution.

That the radicals would do everything in their power to defeat so inequitable an instrument was obvious, but that they would receive help from Stephen Douglas was unexpected. Totally unwilling to have his theories so cavalierly set aside, the senator from Illinois broke with the administration on the issue. James Buchanan tried to threaten him. "Mr. Douglas," he said to the senator, "I desire you to remember that no Democrat ever yet differed from an Administration of his own choice without being crushed." He cited examples dating back to Andrew Jackson, only to be told in no uncertain terms, "Mr. President, I wish you to remember that General Jackson is dead."[4]

Douglas's defection confronted the radicals with a new problem. Should they cooperate with the Little Giant? Was he not on their side in the Kansas struggle? Henry Wilson and Horace Greeley thought so, but most ultras were not so sure. For one thing, they did not trust Douglas; he had caused the whole Kansas trouble with his repeal of the Missouri Compromise, and if he now attempted to curry favor with them, he probably had ulterior

[3] *Cong. Globe,* 34th Cong., 3d Sess., 1031; C. F. Adams–Sumner, May 5, 1857, Sumner Papers; Wilson, *History,* II, 537 ff.; J. M. Walden–Chase, January 14, 1858, Chase Papers, LC.

[4] Rhodes, *History of the United States,* II, 238.

motives. "Never have I seen a slave insurrection before," Wade commented when Douglas first defied the President. Although the Ohioan went to visit the senator from Illinois, he wrote to his wife that while Republicans treated the Democrat courteously, they did not trust him. An election was coming up in Illinois and Douglas merely wanted to be re-elected. Nevertheless, the radicals were willing to let the senator help them. For the moment, they were biding their time.[5]

It was not surprising that these developments upset the Republicans in Illinois. Worried lest they would be left without a party, they sent urgent appeals to Washington to beware. "What does the New-York Tribune mean by it's [sic] constant eulogising, and admiring, and magnifying Douglas?" inquired Abraham Lincoln in a letter to Lyman Trumbull.

> Does it, in this, speak the sentiments of the republicans at Washington? Have they concluded that the republican cause, generally, can be best promoted by sacraficing [sic] us here in Illinois? If so we would like to know it soon; it will save us a great deal of labor to surrender at once.[6]

Trumbull sought to assuage the Illinois party leader. Douglas's action had been so unexpected, he explained, that many Republicans could not refrain from giving him more credit than he deserved. Seward especially had been so anxious for a split within the "so-called democracy," that he and his friends had been "for holding back on our side & letting him take the lead so as to get him committed. . . . Some of our friends here act like fools in running after & flattering Douglas. He encourages it and invites such men as Wilson, Seward, Burlingame, Parrot &c to come & confer with him & they seem wonderfully pleased to go." Promising to do what he could to arrest the movement, Trumbull counseled Lincoln to be patient.[7]

In view of the later controversy about Lincoln's relations with

[5] Thomas, *Lincoln,* pp. 177–8; Ben:Perley Poore, *Perley's Reminiscences of Sixty Years in the National Metropolis* (Philadelphia, 1886), I, 530; Wade–Mrs. Wade, December 20, 25, 1857, Wade Papers.

[6] Lincoln, *Works,* II, 430.

[7] Trumbull-Lincoln, January 3, 1858, RTL.

the radicals, it is interesting to note that the first major problem within the Republican party in which he was involved put him squarely on the side of the most uncompromising elements within the party. To be sure, certain Eastern ultras were willing to yield, but the main opposition to fusion with the Douglas Democrats came from the radicals. On Christmas Day of 1857, Wade explained the situation to Chase: "I do not think any Republican here is at a loss to know the reasons of the course of Douglas," he wrote.

He does not occupy his present position from choice, he is driven to it by the folly and madness of Buchanan under Southern masters. Should Douglas follow in the wake of the Administration and vote to force a Constitution on the people of Kansas against their wish he knows that the whole party at the North would be hopelessly swamped and be even cast out of the Senate. . . . None of us *trust* him. But as he seems just now to be doing a good business for us we think it best to let him have the field & fort . . . What then shall we do. I answer stand proudly by your guns. Roll ever the Republican thunder, avoid all fusion & all compromise. In short, act boldly up to the principles of our good Philadelphia platform, trusting in the strength of our own men and our own principles, and above all not go awhoring after strange gods.

In opposing amalgamation with Douglas's followers, Lincoln could not have asked for more.[8]

Perhaps the firmest opposition to Douglas emanated from Columbus. Chase was not at all willing to sacrifice either party or principle, especially since he harbored presidential ambitions. As early as January, 1858, he agreed with Sumner that it was regrettable to see some Republican statesman and newspapers play into Douglas's hands. Convinced that the Illinois senator was not a suitable ally because of what he had stood for, the governor of Ohio opposed the fusion movement with all his strength. "It is indispensable now," he wrote in May, 1858, to Giddings,

that it should be clearly understood that a great body of the Republicans cannot & will not sacrifice their principles; and it

[8] Wade-Chase, December 25, 1857, Chase Papers, HSP.

should be made clearly to appear that uncertainty in adherence to principle as Republican leaders & the Republican party is far more damaging than the assaults of our opponents.

And he actively supported Lincoln in his senatorial campaign, rendering welcome aid which the candidate never forgot.[9]

Giddings, too, refused to yield to the temptation of making common cause with Douglas. Though he admired the senator's courage and expressed the opinion that in some ways he had more faith in the Little Giant than in "some weak republicans," he wrote a letter to William Dennison of Ohio warning him to co-operate with the anti-Lecompton Democrats, but to leave the Republican party organization intact.[1]

These expressions of firmness were precisely what Lincoln and his friends wanted. And although the danger of a Douglas-Republican fusion was not yet over—there were constant reports of Seward's, Weed's, and Greeley's willingness to sell out the Republicans of Illinois—Lincoln refused to be sidetracked.[2] With the moral support of radicals in all parts of the country, the party remained hostile to the Little Giant. And when Lincoln on June 16, 1858, accepted the Republican nomination for the Senate, he must have been conscious of the help the party's determined wing had given him. His "house divided against itself" speech delivered at the time certainly had a radical tone.

In the meantime, the administration had pushed the bill to admit Kansas under the Lecompton Constitution. Because of Douglas's opposition, the Republicans, radical and conservative, tended to cooperate with him and let him take the limelight. They conferred with him, encouraged him, and promised to make common cause with him. But they did not trust him. In their opinion, the author of the Kansas-Nebraska Act had brought too

[9] Chase-Sumner, January 18, 1858, Sumner Papers; Chase-Giddings, May 5, 1858, Giddings Papers; Lincoln, *Works,* III, 378, 395, IV, 34.

[1] Giddings-Chase, March 18, 1858, Chase Papers, HSP; W. Dennison–Giddings, February 28, 1858, Giddings Papers.

[2] Herndon-Trumbull, December 25, 1857; Norman Judd–Trumbull, March 7, 1858, E. Peck–Trumbull, April 15, 1858, Trumbull Papers, LC; John Wentworth–Lincoln, April 19, 1858, RTL.

much misery upon the country. As Trumbull recalled, by causing the repeal of the Missouri Compromise, Douglas had brought the country to the verge of civil war, and the "people will not forgive him for setting the house on fire, even if he did try to quench the flames before it was entirely consumed."[3]

That the radicals still stood for uncompromising opposition to the slaveholders they showed by their actions in Congress. Greatly encouraged by election results from Kansas, they resolutely fought Buchanan's efforts to have the state admitted under the Lecompton Constitution. Their arguments were strengthened by the fact that the Free-Soilers of Kansas, finally heeding the pleas of Henry Wilson and the *National Era*, had at last decided to participate in territorial elections. They captured the legislature, and although they still refused to vote in the referendum called by the Lecompton convention, a few weeks later in a second election called by the legislature they decisively defeated the constitution.

In spite of this success, to many radicals the outlook for the defeat of Lecompton in Congress did not seem too bright. The administration, which despite the Free-Soilers' boycott considered the first vote on the constitution binding, had patronage, a party organization, and the ruthlessness to push its measures through. John Covode, an active Pennsylvania radical, heard from correspondents in Kansas that the settlers were downcast in expectation of a radical defeat in Washington; Wilson, though unwilling to give up hope, feared the result, and Wade was certain that the President's measure would pass without compromise.[4]

If the radicals were pessimistic, they nevertheless remained pugnacious. In the House, a regular fist fight started when Galusha Grow, the radical whip, stepped over to the Democratic side to confer with John Hickman of Pennsylvania about his objection

[3] Trumbull-Lincoln, January 3, 1858, RTL.
[4] G. W. E. Griffith–Covode, January 3, 1858, Covode Papers, HSWP; Wilson–Sumner, January 18, 1858, Sumner Papers; Wade–T. C. Day, February 15, 1858, T. C. Day Papers, Ohio Philosophical and Historical Society, Cincinnati.

to the Speaker's ruling. "If you want to object, go back to your side of the House, you black Republican puppy," said Lawrence Keitt, a fire-eater from South Carolina. "I will object when and where I please," was the rejoinder. Keitt lunged forward to grab Grow by the throat; the radical defended himself, and a general melee resulted during which congressmen pummeled each other and William Barksdale of Mississippi lost his wig.[5]

In the Senate, too, members almost came to blows, with the radicals bearing the brunt of the attack. In the debates about Lecompton, Senator James S. Green of Missouri called Simon Cameron of Pennsylvania "a damn liar." The Pennsylvanian had implied that his antagonist was no gentleman, and more serious trouble was narrowly avoided when both offered retractions.[6] But the atmosphere remained charged, and a group of radicals decided to take action.

The tense situation in Washington had long irked advanced Republicans. Dueling was considered uncivilized in the North, but the South still adhered to the code. Consequently, when Northerners received a challenge, they were embarrassed. Privately, some were perfectly willing to fight; publicly, however, they neither could nor would sanction the barbarous custom. Rumors of impending duels agitated the capital after the attack on Sumner; both Henry Wilson and Ben Wade were reported ready to give satisfaction. Although Giddings dissuaded both of them, stories subsequently circulated that Wade had given Toombs to understand that he was not only ready to meet him on the field of honor, but that he would choose as his weapon rifles at thirty paces. According to a later account, he had specified that each combatant wear a patch the size of a silver dollar over his heart. He was known as an excellent shot and was never challenged; Anson Burlingame of Massachusetts, however, actually accepted Preston Brooks's demand for satisfaction. Because he named Niagara Falls, Upper Canada, as the meeting place, Brooks,

[5] New York *Evening Post,* February 6, 1858; DuBois and Mathews, *Grow,* p. 173.
[6] New York *Evening Post,* March 17, 1858.

who alleged that he could not travel so far through hostile states, refused. The radicals had proved that they would not shrink from combat.[7]

After the altercation between Cameron and Green, the ultras were to prove again their readiness to fight. Convinced that it was necessary to stop Southern attacks once and for all, three radical senators went so far as to bind themselves to resist further physical aggression. Almost twenty years later, the participants were still so proud of their action that they drew up a memorandum, a copy of which has survived in Chandler's papers. "During the two or three years preceding the outbreak of the slaveholders' rebellion," they wrote:

> the people of the Free States suffered a deep humiliation because of the abuse heaped upon their representatives in both Houses of Congress. This gross personal abuse was borne by many because the public sentiment of their section would have fallen with crushing severity upon them if they had retorted in the only manner in which it could be effectively met and stopped by the personal punishment of their insulters.
> Mr. William H. Seward was the especial object of these insults; and being the admitted leader of the Republicans in the Senate, all men of spirit were insulted through him. . . . On one noted occasion Robert Toombs indulged in such terrible and unjust denunciations of Seward and his followers that the undersigned felt themselves forced to do something to vindicate themselves and their constituents. . . . We consulted long and anxiously. And the result was a League by which we bound ourselves to resent any repetition of this conduct by challenge to fight, and then, in the precise words of the compact, "to carry the quarrel into a coffin."

Conscious of the bloodthirsty ring of this phrase, the signers explained it as the only way in which they could safeguard their manhood in the face of constant threats, and they believed that it had the intended effect. "This arrangement produced a cessation

[7] Giddings–Laura Giddings, May 28, 1856, Julian-Giddings Papers; Giddings-Sumner, July 24, 1856, Sumner Papers; Pierce, *Sumner*, III, 493; Riddle, *Wade*, pp. 245–8; Cincinnati *Daily Gazette*, March 18, 1868; Ashtabula *Sentinel*, June 5, 1856.

of the cause which induced us to make it," they concluded, "and when it became known that some Northern Senators were ready to fight . . . , the tone of . . . insults was at once modified. . . ." Then they certified that but three copies of the memorandum existed, and signed it, Simon Cameron, B. F. Wade, and Z. Chandler. The paper was dated May 26, 1874, and while its contents may have been slightly exaggerated, its substantial authenticity has been generally accepted. James M. Edmunds, the former commissioner of the Land Office and postmaster of the Senate, remembered that Wade let it be known that he would again fight with rifles at twenty paces, with a white paper the size of a dollar pinned over the heart of each combatant. The incident illustrated the spirit of prewar radicalism, even though Simon Cameron, the machine politician from Pennsylvania, was associated with it.[8]

The radicals' struggle against the Lecompton Constitution led to bitter debates in Congress. When Senator James H. Hammond of South Carolina, in a speech in which he praised the allegedly happy lot of Southern slaves and asserted that cotton was king, assailed Northern laborers as "the mudsills of society," Henry Wilson and Hannibal Hamlin immediately sprang to the defense of Northern institutions. Praising the nobility of Northern labor, they boasted of the facility with which the common man could rise in a free state. Toombs attacked the opposition as factious, a characterization which led to heated replies by Wade and Fessenden, the Maine senator telling the Southerner that if he wanted to call a roll of his slaves, he must seek some place other than the Senate chamber. And Chandler delivered his first major speech in Congress.[9]

While their adamant stand showed that the radicals would not yield on fundamentals, it did not mean that they were unreason-

[8] Memorandum, May 26, 1874, Zachariah Chandler Papers, LC; *The Republic*, IV (April, 1875), 194–5; Detroit *Post and Tribune, Chandler*, pp. 143–7; Riddle, *Wade*, pp. 214 ff.

[9] *Cong. Globe*, 35th Cong., 1st Sess., 959–62, 1002–6, 1087 ff.; Wilson, *History*, II, 550–52; Cincinnati *Daily Gazette*, March 11, 1868; New York *Evening Post*, March 17, 1858.

able. Unlike the abolitionists, they were aware of political realities. Consequently, they allowed Douglas to carry much of the burden of the struggle, kept up reasonable relations with their opponents, and even consented to vote for the Crittenden amendment which provided for the submission of the entire constitution to the people. The action disgusted Chase—it meant sacrifice of principle, as he saw it, because in theory at least Kansas might vote for slavery—but it was all part of an arrangement with various opponents of the administration. Having entered into similar combinations in the past himself, the governor of Ohio might have been more understanding.[1]

In the long run, all efforts to block the Lecompton bill proved of no avail. Aided by Northern conservatives afraid of disturbing commercial relations with slaveholders, on March 23, the administration forced the measure through the Senate. But the legislation still had to pass in the House, and the House contained an anti-Lecompton majority. Here too the radicals proved that they were anything but visionary abolitionists. Informed that the only way to defeat the administration was to vote for the House version of Crittenden's proposal, the Montgomery-Crittenden amendment, they came to its support, even Giddings reluctantly voting for it. The maneuver succeeded; the administration refused to accept the amendment in the Senate, and the entire Lecompton proposal was defeated in the House. Radicals had labored with determination to the end to keep "weak brethren" firm.[2]

The result made old Joshua Giddings exceedingly happy. "You are already informed of the result of yesterday . . .," he wrote on April 2 to Chase.

[1] Giddings-Chase, March 18, 1858, Chase—Gerrit Smith, March 30, 1858, Chase—J. J. Crittenden, April 29, 1858, Chase Papers, HSP; Chase-Sumner, September 10, 1859, Sumner Papers; Trumbull-Lincoln, January 3, 1858, RTL; Wade—Mrs. Wade, April 12, 1858, Wade Papers; Sewall, *Hale,* p. 107; DuBois and Mathews, *Grow,* p. 229; Julian, *Giddings,* pp. 346–51.

[2] A. B. Johnson—Sumner, April 1, 1858, Sumner Papers; Giddings-Chase, April 9, 1858, Chase Papers, HSP; Giddings–G. R. Giddings, April 21, 1858, Giddings Papers; Wilson, *History,* II, 557–8; Wade—James Wade, April 1, 1858, Wade Papers.

We are not yet out of the woods yet I hope it may end well . . .
I will endeavor to turn it to the best account in favor of the
radical republicans. It looks now as though the scepter of power
has departed from the democratic party. . . . I hope the Journal
will take the ground that the party are indebted to the radical
portion of the Republican party for its success.

Lovejoy also considered the vote a great triumph,[3] and while
Giddings's claims were exaggerated, there was no denying that
the radicals' refusal to yield on essentials had contributed significantly to keeping the party firm—so firm that even the English
bill, which eventually resulted from the efforts of congressional
committees, ended in failure for the administration. In spite of a
generous offer of land in case the people of Kansas accepted the
Lecompton Constitution, they rejected the proposition.

The radicals' success in blocking the Lecompton Constitution augured well for the elections of 1858. Buchanan had proved
himself so inept and servile to the South that he would have encountered serious difficulties in any case, but since he also had to
contend with a depression which afflicted the country in 1857, his
position was especially weak. The Republicans took advantage of
his troubles, and the radicals again constituted their vanguard.

The most sensational campaign that fall was Douglas's struggle for re-election in Illinois. When Lincoln, despite the opposition of certain Eastern Republicans, challenged the Little Giant,
it was certain that an exciting canvass would follow. And that
Lincoln was a master politician he was to prove in 1858.

In Illinois as elsewhere, the Republican party was divided. The
majority of its supporters was conservative, so much so that
Eastern radicals thought the Republican creed in the state little
better than Douglas's. "At best it is but a white man's party,"
wrote F. W. Bird to Sumner, "& today offers no more hope to the
earnest anti-slavery man than did the Whig party ten years ago."[4]

[3] Giddings-Chase, April 2, 1858, Chase Papers, HSP; Lovejoy–Lucy
Storrs Denham, April 4, 1858, Lovejoy Papers.
[4] F. W. Bird–Sumner, September 14, 1858, Sumner Papers.

But he was not entirely correct. Lincoln was neither an archcon-servative nor an ultraradical. Convinced of the evil of slavery, he was astute enough to know that in a state like Illinois he would have to proceed carefully. Many of the inhabitants were of South-ern origin; imbued with all the prejudices of the frontier as well as those of the South, they generally considered Negroes inferior and would at best respond to appeals to keep territories free in order to make them available to white settlers. Lincoln made the most of this type of argument; but he also refused to give up his princi-ples.

It became evident, when he delivered his acceptance speech, that the future President was not so far distant from the radicals as later observers tended to assume. His insistence that "a house divided against itself cannot stand," that the Union could not endure permanently half slave and half free and that he expected it to cease to be divided, as well as his allegation of a slaveholders' plot against the North and his faith in the ultimate extinc-tion of slavery were all ideas that might have been expressed by any radical. Whatever differences might develop between him and the ultras afterwards, the fact was that, fundamentally, Lincoln and the radicals were looking forward to the same goal: a free democracy untainted by slavery.

Lincoln's skill was severely tested. While Eastern stalwarts deplored the party's lack of antislavery fervor, Illinois conserva-tives complained about its radicalism. Worried about the House Divided speech, they implored him to explain that he did not mean to interfere with slavery in the states, and that he was really not as dangerous as he sounded. But, strengthened by his convic-tions and radical support, he refused to make any retractions. Re-plying to his critic John L. Scripps, who had expressed conservative fears about the candidate's remarks concerning slavery, Lincoln wrote: "The language 'place it [slavery] where the public mind shall rest in the belief that it is in the course of ultimate extinction,' I used deliberately." But he explained that he never meant at the time, nor wished to imply at present, that this sanctioned any power of the federal government to interfere with slavery in the states.[5] His was the doctrine preached by Sumner and Wade, Chandler and Giddings. Only he was more astute. He knew how to use the pressure of the radicals to offset the dead weight of the conservatives and move at his own pace in the direction of progress.

That he was conscious of radical demands as well as of conservative fears he showed in connection with the furor raised by Owen Lovejoy's bid for renomination. Implored to interfere and see to it that a conservative take Lovejoy's place, Lincoln refused. Having been threatened with a bolt by the radicals, he realized the necessity of balancing the two factions. The congressman was renominated, and he corresponded with Lincoln in the most friendly terms.[6]

In the long run, Lincoln succeeded in keeping both wings of the party in his camp. His conservative manager, David Davis, continued as his friend, while Owen Lovejoy deeply appreciated the support which he had received. He told the district convention which nominated him:

> And now I am prepared to say that I am for Lincoln, not because he is an old line whig—to me this is no objection and it is no commendation—but I am for him because he is a true hearted man, and that, come what will, unterrified by power, unseduced by ambition, he will remain true to the great principles upon which the Republican party is organized. I am for him for the same reasons that you and those you represent, are for me.[7]

The radical congressman saw early what many of his colleagues never realized: In Abraham Lincoln they had an ally who would

[5] J. L. Scripps–Lincoln, June 22, 1858, W. Chambers–Lincoln, July 22, 1858, RTL; Lincoln, *Works,* II, 471.

[6] W. H. Lamon–Lincoln, June 9, 1858, Abraham Smith–Lincoln, May 31, June 4, 1858, J. H. Bryant and S. G. Paddock–Lincoln, June 4, 1858, Lovejoy-Lincoln, August 4, 1858, RTL; Lincoln, *Works,* II, 458–9.

[7] David Davis–Lincoln, June 14, 1858, August 2, 3, 15, 1858; Bureau County *Republican,* Extra, June 30, 1858; Chicago *Tribune,* June 9, 1858, RTL.

cooperate with them to the best of his ability. But he would keep his own counsel and act when the time seemed ripe.

Because of the lopsided districting of the state, Lincoln was defeated although the Republicans won a majority of the popular vote. In spite of the dejected letters he received from his supporters, however, he reacted with characteristic courage. "The cause of civil liberties must not be surrendered at the end of *one,* or even one *hundred,* defeats," he wrote. His attitude was not unlike that of many a radical's.[8]

One other campaign that fall which seemed to give the radicals prominence was the New York canvass. In a speech at Rochester, William H. Seward analyzed the points at issue between North and South. "It is an irrepressible conflict between opposing and enduring forces," he said, "and it means that the United States must and will, sooner or later, become either entirely a slave-holding nation or entirely a free-labor nation." Although he had merely expressed his carefully considered opinions of the trends of the time, his opponents were horrified. "The last disastrous defeats of the Northern democracy have emboldened him to throw off the mask, and he now stands boldly before us a more repulsive abolitionist, because a more dangerous one, than Beecher, Garrison or the Rev. Dr. Parker," editorialized the New York *Herald.*[9] To millions of Americans he seemed to be the principal spokesman for the ultras.

But the radicals no longer trusted him. Did he not prevaricate and seek to compromise? And, was he not tied to New York's notorious political manager, Thurlow Weed? "Seward is not doing what he ought to do," William Herndon, Lincoln's radical law partner, had written over a year earlier. "He is getting chilled: he is afraid I fear. Have houris laid their hands upon him and claimed him as their own?" Their fears increased when the New

[8] Horace White–Lincoln, November 5, 1858, David Davis–Lincoln, November 7, 1858, Norman Judd–Lincoln, November 15, 1858, RTL; Lincoln, *Works,* III, 339.
[9] New York *Herald,* October 28, 1858.

Yorker, by speech and vote, had supported an army appropriation bill which other radicals opposed, partially because of their dislike for standing armies, partially because of their apprehension that the military might be used to suppress free soil in Kansas. That he had also supported Buchanan's strong policy toward Great Britain in connection with the perennial problem of searching ships on the high seas did not improve his standing with some extremists, although other radicals joined with him. Severely criticizing the senator's "latitudinarian" views of government, the ultras had correctly assessed his fundamental conservatism years before it became common knowledge. But no open break resulted prior to 1861, and when in 1860 he sought the Republican nomination for the presidency, the Democrats still considered him a "radical abolitionist."[1]

All in all, the elections of 1858 had been most encouraging. Although Joshua Giddings was not renominated, in general the radicals benefited by Republican victories in many Northern states. Among other triumphs, Thaddeus Stevens's return to Congress after an absence of several years was significant. Not only was his great ability recognized at the time—he was even mentioned as a possible candidate for Speaker—but he had won despite the President's effort to defeat him. There was little love lost between Buchanan and his radical fellow townsman, and the administration's failure in the President's home district was a sign of the times. Stevens himself had been confident all along, in spite of the fact that he realized very well that he was "ahead of the people in Anti-Slavery," as he explained the situation to Chase.[2] Such radical representatives as John Covode, Galusha Grow, Owen Lovejoy, and James M. Ashley, among others, were all either elected or re-elected, and before long, Iowa would send

[1] Herndon-Sumner, February 11, 1857, Sumner Papers; New York *Evening Post,* February 3, 5, 17, 1858; J. H. Gibbons–Hale, February 24, 1858, Hale Papers; Giddings-Chase, February 1, June 10, 1858, Chase Papers, HSP; G. A. Nourse–Trumbull, April 27, 1858, Trumbull Papers, LC; New York *Herald,* May 1, 1860.

[2] Giddings-Chase, January 22, 1859, Stevens-Chase, September 25, 1858, Chase Papers, HSP; Stevens-Giddings, n.d., Item No. 1078, Giddings Papers.

to the Senate James W. Grimes, who in spite of his essentially moderate nature was still considered an advanced Republican.

The victories of 1858 did not end the problems troubling the Republican party. Its very size made it inevitable that movements to combine with other opponents of the administration would continue to arise. On the one hand, talk of coalition with Douglas and the anti-Lecompton Democrats had not died down; on the other, conservatives were still actively engaged in watering down Republican principles. Some were ready to revive the old Whig party, especially since Southern ex-Whigs were restive. Most radicals worked indefatigably to defeat these schemes.

The Douglas movement interested not only conservatives, but even such radicals as Henry Wilson. Never reconciled to the failure of Illinois Republicans to endorse the Little Giant, he complained that the party's course in that state was a political crime. Had Republicans only supported the senator, great advantages would have accrued to them, but now Douglas was in a position to dictate terms.[3]

The majority of the radicals, however, totally disagreed, as Chase emphasized when he roundly condemned the Douglas movement. The only reason the senator had ever broken with Buchanan, wrote the governor of Ohio, was that he needed support for his re-election. Fundamentally, the Little Giant was still the candidate of the proslavery party and as such totally unworthy of radical support. A "conspiracy," James M. Ashley termed the Douglas movement, and when in December, 1858, the radicals returned to Washington for the opening of Congress, they were determined to pursue their policies as before. Joshua Giddings, who was about to end his congressional career, emphasized this trend in a letter to Chase. "My active efforts in this city," he wrote, "have been put forth to brace up our men against *concession* and in favor of standing firmly upon our doctrines. I think we shall succeed in this respect. There is far less disposition to modify our platform than I expected to find." Chandler agreed. As he saw it,

[3] E. L. Pierce–Chase, November 5, 1858, Chase Papers, LC.

the old parties' weakness still affected the Democrats. They either had no principles or abandoned them at will. But the Republicans were different and must avoid this pitfall. Men like himself would see to it that they would remain firm.[4]

The radicals were successful. By January, 1859, when Henry Wilson was returned for a second term, the danger of coalition had passed, so that even William Herndon was able to forgive its originators. "I see Wilson is reelected—am glad of it, though I do not much admire him as a warm and chivalrous man . . .," he wrote to Trumbull. "I really wish him success. I have nothing against Wilson and have forgiven the hurt."[5]

One of the reasons for the radicals' opposition to coalition with Douglas was his expansionist foreign policy. Despite the rift between the senator and the administration, both were anxious to bring about the annexation of Cuba. This imperialist venture, certain to add more slave territory to the Union, was anathema to the radicals, who fought it with every weapon at their disposal.

The Buchanan administration again made their task easy. Completely disregarding the stunning defeat which he had sustained in the fall elections, the President prepared a message so truculent that Wade called it "the worst and most dangerous document ever emanating from a President of the United States." Strongly urging the annexation of Cuba and expansion into other parts of Latin America, Buchanan laid the foundation for his lieutenants' demand for $30,000,000 to carry out his imperialist plans. It was the radicals' task to defeat the request.

Because it was no secret that several Republican leaders, Seward and Chandler in particular, were generally in favor of extending the borders of the United States, some Democrats were hopeful of their support. Their actions, however, disappointed the expansionists. Seward prepared a report in which he roundly

[4] Chase-Reed, November 11, 1858, Giddings-Chase, December 12, 1858, Chase Papers, HSP; Ashley-Chase, November 28, 1858, Chase Papers, LC; Chandler–John Clark, December 18, 1858, Chandler Papers.
[5] Herndon-Trumbull, January 27, 1859, Trumbull Papers, LC.

condemned the proposed purchase of Cuba, while Chandler delivered a strong speech denouncing the appropriation of $30,000,-000 "for the right to govern one million of the refuse of the earth."[6]

Southern ultras could not hide their chagrin. Their dissatisfaction became even greater because of Northern advocacy of a homestead bill, which they violently opposed, and Robert Toombs delivered an impassioned harangue against it. Working himself into a fury, he called Seward a demagogue, pounded upon his desk with his fists, and accused Republicans of cowardice. They were skulking on the Cuba issue and shivering in their shoes at its mere mention, all for concern for land for the landless, mere lacklanders, as he put it.

Seward, Wilson, Fessenden, and Wade immediately sprang to their feet, loudly calling upon the presiding officer for a chance to reply. Wade, against whose desk Toombs had inadvertently pushed during his speech, received the floor, and his quick reply delighted the North. "We are shivering in the wind, are we sir, over your Cuba question?" he shouted.

> You may have occasion to shiver on that question before you are through with it. Now, sir, I have been trying here for nearly a month to get a straight forward vote upon this great measure of land to the landless. I glory in that measure. It is the greatest that has ever come before the American Senate, and it has now come so that there is no dodging it. The question will be, shall we give niggers to the niggerless or land to the landless?

Roars of laughter greeted this response, and although the Homestead Bill was lost by the Vice President's casting vote, the Cuba bill was also defeated. The radicals had again shown what they could do.[7]

[6] Richardson, *Messages and Papers of the Presidents*, V, 510 ff.; Wade–James Wade, December 8, 1858, Wade Papers; New York *Herald*, January 21, 25, 26, 1859; Detroit *Post and Tribune, Chandler*, p. 148.

[7] New York *Tribune*, February 26, March 1, 1859; *Cong. Globe*, 35th Cong., 2d Sess., 1354; Isaac R. Sherwood, *Memories of the War* (Toledo, 1923), pp. 2–3.

The other problem which confronted the radicals in 1859 was the possibility of the revival of various conservative coalitions. Not merely in the North, but also in the South there were reports that some former Whigs were anxious to reconstitute their defunct organization in some form, and the Know-Nothings also still had a hold upon many Republicans. To complicate matters even further, the legislature of Massachusetts, anxious to pay its debts to the nativists, authorized the submission to the voters of an amendment to the state constitution for a two years' residence requirement for naturalized citizens before admitting them to the suffrage. At a time when the radicals were trying to attract the Germans in Western states, this action was most embarrassing, and they tried hard to blunt its edge. Henry Wilson denounced it unsparingly; Carl Schurz was invited to address a mass gathering at Faneuil Hall, and leading radical newspapers condemned it. In the long run, these tactics secured the important German vote, but it had again become obvious that radical vigilance was necessary to prevent a lessening of Republican enthusiasm and a watering down of antislavery ideals.[8]

In Ohio, too, dedicated antislavery Republicans were put to the test. Thomas Corwin, a conservative Whig, was making every effort to stage a comeback, capture the Republican party, and return to the United States Senate. His principal opponent for the Senate seat was Salmon P. Chase, who was relinquishing the governorship after a second term. At the state convention, the radicals had succeeded in selecting Ben Wade as the presiding officer; they were able to nominate their gubernatorial candidate, William Dennison, but they failed to obtain a platform to their liking. Adamantly refusing to accept a declaration that the Fugitive Slave Law was unconstitutional, the conservatives scored a victory. A denunciation of the law in general terms was all that could be achieved, and it was only after a hard-fought campaign

[8] J. H. Barrett–Chase, November 30, 1858, Wilson-Chase, May 18, 1859, E. L. Pierce–Chase, April 28, 1859, Chase Papers, LC; New York Evening Post, May 5, 1859; E. L. Pierce–Sumner, April (?), 1859, May 31, 1859, F. W. Bird–Sumner, April 17, 1859, Sumner Papers.

that the radicals succeeded in preparing the way for Chase's election to the Senate.[9]

Whatever the prospects of a conservative revival may have been, they vanished in October, when John Brown's raid ruined all schemes of reconstituting the Whig party. The old man's attempted invasion of Virginia frightened even conservative Southerners, and more and more slaveholders were willing to believe the most blood-curdling stories about Northern Republicans.

The radicals were not at all pleased with the foolhardy enterprise. "The affair at Harper's Ferry is very unfortunate & will be a most effective weapon against the Republican party," wrote one of Julian's correspondents. When Thaddeus Stevens heard of the raid, someone told him, "Why, Mr. Stevens, they will hang that man." He replied heatedly, "Damn him, he ought to be hung." Giddings questioned whether there ever was "such a foolhardy plan as that of Brown's," while James Medill, the radical Chicago editor, believed the incident would put the Republican party on the defensive, scare off all conservatives, and make it impossible for the Southern opposition to cooperate. As Lewis Clephane, Chase's Washington informant, summed it up, "All things seemed to bid fair of the triumphant victory of our party in 1860, until this infernal affair at Harper's Ferry. . . . It certainly will retard the progress of our principles in the slave states for at least ten years.[1]

The radicals' opponents, of course, were unaware of this correspondence. Determined to make political capital of the raid,

---

[9] Chase-Sumner, June 20, 1859, January 20, 1860, Sumner Papers; E. C. Parsons-Chase, July 10, 1859, J. R. French–Chase, July 25, 1859, Chase Papers, LC; Giddings-Chase, June 7, 1859, Chase Papers, HSP; Ashtabula *Sentinel,* May 26, June 16, 1859; Schuckers, *Chase,* p. 194; New York *Evening Post,* October 4, 1859.

[1] A. A. Livermore–Julian, October 22, 1859, Julian-Giddings Papers; W. U. Hensel, "Thaddeus Stevens As a Country Lawyer," *Historical Papers and Addresses of the Lancaster County Historical Society,* X (1905–6), 275; Giddings-Chase, October 20, 1859, Medill-Chase, October 30, 1859, Chase Papers, HSP; L. Clephane–Chase, October 31, 1859, Chase Papers, LC.

they charged the Republicans with complicity in it. "Can any one have read the documents which we have printed . . . and have failed to have brought home to his mind . . . that the whole plot was fully known for the last year and a half to Seward, Sumner, Hale, Chase, Fletcher, Giddings, Sanborn, Howe, and the leading abolitionists on both sides of the Atlantic?" editorialized the New York *Herald* in a sweeping indictment of the entire radical movement. James M. Mason of Virginia and Clement L. Vallandigham of Ohio tried to induce Brown to implicate Giddings among others; Hale was so stung by the accusations that he issued a public denial, offering to go to Virginia and Maryland to prove it, while Giddings threatened a libel suit. Others said nothing; yet millions were told that the radicals had been responsible for the outrages at Harper's Ferry.[2]

Actually, none of the radicals in Congress had had any direct connection with the raid. Like other well-informed men, they had heard of Brown, who had made a rather dubious reputation for himself in Kansas. Some had met him, and several had been solicited for money on his behalf. The mad scheme to invade Virginia, however, had at best been known only to a handful of out-and-out abolitionists. Neither in the November elections nor in the months that followed did the Republicans find the affair as damaging as they had first feared. And when Southerners made a martyr of Brown by hanging him with undue haste, the anti-slavery cause benefited. "O what a gift to this nation has God sent in the heroic soul of John Brown . . ." wrote the Unitarian clergyman James Freeman Clarke to Sumner. "His *action* not a man approves—it was a wild & mad scheme—but his noble spirit is & will be as dear to the South as to the North."[3]

[2] New York *Herald*, October 28, 1859; Julian, *Giddings*, pp. 370–1; Giddings, *History of the Rebellion*, pp. 425–6; New York *Evening Post*, October 31, 1859.
[3] H. Forbes–Sumner, December 27, 1857, J. F. Clarke–Sumner, December 22, 1859, Sumner Papers; Donald, *Sumner*, p. 350; Wilson, *History*, II, 591–4. Gerrit Smith was the only former member of Congress who had some knowledge of Brown's plans.

It was not surprising that the Brown affair embittered the opening sessions of Congress. In the Senate, George M. Mason introduced a resolution of inquiry concerning the raid; in the acrimonious debates which followed, Chandler announced his satisfaction that the abolitionist's execution had shown what the punishment for treason was. Let secessionists take note of the old man's fate![4]

In the House, the situation was even more critical. No organization could be effected for months, because it proved almost impossible to elect a Speaker. John Sherman of Ohio was the Republican candidate, but he had endorsed a book written by Hinton Rowan Helper, a Southern poor white, who had tried to prove that his class suffered because of slavery. Approval of *The Impending Crisis,* as the book was titled, was considered an outrage by Southerners, and since no party had an absolute majority, a deadlock resulted.

In this controversy, the radicals counseled firmness. Wade had vowed opposition to compromise even before the struggle began; in the House, Stevens stood his ground with calmness when Southern fire-eaters, led by Martin J. Crawford of Georgia, rushed at him, threatening him with assassination if he did not retract his words. Former Governor Boutwell of Massachusetts urged an end to defensive tactics, and John A. Bingham, a young Ohioan who sometimes cooperated with the advanced members of the party, was convinced that under no circumstances should the Republicans yield. By and large, however, the radicals exhibited restraint. As long as the party insisted on some Republican candidate, they believed the battle could be won. "I think we shall elect a speaker this week, but probably not Mr. Sherman," wrote Lovejoy in January. "This will be a disappointment but not as bad as to have a democrat." His prediction came true on February 1, when William Pennington, a conservative Republican, was elected. That Lovejoy's analysis had been correct was

[4] *Cong. Globe,* 36th Cong., 1st Sess., 1, 5; New York *Evening Post,* December 8, 1859.

proven by the appointment of several radicals to important committees.[5]

The bitter atmosphere in Congress, however, did not disappear, and the radicals were again able to prove that they could not be intimidated. When Lovejoy, whose denunciations of slavery were especially sharp, stepped across the line to the Democratic side of the House, Roger Pryor of Virginia tried to stop him. A Wisconsin radical, John F. Potter, came to his fellow Republican's assistance; an altercation ensued, and Pryor finally sent a challenge. At this point, Potter turned the tables on the Southerner. Choosing as his weapons bowie knives, he succeeded in ridiculing the whole outmoded code, and Pryor refused to fight.[6] The radicals had scored a telling victory.

By this time, 1860 being an election year, party managers' thoughts were not so much concerned with the speakership and congressional struggles as with the presidency. This problem had caused the radicals much trouble. Both Chase and Seward had been active in seeking the nomination; both were considered radical standard-bearers, but their rivalry had hurt them both. Conservative hopefuls like Edward Bates of Missouri and moderates like N. P. Banks of Massachusetts also had supporters, and unless the contest between Chase and Seward could be resolved, the radicals would go into the convention badly divided. And the Republican nominee was fairly certain of victory because the Democrats, beset by Southern demands for a federal slave code in the territories, and unable to agree on either a platform or a candidate, were hopelessly divided. This situation presented great opportunities for the radicals; possessing neither the unity nor the

[5] Wade–William Schouler, October 24, 1859, Schouler Papers; H. B. Stanton, *Random Recollections* (New York, 1887), p. 208; New York *Evening Post*, December 8, 1859; Boutwell-Sumner, January 21, 1860, Sumner Papers; Bingham-Giddings, January 19, 1860, Giddings Papers; Lovejoy–Lucy Storrs Denham, January ?, 1860, Lovejoy Papers; *Harper's Weekly*, IV (February 18, 1860), 102.

[6] New York *Herald*, April 6, 7, 12, 14, 1860; *Harper's Weekly*, IV (April 14, 1860), 230.

organization necessary for success, however, they were unable to take advantage of it.[7]

When the Republican convention met in May in the Wigwam at Chicago, it turned out that the radicals had not merely two, but three candidates, all working at cross purposes. Seward still competed with Chase, and, much to the Ohioan's disgust, Wade also contended for the nomination. To be sure, the senator denied having had anything to do with the movement on his behalf, but his friends were so active that the Buckeye delegation split. Abraham Lincoln became the beneficiary of these and other rivalries, his nomination being widely interpreted as a concession to conservative opinion because he had carefully avoided extreme statements. Both Seward and Chase were bitterly disappointed. Although they approved of the nominee, they considered him a mere tyro, and not even the selection of the radical Hannibal Hamlin for Vice President could assuage their disappointment.[8]

Even though the radicals had been unable to exert great influence upon the selection of a presidential candidate, they were not totally unsuccessful at Chicago. Anxious to write as inoffensive a platform as possible, and in general more interested in the vital economic issues which had attracted support in the North than in hostility to slavery, the conservatives were busily engaged in putting together planks concerning internal improvements, homesteads, tariffs, and other popular reforms. But when they failed to endorse the "self-evident" truths of the Declaration of Independence, Joshua Giddings immediately rose to move their inclusion.

[7] George Hoadley–Chase, February 6, 1860, Chase Papers, LC; Jacob Brinkerhoff–Hamlin, May 25, 1858, Hamlin Papers, Gamaliel Bailey-Chase, January 16, 1859, Chase-Bailey, January 24, 1859, Medill-Chase, April 26, August 30, 1859, Chase Papers, HSP.

[8] J. W. Webb–Seward, May 14, 1860, Seward Papers; Murat Halstead, *Caucuses of 1860: A History of the National Political Conventions of the Current Presidential Campaign* (Columbus, 1860), pp. 122, 131, 143, 146–7, 149; Chase-Giddings, May 10, 1860, Giddings Papers; Chase–R. C. Parsons, May 30, 1860, Chase Papers, HSP; Chase-Lincoln, May 17, 1860, Trumbull-Lincoln, May 22, 1860, RTL; Thomas, *Lincoln,* p. 216. Seward's famous memorandum of April 1, 1861, advising foreign war as the solution to the secession problem, demonstrated his opinion concerning Lincoln's inexperience.

Voted down, he stalked out of the hall, only to be brought back when his cause had been taken up by the New York reformer, George William Curtis, and the "inalienable rights" of all men declared essential to the preservation of "Republican principles." "I had often seen Mr. Giddings in Congress," recalled the editor Murat Halstead, "but never saw him when his figure appeared so stately, and his snowy head so lofty, as on this occasion." The old radical had been instrumental in forcing the Republican party to remain true to its ideals.[9]

The candidate, too, was not as conservative as some of his backers had hoped. "Mr. Lincoln personally, is unexceptionable," Edward Bates confided to his diary, "but politically, is as fully committed as Mr. Seward is." The radicals' reception of the news from Chicago proved the essential truth of this assessment. The partisans of Seward and Chase were probably happier with Lincoln than they would have been with the rival candidate. As Trumbull, informing the nominee of his popularity in Washington, wrote, "Mr. Wade, Old Ben Wade as we call him, said the election was settled & that our success was certain." The Ohioan sent Lincoln his regards; he wanted the candidate to know that he was "not far from the Kingdom of Heaven" and that he would campaign for him as soon as Congress adjourned. Giddings immediately sent a warm letter of congratulations; he had known and trusted Lincoln ever since the two had served in Congress together over ten years earlier. The radical New England journalist William Schouler expressed his satisfaction; Henry Wilson, David Wilmot, Cassius M. Clay, and Schuyler Colfax all approved, and Gerrit Smith, whose radicalism was hardly distinguishable from out-and-out abolitionism, confirmed Giddings' good opinion of the candidate. "I have read in the newspapers what Lincoln said so wisely and sublimely of the Declaration of Independence," he wrote to the old man. "I feel confident that he is in his heart an abolitionist." Because Smith never voted for any-

[9] Giddings-Julian, May 25, 1860, Murat Halstead–Julian, March 12, 1891, Julian-Giddings Papers; *Proceedings of the First Three Republican National Conventions,* pp. 135 ff., 140 ff.

one who recognized the legality of slavery anywhere, he himself would not cast his ballot for the Republican candidate, but he was certain that "his victory will be regarded by the South as an Abolition victory—not less so than if you [Giddings] yourself were elected President."[1]

To some radicals, Lincoln's success came as no surprise. The Columbus politician Samuel Galloway had written to John Covode in March that Ohio's vote for Chase would only be complimentary, as the "heart of the masses" was "ardent for Lincoln." And while this sentiment was more his own than that of other Republicans, it was evident from the beginning that the Illinois candidate was able to appeal to a wide variety of people. As Galloway himself explained, "I could go cordially for Bates; but there are some of our strong Anti-Slavery men who would not vote for him. . . . That ultra class will vote for Lincoln although they do not like what they term his too liberal views in regard to the Fugitive Slave Law." Trumbull, who was an original Lincoln man, informed him that he was generally considered as radical as Seward; while Richard M. Corwine, a Cincinnati Republican, thought that Lincoln would make an excellent nominee because of his conservatism. The Illinois lawyer was an exceptionally suitable compromise candidate, and his ability to garner support from all factions was widely recognized.[2]

The events which followed the nomination were, in a way, anticlimactic. The Democratic party at Baltimore finally split into two factions, one headed by Stephen A. Douglas and the other by Vice President John C. Breckinridge; remnants of the Whigs

[1] Howard K. Beale, ed., *The Diary of Edward Bates, 1859–1866, Annual Report of the American Historical Association,* IV (Washington, 1933), 129 (hereafter cited as Bates, *Diary*); Chase–R. C. Parsons, May 30, 1860, Chase Papers, HSP; Trumbull-Lincoln, May 18, 22, 1860, Giddings-Lincoln, May 19, 1860, William Schouler–Lincoln, May 21, 1860, David Wilmot–Lincoln, May 21, 1860, C. M. Clay-Lincoln, May 26, 1860, Colfax-Lincoln, May 26, 1860, RTL; Gerrit Smith–Giddings, June 2, 1860, Giddings Papers; Wilson-Stansbury, May 21, 1860, Wilson Papers.

[2] Samuel Galloway–Covode, March 10, 1860, Covode Papers, HSWP; Trumbull-Lincoln, April 24, 1860, R. M. Corwine–Lincoln, April 30, 1860, RTL.

had already nominated John Bell of Tennessee and Edward Everett of Massachusetts on a noncommittal Union-saving platform, and the Republicans' success seemed certain. Under the circumstances, radicals and conservatives cooperated in campaigning for Lincoln. Sumner, who had returned from Europe, delivered election speeches in and out of Congress; John Covode, who had been chairman of an investigating committee, rendered a report severely condemning the peculations of Buchanan's subordinates, and little disunity appeared in Republican ranks. Although James Gordon Bennett predicted a rift between the candidate and the radicals after the election,[3] no great trouble between them was in evidence. Like Lincoln, they considered Southern threats to secede bluff; like Lincoln also, they were determined never to yield on the vital issue of slavery expansion. Having kept their party true to their principles, they were well satisfied when victory was theirs in November.[4] They had reached the goal for which they had worked so long.

[3] Roy Franklin Nichols, *The Disruption of American Democracy* (New York, 1948), pp. 314–22, 340, 331; Sumner, *Works,* V, 191–229, 240–72; Medill-Lincoln, July 5, 1860, E. L. Pierce–Lincoln, July 20, 1860, Amos Tuck–Lincoln, September 8, 1860, Amos Tuck–David Davis, August 24, 1860, Henry Wilson–Lincoln, August 25, 1860, Chandler-Lincoln, August 28, 1860, Chase-Lincoln, November 7, 1860, RTL; Wilson, *History,* II, 701 ff.

[4] Among the victors were not only the national candidates, but also such radical stalwarts as William D. Kelley in Pennsylvania and George W. Julian in Indiana.

CHAPTER

IV

No Compromise!

THE SECESSION WINTER of 1860–61 was a time of crisis, a critical juncture for Northerners as well as Southerners, moderates as well as conservatives. For the radicals, it was a period of testing. In the face of the threatened break-up of the Union, would they succeed in maintaining the principles which they had preached for so long? And if they remained adamant, would they be able to keep their conservative associates from compromising? Above all, should war break out, would they not incur the risk of being held responsible for it? Whatever the answers, it was certain that their actions would be scrutinized by friend and foe alike.

From the very beginning, the radicals had no doubt about their course. Considering the election of Lincoln a vindication of their principles, they were elated by their hard-won victory. "It is a joy to have lived to this day," exulted Joshua Leavitt to Chase, and the Ohioan expressed similar sentiments. "You are President elect," he wrote to Abraham Lincoln.

I congratulate you and thank God. The great object of my wishes & labors for nineteen years is accomplished in the overthrow of the Slave Power. The space is now clear for the establishment of the policy of Freedom on safe & firm grounds.

Carl Schurz, who had become a Republican leader in Wisconsin, was even more enthusiastic. As he put it in a letter to the President-elect, "Yours, dear Sir, is the greatest mission that ever fell to the lot of mortal man: the restoration of original principles in the model Republic of the world." It was an assessment with which many radicals agreed.[1]

But of course the radicals were fully aware of the fact that they would have to guard against new proposals for compromise. With the South threatening to secede and large segments of the population fearful of a collision, talk of additional guarantees to the slaveholders was common. As Trumbull wrote to Chase, he regretted the loss of the House of Representatives. With both Houses against him, the President-elect could do but little, and for him to be compelled to make combinations or form alliances in order to carry measures would be unfortunate. "Mr. Lincoln has it in his power to make a successful administration," the senator added, "if he will only carry out with a firm hand the principles on which he has been elected." Wade, to whom Trumbull had written in similar terms, replied that nothing was more palpably true than the senator's analysis, which, he added, "should be written in letters of gold and placed constantly before the eyes of Mr. Lincoln." If the President-elect acted in accordance with these principles, all would be right. Trumbull promptly sent Wade's letter to Springfield.[2]

Other radicals were equally outspoken. Chandler warned that merchants, afraid for their pocketbooks, would demand concessions, but as a businessman himself, and one who had suffered

---

[1] Joshua Leavitt–Chase, November 7, 1860, John Bingham–Chase, November 6, 1860, C. F. Cleveland–Chase, November 12, 1860, Chase Papers, LC; Chase-Lincoln, November 7, 1860, Schurz-Lincoln, November 7, 1860, RTL; Trumbull-Wade, November 9, 1860, Wade Papers.

[2] Trumbull-Chase, November 8, 1860, Chase Papers, HSP; Trumbull-Wade, November 9, 1860, Wade Papers; Wade-Trumbull, November 14, 1860, Trumbull Papers, LC; Trumbull-Lincoln, December 14, 1860, RTL. Had the South remained in the Union, the Republicans would have been unable to control the 37th Congress.

losses because of the stringency of the uncertain situation, he
believed that he had the right to counsel disregard of their
anguish. "From the days of Carthage to those of James Buchanan,"
he advised Trumbull, "the great mercantile centers have been
peaceable. . . . Yet this spirit has not & *does not* extend beyond
the suburbs of the great commercial marts." John Bingham and
Henry Wilson also strongly emphasized their opposition to compromise, and William Cullen Bryant, the New York poet-editor,
advocated the inclusion of Chase in the Cabinet to ensure a radical
administration. Letters from Washington kept Lincoln advised
of these sentiments.[3]

Actually, the radicals did not have to worry about the President-
elect. As in 1858, he was much more sympathetic to their attitude
than to that of the conservatives. Realizing that the slavery issue
had to be settled once and for all if a solution were ever to be
found, he rejected all requests for concessions on the main question. And because he was subjected to considerable conservative
influence, he made the best possible use of radical counterpressure
to do exactly what he had probably intended all along. The ultras'
agitation must have been convenient for him.

The radicals were soon to be reassured by Lincoln's attitude.
Although he made no public announcements, on December 4 he
granted an interview to Joshua Giddings. The old antislavery
leader had arrived in Springfield at six o'clock in the morning of
the previous day. Safely lodged in the St. Nicholas Hotel, he
wrote home that he could not speak of "Old Abe" yet because he
had not seen him. "If they do not make him play the fool it will
not be for want of effort," he mused, "as allmost [sic] everybody
is doing their best to compromise and break up the party and
disgrace him. . . ." But he had heard that the President-elect bore
himself well, a report which he found accurate when he met
Lincoln. He urged his host to stand firm, advised that at least

[3] Chandler-Trumbull, November 17, 1860, Trumbull Papers, LC;
Bingham-Chase, November 6, 1860, Henry B. Stanton–Chase, December 7, 1860, Chase Papers, LC; Wilson-Chase, December 15, 1860,
Chase Papers, HSP; W. C. Bryant–Lincoln, November 10, 1860, Trumbull-Lincoln, December 2, 4, 1860, RTL.

three radicals be included in the Cabinet, and left with the decided impression that Lincoln's administration would take "radical ground." "I left him with more confidence than I entertained when I went there," Giddings commented afterwards. "I have no doubt that we did the best thing we could when we nominated him." And when in early January Chase visited the President-elect, he too reported that Lincoln was "entirely reliable for the defense of our principles."[4]

In line with their firmly held convictions of the inadmissibility of compromise, the radicals in Congress labored hard to frustrate all efforts at conciliation. In the House, Galusha Grow pushed the Homestead Bill despite Southern opposition; in the Senate, Hale, on December 5, delivered a truculent speech severely castigating the secessionists. Constitutional majorities could not be overturned, he said, and if the incoming administration were to yield, he himself would oppose it. The speech was not very effective, even leading Republicans condemning it, but it was symptomatic of the ultras' attitude.[5]

Buchanan set the stage for the Congressional struggle with his message, in which he denied the legality of secession but refused equally to admit the propriety of squelching it. The President's communication satisfied nobody, Trumbull informed Lincoln on December 4. But he was confident. "A good feeling prevails among Republican Senators," he reported. "The impression with all, unless there be one exception, is that Republicans have no concessions to make or compromises to offer; & that it is impolitic even to discuss making them." Nevertheless, considering the conciliatory efforts of Thurlow Weed, J. W. Webb, and Horace Greeley, all of whom had their own schemes of pacification, wholly inadmissible, he was disturbed because some moderates

----

[4] Giddings–Laura Giddings, December 2, 3, 1860, Julian-Giddings Papers; Giddings–G. R. Giddings, December 10, 1860, Giddings Papers; Giddings–John Allison, December 25, 1860, RTL; Chase–J. S. Pike, January 10, 1861, Pike Papers.

[5] *Cong. Globe,* 36th Cong., 2d Sess., 2, 9; Nichols, *The Disruption of American Democracy,* p. 398; Elihu Washburne–Lincoln, December 9, 1860, RTL.

felt differently. "For Republicans to take steps towards getting up committees or proposing new compromises, is an admission that to conduct the government on the principles on which we carried the election would be wrong," he concluded. In spite of his optimistic assessment of his colleagues' stand, he could not overlook the fact that some of them were ready to make concessions.[6]

Notwithstanding the radicals' disapproval, a committee of thirty-three to seek some solution for the country's troubles was appointed in the House. Chaired by the moderate Republican, Thomas Corwin of Ohio, it nevertheless contained such stalwarts as Mason Tappan of New Hampshire, Justin S. Morrill of Vermont, C. C. Washburne of Wisconsin. To defeat the conservatives, the radicals needed the help of the President-elect; and his aid was promptly given. One of the members, William Kellogg of Illinois, who had originally been enthusiastic about the possibility of compromise, on December 10 received a letter from Lincoln, whom he had asked for advice:

> Entertain no proposition for a compromise in regard to the extension of slavery in the territories. The instant you do, they have us under again; all our labor is lost, and sooner or later must be done over.

Kellogg thereupon resisted concessions; the President-elect's intervention on behalf of the radicals had done its work. And in case there was still any doubt about his position, on the same day Lincoln wrote to Senator Trumbull, instructing him in unmistakable terms:

> Let there be no compromise on the question of extending slavery. If there be, all our labor is lost, and ere long, must be done again. The dangerous ground—that into which some of our friends have a hankering to run—is P. Sov. Have none of it. Stand firm. The tug has to come, & better now, than any time hereafter.

[6] Trumbull-Lincoln, December 4, 1860, RTL. The exception Trumbull mentioned was apparently Senator Dixon of Connecticut. Cf. Trumbull-Lincoln, December 14, 1860, RTL.

On December 13, he repeated his warning to Elihu B. Washburne, another Illinois Republican, whom he advised:

> Prevent, as far as possible, any of our friends from demoralizing themselves, and our cause, by entertaining propositions for compromise of any sort, on 'slavery extension'. . . . On that point hold firm as with a chain of steel.

After such advice, Washburne's brother would not be likely to yield in the committee.[7]

In the Senate, too, the radicals fought compromise in and out of committee. On December 17, Wade rose to deliver a scathing attack on the foes of the Union. Challenging the South to produce examples of instances in which it had been wronged, he pointed out that the government had been in Southern hands for years. And were not Northerners mistreated in the slave states in plain violation of the Constitution? "But what have we to compromise?" he asked.

> Sir, it would be dishonorable to us if we were to listen to a compromise by which he who has the verdict of the people in his pocket, should make his way to the presidential chair. When it comes to that, you have no government. . . . I know not what others may do; but I tell you that, with the verdict of the people given in favor of the platform upon which our candidates have been elected, I would suffer anything to come before I would compromise that away.[8]

The speech was not polished; it was not a great oration, and conservatives of every description denounced it. Most Republicans, however, including the President-elect, generally agreed with its propositions. "Wade's speech today is considered well timed and just what was needed," Washburne informed Lincoln. The Springfield statesman, on the very day on which it was delivered, indicated his assent by thanking Trumbull for enclosing Wade's

---

[7] *Journal of the Committee of Thirty-Three,* 36th Cong., 2d Sess., H.R. Doc. No. 31 (Washington, 1861), pp. 1 ff.; Charles Francis Adams MS Diary, Massachusetts Historical Society, February 8, 1861; Lincoln, *Works,* IV, 150, 151, 153.

[8] *Cong. Globe,* 36th Cong., 2d Sess., 99–107.

letter warning against compromise and signified his complete concurrence.[9]

On the next day, the Senate authorized the appointment of a Committee of Thirteen to deal with the crisis. Every conceivable shade of opinion could be found among its members, who ranged from senators like Jefferson Davis and Robert Toombs, spokesmen for the cotton states, to men like Ben Wade and James W. Grimes, representatives of radical constituencies. Seward was also a member, and his influence was generally considered decisive because he was known to be Lincoln's choice for Secretary of State. If the radicals wanted to prevail, they would again have to rely on the President-elect's help, especially since the plan brought forward by Senator John J. Crittenden of Kentucky seemed very promising. Envisioning, among other changes, a constitutional amendment restoring the Missouri Compromise line, it proposed that south of 36° 30′, both in territory already belonging to the United States and in areas which might be acquired later, slavery was to be protected; north of it, it was to be outlawed. Although the radicals were totally opposed to the scheme, whether or not it would have any chance of acceptance depended on the attitude of the Springfield statesman.

As his letters to Kellogg, Trumbull, and Washburne had already indicated, Lincoln supported the radicals. "If any of our friends prove false, and fix up a compromise on the territorial question, I am for fighting again," he wrote on December 17 to Trumbull. Well could Chase tell Julian that the President-elect would not disappoint the "true Republicans." "He may not be as radical as some of us would wish," added the Ohioan, "but he is, I am confident, perfectly sincere."[1]

Under these circumstances, Lincoln's reaction to the Crittenden

[9] Dwight L. Dumond, *The Secession Movement, 1860–1861* (New York, 1931), p. 162; New York *Herald,* December 18, 1860; Howard Cecil Perkins, ed., *Northern Editorials on Secession* (New York, 1942), pp. 988–9; Washburne-Lincoln, December 18, 1860, RTL; Lincoln, *Works,* IV, 153.

[1] Ibid.; Chase-Julian, December 15, 1860, Julian-Giddings Papers.

Compromise was not very different from the ultras'. To be sure, conservatives were hopeful of an adjustment; he received letters and visitors urging compliance with Crittenden's plan. But the President-elect, cognizant of the radicals' refusal to budge, remained adamant. He was willing to give the South assurances of noninterference with slavery in the states; he was even willing to enforce the obnoxious Fugitive Slave Law, but he was determined not to yield on the crucial question of the extension of slavery. Therefore, when Seward returned to Washington from upstate New York, where Weed had given him word of Lincoln's intentions, it became clear that the compromise would fail. In the Committee of Thirteen, he cast his vote against the proposal; nor was there any agreement on alternative propositions. The radicals had no reason to complain; their resolute stand had facilitated Lincoln's decision to reject vital concessions. And although they might grumble about his willingness to make the Fugitive Slave Law workable, they had every other ground for satisfaction. As Trumbull informed him, "all our friends are delighted at your course as indicated at Springfield."[2]

In the meantime, Buchanan's weakness had become even more painfully manifest. Surrounded by secessionist Cabinet members, friendly with Southern representatives and unable to grasp the necessity for taking a stand, the old man in the White House was clearly unequal to the situation. On December 20, South Carolina finally seceded, and, having led Southerners to believe that he would not countenance any changes in the disposition of the federal forces in Charleston harbor, he was greatly embarrassed when Major Robert Anderson, the Union commander, occupied Fort Sumter. The major, who had ample provocation, had acted in accordance with instructions permitting him to move his troops to a safer base in case of threatening attack, but Southern

[2] Lincoln, *Works*, IV, 156, 158; *Report of the Committee of Thirteen*, 36th Cong., 2d Sess., Sen. Rep. No. 288 (Washington, 1861), pp. 8–13; David M. Potter, *Lincoln and His Party in the Secession Crisis* (New Haven, 1942), pp. 166–76; Trumbull-Lincoln, December 24, 1860, RTL.

associates pressed the President to order Anderson to return to indefensible Fort Moultrie. Upbraided by secessionist sympathizers for an alleged breach of faith, Buchanan seemed irresolute as always, and many observers expected him to yield again.

The President's attitude had always infuriated the radicals; his irresolution during the secession crisis seemed to confirm their worst suspicions. Thaddeus Stevens, who had gone home because of a touch of rheumatism, was uncertain whether to return to Washington before the Christmas holidays. "I do not care to be present while the process of humiliation is going on," he wrote. "Buchanan is a very traitor." That the President was "doubtless guilty of treason" was also Ben Wade's belief, and Lyman Trumbull expressed himself even more forcefully in a letter to Lincoln:

> I am reluctantly compelled to believe that the President means to surrender up the fortications at Charleston when demanded by the Charleston authorities. . . . If the facts turn out as I fear, it will involve the duty of hanging Buchanan, if we are ever in a position to mete out justice to him.

"The President and some of his subordinates seem to be running a race of infamy," complained the New York radical George Opdyke to Chase, to whom he suggested that only a firm policy could prevent complete disaster. And the radicals were worried about the majority in Congress. It seemed to lack both the capacity and will to take action.[3]

In this situation, to the advanced Republicans the muddle concerning the occupation of Fort Sumter seemed fortuitous. Buchanan would have to show his hand; the secession controversy was reaching a climax. "We are all rejoiced at the noble conduct of Maj. Anderson in taking possession of Fort Sumter . . .", wrote Trumbull to Lincoln. "This will probably bring matters to a crisis sooner than Mr. Buchanan expected." That the President-elect would announce his intention of retaking the forts in case

---

[3] Stevens–Edward McPherson, December 19, 1860, Stevens Papers; Wade–Mrs. Wade, December 26, 1860, Wade Papers; Trumbull-Lincoln, December 24, 1860, RTL; George Opdyke–Chase, December 26, 1860, Chase Papers, LC.

of surrender he had already stated on the day before Christmas.[4]

Anderson's move did indeed bring matters to a crisis. Buchanan's Cabinet had been falling apart for a number of days; Secretary of State Lewis Cass having resigned, the President chose Attorney General Jeremiah Black as Cass's successor. This change brought about the appointment of Edwin McMasters Stanton as Attorney General—a reorganization of the Cabinet which was to have far-reaching results. Black himself was opposed to renewed concessions, but Stanton went even further in counseling firmness. An associate of Chase in the 1840's and a foe of slavery since young manhood, he was not the sort of man to yield to Southern pressure. For the time being, he succeeded in preventing additional compromises with the South; he entered into confidential relations with leading Republicans, and together with Secretary of State Black and Postmaster General Joseph Holt he disabused the President of some of his proslavery notions. Emphasizing the impropriety of negotiating with the commissioners sent by South Carolina, he pointed out that no government could afford to give up a national installation in the same week that defalcations involving the Secretary of War had come to light. Buchanan saw the point; declining to hold any intercourse with the commissioners, he refused to order Anderson back. The Secretary of War resigned; Holt became his successor, and eventually John A. Dix, who took over the Treasury, also added new strength to the Cabinet.[5]

If the radicals could welcome the invigorating of the old Cabinet, they were nevertheless uncertain about the new one.

[4] Trumbull-Lincoln, December 27, 1860, RTL; Lincoln, *Works*, IV, 162. Rumors eventually arose that the radicals had had a hand in Anderson's move. According to the *Diary of a Public Man*, Abner Doubleday, a radical officer of the garrison, plotted secretly with Senator Wade to make compromise impossible and to keep Seward out of the Cabinet. There is, however, no contemporary evidence, and the veracity of the "Public Man" has been questioned. Frank Malloy Anderson, *The Mystery of 'A Public Man'* (Minneapolis, 1948), p. 196; Randall, *Lincoln the President*, I, 295.

[5] Nevins, *The Emergence of Lincoln*, II, 358, 375–9; Thomas and Hyman, *Stanton*, pp. 42, 91–104, 109–12.

Unless they could secure the most important posts, all their efforts to keep the party strong might yet prove vain. Accordingly, they exerted their utmost strength to obtain representation in the new administration.

The advanced Republicans' most logical candidate for a Cabinet post was Salmon P. Chase. Widely known throughout the country, experienced as an attorney, senator, and governor, he was considered honest and capable. He would add stature to the new regime, and his appointment would not only give representation to the radicals but to former Democrats as well. The President-elect, who was fully aware of these facts, received letters urging Chase's appointment, and when, on November 24, over thirty prominent Republicans largely of Democratic antecedents met at New York City to consult about the Cabinet, they decided that the Ohioan ought to be Secretary of State. The former Barnburners were especially active in his behalf.[6]

From Lincoln's point of view, however, Chase's claims were less compelling than Seward's. The New Yorker had been the chief contender for the presidential nomination; he was considered a spokesman for the former Whigs, and he was still widely respected as an outspoken antislavery leader. It would never do to overlook him.

Despite Seward's reputation, most radicals, correctly assessing him the emerging leader of the compromise faction within the Republican party, were opposed to his inclusion in the Cabinet. Those ultras especially who had been former Democrats tried to stop him; they were alarmed; they did not trust him, and, taking advantage of Trumbull's fortuitous visit to New York early in December, warned him against the appointment. The Senator from Illinois forwarded their sentiments to Springfield.[7]

[6] W. C. Bryant–Lincoln, November 10, 1860, Dr. H. Wigand–Lincoln, November 9, 1860, E. B. Washburne–Lincoln, December 9, 1860, Medill-Lincoln, December 18, 1860, RTL; H. B. Stanton–Chase, November 30, 1860, December 7, 1860, Chase Papers, LC; Hiram Barney–Chase, November 26, 1860, Henry Wilson–Chase, December 15, 1860, Chase Papers, HSP.

[7] Trumbull-Lincoln, December 2, 1860, RTL; Randall, *Lincoln the President*, I, 258–9.

Lincoln disregarded their advice. Realizing that Seward was an important figure who could not be snubbed, the President-elect offered him the Department of State. But with characteristic political skill he sought to mollify the radical ex-Democrats by making Lyman Trumbull and Hannibal Hamlin privy to his decision. Hamlin was even commissioned to sound out the New Yorker, a task he faithfully carried out, and Seward eventually accepted.[8]

Seward's decision made Chase a promising candidate for the second post. As the New Yorker's conciliatory leanings soon became common knowledge, the former Ohio governor's appointment became especially important for the radicals, and they deluged Lincoln with letters on his behalf. In addition, Chase's moderate views on the tariff would offset Seward's protectionism. Finally, the President-elect decided to sound him out. Conferring with Chase early in January at Springfield, Lincoln queried him about his availability. The Ohioan, who had just been elected to the Senate, hesitated and gave a noncommittal reply, but his friends insisted that he ought to accept. D. N. White, one of his Pennsylvania correspondents, put it succinctly:

> I assure you, my dear sir, that the hearts of thousands of the "radical wing" of the Republican party,—as we are called, which means the real, true, honest Republicans,—are painfully anxious on this subject. In Mr. Lincoln we have confidence. But what can one man do, with a weak-backed . . . Cabinet to contend with. We want a "Radical," to use our weak-kneed brethren's phraseology, in the Cabinet to stand by and stiffen up the President. . . .

This type of pleading had its effect upon the ambitious Chase; Lincoln, who had been continually importuned by leading radicals such as Julian, Andrew, Trumbull, and Hale, decided to make his offer definite, and, despite some last-minute opposition on the part of Seward and high-tariff advocates, the Ohioan became Secretary

[8] Lincoln, *Works*, IV, 149; Hamlin, *Hamlin*, pp. 368–71; Hamlin-Lincoln, December 4, 1860, RTL; Howard K. Beale, ed., *Diary of Gideon Welles* (New York, 1960), II, 388–9 (hereafter cited as Welles, *Diary*).

of the Treasury. Unlike the New Yorker, with whom his relations were strained, he was to represent throughout the next three and a half years, generally without hesitation, the radical cause within the administration.[9]

Because of the possibility of armed conflict, the position of Secretary of War was a most important one. The radicals were anxious to secure it, but eventually it went to Simon Cameron, the Pennsylvania politician whose appointment caused Lincoln more difficulty at the time than any other Cabinet question. Strongly opposed by the faction led by Governor Andrew Curtin in his own state and handicapped by a reputation for financial irresponsibility, Cameron in return for swinging the Pennsylvania delegates to the Illinois candidate, had been promised a post by Lincoln's managers at Chicago. The President-elect had to honor it, although he did so with grave misgivings. And since the Harrisburg politician was not only suspected of dishonesty but was known to support the Crittenden Compromise as well, most radicals were hostile to him. What they could not foresee was that he would eventually make common cause with them.[1]

On the whole, the ultras were not very astute in their attempts to obtain influence in the Cabinet. To be sure, Chandler urged that Wade be made Secretary of War, and Thaddeus Stevens entertained hopes of securing the office for himself, but the radicals also pressed the claims of Gideon Welles, whose appointment was to cause them great trouble. Suggested by Han-

[9] John G. Nicolay and John Hay, *Abraham Lincoln, A History* (New York, 1914), III, 359, 361, 370–2; D. N. White–Chase, February 25, 1861, Chase Papers, LC; Lincoln, *Works,* IV, 171; Washburne-Lincoln, January 10, 1861, Hale-Lincoln, January 19, 1861, J. A. Andrew–Lincoln, January 20, 1861, Trumbull-Lincoln, January 20, 1861, Julian-Lincoln, January 23, 1861, RTL.

[1] J. M. Pomeroy–Lincoln, August 27, 1860, Wilmot-Lincoln, December 12, 1860, Trumbull-Lincoln, December 31, 1860, January 16, 20, 1861, Fessenden-Lincoln, January 20, 1861, Washburne-Lincoln, January 1, 1861, Bryant-Lincoln, January 3, 1861, RTL; Trumbull-Hamlin, January 2, 1861, February 11, 1861, Hamlin Papers; Horace White–Trumbull, January 10, 1861, E. Peck–Trumbull, January 10, 1861, W. Jayne–Trumbull, January 10, 1861, Herndon-Trumbull, January 27, 1861, C. H. Ray–Trumbull, January 16, 1861, Trumbull Papers, LC; Bradley, *Cameron,* pp. 158 ff.

nibal Hamlin to represent the New England states, Welles appealed to Lincoln as a former Democrat and became Secretary of the Navy. His conservatism was so marked, however, that it was not long until he broke with the advanced faction of the party. John Covode proposed the name of the Tennessee loyalist, Emerson Etheridge, another conservative, and George Boutwell that of the moderate Nathaniel P. Banks. And while most radicals overlooked the claims of Henry Winter Davis, the opposition member from Maryland whose vigorous defiance of secessionists would soon make him a leading ultra, they strongly favored his rival, Montgomery Blair, who eventually became Postmaster General. The son of Andrew Jackson's influential collaborator, Francis P. Blair, Sr., Montgomery Blair had greatly impressed them as a border state representative who deserved confidence because of his unconditional unionism.[2] During the Fort Sumter crisis, he justified their trust, but eventually he would prove even more conservative than Seward.

In Cabinet matters, therefore, the extremists were less perspicacious than Lincoln, who appointed conservatives like Edward Bates as well as radicals like Salmon P. Chase, and former Democrats like Gideon Welles as well as former Whigs like William H. Seward, thus achieving his purpose of giving representation to every faction of the party. Because of their failure to assess the appointees correctly, it was not surprising that the radicals, despite their successes, were not satisfied when the final selections were announced. The presence of Cameron in the War Department, as well as the inclusion of conservatives such as Caleb Smith of Indiana as Secretary of the Interior, to say nothing of the powerful position achieved by Seward as Secretary of State, disappointed them. Some said that the Cabinet did not contain three Unionists

---

[2] Chandler-Lincoln, January 21, 1860, S. S. Blair and J. S. Campbell–Lincoln, January 15, 1861, Curtin-Lincoln, January 18, 1861, Boutwell-Lincoln, December 17, 1860, Covode-Lincoln, January 15, 1861, Wade–Preston King, November 10, 1860, Trumbull-Lincoln, December 18, 1860, RTL; A. K. McClure, *Lincoln and the Men of War-Times* (Philadelphia, 1892), pp. 260–1; Hamlin, *Hamlin*, p. 375; H. W. Davis–S. F. DuPont, February 28 or March 1, 1861, DuPont Papers, Eleutherian Mills Library, Wilmington, Del.

as absolute as Dix, Holt, and Stanton; many believed it "indicated a disgraceful surrender to the South," and Thaddeus Stevens, who had long wondered whether the radicals would be able to stand up against Seward's and Cameron's influence, characterized it as an assortments of rivals, one stump speaker from Indiana, and two representatives of the Blair family. But these assessments were incorrect. Having secured Chase's appointment for the Treasury Department, the radicals were actually in a strong position in the Cabinet. Montgomery Blair supported them in the beginning, and Cameron eventually became their ally. Above all, the President continued to sympathize with many of their aims. "On the question of extending slavery under the national auspices," he wrote in February, 1861, to Seward, "I am inflexible. I am for no compromise which *assists* or *permits* the extension of the institution. . . . " Well could the New York *Herald* complain that his Cabinet, judged by the inclusion of Chase and Blair, foreshadowed the "predominance of the radical anti-slavery interest. . . ."[3]

The radicals' success in committing the President-elect to the inclusion of several "advanced" members in the Cabinet and their discovery that he was as much opposed to yielding on fundamentals as they themselves did not end the talk of compromise and concession. To be sure, the Senate Committee of Thirteen failed, but before the same fate overtook the House Committee of Thirty-three, Charles Francis Adams, to his colleagues' utter disgust, had endorsed the admission of New Mexico even if the proposed state should opt for slavery. The Massachusetts Republican had entertained the scheme merely to show the border states how intransigent the deep South really was, as he expected the secessionists to reject the concession, but the radicals were unable to forgive him for his maneuver. "What does Adams mean in voting to admit New Mexico free or slave. . . ?" queried Edward L. Pierce in alarm on December 31, and four days later, he scathingly

[3] Blaine, *Twenty Years of Congress,* I, 285–7; Stevens-Chase, February 3, 1861, Chase Papers, HSP; Lincoln, *Works,* IV, 181; New York *Herald,* March 2, 1861.

contrasted the congressman's weakness with Lincoln's firm position. Sumner was outraged, and not even Adams's more radical stand during January would mollify him. But the committee's efforts eventually came to naught, despite Corwin's effort to rally conservative opinion. The radicals, strengthened by knowledge of Lincoln's support, could no more be induced to cooperate than the representatives from the cotton states. And by February 1, all the southernmost states had left the Union.[4]

The real problem, however, was not Adams's but Seward's. Known as Lincoln's choice for Secretary of State, the New Yorker would be closely watched. He would speak on January 12, and Chase begged him not to countenance any compromise. But Seward had made up his mind. In his speech, he lent his influence completely to the moderate concessions already announced by Adams. He too was ready to vote for the admission of new states, even if they turned out to be slave states.[5]

Seward's action finally revealed beyond doubt what his colleagues had long suspected. Far from being an ultra, the New Yorker was actually a conservative, the leader of those Republicans who sought to contain secession by concessions. As such, he stood within the Republican party as the most powerful antagonist to radicalism. The ultras' plans were the exact opposite of his own, and their reaction to his speech could have been predicted. James M. Ashley remembered years later how he had asked Wade what he thought of it, only to be told, "If we follow such leadership, we will be in the wilderness longer than the children of Israel under Moses." Others heard the Ohioan exclaim, "What a downfall," and he accurately expressed his colleagues' feelings. "Seventeen Senators and fifty-eight representatives stand firm in Washington as they assure me," reported Giddings to his son,

[4] Charles Francis Adams MS Diary, December 21, 26, 27, 28, 29, 1860, Adams Papers; Martin B. Duberman, *Charles Francis Adams, 1806–1886* (Cambridge, 1960), pp. 223–50; Pierce-Sumner, December 31, 1860, January 3, 1861, Sumner Papers; Donald, *Sumner,* pp. 373–82; *Disturbed Condition of the Country,* 36th Cong., 2d Sess., H. R. Report No. 31 (Washington, 1861).
[5] Schuckers, *Chase,* p. 202; *Cong. Globe,* 36th Cong., 2d Sess., 341; Chase-Seward, January (?), 1861, Chase Papers, LC.

and if they continue to do so, the others will yield, and Seward's effort to disband our organization will prove fruitless. The feeling in this Country is up to the fighting point and men are ready to *fight,* but not to compromise. Tell our friends to thank God and take courage.

E. M. Furness, one of Sumner's radical correspondents, sadly confessed to the senator that "within two days I would have lain [sic] down my life, to see Mr. Seward President ... & now I have no words to express my bitter disappointment. How dare he, before God and Christendom, to make a boast of his readiness to sacrifice principle to expediency." Sumner, as he walked away from the chamber, exclaimed, "I knew what was coming, but I confess that I am sad." Chandler commented, "Great God! How are the mighty fallen." Carl Schurz deplored Seward's weakness, and Stevens maintained that he had listened to every word and had heard nothing. Although Lincoln believed the speech might do some good, never again would Seward be considered a radical by Republicans.[6]

Another proposal for compromise engaged the radicals' attention that winter. Late in January, the legislature of Virginia had passed resolutions inviting the other states to meet on February 4 in Washington to consider plans for saving the Union. At first, most extremists, opposing the plan, urged their friends not to participate; as time went on, however, they saw that it would be bad strategy to leave the field entirely to the conservatives. The least that the conference could do would be to secure a respite until March 4, when the Republicans would assume control of the government. But conference or no conference, they were as determined as before to prevent concessions.[7]

[6] J. M. Ashley, "Calhoun, Seward, and Lincoln," *Magazine of Western History,* XIII (November, 1890), 4; Dispatch No. 6, January 15, 1861, Rudolph Schleiden Papers, Staatsarchiv, Bremen, B 13, b 1 a 2, microfilm, LC; Giddings–G. R. Giddings, February 6, 1861, Giddings Papers; E. M. Furness–Sumner, January 14, 1861, Sumner Papers; Joseph Schafer, ed., *Intimate Letters of Carl Schurz, 1841–1869* (Madison, Wis., 1928), pp. 242–3; Lincoln, *Works,* IV, 176.

[7] Robert Gray Gunderson, *Old Gentlemen's Convention: The Washington Peace Conference of 1861* (Madison, Wis., 1961), pp. vii, 6; William Claflin–Sumner, February 7, 1861, John Jay–Sumner, February

The radicals' hesitation was to cause them trouble. Zach Chandler had never been one of the most sagacious ultras. A ruthless politician, he was outspoken and aggressive. Although he had at first questioned the wisdom of Michigan's sending delegates to the Washington conference, he changed his mind, and, on February 11, in a letter as crass as it was offensive, finally urged Governor Austin Blair to have the state participate. "My Dear Governor," he wrote,

> Governor Bingham and myself telegraphed you on Saturday, at the request of Massachusetts and New York, to send delegates to the peace or compromise congress. They admit that we were right, and they wrong, that no Republican State should have sent delegates, but they are here and can't get away. Ohio, Indiana, and Rhode Island, are caving in, and there is some doubt of Illinois; and now they beg us, for God's sake, to come to their rescue and save the republican party from rupture. I hope you will send stiff-backed men or none. The whole thing was gotten up against my judgment or advice, and will end in thin smoke. Still, I hope, as a matter of Courtesy . . . to our erring brethren, that you will send the delegates.
>
> Truly your friend,
Z. Chandler
>
> His Excellency Austin Blair.
>
> P. S. Some of the Manufacturing States think that a fight would be awful. Without a little blood-letting this Union would not be worth a rush.

The letter leaked out and caused a stir in Congress at the time, and even though Chandler cited Thomas Jefferson as an authority for the necessity of some bloodshed every twenty years, ever since it has been cited as proof of the extremists' responsibility for the Civil War. It was, however, Chandler's own expression; many radicals apparently agreed with Chase, who warned sincerely against the danger of civil war.[8]

7, 1861, Sumner Papers; Charles Francis Adams MS Diary, January 28, 1861, Adams Papers; W. Jayne–Trumbull, January 28, 31, 1861, Trumbull Papers, LC; Chase-Giddings, January 31, February 1, 1861, Giddings Papers.

[8] Chandler-Blair, February 11, 1861, Chandler Papers; Detroit *Post*

When on February 4 the conference met, both Northern radicals and Southern extremists worked against its proposed compromises. Michigan, Wisconsin, Minnesota, California, and Oregon, as well as the seceded cotton states, were not represented. In Michigan's case, despite Chandler's repeated appeals for delegates, the members of the legislature, according to Governor Blair, were "so afraid of the shadow of backing down" that they did "not dare do anything." Of the delegates from other states, several were active radicals. Among others, Chase was a member of the Ohio contingent; George Boutwell, John Z. Goodrich, and John Murray Forbes came from Massachusetts; Lot M. Morrill spoke for Maine, and James S. Wadsworth appeared as a member from New York. The delegates visited Buchanan; then the Republicans met, made Chase chairman, and decided to discuss everything in caucus before taking action.

The ultras made their influence felt. Morrill, the new radical senator from Maine, delivered a strong speech in which he made it clear that the North certainly could not agree to any compromise unless the South pledged itself to return to its allegiance, an analysis which almost caused a melee on the convention floor. So haughty was the Southerners' attitude in demanding concessions that even the conservative Senator Solomon Foot of Vermont was critical of the conference. "It is a fraud, a trick, a deception . . . , a device of traitors and conspirators again to cheat the North and to gain time to ripen their conspiracy," he commented. Chase upheld the radical point of view with great dignity by stressing once again the undoubted legality of Lincoln's election. "After many years of earnest advocacy and of severe trial," he said, "we have achieved the triumph of that principle [restriction of slavery]. By a fair and unquestionable majority we have secured that triumph. Do you think we, who represent this

---

and Tribune, Chandler, pp. 189–200; *Cong. Globe,* 36th Cong., 2d Sess., 1370; T. Harry Williams, *Lincoln and the Radicals* (Madison, Wis., 1941), p. 6; L. E. Chittenden, *A Report of the Debates and Proceedings in the Secret Sessions of the Conference Convention for Proposing Amendments to the Constitution of the United States, Held at Washington, D.C., in February, A.D. 1861* (New York, 1864), p. 427.

majority, will throw it away?" Even if Northern delegates consented to do so, their constituents would not uphold them. But
there was no need to be apprehensive. No attack would be made
on slavery within the states, and he declared himself ready to
endorse federal compensation for fugitive slaves. Warning against
the horrors of war, he closed on a note of caution. If Lincoln's
lawful authority were resisted and he fulfilled his oath, war would
be the result. When the conference's recommendations, similar
to the Crittenden proposals in suggesting amendments to divide
slave and free territories along 36° 30′, were not endorsed by
Congress, the radicals, who had opposed them, were satisfied. In
view of the South's refusal to offer pledges of unconditional
loyalty in return for concessions, their attitude was not without
justification.[9]

And so the congressional session drew to a close, with advanced
Republicans fighting to the last against concessions. The only
compromise he would countenance, said Ben Wade, was to
demand two hundred and fifty traitors for hanging and settle for
twenty-five. Neither he nor his friends were able to defeat a
proposed constitutional amendment which would have guaranteed
forever slave property within the states against federal interference, but the amendment was never ratified by the states. The
radicals could congratulate themselves. The concessions they had
feared so much had not been made, and the party stood firm.
Under the circumstances, they could well afford to make a gesture
of their own, and they passed laws for the organization of Colorado, Nevada, and Dakota territories without any reference to
the subject of slavery. Republican governors would at any rate be
in charge of the territorial governments.[1]

[9] Wilson, *History,* III, 84; Blair-Chandler, February 27, 1861, Chandler Papers; Gunderson, *Old Gentlemen's Convention,* pp. 94–5, 105–6;
L. E. Chittenden, *Recollections of President Lincoln and his Administration* (New York, 1891), pp. 20 ff., 32–5, 53–4; Chittenden, *Report,*
pp. 289, 427; LeRoy H. Fisher, *Lincoln's Gadfly, Adam Gurowski* (Norman, Okla., 1964), p. 77.

[1] J. D. Webster–Trumbull, February 7, 1861, Trumbull Papers, LC;
Cong. Globe, 36th Cong., 2d Sess., 1285, 1403; Blaine, *Twenty Years
of Congress,* I, 270.

In the meantime, by a roundabout route the President-elect had arrived in the capital. His stealthy entry greatly upset such ultras as Governor Blair of Michigan, who blamed Lincoln's advisers. He himself would have had the President-elect go through Baltimore in open daylight "if a thousand had to be killed in order to accomplish it." But once the new leader was in Washington, it was possible to make a personal assessment of him. Sumner was at first shocked at his uncouth Western ways, but he was cheered by his attitude. Lincoln was standing firm. As E. L. Pierce wrote to Chase on February 24,

> I have received a most cheering letter from Mr. Herndon. . . .
> Nothing can exceed his testimony to Mr. Lincoln's fidelity to
> our cause in all its purity and breadth—and he quotes his
> declarations up to the very hour he left home.

Lincoln's arrival and support strengthened the foes of compromise in the Peace Convention, and since he was on excellent terms with Trumbull and E. B. Washburne—the two radicals even proposed to arrange for his living quarters in Washington—to say nothing of his confidential relationship with Hannibal Hamlin, there was no evidence of a rift between the President-elect and the more advanced sections of the party, even though some radicals grumbled about the Cabinet.[2]

That the new President knew how to balance the various factions among his supporters in such a way as to satisfy the conservatives while actually favoring the radicals, he showed in the preparation of his inaugural address. At the urging of his conservative friend Orville Browning, he changed the draft of his speech by omitting references to his intentions of reclaiming the public property which had fallen; he accepted many of Seward's careful suggestions, but he also showed the draft to Carl Schurz, the ardent young radical from Wisconsin, to whom he said, "I

[2] Blair-Chandler, February 27, 1861, Chandler Papers; Schurz, *Reminiscences*, II, 240–1; E. L. Pierce–Chase, February 24, 1861, Chase Papers, HSP; Gunderson, *Old Gentlemen's Convention*, pp. 84–5; Washburne-Lincoln, February 19, 1861, RTL.

shall never betray my principles or friends." At least so Schurz remembered it years later, and because Lincoln had not proposed to yield anything substantial, the young man was delighted.[3]

The inaugural address showed Lincoln at his best. Without abandoning the radicals' principal demands, he yet struck a conciliatory tone. Categorically denying the legal right of secession, he declared the Union perpetual. "The power confided to me," he announced, "will be used to hold, occupy, and possess the property, and places belonging to the government, and to collect the duties and imposts" but there need be no war. The government would not assail anybody.

If radicals objected to Lincoln's inclusion of a paragraph welcoming constitutional amendments, they could nevertheless take heart because he had not given up the main point. Slavery would not be expanded, and they knew it. "Our true Republicans are cheered by the firmness of Mr. Lincoln's inaugural, and are full of faith that the mingling of prudence and firmness in carrying out the indicated policy, which we shall have good reason to expect, will bring us through our troubles without disgraceful concessions, and without sacrifice of principle," wrote J. D. Cox, an Ohio Republican, to Chase. The new government was progressive.[4]

From the very beginning, the radicals' influence on the new administration was great. To be sure, the Secretary of State was their antagonist, but the Vice President was in sympathy with their aims. The Secretary of the Treasury represented their interests in the Cabinet, where, for a time, he was strongly supported by Montgomery Blair, then as uncompromising as Chandler and Wade. And in the Senate, which had assembled for a brief special session, they obtained the chairmanships of the most important committees, Sumner securing foreign affairs,

[3] Browning, *Diary*, I, 455; Nicolay and Hay, *Abraham Lincoln*, III, 319–44; Bancroft, *Speeches, Correspondence and Political Papers of Carl Schurz*, I, 179–80.
[4] Lincoln, *Works*, IV, 262–71; J. D. Cox–Chase, March 5, 1861, Chase Papers, HSP.

Wilson the military, Trumbull the judiciary, Wade, territories, Fessenden, finance, Chandler, commerce, and Hale, naval affairs. They had every reason to congratulate themselves.[5]

But the ultras' immediate problem was not a legislative one. It was the executive who would have to decide whether Fort Sumter and other federal installations in the South should be held, reinforced, or abandoned, and it was known that Seward, who, through intermediaries, was in touch with Southern emissaries, was making strenuous efforts to bring about a compromise by surrendering the forts. Would he be able to impose his views upon the administration?

The radicals were seriously worried. "The news that Mr. Lincoln will order Fort Sumter to be evacuated coming soon after the bold statements of his inaugural makes me think of the baby's epitaph—'If so early I must be done for, I wonder what I was begun for,' " wrote F. B. Sanborn, Sumner's extremist friend. The determined members of the party had to do something, and on March 11, the Republican senators held a caucus, its proceedings reported in detail by Rudolf Schleiden, their confidant and Minister Resident of the Hanseatic Republic of Bremen:

> Yesterday afternoon the Republican senators held a so-called caucus. Wade of Ohio made the proposal to repair to the President *in corpore* and to protest against the evacuation. The fort must be held, and if 100,000 men were to lose their lives, he himself was ready to be one of them. Even the prudent Collamer of Vermont was ready to sacrifice at least 1,000 human lives. Chandler of Michigan offered to send provisions to Fort Sumter . . . for $50,000, Simmons of Rhode Island was willing to do it even for $20,000. Finally Sumner and Trumbull succeeded in obtaining a consensus of opinion to the effect that political considerations had to yield in a question which could only be decided by the military authorities, and that it was not at all within the province of the Senate to force its advice upon the administration in this matter. Wade's proposal to send a deputation, as well as many amendents to it, was dropped.

[5] *Cong. Globe,* 36th Cong., 2d Sess., 1446.

But the mood of the Senate was clear, and if Lincoln still had any doubts, Chandler kept urging him to arrest secessionist senators who were delivering disloyal speeches and to destroy the newly established Southern Confederacy.[6]

The Cabinet proved to be the main battleground. There, much to the radicals' dismay, the Secretary of the Treasury, Salmon P. Chase, seemed to be weakening. "Mr. Chase," wrote one of his correspondents, pleading with him for the retention of Fort Sumter, "We have relied on you. How is it we are deceived?" But Blair's strength more than compensated for Chase's temporary indecision. The Postmaster General stood like a rock, and when on March 15 Lincoln polled the Cabinet on the advisability of provisioning the fort, Blair was the only one who gave an unqualified reply in the affirmative. The fort must not be evacuated under any circumstances, he maintained. The South would merely interpret such a move as weakness and the authority of the government would be gone. He even had the assistance of his father, who told the President that evacuation constituted treason. Since all the other Cabinet members either gave negative answers or qualified their statements—Chase stating that he would be opposed to the attempt if it were to cause civil war although he professed to believe this contingency unlikely and so answered in the affirmative—Blair's stand was remarkable. For the time being, the radicals' trust in him had been justified.[7]

The special session of the Senate clearly demonstrated that Republicans agreed with the Postmaster General. Their incisive remarks on the floor set the tone for their caucuses; and a newcomer from Wisconsin, Timothy O. Howe, whom some had distrusted because he had opposed his party's reliance on states' rights arguments to uphold Wisconsin's defiance of the Fugitive

[6] F. B. Sanborn–Sumner, March 12, 1861, Sumner Papers; Dispatch No. 34, March 12, 1861, Schleiden Papers (author's translation); Hamlin, *Hamlin,* p. 397.
[7] T. J. Young–Chase, March 12, 1861, Chase Papers, HSP; F. P. Blair, Sr.–Montgomery Blair, March 12, 1861, RTL; Lincoln, *Works, IV,* 284–5.

Slave Act in the controversy culminating in the case of *Ableman v. Booth,* proved himself a true radical. Painfully affected by the statements of the opposition—he thought its sentiments so monstrous he almost feared that the marble wall would crumble about him—he delivered his maiden speech on March 22–25. Castigating secession in unsparing terms, he declared that no amendments were needed. If all stood by the Constitution, the Union would yet be saved. And on March 28, Senator Trumbull introduced a resolution placing the Senate on record against evacuation. He wanted the Senate to affirm that it was the duty of the President "to use all the means in his power to hold and protect the public property of the United States."[8]

Lincoln observed closely the proceedings in Congress. Fundamentally opposed to his Secretary of State's supine policies, he was totally unwilling to be dominated by him. The President lacked will and had been possessed by radicals and mischievous men, complained his conservative friend, David Davis.[9] But in reality, Lincoln's influence was paramount. He merely permitted the radicals to pave the way for his decisions.

The President kept his head in the Fort Sumter crisis. Beset by trouble, strongly importuned by Seward to abandon the installation on the ground that Southern Unionism must be encouraged, he was well aware of the serious political consequences of evacuation. As William Butler, an Illinois radical, had written to Senator Trumbull,

> Do we surrender Sumter on the ground of expediency or from necessity? If it is done from expediency, I tell you our party will go under. . . . Better try this government now than later.

[8] Howe–Grace Howe, March 9, 1861, Howe–Edward Bates, April 2, 1861, T. O. Howe Papers, Wisconsin Historical Society; *Cong. Globe,* 36th Cong., 2d Sess., 1469–71, 1491–3, 1498 ff., 1519; William H. Russell, "Timothy O. Howe, Stalwart Republican," *Wisconsin Magazine of History,* XXXV (Winter, 1951), 93. The case of *Ableman V. Booth* arose after the defiance of the Fugitive Slave Law by Sherman Booth and the declaration of the State Supreme Court that the federal law was unconstitutional.

[9] H. W. Davis–S. F. DuPont, March 20, 1861, DuPont Papers.

Accordingly, when on March 28 General Winfield Scott advised the surrender of both Fort Sumter and Fort Pickens in Florida, the President called again for the opinions of the Cabinet ministers. What did the members think now? Seward and his allies once more urged surrender, but this time not only did Chase unequivocally join Blair, but they were supported by Cameron and Welles as well.[1]

Lincoln knew he had to do something. The supplies at Fort Sumter were running low, and the installation had either to be provisioned or given up. In the long run, after considerable hesitation, he decided against Seward and carried out the radicals' wishes. He would send provisions to Sumter after giving warning to the South; since he did not intend to send arms as well, if war resulted, it would be the Confederates' fault.

How Lincoln carried out his plans by dispatching naval forces to both Fort Sumter and Fort Pickens, how Seward attempted to frustrate the President's efforts at the last moment by ordering the U.S.S. *Powhatan* to Florida instead of South Carolina, how the Confederate authorities decided to inaugurate war rather than to allow Anderson to be provisioned—all these details have often been described. When the guns opened up on April 12, 1861, on the garrison in Charleston Harbor, they were not to be silenced for four years, over 600,000 Americans would lose their lives, and many more would be maimed and wounded. To what extent were the radicals responsible for this disaster?

It is not surprising that their opponents have always charged them with fomenting war. As early as February 2, 1861, the New York *Herald* printed a headline, "Ultra Republican Schemes to Destroy the Government." The article which followed explained that Lincoln was anxious for a settlement, but that it was well known that there was a large number of Republicans in both

[1] William Butler–Trumbull, March 14, 1861, Trumbull Papers, LC; Richard Current, *Lincoln and the First Shot* (Philadelphia, 1963), pp. 71, 75–81; Cabinet meeting, March 29, 1861, RTL.

Houses who were doing everything in their power to defeat an adjustment of the questions at issue. On March 1, the paper again charged that the radicals were driving the country to war. "Still Harping on War and Blood," read the new article. "The radical, revolutionary republican leaders continue to harp on coercion of the Southern States, bloodshed and war. . . ." And when the conflict had actually broken out, Democratic papers again blamed their most determined antagonists. "When such men as Seward and Chase and Wade and Giddings and Greeley control the administration, what can we expect?" queried the Salem, Indiana, *Washington Democrat.* Except for the inaccuracy concerning the Secretary of State, the charge has been repeated many times since.[2]

It is true that many radicals had long underestimated the danger of secession and civil war. During the crisis of 1850, long before he became more conservative, Charles Francis Adams expressed his disbelief in the likelihood of disunion. At the same time, Edward Wade, who said that his motto was "Liberty first & Union afterward," also professed to see secessionist agitation as a trick. Ten years later, the ultras were still nonchalant about the prospects of separation. "The difficulties in the way of the *seceders* are so great," Sumner on December 16, 1860, wrote to the reformer Samuel G. Howe,

> that I fear we shall not get rid of them *long enough.* My desire is that four or five should go out *long enough* to be completely humbled & chastened & to leave us in control of the government. If they *stay in,* there will be a new Compromise, which I shall . . . fight.

Southern traitors would "howl and rave, like so many devils tormented before their time, but it is all humbug and means nothing

[2] New York *Herald,* February 2, March 1, 1861; Salem, Indiana, *Washington Democrat,* in Howard Cecil Perkins, ed., *Northern Editorials on Secession* (New York, 1942), II, 783; Arnold Whitridge, *No Compromise! The Story of the Fanatics Who Paved the Way to the Civil War* (New York, 1960), pp. 194–5; New York *Herald,* September 20, 1861, May 3, 1862.

and can have no other result, than the ignominy and disgrace of those who resort to it," Ben Wade predicted in November, 1860, giving expression to sentiments which many other radicals substantially shared. And Chandler's "blood-letting" letter certainly also revealed a gross underestimation of the realities of the situation. Only a few extremists grasped how serious things really were.[3]

It is also true that in some ways, several radicals were not as passionately devoted to the Union as their more conservative neighbors. Believing that the American government constituted "mankind's last best hope," they considered its principles of freedom compromised by the continued existence of slavery, an institution they were willing to tolerate only as long as absolutely necessary. Rather than see it perpetuated and strengthened, some were ready to jettison the federal structure. "The threats of dissolution make no impression on us in these 'diggins,'" wrote Edward Wade to Giddings as early as 1850. "We say give us dissolution rather than Slavery extension." In 1854, Sumner declared that if the Union could not exist without a Fugitive Slave Law, it was not worthwhile, a thought his friend Richard Henry Dana echoed two years later during the 1856 campaign. "This *may* be our last national election," he wrote. "Quien sabe? But it is absurd of the majority in numbers & interest to talk of leaving the firm because the minority in numbers & interest insist upon governing." By December, 1860, Giddings had come to the conclusion that if the lower South seceded, it would be just as well, and James Freeman Clarke also envisaged a happy union of free states only.[4]

[3] C. F. Adams–Giddings, January 27, 1850, Edward Wade–Giddings, February 21, 1850, Giddings Papers; George Hochfield, ed., Henry Adams, *The Great Secession Winter of 1806–61* (New York, 1958), p. 12; Sumner–S. G. Howe, December 16, 1860, Boutwell-Sumner, March 25, 1861, Sumner Papers; Wade-Trumbull, November 14, 1860, Trumbull Papers, LC; Hamlin, *Hamlin,* p. 390.

[4] Edward Wade–Giddings, February 21, 1850, Giddings Papers; New York *Tribune,* June 27, 1854; R. H. Dana–Sumner, June 21, 1856, Giddings-Sumner, December 3, 1860, J. F. Clarke–Sumner, December 8, 1860, Sumner Papers.

In the long run, however, most radicals believed in the perpetuity of the Union. "I say," declared Hale on December 5, 1860, in the Senate,

> if . . . with a faithful Government . . . with the blessings of Providence coming down upon us as they are, if at such a time this Confederacy should burst, this glorious fraternity of States be dissevered, and we try, by the doubtful contingencies of separate State action to carry out the great experiment of human liberty, we shall present a most humiliating spectacle.

Twelve days later, Wade made a similar point. "I am for maintaining the Union of these States," he affirmed. "I will sacrifice everything but honor to maintain it."[5] This conviction was the justification for the ultras' refusal to countenance the evacuation of Fort Sumter; it was the reason for their truculence during the crisis. In some ways, the wish was father of the thought. Inexorably opposed to concessions, many radicals honestly thought that their policy was the least risky that could be adopted. If Southern threats were bluff, firmness would set everything right in the shortest possible time, and firmness was exactly what they were preaching. Their innate faith in the perfectibility of the American government triumphed over their temporary doubts.

But the question of their responsibility for war remains to be answered. In spite of the active support of the peace movement by men like Sumner and Giddings, it cannot be denied that, throughout the 1850's, many extremists belittled the horrors of war and delivered bellicose speeches. "Are not Sharp's rifles glorious antislavery documents?" E. S. Hamlin wrote to Sumner in 1855. "I am not frightened by a little blood letting." Great crimes like slavery, he thought, had always been expiated by blood, and America was probably no exception to this rule of history. Jacob M. Howard, later a radical senator from Michigan, agreed. Intensely agitated because of the sack of Lawrence, he unburdened himself to Seward.

> I know of but few instances in history where tyranny has been put down by anything but force & the shedding of blood. Let

[5] *Cong. Globe,* 36th Cong., 2d Sess., 10, 104.

it come. I will bear my part in the responsibility cheerfully—cheerfully if it shall exact my blood or the blood of my sons.

William Herndon, Lincoln's law partner, was likewise given to hyperbole. "I am for striking at the *cause*," he wrote in 1858 to Trumbull,

> and I am this day ready to go further than I have ever gone, if the nigger drivers force Kansas on this free people. I am ready to go any length for self-defense, though that length *should end in war,* bloody and to the hilt.

Chandler's notorious letter to Blair also indicated a callous attitude toward bloodshed, but such occasional expressions are not enough to convict the radicals of war guilt. They were, after all, only reacting to threats.[6]

To assess responsibility for a holocaust like the American Civil War, it is necessary to distinguish between challengers and challenged, aggressors and their opponents. It was not the radicals who had loudly declared that they would break up the Union unless their demands were met; it was not the radicals who had for years uttered threats in and out of Congress, and it was not the radicals who, by refusing to abide by the election results, insisted upon changing the *status quo.* They were not the real aggressors; all they did was react to Southern attacks, unreasonable exactions like demands for a federal slave code in the territories, which they thought unjustified as well as morally reprehensible. And in taking their stand, they were at one with virtually the entire civilized world, which considered slavery a barbarous anachronism. As the fire-eater Lawrence Keitt openly declared in the South Carolina secession convention, "I am willing in this issue to rest disunion upon the question of slavery. It is the great central point from which we are now seceding." Given the uselessness of all concessions made prior to 1860, the ultras' adamant opposition to a renewed compromise was perfectly justified. Agreeing with Lincoln, they believed that the instant a compromise concerning

[6] E. S. Hamlin–Sumner, January 17, 1855, Sumner Papers; J. M. Howard–Seward, May 26, 1856, Seward Papers; Herndon-Trumbull, February 19, 1858, Trumbull Papers, LC.

the extension of slavery were arranged, Southerners would "have us under again; all our labor is lost, and sooner or later must be done over. . . ."[7]

Under these circumstances, the radicals honestly defended their principles as they saw them. They were certain of the moral justification of their course, believed in the necessity of settling the slavery question in such a way as to put the institution on the road to extinction, and refused to yield to threats. If their talk was sometimes unwise, if they underestimated the danger and showed insufficient awareness of the horrors of war, they nevertheless performed a great service for their country. Their backbone enabled Lincoln to stand firm, and his resolution made it possible for him successfully to meet the greatest menace the nation has ever faced.

[7] Edward McPherson, *The Political History of the United States of America During the Great Rebellion* (2d ed., Washington, 1865), p. 17 (hereafter cited as McPherson, *Rebellion*); Lincoln, *Works*, IV, 150.

CHAPTER

V

War and the Struggle Against McClellan

THE OUTBREAK of the Civil War set the radicals astir. Long convinced of the utter incompatibility of slavery and free government, they found their prejudices borne out by events. And the enthusiasm with which Northerners of all political persuasions rushed to the colors augured well for the future. The ultras were no longer alone; they had become the vanguard of the nation.

But it was not only the newly found popularity of their opposition to the slaveholders which cheered the advanced Republicans. The war opened up vistas of success never dreamed of before; slavery itself might be one of its victims. "Only a short time ago, it seemed as if there must be a separation," wrote Sumner to Giddings, "but this generous & mighty uprising of the North seems to menace defeat to the rebels & the extinction of Slavery in blood." The Ohioan replied in the same vein: "Never were the political heavens more bright or auspicious. The first gun fired at Fort Sumpter [sic] rang out the death knell of slavery." Carl Schurz put it even more strongly. Thousands of Democrats were declaring, "Now is the time to remove the cause of all our woes," he said to John Hay, Lincoln's private secretary. "What we could not have done in many lifetimes the madness and folly of the South has accomplished for us. Slavery offers itself more vulnerable to our attack than at any point in any century. . . ."[1]

The radicals' assessment of their possibilities was accurate, and it was this realization that turned even those who had looked forward with equanimity to separation from the South into violent foes of any compromise. Almost overnight, they became the most determined advocates of relentless warfare, the most insistent proponents of unconditional surrender of the South. "Our whole community are quivering under apprehension of a truce or armistice. The most conservative among our loyal men contemplate such a possibility with something akin to horror," wrote William D. Kelley, the Philadelphia radical, to Lincoln.[2] In this belief, the ultras would never waver, and although in 1861 the President did not fully agree with them, in the main, he gradually came to endorse their view. His sense of proportion added a necessary dimension which they lacked.

The radicals' enthusiasm for a speedy and thoroughgoing prosecution of the war became evident at once. Lincoln's call for 75,000 men to suppress the insurrection found them ready. As the Chicago journalist Horace White explained,

> I wrote to the President some time in January that the young men of Chicago would be in at the death to defend his prerogatives *if he would refuse to compromise.* He has kept his promise, & now we are keeping ours. We are drilling every night—over two thousand on the muster rolls—and only eager to hear the second call for troops, which we hope will be for 500,000 men.

Zach Chandler joined with his old opponent, Lewis Cass, for a mammoth war meeting in Detroit, where the two former antagonists appeared arm-in-arm; Ben Wade was active in recruiting

[1] Sumner-Giddings, April 28, 1861, Giddings Papers; Giddings-Sumner, April 30, 1861, Sumner Papers; Hay, *Diaries,* p. 22.
[2] W. D. Kelley–Lincoln, April 27, 1861, RTL.

drives on the Western Reserve and actually tried to enlist; Charles Sumner addressed cheering soldiers in New York, and Hannibal Hamlin traveled to the Empire State to rally support and to take over the government in case of disaster at Washington. In spite of complaints about lack of energy in the capital—some radicals felt that 75,000 troops were not enough and Congress should have been called—the Vice President explained to his wife that allowances should be made for the administration. "They did not know with what promptness the whole north & west were responding," he reasoned. "I now think we will witness more efficiency." Trumbull, too, was hopeful. "Action, efficient, decided bold is what is now wanted everywhere and I feel we are to have it," he wrote to Lincoln.[3] The President had no reason to complain about the enthusiasm of the most extreme wing of the party.

Nevertheless, as the Vice President had already seen, it was clear from the start that Lincoln could not take the radicals' support for granted. Determined to crush the rebellion, the ultras were certain to become impatient if the administration did not seem to move as fast as they deemed proper. They would try to see to it that Lincoln was kept up to the mark. "Measured by the intensity of feeling and a proper appreciation of the crisis, the President and the Cabinet at Washington are far behind the people," editorialized the *New York Times,* a paper of moderate views. The radicals could not be expected to be less demanding.[4]

The physical isolation of Washington during the third week of April made an especially bad impression in the North. Unless communications were reopened, warned Hiram Barney, the radical whom Chase had appointed Collector of the Port of New York, the administration would be severely censured and its moral hold on the country would be lost. Ben Wade, exulting

[3] Horace White–John Nicolay, April 19, 1861, Trumbull–Lincoln, May 15, 1861, RTL; Detroit *Post and Tribune, Chandler.* pp. 204–5; Ashtabula *Sentinel,* April 24, 1861; Sumner, *Works,* V, 492–6; Hamlin, *Hamlin,* pp. 397–404; D. D. Field–Hamlin, April 21, 1861, Hamlin–Mrs. Hamlin, April 23, 25, 28, 1861, Hamlin Papers.
[4] *New York Times,* April 23, 1861.

about the great enthusiasm which prevailed in Ohio, criticized Lincoln severely for negotiating to send troops around Baltimore instead of marching them through the disaffected city. "The South has got to be punished and traitors hung," he concluded,

> if it can be by assent of the President and in a Constitutional way, but the stern demand for justice of a united people cannot and must not be baffled by the imbecility or perverseness of one man though he be the President of the United States.[5]

Some of the ultras were not content to support the war effort from a distance. Early in spring, seeking to infuse the administration with a bellicose spirit, Senators Chandler and Wade arrived in the capital. "Wade and Chandler are here, hot for war," reported Lot Morrill of Maine, who had accompanied his two radical colleagues on a trip to Fortress Monroe, where General Benjamin F. Butler had just taken command. Butler had been a lifelong Democrat; he had even run for governor of Massachusetts on the Breckinridge ticket, but he had made a name for himself by opening communications with Washington and occupying Baltimore in May of 1861. That he had acted against General Scott's orders only increased the extremists' respect for him. On the way back, the senators witnessed some fighting when their transport joined in a gun duel between the U.S.S. *Monticello* and a Confederate battery at Sewall's Point. It was "the best ball playing he had ever seen," commented Chandler.[6]

Despite their feeling that the President might do more than he was doing, during the first months of the war the radicals were careful not to offend him. Realizing that cooperation was essential, they sought to support the administration wherever possible and maintained close personal relations with Lincoln. "When I returned home after the Executive Session, I found

[5] Hiram Barney–Chase, April 23, 1861, Chase Papers, HSP; Wade-Whittlesey, April 30, 1861, Elisha Whittlesey Papers, Western Reserve Historical Association.
[6] Fessenden, *Fessenden*, I, 186; Trefousse, *Butler*, pp. 52 ff., 65–76; Detroit *Post and Tribune*, *Chandler*, pp. 206–7.

nearly all the people sore, and, disheartened . . ." Henry Wilson informed the President on May 16.

> On my return home this week, I find almost everyone hopeful, confident, satisfied. . . . I am sure the people are for prompt and earnest action. They now feel that you are doing the right thing and that all will be done in your power to put down treason.

Chandler, too, addressed Lincoln in a relatively friendly manner. "I should owe you an humble apology for the tone of a dispatch forwarded yesterday, if I had sent it, but I did not," he wrote on June 15. To be sure, he had suggested that martial law be declared immediately in Missouri; that forty more regiments from the Northwest be accepted for service in the border state, and that Governor Claiborne Jackson be hanged at once. But he had only stated what he would do if he had the power, and a friend who sympathized with the sentiments sent off the message. "Pardon me when I say," he concluded, "the People of Michigan think the time has arrived to commence a hanging & so think I." Sumner, who accompanied the Chief Executive on buggy rides, submitted a series of needful measures for the coming special session of Congress, among which were several desired by the administration. The senator from Massachusetts appreciated Lincoln's good qualities.[7]

The special session of Congress, which met on July 4, gave proof of the smooth working of the Republican party machinery. The committees were quickly organized, the radicals not only retaining the important chairmanships in the Senate, but securing crucial positions in the House as well. Galusha Grow was elected Speaker; Thaddeus Stevens became chairman of the Committee on Ways and Means, Owen Lovejoy of the Committee on Agriculture, and James M. Ashley of the Committee on Territories. Even Ben Wade approved of the President's message; both radicals and conservatives supported the necessary war measures, and the two factions approved Lincoln's call for troops during the

[7] Wilson-Lincoln, May 16, 1861, Chandler-Lincoln, June 15, 1861, RTL; Sumner, *Works*, VI, 31; Sumner-Lieber, June 23, 1861, Sumner Papers.

period in which Congress had not been in session. For the first Confiscation Act, freeing slaves employed in war against the Union, the radicals secured almost unanimous Republican support. On the other hand, they reluctantly consented to the Johnson-Crittenden Resolutions which declared that the sole object of the war was the restoration of the Union, and that as soon as this purpose was accomplished, the conflict ought to cease. Much as they disliked the proposition, of all the ultras, only J. F. Potter of Wisconsin and A. G. Riddle of Ohio voted against it in the House, while Stevens and Lovejoy abstained. In the Senate, Sumner did not vote; Trumbull joined four border state senators in opposition, but explained that his attitude was based on technical grounds. The unity of the Republican party, at least for the time being, had been established.[8]

The summer meeting of Congress was highly dramatic. Menaced by enemy forces less than thirty miles across the river, the legislators transacted business virtually on the front line. They frequently visited the army, and when, on July 16, General Irwin McDowell moved forward to give battle, many a civilian went along to watch the imminent defeat of the rebels. That the bellicose radicals were among the sightseers was not surprising; Trumbull, Wade, Grimes, Chandler, and Riddle had taken carriages to accompany the army. But McDowell on July 21 suffered a crushing defeat at Bull Run, and civilians and soldiers alike fled headlong to the safety of the capital.

The group of radical excursionists refused to be stampeded. Trumbull and Grimes had become separated from the others, but Wade, Chandler, and Riddle, pulling their carriage across the road, rifle in hand, attempted to stop the rout. Although one of their friends was shot in the hand, the amateur warriors did not

[8] *Cong. Globe,* 37th Cong., 1st Sess., 17, 21, 61, 110, 219, 431, 434, 442, 448–9; Rhodes, *History of the United States,* V, 437–8; Wade–Mrs. Wade, July 6, 1861, Wade Papers; Blaine, *Twenty Years of Congress,* I, 313 ff., 338–41; A. G. Riddle, *Reminiscences of Men and Events in Washington, 1860–1865* (New York, 1895), pp. 41–3; Frederick W. Seward, *Seward at Washington* (New York, 1891), II, 602.

give up until they were relieved by the Second New York regiment. They returned, infuriated at what they considered military incompetence and certain that they knew more about soldiering than professional officers.[9]

Because of the great disappointment about the defeat, hostile newspapers sought to blame the disaster on some scapegoat, and the radicals were the most available candidates. They had urged the army forward; did they not therefore have to answer for its subsequent defeat? "The responsible parties must be looked for in Congress," charged the independent, anti-Negro and antiradical New York *Herald* after the battle.

> Who are they? They belong to that fanatical abolitionist clique who are laboring . . . to divert this war from its legitimate objective . . . into an exterminating crusade against Southern slavery.

The cry, "Onward to Richmond," was to blame, a slogan coined by a mad "Jacobin club."[1]

These charges against the ultras have often been repeated since. But while it is true that General Scott was prematurely hurried into battle, conservative as well as radical Republicans had been united in the belief that the enemy capital must be seized as quickly as possible. As General James B. Fry, McDowell's Chief of Staff, wrote years later, "Northern enthusiasm was unbounded. 'On to Richmond' was the war-cry. Public sentiment was irresistible, and in response to it the army advanced." If the radicals were guilty of excessive ardor, so was the administration, and so were the conservatives.[2]

From the ultras' point of view, premature marching was not the cause of the reverse. Lack of determination on the part of the

---

[9] Riddle, *Reminiscences*, pp. 52–3; Riddle, *Wade*, pp. 244–5; Ashtabula *Sentinel*, August 1, 1861; Riddle–Mrs. Riddle, July 24, 1861, Riddle Papers; Wade–Mrs. Wade, July 22, 1861, Wade Papers.

[1] New York *Herald*, July 23, 1861.

[2] Randall, *Lincoln the President*, I, 384; James B. Fry, *McDowell's Advance to Bull Run*, in Clarence Buel and Robert Johnson eds., *Battles and Leaders of the Civil War* (New York, 1887–8), I, 176 (hereafter cited as *Battles and Leaders*); Browning, *Diary*, I, 598.

military, if not of the administration, was what was wrong. The
North had been outgeneraled, complained Kinsley S. Bingham,
the radical senator from Michigan; Scott lacked vigor. Chandler
visited Lincoln immediately after the battle and insisted that
thoroughgoing measures be taken at once to show "the country
and the rebels that the government was not discouraged a whit,
but was just beginning to get mad." He thought a call for half a
million additional troops appropriate. Wade, whose cantankerous-
ness was becoming chronic, believed that the troops had behaved
with great bravery but that the officers "were very stupid." "I
must impart some of my courage to the despairing groups around
me," he boasted to his wife. Others heard him exclaim, "I do not
wonder that people desert to Jeff. Davis, as he shows brains, I may
desert myself." And the radicals were more impatient than ever.
As Carl Schurz explained to Lincoln, it did not pay to wait too
long in order to be well equipped. Action was what was wanted.[3]

Fully as aware of the necessity of doing something as were
his advisers, Lincoln sought to remedy the situation by appointing
a new general. The obvious man for the position seemed to be
George Brinton McClellan, who had impressed the radicals as
well as others by his successes in West Virginia.[4] Placing him in
command of the troops near Washington immediately after the
battle, the President showed that the administration responded to
constructive criticism.

The radicals' military judgment, however, was not always
sound. Not only did they soon have reason to rue their support of

[3] K. S. Bingham–Jacob Howard, July 26, 1861, Howard Papers;
Detroit *Post and Tribune, Chandler*, p. 211; Wade–Mrs. Wade, July
22, 1861, Wade Papers; Adam Gurowski, *Diary* (Boston, 1862, New
York, 1864, Washington, 1866), I, 90; Schurz–Lincoln, August 13,
1861, RTL.

[4] Schuckers, *Chase*, pp. 427–8; Riddle, *Reminiscences*, p. 63; Chan-
dler–Mrs. Chandler, July 16, 1861, Chandler Papers; Gurowski, *Diary*,
I, 87; George Nourse–Trumbull, August 16, 1861, Trumbull Papers,
LC; David Donald, ed., *Inside Lincoln's Cabinet: The Civil War Diaries
of Salmon P. Chase* (New York, 1954), pp. 101–2 (hereafter cited as
Chase, *Diaries*); Allen Thorndike Rice, ed., *Reminiscences of Abraham
Lincoln by Men of His Time* (New York, 1886), p. 271.

McClellan, but they also became involved in the controversy between Lincoln and John C. Frémont, a general whom most of them believed to be a genius, when his incompetence was patently clear. Having been appointed to command the Western Department, partially at the behest of the Blair family, the Pathfinder had encountered serious difficulty. His troops were inefficient; all his military skill had not sufficed to prevent the death, at Wilson's Creek, of Major Nathaniel Lyon, one of the foremost upholders of the Union in Missouri, and his rear was rendered insecure by secessionist threats. Harassed and fired by antislavery zeal, on August 31, the general sought to solve his problems by issuing an order freeing all slaves held by rebels within his department. The radicals were delighted.

That Lincoln had to take some type of action was evident. He could neither permit commanders in the field to usurp the functions of the Chief Executive nor allow generals to take premature steps toward emancipation. If he countenanced the proclamation, he would lose the border states. Although he knew very well that he would be severely criticized by the radicals, he decided that he would have to intervene. In characteristic fashion, he gently suggested that Frémont modify the order. Only when the general refused did Lincoln send him a direct order rescinding the proclamation.[5]

Most of the radicals reacted with fury. "The President's letter to Gen. Frémont has caused a funeral gloom over our patriotic city," wrote Joseph Medill to Chase. The war was a slaveholders' rebellion, and until the administration saw the contest in its true light, the blood of loyal men would be shed in vain. Sumner deeply regretted the President's letter. It meant that slavery was not to be touched by martial law, and this fact, he thought, weakened all the armies. Why did not Lincoln use his power properly? A Minnesota editor complained that the President's

[5] Jessie Frémont's Memoirs, p. 252, Frémont Papers; Allan Nevins, Frémont, Pathmarker of the West (New York, 1939), pp. 498–505; John M. Schofield, Forty-Six Years in the Army (New York, 1897), p. 49; Julian, Political Recollections, pp. 198–200; Koerner, Memoirs, II, 167.

action was interfering with recruiting; the Kansas radical, Martin F. Conway, expressed his conviction that the government would have to be "revolutionized," and friends urged Chase not to resign so that at least one great man remained in the Cabinet. His intimate George Hoadly even complained that if the letter to Frémont were an indication of Lincoln's character and policies, he prayed to God to forgive his vote for the President. Wade, so enraged that he wrote an admiring letter to the general, confided to Chandler that Lincoln's views on slavery "could only come of one, born of 'poor white trash' and educated in a slave State." In Missouri as well as elsewhere, the Pathfinder became the idol of the Germans and other radical Unionists.[6]

The criticism of the President did not mean that an unbridgeable gulf had opened up between Lincoln and the radicals. They would continue to work together, even though the President eventually had to dismiss Frémont because of increasing evidence of his maladministration in Missouri. The radicals, at mass meetings, might again bitterly denounce him for replacing the general, but as Chandler himself admitted that Frémont was a failure, Lincoln could afford to discount their strictures. And he saw to it that David Hunter, a general as radical as the Pathfinder, was appointed Frémont's temporary successor.[7]

In the meantime, affairs on the Potomac were also reaching a crisis. Military matters were in a state of flux; although McClellan was in charge of the forces around the capital, old Winfield Scott was still the overall commander. "Old Fuss and Feathers" had been under heavy attack, and McClellan was not

[6] Medill–Chase, September 15, 1861, Chase Papers, HSP; O. Brown–Ramsey, September 19, 1861, Alexander Ramsay Papers, Minnesota Historical Society; Conway-Sumner, October 7, 1861, Sumner-Lieber, September 17, 1861, Sumner Papers; Jessie Frémont's Memoirs, p. 297, Frémont Papers; George Hoadley–Chase, September 18, 1861, Chase Papers, LC; Wade–Chandler, September 23, 1861, Chandler Papers; Koerner, *Memoirs*, II, 167; Nevins, *Frémont*, p. 504.

[7] Ibid., pp. 543–8; Koerner, *Memoirs*, II, 189; New York *Herald*, November 23, 1861; Stevens–Simon Stevens, November 5, 1861, Stevens Papers; Chandler–Mrs. Chandler, October 12, 1861, Chandler Papers; Lincoln, *Works*, IV, 562, V, 1–2.

yet known as the extremists' principal opponent. A change in command might become necessary.[8]

The occasion for the reorganization arose in the fall of 1861. On October 21, a small force commanded by Colonel Edward Baker, Lincoln's friend and a senator from Oregon, had been all but wiped out at Ball's Bluff, a short distance upriver from Washington. Baker was killed, a misfortune which not only proved a heavy personal blow to Lincoln but a challenge to the radicals as well. Baker had endeared himself to them by his reply to Senator Breckinridge of Kentucky, whose antiwar speech in the special session of Congress had been particularly offensive. "What would have been thought," Baker had said,

> if in another Capitol, in a yet more martial age, a senator, with the Roman purple flowing from his shoulders, had risen in his place, surrounded by all the illustrations of Roman glory, and declared that advancing Hannibal was just and that Carthage should be dealt with on terms of peace? What would have been thought, if, after the battle of Cannae, a senator had denounced every levy of the Roman people, every expenditure of its treasure, every appeal to the old recollections and the old glories?

"He would have been hurled from the Tarpeian rock," Fessenden had interjected, in a scene made doubly memorable by the fact that Baker had appeared in full uniform.[9] Now he was dead, and the radicals were deeply stirred. Surely something must be wrong with the military high command.

The disaster at Ball's Bluff proved particularly irritating to Chandler and Wade. The senator from Ohio especially had already developed an attitude of contempt for the administration, which he blamed for dawdling while the enemy was within sight of the

[8] *Battles and Leaders*, II, 114–15; George B. McClellan, *McClellan's Own Story* (New York, 1887), pp. 85, 87; Warren W. Hassler, *General George B. McClellan, Shield of the Union* (Baton Rouge, 1957), pp. 24, 26 ff.; Albert Mordell, compiler, *Selected Essays by Gideon Welles, Lincoln's Administration* (New York, 1960), pp. 60–2 (hereafter cited as Welles, *Lincoln's Administration*).

[9] Blaine, *Twenty Years of Congress*, I, 344–5; Nicolay and Hay, *Abraham Lincoln*, IV, 453–9.

capital. "You could not inspire Old Abe, Seward, Chase, or Bates with a galvanic battery," he had complained to Chandler, to whom he had confessed that it might not be bad if the rebels seized the whole Cabinet, the President, and the capital. Then perhaps the North could make use of instrumentalities equal to the emergency. But even Wade was still willing to cooperate, and after Ball's Bluff, both he and Chandler, accompanied by Trumbull, who had also criticized the Cabinet, arrived at Washington to see what they could do.[1]

At 10 P.M., on October 25, shortly after their arrival, the senators met with McClellan at Montgomery Blair's house. Although they had already lost much of their faith in his skill, they still had hopes that something might be accomplished. They argued, they cajoled, and they pleaded. Wade told the general that he must risk battle even if there were danger of losing it, because new recruits could easily be procured. Nonplused by this argument, McClellan, pointing out that it would be easier to recruit after a victory than after a defeat, averred that he could do nothing as long as General Scott remained in command. The senators left with the understanding that they would make an effort to have the general-in-chief relieved at once.

On the next day, the radicals went to see the President. "This evening the Jacobin club, represented by Trumbull, Chandler and Wade, came up to worry the administration into battle," the moderate John Hay noted in his diary. Chandler told Lincoln that if the extremists' view in favor of an immediate battle were not accepted, he was in favor of sending for Jefferson Davis at once. Precisely what the President said is unknown, but he took advantage of the radicals' advice.[2]

Lincoln made use of the interview in his own way. Although

[1] Wade-Chandler, October 8, 1861, Chandler Papers; Charles B. Smith–Trumbull, August 23, 1861, Trumbull Papers, LC; Wade–Mrs. Wade, October 25, 1861, Wade Papers.
[2] Chandler–Mrs. Chandler, October 27, 1861, Chandler Papers; Chandler–J. F. Joy, October 27, 1861, Joy Papers, Detroit Public Library; Hay, *Diaries*, p. 31; Chandler–H. W. Lord, R. M. Zug Papers, Detroit Public Library; McClellan, *McClellan's Own Story*, pp. 171–2.

Wade thought "Old Abe" was a "fool," and Chandler concluded that the administration was "timid," "vaccillating," and "inefficient," the President skillfully utilized the radicals' importunities to goad on McClellan and to solve the command problem. When after the senators' departure the general appeared and complained about their impetuousness, Lincoln proved sympathetic. But he pointed out that popular impatience was a reality which must be taken into account. Then, on November 1, he accepted Scott's resignation and appointed McClellan in his place. "I should be perfectly satisfied if I thought that this vast increase of responsibility would not embarrass you," he said to the general, only to be assured that McClellan felt a great sense of relief.[3] The President must have thought that he had infused new vigor into the army. What he did not know was that he had merely witnessed the beginning of a long duel between the radicals and McClellan, a struggle in which he was to seek again and again to accomplish his purpose of urging the laggard general forward by using the pressure exerted by the extremists. And since McClellan was generally unwilling to advance, pressure was essential.

Before leaving Washington, the radicals had also secured an interview with Seward and Cameron, upon whom they had again urged the necessity of immediate action. "If we fail in getting a battle here *now*," wrote Chandler, "all is lost." But he thought he had achieved some success. As he explained to Henry W. Lord, the American consul at Manchester,

> Lincoln means well but has no force of character. He is surrounded by Old Fogy Army officers more than half of whom are downright traitors and the other one half sympathize with the South. One month ago I began to doubt whether this accursed rebellion could be put down without a Revolution in the present Administration. Wade, Trumbull, Wilkinson, Pomeroy and myself made a descent upon them and spent two weeks

[3] Wade–Mrs. Wade, October 25, 1861, Wade Papers; Chandler–Mrs. Chandler, October 27, 1861, Chandler Papers; Hay, *Diaries*, pp. 31, 32–3; Lincoln, *Works*, V, 9–10.

with the President, Cabinet, McClellan &c. We raised an awful commotion and I think accomplished our object.[4]

Chandler's optimism was premature. Although he had warned the President that Congress would not furnish the necessary money and men unless a battle were fought before the onset of winter, he soon discovered that McClellan was infinitely more cautious than Scott had ever been. And while Chandler and Wade had long distrusted the "Young Napoleon," as his admirers called the general, not until late fall did he give evidence of the full extent of his shortcomings. He drilled the Army of the Potomac, paraded its divisions, and enjoyed all the pomp and panoply of military display. But the enemy continued to occupy the strategic points south of the capital, and the army would not move forward. That one of his close associates, General Charles P. Stone, had been in command of the ill-fated expedition at Ball's Bluff, did not increase the radicals' confidence in McClellan.[5]

When in December Congress met for the regular session, it was evident that there would be a determined radical drive. Because the President's message was moderate, the New York *Herald* predicted that "under the lead of such revolutionary fanatics as Sumner and Wade in the Senate, and Lovejoy and Stevens in the House," the extremists would attack it most vehemently. In part, this analysis was correct. On December 6, Dr. Charles H. Ray of the Chicago *Tribune,* calling Lincoln "reactionary and feeble," advised Sumner to see to it that Congress goaded him on; on December 9, Thaddeus Stevens in a Republican caucus violently denounced the President, and on the same

[4] Hay, *Diaries,* p. 32; Chandler–Mrs. Chandler, October 27, 1861, Chandler Papers; Chandler–Henry W. Lord, November 16, 1861, R. M. Zug Papers. Morton S. Wilkinson was a radical senator from Minnesota.
[5] Chandler–Henry W. Lord, November 16, 1861, R. M. Zug Papers; Wade–Chandler, October 8, 1861, Chandler–Mrs. Chandler, October 12, 1861, Chandler Papers; Philippe, Comte de Paris, *McClellan Organizing the Grand Army, Battles and Leaders,* II, 118; New York *Tribune,* November 5, 1861; Allan Nevins, *The War for the Union* (New York, 1959), I, 301–2; Alexander McClure, *Recollections of Half A Century* (Salem, Mass., 1902), pp. 344–5.

day Lyman Trumbull heard from home that almost everybody was radical now and critical of the message.[6] In another sense, however, the paper missed the outstanding fact about the relations between the Chief Executive and the ultras: Lincoln's readiness to move with the times.

Throughout the war, the President's dealings with the radicals followed a fairly regular pattern. Fundamentally not averse to their ideas of emancipation and rigorous prosecution of the conflict, he was nevertheless a much more astute politician than any of them. Although he was fully aware of the need to keep pace with the changing demands of the times, he also knew that, if he wanted to succeed in crushing the rebellion, he must retain the support of conservatives in the North and especially in the border states. Consequently, he consistently sought to utilize the radicals' pressure to spur on sluggish generals and politicians, while at the same time moving slowly enough to maintain his influence over conservatives whom he might otherwise alienate completely.

Lincoln's relations with the Joint Committee on the Conduct of the War, especially in its dealings with McClellan, were a case in point. This controversial body, which has been called "a continual embarrassment to the President," "a sort of Aulic Council clothed with authority to supervise the plans of commanders in the field," "a mischievous organization which assumed dictatorial powers," and which has been held responsible for the loss of thousands of lives, was, to be sure, dominated by the radicals from the very beginning.[7] Established as a result of New York Congressman Roscoe Conkling's motion to investigate the causes of the

[6] New York *Herald,* December 5, 10, 1861; C. H. Ray–Sumner, December 6, 1861, Sumner Papers; P. A. Allaire–Trumbull, December 10, 1861, Trumbull Papers, LC. Cf. Arthur Charles Cole, "President Lincoln and the Illinois Radical Republicans," *Mississippi Valley Historical Review,* IV (March, 1918), 417–36, esp. 422–3.

[7] Randall, *Lincoln the Liberal Statesman,* p. 71; William Henry Hurlbert, *General McClellan and the Conduct of the War* (New York, 1864), pp. 160–1; Poore, *Perley's Reminiscences,* II, 103; Edward A. Channing, *A History of the United States* (New York, 1925), VI, 400.

disaster of Ball's Bluff, it was expanded when Chandler introduced a similar resolution in the Senate. After discussion, particularly upon the urging of moderates like Senator John Sherman of Ohio, the upper House decided to extend the investigation into a general survey of the conduct of the war. Conservatives as well as radicals supported the resolution in both Houses, so that the committee was created, according to T. Harry Williams, "the unnatural child of lustful radicalism and confused conservatism." Upon Chandler's suggestion, Wade was appointed chairman, and the Ohioan, Chandler, and Andrew Johnson, then famous as the only Southern senator to have remained loyal after his state seceded, became the senate members of the committee. George W. Julian, who had returned to Congress in 1861, together with John Covode and Daniel Gooch, Banks's successor from Boston, were the Republican members from the House, while Moses Odell, a War Democrat from Brooklyn, represented the opposition. The committee, which held its sessions in secret, brought pressure almost immediately upon the President and the army to make McClellan move.[8] But this was an aim Lincoln shared with the members.

That the "Young Napoleon" was irresolute and a difficult subordinate had become manifest to Lincoln shortly after McClellan's assumption of command. On November 13, the President, who was no stickler for protocol, called upon the general. Not finding him at home, Lincoln and Seward waited for an hour. Then McClellan arrived, but instead of seeing his visitors, he retired. After another half hour, the President again sent word that he was there, only to be told that the general had gone to bed. And

[8] *Cong. Globe,* 37th Cong., 2d Sess., 6, 16, 29, 30, 32, 40, 110; Blaine, *Twenty Years of Congress,* I, 378–9; Williams, *Lincoln and the Radicals,* pp. 62–4; Walter Buell, "Zachariah Chandler," *Magazine of Western History,* IV (1886), 434; *Report of the Joint Committee on the Conduct of the War,* 37th Cong., 3d Sess., No. 108 (Washington, 1863), I, 67 (hereafter cited as *JCCW*); William W. Pierson, "The Committee on the Conduct of the Civil War," *American Historical Review,* XXIII (April, 1918), 558–9; Hans L. Trefousse, "The Joint Committee on the Conduct of the War: A Reassessment," *Civil War History,* X (March, 1964), 6–8.

McClellan's discourtesy and lack of respect were not his worst faults. In spite of favorable weather conditions and his decisive superiority over the enemy, he refused to advance in Virginia. No amount of jogging could dislodge him, although he was well aware of the President's anxiety.[9]

This situation made it possible for Lincoln to put the committee's activities to good use, no matter how rude individual members might be to him. Having begun hearings on the cause of the defeats at Ball's Bluff and Bull Run, the investigators had also utilized the inquiry to determine the reasons for the delay of the Army of the Potomac. Since McClellan had fallen sick on December 20, his subordinates testified first, and what they revealed strengthened the radicals in their conviction that the general was not up to par. While many of his officers, conservatives like William B. Franklin, Montgomery Meigs, and Fitzjohn Porter, among others, testified in his favor, a group of radical generals left no doubt that they disapproved of their commander's hesitation. General James S. Wadsworth was particularly outspoken. There was no question about it, he declared. A forward movement must be undertaken. Morale had never been higher.[1]

This was precisely what the committee—and Lincoln—wanted to hear. The radicals had been convinced for some time that McClellan was no "Young Napoleon." They had attacked him on the Senate floor; they had closely examined committee witnesses about his qualifications, and now they were ready to proceed against him. On December 31, they met with the Chief Executive. "Mr. President," Wade said bluntly, "you are murdering your country by inches in consequence of the inactivity of the military and the want of a distinct policy in regard to slavery." The President allegedly said nothing in reply, but he informed McClellan of the interview.[2]

[9] Hay, *Diaries*, p. 34; Nevins, *War for the Union*, I, 301–2; Lincoln, *Works*, V, 34.

[1] *JCCW*, I, 67, 70, 71, 122–30, 150–60, 170–8, 117–22, 145–50.

[2] *Cong. Globe*, 37th Cong., 2d Sess., 94; Schleiden's Dispatch No. 1, January 6, 1862, Schleiden Papers.

Since the general had not yet recovered, Lincoln did not force a showdown. "I hear that the doings of an Investigating Committee, give you some uneasiness," he wrote to McClellan.

> You may be entirely relieved on this point. The gentlemen of the Committee were with me an hour and a half last night, and I found them in a perfectly good mood. As their investigation brings them acquainted with facts, they are rapidly coming to think of the whole case as all sensible men would.[3]

And while the President, in this instance, apparently stretched the truth for the sake of harmony, the general knew what "all sensible men" thought of the case according to Lincoln: The army must move.

On January 6, the committee met with the entire Cabinet. Again the McClellan problem was discussed, and the ultras found out that no one seemed to have a clear notion of the general's plans. Bitterly arraigning McClellan, Wade insisted upon a radical change of policy. Seward tried to defend the commander, but Chase sympathized with the committee's point of view. The meeting broke up without any definite accomplishments. Before leaving, however, the legislators strongly recommended the appointment of McDowell in McClellan's stead.[4]

Lincoln sought again to utilize the radicals' zeal to spur on his general. "I think you better go before the Committee the earliest moment your health will permit—," he wrote on January 9 to McClellan, "today, if possible." On the same day, he referred to the general-in-chief a copy of a dispatch from General Don Carlos Buell, the hesitant commander in the West, with the "remark that neither he nor [Henry W.] Halleck meets my request to name the DAY when they can be ready to move." It was a pointed reminder.[5]

Although Lincoln was trying his best to induce McClellan to advance, his lack of success was beginning to depress him. "General, what shall I do?" he said to Montgomery Meigs on January

[3] Lincoln, *Works*, V, 88.
[4] Julian, *Political Recollections*, pp. 201–3; Chase, *Diaries*, pp. 57–8.
[5] Lincoln, *Works*, V. 94.

10. "The people are impatient; Chase has no money and tells me he can raise no more; the General of the Army has typhoid fever. The bottom is out of the tub. What shall I do?" Meigs advised him to consult with McClellan's generals.[6]

The President accepted Meigs's advice. Meeting with the general's subordinates and hearing that McDowell had a plan, he told them that if McClellan did not want to use the army, he would like to borrow it. On January 13, he saw them again in the presence of the Cabinet. By this time, however, the general had sufficiently recovered to appear in person. Rudely rejecting McDowell's proposals, he refused to reply to Chase's pointed questions about his plans. But he assured the President that he knew what he was doing and that he had in mind a "particular" time for his military movements. Thereupon Lincoln adjourned the meeting.[7]

McClellan also heeded the President's advice to meet with the committee. In a memorable interview on January 15, he found himself confronted by Chandler and Wade. Asked point-blank why he refused to attack, he replied that he had to prepare the proper routes of retreat. "General McClellan, if I understand you correctly, before you strike at the rebels you want to be sure of plenty of room so that you can run in case they strike back," said Chandler. "Or in case you get scared," interjected Wade. After some more conversation concerning the necessity of keeping routes of retreat open, the general left, with the two radicals convinced that what they had witnessed was "infernal, unmitigated cowardice.[8] In spite of their dislike for Lincoln, the ultras were doing his work for him. His general was in need of prodding.

In other ways, too, the President sought to respond to

[6] "General M. C. Meigs of the Conduct of the Civil War," *American Historical Review*, XXVI (January, 1921), 292.

[7] Henry J. Raymond, *The Life and Public Services of Abraham Lincoln* (New York, 1865), pp. 772–7; McClellan, *McClellan's Own Story*, pp. 155–8; "General M. C. Meigs on the Conduct of the Civil War," loc. cit.

[8] Detroit *Post and Tribune, Chandler*, pp. 224–6.

pressure for a more effective prosecution of the war. The War Department had long caused him misgivings; under the direction of Simon Cameron, it had been conducted very inefficiently and possibly dishonestly. A new Secretary would therefore signify a renewed determination to carry on the war vigorously—an objective all radicals ardently desired. To be sure, Cameron had made a bid for extremist support by publicly endorsing the arming of Negroes, but if a change in the department resulted in the appointment of a proponent of all-out war, the radicals could not object and the Cabinet would be strengthened by the departure of the difficult Pennsylvania boss. Consequently, on January 13, Abraham Lincoln, having sent Cameron as an envoy to Russia, nominated Edwin M. Stanton as his successor. So astute was the new minister that his elevation gratified both McClellan and the radicals.[9]

McClellan soon found out that Stanton was not his friend. From the very beginning, the Secretary, establishing excellent relations with William D. Kelley and John F. Potter as well as with the Committee on the Conduct of the War, cooperated very closely with the radicals. Even before he assumed office, at a breakfast with his predecessor, Chandler, and Wade, he signified his assent to the extremists' views. Once in power, he cemented ever more intimate relations with them. "We must strike hands," he said on January 20 to the chairman of the committee, "and, uniting our strength and thought, double the power of the Government to suppress its enemies and restore its integrity." Lincoln's change in the Cabinet had been beneficial for the radicals.[1]

The arrest of General Charles P. Stone was another example of the administration's collaboration with the radicals. The unfortunate commander, who had been ostensibly responsible for

[9] Thomas and Hyman, Stanton, pp. 133–9; Bradley, *Cameron*, pp. 203 ff.; Sarah Hughes, ed., *Letters and Recollections of John Murray Forbes* (Boston, 1899), I, 236–7; Cameron-Greeley, January 15, 1862, Horace Greeley Papers, New York Public Library; McClellan, *McClellan's Own Story*, p. 153; McClure, *Lincoln and the Men of War-Times*, pp. 158–9; Gurowski, *Diary*, II, 128.

[1] Thomas and Hyman, *Stanton*, pp. 147–8; Henry Wilson, "Jeremiah Black and Edwin M. Stanton," *Atlantic Monthly*, XXVI (July–Decem-

the disaster at Ball's Bluff, was also reputed to have displayed great courtesy toward secessionists, and his very loyalty was being questioned. To make matters worse, after Sumner had attacked him in Congress, he had written the senator a truculent letter, which looked almost as if he were anxious for a duel. In his two appearances before the committee, he was badly hampered because he had neither been informed of the exact charges against himself nor been given an opportunity to cross-examine witnesses. The radicals distrusted him completely; McClellan abandoned him; the administration was suspicious, and finally he found himself under arrest. Seeking unsuccessfully to obtain either a hearing or a release, he remained in detention for the next one hundred and eight-nine days, and even after he was freed, it proved impossible to discover exactly who had arrested him. But it was certain that the committee had sought his ouster; Stanton had cooperated in the miscarriage of justice which resulted, and Lincoln publicly acknowledged his responsibility.[2]

But it was still in his relations with McClellan that Lincoln, despite the radicals' criticism, showed most clearly that he was amenable to their suggestions. He had hardly appointed Stanton, when almost as exasperated as the ultras, he decided to make an all-out effort to force the general to bestir himself. Finally wearied by McClellan's obstinate refusal to march upon the enemy and strengthened by the incessant radical demands for an advance, the President on January 27 issued General Order No. 1, providing for a forward movement on Washington's Birthday. Four days later, he spelled out his directive in greater detail, and al-

ber, 1870), 743–4; John Cochrane, *The War for the Union* (n.p., n.d.), p. 19; Frank Abial Flower, *Edwin McMasters Stanton* (New York, 1905), p. 119.
[2] Blaine, *Twenty Years of Congress*, I, 382–95; Charles Stone–Sumner, December 23, 1861, Sumner Papers; Sumner, *Works*, VI, 145–9; Richard R. Irwin, *Ball's Bluff and the Arrest of General Stone, Battles and Leaders*, II, 123–34; JCCW, II, 265–82, 289–97, 426–33; Bates, *Diary*, p. 229; New York *Tribune*, April 30, 1862.

though the general eventually disregarded the order, he made preparations to attack Richmond by way of Chesapeake Bay and the Rappahannock River in the spring. His continued hesitation brought a reminder from Lincoln on February 8: "Have you determined, as yet, upon the contemplated movement we last talked of?" the President inquired. He was doing his best to spur on the laggard general.[3]

Lincoln's attitude reflected his sympathy with the increasing radical clamor. The army must move, the extremists declared on the floor of Congress; the army must move, concluded the Committee on the Conduct of the War. The blockade of the Potomac was particularly irksome; Moses Odell proposed that something be done about it, and Chandler suggested that the entire committee confer with the Secretary of War. But as Stanton was already in sympathy with McClellan's critics, Wade pointed out that Chandler's motion might be interpreted as a criticism of the patriotic Secretary. Accordingly, the committee decided to congratulate him on the recent victories in the West.

The legislators visited the War Department on February 19. When they broached the matter of the blockade, they found Stanton in full agreement. He did not go to his bed at night "without his cheek burning with shame at this disgrace upon the nation," he said. Since McClellan happened to be in the building at the time, the Secretary called him in.

The interview was again unpleasant. The blockade must be lifted, the committee members averred. McClellan assured them that he was doing his best, but that he must make proper preparations to secure the army's rear. In the words of the committee's journal, Wade

promptly replied that with 150,000 of the most effective troops in the world upon the other side of the Potomac there was no

[3] Lincoln, *Works*, V, 118–25, 130; *War of the Rebellion: A Compilation of the Official Records of the Union and Confederate Armies* (Washington, 1880–1901), Series I, V, 41 (hereafter cited as *O.R.*); McClellan, *McClellan's Own Story*, pp. 162–3.

need of a bridge; they could beat any force the enemy could bring against them; and if any of them came back, let them come back in their coffins.

McClellan made no reply. But he could see that the President had reasons for urging him on.[4]

To circumvent the general's obstructionism, the radicals finally decided that it would be wise to divide the army into *corps d'armée*. Because of seniority, these units would then be commanded by Republican generals, and vigor would be infused into the fighting forces. The only difficulty was that McClellan was resolutely opposed to the scheme.[5]

Lincoln was again not unreceptive to the ultras' plans. When on February 26 the committee came to see him to press for the adoption of the corps organization, he said that he himself had long been in favor of the proposal, although he did not deem it as important as the committee. Since no agreement was reached at the time, on March 4 the radicals, anxious for action, saw the President again. This time he promised to take the proposition "into earnest and serious consideration," and four days later he carried out his pledge. Issuing orders to implement the establishment of army corps, he also set March 18 as the beginning of the campaign. Moreover, he again made certain that the general realized how much distrust he had engendered. As Lincoln explained to McClellan, the plan to move on Richmond by way of the Chesapeake had caused suspicions of a "traitorous" purpose to leave Washington exposed to attack. The general must take every precaution to render the capital secure.[6] The radicals' agitation had borne fruit, and Lincoln was not unhappy about it.

Just how far the President was prepared to cooperate with the ultras he showed when he issued two more directives three days

---

[4] *Cong. Globe,* 37th Cong., 2d Sess., 749; *JCCW,* I, 82–5.

[5] Julian, *Political Recollections,* pp. 204–5; McClellan, *McClellan's Own Story,* pp. 222, 342; Benjamin F. Wade, *Facts for the People* (Cincinnati, 1864), p. 3.

[6] *JCCW,* I, 86–7, 88; *O.R.,* Series I, V, 18, 50, McClellan, *The Peninsular Campaign, Battles and Leaders,* II, 166. The general then submitted his plans to his division commanders who approved.

later. McClellan was relieved of his position as general-in-chief, although he kept the Army of the Potomac. In addition, John C. Frémont, whose dismissal had caused the radicals so much grief, and whose reinstatement they had pursued with singular persistency, was given another command.[7]

McClellan now had no choice but to set his army in motion. If the President needed any excuse for demanding that the general finally initiate the long-promised campaign, the relentless demands of the ultras continued to give it to him, and when, early in March, the Confederates withdrew from Manassas, they furnished new proof of McClellan's caution. The pursuing Federals found that they had been held in check by wooden guns! Obviously, McClellan had grossly overestimated the enemy's strength. "Could the commander be loyal who had opposed all the previous forward movements, and only made this advance after the enemy had been evacuated?" commented George W. Julian. Count Adam Gurowski, the refugee Polish nobleman who was intimate with the radicals, was certain that Louis XV's mistresses would never have dared to appoint such a commander; William P. Fessenden concluded that McClellan was "utterly unfit for his position," and Senator Morton S. Wilkinson wrote to Governor Alexander Ramsay of Minnesota, "The Army of the Potomac although unwieldy in numbers is powerless in action. This result . . . is owing to the imbecility of its commander. I hope that McClellan will redeem himself but I doubt it."[8] Only a successful campaign could restore the general's tarnished reputation.

Many radicals, already convinced of McClellan's lack of skill, were wholly unwilling to entrust the army to him any longer. Attempting their utmost to bring about his removal—the Vice President pleaded with Lincoln to dismiss him while the Secretary

[7] *O.R.*, Series I, V, 50; Wade–C. A. Dana, February 3, 1862, Charles A. Dana Papers, LC; Colfax-Lincoln, March 10, 1862, RTL; Nevins, *Frémont*, p. 554.

[8] Julian, *Political Recollections*, pp. 205–9; Gurowski-Wade, March 14, 1862, Wade Papers; M. S. Wilkinson–Ramsay, April 3, 1862, Ramsay Papers.

of War tried to displace him with the superannuated mystic, Ethan Allen Hitchcock—they were bitterly disappointed when Lincoln permitted him to remain. But the President had to consider the general's political strength. As a member of the opposition party and an opponent of emancipation, he had become the idol of the Democrats and conservatives.[9]

By this time, McClellan had come to the conclusion that not only the radicals, but the President himself had turned against him. At least he blamed them for causing Lincoln to withhold that cordial support which he deemed necessary for success. When, shortly before setting out upon his expedition, he was ordered to release Blenker's division for Frémont's use, he became more convinced than ever. As he surmised correctly, the radicals had had something to do with the matter. They had conferred with Stanton on March 24; a few days later, McClellan was told that the pressure on Lincoln to remove the division was a political maneuver to swell Frémont's command. Since the Pathfinder was getting ready an expedition to liberate Unionist East Tennessee, and since the ultras believed that the 155,000 men McClellan was planning to take with him were too many, it is easy to surmise what was discussed at the Secretary of War's office, even though no records have survived. As McClellan so correctly assessed the situation, the President knew how to cooperate with the radicals.[1]

In his efforts to steer a correct course between radical pressure and conservative influence, Lincoln now embarked upon one of the most controversial incidents of his career. For a long

[9] Schleiden's Dispatch No. 21, March 17, 1862, Schleiden Papers; W. A. Croffut, ed., *Fifty Years in Camp and Field: Diary of Major-General Ethan Allen Hitchcock* (New York, 1909), p. 436; Cyrus Aldrich-Ramsay, April 6, 1862, Ramsay Papers; Columbus *Crisis*, April 2, 1862; Millard Fillmore–J. C. G. Kennedy, March 7, 1862, RTL; New York *Herald*, March 25, 31, 1862; W. J. Howard–Covode, March 18, 1862, Covode Papers, HSWP.

[1] McClellan, *McClellan's Own Story*, pp. 159, 164–5; *JCCW*, I, 90–1; Williams, *Lincoln and the Radicals*, p. 126; Jacob D. Cox, *West Virginia Operations Under Fremont, Battles and Leaders*, II, 278 ff.

time, he had favored a land attack upon Richmond, a movement which would incidentally guarantee the safety of Washington because of its dependence upon large concentrations of troops between the two cities. When he reluctantly approved McClellan's plan for an assault by way of Urbanna and later, the Peninsula, he gave his assent only on condition that sufficient troops be left behind to protect the capital. McClellan had hardly departed when it was discovered that this condition had not been met. As the radical commander of the troops in Washington, James S. Wadsworth, on April 2, pointed out to the Secretary of War, all he controlled was a force of 20,477 men, of whom more than four regiments were to be sent to McClellan! It was evident that this contingent was grossly inadequate; the committee examined Wadsworth on the next day and met with Lincoln that evening.

The President was impressed. Influenced by the facts submitted by the legislators as well as by the Secretary of War, he ordered McDowell's corps detached from the main force of the Army of the Potomac and placed in position south of Washington.[2] Ever since, McClellan and his supporters have been convinced that these arrangements made it impossible for the general to succeed. Some have even charged the radicals with a design deliberately to sabotage the campaign lest McClellan win prior to the achievement of complete emancipation.[3]

These accusations merit serious attention. That McClellan believed himself fatally hampered by the absence of McDowell's corps and Blenker's division is certain, but whether he would have

[2] Henry Greenleaf Pearson, *James S. Wadsworth of Geneseo* (New York, 1913), pp. 118 ff.; *JCCW*, I, 93–4; *Detroit Free Press*, January 10, 1863, Browning, *Diary*, I, 537

[3] New York *Herald*, March 31, July 4, 7, August 2, 1862; New York *World*, January 19, 1863; Philippe, Conte de Paris, *History of the Civil War in America* (Philadelphia, 1876), I, 629; Williams, *Lincoln and the Radicals*, p. 131. Another count against the radicals was the closing of recruiting operations in the states. But recruiting could not affect the army's immediate strength during the campaign, as soldiers had to be trained first. Cf. McClellan, *McClellan's Own Story*, p. 258.

prevailed had he had the additional troops is not so clear. According to his own calculations, the enemy, with 200,000 men, was stronger than the Army of the Potomac with its 150,000, even with the missing troops added. Although these calculations were wholly false, the Confederates never disposing of more than 90,000 during the entire campaign, it is more than likely that the "Young Napoleon," with his habitual tendency of overestimating his opponents, would never have taken Richmond with or without the additional 40,000 soldiers.[4] The radicals' interference merely gave him an excuse for his failure; that it was its real cause is most improbable.

The charge that there was a malicious plot to sabotage McClellan rests on circumstantial evidence and cannot be sustained by concrete facts. There is no doubt that the ultras, anxious to remove the general, assumed a heavy responsibility when, without proper military knowledge, they interfered in army operations. At a time when they were desperately anxious for victory, however, it is most unlikely that they would have risked the entire outcome of the war for imagined political advantages. As Stanton replied at the time to the accusations against him, he could not answer such calumnies publicly, but he would do so in private. After all, he had entered the Cabinet as McClellan's friend. Then Lincoln's General Order No. 1 had not been carried out; the President, attaching only the condition that a sufficient force be left behind to render Washington secure, had given up his own ideas for the general's plans. When it turned out that this had not been done, Stanton ordered McDowell retained, although he continued to give McClellan all the military support possible.[5] The facts were that the "Young Napoleon" was not an outstanding general and that he lacked the daring necessary for success, weaknesses which the radicals recognized at an early time. With Stonewall Jackson ravaging the valley of Virginia, the President had to concern

[4] Ibid., pp. 262 ff.; Hassler, *McClellan*, pp. 107, 139, 188; *Battles and Leaders*, II, 404; Colin A. Ballard, *The Military Genius of Abraham Lincoln* (Cleveland, 1952), p. 73.
[5] Stanton–H. Dyer, May 18, 1862, Stanton Papers.

himself with the safety of the capital. And if the Federal army were ever to win, McClellan would eventually have to be removed.

That McClellan's generalship left much to be desired became apparent almost as soon as he had left Washington. As he slowly moved up the Peninsula, laying siege to Yorktown, a city defended by a mere token force of Confederates, observers were becoming more and more impatient. "The Little Napoleon sits trembling before the handful of men at Yorktown afraid either to fight or to run," wrote John Hay. And not only McClellan's generalship, but also his loyalty was being increasingly questioned. Although these suspicions were totally unfounded—no shred of evidence linking him to the confederates has ever been found—even the conservative Ohio politician Thomas Ewing felt that Lincoln must beware of the general. "He, as well as Beauregard," he wrote, "owes his promotion to Jeff. Davis. And he has done nothing to show ingratitude." As the siege lengthened into weeks, it was not surprising that the radicals shared these views. The general's loyalty was now being openly impugned in the presence of conservative as well as radical Cabinet members.[6]

Still mindful of public pressure, Lincoln sought again to prod his hesitant general. While sending him additional troops, the President insisted that McClellan break the enemy's line at Yorktown at once. On April 9, he wrote to the general again. Explaining his position in detail, he cautioned,

The country will not fail to note—is now noting—that the present hesitation to move upon an entrenched enemy, is but the story of Manassas repeated.

He assured him of his purpose to sustain the army. *"But you must act,"* he admonished.[7]

McClellan, however, continued his leisurely pursuit of the enemy. After capturing Yorktown on May 4, he moved up the

[6] Hay, *Diaries*, pp. 40–1; Thomas Ewing–Lincoln, April 9, 1862, RTL; Bates, *Diary*, p. 253.

[7] Lincoln, *Works*, V, 182, 184–5; Hassler, *McClellan*, p. 91.

Peninsula with great deliberation. His hesitation was infuriating to radicals in Congress as well as in the Cabinet. "McClellan *is a dear luxury*—," Chase wrote to Horace Greeley, "fifty days—fifty miles—fifty millions of dollars—easy arithmetic but not satisfactory. If one could have some faith in his competency in battle—should his army ever fight one—if not in his competency for movement, it would be a comfort."[8]

Fully aware of the problem, Lincoln, mindful of Democratic sympathy for the general, could not interfere until McClellan had shown what he was able to do. And the general was soon put to the test. On May 31–June 1, he fought the battle of Fair Oaks, an indecisive engagement at the very gates of Richmond. Surely he would now move upon the capital with his superior forces and capture it. The rebellion might then be crushed in short order.

But McClellan did nothing of the sort. Having strung out his army in a peculiar fashion on both sides of the Chickahominy, he was engaged by the enemy in a series of battles known as the Seven Days, during which he changed his base from the White House on the Pamunkey to Harrison's Landing on the James. His defensive tactics were brilliant; he performed wonders in logistics, but he never displayed the aggressive characteristics necessary for victory. In fact, he narrowly averted complete disaster, and at the end of the operation he was further from Richmond than he had been at the beginning.

According to McClellan, his misfortunes were due to the administration and especially to the radicals. And he did not hide his chagrin. On June 28, during the Seven Days, he penned a furious letter to the Secretary of War. "I have lost this battle because my force was too small," he complained, charging that he was not responsible for the heavy casualties he had sustained. "I feel too earnestly to-night," he concluded.

I have seen too many dead and wounded comrades to feel otherwise than that this Government has not sustained this army. If you do not do so now the game is lost. If I save this army now, I tell you plainly that I owe no thanks to you or any

[8] Chase-Greeley, May 21, 1862, Chase Papers, LC.

other person in Washington. You have done your best to sacrifice this army.[9]

The letter did not help the general. His failure before Richmond had given pause not only to the radicals, but also to moderate segments of the population. And the ultras were more determined than ever to remove him. Zach Chandler, while in his cups, abused McClellan in public at Willard's Hotel; Chase heard from General E. D. Keyes that Jefferson Davis had "not a greater repugnance to . . . Republicans" than the general, and the Committee on the Conduct of the War opened hearings to investigate the Peninsular campaign. The struggle against McClellan was becoming relentless.[1]

Abraham Lincoln, however, still hesitated. "If I relieve McClellan, whom shall I put in command?" he asked Wade on one occasion when he was being pressed on the matter.

"Why, anybody!" answered the senator.

"Wade," said Lincoln, "anybody will do for you, but not for me. I must have somebody."[2] Well attuned to public opinion, Lincoln had concluded that the time was not yet ripe for the general's removal. But he was willing to entertain the idea.

In order to see for himself, the President next paid a visit to the commander of the Army of the Potomac. Whatever he may have thought of McClellan's strategic capabilities, he found him to be in a politically ambitious mood, when, on July 7, the general handed him the famous Harrison's Bar letter, presuming to lecture him on the necessity of conservative policies. "A declaration of radical views, especially upon slavery, will rapidly disintegrate our present armies," wrote the meddlesome commander, mindful of his Democratic supporters. But the President had not come for political advice. He asked a number of pointed questions and inquired whether it would be possible to remove the army

[9] *O.R.,* Series I, Vol. XI, Part I, 61.

[1] Ewing-Stanton, June 19, 1862, Stanton Papers; Bates, *Diary,* p. 260; E. D. Keyes–Chase, June 17, 1862, Chase Papers, HSP; *JCCW,* I, 260 ff.

[2] Helen Nicolay, *Lincoln's Secretary, A Biography of John G. Nicolay* (New York, 1949), p. 149.

from the Peninsula. He was evidently thinking of terminating McClellan's unsuccessful venture.[3]

As the attacks on the general mounted, the radicals furnished Lincoln with more ammunition against McClellan. Released from a rule of secrecy which had been hurriedly dropped by the Committee on the Conduct of the War, Chandler delivered a philippic in the Senate against the "Young Napoleon." With his great army, why had the general failed? Holding him responsible for the disaster at Ball's Bluff and the siege of Washington, the senator waxed extremely bitter. It was an outrage to accuse the Secretary of War of not supplying reinforcements when McClellan had 158,000 men, he shouted. Privately, he confided to his wife that he considered the general "an imbecile if not a traitor" who ought to "*suffer the extreme penalty of the law.*" William D. Kelley informed Lincoln that Democrats stayed at home and collaborated with the traitorous general in the field while Republicans enlisted—a situation which he thought boded ill for the party. Chase, who assiduously pursued his goal of displacing McClellan by badgering the President, heard that Confederates in Canada had expressed their faith in the "Young Napoleon," while Wade, in a public speech, said the general's forte was "digging and not fighting." "Place him before an enemy," he asserted, "and he will burrow like a wood chuck. His first effort is to get into the ground."[4]

Lincoln, who was now ready to take action, handled the situation with his usual caution. Having already appointed a radical favorite, General John Pope, commander of the Army of Virginia, he called the western commander Henry W. Halleck to Washington as general-in-chief, and on August 3 ordered the Army of the

[3] McClellan, *McClellan's Own Story,* pp. 487–9; Lincoln, *Works,* V, 309–12.

[4] *JCCW,* I, 101; *Cong. Globe,* 37th Cong., 2d Sess., 3386–92; Chase, *Diaries,* pp. 97–8, 102; T. R. Spencer–Chandler July 24, 1862, Chase Papers, HSP; Ashtabula *Sentinel,* July 30, 1862; Chandler–Mrs. Chandler, July 11, 1862, Chandler Papers; W. D. Kelley–Lincoln, July 23, 1862, RTL.

Potomac to be brought back from the Peninsula. As additional troops were being sent to Pope, McClellan's star seemed to be setting, especially since many of his forces were diverted to his rival as soon as they reached Acquia Greek and the vicinity of Washington. To a large extent, the President had again cooperated with the radicals. But, mindful of McClellan's influence with the conservatives and cognizant of his defensive capabilities, he kept him in reserve in case of need.[5]

Misunderstanding Lincoln's motives, the radicals did not believe that this arrangement went far enough. During the last days in August, their favorite, General Pope, was decisively defeated on the old battlefield at Bull Run. As they saw it, however, not Pope but McClellan created the most serious problems because the commander of the Army of the Potomac was not to be trusted. And this assessment seemed to be reinforced by reports that he had not supported Pope to the best of his ability.

It was in the Cabinet that they sought to make their next move. On August 30, Stanton, assisted by Chase, drew up a paper against McClellan, a memorandum which was submitted to other members for signature. The Secretary of the Interior agreed, and so damaged was the general's reputation that even the conservative Attorney General proved sympathetic. After Bates had suggested certain changes, on September 1, together with the authors and Smith, he signed the modified paper. Welles expressed his concurrence but objected to the method, so that only Blair, who was rapidly becoming more conservative, and Seward, who was absent, were opposed. The ultras had garnered support. But at the Cabinet level at least, the movement against McClellan was more than a mere radical plot.

Although Lincoln was in general agreement with the criticism of the general—he said it really seemed to him McClellan wanted Pope defeated—he was not in a position to accede to the Cabinet's

<hr/>

[5] Lincoln, *Works*, V, 287, 312–13; McClellan, *McClellan's Own Story*, pp. 495–6; George B. McClellan, *From the Peninsula to Antietam, Battles and Leaders*, II, 548–9.

demands. Panic was threatening to engulf the defeated army; Lee was preparing to invade Maryland, and unless some general could rally the forces around the capital to stop the advancing enemy, a situation of the utmost seriousness would result. In this emergency, he needed McClellan, whose organizational and defensive abilities were remarkable. Consequently, in the Cabinet meeting of September 2, he not only refused to remove the general, but, pointing out that he could not see who could do the work as well, restored McClellan to effective command.[6]

The President's decision caused great anguish in the radical camp. Extremist Cabinet members fumed; newspapermen complained, and members of Congress were outraged. "Of course the action of the President in placing General McClellan in command without any investigation of the charges so directly affecting him were [sic] not prompted by me," explained Chase to Chandler.

> I thought that there were brave, capable & loyal officers, such as Hooker, Sumner, Burnside and many more who might be named, to whom the command of armies might be more safely & much more properly entrusted. The President thought otherwise, and I must do all I can to make his decision useful to the country.

The Michigan senator was convinced that *"Treason,* rank treason" had caused "our late disaster," and even the moderate John Sherman wrote that he considered the President and McClellan the country's worst enemies. But the conservative press approved of the general's restoration.[7]

McClellan managed to solve the immediate crisis by defeating Robert E. Lee at Antietam. By giving to the North a victory of sorts, he enabled the President to issue the Preliminary Emancipa-

[6] Chase, *Diaries,* pp. 116–20; Welles, *Diary,* I, 93–106; Hay, *Diaries,* p. 45; McClure, *Lincoln and the Men of War-Times,* p. 169.

[7] Chase–John Sherman, September 5, 1862, Chase-Chandler, September 20, 1862, John Sherman–Chase, September 9, 1862, Chase Papers, HSP; Welles, *Diary,* I, 109; H. C. Bowen–Chase, September 13, 1862, S. G. Arnold–Chase, September 16, 1862, Chase Papers, LC; Chandler-Trumbull, September 10, 1862, Trumbull Papers, LC; New York *Herald,* September 4, 1862.

tion Proclamation and to parry the danger of British recognition of the Confederacy. As soon as the battle was over, however, all could see that he had succumbed again to his old faults. Instead of pursuing the enemy, he hesitated, permitting Lee to escape. And, to make matters worse, rumors arose that he was planning to set up a dictatorship!

This situation caused the radicals to redouble their efforts. In the Cabinet, Chase and Stanton led the struggle against McClellan and freely expressed their opinions. The President heard from Major John J. Key that the general had deliberately failed to capture the rebels at Antietam lest the North be enabled to end slavery. The major, who was dismissed for his attitude, maintained without regret that it was the policy of army officers to exhaust both sides and then enforce a compromise which would save slavery. The Vice President, too, urged McClellan's dismissal, while Congressman Kelley told Lincoln that the disastrous results of the October elections in Pennsylvania were due to dissatisfaction with the general.[8]

In the west, where General Don Carlos Buell seemed to copy both McClellan's tactics and politics, similar problems had arisen. "The friends of your administration in Congress . . . ," wrote the radical Samuel Shellabarger to the President on October 22,

> have not abated one tittle of their admiration of the exalted and pure purposes of your . . . earnest and wise efforts for the restoration of the Government. . . . But Mr. Pres. we really fear that, without your fault, the war has drifted into the hands of only semi-loyal men who have no design to whip the rebels.

He begged Lincoln to remove Buell. The President finally dismissed the western commander, but with the November elections in the offing, he could not yet move decisively against McClellan. Nevertheless, at a time when even senators like Fessenden, who was rapidly becoming more moderate, bitterly complained about

---

[8] B. P. Poore–Sumner, September 11, 1862, Sumner Papers; Grimes–Trumbull, October 6, 1862, Trumbull Papers, LC; Chase, *Diaries,* pp. 162–3; Welles, *Diary,* I, 108, 146, 156; Hamlin, *Hamlin,* p. 441; Rice, *Reminiscences of Abraham Lincoln,* pp. 271, 272–80.

the general, it was to be expected that Lincoln would speedily lose faith in him.[9]

The President was again willing to work with the radicals. For the time being, he could not afford to furnish ammunition to the Democrats. Consequently, he asked McClellan again and again to advance; he even visited him at his headquarters, but until the elections were over, he could do no more. On November 5, however, he hesitated no longer. Having concluded that criticism of the laggard commander was justified, he finally removed him from all commands. As he had said to the Cabinet in September, the general was troubled with "the slows."[1]

The radicals were jubilant at the news. "I trust we will see more active operations, and better results," wrote the Vice President on November 10. "Great and holy day! McClellan gone overboard," was Count Gurowski's comment, and Chase expressed his conviction that the army would now advance. Colfax went so far as to send Lincoln a congratulatory telegram, and Fessenden reverted to his radical stance by stating that the general should have been removed long ago.[2] That the radicals had won a great victory was obvious. They had long pressed for McClellan's dismissal; the change had become necessary, and although the President, seeking to utilize the ultras' importunities to impel his commander to speed, had taken his time, when the moment was ripe he had acted. In view of the general's military deficiencies, the country was the net gainer.

[9] Samuel Shellabarger–Lincoln, October 22, 1862, RTL; T. Harry Williams, *Lincoln and His Generals* (New York, 1952), pp. 182–5; Fessenden-Chase, October 23, 1862, Chase Papers, HSP.
[1] Lincoln, *Works*, V, 448, 460–2, 474, 481, 479, 485; Welles, *Diary*, I, 105.
[2] Hamlin–Charles Hamlin, November 10, 1862, Hamlin Papers; Gurowski, *Diary*, I, 313; Chase-Sumner, November 9, 1862, Chase Papers, HSP; Colfax-Lincoln, November 10, 1862, RTL; Hughes, *Letters and Recollections of John Murray Forbes*, I, 336.

VI

The Struggle for Emancipation

JUST AS LINCOLN worked with the radicals in first spurring on and then removing McClellan, so he also cooperated with them in the most controversial issue of the time: the problem of emancipation. Cognizant of the unpopularity of abolitionism and its varieties in the North and determined to retain the loyalty of the border states, at first he sought to exclude it from consideration. But if there was one tenet upon which all radicals agreed it was their demand for an unrelenting war upon slavery. They even maintained that it was impossible to win without it. How Lincoln eventually adopted their point of view without at the same time completely alienating conservatives in the North and the border states was a good illustration of the relationship between the President and the ultras.

It was clear to the radicals from the start that war would hasten the realization of their most optimistic dreams. Sumner, Giddings, and Schurz, to cite only a few, all saw the point, and even moderates like James Hamilton, the son of the first Secretary of the Treasury, who had opposed emancipation before the war because of constitutional scruples, thought that armed rebellion had changed everything. "As soon . . . as the Slave States threw off their allegiance," he wrote afterwards, "freed from my constitutional obligations, I became a most determined abolitionist." At a time when Garrison had come to support the war effort, the difference between abolitionism and radical Republicanism was becoming ever more blurred.[1]

Because of their conviction that emancipation was a *sine qua non* in dealing with the South, the radicals were certain that there could be neither permanent peace nor speedy victory without it. In no way could the President strike "such terror to the whole south as to proclaim the freedom of the slaves of Virginia," Giddings wrote to Chase on May 4, 1861. "Such a proclamation would compel every fighting man to remain at home and look to their negroes instead of going into the army to kill our friends." In a Phi Beta Kappa address at Harvard in June, George Boutwell, making a public demand for emancipation as a means for ending the war, said virtually the same thing. As Charles Sumner phrased it on October 1, at the Republican state convention at Worcester,

It is often said that war will make an end of Slavery. This is probable. But it is surer still that overthrow of Slavery will make an end of the war.[2]

How to convince the President of the feasibility of this policy, however, was a problem. Could Lincoln be won over? Many radicals thought so, and they left no means untried to achieve their purpose. In the Cabinet, Chase had never made a secret of his antislavery convictions; in Congress, Sumner, Chandler, Wade, Stevens, Lovejoy, and other ultras constantly attacked the institution, and in the country at large, radical ministers and newspapers supported them. Martial law was the only way to proceed against

[1] James A. Hamilton, *Reminiscences of James A. Hamilton* (New York, 1869), p. 41; James M. McPherson, *The Struggle for Equality: Abolitionists and the Negro in the Civil War and Reconstruction* (Princeton, 1964), pp. 52–3. Cf. Chapter V.
[2] Giddings-Chase, May 4, 1861, Chase Papers, HSP; Boutwell, *Reminiscences of Sixty Years*, I, 262; Sumner, *Works*, VI, 12.

the "peculiar institution," wrote William E. Channing on April 22, while Ashley avowed that slavery could not, by his vote, be maintained by federal power, when at the same time he would be "called upon to vote men and money without stint to put down the slave masters at the point of the bayonet." Sumner, who never ceased to press for antislavery measures, discussed the subject with Lincoln toward the end of May during a carriage ride. Conceding that the President might be justified in a conservative approach at the time, he nevertheless insisted that a blow be struck against slavery as soon as feasible.[3]

It soon became evident that there might be some justification for the radicals' appeal for emancipation as a war measure. The disposition of fugitive slaves—Negroes who had entered Federal lines—would have to be determined; the administration would have to do something. In May of 1861, the issue became acute near Fortress Monroe, where General Benjamin F. Butler was in command. Confronted with a demand to return fugitive bondsmen to their Confederate owners, he declared them "contraband of war." The term became popular, and the radicals, impressed with the resourcefulness of the formerly Democratic general, were jubilant. "The emancipation of slaves is virtually inaugurated," rejoiced Count Gurowski, while Theodore Winthrop, the novelist on Butler's staff, exclaimed, "An epigram abolished slavery in the United States."[4]

The administration took action in short order. After a Cabinet meeting, in spite of misgivings, the Secretary of War informed

[3] Welles, *Lincoln's Administration*, p. 35; Channing-Chase, April 22, 1861, Ashley-Chase, May 5. 1861, Chase Papers, LC; Sumner, *Works*, VI, 3.

[4] Boston *Daily Evening Transcript*, May 27, 1861; Jessie Ames Marshall, compiler, *Private and Official Correspondence of Gen. Benjamin F. Butler During the Period of the Civil War* (Norwood, Mass., 1917), I, 105–6 (hereafter cited as Butler, *Correspondence*); Trefousse, *Butler*, pp. 78–9; Gurowski, *Diary*, I, 50; Theodore Winthrop, *Life in the Open Air and Other Papers* (New York, 1876), p. 293. Although some doubt has been cast on the accuracy of Butler's story, the fact remains that he popularized the term "contraband."

Butler that his policy had met with approval. Lincoln had demonstrated his flexibility early in the war. [5]

The special session of Congress afforded the radicals a good opportunity to push forward their demands. John Jay, Chase's abolitionist correspondent, advised that Lincoln, in his message, stress the fact that the rebellion was an effort to extend slavery. This would enlighten Europe as well as create sympathy for the government at home. To Lincoln himself, he suggested the propriety of passing a confiscation act. The President's message did not contain any references to emancipation, Lincoln resting his entire case on the ability of self-government to survive, but he was not unwilling to entertain continuing demands for antislavery measures. At any rate, he did not oppose them, and both Houses showed little tenderness for the "peculiar institution." Lovejoy introduced a resolution declaring that it was no part of the duty of soldiers of the United States to return fugitive slaves, a proposition which was adopted by a large vote; Sumner succeeded in obtaining a passport for a colored constituent; Trumbull reported a confiscation act in the Senate, and John A. Bingham took charge of a similar measure in the House. Its provisions were reminiscent of Butler's treatment of Negro slaves as contraband of war.[6]

The antislavery efforts of Congress were not interrupted by the defeat at Bull Run. If anything, the set-back strengthened the radicals' resolve. "We need these reverses to bring our people up to the peril of [not] abolishing slavery," observed Senator Bingham, while Sumner utilized the occasion to remind Lincoln that the time for emancipation had come. And although the Johnson-Crittenden resolutions asserted that the war was not being waged for the purpose of overthrowing the "established institutions" of the states, the Confiscation Act passed with heavy majorities. When he signed it, albeit with misgivings, Lincoln furnished proof of his open-mindedness.[7]

[5] Butler, *Correspondence*, I, 116–17; *O.R.*, Series III, I, 243.
[6] John Jay–Chase, June 4, 1861, Chase Papers, LC; John Jay–Lincoln, June 29, 1861, RTL; Lincoln, *Works*, IV, 421–41; Arnold, *Lincoln*, p. 227; Sumner, *Works*, V, 497–8; Wilson, *History*, III, 237, 240.
[7] K. S. Bingham–Howard, July 26, 1861, Howard Papers; Sumner,

The months following the special session turned out to be frustrating for the advocates of emancipation. First came the revocation of Frémont's order freeing the slaves of Missouri rebels—a directive as exasperating to antislavery stalwarts as its cause had been to the border states. Then came increasingly frequent reports of hostility toward bondsmen in the army; not only was McClellan known to oppose help to runaways, but General Henry W. Halleck, the new commander of the Department of the Missouri, issued an order forbidding them to enter his lines. The antislavery crusade seemed to be lagging.[8]

But the radicals did not propose to allow the country to forget what they considered the primary cause of the war. Determined not to let the cause of emancipation rest, they exerted unrelenting pressure upon the administration. The press was especially outspoken. "The Commander-in-Chief of the armies of the United States, who is at the same time its President, will not forget, we hope, that his official position is in the lead, and not in the rear," was the sentiment of the New York *Evening Post*.

> He should not allow himself to be outstripped by his Cabinet, by Congress, by the Major Generals, and by the people. He is the head of the nation, to which it naturally looks for forward movements. But in the reluctance with which he signed the Confiscation act . . . and in his late modification of Fremont's order, it almost appears as if he desired to go backward.

The President preserved a copy of the article in his papers.[9]

Intellectuals also kept the cause before Lincoln's eyes. George Bancroft, the famous historian who had been a lifelong Democrat and Polk's Secretary of the Navy, on November 15 wrote to the President:

Works, VI, 3; *Cong. Globe*, 37th Cong., 1st Sess., 431, 434; Blaine, *Twenty Years of Congress*, I, 343.

[8] Albert Mordell, compiler, *Civil War and Reconstruction: Selected Essays by Gideon Welles* (New York, 1959), p. 232 (hereafter cited as Welles, *Civil War and Reconstruction*); *O.R.*, Series I, VIII, 370.

[9] Clipping, New York *Evening Post*, September, 1861, RTL.

Your administration has fallen upon times, which will be remembered as long as human events find a record. I sincerely wish to you the glory of perfect success. Civil War is the instrument of Divine Providence to root out social slavery; posterity will not be satisfied with the result, unless the consequence of the war shall effect an increase of free states. This is the universal expectation and hope of men of all parties.

That these sentiments reflected important trends in Congress was known to him. Bancroft had merely emphasized the arguments usually advanced by the radicals.[1]

After the capture in November 1861 of coastal districts in South Carolina, the problem became more critical than ever. "If the President again ignores the *cause* of the *war*," Medill warned Chase, "it is hoped that *you* will not. . . . As the army advances in the cotton states the slaves should be liberated and hired to work the estates of the rebels which should be confiscated." When, on November 13, Colonel John Cochrane, addressing his troops in the presence of the Secretary of War, advocated the use of colored soldiers to suppress the rebellion, Cameron supported him. The Pennsylvanian was becoming Chase's ally in the Cabinet, and Lincoln could hardly afford to disregard the mounting demands for action.[2]

The President's own position on slavery was in fact not as different from the radicals' as has sometimes been assumed. The man who, as early as 1858, had said, "I have always hated slavery, I think as much as any abolitionist," and who, fourteen years after the event, vividly remembered the torment the sight of shackled Negroes on a steamship had caused him as a young man, was no archconservative.[3] He had often expressed his detestation of

[1] George Bancroft–Lincoln, November 15, 1861, RTL.

[2] Medill-Chase, November 25, 1861, Chase Papers, HSP; Frank Moore, ed., *The Rebellion Record, A Diary of American Events* (New York, 1862–7), III, 77, 317; Bates, *Diary*, p. 203. For an excellent account of radical efforts to make Negroes in the captured region self-supporting, cf. Willie Lee Rose, *Rehearsal for Reconstruction: The Port Royal Experiment* (Indianapolis, 1964), esp. pp. 21 ff.

[3] Lincoln, *Works*, II, 492, 320.

Charles Sumner

Early Eastern Radicals in the Senate

John P. Hale

William H. Seward

Salmon P. Chase

Benjamin F. Wade

Early Western Radicals in the Senate

Joshua R. Giddings

George W. Julian

Early Radicals in the House

Henry Wilson

Zachariah Chandler

Lyman Trumbull

Jacob M. Howard

Wartime Radical Leaders in the Senate

Schuyler Colfax

Henry Winter Davis

Owen Lovejoy

Wartime Radi

James M. Ashley

John Covode

aders in the House

William D. Kelley

Benjamin F. Butler

Oliver P. Morton

Timothy O. Howe

George H. Williams

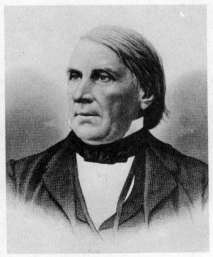

Elihu B. Washburne

Charles D. Drake

Abraham Lincoln

Andrew Johnson

Hannibal Hamlin

Edwin M. Stanton

George S. Boutwell

Prominent

Horace Greeley

Carl Schurz

epublicans

William P. Fessenden

Thaddeus Stevens

Assault on Charles Sumner in the Senate Chamber

Lincoln Visiting McClellan in the Field

The Emancipation Proclamation

Impeachment of President Johnson: The High Court of Impeachment

The Radical Party on a Heavy Grade

the institution and his hope that it would soon disappear. But he knew that it was essential to maintain the nation's unity; the unpopularity of abolition in the North had not abated; nor were the border states entirely secure. In the initiation of antislavery measures, he would have to move with care, relying on his own sense of timing rather than on the impetuous demands of his extremist advisers. Nevertheless, their pressure was useful; nobody knew better than he how to harness it for the purposes of human progress to which he himself was committed.

In November the President showed again that he was responsive to antislavery influences. Replying to Bancroft's letter, he expressed his appreciation of the historian's patriotic activities in behalf of the Unionists of North Carolina. Then he turned to emancipation. "The main thought in the last paragraph of your letter," he wrote, "is one which does not escape my attention, and with which I must deal in all due caution, and with the best of judgment."

A few days later, he demonstrated what he meant by his words. Convinced that the solution of the problem involved gradual, compensated emancipation, he drew up two plans for this purpose. The small border state of Delaware seemed to offer the best prospects; since he was on good terms with its member of Congress, George P. Fisher, he submitted his schemes to Fisher with the recommendation that they be popularized among the members of the legislature. Although these propositions were unsuccessful, the President would seek to resuscitate them many times in the future.[4]

The President's annual message to Congress also contained proof of his willingness to move with the times. Although it did not go as far as many ultras wished—he explicitly cautioned against "radical and extreme measures"—he nevertheless announced, "the Union must be preserved, and hence, all indispensable means must be employed." Recommending the recognition of the two Negro republics of Liberia and Haiti, he emphasized

[4] Ibid., IV, 26; V, 29–31.

the rigorous enforcement of the laws against the international slave trade and suggested that individual states adopt the principles of the Confiscation Act. Persons liberated by such measures might well be colonized in appropriate areas.[5] Since many radicals also believed in voluntary colonization, the President's position was not a very great concession to conservatives.

During the first weeks of the session, few ultras appreciated this fact. Annoyed at the President's deletion of the Secretary of War's recommendation to Congress for the arming of slaves and angry at indications of conservatism in the army, the extremists showed signs of great impatience. As soon as the session opened, the House, led by Thaddeus Stevens, refused to reaffirm the Crittenden Resolution. Stevens also denounced Lincoln in caucus; and in the Senate, Trumbull introduced a stronger confiscation bill. In both chambers, radicals pressed for a variety of antislavery measures. They sought legislation ending the use of the District of Columbia jail for the confinement of fugitive slaves, rescinding army orders against runaways, and abrogating the black code of the District. Even more far-reaching were bills to prohibit slavery in the District and in the territories and to repeal the Fugitive Slave Law. And the Committee on the Conduct of the War, in its interviews with the President, also strongly advocated emancipation.[6]

———————

Nevertheless, the differences between Lincoln and the radicals should not be exaggerated. Thaddeus Stevens might denounce the President, but Charles Sumner had a clearer understanding of Lincoln's purposes. "He tells me that I am ahead of

[5] Ibid., V, 35–53.
[6] "Three Manuscripts of Gideon Welles," *American Historical Review*, XXXI (April, 1926), 487; C. H. Ray–Sumner, December 6, 1861, Charles Stack–Sumner, December 27, 1861, Thomas Reilly–Sumner, December 5, 1861, Sumner Papers; Blaine, *Twenty Years of Congress*, I, 354, 373–5; New York *Herald*, December 10, 1861; Wilson, *History*, III, 260–66, 289 ff., 270 ff., 395, 322; *The American Annual Cyclopaedia and Register of Events of the Year 1862* (New York, 1865), II, 279, 293, 299, 332; Schleiden's Dispatch No. 1, January 6, 1862, Schleiden Papers.

him only a month or six weeks," the senator wrote to Governor John A. Andrew of Massachusetts. And, as events were to show, he was right. Responding to congressional agitation about the use of the district jail for the confinement of slaves, on January 25, 1862, the President caused the marshal of the District to be informed that the practice was to cease. On February 4, mindful of the world-wide condemnation of the international slave trade, he refused to pardon a convicted slaver, Nathaniel Gordon, who was duly hanged after a brief stay of execution, the first man in America to suffer the supreme penalty for this crime.[7] And these actions were only the beginning.

In his efforts to proceed as rapidly against slavery as conditions warranted, Lincoln continued to rely on plans of gradual, compensated emancipation for the border states. In order to realize his design, he again sought to make the most of radical pressure. Beset by conservative advisers who urged him not to touch the "peculiar institution," he would have found it difficult to bring about any progress without constant agitation in and out of Congress. By early March he was ready to act. Concerned about a planned antislavery meeting in New York, he asked Carl Schurz to show him the speech he was planning to deliver. Schurz complied with the request, and the President endorsed the draft. It advocated emancipation in the District of Columbia, the confiscation of rebels' slaves, and compensation for loyal masters. And on March 6, the very day on which the meeting took place at Cooper Union, he sent to Congress a message proposing gradual compensated emancipation in the border states. The President and the demonstrators were pursuing similar goals. "In fact today people talk as though the meeting were an out-and-out administration affair—instead of the bugaboo which had frightened almost all of our editors and politicians almost out of their skins," a New York correspondent informed Charles Sumner the next morning.[8]

[7] Sumner, *Works*, VI, 152; Wilson, *History*, III, 265; Lincoln, *Works*, V, 128–9.

[8] Schurz, *Reminiscences*, II, 320–1; Lincoln, *Works*, V, 144–6; F. W. Ballard-Sumner, March 7, 1862, Sumner Papers. For an example of conservative pressure, even afterwards, cf. Bates, *Diary*, p. 241.

But Lincoln had not merely transmitted his message to please the New York emancipationists; he was really anxious for its success. It was for this reason that he had shown it to Sumner before sending it to Congress, and he now sought to utilize radical impatience to induce the border states to adopt his plans. Meeting with their representatives a few days later, he frankly told them that he was "constantly annoyed by conflicting and antagonistic complaints," on the one side by persons who wanted slaves protected, and on the other, by those who were anxious for the preservation of the rights of the masters. His scheme seemed to him a reasonable solution, and he expressed the hope that it would be accepted. Although the measure failed, and although it did not satisfy the most extreme radicals, the President's intent could not be doubted. He would attempt to attack the institution whenever feasible.[9]

In the weeks that followed, despite conservative pleas that he stand firm, the President continued to give evidence of his willingness to move forward. On April 8, the United States adhered to a treaty for the more efficient suppression of the international slave trade; on April 13, he approved of a new article of war prohibiting the return of fugitive slaves, and on April 16, he signed the bill for abolition of slavery in the District of Columbia.[1]

Emancipation in the capital had long been a subject close to Lincoln's heart. As a co-sponsor, while still an unknown congressman, of a measure to bring about the reform, he could not but sympathize with the achievement of the radicals who piloted it through Congress. Wilson, Wilmot, Wilkinson, Sumner, and Hale in the Senate; Bingham, Ashley, Riddle, and others in the House —all had rendered yeoman service. As finally passed, the bill, providing for the payment of $300 for each bondsman in the District, set aside funds for the colonization of the freedmen with their consent. And so united was the party in favoring the measure

[9] Sumner, *Works,* VI, 391; McPherson, *Rebellion,* p. 210; Nicolay and Hay, *Abraham Lincoln,* V, 212–13; Wilson, *History,* III, 303 ff.
[1] Bates, *Diary,* p. 241; Hicks-Lincoln, March 18, 1862, RTL; Wilson, *History,* III, 352, 296, 284; McPherson, *Rebellion,* pp. 150, 151.

that even Thurlow Weed's conservative organ, the Albany *Evening Journal,* stated:

> Twenty-two Representatives from the Free States voted against expelling Slavery from the National Capital. The bill was no mere "Abolition Scheme." It proposed no outrage upon the rights of individuals. . . . Let these "unfaithful stewards" explain.

The twenty-two were all Democrats.[2]

The President himself, in his message to Congress on the day he signed the bill, made it clear that he agreed with the paper's interpretation. "I have never doubted the constitutional authority of congress to abolish slavery in this District," he declared, "and I have ever desired to see the national capital freed from the institution in some satisfactory way." A few months later, he also signed the measure establishing diplomatic relations with Haiti and Liberia and the bill abolishing slavery in the territories. The Dred Scott decision was dead.[3]

Even in controversies in which the radicals clashed severely with the President, he continued to emphasize his commitment to eventual emancipation. As he had done the previous summer, Lincoln still insisted that he could not possibly allow his generals to take unilateral steps against slavery without his approval. In May, 1862, General David Hunter sought to bring about complete abolition in the Department of the South. Stating that martial law had been declared in the rebellious states comprising his department, he averred that, in a free country, this condition was incompatible with slavery. "The persons in these three States—Georgia, Florida, and South Carolina—heretofore held as slaves," he announced, "are therefore declared forever free."[4]

Although it was widely expected that Lincoln would not sustain the order, Chase, who was about to leave for Philadelphia,

[2] Ibid., p. 212; Wilson, *History,* III, 270–84; Albany *Evening Journal,* April 12, 1862.
[3] Lincoln, *Works,* V, 192; Wilson, *History,* III, 352, 329.
[4] Lincoln, *Works,* V, 222.

earnestly pleaded Hunter's cause with his chief. "It has been made as a military measure to meet a military exigency," he argued,

> and should, in my judgment be suffered to stand upon the responsibility of the Commanding General who made it. It will be cordially approved, I am sure, by more than nine tenths of the people on whom you must rely for support of your administration.

But the radicals had little hope. "Mr. Lincoln will undoubtedly revoke General Hunter's proclamation . . . ," Senator Howard predicted in a letter to Governor Blair.

> That step will *reduce* to slavery some million of human beings & add confidence but not strength to the rebels. *Dieu dispose.* Tell our people to bear it as well as they can.

Carl Schurz, too, realized that the President might not sustain the order; he only asked Lincoln not to "tie our hands" for the future. Something very much like the proclamation would soon become necessary again.[5]

The radicals' fears were justified. On May 19, convinced of the overriding necessity of maintaining control over political matters himself and beset by conservative protests, the President counter-manded the order. As he explained to Chase, "No commanding general shall do such a thing, upon my responsibility, without consulting me." In his own proclamation, however, he again referred to his recommendation that the federal government cooperate with any state which might adopt a gradual scheme of abolition. "You can not, if you would, be blind to the signs of the times . . . ," he exhorted the people concerned.

> This proposal makes common cause for a common object, casting no reproaches upon any. . . . Will you not embrace it? So much good has not been done, by one effort in all past time, as, in the providence of God, is now your high previlege [sic] to do. May the vast future not have to lament that you have neglected it.

[5] Chase-Lincoln, May 16, 1862, Schurz-Lincoln, May 16, 1862, RTL; Howard-Blair, May 17, 1862, Austin Blair Papers, Detroit Public Library.

And two days later, he signed a bill providing for the education of Negro children in the District of Columbia.[6]

The radicals were extremely bitter about the revocation. Of course Lincoln overruled Hunter's order, mused Count Gurowski,

> It was too noble, too great for the tall Kentuckian. Henceforth every Northern man dying in the South is to be credited to Mr. Lincoln.

"A more injudicious and unjust edict has not been issued since the war began," complained Medill to Chase. And the Secretary himself was most uneasy about it. As he wrote to Horace Greeley, "I have not been so sorely tried by anything here . . . as by the nullifying of Hunter's proclamation."[7] But the President had again displayed his sense of timing. The pressures upon him had been great, and he had really had no alternative but to revoke the order.

Carl Schurz fully understood the Executive's position. Although a radical himself, he assured Lincoln that he still had the utmost confidence in his policies. "You told me a week ago," he wrote,

> in the course of our confidential conversation, that you expected to be left without support at the next congressional elections by the Republican party as well as by the Democratic; by the latter, because you were too radical and by the former, because you were not radical enough. It is indeed true, that misunderstandings between yourself and the Republicans may possibly arise. After you had explained your policy to me the other day I left you perfectly happy and contented, fully convinced that, in spite of appearances to the contrary, you were determined to use all your constitutional power to deliver this country of the great curse, and so I would receive all your acts and manifestations with the utmost confidence.

Schurz had gauged Lincoln correctly.[8]

That the radicals were not pleased with the repeal was not

[6] Peter Sturtevant–Lincoln, May 16, 1862, Reverdy Johnson–Lincoln, May 16, 1862, RTL; Lincoln, *Works,* V, 219, 222–4; Wilson, *History,* III, 266.

[7] Gurowski, *Diary,* I, 210–11; Medill-Chase, May 30, 1862, Chase Papers, HSP; Chase-Greeley, May 21, 1862, Greeley Papers.

[8] Schurz-Lincoln, May 19, 1862, RTL.

surprising. In their opinion, the time for half measures was gone, and nothing but complete emancipation would satisfy them. "The most determined abolitionists everywhere," wrote Rudolf Schleiden to his government on March 31,

> do not believe in the restoration of the Union without previous emancipation. As Senators Wade and Sumner told me only a few days ago, they are expecting that the South, even after the complete destruction of its military formations, could not be subjugated, in any case could not be kept in subjection, without the abolition of slavery everywhere. Consequently, as soon as the present season causes a lengthy period of military inactivity, the financial situation will force the administration and Congress to decide whether the independence of those states which have not yet been conquered by that time should be recognized, or whether universal emancipation should be declared, and, [with the North] strengthened by this weapon, the South should be militarily put under the yoke.[9]

Given this conviction, the radicals, the men Schleiden was referring to, left no opportunity unexploited to air their views and exert pressure upon the President. Chase and Stanton upheld the antislavery position in the Cabinet; religious bodies sent resolutions to the White House, and Congress resounded to speeches emphasizing the necessity of striking at the "peculiar institution." The Boston abolitionist Wendell Phillips was even received on the Senate floor. While Lincoln might revoke Hunter's order, he knew that eventually he would have to issue one much like it.[1]

The principal legislative assault on the institution was the second Confiscation Act. Introduced in December by Lyman Trumbull in the Senate and by Thomas Elliot of Massachusetts, among others, in the House, the measure was debated for months.

---

[9] Dispatch of March 31, 1862, Schleiden Papers (author's translation).

[1] Chase-Lincoln, May 16, 1862; Resolution of Cleveland Congregational Conference, April 18, 1862, Cuyahoga and Lorraine Counties Congregational Church Conference (Samuel Wolcott)–Lincoln, April 18, 1862, Resolutions of General Assembly, Presbyterian Church, May 21–30, 1862, RTL; Thomas and Hyman, *Stanton*, pp. 229–30; Sumner, *Works*, VI, 395–438, 474–86; *American Annual Cyclopaedia*, 1862, II, 342; W. P. Phillips–Sumner, April 8, 1862, Sumner Papers; Oscar Sherwin, *Phillips*, p. 459.

As it finally emerged from the committees in both Houses, it provided for the confiscation of rebel property and the emancipation of slaves belonging to disloyal persons. In addition, the President was authorized to employ Negroes to suppress the insurrection. Former slaves would soon serve in the Union army.[2]

Because of the President's reluctance to sign a bill which had caused much wrangling between radicals and conservatives, the passage of the measure has often been cited as an example of the tension between the extremists and the White House.[3] That there was trouble between Lincoln and the ultras is undeniable. In the long run, however, the President, despite urgent pleas that he veto the pending legislation, gave it his approval. And as he did so, he showed again where his sympathy lay.

The necessity for cooperation was appreciated by congressional leaders as well as by the President. To be sure, it had to be on the level of a common denominator, one far less advanced than many radicals wished, but it could be achieved. As John Bingham, the Ohio congressman who was one of the bill's chief sponsors in the House, observed on December 19,

> I think Congress ought to act & not find fault with the President. . . . Congress may liberate all Slaves on the ground that it is necessary to the public defense in this time of Domestic Rebellion, for the reason that retained by their Rebel Masters they are employed to Supply Bread or fight battles for the Rebels—whereas if liberated & taken from the Rebels they may fight or work for the cause of Liberty. . . . I think all the Slaves ought to be declared free by law of Congress . . . but I cannot get such a bill through now & therefore I provide for emancipating all held by Rebels. . . . "[4]

In this endeavor, he succeeded.

[2] J. G. Randall, "Some Legal Aspects of the Confiscation Acts of the Civil War," *American Historical Review,* VIII (1912), 80–1; Sumner, *Works,* VII, 3; *American Annual Cyclopaedia,* 1862, II, 276, 277; *Cong. Globe,* 37th Cong., 2d Sess., Ap., 412–13.

[3] Williams, *Lincoln and the Radicals,* pp. 164–6; Randall, *Lincoln the President,* II, 228–9; Hesseltine, *Lincoln and the War Governors,* pp. 241–3. These authors stress the controversy between Lincoln and the radicals.

[4] John Bingham–Giddings, December 19, 1861, Giddings Papers.

The constitutionality of various sections of the bill caused difficulty from the beginning. To what lengths could a republican government go in confiscating private property? How did the constitutional prohibition of forfeiture beyond a person's natural life affect the problem? Could slavery be attacked directly by Congress? Were there no limits to legislative power—or should the President be left free to move at his own discretion? All these questions troubled Lincoln; thoroughly debated in and out of Congress, they led to a division among the radicals themselves. By and large, the ultras, those who were to remain in the vanguard of the movement, favored unconditional confiscation and emancipation; while another faction, represented especially by Senator Fessenden of Maine, although they did not oppose the principle of the forfeiture of rebel property, agreed with the conservatives that constitutional safeguards were of the utmost necessity. As usual, Lincoln took a cautious position. Generally in sympathy with the moderates, though in agreement with the radicals' final goals, he nevertheless moved in such a way as to maintain party unity. And that way was forward.

The differences among the Republicans became fully manifest when in the spring of 1862 the bill was discussed in the Senate. As radical a senator as Sumner was perplexed about his course. Should he go for confiscation of the property of all leaders of the Confederacy? Should he strive for the emancipation of all slaves? (He thought he was very certain on this point). Should confiscation apply merely to personal property or to land as well? He would eventually favor the application of the full rigor of the law, but other Republicans, even some formerly acting with the radicals, were not so sure. Senators James R. Doolittle of Wisconsin and Edgar Cowan of Pennsylvania, especially, were worried about the constitutional provision that no attainder of treason should "work . . . forfeiture except during the Life of the Person attained"; James Dixon of Connecticut and Orville Browning of Illinois were concerned about congressional infringement of the President's powers, and Fessenden supported them. With the war seemingly entering a revolutionary stage, some Republicans, many of them fundamentally moderate or conservative, were having second thoughts.[5]

This was not true of the ultras. Ceaselessly advocating the most rigorous, far-reaching bill obtainable, they sought to refute the arguments of more conservative colleagues. As a former Whig, Wade could not understand why it had been asserted that the President should have more power over forfeitures of property than Congress; as a long-time radical, he wanted slavery eradicated. Before the war, much as he hated it, he had been willing to let the institution alone in the states. But the rebellion had changed all that; he was no longer bound. Progress could not be stopped, he asserted, and unless he had mistaken Him greatly, God was "at least a gradual emancipationist."[6]

In their anxiety to rush the bill through, some ultras clashed sharply with their colleagues. Wade went so far as to accuse all those favoring referral to a select committee of helping the opposition, a charge which Lafayette Foster of Connecticut indignantly rejected. Even Sumner, who was as committed to the bill as Wade, thought the Ohioan had gone too far, but the chairman of the Committee on the Conduct of the War was irrepressible. In a bitter debate with Fessenden, he made a host of enemies for himself. Because of Trumbull's skill and diplomacy, the measure finally carried. But the Senate version, carefully safeguarding due process and granting some leeway to the President, was considered so weak by some radicals that Chandler actually voted against it.[7]

In the meantime, after several setbacks, the House, asserting the supremacy of Congress over the President, had passed a slightly stronger measure, which was based on the premise that the rebels were belligerents who could be prosecuted as such. When the

[5] Sumner-Lieber, April, 1862, Sumner Papers; New York *Herald*, May 3, 1862; *New York Times*, June 26, 1862; *Cong. Globe*, 37th Cong., 2d Sess., 2959 ff.; 2928 ff.; 3000 ff.

[6] *Cong. Globe*, 37th Cong., 2d Sess., 1916–19.

[7] Ibid., pp. 1957, 2202–4, 3000–6; New York *Herald*, June 30, 1862; *American Annual Cyclopaedia*, 1862, 370.

representatives, by overwhelming majorities, refused to accede to the Senate bill, the ultras were delighted. "I am glad the House had the manhood to scornfully reject the miserable abortion bill of the Senate, which is but a mockery and insult to the country," wrote Medill to Trumbull. Eventually, however, a committee of conference worked out a new compromise which retained features of both measures. The result was the final bill which was stronger than the Senate version but weaker than that of the House. This time, even Chandler voting "aye," all but a few lone Republicans in both chambers supported the measure.[8]

But of course the bill still had to receive the President's approval. Fully aware of Lincoln's constitutional scruples, the conservatives had not given up hope of winning him over to their point of view. July 13, the day following the bill's passage, was a Sunday. After church, Browning, who had opposed the final version, visited Seward. Weed was present, and the three men agreed: The President must veto the legislation. On the next day, Browning, having secured an interview with Lincoln himself, told him that he must stand pat. His course upon the measure would determine whether he was to control the "abolitionists," or whether they were to control him. At least the senator thought so, and Lincoln promised to give the matter his mature consideration.[9]

The President was as good as his word. Consider the bill he did, and he found many things which he disliked. The principle of emancipation, however, was not one of these. Only two days earlier, on July 12, Lincoln had made this clear in an interview with border state representatives. After having again pleaded with them to accept the principle of gradual, compensated disappearance of slavery, he skillfully attempted to explain his own problems. But he did not denounce the radicals; he sought to make the most of their arguments. As he put it:

[8] Ibid.; Wilson, *History*, III, 339–46; Medill-Trumbull, July 4, 1862, Trumbull Papers, LC.; Trumbull–Mrs. Trumbull, July 12, 1862, Trumbull Papers, Illinois State Historical Library, Springfield; *Cong. Globe*, 37th Cong., 2d Sess., 3266–7, 3275–6.
[9] Browning, *Diary*, I, 558.

I am pressed with a difficulty not yet mentioned—one which threatens division among those who, united are none too strong. An instance of it is known to you. Gen. Hunter is an honest man. He was, and I hope, still is, my friend. I valued him none the less for his agreeing with me in the general wish that all men everywhere, could be free. He proclaimed all men free within certain states and I repudiated the proclamation. . . . Yet in repudiating it, I gave dissatisfaction, if not offence, to many whose support the country can not afford to lose. And this is not the end of it. The pressure, in this direction, is still upon me, and is increasing. By conceding what I now ask, you can relieve me, and much more, can relieve the country, in this important point.

He also used the opportunity to send to Congress another message recommending legislation to bring about gradual, compensated emancipation.[1]

Because of his desire to proceed in a constitutional manner, Lincoln asked both Houses to remain in session until they had heard from him. Letting it be known that he could not approve of the Confiscation Bill if it violated the constitutional provision against forfeiture of property beyond a person's natural life or the prohibition of *ex post facto* legislation, he obtained his way. Congress passed the necessary explanatory resolutions, and the President signed the bill. At the same time, he sent the legislators the veto message which he would have written had they not heeded his admonition.[2]

This unusual procedure angered the radicals. Often products of the old Whig philosophy of resistance to strong executives, they had no patience with presidential interference, especially in matters concerning slavery. Disappointed about their failure to block the explanatory resolution, they were provoked again by the President's message. The feeling in Congress was intense; members denounced Lincoln's action, and Wade said the country was going to hell. The scenes witnessed in the French Revolution, he

[1] Lincoln, *Works*, V, 317–19, 324–5.
[2] Ibid., p. 326; *New York Times*, July 16, 1862; *Cong. Globe*, 37th Cong., 2d Sess., 3374–83; New York *Tribune*, July 18, 1862.

predicted, were nothing in comparison with what would be seen in America.[3]

In reality, however, the radicals did not have much reason to complain. Even a cursory perusal of the President's message showed again how close he was to their point of view. "There is much in the bill to which I perceive no objection," he declared. He agreed with the principle of confiscating rebel property; he thought it right that traitors should forfeit their slaves; and he did not believe that slaves confiscated by the government could ever be reduced to bondage again. Finally, he even endorsed the section permitting him to raise colored troops. He was rapidly approaching the point where he would be ready to sign an emancipation proclamation of his own—an attitude which Charles Sumner, for one, appreciated. Although he disagreed with the President's objections, he was satisfied with Lincoln's stand on slavery. "But whatever the difference between the President and Congress," he said in the Senate,

> there are two points on which there is no difference. Blacks are to be employed, and slaves are to be freed. In this legislative proclamation the President and Congress will unite. Together they will deliver it to the country and to the world.[4]

As the promulgation of the Emancipation Proclamation was probably one of the most famous single episodes of Lincoln's administration, it was also one of the best illustrations of the skillful way in which the President balanced the conservatives' caution with the radicals' urgency. Radical congressmen, radical Cabinet members, radical newspapermen had pleaded with Lincoln and cajoled him for months to free the slaves; their conservative counterparts had urged him to do the exact opposite. One faction in effect stated that the war could not be won unless he emancipated the Negroes; the other told him that all would

---

[3] Julian, *Political Recollections,* pp. 219–20.
[4] Lincoln, *Works,* V, 328–31; *Cong. Globe,* 37th Cong., 2d Sess., 3382.

be lost if he failed to safeguard the "peculiar institution."[5] That the President managed, in the main, to implement the policies demanded by the former without completely repelling the latter was a gift which made him an outstanding leader. It was also an ability which made it possible for him to prevail.

On June 18, alerted to the increased demand for action, while the Confiscation Bill was still pending, Lincoln invited Hannibal Hamlin for supper at the Soldiers' Home. After the meal, the President took his guest into the library. Telling Hamlin that he had finally decided to take the advice of friends like the Vice President, he revealed his secret. He would liberate the slaves. Then, inviting criticism, he read a draft of the Preliminary Emancipation Proclamation. Hamlin, one of the leading radicals, was delighted, and Lincoln accepted two of his three critical comments.[6]

Since Lincoln did not make public his decision to issue the proclamation, the pressure upon him continued. On June 20, he was again asked, this time by a delegation of Progressive Friends, to make an end of slavery. Cordially welcoming the petitioners, he told them that he agreed with their goal. He too wanted to see slavery abolished, but he disagreed about the ways in which this object was to be accomplished. And diplomatic as he was, he still kept conservatives satisfied. When his old friend Orville Browning, whose conservative stand in Congress had made him one of the radicals' chief antagonists, paid him a visit a few days later, he reassured the senator. The President said no Negro was to be armed for the time being; nor did he believe that Congress had any power to deal with slavery within the states.[7]

But the radicals did not permit Lincoln to forget their main objective. On July 4, Sumner pleaded with him to make the national holiday even more famous by freeing the bondsmen; on

[5] John Hope Franklin, *The Emancipation Proclamation* (Garden City, 1963), pp. 15–30; Lincoln, *Works,* V, 343; Bates, *Diary,* p. 241; Sumner, *Works,* VI, 16, 3.

[6] Hamlin, *Hamlin,* pp. 428–9.

[7] Lincoln, *Works,* V, 278–9; Browning, *Diary,* I, 555.

July 11, Governor Richard Yates of Illinois expressed his conviction that "conservative policy" had utterly failed to reduce traitors to obedience, and that Negro troops must be raised.[8] The President, in the meantime, was carefully watching the progress of the Confiscation Bill in Congress.

In the days that followed, Lincoln sent to both Houses his scheme for gradual emancipation, held his interview with the border state representatives, and signed the Confiscation Bill. He also put his signature to a measure granting freedom to slaves and their families serving with the Union forces. When Congress finally adjourned, Republican members of the House and Senate joined in an Address to the Loyal People of the United States. Exhorting Americans to support the administration, the legislators prayed for a speedy end of slavery.[9]

By this time, the President had discussed the proclamation with members of his Cabinet. He first broached the subject to Seward and Welles on July 13, when he was riding in a carriage with them to attend the funeral of one of Stanton's children. The full Cabinet considered it on July 22, Seward expressing his opinion that Lincoln had better await a victory before issuing any such document. Blair, now in complete sympathy with the conservatives following his family's break with Frémont, warned that it would result in the loss of the November elections.[1] But even his most cautious advisers could see that none of their objections would keep the President from holding to his course.

The period between this session and the promulgation of the

[8] Franklin, *The Emancipation Proclamation*, p. 24; Yates-Lincoln, July 11, 1862, RTL.

[9] Lincoln, *Works*, V, 324–5, 317–19, 328; Dudley Taylor Cornish, *The Sable Arm: Negro Troops in the Union Army, 1861–1865* (New York, 1956), p. 46; New York *Tribune*, July 19, 1862.

[1] Welles, *Diary*, I, 70–1; F. B. Carpenter, *Six Months at the White House with Abraham Lincoln* (New York, 1867), p. 21; The Cabinet on Emancipation, July 22, 1862, note in Stanton Papers. On July 20, Chase wrote to R. C. Parsons: "The Slavery question perplexes the President almost as much as ever and yet I think he is about to emerge from the obscurities where he has been groping into somewhat clearer light. . . . So you see the man moves." Chase-Parsons, July 20, 1862, Chase Papers, HSP.

Preliminary Emancipation Proclamation on September 22 was one of suspense for radicals and conservatives alike. Those who were not privy to the secrets of the administration stepped up their pressure either to emancipate or to protect slavery. Petitioners and petitions came to Lincoln in a never-ending stream. Robert Dale Owen, the famous reformer, wanted him to do something at once; his Kentucky friend James Speed warned against any interference with slavery, the abolitionist Henry B. Stanton badgered the Vice President to carry the revolution forward, while the conservative Maryland Unionist Reverdy Johnson begged the President not to undermine the local institutions of the states. Harshly castigating the radicals, Edgar Cowan told Lincoln that he could no more attack bondage in the South than Christianity in the North; Zach Chandler, on the contrary, maintained that even he had been lagging behind the people in antislavery zeal.[2] And the problem of Negro troops also demanded solution. Should Lincoln accept the offers of colored soldiers? Radicals were emphatic in their insistence that he do so; their opponents predicted dire calamity if he did. In the end, Ben Butler resolved the question in New Orleans by mustering in a regiment of free Negroes who had been armed by the Confederacy. Until the policy became nation-wide, however, the President had to be circumspect. Although he would eventually endorse the use of Negro soldiers, he still thought colonization was the best answer to the race problem.[3]

Lincoln's faith in colonization did not place him in a position of sharp antagonism toward all radicals, since many of them had favored this solution at one time or other.[4] To be sure, Chase had

[2] Owen-Stanton, July 23, 1862, Stanton Papers; Speed-Lincoln, July 28, 1862, Edgar Cowan–Lincoln, August 8, 1862, Chandler-Lincoln, August 8, 1862, RTL; H. B. Stanton–Hamlin, July 24, 1862, Hamlin Papers; Lincoln, *Works*, V, 343.

[3] Yates-Lincoln, July 11, 1862, RTL; New York *Tribune*, July 19, 1862; New York *Evening Post*, July 10, 1862 (clipping in RTL); Chase, *Diaries*, pp. 95–100; New York *Herald*, July 19, 1862; Benjamin F. Butler, *Butler's Book* (Boston, 1892), pp. 492–4; Lincoln, *Works*, V, 370–5.

[4] W. G. Snethen–Trumbull, December 8, 1861, Trumbull Papers,

become critical of it, but given the state of race relations at the time, the idea was widespread, as the President, on August 14, emphasized to a group of visiting colored delegates. Many a radical would have told them the same thing. Senator Pomeroy of Kansas was even then considering taking charge of a colony to be established at Chiriqui.[5]

The controversy seemed to reach a climax on August 19, when Horace Greeley, in the New York *Tribune,* published his Prayer of Twenty Millions. A broad attack on the President's conduct of the government, the Prayer not only accused Lincoln of negligence in enforcing the Confiscation Act, but also asserted that slavery and the restoration of the Union were incompatible. The President's reply has often been quoted. He emphasized that if he could save the Union without freeing any slave, he would do it; if he could save it by freeing all the slaves, he would do it, and if he could do it by freeing some and leaving others in slavery, he would do that too. What has sometimes been forgotten, however, is Lincoln's concluding sentence. "I have here stated my purpose according to my view of *official* duty," he wrote, "and I intend no modification of my oft-expressed *personal* wish that all men, everywhere, could be free."[6] The gap between him and the radicals was not so large after all, especially since he had already written his Emancipation Proclamation. All that remained to be done was to find the correct time to publish it.

The end of August was hardly the proper moment for any revolutionary steps. Because of Pope's defeat at Manassas, any declaration freeing slaves would have had little effect, and Lincoln knew it. To be sure, the radicals were still impatient. A mammoth war meeting took place at Boston, where Frémont called for immediate emancipation. Sumner, who sent his endorsement of these demands to the White House, wanted Preston King

LC; Dennison-Wade, February 6, 1860, Wade Papers; New York *Tribune,* March 13, 1860, January 17, 1851; Chase-Douglass, May 4, 1850, Stevens-Chase, August 25, 1862, Chase Papers, HSP.

[5] Chase–E. L. Pierce, August 2, 1862, Chase Papers, LC; Lincoln, *Works,* V, 370–5; New York *Herald,* August 26, 1862.

[6] Lincoln, *Works,* V, 388–9.

to intercede with the President. King told him that Lincoln was already familiar with the New Yorker's views, but religious denominations again implored Lincoln to initiate general emancipation. And the other side was active too. Before leaving the capital, border state representatives cautioned the President not to yield to the radicals, Senator John B. Henderson of Missouri especially imploring him not to listen to them, while Governor Hamilton Gamble of the same state issued a warning of his own.[7] Lincoln was again biding his time. But he was still moving forward— slowly, deliberately, in his own good time, yet forward just the same.

During the first three weeks of September, events were moving swiftly. Lee invaded Maryland; McClellan prepared to stop him, and the armies clashed at Antietam. Robert Dale Owen, approaching Chase with a scheme for immediate emancipation, requested that it be passed on to the President. On September 17, the reformer sent an appeal to Lincoln himself. The sixty days' grace given by the Confiscation Act were rapidly approaching their end, he pointed out. Something must be done. Why not issue a proclamation freeing all the slaves and promising compensation to loyal owners? Freedmen might then be drafted for government service.[8]

Whether or not the President was impressed with Owen's proposal, he had now come to the conclusion that the time for issuing his proclamation had arrived. In a Cabinet meeting on September 22, he revealed that when the rebel army had been at Frederick, he had determined to publish an emancipation procla-

[7] Boston *Journal,* August 29, 1862; King-Sumner, August 30, 1862, Sumner Papers; Resolutions, Spring Street Congregational Church, Milwaukee, September 5, 1862; Resolutions, Methodist Episcopal Church, Cincinnati Conference, September 8, 1862; Congregational Church, Massachusetts General Conference, Newton, September 12, 1862; Indiana Conference, Wesleyan Methodist Church, September 12, 1862; Garrett Davis, R. A. Buckner, J. B. Huston–Lincoln, September 6, 1862; J. B. Henderson–Lincoln, September 3, 1862, Hamilton Gamble–Lincoln, September 9, 1862, Sumner-Lincoln, August 29, 1862, RTL; Lincoln, *Works,* V, 418–25.

[8] R. D. Owen–Chase, September 15, 1862, Chase Papers, HSP; R. D. Owen–Lincoln, September 17, 1862, RTL.

mation as soon as the Confederates were driven out of Maryland. "I said nothing to anyone," he confessed, "but I made the promise to myself, and . . . to my Maker. The rebel army is now driven out, and I am going to fulfill that promise." Although he had called the secretaries together to show them what he had written, he had made up his mind. The proclamation would be published, and all the Cabinet could do was to make suggestions about form.[9]

The Preliminary Emancipation Proclamation which he then promulgated fell far short of the expectations of the most determined antislavery forces. Promising an amnesty to all insurgents who would lay down their weapons within ninety days, it offered freedom merely to the slaves of those still in arms against the government after that time. Because it excluded virtually all conquered areas, even if the final proclamation should go into effect it would at first free few Negroes. But it was clear that for slavery, it was the beginning of the end. "This was a most wonderful history of an insanity of a class that the world had ever seen," commented Chase.

> If the slaveholders had staid [sic] in the Union they might have kept the life in their institution for many years to come. That what no party and no public feeling in the North could ever have hoped to touch they had madly placed in the path of destruction.

And while Count Gurowski, acrimonious as ever, denounced the conditional aspects of the document, even Ben Wade was moved to exclaim, "Hurrah for Old Abe and the *proclamation*." Congratulating the President, Hannibal Hamlin wrote:

> It will stand as the great act of the age. It will prove to be wise in Statesmanship, as it is Patriotic. It will be enthusiastically approved and sustained . . . God bless you for the great and noble act.

Sumner delivered an oration in its praise; Gerrit Smith sent Lincoln his blessings, and one of Thaddeus Stevens's correspondents rejoiced that the manifesto had given proof of the President's

[9] Welles, *Diary*, I, 142–4; Chase, *Diaries*, pp. 149–52.

agreement with the radicals.[1] The proclamation was a success.

Whether Lincoln would have been willing or able to issue the proclamation without radical prodding, however, is questionable. Confronted with difficulties, dubious about his own constitutional powers, and anxious to avoid offense to the border states, the President needed the ultras' help in order to commit himself. "In Lincoln's desk the Emancipation Proclamation would probably have remained had it not been for the increased activities of the radicals . . .," William Best Hesseltine, a historian by no means sympathetic to the ultras, has written, and his conclusion is supported by the evidence. As Julian, a contemporary observer, reminisced afterwards, "It was in yielding to this [radical] pressure that he finally became the liberator of the slaves through the triumph of our arms which ensued." And considering the relationship between Lincoln and Thaddeus Stevens, perhaps one of the most representative radicals in the House, Alexander K. McClure, the Pennsylvania newspaperman, stated: "Had Stevens not declared for the abolition of slavery as soon as the war began, and pressed it in and out of season, Lincoln would not have issued his Emancipation Proclamation as early as September, 1862." Carl Schurz, also remembering Lincoln's dependence on the radicals, was particularly impressed with Sumner's influence. He wrote:

> Lincoln regarded and esteemed Sumner as the outspoken conscience of the advanced anti-slavery sentiment, the confidence and hearty cooperation of which was to him of the highest moment in the common struggle. While it required all his fortitude to bear Sumner's intractable insistence, Lincoln did not at all deprecate Sumner's agitation for an immediate emancipation policy, even though it did reflect upon the course of the administration. On the contrary, he rather welcomed everything that would prepare the public mind for the approaching development.[2]

[1] Hay, *Diaries*, p. 50; Gurowski, *Diary*, I, 277; Wade-Julian, September 29, 1862, Julian-Giddings Papers; Hamlin-Lincoln, September 25, 1862; Gerrit Smith–Lincoln, October 9, 1862, RTL; Sumner, *Works*, VII, 191–236; S. S. Blair–Stevens, November 8, 1862, Stevens Papers.

[2] Hesseltine, *Lincoln and the War Governors*, p. 249; Julian, *Political Recollections*, p. 227; McClure, *Lincoln and the Men of War-Times*, p. 262; Schurz, *Reminiscences*, II, 317.

The reaction of the conservatives furnished further proof of Lincoln's skill. He had timed his move correctly, and although he had yielded to the radicals, he had done so without causing a major rift in the country. To be sure, much of the Democratic opposition violently denounced the step, but even the New York *Herald,* critical of the administration as it was, emphasized the conservative aspects of the proclamation. The South could save its institutions by surrendering before January 1, the paper pointed out. Let the deluded section make the most of it! And with the opposition newspaper so understanding, conservative Republicans had to acquiesce. In the Cabinet, Seward, Blair, and Bates, continued to cooperate with the President; in the country, their sympathizers followed suit. "And now a word as to the Proclamation," wrote Senator Ira Harris of New York,

> I was startled when I first saw it. But it did not take me long to get reconciled to it, and now I find, every day, that men vastly more conservative than I have ever been are giving us their adhesion to the proclamation. . . . It makes the men of extreme views exceedingly well satisfied with themselves, and nobody, except Democrats who want to be dissatisfied, find any fault. Those who have been clamoring for a policy have got it.[3]

The interaction between the radicals and the President—a relationship marked by similar goals but different methods—had proven productive of great good.

[3] Charles A. Dana, *Recollections of the Civil War* (New York, 1899), p. 180; New York *World,* September 24, 1862; New York *Herald,* September 23, 27, 1862; Ira Harris–Lincoln, October 2, 1862, RTL.

VII

Cooperation
for Victory

LINCOLN'S PROMULGATION of the Preliminary Emancipation Proclamation and his dismissal, little more than six weeks later, of General McClellan, emphasized more clearly than anything up to that time the similarity between his and the radicals' war aims. Like them, he was determined to carry on the conflict as rigorously as necessary. The administration, as well as the most extreme wing of the party, was now committed to a remorseless struggle for reunion and the end of slavery.

To secure these ends, the President and the radicals continued to work together—unwillingly, at times, but effectively just the same. Although the advanced Republicans were often far ahead of the administration, in the end, Lincoln generally caught up with his critics. The ultras' impetuousness mitigated by his caution was an exceptional combination.

It is not surprising that the collaboration between the President and the radicals has often been overlooked. The evidence of constant quarrels between them is there for all to see. Newspapers were full of it at the time; foreign diplomats reported it to their governments, and historians have commented upon it since.[1] But in recounting these differences, they have neglected the central factor in the relationship between Lincoln and his radical critics, the similarity of their aims, and the masterful way in which the President made use of extremist demands to obtain reforms which he considered desirable.

The struggle against slavery furnished the best example of this cooperation after September, 1862, as well as before. To be sure, Lincoln had published his Preliminary Emancipation Proclamation, but would he be able to carry it out? Would conservative pressures permit him, on January 1, 1863, to free Confederate slaves as he had promised? In the difficult months preceding the target date, some observers doubted it.

It was to be expected that conservatives would disparage the emancipation policy. Opposition newspapers castigated it in no uncertain terms. But some critics went even further. Republican setbacks during the fall elections gave rise to conservative hopes that the President would have to reconsider. Lincoln would have to postpone the proclamation, wrote the New York *Herald.* The President's friend, Orville Browning, told him that the document was responsible for the Democratic successes, and even Fessenden criticized it as a *brutum fulmen.* "The New Policy Not a Finality," read a headline in the Washington *National Intelligencer,* which explained that emancipation on January 1 was not at all certain. To drive the point home, when Congress met, Representative George Yeaman of Kentucky offered a resolution castigating the proclamation as "not warranted by the Constitution," "not calculated to hasten the restoration of peace," "not well chosen as a war measure," and "an assumption of power dangerous to the rights of citizens and to the perpetuity of a free people." As late as

---

[1] For example, New York *Herald,* May 20, June 27, July 17, 18, 1862, January 20, November 20, December 11, 1863; New York *World,* December 1, 1862, January 20, May 25, 1863; Albany *Evening Journal,* December 22, 1862; Dispatches of February 10, 16, 1863, Schleiden Papers; Williams, *Lincoln and the Radicals,* passim; Randall, *Lincoln the Liberal Statesman,* pp. 69 ff.; Hesseltine, *Lincoln and the War Governors,* pp. 356–7.

December 27, some people were still wondering about the President's intentions.[2]

Under these circumstances, Lincoln needed support, and as so often, he obtained it most noticeably from the radicals, whose most cherished beliefs were at stake.

In point of time, one of the first efforts to sustain the new policy was undertaken by the Northern governors who on September 26 came to see Lincoln. Having met at Altoona, Pennsylvania, in order to induce the President to issue an emancipation proclamation and to urge him to remove McClellan, the executives arrived at a time when their first objective had already been met. The "Young Napoleon," it is true, was still in command, but since moderates at Altoona had prevented the adoption of any resolutions censuring the general, the interview was held under favorable circumstances. Requesting the publication of a call for 100,000 volunteers, Lincoln's visitors offered their congratulations on the proclamation. Although the New York *Herald* complained of a "Roundhead Conspiracy," the meeting was amicable, the President thanking his callers for their support and promising them to take their suggestions under consideration.[3] It was clear to him that the interview would have been less cordial without the proclamation.

The radicals' enthusiastic reception of the document also strengthened the President's hand. Amid the welter of criticism, expressions of approval from men like Hamlin, Chase, and Sumner must have afforded relief. And Lincoln knew that the friends of emancipation would not countenance retreat, even had he been so inclined.

But the President was not at all disposed to abandon his policy.

[2] Washington *National Intelligencer*, September 23, November 1, 1862; New York *World*, September 24, 1862; New York *Herald*, October 19, 1862; Browning, *Diary*, I, 587–90; McPherson, *Rebellion*, p. 229; Allan Nevins and Milton Halsey Thomas, eds., *The Diary of George Templeton Strong* (New York, 1952), III, 282 (hereafter cited as Strong, *Diary*).

[3] Hesseltine, *Lincoln and the War Governors*, pp. 253–61; McClure, *Lincoln and the Men of War-Times*, pp. 248–9; Chase, *Diaries*, pp. 160–1; Lincoln, *Works*, V, 441; New York *Herald*, September 26, 1862.

On the contrary, in his message to Congress, he included a suggestion for an antislavery amendment envisioning compensation for losses incurred by loyal owners if by 1900 they abolished the institution. Chase, to whom he showed the message prior to its delivery, doubted that the proposition would be favorably received. However, since it prohibited the re-enslavement of those already freed "by the chances of war," even he could not deny that it presaged final emancipation.[4]

In spite of its obvious antislavery tone, the message could be interpreted as a retreat from Lincoln's announced stand on the slavery question. If it was really a backward step, however, it did not mean that he was abandoning his purpose. He believed in the proclamation; as he told visiting Kentucky Unionists, he would rather die than take back a word of it. If he seemed hesitant, he was acting for political reasons. And the radicals showed again that he could rely on them. So well had they done their work that the Republicans, by the overwhelming division of 75–47, virtually all members of the party voting yea, promptly tabled Yeaman's resolution. In addition, they secured specific support. A resolution asserting that the proclamation was an expedient war measure, warranted by the Constitution, was adopted by a vote of 78–52.[5]

In order to make certain that the Emancipation Proclamation was issued on New Year's Day, the radicals continued their clamor up to the end. Strengthened by the congressional resolution favoring the policy, they did not allow their opponents to steal a march on them. One hundred and forty-six presidential electors from New York and many others from Massachusetts asked Lincoln to carry out his announced purpose on time; Sumner repeatedly saw him for the same reason, and the Society of Friends in Iowa sent him resolutions favoring the proclamation. At the same time, Robert Dale Owen, stressing the diplomatic benefits to be expected from emancipation, sent appeals to both Seward and

[4] Lincoln, *Works,* V, 529–32; Chase-Lincoln, November 28, 1862, RTL.

[5] New York *Herald,* December 2, 1862; Benjamin Quarles, *Lincoln and the Negro* (New York, 1962), p. 134; Lincoln, *Works,* V, 503; McPherson, *Rebellion,* p. 229.

Chase. Consequently, Lincoln could disregard last-minute conservative appeals to dissuade him, whether they took the form of private pleas, like Orville Browning's efforts to intervene, or public attacks, like Congressman Yeaman's bitter speech in the House of Representatives. "The President says he could not stop the Proclamation if he would, and he would not if he could," wrote Sumner on December 28.[6] Hesitant as he had been about the wisdom of publishing the document, Lincoln had made up his mind. And once he had decided, he was known to be firm if he could count on effective backing. The radicals furnished it to him.

On January 1, the President issued the Emancipation Proclamation. After quoting appropriate passages from the preliminary manifesto, by virtue of his power as commander-in-chief of the army and navy, he declared that all slaves in states and parts of states still in rebellion, "are, and henceforward shall be free," enjoined freedmen to abstain from violence, and announced that they would be received into the armed services. Upon Chase's last-minute advice, Lincoln added the conclusion,

And upon this act, sincerely believed to be an act of justice, warranted by the Constitution, upon military necessity, I invoke the considerate judgment of mankind, and the gracious favor of Almighty God."[7]

The proclamation, with all its imperfections—in the main, it still applied only to areas not yet under Union control—constituted not merely a great victory for the radicals, but also an excellent example of the interaction between extremist pressure, conservative counterpressure, and executive reaction to both.

It was recognized at the time that the radicals had played a large role in the events leading to the publication of the Emancipation Proclamation. Bitterly hostile, the New York *World* condemned the President "and the radical clique with which he now sur-

[6] Petitions in RTL, December 24, 27, 1862; Hughes, *Letters and Recollections of John Murray Forbes,* I, 347–9, 352; R. D. Owen–Chase, December 29, 1862, Chase Papers, HSP; R. D. Owen–Seward, December 29, 1862, RTL; Browning, *Diary,* I, 606–7; *Cong. Globe,* 37th Cong., 3d Sess., 130–7.

[7] Lincoln, *Works,* VI, 26–30; Welles, *Diary,* I, 210; Boutwell, *Reminiscences of Sixty Years,* II, 17.

rounds himself" for replying with the promulgation of an emancipation manifesto to conservative demands for moderate policies.
The New York *Herald,* equally opposed, charged that the ultras
had forced Lincoln to sign the document, and more impartial
observers like the well-informed minister from Bremen, Rudolf
Schleiden, substantially agreed. "His [Lincoln's] decision seems to
have been caused chiefly by the apprehension that the extreme
Republican party would overthrow him if he reneged," he reported. But the envoy as well as the opposition press overlooked
one essential point. As Lincoln had said to Sumner, he could not
stop the proclamation if he would, and he would not if he could.[8]

Once the Emancipation Proclamation had been published, radical support enabled Lincoln to stand firm in carrying it out. Conservatives had not given up the idea that somehow or other the
President might still be swayed from his purpose. As Charles
Sumner complained in August, 1863,

> I find everywhere consternation at the idea that the Proclama-
> tion can be forgotten or abandoned. . . . Mr. Seward's speech has
> had a tendency to excite distrust, which has been increased by
> reports that some of the cabinet wished the Govt. to turn from
> the Proclamation. Mr. Thurlow Weed has increased these
> anxieties by the overtures which he has made in the *Evening
> Journal.*

But his fears were unfounded. His plea to do justice to the black
man was only one of many factors influencing the President.
There were reports of the good effects of the policy upon foreign
relations—news which the radicals were quick to emphasize—
and ultras throughout the country delivered speeches praising
emancipation. Lincoln did not have to move backward. Again and
again he stressed his determination not to retract, and even
though conservatives like Senator Dixon continued to admonish
him to remain true to the principles announced at his inauguration, he stood by the proclamation.[9]

[8] New York *World,* January 8, 1863; New York *Herald,* January 20,
1863; Dispatch of January 2, 1863, Schleiden Papers (author's translation); Hughes, *Letters and Recollections of John Murray Forbes,* I,
352.

[9] Sumner-Lincoln, August 7, 1863; Dixon-Lincoln, November 14,

In the same way that the radicals were instrumental in reinforcing the President's commitment to emancipation, they also made possible the success of other measures designed to elevate the Negro. Ever since the beginning of the war, some ultras had advocated the use of colored troops. Gradually, these demands had become more and more insistent. Although Hunter's efforts to recruit freedmen proved premature, the Militia Act of July, 1862, provided for the employment of Negro soldiers, and some colored units, including Butler's force in New Orleans, were raised during the second half of the year. But Lincoln was still hesitant. Worried about popular prejudice, he wanted to be certain, and it was not until January, 1863, that he finally decided that the right time had come. As the proclamation contained a paragraph endorsing the proposal, Negro troops were mustered into the service with ever-increasing frequency. Constant radical propaganda, including the intervention of the Vice President, whose son volunteered for the command of one of the new units, facilitated this decision. By the spring of 1863, the President himself encouraged governors and generals to enlist freedmen.[1]

Many different antislavery reforms prevailed because of the cooperation between the President and the radicals. The prohibition of discrimination in Washington streetcars, a War Department General Order permitting the freeing of slaves, the repeal of the Fugitive Slave Law, the prohibition of the interstate slave trade, provisions for equal pay for colored soldiers and freedom

---

1863, RTL; C. D. Cleveland–Chase, February 5, 1863, Chase Papers, HSP; Koerner-Trumbull, March 22, 1863, Trumbull Papers, LC; Lincoln, *Works,* VI, 63–5; *Buler's Book,* p. 567; Cincinnati *Daily Gazette,* June 18, 1863; Washington *National Intelligencer,* September 18, 1863; Lincoln, *Works,* VI, 358, 406–10; VII, 36–53, 281.

[1] William Holliday–Blair, April 22, 1861, Austin Blair Papers; J. A. Hamilton–Chase, November 20, 1861, Chase Papers, HSP; S. R. Curtis–Trumbull, December 19, 1861, Trumbull Papers, LC; Hamilton, *Reminiscences,* p. 529; Cornish, *The Sable Arm,* p. 46; Quarles, *Lincoln and the Negro,* pp. 153 ff; G. S. Denison–Chase, August 11, 1862, Chase Papers, LC; J. M. Forbes–Sumner, November 29, 1862, Sumner Papers; Hamlin, *Hamlin,* pp. 431–3; Theodore Tilton–Lincoln, February 3, 1863, RTL; Lincoln, *Works,* VI, 149–50, 154–5; Allan Nevins, *The War for the Union* (New York, 1960), II, 512 ff.

for their families—all these were ceaselessly advanced by the radicals. The President, who approved of all of them, promptly signed those requiring his assent.[2] Whether he would ever have had the chance to do so without the extremists' efforts remains doubtful.

That the President, who detested slavery, was wholly in sympathy with measures to uplift the Negro he proved again and again. In July, 1863, he had under consideration a scheme for the reconstruction of Arkansas. But he stated unequivocally,

> The Emancipation Proclamation applies to Arkansas. I think it is valid in law, and will be so held by the courts. I think I shall not retract or repudiate it. Those who shall have tasted actual freedom I believe can never be slaves, or quasi-slaves again.

Three weeks later, he endorsed a colored ministers' committee's request for Negro chaplains, and then made his sentiments known again in a letter to James C. Conkling, a Springfield acquaintance, who had invited him to attend a Union mass meeting in Illinois. "You are dissatisfied with me about the negro," he wrote,

> Quite likely there is a difference of opinion between you and myself upon that subject. I certainly wish that all men could be free, while I suppose you do not. . . . You dislike the emancipation proclamation; and, perhaps, would have it retracted. You think it is unconstitutional. I think differently.

And as he put it so clearly when speaking of the differences between the radicals and conservatives in Missouri,

> I believe, after all, those radicals will carry the state, and I do not object to it. They are nearer to me than the other side, in thought and sentiment, though bitterly hostile personally. They are utterly lawless—the unhandiest devils in the world to deal with—but after all, their faces are set Zionwards.

The man who, speaking to two visitors from Kentucky, on April 4, 1864, said, "I am naturally anti-slavery. If slavery is not wrong, nothing is wrong," was no friend of the peculiar institution. Care-

---

[2] Sumner, *Works*, VIII, 103–4, 403–18; *O.R.*, Series III, III, 148–64; Horace Greeley, *The American Conflict* (Hartford, 1866), II, 267, 269; Wilson, *History*, III, 354–6, 373–9, 394–6, 403–14.

ful as he was, he welcomed progress. There was a place for radical concepts in Lincoln's scheme of things.[3]

It may be objected that the President was not fully in control of the situation, that he was simply being pushed by the radicals into adventures which he fundamentally disliked. Such an explanation does not accord with the evidence. He had learned much since his arrival in the capital. Deeply conscious of his prerogatives as well as of his responsibilities, he maintained his supremacy in the Cabinet, and he jealously safeguarded his rights as Commander-in-Chief. In his relations with his critics, he retained the upper hand throughout. "You may talk as you please of the Abolitionist Cabal directing affairs from Washington . . .," John Hay in September, 1863, pointed out to John G. Nicolay. "The old man sits here and wields like a backwoods Jupiter the bolts of war and the machinery of government with a hand equally steady and equally firm."[4]

The Secretary's analysis was borne out by facts. If Congress tried to interfere, Lincoln stood his ground. If he found a general wanting, he recalled him, and no amount of radical agitation could change his mind. Conversely, if a general was merely under attack because of his politics, the President would not remove him. He was perfectly capable of finding his own commanders. The Committee on the Conduct of the War was not always consulted.

The most obvious example of Lincoln's independence was his handling of the Cabinet crisis of December, 1862. The effort of Congress to oust Seward from Lincoln's official family has often been cited as an instance of the bitterness between the President and the radicals. David Donald has demonstrated that such an interpretation is exaggerated; moderates as well as ultras joined in the Caucus, and a conservative, Jacob Collamer of Vermont,

---

[3] Lincoln, *Works*, VI, 358–9, 406–10, VII, 281; Hay, *Diaries,* p. 108; cf. David Donald, *Devils Facing Zionwards,* in Grady McWhiney, ed., *Grant, Lee, Lincoln and the Radicals: Essays on Civil War Leadership* (Chicago, 1964), pp. 72–91. Cf. Richard N. Current, *The Lincoln Nobody Knows* (New York, 1958), p. 235.

[4] Hay, *Diaries,* p. 91.

chaired the committee which presented the grievances.[5] Nevertheless, the radicals played a leading role in the controversy.

The extremists had been dissatisfied with Lincoln's official family for a long time. As early as July 28, 1861, Trumbull sharply criticized the department heads; three days later, one of John Covode's correspondents expressed the opinion that the country had confidence in Lincoln and General Scott, but none in the Cabinet, and that August, newspapers carried reports about the radicals' disappointment with the conservative members of the administration. At first, Welles and Cameron were the chief targets of criticism; by 1862, however, Seward had become the ultras' principal antagonist. In September, a committee representing the views of five New England governors came to Washington to air the opposition to the Secretary of State, and after the Democratic victories in October, Stevens expressed the opinion that there was no hope without a new set of ministers. A few weeks later, he was even more explicit. "It were a great blessing if Seward could be removed," he wrote. "It would revive hope, now nearly extinct. But I fear it cannot be done." So critical had the Secretary's position become that even a moderate like William P. Fessenden speculated about the possibility of his ouster. And Chase had long been complaining that the Cabinet did not meet as a unit.[6]

When on December 16, a caucus of Republican senators met to consider the recent disaster at Fredericksburg, where McClellan's successor, Ambrose Burnside, had suffered a serious reverse, no one defended the Secretary of State. Wade, Trumbull, Wilkinson, and Grimes, among others, all attacked Seward, whose

[5] Williams, *Lincoln and the Radicals,* pp. 208–15; Burton J. Hendrick, *Lincoln's War Cabinet* (Boston, 1946), pp. 334 ff.; Thomas, *Lincoln,* pp. 351–4; Randall, *Lincoln the President,* II, 242–9; David Donald, *Lincoln Reconsidered* (New York, 1956), pp. 113–14.

[6] Trumbull–Mrs. Trumbull, July 28, 1861, Trumbull Papers, ISHL; B. F. Stein–Covode, July 31, 1861, Covode Papers, HSWP; New York *Herald,* August 27, 1861; Chase, *Diaries,* pp. 128–30. Stevens–S. Stevens, October 27, November 17, 1862, Stevens Papers; Hughes, *Letters and Recollections of John Murray Forbes,* I, 337; Chase-Greeley, September 7, 1862, Greeley Papers; Chase, *Diaries,* p. 144; Chase–John Sherman, September 20, 1862, Chase Papers, HSP. The governors had met in conference at Providence, R.I.

usefulness to the administration they questioned, and on the next day, Jacob Collamer was appointed chairman of a committee to lay the senators' grievances before the President.

On December 18, the congressional group arrived at the White House, where it conferred with Lincoln for three hours. Insisting upon vigorous prosecution of the war, the committee presented a paper calling for unity in the Cabinet and the concurrence of ministers and generals in these sentiments; Wade blamed recent defeats on the prevalence of Democratic officers in the army, and Grimes remarked that the Secretary of State had lost the country's confidence.

Lincoln refused to be overawed. Although Seward immediately handed in his resignation, the President, consulting with the Secretaries on the next day, invited them to meet with the committee that evening. When the interview took place, Chase was embarrassed by direct questions about the functioning of the Cabinet, and the result was that he too asked to be relieved. "Now I have the biggest half of the hog," said Lincoln, who refused to accept either resignation. The crisis came to an end, the President having shown his independence without wholly alienating the radicals. "Old Abe promises to stand firm & I think he will," wrote Chandler to the governor of Michigan shortly afterward. "We shall get rid of his evil genius, Gov. S., eventually if not now. . . . Without him Old Abe is naturally right."[7]

Just as he had revealed his independence in the Cabinet crisis, so the President kept the army strictly under his own control. Although Frémont was one of the radicals' favorite generals— he had been restored to command in the spring of 1862 because of their clamor—he failed to make good. After refusing a subordinate command, in June, 1862, he was relieved for the last time, his friends' efforts notwithstanding. When Julian in March,

---

[7] Browning, *Diary,* I, 596–603; Bates, *Diary,* 269–71; Welles, *Diary,* I, 194–206; Fessenden, *Fessenden,* I, 231–51; Hamlin–Mrs. Hamlin, December 19, 1862, Hamlin Papers; Chandler–Austin Blair, December 22, 1862, Austin Blair Papers. The radicals continued their efforts to dislodge Seward long afterward. Cf. New York *Herald,* February 12, 1863.

1863, told Lincoln that no appointment would stir the country as much as the Pathfinder's, the President quickly put him in his place. It would "stir the country on one side," he replied, "and stir it the other way on the other. It would please Frémont's friends, and displease the conservatives." No matter how much the radicals tried, Frémont was never given active command again.[8]

On the other hand, General Halleck, whom Lincoln had brought to Washington as general-in-chief remained in office despite the radicals' agitation against him. Notoriously indecisive, Halleck was not the sort of man to appeal to Republicans dedicated to a vigorous prosecution of the war. "Give Halleck 20,000 men and he couldn't raise three sitting geese," complained Wade. But Lincoln found the scholarly general useful.[9]

Another example of Lincoln's independence was his refusal to permit General Butler to return to New Orleans. The former Massachusetts Democrat had endeared himself to the radicals not merely because of his insistence upon treating certain fugitive slaves as contraband of war, but also because of his forceful administration of the Crescent City. He had cowed secessionists, threatened to treat any Southern lady insulting his soldiers "as a woman of the town plying her avocation," and executed a Southern sympathizer who had torn down the American flag. That he was outlawed by Jefferson Davis only made him more popular in the North. But he had also caused difficulties for his own government. His high-handed treatment of foreign consuls as well as persistent rumors of corruption had undermined his position, and in December, 1862, he was recalled.

When Butler left his command in Louisiana, he left behind his old party affiliations as well. Although he had already partially separated himself from his Democratic associates by his original solution of the contraband problem, his real conversion took place

[8] Nevins, *Frémont*, pp. 562–63; Jessie Frémont's Memoirs, pp. 300–1, Frémont Papers; Julian, *Political Recollections*, pp. 229–30.

[9] Gurowski, *Diary*, III, 297; Chase, *Diaries*, p. 148; Stephen E. Ambrose, *Halleck: Lincoln's Chief of Staff* (Baton Rouge, 1962), pp. 61, 103, 161.

in New Orleans. Forced by circumstances to rely on the most radical measures to keep the city under control—his levy of a colored regiment was an example—he found that the ultras in Louisiana as well as their sympathizers in the North were his firmest supporters. And since he suspected that Seward had had a great deal to do with his recall, he naturally turned to the Secretary's opponents for help.

Butler's new friends immediately rallied to his cause. "All the hearts in the country resounded with Butler," wrote Count Gurowski, who was convinced that the conservatives were to blame for the general's recall. Chase vigorously defended him; the Committee on the Conduct of the War gave him a favorable hearing; the press bestowed lavish praise, and Congress as well as various state legislatures voted him resolutions of thanks. The general became a full-fledged radical.[1]

The President realized that he could not simply let Butler leave without another assignment. Summoning him to Washington, Lincoln asked the general whether he would not consider a command in the Mississippi Valley, where he could raise an army of Negro troops. But when Butler, demanding to know why he had been recalled, insisted on his return to Louisiana, the President refused. Having just appointed General Banks for the position, he could not suddenly reverse himself. No matter how popular he was with the radicals, Butler would have to bide his time.

In the months that followed, the ultras repeatedly sought to have the general restored. Sharing Count Gurowski's conviction that the displaced commander had fallen victim to conservative intrigue, they believed that he was the ideal man to administer disaffected areas. Receiving assurances of support from Sumner

[1] Trefousse, *Butler,* pp. 107–34; Gurowski, *Diary,* II, 65; Chase-Denison, January 19, 1863, George S. Denison Papers, LC; Butler, *Correspondence,* II, 541–3; *JCCW,* III, 353–64; Boston *Commonwealth,* January 10, 1863; Boston *Daily Advertiser,* January 5, 13, 1863; Boston *Daily Journal,* January 13, 14, 1863; *New York Times,* January 3, 14, 1863; New York *Tribune* (Weekly), January 10, 17, 1863; *Cong. Globe,* 37th Cong., 3d Sess., 222–3, 236; notification of actions of legislatures of Ohio and Massachusetts, January 20, 30, 1863, in Butler Papers, LC.

and Chase, he delivered radical speeches in various cities. When, in February, Butler came to Washington, the President, who a few weeks earlier had actually prepared orders restoring him, seemed friendly. Again drawing up draft orders, this time for an inspection trip to the Mississippi valley, he discussed the general's problems. But nothing was decided. Lincoln never issued the orders. Remaining deaf to pleas to send Butler back to New Orleans, denying requests to give him an opportunity to enforce the draft in the North, and resisting pressure to let him take over the administration of Missouri, the President even withdrew the offer to let him raise colored troops in the Mississippi valley. While he finally permitted the general to try his hand once again by giving him the command of the Army of the James—Lincoln was too astute to alienate so powerful a politician—he never permitted him to realize his first ambition, to resume his post in Louisiana.[2]

Another one of the radicals' protégés, General Burnside, fared even worse. In spite of persistent effort in his behalf—the Committee on the Conduct of the War gave him a clean bill of health after the Battle of Fredericksburg—he had to go. When troubles with his subordinates proved him to be incapable of leading a large army, Lincoln properly dismissed him, and although the committee conducted another investigation and again sought to exonerate him, the President was not inclined to take him back.[3]

Fighting Joe Hooker was Burnside's successor. Talking like a radical, he proposed to spare no efforts to move upon the enemy, and he soon secured the ultras' firm friendship. When he lost the Battle of Chancellorsville, they saw to it that he was relieved of

[2] J. W. Turner–A. J. Butler, January 4, 1863, Butler Papers; Trefousse, *Butler*, pp. 135–40; Butler, *Correspondence*, II, 570–71, 584, III, 118–19, 139–41; Lincoln, *Works*, VI, 73–4, 100; E. B. Washburne–Lincoln, April 9, 1863, W. A. Hall–Lincoln, July 15, 1863, Robert Maxwell–Lincoln, July 15, 1863, RTL; Boutwell-Sumner, May 8, 1863, Sumner Papers; *O.R.*, Series I, XXII, Part II, 581, 604.

[3] Chandler–Mrs. Chandler, December 18, 21, 1862, Chandler Papers; *New York Times*, December 22, 1862; New York *Tribune*, December 24, 1862; Cochrane, *The War for the Union*, pp. 51–3; *O.R.*, Series I, XXI, 1004; *JCCW*, I, 52–60.

all blame, Wade and Chandler traveling to Falmouth to investigate. Upon their return, they brought back such encouraging reports that news about the fighting ability of the Army of the Potomac became favorable once again. Even the President shared for a while in the renewed optimism, but when Hooker seemed incapable of dealing with Lee's invasion of Pennsylvania, Lincoln replaced him with George Gordon Meade. The radicals were powerless to save their favorite.[4]

Meade's subsequent career furnished another excellent example of Lincoln's independence in dealing with the army. To be sure, the general won the Battle of Gettysburg, but, failing to follow up his victory, he permitted Lee to escape. Slow, deliberate and conservative, he possessed many of McClellan's characteristics and gathered about himself the friends of the former commander of the Army of the Potomac. Under these circumstances, the radicals inevitably turned against him, and since he had many enemies, he was soon under incessant attack. The most important of Meade's opponents was General Daniel Sickles, a New York politician who had lost his leg at Gettysburg. Blamed for moving his Third Corps too far forward, Sickles countered with charges that Meade had been in favor of a general retreat. The radicals were willing to listen to these complaints.[5]

When the Committee on the Conduct of the War was reestablished by the Thirty-eighth Congress, the ultras, led by Chandler, Wade, and Wilkinson, sought actively to replace the commander of the Army of the Potomac. Summoning Sickles as well as other hostile witnesses, they thought they had gathered enough evidence to submit the case to the President, whom they visited on March 3, 1864. Insisting that Meade must be relieved, they suggested that Hooker might take his place. But they con-

[4] Lincoln, *Works,* VI, 78–9; Williams, *Lincoln and the Radicals,* pp. 266 ff.; Dispatch of May 19, 1863, Schleiden Papers; Sumner-Lieber, May 19, 1863, Sumner Papers; Nicolay and Hay, *Abraham Lincoln,* VII, 226.

[5] W. A. Swanberg, *Sickles the Incredible* (New York, 1956), pp. 175 ff., 189–92, 194 ff., 238–9; George Meade, *The Life and Letters of George Gordon Meade* (New York, 1913), II, Chs. II–IV; Freeman Cleaves, *Meade of Gettysburg* (Norman, Okla., 1960), pp. 216, 225 ff.

ceded that the choice was Lincoln's responsibility, and the President remained noncommittal.

The campaign against Meade continued, in the newspapers as well as in the committee. When the general came to Washington in person to defend himself, he found that a majority of the investigators were implacably hostile. No matter how much the radicals complained, however, Lincoln refused to comply with their wishes.[6]

Perhaps the best instance of the President's complete control was his elevation of General U. S. Grant to supreme command. The general, who had had Democratic leanings before the war, had not been the radicals' favorite. In the 1850's, he had been involved in a lawsuit with Zach Chandler; in 1862, he aroused his opponent's suspicions because of his shortcomings at Shiloh, and in the spring of 1863, he failed to take Vicksburg as speedily as his critics thought desirable. Shortly after the Battle of Chancellorsville, a group of disgruntled legislators appeared at the White House. "Mr. President," said Ben Wade, acting as their spokesman, "I have called to ask you to relieve Grant. He is doing nothing. His hospitals are filled with sick. His army is wasting away."

"Senator, that reminds me of a story," was the reply.

"Bother your stories, Mr. President. That is the way it is with you, sir. It is all story, story. You are the father of every military blunder that has been made during the war. You are on the road to h—l, sir, with this Government, and you are not a mile off this minute."

"Wade, that is about the distance from here to the Capitol," rejoined Lincoln, and Grant not only remained in command but soon proved himself indispensable. On July 4, Vicksburg fell to him; in the fall, his armies won a series of brilliant victories at Chattanooga, and it became apparent that he was the President's

[6] *Report of the Joint Committee on the Conduct of the War,* 38th Cong., 2d Sess., Sen. Rep. No. 142 (Washington, 1865) [hereafter cited as *JCCW* (*1865*)], I; New York *Tribune,* March 6, 8, 1864; Meade, *Life and Letters of George Gordon Meade,* II, 172–3, 176; Williams, *Lincoln and the Radicals,* pp. 338 ff.

choice for general-in-chief. Since he had proved that he could fight, most radicals quickly endorsed him, but they had little to do with the President's decision. The Committee on the Conduct of the War was not even consulted. It was investigating matters connected with heavy ordnance and frauds concerning ice contracts at the time.[7] Lincoln was the Commander-in-Chief of the army and navy, and while he utilized the radicals' zeal when it suited him to do so, he saw to it that he remained President in fact as well as in name.

The President's independence, however, did not lessen his reliance upon the radicals for support in the prosecution of the war. In the army, in Congress, in elections, and in rallying public opinion, they gave him valuable aid, and it would be totally misleading to overlook it.

The frustration of McClellan's efforts to return to active command is a case in point. That the radicals were determined to prevent it is well known; that their desires corresponded to the President's own is less frequently mentioned.

The movement for the general's recall began immediately after his removal. At the time of the Cabinet crisis, his supporters pointed out the need for his restoration. There was even talk of dictatorial powers, and in February, 1863, Chase was warned that the general needed some sort of employment if he were not to become dangerous. Trumbull heard of a plot to oust the President in order to install McClellan as a military dictator, and General Butler also cautioned against the "Young Napoleon's" wiles. Nevertheless, when, in the summer of 1863, Lee invaded Pennsylvania, many public figures frantically urged Lincoln to call upon the general to save them.[8]

[7] George, Chandler, pp. 212–13; M. A. De Wolfe Howe, ed., *Home Letters of General Sherman* (New York, 1909), p. 278; Charles C. Coffin, *Abraham Lincoln* (New York, 1893), pp. 367–8; J. M. Scovel, "Sidelights on Lincoln," *Overland Monthly,* XXXVIII (October, 1901), 267 (slightly different quotes); Blaine, *Twenty Years of Congress,* I, 509–11; Sumner-Lieber, December 28, 1863, Sumner Papers; *Cong. Globe,* 38th Cong., 1st Sess., p. 797; *JCCW* (1865), II, 1–179, III, 21–100. Stevens opposed the creation of the rank of Lt. General.

[8] Bates, *Diary,* p. 270; John Jay–Chase, December 15, 1862, H. C. Bowen–Chase, February 6, 1863, Chase Papers, LC; G. F. Allen–Trum-

Faced with this determined activity on the part of McClellan's backers, Lincoln had to be wary. After having repeatedly tried out the hesitant general, again and again he had found him wanting, and he certainly had no desire to reinstate him. If he was able to withstand the entreaties of McClellan's friends, he was materially helped by the radicals.

The ultras missed no opportunity to foil the general's supporters. When, after the Battle of Fredericksburg, the Senate passed a resolution charging the Committee on the Conduct of the War with an investigation of the disaster, the members traveled to army headquarters at Falmouth to take testimony. But they did not seek to destroy Burnside, who had taken McClellan's place. Freely admitting his difficulties, the defeated general cooperated and appeared to be in sympathy with the radicals. The investigators consequently absolved him from all guilt, and Lincoln, who had appointed him in the first place, was able to retain him a bit longer. Burnside's troubles could not be allowed to redound to McClellan's profit.[9]

The committee next turned its attention to a renewed investigation of the Peninsular Campaign. Determined to highlight McClellan's incompetence once and for all, the investigators gave free rein to general after general who testified that the "Young Napoleon" had been less than efficient in handling the assault upon Richmond. Although the luckless commander was permitted to defend himself, his statements were inept. "If ever a man was condemned out of his own mouth he was. . . . His testimony condemns himself," observed General Samuel P. Heintzelman, one of his former corps commanders. When the committee published its report, it made the most of its findings. The document was a devastating attack upon McClellan.[1]

---

bull, February 22, 1863, Trumbull Papers, LC; Butler-Wilson, February 22, 1863, Henry Wilson Papers; A. K. McClure–Lincoln, June 30, July 1, 1863, J. Edgar Thompson–Lincoln, June 30, 1863; Edward Everett–Lincoln, June 16, 1863, James Dixon–Lincoln, June 28, 1863, RTL.

[9] Chandler–Mrs. Chandler, December 18, 21, 1862, Chandler Papers; *JCCW*, I, 51–7, 643–56; New York *Tribune*, December 24, 1862.

[1] *JCCW*, I, 302–641; 4–37; Samuel P. Heintzelman, MS Diary, March 3, 1863, Heintzelman Papers, LC.

The report served the President well. Speaking to the journalist Noah Brooks shortly before the Battle of Chancellorsville, aboard a steamer in the Potomac, he said, "I kept McClellan in command after I had expected that he would win victories, simply because I knew that his dismissal would provoke popular indignation and shake the faith of the people in the final success of the war." But having discharged the general, he had no desire to have him back. When, a few months later, Brooks asked him about his intentions in view of rumors of McClellan's recall, he reminded the newspaperman of the interview aboard the steamer. He had neither changed his mind nor did he have any intentions of doing so. As John C. Ropes, who later became a military historian, wrote on January 1, 1863, the country had suffered greatly from mixing up war with politics—a grievous fault for which McClellan's friends were much more responsible than his enemies. "The cry of the so-called radical party has always been to push forward, do something—yet the uniform charge against them has been that they wish to prolong the war till Slavery can be overthrown." Lincoln, like the radicals, was done with McClellan.[2]

In Congress, too, Lincoln was able to work with the extremists. It has recently been emphasized that an amazing degree of unity between advanced and moderate Republicans existed. The first and second Confiscation Acts, the bill emancipating slaves in the District of Columbia, legislation abolishing the institution in the territories—all these reforms received the votes of almost every Republican in both Houses. But while they were a tribute to party unity, they were usually furthered by the radicals who were in charge of the most important committees.[3]

[2] Brooks, *Washington in Lincoln's Time*, p. 26; Worthington C. Ford, ed., *War Letters of John Chipman Gray and John Codman Ropes* (Boston, 1927), pp. 49–50.

[3] Donald, *Lincoln Reconsidered*, pp. 11–12; Donald, *Devils Facing Zionwards*, loc. cit., p. 79; McPherson, *Rebellion*, pp. 195–7, 211–12, 254–5; *Cong. Globe*, 37th Cong., 1st Sess., 17, 21. Although the actual division of the Republican party was more complicated than the simple radical–moderate–conservative scheme, cooperation between the groups

The radicals' zeal was particularly evident when it came to giving the administration what it most desperately needed: men and money. The speed with which the President's emergency measures in 1861 were endorsed was a good beginning, and with the radical Henry Wilson as chairman of the Senate's military affairs committee, one enlistment bill after the other, including the conscription law of 1863, secured congressional approval. In the Thirty-eighth Congress, the radicals took over the House committee on military affairs as well, and Robert C. Schenck, the new chairman, cooperated effectively with both Wilson and the President. Congress saw to it that the army was kept strong.[4]

Money, too, was supplied to the administration without stint or hesitation. In Thaddeus Stevens as chairman of the Ways and Means committee of the House, the Executive had a redoubtable representative in Congress who never failed to produce the desired funds. That Stevens was often critical of the President is true; but his strictures never led him to slacken in his enthusiasm for providing the sinews of war. And so skillful was his management that his measures usually carried. As was widely recognized at the time, he had few peers in parliamentary maneuvering.[5]

Because of their unwavering advocacy of stringent war measures, the radicals often incurred the public's ire. So prominently were they identified with the unpopular conscription act of 1863 that they were among the principal targets of rioters who sought to resist the draft. The extremists were merely getting a "taste of their own medicine," commented the Democratic New York *World* in an article on the disorders in the metropolis, where the collector's office, Frémont's house, the New York *Tribune,* and

---

still prevailed. Cf. Allen G. Bogue, "Bloc and Party in the United States Senate: 1861–1863," *Civil War History,* XIII (September, 1967), 221–41.

[4] *Cong. Globe,* 37th Cong., 1st Sess., 442, 448–9; Seward, *Seward at Washington,* II, 602; Nevins, *The War for the Union,* I, 199; Randall, *Lincoln the President,* II, 290–2; McPherson, *Rebellion,* pp. 115–17; Blaine, *Twenty Years of Congress,* I, 499; Nicolay and Hay, *Abraham Lincoln,* VII, 4.

[5] Blaine, *Twenty Years of Congress,* I, 325–6, 421–5; Nevins, *The War for the Union,* I, 199; Washington *National Intelligencer,* September 23, 1863; Brodie, *Stevens,* pp. 150–3.

other buildings identified with radicals were seriously endangered. Nevertheless, the ultras did not draw back. Suggesting stern measures to quell the revolt, they demanded that the administration enforce its authority. "The Government must execute the laws or it will not & ought not be respected here or elsewhere," Collector Barney wrote to Chase.[6]

The radicals also lent their influence to other measures necessary for the prosecution of the war. Senator Wade, one of Lincoln's most stringent critics, took charge of legislation creating the position of Assistant Secretary of War and a bill granting the President authority to seize and assume control of railroad lines. He also defended the administration as well as himself in replying to attacks upon the irregular proceedings leading to the imprisonment of General Stone. Charles Sumner, as chairman of the Foreign Affairs Committee in the Senate, contributed largely to the peaceful settlement of the *Trent* affair, an incident involving the seizure on the high seas of two Confederate commissioners traveling on a British ship, while Thaddeus Stevens introduced, and George W. Julian strongly urged, the passage of the Habeas Corpus Act. The ultras were the most zealous Republicans.[7]

One of the most important services the extremists rendered to Lincoln was their adroit use of propaganda. That the great radical newspapers—the New York *Tribune,* the Chicago *Tribune,* the *Missouri Democrat,* the Cincinnati *Gazette,* and the Washington *Chronicle*—sought to inspire patriotic fervor and that ministers like Henry Ward Beecher would do their utmost to fire their congregations with enthusiasm for the country was to be expected, but that Congress itself would take a hand in rallying public opinion was something new.

The propaganda activities of Congress centered in the Com-

[6] New York *World,* July 25, 1863; Strong, *Diary,* III, 335–40; John Jay–Stanton, July 16, 1863, Stanton Papers; D. D. Field–Chase, July 15, 1863, Hiram Barney–Chase, July 18, 1863, Chase Papers, HSP.

[7] *Cong. Globe,* 37th Cong., 2d Sess., 386, 409, 427 ff., 511 ff., 1662–8, 1678 ff., 1733–5; 3rd Sess., 1064–9, 1435, 1479; Stanton-Wade, January 27, 1862, Stanton Papers; Sumner, *Works,* VI, 161; Schurz, *Reminiscences,* II, 317–18; McPherson, *Rebellion,* pp. 183–7.

mittee on the Conduct of the War. Because of its duties to investigate military affairs, it had access to information eagerly awaited by the public, a circumstance which the radical committee members exploited fully. Certain that their reports would be widely read, they saw to it that their findings bolstered firm Union attitudes.

Their first report dealt with barbarities at Bull Run. Having been charged with an investigation of alleged brutalities, the members of the committee journeyed to the site of the battle. Interviewing survivors, the investigators pieced together a report of harrowing atrocities—of prisoners abused, bodies mutilated and left naked upon the field, even of skulls allegedly made into trinkets. "The members of your committee might content themselves by leaving this testimony to the Senate and the people without a word of comment," wrote the chairman,

> but when the enemies of a just and generous government are attempting to excite the sympathy of disloyal men in our own country, and to solicit the aid of foreign governments by the gravest misrepresentations of the objects of the war . . . this, the most startling evidence of their insincerity and inhumanity, deserves some notice at our hands.

Then, launching into a passionate indictment of the leaders of the rebellion, he warned the people to remain on guard against the restoration of such men to power. The report created a sensation; newspapers across the country cited it, and the fighting spirit of the North received a needed boost.[8]

The committee's final reports were more comprehensive. Submitted to the public after the Thirty-seventh Congress had adjourned, the first sets dealt with a variety of subjects, including the operations of the Army of the Potomac, the Battle of Ball's Bluff, and the operations of the Western Department—all presented from the radical point of view. They castigated McClellan and his

---

[8] T. Harry Williams, "Benjamin F. Wade and the Atrocity Propaganda of the Civil War," *Ohio State Archæological and Historical Quarterly*, XLVIII (January, 1939), 33–43; *JCCW*, III, 449–91, esp. 455; New York *Tribune*, May 1, 1862; Cincinnati *Daily Gazette*, May 5, 1862.

supporters, upheld Butler, and exonerated Burnside and Frémont. But they also praised the administration and sounded a call for victory. "The past, notwithstanding its errors and reverses, is full of encouragement, and gives full assurance of final success," stated the preamble. "No great war was ever conducted by any people or Government without great mistakes. . . ." Presenting the first full evidence of the country's sacrifices and efforts, and widely reprinted, the reports were designed to contribute substantially to the strengthening of morale.[9]

Early in 1864, the reconstituted committee published another impressive document. This time, the Senate had charged it with the investigation of reputed atrocities at Fort Pillow, where Confederate troops commanded by General Nathan Bedford Forrest had allegedly massacred prisoners of war. Senator Wade and Representative Gooch traveled west; what they found profoundly disgusted them. Forrest's men had apparently killed their captives with wanton savagery. There were reports of living prisoners buried with the dead, Negro soldiers tortured to death, and brutal barbarities inflicted upon Tennessee Unionists. After describing the capture of the Federal forces, the committee's report stated:

> Then followed a scene of cruelty and murder without a parallel in civilized warfare, which needed but the tomahawk and scalping knife to exceed the worst atrocities ever committed by savages. The rebels commenced an indiscriminate slaughter, sparing neither age nor sex, white or black, soldier or civilian.

So persuasive was the document that even the conservative Attorney General noted in his diary that the investigators had revealed "a cruel barbarity on the part of the enemy even worse than had been reported." Shortly afterwards, the members of the committee published still another summary of their findings, a gruesome description of the emaciated conditions of returning prisoners of war, whose pictures they sent to the President as well as to the newspapers. The effect was predictable. The nation's

[9] *JCCW*, I, 1–66; II, 4–18; III, 3–6; New York *Tribune*, April 1, 6, 1863. The *Tribune* published the first one in pamphlet form.

determination to overcome the perpetrators of these disasters could only be increased by the committee's propaganda.[1]

In support of the war effort, the radicals also organized Loyal Leagues in various Northern cities. With their brother institutions, the Union League clubs, these patriotic societies engaged in propaganda, sought to strengthen the national cause, and assisted in raising troops. Eventually, they spread to the South, where they became a powerful adjunct of the Federal forces.[2]

Because the radicals were often the most ardent Republicans and frequently furnished leadership for the party, they performed yeoman service for the administration during the frequent wartime election campaigns. Differences between Lincoln and the ultras were common knowledge, but the fact remained that these disagreements were minor when compared with the Democratic threat to the government. No matter how radical the Republican nominees, their victories were the administration's successes, and their defeats its disasters.

As early as 1861 the mutual dependence of the extremists and the government during election campaigns became evident. "The elections are approaching . . . ," wrote the radical New York *Tribune* on September 1. "If the rebellion is to be put down, the Administration must not only have men and money, but confidence and obedience." On election day, Horace Greeley again admonished his readers. "The Union State ticket was nominated and will be supported on the simple platform of STANDING BY THE GOVERNMENT IN THE UNITED STATES IN ITS PRESENT

[1] 38th Cong., 1st Sess., H. R. Report No. 65, *Fort Pillow Massacre* (Washington, 1864), esp. pp. 4–5; H. R. Report No. 67, *Returned Prisoners* (Washington, 1864); Bates, *Diary,* p. 365; Wade-Lincoln, May 20, 1864, J. G. Nicolay Papers, LC; Cincinnati *Daily Gazette,* June 3, 1864.

[2] Henry W. Bellows, *Historical Sketch of the Union League Club of New York* (New York, 1879), pp. 3 ff., 32, 53 ff.; Walter Lynwood Fleming, *Sequel to Appomattox* (New Haven, 1919), pp. 174 ff.; Roberta F. Carson, "The Loyal League in Georgia," *The Georgia Historical Quarterly,* XX (June, 1936), 125–53, esp. 125–7. Cf. Guy James Gibson, Lincoln's League: The Union League Movement During the Civil War, unpublished doctoral dissertation, University of Illinois, 1957, pp. 532–3.

ARDUOUS STRUGGLE WITH ARMED TREASON." In Massachusetts, a radical like Charles Sumner delivered the principal address at the state convention, and although its emancipationist stance contrasted with the President's revocation of Frémont's edict, the senator's old friend A. B. Johnson conceded that he could work with the administration. "The speech and the policy are regarded here by some as in opposition to the position of the President," he wrote. "But I am satisfied that both President and Cabinet will follow where the public lead." In Ohio, Ben Wade and John A. Bingham, actively campaigning for the newly formed Union ticket, pleaded for close cooperation with the national government; the slate won, and the Buckeye State was temporarily safe for the President's party. In other states also, radical successes were Republican successes. The administration could take satisfaction in the outcome of the off-year canvass.[3]

In the following year, conditions were less favorable for the party in power. In the crucial fall elections, especially, the administration was hard-pressed. Disappointment with the slow progress of the war, frustration with McClellan's failure to capture Richmond, and dissension caused by the Emancipation Proclamation all made the outcome of the contest dubious. The Republican party needed all the help it could muster.

The radicals were again in the forefront of the struggle. Even before the beginning of the fall campaign, Sumner had emphasized his full support of the administration. "Your criticism of the President is hasty," he replied on June 5 to one of Lincoln's detractors,

> I am confident, if you knew him as I do, you would not make it. The President cannot be held responsible for the misfeasance of subordinates, unless adopted, or at least tolerated . . . by him. . . .
>   Could you—as has been my privilege often—have seen the President, while considering the great questions on which he has already acted, beginning with the invitation to emancipa-

[3] New York *Tribune,* September 1, November 5, 1861; October 19, 28, November 7, 1861; A. B. Johnson–Sumner, October 4, 1861, Sumner Papers; Emilius O. Randall and Daniel Ryan, *History of Ohio* (New York, 1912), IV, 174; George H. Porter, *Ohio Politics During the Civil War Era* (New York, 1911), pp. 88–9.

tion in the States, the Emancipation in the District of Columbia, and the acknowledgement of the Independence of Hayti and Liberia, even your zeal would be satisfied; for you would feel the sincerity of his purpose to do what he can to carry forward the principles of the Declaration of Independence.[4]

While Sumner's endorsement of the President went further than some of his colleagues might have thought justified, they nevertheless could not quarrel with him about the basic point. The government must be supported against its Democratic opponents.

Perhaps the most crucial contest in the fall of 1862 was the New York campaign. Always powerful in the Empire State, the Democrats, coalescing with a remnant of the conservative Constitutional Union party, had nominated Horatio Seymour. The candidate was an able and popular lawyer, who, though personally loyal, had a wide appeal to the peace wing of the organization. Undaunted by this challenge, the ultras insisted upon choosing as their standard-bearer General James S. Wadsworth, a wealthy landowner from Geneseo who had proved his devotion to radicalism in Washington during the course of the controversy with McClellan. To the New York *Herald,* the general's nomination signified the radicals' take-over of the Republican organization— the paper even expressed the opinion that Lincoln would be glad to see him defeated. Considering the Democrats' bitter anti-administration platform, however, Lincoln had no choice but to rely on the leaders of his own party, no matter how radical they might be. This he did, and the extremists waged a determined campaign, importing such national figures as Governor Yates of Illinois to help elect the general. If the visiting statesman criticized the President for not moving fast enough, his efforts were nevertheless part of a contest to sustain the administration and the Emancipation Proclamation. As General Wadsworth himself said at Cooper Union:

I do not believe that even in this heated canvass any man has dared to stand up before you and say that Abraham Lincoln is not an honest man, honestly striving to save his country. . . .

[4] Sumner, *Works,* VI, 116–17.

What can any honest patriot . . . do but sustain and strengthen Abraham Lincoln? Let him be sustained. . . . Gentlemen, I stand by Abraham Lincoln.

When the general lost, his defeat was a blow for the administration as well as for his radical friends.[5]

In Pennsylvania, the Republican party was also in trouble. The radicals worked hard—the governors' meeting at Altoona was credited with preventing a complete disaster—and the defeat of such stalwarts as Speaker Galusha Grow and Congressman Edward McPherson was as serious a setback for the administration as the victory of Representatives William D. Kelley, Thomas Williams, John M. Broomall, and Thaddeus Stevens—ultras one and all— was a source of consolation for it.[6]

In the Northwest, despite the prevalence of a great deal of conservative sentiment, the radicals also played a leading role in the fall campaign. In Michigan, Zach Chandler, up for re-election himself and under attack, virtually took charge of the struggle against the conservatives, his well-organized machine and energy making possible a major effort to achieve a Republican success. "I am all right if we carry the State," he wrote to Trumbull, whom he asked to help in the canvass, "but the Browning-Cowan faction are trying to get up an anti-confiscation no party union with the Locos. We shall take square ground upon confiscation & *the* use of all the elements which God and nature have placed in our hands to crush this rebellion." Trumbull as well as other party stalwarts came to assist the senator. When in November the Republicans

[5] De Alva Stanwood Alexander, *A Political History of the State of New York* (New York, 1909), III, 37–45; *The American Annual Cyclopaedia,* 1862, pp. 654–6; New York *Herald,* September 6, November 3, 1862; John H. Krenkel, ed., Richard Yates and Catherine Yates Pickering, *Richard Yates, Civil War Governor* (Danville, Ill., 1966), p. 180; *New York Times,* September 28, October 2, 13, 26, 30, 31, 1862; Strong, *Diary,* III, 270, 272.

[6] *The American Annual Cyclopaedia,* 1862, pp. 703–5; *New York Times,* October 15, 1862; Stevens-McPherson, October 30, 1862, Stevens Papers; A. K. McClure, *Old Time Notes of Pennsylvania* (Philadelphia, 1905), I, 559–60; Stanton Ling Davis, *Pennsylvania Politics, 1860–1863* (Cleveland, 1935), p. 263; Konkle, *The Life and Speeches of Thomas Williams,* II, 479–81. Despite the author's disclaimer, Williams was a radical.

scored a victory, they contributed greatly to offsetting the party's losses in other states and saving a congressional majority for the administration. Incidentally, despite a determined effort by a former collaborator, James F. Joy, to defeat him, on January 8, 1863, Chandler was also re-elected. His return to the Senate was a triumph for the organization.[7]

In Iowa, in 1862, the Republicans prevailed. But as Grimes informed Chase,

> We took the bull by the horns and made the proclamation an issue. I traversed the State for four weeks, speaking every day and the more radical I was the more acceptable I was. The fact is we carried the State by bringing the radical element to the polls.[8]

Conditions were different in Indiana. A powerful opposition made things very difficult for the Republicans, and the hard work performed by radicals like Julian and Colfax was indispensable for whatever successes the party managed to achieve. Although most of the congressmen elected in 1862 turned out to be Democrats, both Colfax and Julian retained their seats. Their defeat would have resulted in the return of avowed enemies of the administration.[9]

The President had reasons to be particularly worried about Illinois. Under radical leadership, the state Republican convention endorsed the Emancipation Proclamation, but dissatisfaction was rife, and the Democrats carried the day. Of five Republican congressmen to be returned, three—Owen Lovejoy, Elihu B. Washburne, and John F. Farnsworth—were more or less

[7] Detroit *Post and Tribune, Chandler,* pp. 250–1; Harris, *Chandler,* pp. 65–7; Chandler-Trumbull, September 17, 1862, Trumbull-Chandler, September 28, 1862, Trumbull Papers, LC; Trumbull-Chandler, November 9, 1862, M. S. Wilkinson–Chandler, October 20, 1862, Chandler–Mrs. Chandler, January 8, 1863, Chandler Papers; George, *Chandler,* pp. 132–4.

[8] Salter, *Grimes,* pp. 217–18.

[9] *The American Annual Cyclopaedia,* 1862, pp. 527–9; Riddleberger, *Julian,* pp. 173–4; O. J. Hollister, *Life of Schuyler Colfax* (New York, 1886), pp. 196–9.

radical. Their successes were among the few consolations for Lincoln in his home state.[1]

In Ohio, too, the administration found itself in difficulty. By no means as radical as its senior senator, Ben Wade, the state had already demonstrated its dissatisfaction with extremist leadership when the Union legislature, chiefly because of his radicalism, had refused to re-elect him. While no rival had yet been put in his place—the senatorial election had simply been postponed—the archradical's chances of returning to the Senate seemed slight. Nevertheless, refusing to compromise, he sent an ultra-emancipationist letter to the Republican convention. But while he chided the President for not having moved ahead faster, he also expressed his conviction that Lincoln would carry out the people's wishes, and the convention promptly endorsed the administration. When the Democrats won the election and John A. Bingham as well as Samuel Shellabarger among others, were defeated, an utter rout for both extremists and the President was averted only because James M. Ashley, Robert C. Schenck, and James A. Garfield, then considered radical, were among the five Republicans to survive the Democratic tide. And when the outgoing legislature finally re-elected Wade, it became evident that whatever successes the administration party had achieved in the Buckeye State were largely radical victories as well.[2]

In the post-mortem of the defeats, there was general agreement that radicalism had been one of the issues. But whether the voters had rejected radical proposals or whether they had expressed dissatisfaction with the administration's allegedly hesitant attitude

[1] *The American Annual Cyclopaedia,* 1862, pp. 518–19; Cole, *The Era of the Civil War,* pp. 296–8; Magdol, *Lovejoy,* p. 372; Charles A. Church, *History of the Republican Party in Illinois, 1854–1912* (Rockford, Ill., 1912), p. 89, contains the results. After Lovejoy's death in 1864, another radical, Ebon C. Ingersoll, took his place.

[2] Cincinnati *Daily Gazette,* February 14–March 28, 1862; Ashtabula *Sentinel,* September 10, 1862; John Bingham–Giddings, November 3, 1862, Giddings Papers; Shellabarger–Chase, October 15, 1862, Chase Papers, LC; New York *Tribune,* October 18–20, 1862, January 23, 1863. Riddle was not even renominated; Chase-Parsons, October 9, 1862, Chase Papers, HSP. For the make-up of the 38th Congress, cf. Blaine, *Twenty Years of Congress,* I, 497–502.

was a question upon which radicals and conservatives came to diametrically opposite conclusions. Immediately after the Democratic sweep in October in Pennsylvania, Indiana, and Ohio, the New York *Herald* attributed the administration's troubles to its yielding to extremists. After the November elections, the paper repeated its assertions. "The State of New York has given the finishing blow to our radical abolitionists . . . ," it stated.

> They must now be removed into the background. Their overthrow will revive the hopes of the Union men of the South, and, with the dispersion of the rebel army of Virginia, we may now expect a general Southern reaction in favor of the Union, which will speedily end this rebellion.

Orville Browning, equally conservative, made a similar appraisal. "Badly beaten by the Democrats," he wrote in his diary. "Just what was to be expected from the insane ravings of the Chicago Tribune. . . ." A few weeks later, he told Lincoln that the Emancipation Proclamation was to blame for the revival of the opposition party.[3]

The radicals, however, had entirely different ideas about the meaning of the elections. "In this State, we are used up horse, foot & wagons," reported Lyman Trumbull to Chandler.

> Hundreds of Republicans who believed that their sons and relatives were being sacrificed to the incompetency, indisposition or treason of pro-slavery Democratic generals, were unwilling to sustain the administration which allowed this. I felt myself . . . that it was an uphill business to attempt to sustain the Administration, & nothing but the belief that to suffer the Government to get into the hands of the Democracy would be worse enabled me to do it at all.[4]

Other ultras agreed with the Senator from Illinois. "The Democrats are making capital on the ground of our imbecility more than our radicalism," wrote Justin Morrill to Chase, an assessment with which the secretary's Ohio correspondents heartily concurred. According to R. C. Parsons, dissatisfaction with the man-

[3] New York *Herald,* October 16, 18, 19, November 5, 1862; Browning, *Diary,* I, 582, 588–90.
[4] Trumbull-Chandler, November 9, 1862, Chandler Papers.

agement of the war caused the defeat; another Buckeye Republican thought want of confidence in the administration and do-nothing generals were the cause of the disaster. Adam Gurowski blamed the setback on the President and lack of principles, while Sumner wrote to Lincoln that only "the most unflinching vigor, in the field and in council," could counteract the losses. As Carl Schurz summed up the radicals' conclusion in a letter to the President,

> The defeat of the administration is the administration's own fault. It admitted its professed opponents to its counsels. It placated the army . . . into the hands of its enemys [sic] . . . . It forgot the great rule, that, if you are true to your friends, your friends will be true to you, and that you make your enemies stronger by placing them upon an equality with your friends.

Carefully examining these assessments, Lincoln replied that he was not at all certain Republican generals were much better than Democratic ones. At any rate, he must continue to seek to suppress the rebellion by relying on the whole people, not merely the Republicans. Whatever his sentiments, however, he had been shown that the weakened party needed the support of its most zealous members. And much as the radicals might complain, they too had to continue to work with the President, as Schurz admitted in another letter. "You must forgive something to the sincerity of my zeal," he wrote, "for there is no living being on this continent, whose wishes for the success of your administration are more ardent than mine."[5]

The elections of 1863 again demonstrated the interdependence of the radicals and the government. In Ohio, especially, Republican success was vital, because the opposition had nominated for governor Representative Clement L. Vallandigham, the country's most notorious peace Democrat. After delivering an intemperate antiwar speech at Mount Vernon, the congressman had been

[5] Justin Morrill–Chase, October 27, 1862; R. C. Parsons–Chase, October 21, 1862, S. G. Arnold–Chase, October 20, 1862, Chase Papers, LC; Gurowski, *Diary*, I, 300–1, 312; Sumner-Lincoln, November 8, 1862, Schurz-Lincoln, November 8, 20, 1862, RTL; Lincoln, *Works*, V, 493–5.

arrested by General Burnside for violating General Order No. 38, an edict prohibiting disloyal utterances. Found guilty by a military commission, he was sentenced to imprisonment for the duration of the war. Lincoln changed the punishment to exile in the Confederacy, but Vallandigham, escaping from the South, had turned up in Canada, where he accepted the nomination and waged an active campaign. His triumph would have constituted a major disaster for the national cause.

In this emergency, radicals and conservatives alike loyally cooperated with the administration. Once again making a War Democrat, John Brough, their candidate, they presented a united front to the opposition. "The Administration will regard the nomination of Brough by the State Convention yesterday as an earnest approval of the most vigorous policy for prosecuting the War & not as a disapproval of the policy of General Burnside," former Governor Dennison and Senator Wade wrote to Lincoln. Ashley, too, heartily endorsed Brough, and both conservatives and radicals agreed that Vallandigham must not be allowed to return. As Ben Wade and John Sherman told Lincoln, violence would be the result of his reappearance, while Ashley warned that the Republican cause would be jeopardized. Vallandigham was accordingly kept out of Ohio, where the radicals took a prominent part in the canvass. Governor Yates of Illinois lent his aid, General Butler was active, and Ben Wade delivered speeches boasting of his extremism and pointedly defending his party's record. When Vallandigham was beaten, both the President and the radicals were doubtless relieved.[6]

In Pennsylvania, too, an important contest took place in 1863, when Judge George W. Woodward of the state supreme court challenged Governor Andrew G. Curtin's bid for re-election. Again the radicals did their best to sustain the Republican ticket,

[6] George Fort Milton, *Abraham Lincoln and the Fifth Column* (New York, 1962), pp. 125–45; William Dennison and Wade–Lincoln, June 18, 1863, Ashley-Lincoln, June 23, 1863, RTL; Ashley-Chase, June 23, 1863, Chase Papers, LC; John Sherman, *Recollections,* I, 324; George H. Porter, *Ohio Politics During the Civil War Period* (New York, 1911), p. 179; Butler, *Correspondence,* III, 112–13; Cincinnati *Daily Gazette,* September 26, 1863.

Thaddeus Stevens going so far as to ask Chase to mobilize the Treasury clerks to enable them to take part in the election. The Maryland radical Henry Winter Davis spoke in Philadelphia, and the outcome was favorable, as it was in other states. "Hurrah for New York Ohio & Pen," wrote Chandler to Governor Blair. "Copperheads at a discount there." His sentiments could only have been shared by the President.[7]

Even in safe states, at election time the radicals firmly adhered to the government. "Gentlemen," said Henry Wilson in September, 1863, when addressing the Massachusetts Republican Convention at Worcester,

> you are here to support Abraham Lincoln's administration without qualification or reservation. You are here to stand by it, to let him feel that he can lean upon old Massachusetts and find that every throb of her heart is true to the Constitution and the Union. And . . . we have in the President's chair as ardent a lover of humane liberty as treads the soil of North America.

The convention adopted resolutions pledging its unwavering support to the government and the Emancipation Proclamation, renominated John A. Andrew, and listened to radical speeches. And the Bay State responded handsomely.[8]

When, in December, 1863, the Thirty-eighth Congress met, the ultras and the administration collaborated again. To some degree, Republican gains in the border states, where such radicals as Henry Winter Davis and B. Gratz Brown had conducted successful campaigns, had offset losses elsewhere, so that the government party, despite severe losses, was able to retain a working

[7] McClure, *Old Time Notes of Pennsylvania,* II, 52–60; Stevens-Chase, September 21, 1863, Chase Papers, HSP; Philadelphia *Inquirer,* September 17, 1863; Chandler-Blair, November 5, 1863, Austin Blair Papers; *Speeches and Addresses Delivered in the Congress of the United States, and on Several Public Occasions, by Henry Winter Davis, of Maryland* (New York, 1867), pp. 306–37 (hereafter cited as Davis, *Speeches*).

[8] Washington *National Intelligencer,* September 28, 1863; New York *Tribune,* September 25, 1863; Edith Ellen Ware, *Political Opinion in Massachusetts During the Civil War and Reconstruction* (New York, 1916), pp. 116 ff.

majority in both Houses. Sumner, Wade, Chandler, Ashley, Lovejoy, Julian, and Stevens, to mention only a few outstanding radicals, had all been re-elected, and the party had been strengthened by the entry into Congress of such advanced Republicans at that time as Robert C. Schenck of Ohio and Thomas Williams of Pennsylvania. The leaders of the administration party, of whom Stevens was recognized as paramount even by the opposition, made arrangements to organize Congress in such a way as to assure the success of the national cause. Because of Grow's defeat, a new Speaker had to be chosen, and the radicals saw to it that Schuyler Colfax, who sympathized with them, obtained the influential post.[9]

The control of the speakership was important. Rumors had long circulated that Emerson Etheridge, the clerk of the House, who was violently opposed to the radicals and to the Emancipation Proclamation, was ready to exclude Republican members by charging that their election certificates were not in proper form. Because this plan could be frustrated by the Speaker, as soon as Lincoln heard of Colfax's election, he asked him to make sure to have all the available voting strength ready to counter any untoward moves which Etheridge might attempt. Like the radicals, the President was not prepared to let conservative opponents take over.

Whether there had been a plot or not, Etheridge's days were numbered. With Stevens's help, Edward McPherson, the defeated Pennsylvania ultra, became the new clerk, and in view of Etheridge's attitude—he had delivered a vehement harangue against Lincoln during the summer—the President could not have been too unhappy about this arrangement.[1]

In the distribution of committee chairmanships also, the radicals and the administration worked together. Without opposition

[9] Blaine, *Twenty Years of Congress,* I, 497–502; W. R. Stracher–Lincoln, November 13, 1863, RTL; Randall, *Lincoln the President,* III, 287.
[1] Unsigned memorandum to Hay, December 6, 1863, Nicolay Papers; Hay, *Diaries,* p. 123; New York *Tribune,* September 30, 1863; Stevens–McPherson, November 15, 1863, Stevens Papers; McPherson, *Rebellion,* p. 1. I am indebted to Professor Harold M. Hyman for information concerning the Etheridge plot.

from the White House, the most important positions went to the most advanced members of the party. Sumner, Chandler, Wilson, Trumbull, and Wade retained their posts in the Senate; in the House, Stevens continued as chairman of the Committee on Ways and Means, Schenck took charge of military affairs, Davis of foreign relations, Julian retained public lands, and Ashley, territories. A recent radical arrival from Iowa, James F. Wilson, became the head of the Committee on the Judiciary.[2] But the radicals' prominence in Congress did not lessen the legislature's support of Lincoln's war measures. In the new Congress as in the old, men and money were supplied without trouble, and antislavery measures passed as easily as before.

Lincoln's cooperation with the radicals, then, was a voluntary relationship in which he always retained the upper hand. Pursuing the same goals of emancipation and total victory, both sought to make the army as efficient as possible and hoped to employ Negro troops to the best advantage. More astute and possessed of better political instincts than the radicals, Lincoln moved more cautiously. Eventually, however, he accomplished practically everything the advanced members of his party wanted. They, in turn, supported his most vital measures, constituted the shock troops of the Republican party, and provided a spur for laggard generals and politicians. If and when they went too far, the President stopped them. But he needed them as much as they needed him.

[2] *Cong. Globe,* 38th Cong., 1st Sess., 16, 18.

VIII

The Problem of Wartime Reconstruction

DURING THE ENTIRE CIVIL WAR, there was no more crucial problem testing the relationship between Lincoln and the radicals than reconstruction. How the seceded states were to be brought back into the Union, who was to restore them, and who was to govern them after their return—all these were questions about which there was little agreement. Because of the dramatic clashes between the President and the most advanced wing of his party, many observers have concluded that, had he lived, Abraham Lincoln would have experienced the same troubles as Andrew Johnson, that his approach to reconstruction was identical with his successor's, and that the radicals would have broken with the former as completely as they did with the latter.[1]

But is such an interpretation justified? Did Lincoln really con-

[1] Cf. Williams, *Lincoln and the Radicals,* p. 384; William Starr Myers, *The Republican Party* (New York, 1931), pp. 146–7; cf. Lloyd Paul Stryker, *Andrew Johnson: A Profile in Courage* (New York, 1929), pp. 202 ff.

sistently oppose the radicals' proposals for reconstruction or did he manage to cooperate with them? Was his reconstruction policy fixed or was it flexible? And if it was flexible, to what degree did he allow the radicals to pave the way for it? To find the answers to these questions, the wartime policies of both the ultras and the President deserve careful examination.

For a long time the radicals had been pondering the question of reconstruction. To most of them, the key to the problem lay in Article IV, Section 4, of the Constitution, providing that "The United States shall guarantee every State in this Union a Republican Form of Government." As early as 1850, one of Chase's correspondents pointed out to him that the article made slavery illegal in all but the original states. Was not "the peculiar institution" incompatible with Republican government? In 1858, Theodore Parker, applying the clause even to the original states, made the same point, and Wendell Phillips alerted Sumner to it. When the Southern states seceded, the article assumed new importance, Unionists in western Virginia invoking it to demand federal assistance. In a pronounced assertion of national power, James Hamilton in December, 1860, characterized South Carolina's contemplated action as "State Suicide," a concept which led to the idea that insurrectionary commonwealths reverted to the status of territories. Some observers went further—as early as January, 1861, the notion that rebellious states could be held as "conquered provinces" was bruited about, and several radicals proposed that Yankee emigration into the border states as well as into Texas and Virginia would be the way to secure these areas. For the ultras, emancipation was a *sine qua non* of reconstruction.[2]

Abraham Lincoln's notions of reconstruction were ostensibly

[2] J. M. McCormick–Chase, September 16, 1850, Theodore Parker–Chase, March 9, 1858, Chase Papers, LC; Wendell Phillips–Sumner, June 2, 1858, Sumner Papers; Hamilton, *Reminiscences,* p. 455; Lucian Barbour–Trumbull, January 18, 1861, W. B. Slaughter–Trumbull, February 16, 1861, Trumbull Papers, LC; Eli Thayer–Lincoln, October 12, 1861, J. A. Andrew–Gustavus Fox, November 27, 1861, RTL; Charles Henry Ambler, ed., Anna Pierpont Siviter, *Recollections of War and Peace, 1861–1868* (New York, 1938), p. 51.

different. Much as he detested slavery, at the time of the secession crisis he did not believe that the federal government possessed the right to interfere with the domestic institutions of the states, a point which he stressed in his first inaugural as well as on July 4, 1861, in his message to Congress. "Lest there be some uneasiness in the minds of candid men," he said,

> as to what is to be the course of the government, towards the Southern States, *after* the rebellion shall have been suppressed, the Executive deems it his duty to say, it will be his purpose then, as ever, to be guided by the Constitution, and the laws; and that he probably will have no different understanding of the powers, and duties of the Federal government, relatively to the rights of the States, and the people, under the Constitution, than that expressed in the inaugural address.

But the word "probably" was indicative of his thinking.[3]

To induce the President to alter his views, much preliminary work was needed, a task the radicals readily performed. As chairman of the House Committee on Territories, James M. Ashley had secured a vantage point in matters dealing with the seceded states, and he made the most of it. Introducing in July, 1861, a bill for the establishment of temporary provisional territorial governments in districts conquered from the insurgents, he set the pattern for congressional reconstruction. Although the bill, as well as a similar measure which he advocated in December, was tabled, the broad outlines of the radical program were plain for all to see.[4]

The President did not have to rely on Congress alone for an exposition of radical views. His own Secretary of the Treasury was in full accord with Ashley's position. When in December, 1861, the congressman, accompanied by Senator Wade, called on Chase, the secretary became specific. As he recorded the visit in his diary,

> To both of them I gave my views in brief as to the relations of the insurrectionary States to the Union; that no State nor any portion of the people could withdraw from the Union or absolve

[3] Lincoln, *Works,* IV, 263, 439.
[4] Paddock, An Ohio Congressman in Reconstruction, pp. 9, 12.

themselves from allegiance to it; but that when the attempt was made, the State government was placed in hostility to the Federal Government, the State organization was forfeited and it lapsed into the condition of a Territory with which we could do what we pleased; . . . that those States could not properly be considered as States in the Union but must be readmitted from time to time as Congress should provide.

Wade and Ashley expressed their full concurrence.[5]

For the radicals the reduction of the insurgent states to territorial status was so important because they believed that this policy would make it possible for the federal government to abolish slavery in them. To make this point clear, Charles Sumner, on February 11, 1862, introduced eight resolutions expressing his theory that the seceded states, having committed suicide, had forfeited all rights and were therefore territories. To protect the republican form of government, Congress had to take charge. Lest there be any doubt what Congress ought to do in these territories, the senator included resolutions ending slavery in them. But neither the Senate nor the House was as yet willing to accept so advanced a doctrine.[6]

In the meantime, under the pressure of events, the President was already abandoning his conservative stance. After large portions of Tennessee had been conquered, he too sought to secure republican government for the state by appointing Andrew Johnson military governor. Johnson could be expected to be acceptable to the radicals; as the only Southern senator who refused to go with his state, he had given ample proof of his loyalty and was a member of the Committee on the Conduct of the War. Although Lincoln's move did not suit the advanced members of his party— they considered it an executive usurpation of legislative functions—it was nevertheless a good indication of the President's willingness to experiment. That he was not going to adhere strictly to the stand laid carefully down in his first inaugural

[5] Chase, *Diaries,* pp. 50–1.
[6] Sumner, *Works,* VI, 301–5.

address he showed by appointing military governors for Arkansas, North Carolina, and Louisiana as well.[7]

It was not only in dealing with conquered areas that the President demonstrated how flexible his policy was. The border states, in many ways, became a testing ground for reconstruction policies. Their divided loyalties, the presence of slavery, and their fierce factionalism created conditions which forced the President to abandon his earlier caution. They also furnished experience for the radicals who received valuable aid from unconditional Unionists. The interaction between Lincoln and his critics frequently made it possible for both not merely to retain the border's loyalty but eventually to bring about the abolition of slavery as well.

How readily the President was willing to endorse plans different from his own could be seen in the northwestern part of Virginia. Owning few slaves and trading with the North as well as with other sections, the inhabitants of the area had long resented tidewater domination. Their unionism was genuine and when Virginia seceded, they set up at Wheeling a restored government which promptly demanded and received Lincoln's protection. Its senators and representatives were seated in Congress, a process in which Wade, as chairman of the Senate Committee on Territories, took a leading part.

The more extreme Unionist leaders in Wheeling, however, were not satisfied. Anxious for the organization of a separate state, they believed that civil war and secession had given them an opportunity. But because of its doubtful constitutionality, a statehood bill would doubtless encounter trouble in Congress. Its advocates needed allies in Washington. And these allies were radicals.

The extremists could see many advantages in the statehood movement. Francis Pierpont, the governor of Restored Virginia, had impressed them with his vigor at the time of his defiance

---

[7] Nicolay and Hay, *Abraham Lincoln,* VI, 344–6; G. B. Cheever–Sumner, March 5, 1862, Sumner Papers.

of the Old Dominion. Since he favored separation, which had been endorsed by a popular vote, they were anxious to oblige the West Virginia loyalists. At any rate, the change would lead to eventual emancipation.[8]

The chairman of the Senate Committee on Territories promptly prepared a bill for the admission of the new state. But he ran into trouble. Because the measure provided merely for gradual emancipation, Charles Sumner, supported by a few other radicals, opposed it. Wade then arranged for a compromise providing for eventual freedom for all slaves, and on July 14, 1862, the Senate passed the bill. In December, the House followed suit, Thaddeus Stevens making it clear that he was voting in the affirmative not because he thought the legislation constitutional, but because he considered it a war measure.[9]

Would the President sign the bill? Known to be of doubtful constitutionality, bitterly fought by conservatives and not even endorsed by all ultras, it would make a mockery of the pretensions of the advocates of states' rights. Lincoln had always been understood to be opposed to radical measures of reorganization. His reaction to the scheme would be significant. Would he maintain his position?

The President was willing to fit his theories to the occasion. Spurred on by Governor Pierpont, he polled the members of his Cabinet, to whom he submitted two questions: "1st. Is the said Act constitutional? 2d. Is the said Act expedient?" When he received contradictory replies, Welles, Blair, and Bates opposing, Seward, Chase, and Stanton favoring the measure, he sided with those proposing a radical solution. On December 31, 1862, he

[8] Blaine, *Twenty Years of Congress*, I, 459 ff.; Siviter, *Recollections*, p. 96; Richard Orr Curry, *A House Divided: Statehood Politics and the Copperhead Movement in West Virginia* (Pittsburgh, 1964), pp. 69–89; Charles Henry Ambler, *West Virginia, The Mountain State* (New York, 1940), Ch. XVIII–XXI.

[9] Charles H. Ambler, *Waitman Thomas Willey* (Huntington, W. Va., 1954), pp. 79–80; *Cong. Globe*, 37th Cong., 2d Sess., 2941, 3037–8, 3308–20; New York *Tribune*, June 24, July 15, 1862; Blaine, *Twenty Years of Congress*, I, 460–6. Other radicals, including Ashley and M. F. Conway, voted against the bill, Conway refusing to sanction another slave state. Brooks, *Washington in Lincoln's Time*, p. 107.

signed the bill. In one of the first controversies about the restoration of a state, he had taken the advanced view.[1]

The clearest example of the President's willingness to experiment in slave states occurred in Missouri. It was in this border commonwealth that his pragmatic approach in dealing with both radical and more conservative reconstructionists was put to its most severe test. Almost from the very beginning of the secession crisis, Unionists in the state had been divided into moderates and radicals, who, while cooperating against Southern sympathizers, nevertheless bitterly resented one another. The moderates, who soon became virtually indistinguishable from conservatives, were led by Hamilton Gamble, a respected jurist, and William S. Harney, the federal commander in St. Louis; the radicals, by Francis P. Blair and Nathaniel Lyon. Lyon was a zealous red-bearded captain from Connecticut whose military skill contributed significantly to the defeat of the secessionists; Blair, the best-known Republican in Missouri, had excellent connections in Washington, where his brother was a member of Lincoln's Cabinet. By giving him permission to remove Harney, Lincoln sided with Blair in the first round of the struggle, and for the moment, the radicals were triumphant. But when, shortly afterwards, Frémont took command and began to quarrel with Blair in turn, the situation changed. The former radical leader now made common cause with the moderates who had just inaugurated Gamble governor; Frémont became the hero of the ultras, especially the numerous Germans, and the contentions of the Claybanks and the Charcoals, the new names for the two factions, rent the entire state. Lincoln's revocation of Frémont's emancipation order and his dismissal of the Pathfinder seemed to place him squarely on the Claybank's side.[2]

[1] Francis Pierpont–Lincoln, December 18, 20, 1862, RTL; Lincoln, *Works,* VI, 17, 26–8.

[2] MS Autobiography of Charles D. Drake, Historical Society of Missouri, pp. 671 ff., 697 ff.; William E. Parrish, *Turbulent Partnership: Missouri and the Union, 1861–1865* (Columbia, Mo., 1963), pp. 15–32, 33–76; Edward Conrad Smith, *The Borderland in the Civil War*

But the President's action had not been caused by his disapproval of the radicals' aims. Responsible for the safety of the nation, he could not disregard the opposition to Frémont's action, which was especially strong in the border states.[3] When the time was ripe, he himself would go much further.

During the next few years, the controversies in Missouri became chronic. B. Gratz Brown, the editor of the St. Louis *Democrat,* and Charles D. Drake, "a little, fiery debater, intensely earnest and radical," emerged as the spokesmen for the Charcoals, who favored immediate rather than gradual emancipation, opposed Gamble and Blair, and generally believed Lincoln to be their nemesis. While keeping the state in turmoil, they also furnished the leadership for emancipation, Brown himself advocating Missouri's inclusion in the President's proclamation. And they enjoyed close relations with the radicals in Congress.[4]

Lincoln soon found himself sorely tried by the feud. Harassed by both factions, urged to take action against either one or the other, he attempted to bring them together. "I am having a good deal of trouble with Missouri matters . . . ," he wrote on January 5, 1863, to the radical General Samuel R. Curtis.

> One class of friends believe in greater severity, and another in greater leniency, in regard to arrests, banishments, and assessments. As usual in such cases, each question the other's motives. . . . Now, my belief is that Gov. Gamble is an honest and true man, not less so than yourself; that you and he could confer together on this, and other Missouri questions with great advantage to the public; that each knows something which the other does not, and that, acting together, you could about

---

(New York, 1927), pp. 226–62; Thomas L. Snead, *The First Year of the War in Missouri, Battles and Leaders,* I, 273; Nevins, *The War for the Union,* I, 120–9; Norma Peterson, *Freedom and Franchise, The Political Career of B. Gratz Brown* (Columbia, Mo., 1965), pp. 106–9.

[3] Lincoln, *Works,* IV, 531–3.

[4] Schofield, *Forty-six Years in the Army,* pp. 56–7; Howard, *Civil-War Echoes,* p. 67; Peterson, *Freedom and Franchise,* pp. 106–9, 121; George Hoadly–Chase, September 18, 1861, in Chase, *Diary and Correspondence,* pp. 503–5; B. G. Brown–Wilson, December 6, 1862, Henry Wilson Papers.

double your stock of pertinent information. May I not hope that you and he will attempt this?

To Brown, who protested that Curtis was openly in the interests of freedom, while the governor was "secretly in the service of slavery," he wrote that he took no part between his friends in Missouri, of whom he considered the radical leader one. Although he affirmed again and again that he wished to keep out of the quarrel, he incurred the radicals' ire when, in May, he replaced Curtis with John M. Schofield. No matter how much he protested that Schofield had been sent to Missouri to settle the controversy, they were convinced that Lincoln backed their opponents.[5]

The more conservative Unionists, however, were by no means satisfied. In spite of the President's well-known preference for a feasible emancipation policy, they adopted a measure so gradual as to be wholly impracticable. Moreover, Governor Gamble was insulted because Lincoln characterized him as the head of one of the state's factions.[6]

The radicals sought to make the most of their antagonists' predicament. As Drake in August, 1863, informed the President, Gamble did indeed represent nothing but a faction. Lincoln ought to give his support only to loyal people. Brown also appealed to Lincoln to rely on the unconditional emancipationists and dismiss Schofield, and after the population had become incensed because of William Quantrill's raid on Lawrence, Kansas, where the Confederate marauder had committed acts of barbarity, a radical convention met at Jefferson City. Adopting fiery resolutions favoring immediate emancipation, the gathering appointed a delegation to go to Washington and bring about General Schofield's recall.[7]

[5] Lincoln, *Works*, VI, 36–7, 42, 178, 211–12, 218–19; B. G. Brown–Nicolay, November 25, 1862, RTL; Bates, *Diary*, p. 294; W. P. Mellen–Chase, August 6, 1863, Chase Papers, HSP.

[6] Nicolay and Hay, *Abraham Lincoln*, VII, 208–10; Gamble-Lincoln, July 13, 1863, RTL.

[7] C. D. Drake–Lincoln, August 11, 1863; B. G. Brown–Lincoln, September 9, 1863, James O. Broadhead–Bates, September 22, 1863, Broadhead–M. Blair, September 22, 1863, RTL; Nicolay and Hay, *Abraham Lincoln*, VII, 210 ff.; Washington *National Intelligencer*, September 9, 1863; MS autobiography of Charles D. Drake, pp. 715 ff.

Lincoln dealt skillfully with the delegates. Tactfully pointing out that he considered them true friends of the administration, he reminded them that he still preferred gradual rather than immediate emancipation and that he could not remove Schofield without cause. In a formal reply, which he sent later, he was more explicit. He took notice of their demands that Schofield be replaced with Butler, that Governor Gamble's conservative state forces, the Enrolled Militia, be disbanded, and that only properly qualified voters be admitted to the polls. Nevertheless, he concluded that the facts presented to him did not warrant his compliance. "The radicals and conservatives," he wrote,

> each agree with me in all things, and disagree in others. I could wish both to agree with me in all things; for then they would agree with each other, and would be too strong for any foe from any quarter. They, however, chose to do otherwise, and I do not question their right. I shall do what seems to me my duty. I hold whoever commands in Missouri, or elsewhere, responsible to me, and not to either radicals or conservatives. It is my duty to hear all; but at last, I must, within my sphere, judge what to do, and what to forbear.

"God bless Abraham Lincoln," commented the *National Intelligencer.* "He has routed the Jacobins, horse, foot, and dragoons."[8]

The paper was mistaken. The President did not intend to rout the radicals; nor had he done so. As he told the Attorney General after meeting with the Missouri delegation, he really thought "some of them were . . . pretty good men, if they only knew how!" To Schofield, he gave instructions to prevent illegal voting—an order favoring the radicals because it affected largely returned secessionists. And when Governor Gamble demanded federal protection against his extremist opponents, Lincoln refused. "You tell me 'a party has sprung up in Missouri, which openly and loudly proclaims the purpose to overturn the provisional government by violence,'" he wrote.

[8] Lincoln, *Works,* VI, 499–504; Washington *National Intelligencer,* October 29, 1863.

Does the party so proclaim, or is it only that some members of the party so proclaim? If I mistake not, the party alluded to recently held a State convention, and adopted resolutions. Did they, therein declare violence against the provisional State government? No party can be justly held responsible for what individual members of it may say or do.

It was clear to him that public opinion in the West was turning toward the Charcoals, a trend which did not particularly alarm him. As he made clear to John Hay, they were nearer to him than more conservative Republicans.[9]

The fall election resulted in a very narrow moderate victory, and shortly afterwards, the legislature elected two Republican senators. That one of them, B. Gratz Brown, was a radical, and the other, John B. Henderson, a moderate, seemed providential to the President. "I understand, this is one and one," he commented. "If so, it is knocking heads together to some purpose." And the purpose was very clear. As he said to John Hay while talking about the Missouri problem:

> . . . these radical men have in them the stuff which must save the State and on which we must mainly rely. They are absolutely uncorrosive by the virus of secession. . . . While the conservatives, in casting about for votes to carry through their plan, are tempted to affiliate with those whose record is not clear. If one side must be crushed out and the other cherished, there could be no doubt which side we would choose as fuller of hope for the future. We would have to side with the radicals.[1]

Although the ultras failed to appreciate him, in December he proved this commitment by finally recalling Schofield. In 1865, the triumphant Charcoals brought about emancipation, an end result made possible by their efforts as well as by the President's willingness to experiment in the remaking of a state.[2]

[9] Bates, *Diary*, p. 308; Lincoln, *Works*, VI, 492–3, 526–7; Gamble-Lincoln, October 1, 1863, RTL; Hay, *Diaries*, pp. 101, 108.
[1] Parrish, *Turbulent Partnership*, pp. 171–3; Lincoln, *Works*, VII, 13; Hay, *Diaries*, p. 135.
[2] Lincoln, *Works*, VII, 78–9; Parrish, *Turbulent Partnership*, pp. 200–1; Bates, *Diary*, p. 439.

If Lincoln demonstrated his pragmatism in dealing with the radicals' program in Missouri, he also gave evidence of his skill in Maryland. Like other border commonwealths, the state had been divided in sentiment at the time of the outbreak of war. Aided by the federal government, the Unionists in 1861 squelched the secession movement, but they were beset by factionalism. One group was eventually identified with Postmaster General Montgomery Blair; the other made common cause with Henry Winter Davis, the unconditional Unionist from Baltimore.[3]

Davis was a remarkable man. Handsome, buoyant, and irrepressible, he impressed foe and friend alike with his classic features, black, curly hair, and winning oratory. "My son, beware of the follies of Jacksonism," his father had told him, and the son never forgot it. To him, Democrats seemed the cause of every evil, and when the old Whig organization collapsed, Davis collaborated with the Know-Nothings in order to continue the struggle against the hated "Locos." After his election to Congress, he cast the decisive vote for Pennington which broke the deadlock in the speakership controversy of 1860. During the secession debates, he thundered against disunion, but in spite of his hatred for the Democrats, in 1860 he opposed the Republican ticket in Maryland in order to strengthen Breckinridge's opponents. The result was that local Republicans blamed him for siphoning off almost 9,000 votes which went to Bell instead of Lincoln. Nevertheless, rejoicing at Lincoln's election, as an outspoken Southern Unionist he had hopes of joining the new Cabinet.[4]

[3] Charles L. Wagandt, *The Mighty Revolution: Negro Emancipation in Maryland, 1862–1864* (Baltimore, 1964), pp. 15–28; *O. R.*, Series I, II, 568, 601.

[4] Brooks, *Washington in Lincoln's Time*, pp. 28, 183; Howard, *Civil-War Echoes*, p. 133; Adams, *The Great Secession Winter of 1860–61*, pp. 17–18; Boutwell, *Reminiscences of Sixty Years*, II, 2; Bernard Steiner, *Life of Henry Winter Davis* (Baltimore, 1916), pp. 7–63, 144 ff., 189, 216; Davis–S. F. DuPont, October 18, November 7, 1860; W. G. Snethen–Chase, November 14, 1860, Chase Papers, LC; W. G. Snethen–Trumbull, November 21, 1860, Trumbull Papers, LC; W. G. Snethen–Hale, November 24, 1860, Hale Papers.

Davis was slated for disappointment. His archrival, Montgomery Blair, became Postmaster General, and the Maryland orator was very resentful. But he campaigned enthusiastically for the national cause. Although he lost in the congressional race in June, he polled a large enough vote to feel encouraged about the prospects of the Union in Maryland, and when the state was finally secured by a combination of political finesse and military force, he continued his association with the Republican party. But he was not yet an uncompromising extremist; in December, 1861, he condemned Frémont, immediate emancipation, and territorial rule for the South; in May, 1862, he called immediate abolition impolitic, and as late as October, 1862, he still considered it impossible to govern the South by force. Only when the Blairs became more and more closely identified with gradual emancipation and conservatism did he embrace the advanced doctrines for which he was to become famous.[5]

After the promulgation of the Emancipation Proclamation, the stage was set for the assault upon slavery in Maryland as well as elsewhere. Running in a primary against Thomas Swann, a conservative Unionist, Davis assumed a radical stance, won nomination, and emerged as an "unconditional Unionist," the name favored by Maryland ultras, who eventually became the advocates of immediate emancipation. Despite Davis's personal rancor toward him, Lincoln was not unsympathetic. "As you ask my opinion," he wrote to Davis on March 18,

I give it that the supporters of the war should send no man to Congress who will not go into caucus with the unconditional supporters of the war. . . . Let the friends of the government first save the government, and then administer it to their own liking.[6]

In the meantime, Davis's antagonist, Montgomery Blair, had become one of the ultras' chief opponents. Enmeshed in intrigue

[5] Davis–S. F. DuPont, March 12, 1861, August 25, October 11, December 18, 1861, Davis–Mrs. S. F. DuPont, May 20, 1862, October 20, 1862, DuPont Papers; Steiner, Davis, pp. 194–6.
[6] Ibid., pp. 216 ff.; W. G. Snethen–Chase, June 5, 1863, Chase Papers, LC; Lincoln, Works, VI, 140–1.

against Chase, during the fall campaign he delivered a speech at Rockville in which he savagely attacked radical policies and their proponents. Davis, already outraged at the recall of his friend Admiral S. F. DuPont, who had failed to take Charleston harbor, became increasingly bitter against the administration, and other radicals shared his dismay. "If the President persist in retaining such men as Blair and Seward," wrote Stevens to Sumner after the Rockville speech, " we must take care that his reign shall not be prolonged. We must think of a successor." Davis could not have agreed more.[7]

The President, however, did not merit these strictures. Although refusing to disavow Blair, he nevertheless expressed his opinion that Davis was the candidate of the Union party and must be sustained. The controversy was merely one of form, he explained. Anxious for the abolition of slavery in Maryland, he needed the radicals' push as well as the conservatives' pull. The former would work for reform while the latter would keep the opposition in line. Accordingly, he generally sustained General Robert C. Schenck's vigorous measures of military interference with the elections, in spite of Governor Augustus W. Bradford's strong protests against a loyalty oath for prospective voters. With the aid of such devices, in November the unconditional Unionists were largely successful, and Davis was elected to Congress without opposition.[8]

During the next year, the Maryland radicals succeeded in

[7] M. Blair–Lincoln, April 27, 1863, Chase-Lincoln, October 5, 1863, Kelley-Lincoln, October 21, 1863, RTL; *Speech of the Hon. Montgomery Blair (Postmaster General), on the Revolutionary Schemes of the Ultra Abolitionists, and in Defense of the Policy of the President. Delivered at the Unconditional Union Meeting Held at Rockville, Montgomery Co., Maryland, on Saturday, October 3, 1863* (New York, 1863); Davis–S. F. DuPont, July 11, November 4, 1863, DuPont Papers; Stevens-Sumner, October 9, 1863, Sumner Papers; William Ernest Smith, *The Francis Preston Blair Family in Politics* (New York, 1933), II, 126, 236.

[8] Hay, *Diaries*, pp. 105, 112–13; Lincoln, *Works*, VI, 555–8; Washington *National Intelligencer*, November 5, 6, 9, 1863; Nicolay and Hay, *Abraham Lincoln*, VIII, 460 ff. Lincoln revoked that part of Schenck's order which permitted provost marshals to arrest secessionists at the polls, but confirmed their right to require an oath of allegiance of voters whose loyalty had been challenged.

securing a constitutional convention, which endorsed immediate emancipation, and in the fall of 1864, to Lincoln's great delight, the electorate ratified it. "Winter Davis is taking the stump . . . ," said John Hay to his chief shortly before the election. "I doubt if his advocacy of you will be hearty enough to be effective."

"If he and the rest can succeed in carrying the State for emancipation, I shall be very willing to lose the electoral vote," was the reply. Davis' part in bringing about the reform was crucial, and the President had again shown how ready he was to experiment.[9] In matters of reorganizing slave states, he knew how to put the radicals' energy to good use.[1]

In other parts of the country as well as in the border states, the radicals never fully appreciated the President's pragmatism. In 1862, many of his ideas about reconstruction had been put into practice. Not only in Tennessee, where Andrew Johnson wielded power as military governor, but also in North Carolina and Arkansas, a beginning had been made.[2] None of these experiments met with the ultras' favor. "If something be not speedily done by Congress, the prospect before us is dark indeed," wrote one observer to Charles Sumner on March 5, 1862. "The recent action of the President, in taking into his hands the government of Tennessee . . . involves a palpable usurpation of the Legislative power of our government." Lincoln should have asked Congress to provide for a territorial code for the conquered state. And while many radicals disliked any assumption of executive power on principle, they were also concerned about a more practical issue: the question of emancipation. At first, the President's scheme

[9] Wagandt, *The Mighty Revolution,* pp. 246 ff.; Hay, *Diaries,* p. 216; Brooks, *Washington in Lincoln's Time,* p. 183.

[1] The factionalism of the Republican party in Kentucky was not so evident. The party was not strong enough. For a history of the state during the Civil War, cf. Ellis Merton Coulter, *The Civil War and Readjustment in Kentucky* (Chapel Hill, N. C., 1926).

[2] Reinhard H. Luthin, *The Real Abraham Lincoln* (Englewood Cliffs, N. J., 1960), pp. 473–4, 477–9, 482–5.

did not provide for the abolition of slavery, either gradual or immediate.[3]

Lincoln's plan encountered difficulties from the start. Edward Stanly, the military governor of North Carolina, was a conservative. Hardly had he arrived in the state than he closed the colored schools and sought to enforce the Fugitive Slave Law. While newspapers protested, Sumner delivered a philippic in the Senate, where a resolution of censure was introduced. For the time being, Lincoln refused to recall Stanly, but he was not going to commit a similar error again. Having decided to promulgate the Emancipation Proclamation, he was rapidly coming to see the importance of one of the ultras' main objections to his plan. He determined to insist upon emancipation himself.[4]

Unlike his radical critics, Lincoln moved forward cautiously, and it was not until almost a year had passed that he committed himself.[5] After seeing to it that elections for Congress were held in New Orleans, where, in December, 1862, two representatives were chosen and seated, and after replacing Butler with Banks, he evinced interest in restoring the state government. This project was complicated by a division of opinion among local Unionists. The conservatives, anxious to save slavery, favored the retention of the old constitution of 1852; their opponents, eager to abolish the "peculiar institution," wanted to write a new basic law. In this controversy, Lincoln unhesitatingly chose the side of the foes of slavery. Rejecting the conservatives' request in June, 1863, for the readmission of the state under the old charter, in

[3] Nicolay and Hay, *Abraham Lincoln*, VI, 344–6; G. B. Cheever-Sumner, March 5, 1862, Sumner Papers; Welles, *Lincoln's Administration*, p. 83.

[4] New York *Herald*, June 4, 5, 6, 1862; *New York Times*, June 4, 1862; *Harper's Weekly*, VI (June 21, 1862), 386; Sumner, *Works*, VII, 112–19; Lincoln, *Works*, V, 259–60.

[5] With General Butler's approval, in June 1862, Lincoln appointed George S. Shepley military governor of Louisiana. When Reverdy Johnson in July reported that Union feeling was being crushed because of talk of emancipation, Lincoln wrote him that he would not "surrender this game leaving any card unplayed." Trefousse, *Butler*, p. 126; Lincoln, *Works*, V, 342–4.

August he explained his position more fully to General Banks. He would be very glad for Louisiana to adopt a new constitution ending slavery, he wrote, suggesting that at the same time the state "adopt some practical system by which the two races could gradually live themselves out of their old relation to each other, and both come out better prepared for the new. Education for the young blacks should be included in the plan." As he pointed out, "as an anti-slavery man I have a motive to desire emancipation, which pro-slavery men do not have."[6]

The conservatives had not yet given up. Seeking to save as much of the old order as possible, in November they attempted to hold an election in accordance with the old constitution. Their maneuver proved abortive, and the President instructed General Banks to move as quickly as possible toward a reorganization of the government. "If a few professedly loyal men shall draw the disloyal about them, and colorably set up a State government, repudiating the emancipation proclamation, and re-establishing slavery, I can not recognize or sustain their work," he wrote. The new state of Louisiana would be a free state.[7]

The radicals again facilitated Lincoln's conversion to reconstruction with emancipation. Committed to congressional control of reconstruction to bring about freedom for the slaves, they made every effort to promote their program. Sumner continued to advocate his state-suicide theory, which, in October, 1863, he set forth at great length in an article in the *Atlantic Monthly*. Chase, favoring the extension of the areas affected by the Emancipation Proclamation, publicized similar ideas, and Thaddeus Stevens in January, 1863, delivered an incisive speech in the House in which he called the Southern states conquered provinces.

[6] Ibid., pp. 462–3; VI, 287–9, 364–5; New Orleans *Delta,* December 4, 1862; Butler, *Butler's Book,* p. 523; Willie Malvin Caskey, *Secession and Restoration in Louisiana* (Baton Rouge, 1938), pp. 55 ff.; Gerald M. Capers, *Occupied City: New Orleans under the Federals, 1862–1865* (Lexington, Ky., 1965), pp. 128–32.

[7] Nicolay and Hay, *Abraham Lincoln,* VIII, 424 ff.; Thomas Durant–Lincoln, October 23, 1863, G. S. Shepley–Lincoln, October 29, 1863, RTL; Lincoln, *Works,* VII, 1–22.

Widespread criticism of General Banks, who tended to be more moderate than his predecessor, was also due to the persistence of radical influence. In August, 1863, William Whiting, the astute Solicitor of the War Department, wrote to the Philadelphia Union League that the abolition of slavery must be made a condition for readmission. No matter how much the conservatives might badger Lincoln, there was never any lack of radical counterpressure. The President again made the best of both.[8]

Lincoln's response to these conflicting influences was contained in his annual message to Congress on December 8, 1863. Taking great pride in the progress of emancipation and the enrollment of Negro troops, he declared:

> I shall not attempt to retract or modify the emancipation proclamation; nor shall I return to slavery any person who is free by the terms of that proclamation, or by any of the acts of Congress.

Then he set forth a plan under which the states might be reconstructed. Offering amnesty to all except high Confederate officials and their abettors, he proposed to re-establish state governments as soon as ten per cent of the legal voters had taken the required oath of allegiance. Although he refused to turn over control to Congress, as the radicals wished, he insisted on compliance with the Emancipation Proclamation and the Confiscation Acts. But as yet he did not ask for abolition of slavery in areas where the Emancipation Proclamation did not apply—an omission which was bound to irk the ultras.

The reactions to the proposal were mixed. While the Chicago *Tribune* praised Lincoln's insistence upon the Emancipation Proclamation, Chase and other radicals were perturbed. The President's mind worked in the right direction, wrote Henry Ward

[8] Sumner, *Works,* VII, 162, 493–546; Chase, *Diaries,* pp. 143, 178–9, 188–9, 191–7; Chase–N. B. Buford, October 11, 1862, Chase–George Denison, January 19, 1863, B. F. Flanders–Chase, April 30, 1863, Chase Papers, HSP; New York *World,* January 9, 1863; Daniel Ullman–Hamlin, June 10, 1863, Hamlin Papers; J. W. Shaffer–Butler, October 2, 1863, Butler Papers; New York *Herald,* August 11, 1863.

Beecher to the Secretary, but seldom "clearly and cleanly." Senator Dixon, on the other hand, welcomed the message. The radicals' support of the scheme, he informed Henry Raymond, the editor of the *New York Times,* was rather forced. "They cannot very well oppose it, while they must see that it is utterly incompatible with their favorite theory." The best analysis was given by the New York *Herald,* which wrote:

> The art of riding two horses is not confined to the circus. . . . President Lincoln . . . has for some time been riding two political horses, and with the skill of an old campaigner, he whips them—the radical horse "a leetle ahead"—through his message. . . . During the last two or three years he has given us some marvellous surprises in bringing forward the radical horse in front when it was supposed he had been hopelessly dropped behind.[9]

The President's amnesty proclamation furnished a basis for the reconstruction of Louisiana. After Lincoln, much to the radicals' dismay, had put Banks completely in charge of the "free state" reorganization there, the general prepared for elections. As in other Southern states, however, factionalism had become endemic. Three groups vied for control, a radical segment lead by Congressman B. F. Flanders, a moderate wing supporting his colleague Michael Hahn, and the conservative remnant backing J. Q. A. Fellows. Although both moderates and radicals favored emancipation, they differed on the question of freedmen's rights, some of the more advanced Republicans going so far as to contemplate Negro suffrage. Since Lincoln, anxious to establish a government as quickly as possible, supported Banks, Hahn, and the moderates, Louisiana radicals tended to make common cause with Chase and his allies. Hahn was elected, and after the new government was inaugurated, a constitutional convention met which abolished

⁹ Lincoln, *Works,* VII, 48–56; Chicago *Tribune,* December 14, 1863; Beecher-Chase, December 28, 1863, Chase Papers, LC; James Dixon–Raymond, December 13, 1863, Henry Raymond Papers, New York Public Library; New York *Herald,* December 11, 1863.

slavery. Much as the ultras disliked the new regime, Lincoln believed that it contained the kernel of future success.[1]

But the President was again willing to listen to radical proposals. Gradually but surely, he was moving toward the acceptance of one of the most controversial measures for reconstruction, the enfranchisement of the colored race.

The issue of Negro suffrage was fraught with great difficulty. While some abolitionists had insisted upon the reform for some time, as long as most nonwhites remained in bondage, the question of giving them the vote seemed remote. By the end of 1863, however, such leading radicals as Salmon P. Chase and Charles Sumner stood committed to the innovation. After having recommended it to his followers in New Orleans, on December 29, the Secretary of the Treasury wrote to Greeley, "I find that almost all who are willing to have colored men fight are willing to have them vote." He advocated enfranchising literate Negroes both in Louisiana and Florida, and his supporters gradually accepted his advice. Sumner, who had long fought for the Negroes' equality before the law—as witnesses in the courts, as passengers in public conveyances, and as carriers of United States mail—early in 1864 raised the question by moving an amendment for universal suffrage in the new territory of Montana. In view of the Southern Unionists' weakness, the necessity of enfranchising some freedmen in order to maintain control was evident.[2] But popular prejudice was difficult to overcome. Even most Northern states still discriminated against nonwhites.

[1] Lincoln, *Works*, VII, 89–91, 486–87; T. J. Durant–Chase, January 16, March 5, 1864, John Hutchins–Chase, February 12, 1864, Chase Papers, LC; B. F. Flanders–Chase, January 23, 24, February 26, 1864, Chase Papers, HSP; J. McKaye–Sumner, February 5, 1864, Sumner-Lieber, May 4, 1864, Sumner Papers; Nicolay and Hay, *Abraham Lincoln*, VIII, 431–7; Charles H. McCarthy, *Lincoln's Plan of Reconstruction* (New York, 1901), pp. 69 ff. Banks finally decided to suspend only parts of the old constitution—those sanctioning slavery.

[2] McPherson, *The Struggle for Equality*, pp. 24–5; Chase–Greeley, December 29, 1863, Greeley Papers; L. D. Stickney–Chase, January 11, February 24, 1864, John Hutchins–Chase, February 24, 1864, Chase Papers, LC; Sumner, *Works*, VI, 384, 442; VII, 152–62, 236–43.

In spite of these complications, Lincoln was not far behind his radical critics. Sometime in January, 1864, in a letter to General Wadsworth, he wrote:

I cannot see, if universal amnesty is granted, how, under the circumstances, I can avoid exacting in return universal suffrage, or, at least, suffrage on the basis of intelligence and universal military service.

The ultras' agitation had not been in vain, and when the new government of Louisiana was inaugurated, the President advised Governor Hahn:

I congratulate you on having fixed your name in history as the first free-state Governor of Louisiana. Now you are about to have a Convention which, among other things, will probably define the elective franchise. I barely suggest for your private consideration, whether some of the colored people may not be let in—as, for instance, the very intelligent, and especially those who have fought gallantly in our ranks. They would probably help, in some trying time to come, to keep the jewel of liberty within the family of freedom. . . .

The suggestion was disregarded; Lincoln, however, would recur to it at a later time.[3]

But the President's open-mindedness did not mollify the radicals. As soon as his message containing the amnesty proclamation had been received in Congress, Henry Winter Davis, whose differences with Lincoln were notorious, moved that those parts dealing with reconstruction be referred to a select committee. The

[3] Lincoln, *Works*, VII, 101–2, 243. The authenticity of the complete Wadsworth letter, the date of which is not certain, has been questioned. In the version cited, two additional paragraphs appear, in which Lincoln comes out unequivocally for "civil and political equality of both races." Even those who deny their authenticity, however, concede that the first two paragraphs expressed Lincoln's views. Ludwell E. Johnson, "Lincoln and Equal Rights: The Authenticity of the Wadsworth Letter," *Journal of Southern History*, XXXII (February, 1966), 83–7; cf. Harold M. Hyman, "Lincoln and Equal Rights for Negroes: The Irrelevancy of the 'Wadsworth Letter,' " *Civil War History*, XII (September, 1966), 258–66.

motion carried; Davis became the committee's chairman, and he prepared the reconstruction bill bearing his name.

Davis's measure showed again that the radicals were not totally impractical. Although many of them were anxious to build up a loyal and Republican South based on Negro suffrage, they realized that the time was not yet ripe for such an innovation, and the bill confined the electorate to whites. It asserted the supremacy of Congress, specifically outlawed slavery, and required a fifty per cent majority rather than ten per cent of the voters to approve the new governments. It also differed from Lincoln's plan by more rigidly excluding Confederate sympathizers by means of an "iron-clad oath." Potential voters had to swear that they had never voluntarily borne arms against the United States or given aid to the enemy. Stevens disliked the bill because he believed that it was not stern enough; a Senate committee attempted to add a Negro suffrage amendment, but in the long run, managed by Davis in the House and Wade in the Senate, it passed both chambers with impressive majorities. Almost the entire Republican party endorsed it.[4]

Save for the rigid assertion of congressional authority over reconstruction, there was nothing in the bill with which the President could not have agreed. But he had announced his policy, which several states had already begun to implement. It was therefore a moot question whether he would consent to it. Congress was ready to adjourn on the Fourth of July; early in the morning, Lincoln rode to the capitol to examine and sign bills. Sumner, Boutwell, and Chandler pleaded with him, the Michigan senator especially seeking to influence him. If the measure were vetoed, it would put a terrible burden on the party. But Lincoln remained calm. "Mr. Chandler," he said, "this bill was placed before me a few minutes before Congress adjourns. It is a matter of too much importance to be swallowed in that way."

[4] McPherson, *Rebellion,* pp. 317–20; New York *Tribune,* May 3, 5, June 30–July 5, 1864; Cox, *Three Decades of Federal Legislation,* pp. 339 ff.

"If it is vetoed it will damage us fearfully in the Northwest. It may not in Illinois; it will in Michigan and Ohio. The important point is that one prohibiting slavery in the reconstructed States."

"That is the point on which I doubt the authority of Congress to act."

"It is no more than you have done yourself."

"I conceive that I may in an emergency do things on military grounds which cannot be done constitutionally by law."

"Mr. President I cannot controvert y[ou]r position by argument. I can only say I deeply regret it." Then the senator left.

The President refused his assent. As he pointed out to John Hay, the radicals had never been very friendly to him; the controversy about the bill would not make much difference, and he was unwilling to admit that the Southern states were not in the Union. A few days later, he published a message which explained the reasons for his stand.[5]

The radicals reacted violently. In their fury about his refusal to sign the bill, they lost all sense of proportion. "What an infamous proclamation!" wrote Thaddeus Stevens.

> The Prest. is determined to have the electoral votes of the seceded States.... The idea of pocketing a bill & then issuing a proclamation as to how far he will conform to it is matched only by signing a bill and then sending in a veto. How little of the rights of war and the law of nations our Prest. knows!

Garfield, Sumner, Schenck, and Pomeroy, among others, all severely condemned Lincoln, and eventually Wade and Davis would sign their notorious manifesto impugning the Chief Executive. The rift between the radicals and the White House appeared to be complete.[6]

At first sight, the controversy about the Wade-Davis Bill might seem to prove the thesis that there was an unbridgeable gulf between Lincoln and the radicals. In reality, however, it showed again that the President was not at all unwilling to listen to

[5] Hay, *Diaries*, pp. 204–6; Lincoln, *Works*, VII, 433–4.
[6] Stevens-McPherson, July 10, 1864, Stevens Papers; Chase, *Diaries*, pp. 230–2.

radical objections and make the most of them. Although he had told Chandler in no uncertain terms that he did not believe that Congress had the power to abolish slavery in the seceded states, he not only called the bill "one very proper plan for the loyal people of any State choosing to adopt it," but also advocated a constitutional amendment prohibiting the institution. And in the peace negotiations which he was carrying on through two emissaries to Richmond, as well as at Niagara Falls, he also made it clear to the Confederates that he would not accept any terms which did not include emancipation as well as reunion. His position was not very far from the radicals'.[7]

In order to understand the bitterness created by the veto of the Wade-Davis Bill, it must be remembered that 1864 was a presidential year. And the relationship between Lincoln and the radicals was strained by the contest as it had never been before.

That the radicals would have liked to substitute some other candidate for Lincoln was no secret. As early as May, 1863, the New York *Herald* observed that the ultras were anxious to put Chase into the White House, while the moderates wanted to renominate Lincoln. Chase's ambition was notorious; a presidential hopeful in 1856 and 1860, he was certain to be receptive to a renewed movement on his behalf. Other candidates were also mentioned, but from the very beginning, many observers doubted the feasibility of changing standard-bearers in the middle of a war. Comparing Lincoln with any would-be successors, in August, 1863, Jesse Fell wrote to Trumbull, "We have tried the former; know what he is; know that he is both honest and patriotic; that if he don't go forward as *fast* as some of us like, he *never goes backward;* and my impression is . . . that he will be a very formidable candidate."[8]

[7] Hay, *Diaries,* pp. 204–6; Lincoln, *Works,* VII, 433–4, 435, 452; James R. Gilmore, *Personal Recollections of Abraham Lincoln and the Civil War* (Boston, 1898), pp. 239 ff.; William Harlan Hale, *Horace Greeley* (New York, 1950), pp. 280–4.

[8] New York *Herald,* May 26, 1863; E. B. Crocker–Chase, June 27, 1863, Chase Papers, LC; William Frank Zornow, *Lincoln & the Party*

The Illinois politician was right about the President. Popular with the people as well as with the soldiers and strengthened by his control of the patronage, he was in an excellent position to secure his renomination. He professed to be unconcerned about Chase's efforts—"if he becomes President, all right," Lincoln said. "I hope we may never have a worse man."—but he kept a close watch on Treasury appointments. As was his habit, he allowed the Secretary great leeway, but he also permitted the Blairs and others to attack his rival. The result was that Chase's chances declined. "The taste of eating a man's bread and stabbing him at the same time may be questioned . . . ," observed David Davis. "Chase is doomed to disappointment. . . . The politicians . . . would put Mr. Lincoln aside if they dared. They know their constituents don't back them, and hence they gamble rather than make open war." And although Chase's managers remained active, even Count Gurowski admitted that the radicals, whom he considered "the purest men in Congress," were beginning to "cave in, and to be reconciled to the idea of accepting the reelection of Lincoln as an absolute necessity." The pressure from the electorate and the White House was too great.[9]

Nevertheless, some of the more ardent ultras refused to give up. Determined to prevent the President's renomination, they circulated a memorandum signed by Senator Pomeroy, which asserted that Lincoln's re-election would be almost impossible. The circular also complained about the President's predilection for compromise and maintained that Chase had shown unexpected strength. But its publication was most embarrassing to the Secretary, who denied all knowledge of the affair, and shortly after-

Divided (Norman, Okla., 1954), pp. 22 ff.; Jesse Fell–Trumbull, August 16, 1863, Trumbull Papers, LC.

[9] J. M. Palmer–Trumbull, December 18, 1863, Norman Judd–Trumbull, January 2, 1864, Trumbull Papers, LC; William Claflin–Sumner, December 18, 1863, Sumner Papers; Hay, *Diaries*, pp. 109–10; New York *Herald*, October 20, 1863; David Davis–Rockwell, January 24, 1864, Davis Papers; Heaton-Chase, January 14, 1864, Chase Papers, HSP; Gurowski, *Diary*, III, 60.

ward, the Ohio legislature endorsed Lincoln's renomination. The Treasury head had to withdraw from the race.[1]

Chase's declination did not end the attempts to displace the President. Some ultras favored Ben Butler; others preferred Frémont, and even Chase's partisans continued to hope for a change in the Secretary's fortunes. Grant, too, appealed to some Republicans, provided the Democrats did not nominate him first. Then Francis P. Blair, Jr., in the House delivered a slashing attack on Chase, the radicals, and their reconstruction policies. Outraged, the ultras wanted Lincoln to disavow him. But the President refused, and his extremist opponents were more indignant than ever.[2]

Since the Republican convention was scheduled to meet on June 8, the radicals had to work fast if they wanted a new candidate. After they had tried unsuccessfully to postpone the meeting, they entertained new hopes when, in May, a group of disgruntled extremists nominated Frémont on a separate ticket. The third party might induce the regulars to consider the nomination of somebody more acceptable to the advanced wing than the President. But no one of national importance endorsed the Pathfinder; Lincoln's popularity with the rank and file could not be denied, and no suitable alternatives were available. Chase had withdrawn; Butler had suffered a setback before Richmond, and Grant had not proved interested. When the Union convention met at Baltimore, Lincoln was easily renominated. Even the radical delegation from Missouri, bitterly opposed to the President and seated only after a struggle with conservative rivals, in the end fell in line.[3]

[1] Circular of February, 1864, enclosed in M. M. Brien–Lincoln, February 23, 1864, RTL; Lincoln, *Works*, VII, 200–1, 212–13; Brooks, *Washington in Lincoln's Time*, pp. 127–9; R. C. Parsons–Chase, March 2, 1864, Chase Papers, LC.
[2] Boston *Commonwealth*, March 25, 1864; Butler, *Correspondence*, III, 513; Sherman Booth–Chase, May 2, 1864, R. C. Parsons–Chase, May 16, 1864, Chase Papers, LC; McClure-Stevens, March 9, 1864, J. A. Hiestand–Stevens, May 29, 1864, Stevens Papers; E. H. Spahr–Sherman, May 6, 1864, A. Denny–Sherman, May 22, 1864, John Sherman Papers; New York *Herald*, April 25, 1864; Ashley-Lincoln, May 3, 1864, RTL.
[3] Welles, *Lincoln's Administration*, pp. 142 ff.; S. N. Pettis–Lincoln, June 1, 1864, RTL; Zornow, *Lincoln and the Party Divided*, pp. 87–104;

The radical agitation, however, had not been in vain. Its very strength made it easier for Lincoln to realize one of his most important projects, the abolition of slavery by constitutional amendment. He himself induced the chairman of the Republican National Committee to see to it that the platform included the reform, and the result was that the party went before the voters with a radical program. If the President could win re-election, keep control of the organization, and fulfill the promises of the platform, slavery would finally be abolished in the United States. The radicals' first objective would be achieved, and Abraham Lincoln would become the instrument of its success.[4]

Whether the President would prevail was highly problematic. While the convention had emphasized the Unionist character of the ticket by giving second place to Andrew Johnson, a former Democrat as well as a Southern loyalist, the fortunes of the organization soon hit a wartime low. As Grant's heavy losses in his campaigns against Richmond contributed to war-weariness, Lincoln's prospects became less and less favorable, and the radicals were acutely unhappy.

The ultras' disappointment was not quite rational. "To reconcile them to Old Abe," the New York *Herald* pointed out, "all that they could have asked for . . . is conceded in the platform . . . ; but still they regard themselves the victim of a bad bargain." Distraught and blinded by their zeal, they again failed to assess the President properly. When, at the end of the month, Lincoln accepted Chase's resignation, they were even more dismayed. Refusing to see that the Secretary himself had brought about his differences with the President about patronage and other matters, they were doubly offended when Lincoln tried to nominate the war Democrat, David Tod, for the vacant Cabinet post. Fessenden, who finally took over the Treasury, was still considered

<hr />

Trefousse, *Butler,* p. 161; Simeon Nash–Chase, June 10, 1864, Chase Papers, LC. For the view that Lincoln's popularity was less certain than his political skill, cf. Donald, *Lincoln Reconsidered,* pp. 64 ff.

[4] Arnold, *The History of Abraham Lincoln and the Overthrow of Slavery,* pp. 357–8.

friendly to them, but they could not always rely on him. Their influence in the Cabinet had declined.[5]

A few days later, Lincoln pocketed the Wade-Davis Bill. This action, which angered even the moderates, infuriated the ultras. The chief motive for the veto was "to keep open the field to supply by sham states any deficiencies in the votes of the real states," commented Henry Winter Davis, predicting possible civil war for the presidency unless there was a revolt against Lincoln's nomination. Other radicals shared many of his apprehensions, and a widespread movement to bring about the President's withdrawal began to take shape.[6]

Winter Davis's fears and impetuousness led him to undertake a step which was to cut short his congressional career. Filled with hatred for the President and worried about the dwindling prospects of the party, he composed a protest in which Senator Wade joined. Published on August 5 in the New York *Tribune,* the Wade-Davis Manifesto was a remarkable document. Castigating the party's nominee in most severe terms, it accused him of holding the electoral votes of "the rebel States at the dictation of his personal ambition," of defying the judgment of Congress, and of exercising "dictatorial usurpation" in Louisiana. "But he must realize that our support is of a cause and not of a man," the authors continued,

> that the authority of Congress is paramount and must be respected . . . ; and if he wishes our support, he must confine himself to his executive duties—to obey and execute, not make the laws—to suppress by arms armed rebellion, and leave political reorganization to Congress.[7]

The appearance of this unprecedented attack at first seemed to complicate Lincoln's task greatly. But he had handled the radicals

[5] Luthin, *Lincoln,* pp. 517–18; Thomas, *Lincoln,* pp. 428–32; New York *Herald,* June 11, July 2, 1864; Chittenden, *Recollections of President Lincoln and His Administration,* pp. 370 ff.; Chase, *Diaries,* pp. 223–6, 231; Jellison, *Fessenden,* p. 144.

[6] Davis–S. F. DuPont, July 7, 1864, DuPont Papers; Stevens-McPherson, July 10, 1864, Stevens Papers; Brooks, *Washington in Lincoln's Time,* p. 121; Zornow, *Lincoln & the Party Divided,* pp. 110–11; Butler, *Correspondence,* IV, 465, 534–6.

[7] New York *Tribune,* August 5, 1864; Trefousse, *Wade,* pp. 226–7.

in the past, and he would know how to deal with them again. Disappointed as he was, he told a characteristic story. The manifesto was not worth fretting about, he said.

> It reminds me of an old acquaintance who, having a son of a scientific turn, bought him a microscope. The boy went around, experimenting with his glass upon everything that came his way. One day, at the dinner table, his father took up a piece of cheese. "Don't eat that, father," said the boy; "it is full of wrigglers." "My son," replied the old gentleman, taking at the same time a huge bite, "let 'em *wriggle;* I can stand it if they can."[8]

The President was right. While Democratic and opposition newspapers applauded, Republicans were dismayed. "It seems to me nobody has done such an infamous thing since the war began," E. Stansbery, one of his acquaintances, wrote to Sumner. The *New York Times* characterized the manifesto as "by far the most effective Copperhead campaign document thus far issued," and even outspoken radicals were critical. When Gerrit Smith wrote a public letter deprecating it and the *Anti-Slavery Standard* as well as the New York *Tribune* and the Washington *Daily Morning Chronicle* failed to endorse it, it became evident that Wade and Davis had blundered.[9]

In spite of the manifesto's unpopularity, various radical factions still sought to induce the President to withdraw. While James M. Ashley was thinking of making common cause with the war Democrats, George Opdyke, David Dudley Field, Henry Winter Davis, Theodore Tilton, and others, in a series of conferences in New York, made plans for a new convention to be held in September, when they hoped to replace Lincoln with Butler, Chase,

[8] Carpenter, *Six Months at the White House*, p. 145.
[9] New York *World*, August 6, 1864; E. Stansbury–Sumner, August 10, 1864, Sumner Papers; *New York Times*, August 12, 13, 1864; New York *Tribune*, August 5, 17, 1864; Blaine, *Twenty Years of Congress*, II, 43–5; Washington *Morning Chronicle*, August 6, 1864.

or some other candidate. Convinced that the President could not win, they believed such a course offered the only remaining chance of Republican success.[1]

Events soon proved the ultras mistaken. Shortly after the Democrats on August 29 nominated McClellan on a platform declaring the war a failure, Sherman took Atlanta. Farragut had already won his victory in Mobile Bay, and later in September, Sheridan decisively defeated the Confederates in the valley of Virginia. The Democrats' analysis was evidently false; moreover, against Mc-Clellan, many radicals were willing to support almost anybody. "It may be that Mr. Lincoln will see that we shall all be stronger and more united under another candidate," commented Charles Sumner. "But if he does not see it so, our duty is nevertheless clear to unite in the opposition to the common enemy."[2]

The re-establishment of Republican unity proved once again that the President and the radicals were generally able to reach some kind of accommodation. Because of Frémont's candidacy, McClellan's defeat might yet be put in doubt, unless the Pathfinder could be persuaded to withdraw. To bring about this result, the President might make concessions, a point which was not lost on Senator Chandler. Even while other extremists were still seeking to displace Lincoln, Chandler had begun to busy himself to achieve a compromise involving Montgomery Blair's dismissal in return for Frémont's retirement. Traveling to Washington late in August, the senator secured promises from the White House. Then he went to Philadelphia and New York to obtain Frémont's consent, only to find that the Pathfinder would not commit himself until he had conferred with friends. Finally, much to Chandler's chagrin, he decided to withdraw unconditionally. To prevent a

[1] Ashley-Chase, August 5, 1864, Chase Papers, LC; Ashley-Butler, August 5, 1864, Butler Papers; Butler, *Correspondence,* V, 67–8, 81, 116 ff.; H. W. Davis–S. F. DuPont, August 5, 10, 18, 24, 25, 27, 31, 1864; DuPont Papers; H. W. Davis–Chandler, August 24, 1864, Chandler Papers.

[2] Welles, *Lincoln's Administration,* pp. 200 ff.; New York *Sun,* June 30, 1889; Theodore Tilton–Nicolay, September 6, 1864, RTL; Davis–S. F. DuPont, September 19, 1864, DuPont Papers.

last-minute debacle, the senator rushed back to see Lincoln. Frémont's action had made it incumbent upon the President to carry out his part of the bargain, he argued, and in spite of some hesitation—the Pathfinder's letter of withdrawal had been couched in most ungracious language—Lincoln agreed. He dismissed Blair, and the radicals, including Davis and Wade, rallied to the party's support.[3]

Once the radicals had made up their minds that Lincoln could not be displaced, much as they distrusted him, they became once again the most active workers for the ticket. Wilson had long counseled unity and exerted himself for victory; Sumner, in campaign speeches, emphasized that only the Republican party with Abraham Lincoln at its head would be able to carry out "the utter and complete extirpation" of slavery; Thaddeus Stevens, enlisting Carl Schurz's help, contributed his great talents to securing success, and Julian, though he considered "Old Abe . . . rather a burden than a help," wrote to Sumner that he was "at work in good earnest for the *cause*." Chase loyally cooperated, and Wade, who wished "the d---l had Old Abe," energetically attacked McClellan and everything he stood for. Even Henry Winter Davis, who had himself failed of renomination, delivered effective speeches. "The radicals decided these October elections," mused Count Gurowski, "and their casting vote will decide the great November election." And while the crotchety count was undoubtedly exaggerating, there was a kernel of truth in his remarks. Both Lincoln and the radicals rejoiced at the party's victory on November 8. Francis Lieber, who had been anxious to displace

[3] Chandler–Mrs. Chandler, August 27, September 2, 6, 8, 18, 24, 1864, Wade-Chandler, September 15, October 2, 1864, Frémont-Chandler, May 23, 29, 1878, Chandler Papers; H. W. Davis–S. F. DuPont, September 19, 28, or 29, 1864, Dupont Papers; Chandler-Blair, September 29, 1864, Austin Blair Papers; Gurowski, *Diary*, III, 358–59; Winfred A. Harbison, "Zachariah Chandler's Part in the Reelection of Abraham Lincoln," *Mississippi Valley Historical Review*, XX (September, 1935), 267–76; H. W. Davis–Stevens, September 30, 1864, Stevens Papers.

the President two months earlier, now hoped that history would refer to the canvass as "The Great and Good Election of 1864."[4]

In this hard-won triumph, Lincoln had again proved himself a master politician. Overcoming all opposition, he not only prevailed, but retained control of the party machinery. But as on previous occasions, he did not achieve this success by simply standing still. Because he himself was willing to adopt portions of the radicals' program by insisting on unconditional emancipation, he was able not merely to reach an agreement with them but also to further the enactment of another reform. And although he was compelled to reconstruct his Cabinet, he could nevertheless take pride in the final victory in the battle against human bondage —a cause which was almost as important to him as to the extremists. As Carl Schurz, rejecting Frémont's claims, pointed out in October, "The main thing is that the policy of the government moves in the right direction—that is to say, the slaveholder will be overthrown and slavery abolished."

The impact of this relationship was not lost on the conservatives. After Blair's dismissal, Bates expressed the opinion of many of his associates when he observed that the ultras were hoping to become the controlling element. "Perhaps their success is a melancholy defeat for their country," he reflected.

> I think Mr. Lincoln could have been elected without them and in spite of them. In that event, the Country might have been governed free from their *malign* influences, and more nearly in conformity with the constitution.[5]

What he was unwilling to admit was that the President had made

[4] Henry Wilson–Lincoln, September 5, 1864, RTL; Sumner, *Works,* IX, 67–82; Schurz, *Reminiscences,* III, 101; Butler, *Correspondence,* V, 151; Julian-Sumner, September 4, 1864, Sumner Papers; Chase, *Diary and Correspondence,* pp. 449–51; Chase, *Diaries,* p. 258; Wade-Chandler, October 2, 1864, Chandler Papers; Cincinnati *Gazette,* October 20, 25, 1864; *New York Times,* September 22, 23, 1864; New York *Tribune,* October 28, 1864; Gurowski, *Diary,* III, 371; Strong, *Diary,* III, 512.

[5] Schafer, *Intimate Letters of Carl Schurz,* pp. 306–7; Bates, *Diary,* pp. 412–13.

no substantial concessions that he was not perfectly ready to make. Unlike the Attorney General, Lincoln was no conservative.

How thoroughly Lincoln was committed to progress, he showed soon after the election. Determined to end slavery once and for all by constitutional amendment, he employed his vast powers to make the measure's success possible. And again, he cooperated closely with the radicals.

In bringing about the success of the Thirteenth Amendment, the radicals played an important role. As the most prominent advocates of emancipation, they had prepared Congress and the people for the acceptance of the reform. If they believed other measures more efficient for their purposes, they nevertheless took a decisive part in pushing the amendment through both Houses, until finally Lincoln was enabled to exert his powers to the fullest and become the Great Emancipator in fact as well as in name.

As early as December 4, 1863, Representative Isaac N. Arnold of Illinois urged the President to include in his annual message a proposition for an antislavery amendment. Lincoln failed to heed the advice, but ten days later, James M. Ashley introduced into the House a resolution calling for the constitutional change. In the Senate, John B. Henderson reported a similar measure, which radicals like Sumner, Trumbull, and Wilson drove to a successful conclusion. Although Sumner complicated matters by holding out for a different version, on April 8, 1864, the amendment received the necessary two-thirds vote of the Senate.

The progress of the amendment in the Upper House was a godsend for Lincoln, who now exerted his influence to incorporate it in the Union party platform. And although Ashley, despite all efforts, failed to muster the required two thirds in the House, the President used his influence to further its final success. Foreseeing the need for an additional state to secure ratification, he employed his patronage to facilitate the admission of Nevada. In his annual message on December 6, 1864, he not only included a specific recommendation for the amendment, but repeated his previous declaration that he would neither retract the Emancipation Proclamation nor return to slavery any persons already free. "If the people should, by whatever mode or means, make it an Executive duty to re-enslave such persons, another, and not I must be their instrument to perform it," he declared. Although the composition of the House had not changed significantly since the previous summer, the elections and the satisfactory progress of the war had strengthened the Republicans' position. If worst came to worst, after March 4, the President could always call the new Congress into special session. There were reports that he was willing to do it.[6]

With Lincoln's aid, Ashley carefully planned his strategy. Ready to call for a vote in January, he enlisted support of the White House. "*You* must help us [with] *one* vote," he wrote. "Don't you know of a sinner in the opposition who is on praying ground?" When, on January 6, he delivered a final appeal for the measure, he invoked the President's prestige once more. " '*If slavery is not wrong, nothing is wrong.*' Thus simply and truthfully hath spoken our worthy Chief-Magistrate," he said, pleading for the immediate adoption of the amendment. On January 24, again sending out printed circulars, he informed all Republicans that their presence on the thirty-first was essential, because a sufficient number of Democrats would absent themselves or vote aye to pass the measure. He knew what he was talking about. While radical colleagues were tirelessly working for the reform, Thaddeus Stevens particularly pressing for it, the President was employing his influence and patronage to enlist conservative Republicans to further it and even managed to induce wavering opposition members to fall in line. Amid intense excitement, the resolution proposing the amendment passed. Members on the

[6] I. N. Arnold–Lincoln, December 4, 1863, RTL; Arnold, *The History of Abraham Lincoln and the Overthrow of Slavery*, pp. 346–58; McClure, *Lincoln and the Men of War-Times*, p. 98; Pierce, *Sumner*, IV, 184–5; Sumner, *Works*, VII, 347–401; Dana, *Recollections of the Civil War*, pp. 174–8; Lincoln, *Works*, VIII, 149–52; Schurz–Elihu B. Washburne, January 18, 1865, Washburne Papers, LC; J. G. Randall and Richard N. Current, *Lincoln the President: Last Full Measure* (New York, 1955), pp. 298–307. Sumner believed that the amendment ought to assert universal equality before the law.

floor echoed the galleries' cheers; congressmen embraced one another, and some wept like children. It was a great day for all Republicans, and for none more than for the radicals. The reform for which they had labored for so long had finally succeeded. With the President's help, they had killed the "peculiar institution," and reconstruction would bring freedom for the slaves. After the election as before, the interaction between Lincoln and the ultras had been productive of great progress.[7]

How little the effort to displace him had affected the President in his willingness to cooperate with the radicals he had already proved early in December. Chief Justice Roger B. Taney's death had created a vacancy on the Supreme Court, and because of the importance of pending constitutional questions about reconstruction, Lincoln's choice of a successor would be a matter of great significance. Considering Chase eminently fitted for the position, prior to the change in the Treasury Department, the President had given Charles Sumner an implied promise to appoint the Secretary, a commitment which he adhered to even afterward. When Taney died, however, the conservatives made every effort to change Lincoln's mind. Attorney General Bates wanted the post himself; others implored the President to appoint Associate Justice Noah Swayne, and even Montgomery Blair was an aspirant for office. But Lincoln stood firm. Constantly reminded by Sumner and other radicals of Chase's availability, on December 6, he appointed the former Secretary Chief Justice of the United States. Radicals hailed the event as a great victory.[8]

[7] Ashley-Lincoln, December 25, 1864, RTL; *Speech of Hon. J. M. Ashley, of Ohio, Delivered in the House of Representatives on Friday, January 6, 1865, On the Constitutional Amendment for the Abolition of Slavery* (New York, 1865), p. 3; printed circular, January 24, 1865, in Ignatius Donelly Papers, Minnesota Historical Society; Arnold, *The History of Abraham Lincoln and the Overthrow of Slavery*, pp. 358–64; John Hamilton–Chase, January 27, 1865, Chase Papers, LC; "George W. Julian's Journal—The Assassination of Abraham Lincoln," *Indiana Magazine of History*, XI (December, 1915), 327; Ashley, "Governor Ashley's Biography and Messages," loc. cit., pp. 173–83.

[8] Sumner-Lieber, October 14, 1864, Sumner Papers; Chittenden, *Recollections of President Lincoln and His Administration*, pp. 380–4;

The reconstruction problem, however, remained to be solved. Lincoln still stood behind the state governments which had begun to function in Arkansas and Louisiana in accordance with his plan. Although Congress, which had refused to admit the Arkansas congressmen-elect in the long session, proved unwilling between December and March, 1865, to seat those from Louisiana, he would not abandon his scheme. In addition to the conflict about authority between the legislative and executive branch, the issue in dispute involved the position of the Negro: the final abolition of slavery prior to the passage of the Thirteenth Amendment, and an extension of civil rights afterward. Just as Lincoln had yielded on the former, he stood ready to give way on the latter. He knew as well as his critics that Republican control of Southern states was almost impossible as long as freedmen remained disenfranchised, and shortly before his death he prepared to catch up with the radicals once again.[9]

The advanced Republicans had never permitted the President to forget their demands. The election was hardly over when Charles Sumner wrote to him:

> I venture to suggest whether the whole subject of "terms of reconstruction" does not properly belong to Congress. I make this remark with no other object than to secure harmony & unity. in our public counsels, which will render the Govt. irresistible.[1]

Browning, *Diary*, I, 686–7; F. P. Blair, Sr.–Hamlin, November 22, 1864, Hamlin Papers; Bates-Lincoln, October 13, 1864, Stanbery-Lincoln, October 31, 1864, Geiger-Lincoln, October 28, 1864, M. Waite–Lincoln, October 22, 1864, James Joy–Lincoln, October 31, 1864, Kelley-Lincoln, October 13, 1864, Colfax-Lincoln, October 23, 1864, Sumner-Lincoln, October 24, 1864, J. S. Morrill–Lincoln, November 2, 1864, RTL; Sumner-Chase, November 20, 1864, Chase Papers, HSP; Schuckers, *Chase*, pp. 487–8; Brooks, *Washington in Lincoln's Time*, pp. 174–7. The appointment of two radicals, William Dennison and James Harlan as Postmaster General and Secretary of the Interior, also showed that Lincoln was still cooperating. LaWanda and John H. Cox, *Politics, Principle and Prejudice, 1865–1866* (New York, 1963), pp. 42–43.

[9] William Best Hesseltine, *Lincoln's Plan of Reconstruction* (Tuscaloosa, Ala., 1963), p. 107; Sumner, *Works*, IX, 1–25.

[1] Sumner-Lincoln, November 20, 1864, RTL.

And while the President was by no means ready to accept this interpretation, he was not at all unwilling to accommodate his critics.

The reconstruction question came up as soon as Congress assembled in December, when it refused to accept the credentials of the Louisiana members, Wade in the Senate and Davis in the House presenting memorials against their admission. Neither the President nor the radicals, however, were anxious to bring about a breach between the White House and the Capitol, so that Ashley on December 14 introduced a new reconstruction measure which bore much greater similarity to Lincoln's scheme than did the Wade-Davis Bill. Scrapping the ten per cent provision, it proposed recognition of the Louisiana government while stipulating for the abolition of slavery. Lincoln immediately expressed his qualified agreement.[2]

It was evident that Negro suffrage complicated the Louisiana question. "The ballot for the negro is their only safety," wrote B. F. Flanders to Chase on January 10, 1865, "but I have little hope of that. Recognition of the present State Government would make that act of right, justice and safety, impossible for years to come." The Chief Justice agreed that it would be criminal not to give the vote to freedmen, and William D. Kelley proposed an amendment to Ashley's bill incorporating the reform. He could rely on radical support.

Because of a total lack of unanimity, Ashley's bill failed, and the controversy was not settled during Lincoln's lifetime. In February, Congress by overwhelming majorities voted to exclude Southern electoral votes from the presidential count and engaged in lengthy debates about Ashley's measure, the original Wade-Davis Bill, and various substitutes. The contest became so heated that one of the Louisiana claimants physically assaulted Kelley; however, none of the bills was brought to a vote before the session expired. "We killed the Louisiana Bill yesterday morning so dead

---

[2] McCarthy, *Lincoln's Plan of Reconstruction*, pp. 289 ff.; 341 ff.; Ashley's bill in RTL, December 15, 1864; Hay, *Diaries*, p. 244; H. W. Davis–S. F. DuPont, December 20, 1864, DuPont Papers.

that it will not pass this session," Chandler wrote to his wife. But the civil rights problem constituted a possible opening for compromise, and Lincoln was quick to seize upon it.[3]

The President, for the last time, gave every sign of attempting once more what he had accomplished so often in the past. Pushed forward by the radicals and held back by the conservatives, he proceeded to take steps at the right time and move in the direction of the extremists. Explaining the Louisiana problem in November to General Stephen A. Hurlbut, he had already stressed his concern for the rights of the freedmen. The state's new constitution, he emphasized, was "better for the poor black man than we have in Illinois." In March, he unhesitatingly signed the bill establishing a Freedmen's Bureau, a measure which the ultras had agitated for a long time to assist the powerless in the South.[4] In the spring of 1864, he had privately communicated his ideas on the suffrage to Governor Hahn; now, after the radicals had campaigned for the reform without let-up, he believed the time ripe for endorsing it in public. After receiving a letter from the Chief Justice pleading for the enrollment of loyal citizens without regard to complexion, Lincoln prepared to deliver what proved to be his last public speech. The date was April 11, 1865; Lee had surrendered his army, and the war was virtually over. Speaking of reconstruction, the President said:

> The amount of constituency, so to speak, on which the new Louisiana government rests, would be more satisfactory to all, if it contained fifty, thirty, or even twenty thousand, instead of only about twelve thousand, as it does. It is also unsatisfactory to some that the elective franchise is not given to the colored man. I would myself prefer that it were now conferred on the

[3] B. F. Flanders–Chase, January 10, 1865, Chase Papers, HSP; Schuckers, *Chase*, p. 514; McCarthy, *Lincoln's Plan of Reconstruction*, pp. 289 ff., 304–17; Nicolay and Hay, *Abraham Lincoln*, IX, 449–56; Chandler–Mrs. Chandler, February 27, 1865, Chandler Papers.

[4] Lincoln, *Works*, VIII, 106–8; Blaine, *Twenty Years of Congress*, II, 163; La Wanda Cox, "The Promise of Land for the Freedmen," *Mississippi Valley Historical Review*, XLV (December, 1958), 413–40; John G. Sproat, "Blueprint for Radical Reconstruction," *Journal of Southern History*, XXIII (February, 1957), 25–44; McPherson, *The Struggle for Equality*, pp. 178–91.

very intelligent, and on those who serve our cause as soldiers. Still the question is not whether the Louisiana government, as it stands, is quite all that is desirable. The question is, "Will it be wiser to take it as it is, and help to improve it?"

The President was approaching the radicals' position on reconstruction, and after the Cabinet meeting on the next day, Attorney General James Speed told Chase, "He never seemed so near our views." In December, the hostile Count Gurowski had written, "The great shifter, the great political shuffler, Abraham Lincoln, some day or other will turn up a radical."[5] His prediction, if not his assessment, was correct. As long as Lincoln's leadership prevailed, the radicals were able to bring about progress. Without him, things were going to be greatly different.

[5] Chase-Lincoln, April 11, 1865, RTL; Lincoln, *Works*, VIII, 399–405; Schuckers, *Chase*, pp. 578–9; Gurowski, *Diary*, III, 51. Lincoln demonstrated his skillful handling of both radicals and their opponents during his last days by not only moving in the direction of the former, but also keeping the latter satisfied by giving them patronage. Cf. Harry J. Carman and Reinhard H. Luthin, *Lincoln and the Patronage* (New York, 1943), pp. 314–15.

IX

The Break
with Johnson

ON GOOD FRIDAY, April 14, 1865, George W. Julian returned to Washington from Richmond, where the Committee on the Conduct of the War had been engaged on a fact-finding trip. Reaching the capital at 7 p.m., he went home and retired at ten thirty. Shortly afterward, he heard a loud knocking at the door. Assassins were about to take the town, he was told: the President and Secretary of State had been assaulted. Still half asleep and frightened, he felt himself growing "suddenly cold, heartsick, and almost helpless." At seven thirty in the morning, the tolling of the bells announced Lincoln's death. "Deep sorrow and revenge are almost universal feelings here, and I fear we are on the verge of a new & more terrible war than ever," Julian wrote to his wife. "Humanitarianism, I think, has met with a terrible shock."[1]

Humanitarianism had indeed met with a terrible shock. Lincoln's death removed from the helm the one man who had proved that he knew how to translate the radicals' demands into effective action. Many years later, Julian sorrowfully recalling that

---

[1] "George W. Julian's Journal . . . ," loc. cit., p. 334; Julian–Mrs. Julian, April 15, 1865, Julian Papers.

several of his colleagues at the time had been happy that the assassination had put an end to Lincoln's effort to implement conciliatory policies, commented:

> It was forgotten in the fever and turbulence of the moment, that Mr. Lincoln, who was never an obstinate man, and who in the matter of his Proclamation of Emancipation had surrendered his own judgment under the pressure of public opinion, would not have been likely to wrestle with Congress and the country in a mad struggle for his own way.

What Andrew Johnson would do was unknown.[2]

At the time of the assassination, few radicals were able to assess the crime in its true proportions. The members of the Committee on the Conduct of the War had rushed back from Richmond deeply distrustful of Lincoln. Having heard that he had given permission to General Geoffrey Weitzel, the Federal commander in the city, to permit the assembly of the Confederate legislature of Virginia, they had returned determined to protest. What they did not understand was the fact that the President had issued the directive under entirely different circumstances prior to Lee's surrender in hopes of bringing about an end to the war. But the Army of Northern Virginia laid down its arms at Appomattox; peace seemed imminent. Having long recognized the Pierpont administration in the Old Dominion and fully aware of radical opposition to the summoning of any "rebel" legislature, Lincoln reversed his instructions. The members of the committee could have continued their Southern trip; in spite of their fears, the President had again shown his willingness to move with events. But as they had always distrusted his efforts to bring about a negotiated peace—they had criticized F. P. Blair's trip to Richmond at the beginning of the year as well as the Hampton Roads conference between Lincoln and high Confederate officials in February—so they again misjudged his last attempt at peacemaking.[3]

[2] Julian, *Political Recollections*, p. 256.
[3] "George W. Julian's Journal . . . ," loc. cit., pp. 332–3; undated statement in the papers of B. B. French, entitled, "Facts worthy of

Lincoln's murder had a peculiar effect on the radicals. At a caucus in Washington, the participants could hardly hide their satisfaction at the turn of events. "Hostility towards Lincoln's policy of conciliation and contempt for his weakness were undisguised," commented Julian. "The universal feeling among radical men here is that his death is a god-send." The Massachusetts antislavery stalwart, F. W. Bird, expressing hope that Johnson would surround himself with wise advisers, added, "God alone is great," while George Loring, another Massachusetts politician, experienced a similar reaction. "Had another compromise been commended?" he queried. "And did God stand between it & his people?" Outwardly, the radicals preserved the proprieties. But their feelings could scarcely be concealed.[4]

In order to safeguard their interests, the ultras sought to re-establish their cordial relations with Andrew Johnson. They had thought well of him when he, alone among Southern senators, remained loyal in 1861; they had appreciated his service on the Committee on the Conduct of the War, and they knew that he had a reputation for strength. "They [the assassins] have assaulted their two best friends in the Government," commented General Heintzelman. "Andy Johnson is perfectly rabid and radical." James M. Ashley agreed. "The prayer of every loyal heart in this nation is, that God will bless, preserve and keep you from harm," he wrote to the President on the day of his accession to office. "I hope it is all for the best. You have been called by a most solemn event and in a perilous hour to discharge the most responsible office on earth." And the Committee on the Conduct of the War immediately asked Johnson for an interview.[5]

record," New York Historical Society; Randall and Current, *Lincoln the President*, pp. 354–6; *New York Times*, February 3, 7, 1865; Cincinnati *Gazette*, February 18, 1865.

[4] "George W. Julian's Journal . . . ," loc. cit., pp. 334–5; F. W. Bird–Sumner, April 15, 1865, Sumner Papers; George Loring–Butler, April 18, 1865, Butler Papers.

[5] Kenneth Stampp, *The Era of Reconstruction, 1865–1877* (New York, 1865), pp. 50–1; Sumner, *Works*, IX, 1; Samuel Heintzelman,

During the afternoon of April 15, Julian, Wade, Chandler, John Covode, and Judge David K. Cartter of the Supreme Court of the District of Columbia caucused in Washington. Betraying such ill-concealed satisfaction that even Julian thought their behavior disgusting, they sought to induce Samuel Wilkeson, the Washington correspondent of the New York *Tribune,* to prevail upon Horace Greeley to abandon his conciliatory tone. They also agreed that Johnson ought to appoint a new Cabinet. They would urge him to offer the State Department to Ben Butler; John Covode was their choice for Postmaster General.

On the next day, Easter Sunday, the members of the Committee on the Conduct of the War met with the new President. In a much-quoted interchange, the chairman addressed him: "Johnson, we have faith in you. By the gods, there will be no trouble now in running the government." The President replied that he was much obliged, and that he could only say:

> You can judge my policy by the past. Everybody knows what that is. I hold this: Robbery is a crime; rape is a crime; murder is a crime; *treason* is a crime, and *crime* must be punished. The law provides for it and the courts are open. Treason must be made infamous and traitors impoverished.

Greatly encouraged, the legislators left.

After their interview, the radical leaders met with General Butler, who expressed the opinion that the President must not "administer on the estate of Lincoln but on that of the Government, and select new men to do it." Charles Sumner was more specific. That very evening, he called on Stanton, who had drawn up a provisional plan for reconstruction. Taking advantage of Welles's presence, the senator emphasized the need for Negro suffrage.[6]

In the days that followed, there were frequent meetings between

---

MS Diary, April 15, 1865, Heintzelman Papers; Ashley-Johnson, April 15, 1865, Johnson Papers, LC; *JCCW* (*1865*), I, xxxvi.

[6] "George W. Julian's Journal . . . ," loc. cit., pp. 334–5; Welles, *Diary*, II, 291.

Johnson and various radicals. According to James G. Blaine, the President asked Wade what he would do if he were in his place, only to be told that the senator would either force into exile or hang about ten or twelve of the worst rebels, perhaps by way of good measure, thirteen, a baker's dozen. The President thought more ought to be executed, but Wade was opposed to large-scale vengeance. It would only cause an unfavorable reaction in the North. And although the radicals were fully aware of Johnson's friendly relations with the Blairs, they hoped to be able to counteract the family's conservative influence. The new Chief Executive's hatred for the Southern aristocracy was well known, and he invited General Butler to draw up a plan for the punishment of Confederate leaders. The general promptly complied.[7]

If the radicals were pleased with their first interviews with the new President, his actions during the next few weeks seemed to confirm their expectations. Shortly after Johnson's accession, General William T. Sherman negotiated surrender terms with General Joseph E. Johnston. Already dissatisfied with Grant's leniency at Appomattox, the ultras deeply distrusted Sherman, who, they feared, would try to be even more conciliatory than the lieutenant general. When the text of the convention became known in Washington, it confirmed the radicals' worst apprehensions. Thinking that he was carrying out Lincoln's wishes, Sherman had negotiated an agreement based upon the immediate restoration of full civil rights to the Confederates, including the recognition of the insurgent state legislatures!

Sherman's course infuriated the radicals. Characterizing the General's conduct as "in the highest degree criminal," Boutwell advocated a court-martial; Congressman Samuel Hooper acccused Sherman of delusions of grandeur, and the Committee on the Conduct of the War decided to postpone its adjournment in order to summon him. Even Senator John Sherman, the general's

[7] Julian–Mrs. Julian, April 17, 1865, Julian Papers; Browning, *Diary,* II, 22; Chandler–Mrs. Chandler, April 23, 1865, Chandler Papers; Blaine, *Twenty Years of Congress,* II, 14; Butler, *Correspondence,* V, 602–5; H. W. Davis–S. F. DuPont, April 22, 1865, DuPont Papers.

brother, expressed dismay. But to the radicals' great satisfaction, the Cabinet unanimously disapproved the proffered convention. As Chandler exulted to his wife, the President not only listened intently to his protest against Sherman's terms, but "took hold of the matter and condemned it worse than I did." Apparently the new Chief Executive was eager to cooperate.[8]

To most ultras, cooperation meant sympathy for Negro suffrage. While some radicals were willing to consider restricting the vote to those of both races who could read and write, in general they believed that impartial suffrage was not only an indispensable part of republican government, but that it was essential if the gains of the Civil War were not to be lost. "Looking at the matter for white men and not for the negro," wrote Horatio Woodman to Charles Sumner on April 24, "I should say that, if there is no other clear guarantee against the old oligarchy in each state getting control again, then either keep them out of Congress, or find a way to let negroes vote, and this practically not theoretically or philanthropically." Although Sumner could not be swayed by such an argument—he was completely dedicated to the principle of racial equality—there was little question about its relevance.[9] If the South were to be reconstructed without the freedmen's votes, only Democrats would be elected, and the Republican party would lose its majority in Congress. To make matters worse, after the next census, the lapse of the three-fifths compromise would give the South greater representation than ever before. Such a development

[8] William T. Sherman, *Memoirs of General William T. Sherman* (New York, 1913), II, 326–41, 346–57; Bancroft, *Speeches, Correspondence, and Political Papers of Carl Schurz*, I, 252–3; "George W. Julian's Journal . . . , loc. cit., p. 337; Boutwell–Sumner, April 26, 1865, Samuel Hooper–Sumner, April 24, 1865, Sumner Papers; Julian–Mrs. Julian, May 6, 1865, Julian Papers; John Sherman–Stanton, April 27, 1865, Stanton Papers; Chandler–Mrs. Chandler, April 23, 1865, Chandler Papers.

[9] Butler, *Correspondence*, V, 652; C. A. Dana–Sumner, September 1, 1865, Sumner Papers; J. W. Webb–Johnson, August 14, 1865, Wade Papers; Eric McKitrick, *Andrew Johnson and Reconstruction* (Chicago, 1960), pp. 55–8; Horatio Woodman–Sumner, April 24, 1865, Sumner Papers; Schurz, *Reminiscences*, III, 246.

would spell complete disaster, not merely for the dream of human rights for the liberated slaves, but also for the political fortunes of the party which had led the nation to victory. That any party in power, radical or not, would voluntarily consent to political suicide was not to be expected.

In the first days after the assassination, Sumner, who saw Johnson frequently, believed that the President favored universal suffrage. Late in April, the senator, accompanied by the Chief Justice, visited the Chief Executive. Chase was about to undertake a trip to the South, and Sumner understood that Johnson had authorized the Justice to promote reorganization without distinction of color. "I had looked for a bitter contest on this question," he wrote to Francis Lieber, "but with the President on our side it will be carried by simple *avoirdupois!*" Even the Massachusetts abolitionist George L. Stearns, emphasizing as he did the need for immediate enfranchisement of all Negroes, rejoiced that Johnson had advanced to "this position."[1]

Appearances, however, were deceiving. Johnson was not the radical some ultras believed him to be. The President was not only not an extremist, he was not even a bona fide Republican. A poor boy who had made good, he could never forget his humble origins, his hard lot as a tailor's apprentice, his running away from his master, his rise to state and national fame as a representative of the small East Tennessee craftsmen and farmers with whom he closely identified. Like these constituents he had always favored homestead legislation, opposed the slave-holding aristocracy, and maintained his fierce loyalty to the Union. But his love for the Union was part and parcel of his reverence for the Constitution of what he believed to be a simple agrarian republic based on sovereign states. The Negro had no real place in his scheme of things, and he never understood that the war had wrought tremendous transformations, social and industrial as well as constitutional, in America. The radicals' failure to assess Johnson

[1] Sumner-Lieber, May 2, 1865, G. L. Stearns–Sumner, May 8, 1865, Sumner Papers.

correctly was to have more serious consequences than their lack of understanding of Lincoln.[2]

Ironically, the ultras themselves bore some responsibility for the Tennessean's elevation to the Vice Presidency. The exact reasons for Hannibal Hamlin's replacement as Lincoln's running mate are still disputed, but it is certain that in 1864 Charles Sumner and the New England delegation had not been averse to the change. Sumner, who disliked Fessenden, had been anxious for Hamlin to take the place of the senator from Maine, and New England had not supported the Vice President effectively. Thaddeus Stevens, opposing these maneuvers from the start, had actively favored Hamlin. According to Alexander McClure, he had commented, "Can't you find a candidate for Vice President in the United States without going down to one of those damned rebel provinces to pick one up?" Henry Winter Davis, too, had distrusted Johnson, but other radicals had not made an issue about the nomination.[3]

Stevens and Davis had been more farsighted than their colleagues. In 1861, Johnson's famous resolution had asserted that the aim of the war was the preservation of the Union "with all the dignity, equality, and rights of the several States unimpaired," and there was no evidence that he had ever changed his mind. To be sure, he had voted for the Confiscation Acts, served on the Committee on the Conduct of the War, and administered Tennessee with an iron hand. But in November, 1863, he had written to Montgomery Blair that he hoped the President would not be committed to the notion of states relapsing into territories, and in

[2] Cf. Stampp, *The Era of Reconstruction,* pp. 55 ff.; George Fort Milton, *The Age of Hate, Andrew Johnson and the Radicals* (New York, 1930), pp. 59–97; Stryker, *Johnson,* pp. 1–12, 17–35.

[3] Hamlin, *Hamlin,* pp. 461–90, maintains that Lincoln was not involved in the change; McClure, *Lincoln and the Men of War-Times,* pp. 104 ff.; disagrees. A. H. Rice–Hamlin, June 13, 1864, Albert Smith–Hamlin, June 13, 1865, Robert Beale–Hamlin, June 5, 1864, Hamlin Papers; McClure, *Lincoln and the Men of War-Times,* p. 260; H. W. Davis–S. F. DuPont, June 4 or 5, 1864, DuPont Papers; Wilson, *History,* III, 578.

July, 1864, he had expressed his satisfaction with the pocket veto of the Wade-Davis Bill. Although he had believed strongly in taking all measures necessary to suppress the rebellion, he had never been an advocate of equal rights. Years later, Frederick Douglass maintained that the Vice President had been unable to hide his aversion to nonwhites when he spotted the Negro leader on inauguration day.[4]

Whatever the evidence, Sumner and his friends were somewhat contrite when, during the inauguration, the Vice President appeared to be intoxicated. In a caucus held shortly afterwards, they actually pressed for a motion demanding Johnson's resignation. When Wade, King, and Doolittle opposed it, however, it came to naught. Wade liked the former tailor from Tennessee who had fought with him for the Homestead Bill and had served with him on the Committee on the Conduct of the War. Believing "it wiser to take a more forbearing course," the members of the caucus took no action.[5]

The administration's honeymoon was to be short. On May 9, Johnson recognized Governor Pierpont's regime in Virginia. Although the state presented a special case because of the existence of the Alexandria government, the radicals were worried. "I see the President is precipitating things," Stevens wrote to Sumner.

> I fear before Congress meets he will have so bedeviled matters as to render them incurable. It would be well if he would call an extra session of Congress. But I despair of resisting Executive influence.

Carl Schurz warned Sumner that efforts were being made to hurry Southern states back into the Union, while Wade expressed

---

[4] Johnson–M. Blair, November 24, 1863, Johnson-Lincoln, July 13, 1864, RTL; Douglass, *Life and Times of Frederick Douglass,* p. 371.

[5] Chandler–Mrs. Chandler, March 6, 1865, Chandler Papers; Howe–Grace Howe, March 5, 1865, Howe Papers; Sumner-Lieber, March 8, 1865, Sumner Papers; A. G. Browne–Andrew, March 21, 1865, John A. Andrew Papers, Massachusetts Historical Society; H. W. Davis–S. P. DuPont, April 22, 1865, DuPont Papers; Welles, *Civil War and Reconstruction,* p. 215.

dismay that Johnson had not yet reorganized his Cabinet. Nevertheless, both Sumner and Wade still defended the Chief Executive. In a caucus on May 12 at the National Hotel, they insisted Johnson was in no danger. They were certain that he favored Negro suffrage.[6]

The ultras' continued faith in Johnson did not mean that they had abandoned their program. Just as they had succeeded in popularizing it during Lincoln's administration, so they tried again to prepare the President's way, by pressure as well as by propaganda. Kelley, who invoked Lincoln's authority in a public address pleading for Negro suffrage, strongly urged the President to adopt the reform. Sumner constantly advised the same thing, and Stevens on May 16 warned Johnson that reconstruction was a subject within the competence of the legislative branch. "While I think we shall agree with you almost unanimously as to the main objects you have in view," he wrote, "I fear we may differ as to the manner of effecting them." Let the President call a special session of Congress. Chase also offered advice. Before leaving for the South, he told Johnson the people of the former Confederate States ought to be directed to recognize Negroes as citizens with the right to vote, an idea he continued to advocate in letters from South Carolina. Even in Johnson's own Cabinet, Stanton, Dennison, and Speed favored enfranchising the Negroes and said so. And on May 22, the Committee on the Conduct of the War issued its final reports.[7]

The committee's 1865 reports, like those in 1863, constituted

[6] Richardson, *Messages and Papers of the Presidents*, VI, 337; Stevens-Sumner, May 10, 1865, Sumner Papers; Bancroft, *Speeches, Correspondence, and Political Papers of Carl Schurz*, I, 254–5; Wade-Butler, May 9, 1865, Butler Papers; Julian, *Political Recollections*, p. 263.

[7] Philadelphia *Daily Telegraph*, April 26, 1865; Pierce, *Sumner*, IV, 241; Kelley-Johnson, May 12, 1865; Stevens-Johnson, May 16, 1865, Johnson Papers; Schuckers, *Chase*, p. 521; Chase, *Diaries*, p. 270; Welles, *Diary*, II, 301–2; *New York Times*, May 23, 1865. James Speed became Attorney General after the resignation of Edward Bates.

an all-out defense of the radical position. Some of them had appeared in newspapers before, but the impact of the publication of the entire set was notable. Wade and his associates had labored diligently to present their side of the story. Reminding the public of the horrors of the rebellion, they expressed great pride in the nation's accomplishments. They counterbalanced condemnation of conservative generals like Meade, Banks, and McClellan with praise for radicals like Burnside, Hooker, and Butler. And as if to highlight the importance of Negro aid in the rebuilding of the nation, they severely censured Meade's failure to rely fully on colored troops during the Battle of the Crater at Petersburg. So enthusiastically did radical newspapers welcome the reports and praise the committee's work that observers might well have concluded that its members were among the most farsighted statesmen in the country.[8]

Unlike his predecessor, however, Johnson was not openminded. Unwilling to profit from the radicals' suggestions, he began to show that his conception of reconstruction was entirely different. When speaking about punishment for the leaders of the Confederacy, he had sounded radical enough, but when it came to the rebuilding of the nation, he was determined to carry out a plan which he believed to have had Lincoln's sanction: the restoration of all the Southern states within the shortest possible time. Since Negro suffrage would only stand in the way, he was loath to complicate his efforts with a proposal so unpopular in the South. What he forgot was that Lincoln had always insisted on flexibility, that he had conceived of his plan as merely one of several possibilities, and, above all, that he had always welcomed constructive criticism.

In spite of his recognition of Virginia, in the early spring of 1865 Johnson's true intentions were still unknown. On May 29, however, when he issued a general amnesty proclamation and

[8] *JCCW* (*1865*); portions of the report on the Petersburg mine disaster had appeared in February. New York *Tribune,* February 7, 1865. For the reception of the final reports, cf. New York *Tribune,* May 19, 23, 31, 1865; Cincinnati *Daily Gazette,* May 20, 23, 1865.

appointed William W. Holden provisional governor of North Carolina, the outlines of his scheme began to emerge. Scrapping Lincoln's ten-per-cent provision and adding to the list of persons exempted from the amnesty those whose taxable property amounted to more than $20,000, he called for rapid reestablishment of regular government. The governor was to supervise the calling of a convention based on the old electorate; a loyal administration was to be revived, and the state restored to its normal relation to the Union.[9]

The radicals were horrified. "Shall we acquiesce in the policy of the administration," wrote the Missouri congressman, Benjamin Loan, to Sumner,

> or shall we adhere to our former views that Congress alone is authorized to deal with the subject of reconstruction and that our safety and the peace of the country requires us to disenfranchise the rebels and to enfranchise the colored citizens in the revolted states and thereby confide the political power therein to local and therefore safe hands.

Much as he deprecated the existence of differences between the Executive and "the radical union members of Congress," he believed it to be much more disastrous to abandon "our principles." Stevens queried whether there was any possibility of devising a plan to arrest the government "in its present ruinous career"; Schurz sounded the alarm to Sumner, and the senator from Massachusetts himself called on Wade to deliver a speech or write a letter to set Johnson straight. "How easy it was to be right," he commented. "The President seems to have made an effort to be wrong." To Stevens, whom he asked to see Johnson, he sent an urgent plea for speeches and action. "The North was ready for the true doctrine and practice," he complained. "It is hard—very hard to be driven to another contest." Henry Winter Davis, asserting that Negro suffrage was absolutely essential despite the North Carolina Proclamation, proposed a constitutional amendment to secure it, while Jacob Howard expressed the opinion that Congress

[9] Richardson, *Messages and Papers of the Presidents,* VI, 310–14.

would "have the d---l to pay with . . . rebel states" because of the President's policy.[1]

But the ultras still had hope. It seemed incredible that the President was permanently lost to them. Only recently he had appeared to be one of them; obviously he was merely surrounded by bad advisers. What was needed was counteraction, and the leading radicals sought to supply it. To stop the President's scheme, they still believed that the same sort of effort they had made before would be effective. Urging, cajoling, organizing in favor of universal suffrage might bring about the desired result. They had often succeeded in changing Lincoln's mind; why should they not succeed with Johnson?

They did not waste any time. On June 1, Sumner delivered a eulogy on Lincoln before the municipal authorities of Boston. Using the occasion to stress the murdered hero's devotion to the Declaration of Independence and his commitment to emancipation, the senator argued that the only way in which Lincoln's ideas could be perpetuated was through universal suffrage. On the Fourth of July, Henry Winter Davis at Chicago eloquently pleaded for enfranchisement of the freedmen, and Ben Butler went even further. The flamboyant general, who in January had been summarily relieved after his failure to capture Fort Fisher, had lost none of his confidence. In a speech on June 17 at Lowell, Massachusetts, he recommended that forfeited lands be distributed among colored veterans. While the Union League Club of New York passed resolutions endorsing equal voting rights in the South, the old abolitionists, especially Wendell Phillips, were indefatigably active on behalf of universal suffrage. They even contributed to the establishment of the new weekly magazine,

[1] Benjamin Loan–Sumner, June 1, 1865, Stevens-Sumner, June 3, 1865, Davis-Sumner, June 22, 1865, Howard-Sumner, June 22, 1865, Sumner Papers; Bancroft, *Speeches, Correspondence, and Political Papers of Carl Schurz*, I, 258–60; Sumner-Wade, June 9, 12, 1865, Wade Papers; Sumner-Stevens, June 19, 1865, Stevens Papers.

The Nation, in the hope that the editor, E. L. Godkin, would popularize the cause.[2]

The radicals did not confine themselves to propaganda alone. Seeking to dissuade Johnson from his course by direct appeals, they freely offered their advice. Within a few days of the publication of the North Carolina proclamation, Carl Schurz warned the President that his policy was dangerous. It was necessary to have all loyal inhabitants vote for state conventions, he advised, suggesting that the idea be incorporated in the forthcoming proclamation reorganizing South Carolina. Robert Dale Owen, in a nineteen-page letter, cautioned the President not to overlook the implications of the lapse of the three-fifths compromise. Negro suffrage was the only answer, he pleaded, pointing out that it was "not conceivable that Northern voters, fresh from victory," would agree "that the men they conquered shall have three votes for President and Representative to their one." Stevens urged Johnson to hold his hand and wait the action of Congress; Maryland Republicans warned against the conservatives, and Sumner and Chase persisted in reminding the administration of their belief in votes for all loyal citizens. At the end of the month, Wade, Stevens, and Henry Winter Davis came to Washington in person to win over the President. Wade especially had no desire to break with him.[3]

But the President did not react to pressure as Lincoln had responded. Although he still sought to assuage his critics—Secretary of the Interior James Harlan tried to convince the radicals of

[2] Sumner-Wade, June 12, 1865, Wade Papers; Sumner, *Works,* IX, 367–428; *The Fourth of July in Chicago: Oration of Henry Winter Davis of Maryland, Delivered at the Great Sanitary Hall, July 4, 1865* (Chicago, 1865); *New York Times,* June 3, 19, 1865; Bellows, *Historical Sketch of the Union League Club of New York, p.* 87; McPherson, *The Struggle for Equality,* pp. 320 ff.; William M. Armstrong, *E. L. Godkin and American Foreign Policy, 1856–1900* (New York, 1957), pp. 18–19.

[3] Schurz-Johnson, June 6, 1865, R. D. Owen–Johnson, June 21, 1865, Stevens-Johnson, July 6, 1865, W. G. Snethen–Johnson, July 19, 1865, Sumner-Johnson, June 30, 1865, Johnson Papers; Welles, *Diary,* II, 343, 325; Welles, *Civil War and Reconstruction,* p. 215.

the purity of Johnson's intentions—he extended the application of his plan of reconstruction to the remaining Southern states. In those commonwealths in which Lincoln had inaugurated the process, Johnson maintained the governments already in power; but unlike the Great Emancipator, he did not attempt to compromise the differences between the various local factions. His sympathies were with the conservatives, and he made so little effort to hide this fact that in Louisiana, even the moderate Michael Hahn found the new government distasteful. J. Madison Wells, his more conservative successor as governor, enjoyed Johnson's full support.[4]

How hostile the President was to the radicals he showed in August. In a letter to William L. Sharkey, his own appointee as governor of Mississippi, he made it clear that he expected the state to adopt the Thirteenth Amendment. Then he turned to the problem of the suffrage. "If you could extend the elective franchise to all persons of color who can read the Constitution of the United States in English and write their names," he suggested,

> and to all persons of color who own real estate valued at not less than two hundred and fifty dollars and pay taxes thereon, you would completely disarm the adversary. . . . This you can do with perfect safety. . . . And as a consequence, the radicals, who are wild upon negro franchise, will be completely foiled in their attempts to keep the Southern States from renewing their relations to the Union. . . .

The ultras could still try to pave the way, but there was no executive ready to follow where they were leading.[5]

In view of the multiplying signs of Johnson's true intentions, the radicals' extreme caution—their reluctance to believe

[4] James Harlan–E. B. Washburne, June 12, 1865, Washburne Papers; Harlan-Sumner, June 15, 19, 1865, Michael Hahn–Sumner, October 6, 1865, Sumner Papers; Madison Wells–Johnson, July 5, 1865, Johnson Papers; Stryker, *Johnson*, pp. 219–20.

[5] Walter Fleming, *Documentary History of Reconstruction* (New York, 1906), I, 177.

that the President had really left them—is remarkable. James Harlan, the sympathetic Secretary of the Interior, expressing his conviction that everything would turn out all right, cautioned them not to drive Johnson into the arms of the Democrats. Republicans must not break with the President lest the opposition benefit—this was the position taken not merely by Secretary Harlan, but also by others. Perhaps the North Carolina scheme was merely temporary, thought Boutwell, and Howard agreed with him. When Wade came to Washington in June, he indulged in hopes "that the President might be brought into the views of the Radicals"; Trumbull announced that he was a Johnsonian, and Henry Wilson stressed the necessity of attempting to stand by the administration. In July, even Thaddeus Stevens offered friendly advice to the White House; nor did he fail to express faith in the President when on September 7 he developed fully his own plan of reconstruction, confiscation of land and its distribution to freedmen. Johnson, he said, would eventually agree. Butler also argued that differences with the President did not necessarily constitute a deep disagreement, and James Medill warned Johnson not to "show so much eagerness to rush into the embrace of the '$20,000' rebels." They could not be relied upon. "Better stick close to old friends who carried you into the White House than to exchange them for Copperheads & rebels . . . ," he admonished. "The great doctrine of *equal rights* is bound to prevail. It is your high privilege to lead the column." In October, the abolitionist Moncure Conway still had a good word to say about the President; in November, while J. M. Howard counseled that radicals do all in their power to prevent a rupture, Henry Winter Davis was trying to reach an agreement with the White House, and when in December Congress met, Sumner and Stevens visited Johnson. They all tried to stay the impending rift.[6]

[6] Harlan-Sumner, August 25, 1865, Boutwell-Sumner, June 12, 1865, Charles Dana–Sumner, September 1, 1865, Howard-Sumner, July 26, 1865, Wilson-Sumner, September 9, 1865, M. Conway–Sumner, October 16, 1865, Howard-Sumner, November 12, 1865, Sumner-Lieber, December 3, 1865, Sumner Papers; Welles, *Civil War*

But in spite of their reluctance to break with Johnson, many ultras were becoming increasingly discouraged during the late summer and fall. "The President has evidently gone away from the true path for good," Chase's son-in-law informed him in September. "I fear we are ruined," wrote Stevens to Sumner in October, when Sumner regretfully stated that he had hoped for peace and tranquillity but that he was still doomed to "strife and controversy." Wade was so disgusted that he contemplated a Negro insurrection in the South. "After all it may be that President Johnson means well in all that he has been doing," he wrote. "If so it is but an additional proof that the road to hell is paved with good intentions."[7]

———————

Prospects were not quite so unpromising as the radicals feared. Butler had for some time entertained hope that the "rebels" would behave "so outrageously as to awaken the Government and the North," and his wish soon came true. The new regimes established by Andrew Johnson not only showed little grace in repealing the secession ordinances and ratifying the antislavery amendment, but drew up black codes so harsh as to constitute thinly veiled attempts to reinstitute slavery. Some governors delivered contumacious speeches, while the legislatures sent to the Senate unpardoned Confederates of high rank, including the former Vice President of the Confederacy, Alexander H. Stephens. The President's policies had shortcomings.[8]

Making the most of Southern defiance, the radicals sought to convert as many people as possible to a more thorough method

———————

and Reconstruction, p. 215; Stevens-Johnson, July 6, 1865, Medill-Johnson, September 15, 1865, Johnson Papers; Welles, *Diary*, II, 322; Benjamin B. Kendrick, *The Journal of the Joint Committee of Fifteen on Reconstruction* (New York, 1914), p. 139.

[7] William Sprague–Chase, September 6, 1865, Chase Papers, LC; Stevens-Sumner, October 7, 1865, Howard-Sumner, November 12, 1865, Wade-Sumner, November 1, 1865, Sumner Papers; Sumner-Chase, October, 1865, Chase Papers, HSP.

[8] Butler-Wade, July 26, 1865, Wade Papers; *New York Times*, July 20, 1865; John Hope Franklin, *Reconstruction After the Civil War* (Chicago, 1961), pp. 40–53.

of reconstruction. In an address at his home, Thaddeus Stevens advocated not merely civil rights for Negroes, but demanded that the property of all insurgents worth more than $10,000 be confiscated, their lands to be parceled out to freedmen in forty-acre lots and the rest to be used to pay off the national debt. Sumner continued to agitate for Negro suffrage; Colfax warned the South that it must furnish some proof of sincerity before it could be restored to full fellowship; and Butler demanded that colored veterans at least be given the franchise. "We, the Union men of Massachusetts also endorse President Johnson's policy as we understand it," he said, explaining that if Johnson could determine that certain rebels could vote, he could also enfranchise the Negroes.[9]

But the President refused to listen. Reassured by conservatives that the radicals constituted only a small and malignant faction, he insisted on pressing his program upon Congress and implemented it by granting pardons on a large scale. Fundamentally a Jacksonian Democrat firmly wedded to the federal system and white supremacy, in the long run, he dreamed of bringing about a new coalition of conservative Republicans and Democrats with himself as leader.[1]

Johnson's plans were by no means farfetched. Tired of war, weary of racial problems, and anxious to see peace and tranquility restored, the majority of American voters would probably gladly have endorsed any scheme that promised to bring to an end the issues of the "great rebellion." Senator Doolittle estimated that two thirds of all Republicans would follow the President, influential newspapers like the New York *Herald* welcomed the formation of a constitutional party sustaining him, and in the fall elections, several Northern states defeated propositions

[9] *New York Times,* September 10, 1865; Sumner, *Works,* IX, 437–88; New York *Herald,* November 19, 1865; *Commonwealth,* September 23, 1865.

[1] *New York Times,* June 20, 22, 23, 27, 30, 1865; Jonathan T. Dorris, *Pardon and Amnesty Under Lincoln and Johnson: The Restoration of the Confederates to Their Rights and Privileges* (Chapel Hill, 1953), pp. 140, 314 ff.; Cox and Cox, *Politics, Principle, and Prejudice,* pp. viii, 172 ff.

to enfranchise the Negroes.[2] With some skill and finesse, he might have succeeded.

But was his success desirable? That his program left much to be desired has been pointed out many times. John Hope Franklin has termed it "Reconstruction: Confederate Style"; W. E. B. Du Bois, in his book, *Black Reconstruction,* has called the chapter dealing with it, "Looking Backward," and Kenneth Stampp has been equally emphatic in denouncing the "pattern of disenfranchisement, discrimination, and segregation," which the Johnson governments inaugurated. It was not for doctrinaire reasons that the advanced Republicans broke with the President; the evidence that their efforts were needed was overwhelming.[3]

The war was hardly over when Southern Unionists pleaded for protection. "The Union men of this State are more troubled by the arrogance of the recently returned rebel soldiers & others from Richmond than they were by the armed guerillas a month ago . . . ," wrote Virginia Republican John C. Underwood to Chase on April 28, 1865. "It seems to me that a *little* vigor now would be worth more than *much* hereafter." Moncure Conway a few months later found similar conditions in the Old Dominion, and newspapers showed that in North Carolina, too, Negroes and Unionists were in a precarious situation. In South Carolina, according to General Quincy A. Gillmore, there were simply not enough loyal people to warrant speedy restoration; the whites resented emancipation, put their hopes in Johnson and his appointees, and the Negroes were worried. In the Sea Islands, returned Confederate soldiers appeared to be as rebellious as in 1861; John Covode found reaction gaining the upper hand in Louisiana, and Carl Schurz reported doleful conditions in Georgia and Mississippi. "It is important that the Government as well as the people should understand that things are very far from being ripe

[2] J. R. Doolittle–Johnson, September 2, 1865, Johnson Papers; New York *Herald,* September 18, October 16, 1865; McPherson, *The Struggle for Equality,* pp. 333–4.

[3] Franklin, *Reconstruction After the Civil War,* p. 53; W. E. Burghardt Du Bois, *Black Reconstruction* (New York, 1935), pp. 128 ff.; Stampp, *The Era of Reconstruction,* p. 82.

yet for the restoration of civil government," he wrote to Sumner. Even the conservative Secretary of the Navy considered the "tone and sentiment of the people of the South . . . injudicious and indiscreet," and the *New York Times,* one of the leading nonradical organs, printed reports of atrocities against freedmen.[4]

Conditions did not improve with the passage of time; if anything, they became worse. In August, Thomas W. Conway, Assistant Commissioner of the Freedmen's Bureau at New Orleans, put the matter bluntly in a letter to Chase. "I am convinced by a thousand facts . . .," he wrote,

> that unless something like Mr. Sumner's plan of reducing the rebel states to a territorial basis [is adopted], we shall have endless anarchy and revolution. What may we not expect a year or two hence, when our bayonets are withdrawn, if now, right in their presence, police juries and civil court, enact laws and ordinances every whit as bad as was the famous 'Black Code'?

In Mississippi, Trumbull learned, the state convention was as proslavery as its secessionist predecessor. In North Carolina, averred a local Unionist, men of his persuasion were lost should Congress admit "rebels" and modify the test oath. So bad was the situation in the state that even Governor William W. Holden, himself Johnson's appointee, warned the President to beware of a resurgence of secessionist activity. Benjamin Truman, whom the President himself had sent to the South to furnish a conservative corrective to radical reports, emphasized that in the Georgia convention, "the utmost malignity and meanness and ingratitude were manifest." And in Texas, where no government had been organized by the time Congress met, things were no better. "If Congress does not promptly rescue us from a premature organization," a local correspondent warned Chase, "we shall be placed

[4] J. C. Underwood–Chase, April 28, 1865, Chase Papers, LC; Moncure Conway–Sumner, July 29, 1865, Sumner Papers; *New York Times,* June 26, August 1, 1865; Q. A. Gillmore–Chase, August 22, 1865, Chase Papers, HSP; M. S. Littlefield–Trumbull, May 8, 1865, Trumbull Papers, LC; Covode-Wade, July 11, 1865, Wade Papers; Bancroft, *Speeches, Correspondence, and Political Papers of Carl Schurz,* I, 267–8; Welles, *Diary,* II, 347–8.

bound hand and foot in the hands of our old political opponents." The former Southern slaveholder who wrote Stevens that it would be barbarous to leave the Negro to be dealt with by those whose prejudices were of the most bitter character against him was right. As he put it, "Whatever genuine Union sentiment was forming and would in time have grown up, has been checked by Mr. Johnson's course."[5]

In view of these circumstances, the radicals had every reason to act. And once they had made up their minds that the President's course must be arrested, they did their work thoroughly. By incessantly keeping the problem of government by unrepentent "rebels" before the people, they put Johnson's actions in an impossible light, and by occasionally playing down their demands for Negro suffrage, they enlisted moderate support. All in all, they enabled the electorate gradually to come up to their position. In this way, they managed to undo Johnson's scheme of reconstruction; they even succeeded in embedding long-range gains in the Constitution; in the absence of a great leader in the White House, however, despite all appearances, they were unable to prevail in the end.

The radicals' parliamentary skill had impressed observers ever since the meeting of Congress in December, 1865. A minority within their own party, lacking firm organization and not even clearly defined as a group, under Thaddeus Stevens's leadership they devised the strategy of referring all matters concerning restoration to a Joint Committee of Fifteen on Reconstruction. Pending its decisions, no representative from any formerly insurgent state could be admitted. How Congress assembled, how the clerk of the House of Representatives, Stevens's friend Edward McPherson, read the roll omitting all Southern claimants, includ-

[5] T. W. Conway–Chase, August 8, 1865, W. Alexander–Chase, December 21, 1865, Chase Papers, LC; C. E. Lippincott–Trumbull, August 29, 1865, Trumbull Papers, LC; Holden-Johnson, October 5, 1865, B. Truman–W. A. Browning, November 9, 1865, Johnson Papers; R. W. Flournoy–Stevens, November 20, 1865, Stevens Papers.

ing even the unquestionably loyal Horace Maynard of Tennessee, and how the House was organized without the Southern members has often been told. Thaddeus Stevens has justly been credited with the strategy which was adopted, but the onus for the break with Johnson has generally been placed upon the radicals.[6]

In reality, in spite of their disappointment, the ultras were still willing to come to an agreement with the White House. Stevens himself, on the Wednesday before the opening of Congress, visited the President to see whether Johnson would not cooperate. Sumner, too, made it clear that he wanted to cultivate friendly relations with the Chief Executive. He said so to George Bancroft, the historian who had just prepared Johnson's annual message, and on December 3, went to the White House, where he conversed with the President for two and a half hours. The interview began pleasantly enough, but Sumner concluded that his host did not understand the situation. That the President used Sumner's hat, which was on the floor next to the senator's chair, as a spittoon, did not improve matters. Nevertheless, Horace Greeley wrote to Speaker Schuyler Colfax, "I pray you to take care that we do nothing calculated to drive the President into the arms of our adversaries. Let us respect his convictions and thus impel him to respect ours." Ben Wade also tried to see the President once more, but he found the antechamber so full of Democrats and Confederate sympathizers that he concluded his mission was fruitless.[7] Supported by Democrats, Southerners, and some conservative Republicans who sympathized with his policies and opposed the radicals' insistence on further protection for the freedmen, Johnson was determined to have his own way.

[6] Milton, *The Age of Hate*, pp. 265–8; Stryker, *Johnson*, pp. 231–6; Howard K. Beale, *The Critical Year, A Study of Andrew Johnson and Reconstruction* (2d ed., New York, 1958), pp. 74–5; William Archibald Dunning, *Reconstruction, Political and Economic, 1865–1877* (New York, 1907), pp. 51 ff.

[7] Kendrick, *The Journal of the Joint Committee of Fifteen on Reconstruction*, p. 139; Bancroft-Johnson, December 1, 1865, Johnson Papers; Sumner-Lieber, December 3, 1865, Sumner Papers; Greeley-Colfax, December 11, 1865, Greeley Papers; *New York Times*, November 8, 1867.

But the radicals were not disposed to give in. While the most advanced Republicans—men like Ashley, Sumner, Stevens, Wade, Wilson, and Chandler—were not representative of the aspirations of the average member of the party, they knew that their insistence on safeguarding the Negroes' rights lest former "rebels" join hands with the Democrats enjoyed the support of the broad majority of their colleagues in and out of Congress. Accordingly, while they saw to it that their ultimate aims were publicized, many of them were willing to settle for far less.

The radical leaders worked ceaselessly to popularize their ideas. In an article entitled, "Clemency and Common Sense," in the *Atlantic Monthly* of December, 1865, Sumner argued that justice demanded protection for friends and allies. They must not be handed over to the "tender mercies of . . . pardoned criminals," he maintained, emphasizing that clemency had limitations. Carl Schurz's report on conditions in the South, which asserted that former Confederates were neither loyal nor disposed to grant elementary rights to their former slaves, pointed to Negro suffrage as a solution. The document was widely circulated, and stories of outrages in the Southern states appeared in radical newspapers. Northern readers might not care for Negro suffrage, but they had no desire to see their Southern adversaries reassert themselves.[8]

The most effective arena for propaganda was the floor of Congress, where the radicals were helped by the provocative presence of many Southern claimants for membership who nine months earlier had still served in the Confederate army. On the very first day of the session, Sumner offered resolutions to extend the suffrage to Southern freedmen; Wade in the Senate introduced a bill to enfranchise the Negroes in the District of Columbia, and Kelley soon sponsored the measure in the House. On December 18, Thaddeus Stevens delivered a speech calling for the reduction of the former insurgent states to territorial status; they could not

[8] Sumner, *Works,* IX, 503 ff.; X, 47–54; Schurz, *Reminiscences,* III, 204–9; *Commonwealth,* October 7, 1865; *Independent,* January 25, February 19, 1866.

regain representation in Congress, he maintained, until the Constitution was amended to eliminate the three-fifths clause. "This is not a 'white man's Government' . . . ," he thundered. "To say so is political blasphemy, for it violates the fundamental principles of our gospel of liberty." He himself advocated homesteads for Negroes. On the next day, Sumner characterized Johnson's state paper and General Grant's moderate report, which accompanied it, "a whitewashing message," and called for the reading of Schurz's findings instead. Then, on the twentieth, he delivered a speech calling for complete enfranchisement of the freedmen. On December 19, Ashley introduced a bill providing for reconstruction based on Negro suffrage; on January 8, Shellabarger announced to the House that no state could be readmitted until it had given proof of loyalty; on the tenth, Kelley called for universal suffrage, and on the same day, Timothy O. Howe introduced in the Senate resolutions for the establishment of provisional governments in the "districts" embracing the former Confederacy. He too explained them carefully in a supporting speech. And on February 22, the Maryland ultra J. A. J. Creswell, amid imposing ceremonies on Capitol Hill, delivered a eulogy on the recently deceased Henry Winter Davis, who had been considered one of the radicals' chief oracles. Since many of these speeches went out into the country in pamphlet form, no one could doubt which way the radicals wanted to go.[9]

But in spite of these assaults on the President's program, the radicals were still hopeful of coming to terms with him. Always

[9] *Cong. Globe*, 39th Cong., 1st Sess., 1–2, 10, 72, 78–9, 90–7, 142–5, 181–3, 162, 163–7; Steiner, *Davis*, pp. 285–7; *Speech of the Honorable Charles Sumner, of Massachusetts, on the Bill to Maintain the Freedom of the Inhabitants in the States Declared in Insurrection and Rebellion by the Proclamation of the President of July 1, 1862, Delivered in the Senate of the United States, December 20, 1865* (Washington, 1865); *Speech of the Hon. S. Shellabarger, of Ohio, Delivered in the House of Representatives, January 8, 1866* (Washington, 1866); *Suffrage in the District of Columbia*, pamphlet of Kelley's speech, January 6, 1866 (n.p., n.d.); Welles, *Diary*, II, 438.

having differed with the Executive, many of them could not see that their controversies with Johnson were of a nature entirely dissimilar from previous misunderstandings with Lincoln. As Boutwell on December 29 wrote to Butler, "There is a clear way for the President if he can only be induced to take it without any inconsistency on his part." A few days later, the ultraradical *Independent* praised Johnson highly for permitting Negroes as well as whites to visit him at the White House on New Year's Day; the House passed a resolution of confidence in the President's willingness to join with Congress in restoring the Southern states, and on Thaddeus Stevens's motion, a subcommittee of the reconstruction committee waited upon Johnson to seek his cooperation. The interview was a friendly one, the President conveying the impression that he would not move precipitously. Robert C. Schenck, in a speech at Columbus advocating an amendment to repeal the three-fifths compromise, also voiced the opinion that Congress and the President would come together in demanding the change. And while Sumner bitterly condemned the administration's policy, he too told the Secretary of the Navy that Congress would commence no war upon the President. Toward the end of the month, at a party given by Senator Ira Harris of New York, Wilson also met Welles. Taking the Secretary aside, he asked whether a break was intended. And as late as February 10, Julian went to see the Chief Executive. "I think I shall have no trouble with him for a while at least," he informed his wife. For a group which was allegedly aggressive, the radicals showed remarkable patience.[1]

It was in the Cabinet that the radicals' forebearance was most notable. To be sure, Seward, Welles, and Hugh McCulloch, Fessenden's successor in the Treasury, sympathized with Johnson's program, but the other members were either hostile or lukewarm

[1] Boutwell-Butler, December 29, 1865, Butler Papers; Edward McPherson, *The Political History of the United States During the Period of Reconstruction* (3d ed., Washington, 1880), p. 111 (hereafter cited as McPherson, *Reconstruction*); Kendrick *The Journal of the Joint Committee of Fifteen on Reconstruction*, pp. 39–40; *Independent*, January 4, 1866; New York *Herald*, January 6, 1866; Welles, *Diary*, II, 415, 393, 397, 421–2.

to it. Secretary of the Interior Harlan tried to bridge the gap between his radical friends and his chief; Postmaster General Dennison and Attorney General Speed did not resign until the summer of 1866, and Secretary of War Stanton, secretive and deep within the radicals' confidence, also waited for the President to make the decisive move. The extremist members made every effort to keep the peace. They were singularly unsuccessful.[2]

Perhaps the best indication of the lengths to which Johnson would go in his refusal to heed his party was his veto of the Freedmen's Bureau Bill. Drawn up by Lyman Trumbull, the measure could not be considered extreme. The senator from Illinois, one of the least doctrinaire radicals if a radical at all, had shown during the 1862 debates about the Confiscation Bill that he was anything but an ultra. In fact, by 1866, he could well be called a moderate, and in December and January, he sought to act as a peacemaker. His bill, which would merely have extended the life and expanded the functions of the Freedmen's Bureau, passed by large majorities. To make certain of the President's assent, some radicals proposed the admission of Tennessee as a *quid pro quo*. But Johnson was adamant. No matter that Stanton, Speed, and Harlan expressed regret; no matter that even the sympathetic Gideon Welles was disturbed at Trumbull's probable alienation, the President, convinced of the soundness of his constitutional views which were shared by many conservatives afraid of the expansion of federal power, insisted on a veto. Contrary to his collaborators' advice, he made his message unnecessarily offensive by casting doubt on Congress's right to legislate as long as any states were unrepresented. Calling attention to the principle of "no taxation without representation," he declared:

> I would not interfere with the unquestionable right of Congress to judge, each House for itself, "of the elections, returns, and qualifications of its own members"; but that authority cannot

[2] Ibid. pp. 481–2, 523–5; Browning, *Diary*, II, 74; Harlan-Sumner, September 11, 1865, Sumner Papers; Harlan-Trumbull, February 26, 1866, Trumbull Papers, LC; Thomas and Hyman, *Stanton*, p. 465; Milton, *The Age of Hate*, p. 340.

be construed as including the right to shut out in time of peace
any State from the representation to which it is entitled. . . .

Then, to make matters worse, on Washington's Birthday, he
publicly called Sumner, Stevens, and Wendell Phillips traitors.[3]

Johnson's remarks were widely denounced—dastardly, the
Commonwealth called them—but some radicals still hoped for
a settlement. Trumbull was working on a civil rights bill which
he repeatedly submitted to the President for his approval; Senator
William M. Stewart of Nevada brought forward a double proposal for universal amnesty coupled with universal suffrage, and
Chase was sanguine that the differences between the executive and
legislative departments might still be reconciled. "I see no reason
why they may not be with good intention on both sides," he wrote
on March 14. Johnson, however, persisted in his course. Possibly
emboldened by the fact that the Senate had sustained his veto of
the Freedmen's Bureau Bill, he took a dim view of the Civil
Rights Bill which sought to guarantee the freedmen's privileges
of citizenship. That the radicals were gaining strength because of
the ejection of Senator John P. Stockton of New Jersey did not
faze him. Disapproving of the measure on principle and determined to have his own way, on March 27 he vetoed it.[4]

The excitement which followed, the speedy repassage of the
bill in the House, and the dramatic scene in the Senate, where
Wade announced his willingness to take advantage of the absence
of a sick colleague "if God Almighty has stricken one member so

[3] Krug, *Trumbull*, p. 190; A. C. Fuller–Trumbull, December 27,
1865, F. A. Eastman–Trumbull, January 4, 1866, D. L. Phillips–
Trumbull, January 7, 1866, N. Bateman–Trumbull, January 15, 1866,
Trumbull Papers, LC; Blaine, *Twenty Years of Congress,* II, 162–70;
Welles, *Diary,* II, 434–5; John H. and LaWanda Cox, "Andrew John-
son and His Ghost Writers," *Mississippi Valley Historical Review,*
XLVIII (December, 1961), 460–79; Richardson, *Messages and Papers
of the Presidents,* VI, 403–4.

[4] *Commonwealth,* February 24, 1866; *Cong. Globe,* 39th Cong.,
1st Sess., 1766; White, *Trumbull,* pp. 257 ff.; George Rothwell Brown,
ed., *Reminiscences of Senator William M. Stewart of Nevada* (New
York, 1908), pp. 215–18; Chase–Nettie Chase, March 14, 1866,
Chase Papers, LC; Richardson, *Messages and Papers of the Presidents,*
VI, 405.

that he cannot be here to uphold the dictation of a despot"—all these events showed that the breaking point had been reached. But although the radicals were now referring to Johnson in increasingly harsh terms, not all of them had given up hope. The reconstruction committee in general and Stevens in particular proved so amenable to suggestions that Sumner was outraged. First Stevens was willing to accept Robert Dale Owen's proposal to postpone Negro suffrage until 1876; then he agreed to scrapping the idea altogether in favor of a simple permission for Congress to reduce representation in states which discriminated against freedmen. Butler also tried to draw up a compromise solution which he urged upon the President, and the Senate changed the proposed clause disqualifying Confederate officers until 1870 to a provision giving Congress the power to pass an amnesty by a two-thirds vote. Both Houses finally accepted the Fourteenth Amendment in its present form, and Senator Edwin D. Morgan of New York asked Welles whether he did not think that the differences between Congress and the President were now very minor. The constitutional change was widely regarded as moderate, so that Johnson might easily have endorsed it. But he rejected it. The breach which resulted was largely of his own making.[5]

In assessing the causes and result of the rupture, the radicals' reluctance to bring it about must be taken into account. Far from seeking to create turmoil, they exhausted every means of coming to an agreement; had Johnson been as astute as his predecessor, he too might have worked out some compromise with his critics. After all, it was not for obscure doctrinaire reasons that they disagreed with him; they were worried about their party's future, an apprehension which many moderates shared.

[5] Stryker, *Johnson*, pp. 289–91; Robert Dale Owen, "Political Results from the Varioloid," *Atlantic Monthly*, XXXV (June, 1875), 660–70; Kendrick, *The Journal of the Joint Committee of Fifteen on Reconstruction*, pp. 115 ff.; Blaine, *Twenty Years of Congress*, II, 205–14; Sumner, *Works*, X, 282–337, 375–6; New York *Herald*, April 25, 30, June 15, 1866; *Commonwealth*, May 5, 1866; Welles, *Diary*, II, 521; S. J. Field–Chase, June 30, 1866, Chase Papers, LC.

Had they been motivated by financial issues, they could not have cooperated with each other—Sumner, Chandler, Davis, Julian, and Chase favoring hard money, while Stevens, Wade, and Butler identified themselves with greenbackism. On economic issues also, they did not see eye to eye; low tariffs appealed to Sumner, Trumbull, Julian, and Medill; protection, to Kelley, Stevens, Chandler, Wade, and Butler.[6] The one aim shared by all these leaders was the effort to protect the Negro, whether for humanitarian or political reasons. This could only succeed through the Republican party, and the Republican party could only succeed if it were accomplished. Any break with the President, the organization's titular leader, would merely complicate matters.

The importance of this consideration was never in doubt. "I am weak enough to prefer my *friends* though black to my *enemies* though white," wrote Howard on July 26, 1865.

> It is not to be denied that we have few friends in the rebel states but the blacks. If their former masters don't like to vote with them let them imigrate [sic]. The country will be better for it.—But their real object is to keep up an antagonism against the loyal states—to get control of the rebel states—to oppose the payment of the war debts of those states, & finally to compel Congress to pay not only these debts but the whole Confederate debt.

And Wade, after his return from Washington that month, put it more succinctly. "To me, all appears gloomy," he wrote to Sumner, "the President is pursuing . . . a course . . . that can result in nothing but consigning the great Union, or Republican party, bound, hand and foot, to the tender mercies of the rebels we have so lately conquered in the field, and their copperhead allies in the

---

[6] Sumner, *Works,* VI, 320 ff., IX, 26–7; George, *Chandler,* pp. 271 ff.; Steiner, *Davis,* p. 322; Julian, *Political Recollections,* pp. 365, 274; Schuckers, *Chase,* p. 239; Brodie, *Stevens,* pp. 171–2; Trefousse, *Butler,* pp. 187, 193–4, 251; Trefousse, *Wade,* pp. 309, 365, 285, 295; Ray-Trumbull, February 2, 1866, Medill-Trumbull, July 1, 1866, Trumbull Papers, LC; Detroit *Post and Tribune, Chandler,* pp. 159 ff.; Coben, "Northeastern Business and Radical Reconstruction," loc. cit.; Linden, Congressmen, Radicalism and Economic Issues, esp. pp. 21 ff.

North." To prevent these developments, the radicals had no choice but to resist the President.[7]

So it was that during his first year in office, Johnson proved conclusively that his approach to national problems was entirely different from Lincoln's. Unlike his predecessor, he had stood still instead of availing himself of radical advice. Stubborn, opinionated, and, because of his humble Southern antecedents totally out of sympathy with the basic radical goals of human equality, he could neither cooperate with the extremists nor implement successfully a policy of his own. Carl Schurz, who was a keen analyst of character, emphasized this essential difference between the two Presidents in his memoirs. "It was pretended at the time," he recalled,

> and it has since been asserted by historians and publicists that Mr. Johnson's Reconstruction policy was only a continuation of that of Mr. Lincoln. This was true only in a superficial sense, but not in reality. Mr. Lincoln had indeed put forth reconstruction plans which contemplated an early restoration of some of the rebel States. But he had done this while the Civil War was still going on, and for the evident purpose of encouraging loyal movements in those States and of weakening the Confederate State government there by opposing to them governments organized in the interest of the Union. . . . So long as the rebellion continued in any form and to any extent, the State governments he contemplated would have been substantially in the control of really loyal men who had been on the side of the Union during the war. Moreover, he always emphatically affirmed in public as well as in private utterance that no plan of reconstruction he had ever put forth was meant to be "exclusive and inflexible." . . . Had he lived, he would have as ardently wished to stop bloodshed and to reunite as he ever did. But is it to be supposed for a moment that, seeing the late master class in the South . . . intent upon subjecting the freedmen again to a system very much akin to slavery, Lincoln would have consented to abandon those freedmen to the mercies of that master class? . . .

[7] Howard-Sumner, July 26, 1865; Wade-Sumner, July 29, 1865; Sumner Papers; Shelby M. Cullom, *Fifty Years of Public Service: Personal Recollections of Shelby M. Cullom* (Chicago, 1911), pp. 145–6.

To assert in the face of all this that the Johnson reconstruction policy was only Lincoln's policy continued, is little less than a perversion of historical truth.

On February 19, 1866, Senator Richard Yates of Illinois admonished Johnson to do what Lincoln had always done, "the right thing at the right time, in the right way, and at the right place." But Johnson was incapable of doing so. It may well be that John Wilkes Booth accomplished more than he has been given credit for. Possibly the Southern way of life was the chief gainer in the change of Presidents.[8]

[8] Schurz, *Reminiscences*, III, 221; *The Only Salvation: Equality of Rights* (Pamphlet, n.p., n.d., with Senate speech of Senator Richard Yates, February 19, 1866).

CHAPTER

X

The
Difficulties of
Success

THE PRESIDENT'S ADAMANT STAND in the winter
and spring of 1866 created a wholly unprecedented situation. "If
the Johnsonian policy were carried out to the fullest extent, the
supremacy of the Republican party in the councils of the Nation
would be at stake," wrote Illinois congressman Shelby S. Cullom,
and his analysis was correct. Either the President would have to be
blocked or the Democrats would return to power. So impossible
did Johnson's course appear to almost all Republicans that with
very few exceptions they began to cooperate with their most advanced colleagues. In the broadest sense of the term—opposition
to the President's reconstruction policies—they became radicals
themselves.[1]

---

[1] Cullom, *Fifty Years of Public Service*, pp. 145–6. "The President
seemed to have no comprehension of the fact that with inconsiderable
exceptions the entire party was composed of Radicals," wrote James
G. Blaine in his *Twenty Years of Congress*, II, 82. Gideon Welles, too,
used the term to include most members of the party as time went on.
Welles, *Diary*, II, 447, 479, 633–4. Cf. W. R. Brock, *An American*

This development created great difficulties for the radical leaders. No longer able to act out their accustomed role as spokesmen for a pressure group, they would have to seek to give positive direction to a large political party. And this organization, made up of diverse elements which could agree only on the common partisan need to check the President, was faced with the necessity of taking charge of the government. It was a task of such magnitude that it is not surprising that the radicals failed. What is astonishing is that they accomplished anything at all.

The radicals' problems in 1866 were almost insuperable. The restoration of normal conditions in the war-ravaged Southern states would have been difficult even had Congress been able to count on the Executive; with the two branches of government working against each other, the task became infinitely more complicated. In some way, almost four million freedmen who had been emancipated but not given equal rights had to be fitted into a society which was as prejudiced against them as they were unaccustomed to it. Generations of bondage had ill prepared them for the struggle for existence, and their former masters were only slightly less hostile to them than the great mass of poorer whites. Governments had to be restored in areas where few loyal Southerners could be found; outspoken local Unionists, both native scalawags and immigrant carpetbaggers, had to be protected; a depleted economy had to be reanimated and normal channels of trade restored. That the United States was, at the same time, developing into one of the world's industrial giants did not make the staggering task of reconstruction easier.

To solve problems of this magnitude, strong, determined direction was necessary—leadership that knew what it wanted, was aware of where it was going, and could rely on unquestioned parliamentary support. But although men like Stevens and Sumner were quite aware of their purpose, they could not be certain of where they were going because they were unable to achieve

Crisis, Congress and Reconstruction, 1865–1867 (London, 1963), p. 69.

unanimity among their allies; nor could they command unquestionable support because for every bill it was necessary to secure a two-thirds vote in both Houses to override the President's vetoes. Stevens soon learned what Sumner never understood. Instead of boldly challenging conservative measures in order to prod Congress and the President forward, the radicals now had to be careful to marshal as many votes as possible so as to achieve anything at all.

The very size of the Republican party presented difficulties almost unknown to the smaller radical pressure group of former years. The organization was not merely split into radicals, moderates, and conservatives; the radicals themselves were divided. One convenient classification is the scheme prepared by David Donald, who has distinguished conservatives, moderates, independent radicals, Stevens radicals, and ultraradicals. The conservatives cooperated with Johnson; the moderates were willing to settle for measures like the Fourteenth Amendment; the Stevens radicals were prepared to yield on lesser issues in order to secure vital legislation, while the ultras were unwilling to compromise and favored the most extreme measures of reconstruction. The independent radicals were unpredictable. Other classifications have also been suggested. Robert P. Sharkey, in an attempt to group radicals in accordance with their economic views, has called those favoring protectionism and soft money "true ultras," as distinct from "political radicals," a concept which is similar to Louis M. Hacker's "Old" and "New" Radicals. Patrick Riddleberger has differentiated between those extremists who were primarily reformers and those who were party regulars first, and Sister Mary Karl George has contrasted political with economic humanitarians. The threefold distinction among radicals, moderates, and conservatives, has almost become traditional, but, as W. R. Brock has pointed out, none of these lines was hard and fast. Men could be radical on one issue, and moderate or even conservative on another.[2]

[2] Donald, *The Politics of Reconstruction, 1863–1867*, pp. 59–64; Robert P. Sharkey, *Money, Class, and Party, an Economic Study of the*

For this reason, it is difficult to speak of clearly defined groupings within the Republican party. Confining the word "radical" to the issues of racial adjustment, for purposes of convenience, the main outlines of David Donald's categories may be used. His ultras were the doctrinaire, impractical radicals, whose intransigence was compounded, after the passage of the Thirteenth Amendment, by the virtual disappearance of the distinctions between themselves and the former abolitionists. Senators like Charles Sumner and congressmen like James M. Ashley, urged forward by agitators like Wendell Phillips, frequently embarrassed their allies by their inflexibility.[3] Their insistence on complete and immediate racial equality, no matter what the cost or the political consequences, was their distinguishing characteristic, which separated them from the practical radicals, who often shared their philosophy but employed different methods. This second group, represented by men like Thaddeus Stevens and Samuel Shellabarger in the House, and Benjamin F. Wade and Zachariah Chandler in the Senate, had a better grasp of immediate political advantages and was willing to compromise on such issues as the admission of western territories with or without Negro suffrage. Then there were the moderates, Republicans like Trumbull, Fessenden, Sherman, and Grimes in the Senate, and Bingham, Blaine, and Schenck in the House, who stressed the importance of the protection of Negroes in the South but were unwilling to go to extremes to achieve it. Finally, of course, there was the corporal's guard of Republican conservatives who sup-

---

Civil War and Reconstruction (Baltimore, 1959), pp. 281–2; Louis M. Hacker, *The Triumph of American Capitalism* (New York, 1946), pp. 340–2; Patrick Riddleberger, "The Break in the Radical Ranks; Liberals Versus Stalwarts in the Election of 1872," *Journal of Negro History*, XIV (April, 1959), 136–57; Riddleberger, "The Radicals' Abandonment of the Negro During Reconstruction," loc. cit.; George, Chandler, p. 193; Brock, *An American Crisis*, pp. 73–5; Edward L. Gambrill, "Who Were the Senate Radicals?" *Civil War History*, XI (September, 1965), 237–44, esp. 240 ff. Cf. also McKitrick, *Andrew Johnson and Reconstruction*, pp. 53 ff.

[3] T. W. Higginson–Sumner, February 18, 1866, Wendell Phillips–Sumner, April 23, 1866, Frederick Douglass–Sumner, October 19, 1866, Sumner Papers; Sherwin, *Phillips*, pp. 538 ff.

ported Johnson—Edgar Cowan, James Dixon, James R. Doolittle, and Daniel S. Norton in the Senate, and to some degree, Henry Raymond and a few others in the House. How changing these alignments were may be seen in part by Professor Donald's apt characterization of some radicals as "independent."[4]

This division was not the only source of Republican disunity. In addition to differences about reconstruction, the radicals failed to achieve cohesion on most other problems. Unable to find any common ground about the tariff and financial affairs before the war, when some had been neo-Hamiltonian Whigs, and others, laissez-faire Democrats, and unable to agree on economic policy during the conflict, they could never reconcile their disagreements afterward. As the greenback issue became more and more important, the hard-money stand of Chandler, Sumner, Julian, and Schurz contrasted ever more sharply with Butler's, Stevens's, and Wade's espousal of the cheap currency. That some radicals endorsed a fairer distribution of the proceeds of labor, votes for women, and the confiscation of property heightened these disagreements.[5]

When all these differences are taken into account, what common radical goals and common radical motives remain to explain the policies of the radical Congresses between 1866 and the end of Reconstruction?

The answer to these questions seems fairly simple. As for years past, the common denominator of the thinking of all radicals and even to some degree of the moderates was the desire to grant a modicum of protection to freedmen and loyalists in the South and to enable the freedmen to become full-fledged citizens. Convinced that only the Republican party could realize these aims, most Re-

[4] Cf. Donald, *The Politics of Reconstruction*, pp. 100–5.
[5] Coben, "Northeastern Business and Radical Reconstruction: A Re-examination," loc. cit.; Irwin Unger, *The Greenback Era: A Social and Political History of American Finance, 1865–1879* (Princeton, 1965), pp. 83, 88, 260; Chandler-Butler, June 4, 1866, Butler Papers; Howe-Rublee, January 15, 1868, Howe Papers; Montgomery, *Beyond Equality*, pp. 86 ff., 34 ff.; Montgomery, *Labor and the Radical Republicans*, pp. 112, 414; *New York Times*, June 20, July 1, 1867.

publicans found it easy to strive for moral advances which were political advantages as well.[6]

In seeking these aims, the desire for vengeance was hardly the determining factor. Four years of civil war had left their legacy of hatred, but rarely in the history of unsuccessful rebellions has the defeated faction been treated so leniently. Not one highly placed Confederate official was executed, not even Jefferson Davis, who was released on bail after two years in prison. Southern generals suffered no deprivation of freedom; Southern congressmen were generally unmolested, and no proscriptions of conquered leaders disfigured the records of American jurisprudence. While it may be argued that President Johnson's unprecedented pardoning policy contributed significantly to this result, there is abundant evidence that most radicals were not bloodthirsty.

Charles Sumner was the foremost radical advocate of magnanimity. Unlike many of his colleagues, he took this stand while the war was still going on, when he opposed resolutions of retaliation upon prisoners of war for the indignities inflicted upon Union soldiers in the hands of the Confederacy. Resisting the arguments of his political collaborators, he exclaimed:

> A humane and civilized people cannot suddenly become inhumane and uncivilized. . . . We cannot be cruel, or barbarous, or savage, because the Rebels we now meet in warfare are cruel, barbarous and savage. We cannot imitate the detested example.

He succeeded in defeating the resolutions, and shortly afterward introduced new ones prohibiting the display in the Capitol of pictures of victory in battle with fellow citizens. His attitude did not change during Reconstruction. The exile of a hundred to five hundred leading Confederates was his idea of punishment, and with indignation he rejected imputations of vengefulness. When,

[6] In arguing for his Reconstruction Act, Thaddeus Stevens, on January 3, 1867, said: "It would insure the ascendency of the Union party. Do you avow the party purpose? exclaims some horror-stricken demagogue. I do. For I believe, on my conscience, that on the continued ascendency of that party depends the safety of this great nation." *Cong. Globe*, 39th Cong., 2d Sess., 252; cf. Schurz, *Reminiscences*, III, 218–19.

in 1872, he expressed "deep felt satisfaction" that no citizen "who drew his sword against the liberty and life of the nation" had "suffered by the hand of the executioner," he was merely re-emphasizing what he had always stood for.[7]

Other radicals were equally opposed to revenge. Chase, knowing full well that his action would make a trial of Jefferson Davis difficult, refused to hold court in Virginia. He professed kindly feelings for the South, and his leniency was so well known that he was warned it would do him harm in his quest for the presidency. Horace Greeley not only advocated universal amnesty but acted upon his principles when he went bail for the former President of the Confederacy. Henry Wilson interceded in behalf of Davis, asked Johnson to ease the lot of Alexander H. Stephens, and recommended that C. C. Clay be released on parole. The people of the North, he told Southern audiences in 1867, had no feeling of hatred or revenge; they merely wanted to elevate the lowly. Even Parson William G. Brownlow, the fire-eating radical reconstruction Governor of Tennessee, sought to help Henry S. Foote, while Secretary of War Stanton, upon hearing that Jefferson Davis was in irons, ordered the shackles removed. Trumbull and Hamlin resisted demands for punishment of Confederates, and many former abolitionists, now cooperating with the radicals, were equally opposed to bloodletting.[8]

What most radicals wanted was a symbolic act rather than a general policy of proscription. After the assassination of Lincoln, Henry Winter Davis warned Johnson not to try the murderers by

[7] Sumner, *Works*, IX, 206–27, 333–5; Sumner-Lieber, August 2, 1865, Providence *Journal*, August 3, 1872, Sumner Papers; Welles, *Diary*, II, 397.
[8] Charles Warren, *The Supreme Court in United States History* (Boston, 1926), II, 421; W. P. Mellen–Chase, July 11, 1867, Chase Papers, LC; Hay, *Diaries*, pp. 274–5; Greeley–Chase, November 22, 1866, Chase Papers, HSP; Hudson Strode, *Jefferson Davis, Tragic Hero* (New York, 1964), pp. 306–11; Wilson-Johnson, August 14, 1865, March 3, 1866, Johnson Papers; Washington *Chronicle*, April 23, 1867, Foote, *Casket of Reminiscences*, p. 229; Stanton–N. A. Miles, May 28, 1865, Stanton Papers; Trumbull–Mrs. Gary, June 27, 1866, Trumbull Papers, LC; Hamlin, *Hamlin*, p. 509; McPherson, *The Struggle for Equality*, pp. 314–16.

a military commission. Hand them over to a court, he urged. The people wanted justice, not vengeance, and he scoffed at reports that Jefferson Davis had been implicated in the plot. His friend Wade, who during the war had been insistent in demands for retaliation, afterwards also was not interested in large-scale executions. Not only did he seek to dissuade the President from hanging too many Confederates, but he opposed the supreme penalty for Mary E. Surratt, accused on insufficient evidence of complicity in Lincoln's assassination. As he pointed out in December, 1866, he was not the advocate of any greater vigor than was necessary for general security. Chandler, who was more extreme, also did not intend to go beyond the execution of a few leading Southerners and was worried about Johnson's sanguinary talk. The *Independent* aptly characterized the radicals' attitude when its correspondent summed up the reaction to Jefferson Davis's release on bail. "There is evidently a general feeling of disappointment at the result," he reported. "I do not think there was a strong demand for his punishment; but a very large class of earnest Republicans earnestly desired his conviction for treason."[9]

Thaddeus Stevens approximated much more closely the traditional concept of radical vindictiveness. Undoubtedly favoring stern punishment at least for the leaders of the Confederacy, he was capable of opposing appropriations to rebuild flood-ravished dikes in Mississippi and was the only man in Congress to rejoice at the execution of the Emperor Maximilian in Mexico. But was the sardonic old man, crippled and often plagued by ill health, spurred on merely by an abounding hatred of the South? Was he only trying to seek revenge for the wartime destruction of his iron works near Gettysburg? Although these explanations have been offered, they seem no more adequate to tell the whole story than similar attempts attributing his actions to the influence of his putative mulatto mistress or to his alleged concern for the expan-

[9] H. W. Davis–Johnson, May 13, 1865, Johnson Papers; Davis–S. F. DuPont, May 18 or 19, 1865, DuPont Papers; *Cong. Globe,* 38th Cong., 2d Sess., 363 ff.; 39th Cong., 2d Sess., 163; Blaine, *Twenty Years of Congress,* II, 14–15; Riddle, *Wade,* p. 269; Detroit *Post and Tribune, Chandler,* pp. 284 ff.; *Independent,* May, 30, 1867.

sion of Northern business at the expense of the South. He was a complex human being, tortured in body and mind, to be sure, but nevertheless able to seek sensible solutions. Like other radicals, he shared the general desire for a few symbolic prosecutions of leading insurgents. But not even he advocated the execution of more than a handful of Confederate officials. At the time of Lincoln's assassination, he refused to be stampeded into a belief in Jefferson Davis's complicity in the crime, and in 1865, at Lancaster, he said:

> I am not fond of sanguinary punishments, but surely some victims must propitiate the manes of our starved, murdered slaughtered martyrs. . . . Policy if not justice would require that the poor, the ignorant and the coerced should be forgiven.

His one abiding passion was equality; he himself wrote his epitaph on his tombstone in a Negro cemetery:

> I repose in this quiet and secluded spot, not from any natural preference for solitude, but finding other cemeteries limited as to race, by charter rules, I have chosen this that I might illustrate in my death the principles which I advocated through a long life, equality of man before his Creator.[1]

Conviction often cost the radicals dear. In spite of charges by the opposition, political self-seeking was not the chief motive impelling radical statesmen any more than vindictiveness. While it is true that the elevation of Negroes in the South and their eventual enfranchisement would provide a useful power base for the Republican party, championship of racial equality in the North was not popular and endangered the success of candidates favoring it. "I am well aware that there is in Oregon a widespread prejudice against the negroes," wrote George H. Williams, the Sunset State's radical senator, on June 20, 1866,

[1] Brodie, *Stevens,* pp. 224, 295, 305–7, 366; McClure, *Lincoln and the Men of War-Times,* p. 256; Thompson Powell-Stevens, February 22, 1866, Stevens Papers; Robert Selph Henry, *The Story of Reconstruction* (Indianapolis, 1938), p. 49; Stewart, *Reminiscences,* p. 205; Beale, *The Critical Year,* pp. 225, 267–8; Hacker, *The Triumph of American Capitalism,* p. 340; *New York Times,* September 10, 1865. Both Beale and Hacker emphasize economic factors.

& I have no doubt that my course in reference to the Freedmen's Bureau & Civil Rights Bill will be unsatisfactory to some of my friends. But it seemed to me that both these measures were demanded by the plainest dictates of humanity & justice.

Carl Schurz and other radicals also commented on the unpopularity of measures favoring the Negro; as time went on, the problem of Northern prejudice became more and more difficult, and by 1867, it was to cost the Republicans control of important state legislatures. Whatever faults the radicals may have had, they were sincere in their commitment to human rights. What they were seeking was neither vengeance nor crass political gain; they wanted security for their experiment in modern democracy.[2]

To achieve this security, the radicals made every effort to retain moderate support. Although most of them believed that impartial suffrage was as necessary for their safety as it was desirable on principle, leaders like Stevens were prepared to settle for far less. If they wanted to be certain of sufficient votes to override the President's vetoes, they had to compromise, and they consistently attempted to do so.

The Fourteenth Amendment furnished abundant proof of their disposition to cooperation. In the complicated negotiations leading to its passage the radicals in general and Stevens in particular yielded again and again. Henry Wilson exerted all his strength in its behalf; Stevens and Chase urged Sumner to support the measure, and they compromised their principles to such an extent that they infuriated the doctrinaires. That it was not a perfect solution to the country's problems no one knew better than Stevens himself. But the need was pressing; it was necessary to secure two thirds of both Houses, and the amendment seemed to offer a modicum of protection for Republican interests.[3]

[2] Williams–M. P. Deady, June 20, 1866, Matthew P. Deady Papers, Oregon Historical Society; Schurz, *Reminiscences,* III, 246; N. L. Mayo–Trumbull, May 1, 1866, Trumbull Papers, LC; John Cochrane–Washburne, November 4, 1867, Washburne Papers; Stevens–F. A. Conkling, January 6, 1868, Stevens Papers. Cf. Note 6, page 341.
[3] Boutwell, *Reminiscences of Sixty Years,* II, 37, 42–7; Julian, *Political Recollections,* pp. 272–3; Blaine, *Twenty Years of Congress,*

It was recognized at the time that the constitutional change was hardly the radicals' idea of a good measure. With considerable exaggeration, the New York *Herald,* predicting the amendment's acceptance, stated: "Congress . . . in rejecting the violent and obnoxious ideas and propositions of Thaddeus Stevens, and in adopting the policy of President Johnson, has saved the republican party." The moderate Governor Jacob Cox of Ohio explained to Johnson that the state's Republican platform was an attempt to compromise because it merely endorsed the amendment, and doctrinaire radicals everywhere were dismayed. "The Glory and Shame of Congress," was the title of the *Independent*'s summary of the achievements of the legislators, the "glory" of their resistance to Johnson, and the "shame" of their abandonment of impartial suffrage. Wendell Phillips was outraged and praised Sumner, who deplored the failure to provide votes for Negroes, while Julian felt so resentful about it that years later he still vented his spleen in his memoirs. As George Boutwell pointed out, however, "it was impossible in 1866 to go farther than the provisions of the Fourteenth Amendment."[4] Making the Negroes citizens, requiring the states to observe due process of law, and giving Congress power to reduce the representation of any state restricting the right of suffrage, the measure was liberal enough to include a clause enabling Congress to grant an amnesty to leading former Confederates. Its very moderation guaranteed Republican unity, and Stevens, if not Sumner and his admirers, realized that he

---

II, 193–214; Theodore Tilton–Sumner, February 3, 1866, Chase-Sumner, March 9, 1866; Wendell Phillips–Sumner, March, 17, 24, April 30, 1866, Stevens-Sumner, March 3, 1866, endorsing letter from C. W. Wardwell to Stevens, Sumner Papers; Pierce, *Sumner,* IV, 276–83; Brodie, *Stevens,* pp. 266–71; Woodburn, *Stevens,* p. 418; Joseph B. James, *The Framing of the Fourteenth Amendment* (Urbana, 1956), p. 191; Paddock, An Ohio Congressman in Reconstruction, p. 29. The amendment did, however, include some of the fundamental radical constitutional notions. Jacobus ten Broek, *The Antislavery Origins of the Fourteenth Amendment* (Berkely, 1951), esp. p. 218.

[4] New York *Herald,* June 15, 1866; Cox-Johnson, June 21, 1866, Johnson Papers; *Independent,* August 2, 1866; Wendell Phillips–Sumner, March 17, 1866, Sumner Papers; Julian, *Political Recollections,* pp. 272–3; Boutwell, *Reminiscences of Sixty Years,* II, 41.

could not act as the head of a pressure group and hammer out constructive legislation at the same time.

The moderates and less extreme radicals were generally satisfied with the proposed adjustment. Even while it was still under consideration, Ebenezer Peck, an experienced Illinois politician, expressed his gratitude that Negro suffrage was not part of it; Horace White, who personally considered the measure "a politician's dodge rather than the work of statesmen," was convinced that the party could carry it in his home state, and Associate Justice Stephen J. Field was equally pleased. "The proposed amendments to the Constitution . . . ," he wrote to Chase,

> appear to me just what we need. I think all members of the Union party can unite cordially in their support. If the President withhold his approval he will sever all connection with the Union party. . . . The American people do not intend to give up all that they have gained by the war—and they do intend that loyal men shall govern the country.[5]

Under normal circumstances, the amendment might indeed have become a basis for an eventual settlement. Many radicals expected that it would, although they would then have been prepared for agitation for further reform.

But times were not normal, and Johnson not only refused to accept the measure, but actively worked against it. At the same time, he reconstructed his Cabinet by placing conservatives into the portfolios made vacant by the resignations of Harlan, Dennison, and Speed, who were unable to collaborate with him any longer. Finally, he sought to organize a new political grouping.[6] By doing so, he handed the entire Republican party, not merely the radicals, a campaign issue, and they made the most of it. He also made it possible for them to induce Congress to go further than the amendment. By refusing to cooperate, however, he again

[5] E. Peck–Trumbull, May 8, 1866, Horace White–Trumbull, May 31, 1866, Trumbull Papers, LC; D. D. Field–Chase, June 30, 1866, Chase Papers, LC.

[6] McKitrick, *Andrew Johnson and Reconstruction,* p. 357; Milton, *The Age of Hate,* pp. 340–1.

forced them to seek accommodations with the moderates. They would still have to mute their demands and curtail their activities as trailblazers.

During the elections of 1866, the radicals played their role with great skill. Johnson's efforts to build up a new party failed, partly because even those sympathetic to him were opposed to cooperation with the Democrats. The Philadelphia National Union convention as well as the Cleveland gathering of soldiers and sailors called by his followers merely served as models for rival meetings at Philadelphia and Pittsburgh, gatherings in which radicals of all shades successfully collaborated with less advanced Republicans. They even allowed the moderates to write resolutions omitting references to universal suffrage. In such an atmosphere, Sumner's and Butler's continued advocacy of the reform could not dominate the campaign any more than Stevens's assertion that equality before the law was the fundamental Republican creed. Johnson's foolish behavior—his "swing-around-the-circle" to Illinois, his provocative speeches, and his lack of dignity—furnished ammunition to his enemies. Permitting himself to be led on by hostile crowds, he became abusive, and Mary Lincoln complained that he had by his presence "desecrated" her husband's last resting place. These circumstances facilitated the radicals' task; as in the past, they were among the most sought-after speakers, and the results justified their efforts. Over two thirds of the new members of Congress were opposed to the President.[7]

Considering their successes in the campaign, the radicals continued to move with circumspection. It is true that Stevens, returning to Washington for the opening of Congress, remarked

---

[7] David Davis–J. Rockwell, August 9, 1866, Davis Papers; Beale, *The Critical Year*, pp. 131 ff., 184–7, 363 ff.; Dunning, *Reconstruction*, pp. 75–8; McPherson, *Reconstruction*, pp. 241–3; *Commonwealth*, August 24, 1866; Sumner, *Works*, XI, 1–39; *The Pending Canvass. Speech of the Honorable Thaddeus Stevens, Delivered at Bedford, Pennsylvania, on Tuesday Evening, September 11, 1866* (Lancaster, 1866), esp. pp. 11–12; McCulloch, *Men and Measures of Half a Century*, p. 397; Mary Lincoln–Sumner, September 10, 1866, Sumner Papers; *Independent*, November 8, 1866.

that he was "altogether too conservative last session, but that he intended this session to be very radical in his views." In general, however, the advanced Republicans did not lose sight of their dependence upon moderate support. Talk of compromise had not yet ceased, and despite all indications to the contrary, some practical radicals were still considering the possibility of ratification of the Fourteenth Amendment as a basis for final settlement.[8]

Whether or not the acceptance of the amendment entitled the Southern states to full representation was a question which had long divided the radicals. The companion measure which Stevens had reported from his committee, a bill setting forth the conditions required for restoration, had not been passed, and Congress, despite warnings, had adjourned without spelling out the exact procedure of Reconstruction. Yet to some radicals, the amendment itself clearly seemed to imply that acceptance would ensure restoration. This was Chase's view, and he fully expected that the states would give their consent. During the fall campaign, B. R. Cowan, the chairman of the Ohio Republican executive committee, had suggested to Governor Marcus Ward of New Jersey that the leading Southern supporters of Johnson's policy be informed of the finality of the amendment so that they might secure its adoption. The plan, he had written, was Governor Dennison's, and although he himself was in no hurry to see the seceded states come back, he nevertheless had felt bound. "Having adopted the Congressional plan as our platform . . . ," he concluded, "we cannot go back on it to require new conditions, with propriety, unless the South shall furnish us the excuse, by further outrages." It was a point of view reinforced by the actions of Governor Brownlow of Tennessee. After calling his legislature into session, he had seen to it that the proposal was quickly ratified, and when Congress had thereupon readmitted the state, it appeared to endorse the governor's interpretation. But the more doctrinaire radicals had differed, Sumner having tried to block the admission of Tennessee until she

[8] New York *Herald,* November 30, 1866; *Independent,* November 29, 1866, February 1, 1867; John Bright–Greeley, November 28, 1866, Greeley Papers.

had conferred impartial suffrage upon her citizens, a position in which he had been supported by B. Gratz Brown and others. It was evident that far harsher terms would be offered if the Southern states did not accept the amendment.[9]

This threat was clearly recognized at the time of the election campaign, when Northern papers warned the South that it had better comply or face worse conditions. But not even the successful outcome of the canvass solved the problem. Although the New York *Herald* informed its readers that the radical victory had made the acceptance of the amendment certain, there was no indication that the President would yield.[1]

The radicals themselves were still divided about the measure. In a debate in the Senate on December 14, Wade declared unequivocally that the amendment, if accepted, would entitle the Southern states to return. Sumner again dissented. "I do not agree with the Senator," he said.

> I distinctly stated, when the Amendment was under discussion, that I did not accept it as a finality, and that, as far as I had a vote on this floor, I would insist that every one of these States, before its Representatives were received in Congress, should confer impartial suffrage, without distinction of color.

But the Ohioan would not concede the point. "I cannot see how the Senator could have misled the Southern States with that," he declared.

> When they complied with all we asked of them in the constitutional amendment I supposed we could not refuse to let them in on these terms. If the Senator did not intend that they should have the benefit of what we had done by compliance with the

[9] James, *The Framing of the Fourteenth Amendment*, p. 169; McPherson, *Reconstruction*, pp. 103–4; Medill-Trumbull, July 17, 1866, Trumbull Papers, LC; Chase–Kate Chase, June 15, 1866, Chase–Nettie Chase, October 15, 1866, Chase Papers, LC; B. R. Cowan–Marcus Ward, October 11, 1866, Ward Papers; McKitrick, *Andrew Johnson and Reconstruction*, p. 361; Sumner *Works*, X, 490–4, 502–3. Boutwell, Kelley, Julian and Thomas Williams were among those in the House voting against the admission of Tennessee. *Harper's Weekly*, X (August 4, 1866), p. 483.

[1] New York *Herald*, October 2, November 8, 1866.

terms on their part it seems to me there was something wrong. I intended to let them in on the terms we prescribed. I did not ask for more, and I would not be satisfied with less; and if now they should comply with them it would be bad faith in me to refuse to admit them. Certainly, I am as much for colored suffrage as any man on this floor, but when I make such an agreement as that I stand by it always.[2]

These expressions of opinion were a good indication of the divided counsel even among the most important radicals. They also showed that Southern acceptance of the amendment would, in all likelihood, have ended Reconstruction. The doctrinaires who supported Sumner did not have the strength to keep the Southern states out.

The practical radicals' willingness to abide by the amendment and to proceed with caution was also underlined by their excursion to New Orleans during the Christmas recess of 1866. Wade and Henry Lane of Indiana were the most prominent members of the congressional travel group, which was frequently called upon to address Southern audiences. In Memphis, the Ohio senator declared that Congress was charged with the responsibility for the destinies of the nation. "Now let me say that I do know," he continued,

that the great body of which I am a humble member has no resentments toward the people of any portion of this country— none at all. They will indulge in no vindictive legislation. They will be guided by their sense of security and justice—nothing else.

Congress would not reconsider, however. The South would have to accept the Fourteenth Amendment.

Similar speeches in Mississippi and Louisiana underscored the visiting statesmen's attitude, and, by and large, their reception was not unfriendly. "Yes," said Senator Lane to one Southerner, "We find after all that you're not so hard hearted, and we hope that you'll also discover that we radicals don't wear horns." When the party returned, the New York *Herald* reported that the amendment was still a possible solution of the nation's problems.[3]

But time was running out, and one Southern state after another, encouraged in its resistance by Johnson, rejected the measure. The feeling that something more was needed to guarantee security for the nation and safety for the Negroes became more widespread, not merely among radicals, but among moderates as well. "I feel that if the Southern States should adopt the Constitutional Amendment within a reasonable time we are morally bound to admit them to representation. If they reject it then I am in favor of striking for impartial suffrage though I see that such a course is beset with grave dangers," commented James A. Garfield on New Year's Day, 1867. What made his opinion significant was that he was anxious for them to accept, an attitude shared by Grant. As the general told Johnson, the President ought to endorse the change. Otherwise Congress would impose harsher terms. Of the soundness of this advice, the radical Washington *Daily Morning Chronicle* furnished abundant proof. "We have proposed to treat with illegal state governments, offering terms imperfect as to justice and the national security, but distinguished for generosity to them," suggested the paper in an article reprinted from the Cincinnati *Gazette.*

> We next go to the people, and offer them a legal reconstruction of government on terms better adapted to national and personal security, but still abounding in magnanimity to them. If they reject, we shall have no recourse but to govern them by United States laws until a loyal generation shall grow up.

And during a January meeting of the Republican National Committee, while chairman Marcus Ward still expressed his conviction that the voters had approved of the Fourteenth Amendment as the best possible settlement, he indicated that in the long run, impartial suffrage would have to be added. The President's intran-

[3] Washington *Daily National Intelligencer* January 3, 5, 1867; December 31, 1866; New York *Herald,* December 27, 1866, January 4, 1867.

sigence was paving the way for sterner measures.[4]

And sterner measures seemed necessary. If during 1865 the Johnson governments had shown great shortcomings, by the end of 1866 they had been thoroughly discredited. Day after day, Republican congressmen and publicists heard about new outrages. "The President's policy has crushed all the hopes of Unionmen in this State," a Louisianian reported to Trumbull.

> The whole of the offices are filled . . . by Confederate officers and they are decidedly more defiant than they were at any time during the Rebellion. The Union men are despised shunned and persecuted throughout the State and I predict that hundreds will be compelled to leave here as soon as the military are withdrawn.

In Alabama, a former constituent complained that the President's policies "and extreme favoritism to open enemies of the Government" had brought back a state of anarchy "which must sooner or later bring on open feudes [sic]" between Northerners and Southerners. A Texan, detailing similar circumstances to Chase, wrote,

> We in Texas are in nearly the same condition as in the spring of 1861. Public sentiment is as hostile to Congress as it then was to the U.S. Government. While the President has made loyalty odious and treason respectable, Congress has done nothing for our practical relief.

Governor E. M. Pease confirmed the existence of this state of affairs to Gideon Welles, whom he told that the only way Union men could live in Texas was under the protection of the army. From Georgia, Greeley heard that the Unionists were wholly without influence. "One year ago," his correspondent wrote him,

> rebels were respectful, nay, deferential to Union men of character. That is no longer the case. The timid Unionists are enrolling themselves among the Democrats & administration men.

[4] Mary L. Hinsdale, ed., *Garfield-Hinsdale Letters, Correspondence Between James Abram Garfield and Burke Aaron Hinsdale* (Ann Arbor, 1949), p. 88; Welles, *Diary*, III, 7–8; Washington *Daily Morning Chronicle* January 1, 1867; MS of remarks "Read by Marcus L. Ward at Meeting of National Republican Committee at Washington, January 1867," Ward Papers.

He considered Congress the only remaining hope. After the July New Orleans riot, in which radicals and Negroes were killed, Washburne learned that Florida Unionists thought their continued residence in the state impossible. "So soon as it is understood that the military is to sustain the civil authorities and not act independent of the said authorities, the Union men better get out," Daniel Richards, a leading radical politician in the state, informed him. Similar news came from other states, and finally even original Johnson supporters believed the time had come for action. When Chase visited Sumner in December, he met ex-Governor Holden and several of his followers. To quote the Chief Justice,

> They were all satisfied that the Experiment had failed & were anxious that Congress should interfere by an enabling act authorizing the people black & white to vote for members of a Convention who might form a state constitution of Republican Government.[5]

If the Southern Unionists' condition was perilous, the Negroes' was worse. Terrorized and often in fear of their lives, they clearly needed protection. While the damaging testimony taken by the Reconstruction committee could be dismissed as propaganda, the riots in Memphis and New Orleans with their large loss of life unmistakably demonstrated the freedmen's insecurity. Congress would have to do something; the radicals were now in a position to see to it that it did.[6]

But how to proceed was still a problem. The election victory

[5] A. P. Fields–Trumbull, May 19, 1866, Jonathan Roberts–Trumbull, April 21, 1866, John Dietrich–Trumbull, July 16, 1866, Trumbull Papers, LC; William Alexander–Chase, July 17, 1866, Chase–Nettie Chase, December 12, 1866, Chase Papers, LC; Welles, *Diary,* II, 568; Joshua Hill–Greeley, September 22, 1866, Greeley Papers; D. Richards–Washburne, September 11, 1866, Washburne Papers; D. B. Thomas–Stevens, February 25, 1866, J. H. Aughey–Stevens, February 27, 1866, Marion Roberts–Stevens, May 15, 1866, M. L. Mallet–Stevens, May 28, 1866, Stevens Papers; E. Cushing–Sumner, November 30, 1866, Sumner Papers.

[6] Beale, *The Critical Year,* pp. 93–4; Franklin, *Reconstruction After the Civil War,* pp. 58, 62–4; *Independent,* May 17, August 16, 1866; P. H. Sheridan, *Personal Memoirs of P. H. Sheridan* (New York, 1866), II, 233–42.

of 1866 had not ended the factionalism which plagued the Republican party, neither among the members of the organization in general nor among the radicals in particular. The finality of the Fourteenth Amendment was not the only disputed issue between them; at every step politically minded managers had to encounter the obstruction of the doctrinaires as well as the hesitation of the moderates. Under these circumstances, they had to be satisfied with every piece of legislation they were able to obtain. To ask for more was useless.

The admission of new states was a case in point. While the Republicans had a two-thirds majority, some of the moderates were not entirely reliable. Additional radical members, especially in the Senate, would strengthen the anti-Johnson wing, and since Colorado and Nebraska had taken preparatory steps for statehood, there was a possibility that they would supply them. Consequently, though there was some question about the exact number of inhabitants in Colorado, by 1866 both Houses were considering bills for the admission of the two commonwealths. But the process ran into a snag. Doctrinaire Republicans, led by Sumner, refused to overlook the white suffrage restrictions in the prospective state constitutions. Oblivious of the virtual absence of Negroes in the West and totally uninterested in pressing political considerations, Sumner exerted all his talents against the admission bills. Although both passed in the end, because of the combined opposition of doctrinaires and moderates, there were not enough votes to override the President's veto.[7]

In December, 1866, the radicals introduced the subject again. But as before the suffrage problem complicated passage; Sumner still fulminated against the abandonment of principle. Although Wade told him bluntly that the four new senators were needed in order to secure human rights in the entire country, the self-

[7] Blaine, *Twenty Years of Congress*, II, 274 ff.; New York *Tribune*, January 19, March 14, April 26, July 28, 1866; Sumner, *Works*, X, 346–74; Elmer Ellis, "Colorado's First Fight for Statehood, 1865–1868," *The Colorado Magazine*, VIII (January, 1931), 23–30; Victor Rosewater, "The Political and Constitutional Development of Nebraska," Nebraska State Historical Society, *Transactions and Reports*, V (1893), 240–66.

righteous orator refused to be convinced until his views had received at least partial recognition in the pending legislation. To complicate matters further, Lafayette Foster, the President *pro tem* of the Senate, was retiring; as the law then stood, in the absence of a Vice President, the office carried with it succession to the presidency. As the debates on the admission of the territories proceeded, there was more and more talk of Wade's elevation to the vacant post, a state of affairs which made the senator's position difficult. As chairman of the Committee on Territories, he was in charge of legislation for the admission of new states; as probable Vice President, he himself was suspected of harboring personal ambitions because of the possibility of the impeachment of Johnson. Finally, Nebraska was admitted despite the President's veto, but the Colorado bill failed. Although both Houses passed it, the necessary votes to override the veto could not be secured. During the night of February 28, when he thought an opportunity for a favorable vote was at hand, Wade unsuccessfully tried to hurry the measure through the Senate. "There are peculiar reasons which connect themselves with the Senator from Ohio, which draw some attention to him, and to the course he is pursuing on this occasion," said the conservative Senator Doolittle. "We all know, that Senator, in pressing this matter of Colorado, has said over and over that his purpose was to reinforce a majority in this body, already more than two-thirds. And for what, sir?" That Wade had not yet been elected—Fessenden strenuously opposed him—made no difference; that the radicals were really anxious to secure their program was less dramatic than the imputation of self-seeking which has stuck to Wade ever since. Colorado had to wait over ten years more until she was admitted to the Union. Had Sumner not held up the passage of the original bill, the result might have been different.[8]

Another example of the radicals' difficulties was the wording

[8] New York *Tribune*, December 6, 8, 11, 15, 1866, January 4, 10, 15, 29, 30, February 8, March 1, 2, 1867; Hay, *Diaries*, p. 263; David Miller DeWitt, *The Impeachment and Trial of Andrew Johnson* (New York, 1903), pp. 158 ff., 169–77; *Cong. Globe*, 39th Cong., 2d Sess., 1922.

of the Tenure-of-Office Bill. Because of the widespread desire to curb the President's use of patronage, George H. Williams of Oregon on December 3, 1866, introduced into the upper House a measure to require the Senate's consent to the removal of federal officials. Although Williams's radicalism was beyond question, he had not included Cabinet officers in his bill. Discussion ensued, and when Timothy O. Howe sought to remove this exclusion, not only the moderates, but Williams as well as Yates joined with the administration forces to defeat his amendment. Under the leadership of another radical, Thomas Williams of Pennsylvania, the House of Representatives passed a bill which did cover the Cabinet. The Senate, however, refused to yield. It was not until John Sherman had worked out an ambiguous compromise formula, providing that the Secretaries were to hold office "for and during the term of the President by whom they may have been appointed, and for one month thereafter," that the legislation received the requisite majorities in both Houses. Whether the final version was really applicable to such controversial figures as Edwin M. Stanton, the Secretary of War, who represented the radicals in the Cabinet, was dubious.[9]

In spite of these complications, the radical leaders were determined to press forward. The South was evidently not going to accept the Fourteenth Amendment; Johnson refused to yield, and the electorate had shown that it would sustain more thoroughgoing measures. Careful not to alienate the moderates, the advanced Republicans took advantage of Johnson's unpopularity to pass, over his veto, a bill for Negro suffrage in the District of Columbia. Because of the President's intransigence, they also found it possible to convince their colleagues of the necessity of further measures to curb him. To ensure continued congressional supervision, they fixed the time for the assembly of the Fortieth Congress for March 4, immediately after the adjournment of the

[9] Blaine, *Twenty Years of Congress*, II, 270–4; *Cong. Globe*, 39th Cong., 2d Sess., 2, 17, 382, 547–50, 939–44, 969–70, 966 ff., 1246, 1340, 1514, 1518.

Thirty-ninth; in order to safeguard the army from interference, they directed that the President could issue orders only through the general-in-chief, U. S. Grant, who had to be stationed in Washington. These successes as well as the Tenure-of-Office Act showed the skill of the radical leadership.[1] The most important bill enacted that winter, however, was the Reconstruction Act. It was the answer to the President's contumacy. Designed to safeguard Southern Unionists and Negroes as well as the supremacy of the Republican party, it finally realized one of the basic radical goals: votes for Negroes, at least in the South. Its ultimate passage, however, was made possible not by radical pressure, but by the President's own resistance to his party.

Although Thaddeus Stevens was the universally acknowledged radical leader in the House, he had not been in favor of the Reconstruction Act as it finally emerged. His plan was to place the unreconstructed states under a military government and to await events. At most he was willing to further a separate bill for the Reconstruction of Louisiana. Running into opposition in the House, where James G. Blaine and others sought to provide for a scheme of restoration as well as military rule, the tenacious party manager succeeded in beating down the opposition. But as usual, the radicals were not united. When the moderate Senator Sherman renewed the reconstruction proposals in the Senate, they carried, even Sumner supporting them. Stevens made one last effort to beat down the amendment by seeing to it that the House refused to concur—in the crucial ballot, the extreme radicals joined with the Democrats in voting against the Senate version. But the session was drawing to a close; if Andrew Johnson was to be prevented from pocketing the bill, if any legislation at all was to be passed, some action would have to be taken. The Senate insisted, some of the most radical members again urging haste and steadfastness, and Stevens yielded. He knew when he had to compromise, and even the most doctrinaire radicals rallied for a record vote of 128–46, only five conservatives voting with the Democrats.

---

[1] Franklin, *Reconstruction After the Civil War,* pp. 70–2.

The resultant measure was a patchwork. Dividing the South into five military districts, it declared the Johnson governments illegal and provided for a process of Reconstruction based on Negro suffrage, disfranchisement of leading Confederates, and the ratification of the Fourteenth Amendment. That the President vetoed it made no difference, since Congress immediately overrode his objections. It is conceivable, however, that a more united party with executive support might have produced a more workable bill.[2]

In the Fortieth Congress, the radicals' majority was even more pronounced than in the Thirty-ninth. But the problems created by this accretion of strength were also greater. Relations with the moderates were strained at the very beginning of the session, when Benjamin F. Butler, now a radical representative from Massachusetts, started a dramatic row with John Bingham, who was becoming more and more cautious. In a dispute about a bill for the relief of the Southern poor, Butler questioned Bingham's fairness. The Ohio representative lost his temper. Accusing ths general of having voted fifty times for Jefferson Davis as his candidate for President, he replied that he repelled with contempt "any utterance of that sort from any man, whether he be the hero of Fort Fisher not taken or Fort Fisher taken." Equally enraged, Butler shouted that he had done his part during the war, but that "the only victim of the gentleman's prowess . . . was an innocent woman hung upon the scaffold." The allusion referred to Mary Surratt, executed after a trial by a military commission in which Bingham, as one of three prosecutors, had played an important part. Butler had just discovered that Lincoln's assassin's diary had been mutilated, so that President Johnson never saw certain passages which might have proved Mrs. Surratt's probable ignorance of the plot to kill rather than to kidnap the victim. "Who spoliated that book," the general roared.

[2] Blaine, *Twenty Years of Congress,* II, 250–62; *Cong. Globe,* 39th Cong., 2d Sess., 250 ff., 817, 1037, 1073–80, 1173–83, 1206–10, 1215, 1302 ff., 1360 ff., 1364–99, 1459, 1467–9, 1315 ff., 1320, 1340, 1400, 1555 ff., 1625, 1645.

Who suppressed that evidence? Who caused an innocent woman to be hung when he had in his pocket the diary which had stated at least what was the idea and the purpose of the main conspirators in the case?

That the extremist Butler accused the moderate Bingham of undue harshness also showed how difficult it was to keep the party united. And a few months later, Chandler mercilessly attacked Fessenden as a Republican conservative, a "species" he called a "hybrid" with "no power of reproduction." The Senator from Maine responded in an angry rebuttal.[3]

Among themselves, the radicals were also still divided. Just as they had differed about the best measures to be adopted, so they disagreed about the best way to secure Southern compliance. In order to explain congressional policies to the people of the former Confederacy, in the spring and summer of 1867 a number of statesmen traveled to the disaffected section. Oliver P. Morton of Indiana, who had joined the radicals in 1866, told his listeners in Arkansas that they should have accepted the Fourteenth Amendment. Now they would have to comply with the Reconstruction acts; if they did not, more onerous conditions would be imposed. Henry Wilson sought to be especially reasonable. Let the acts be carried out, he counseled; if the Southern states responded in good faith, there would be no question about their speedy restoration. But his line of reasoning did not suit other radicals. "For the Lord's sake get Wilson of Massachusetts home," wrote the extremist General James A. Brisbin to his friends in Congress. "He is doing incalculable harm." While Wade, commenting that Wilson had always been "a —— fool," advised Chandler to issue a card announcing that the senator did not speak for the party, Stevens publicly repudiated him. Many conditions would have to be met before a state could came back, he announced; and at Mobile, William D. Kelley so offended a Southern audience that he was physically assaulted.[4]

[3] *Cong. Globe,* 40th Cong., 1st Sess., 256–64, 749 ff.; Trefousse, *Butler,* pp. 191–2.

[4] Washington *Daily Morning Chronicle,* April 23, 1867; *Independent,* May 2, 1867; J S. Brisbin–Wade, April 30, 1867, Wade-

The patchwork of Reconstruction caused by the party's difficulties had to be pieced together in three supplementary acts passed by Congress during 1867 and 1868. In March, 1867, it became necessary to enable the commanding generals of the Southern military districts to take steps needed to initiate the process of Reconstruction; in July, another bill with additional power for the commanders had to be passed in order to nullify the Attorney General's opinion restricting their right to deal with the state governments, and in March, 1868, a fourth measure made possible the ratification of the new state constitutions by the majority of votes cast rather than by over fifty per cent of those registered. These piecemeal steps all caused dissension; they were the most that could be secured at the time, but they could not ensure the full and permanent integration of the Negro into society.[5]

In the long run, the South had little choice but to submit to these measures. In the North, however, conditions were different. The frequent elections in many states constantly kept the radicals on guard. As long as they had merely been a pressure group, temporary defeats in local canvasses were not fatal, but when they had become the leaders of a congressional coalition attempting to exercise executive as well as legislative powers, they could ill afford electoral setbacks. And considering the great variety of opinions represented in their ranks, they were bound to offend sundry interests which would endanger their cause at the polls.

Wilson, Kelley, and Morton had not been the only congressional travelers in 1867. A group of statesmen, among whom Wade, Trumbull, Chandler, Howe, and Creswell were especially prominent, took a trip to the West in May and June, and the reports which circulated about their activities were extemely

---

Chandler, n.d., endorsing it, Chandler Papers; New York *Herald*, April 28, May 10, 17, 1867; William Dudley Foulke, *Life of Oliver P. Morton, Including His Important Speeches* (Indianapolis, 1899), I, 466 ff., II, 6.

[5] McPherson, *Reconstruction*, pp. 191–4, 335–7; *Harper's Weekly*, XI (June 15, 29, July 6, 1867), 370–1, 402, 418.

damaging. Wade's actions were under special scrutiny; newly elected by his colleagues as President *pro tem* of the Senate, he was next in line for the presidency. At Lawrence, Kansas, he delivered an impromptu speech in which he not merely threatened that "another turn would be given to the screw" if the South did not accept the Reconstruction acts, but also expressed the opinion that while radicalism was righteousness, conservatism was hypocrisy and cowardice. Then, to prove his point, he called attention to the pressing problem of maldistribution of property, the necessity of improving the relations between capital and labor, and the need for woman suffrage. Upon his return, despite severe criticism, he repeated some of these assertions in an interview with the Cincinnati *Commercial.* Eastern businessmen were horrified; the conservative press had a field day, and Thaddeus Stevens told a reporter of the New York *Herald* that he did not think Johnson would be impeached as long as Wade was his successor. And since Ohio was about to go to the polls, the reputation of its senior senator, whose fate would then also be decided, was of no small concern to the radicals.[6]

This unfavorable publicity did not help the cause during the elections of 1867. If these contests proved anything, they showed that the radicals, often charged with interest in nothing but "power and office," were truly committed to the principle of impartial suffrage. The proposal was unpopular; they knew it; yet they made it their campaign issue.

Early in September, it became evident that things were not going well. The Democrats won in California, gained votes in Maine, and defeated the candidate for territorial delegate in Montana. During the next month, the radicals suffered a major

[6] Washington *Daily National Intelligencer,* June 6, 13, 29, 1867; *New York Times,* June 8, 12, 20, July 1, 6, 1867; New York *Herald,* June 27, July 16, 1867; *New York Tribune,* June 13, 14, 1867; Hans L. Trefousse, "Ben Wade and the Failure of the Impeachment of Johnson," *Historical and Philosophical Society of Ohio Bulletin,* XVIII (October, 1960), 24–52; William Frank Zornow, " 'Bluff Ben' Wade in Lawrence, Kansas: The Issue of Class Conflict," *Ohio Historical Quarterly,* LXV (January, 1956), 44–52.

disaster in Ohio. Before the start of the campaign, moderates had opposed the inclusion of a Negro suffrage plank in the Republican platform, but their rivals insisted on endorsing an impartial voting amendment to the state constitution. Making the most of their opportunity, the Democrats pulled through the streets wagons filled with girls dressed in white, bearing banners with the inscription, "Fathers, save us from negro equality." These appeals to prejudice were effective; little that the Republicans could do could counteract them. In vain did Wade urge the voters to overcome bigotry—they were not to blame for prejudice, he told them, but they were to blame if they suffered what they knew to be prejudice to prevail on them to do injustice to others. In vain did the Chief Justice call on his fellow citizens to sustain the party; in vain did leading radicals seek to rally the flagging voters. The suffrage amendment was defeated, and while the Republicans barely elected Rutherford B. Hayes governor, they lost the state legislature which would have to elect the new United States senator. Wade's career was drawing to a close.[7]

That the suffrage problem was chiefly responsible for the setback was the general consensus. "The 'Amendment' caused our defeat," wrote R. C. Parsons to Sumner, and John Sherman agreed with this analysis. "Honor to Ohio," commented the New York *Tribune.*

> The Republicans . . . with everything at stake, including Mr. Wade's seat in the Senate, accepted—in fact challenged—an issue which they might have postponed, and thus transformed into a hazard what before was a certainty.

In Pennsylvania, too, the Republicans lost, and local observers were certain that the defeat was "owing simply and purely to the question affecting our sable brother." It was a severe disappoint-

[7] *Harper's Weekly,* XI (September 28, October 26, 1867), 610–11, 674–5; P. B. Cole–Sherman, June 16, 1867, John Sherman Papers; Cincinnati *Gazette,* June 20, August 21, 23, September 18, 23, 26, October 10, 16, 1867; *Independent,* October 10, 1867; Clifford H. Moore, "Ohio in National Politics, 1865–1896," *Ohio State Archaeological and Historical Quarterly,* XXXVII (April–July, 1928), 247.

ment, but the radicals had proved their readiness to bring on sacrifices for their ideals.[8]

What followed was almost anticlimactic. Negro suffrage amendments were defeated in Kansas and Minnesota as well as in Ohio; the Democrats won in New York, New Jersey, and Maryland, and the Republicans also suffered losses in other states. The radicals would have to exercise caution.[9]

While the suffrage question had undoubtedly been the main cause of the Republicans' reverses, their dissensions had also contributed to their weakness. "A class of our people want . . . quiet and don't like Ben Butler and Ben Wade & the radicals, while another set don't like Fessenden & the conservatives," observed John Sherman, and *Harper's Weekly* offered a similar analysis:

> For ourselves . . . while declaring our admiration for the indominable tenacity to principle of Mr. Thaddeus Stevens, we have more than once expressed distrust of his capacity as a party chief. Of General Butler and Mr. Ashley we said a month ago, as often before, that whatever their ability and party service, "they are not men in whose wisdom the sober, thoughtful, influential body of the people confide." Certainly Mr. Wade and Mr. Chandler, with all respect for the sincerity of their convictions and the ardor of their eloquence do not inspire an equal respect for their good sense, which is an indispensable quality of a party leader.

And while the distrust of many of the radical leaders was bad enough, such extraneous issues as prohibition and greenbacks, which divided both moderates and radicals, further complicated matters.[1]

[8] R. C. Parsons–Sumner, October 10, 1867, Sumner Papers; John Sherman–Colfax, October 20, 1867, Colfax Papers, U. of Rochester; New York *Tribune,* October 12, 1867; M. R. Thayer–Washburne, October 10, 1867, Washburne Papers.

[9] *Harper's Weekly,* XI (November 23, 30, 1867), 738, 755; Fernand Baldensperger, ed., Georges Clemenceau, *American Reconstruction* (New York, 1928), p. 134 (hereafter cited as Clemenceau, *American Reconstruction*).

[1] John Sherman–Colfax, October 20, 1867, Colfax Papers, UR; *Harper's Weekly,* XI (October 26, November 23, 1867), 674, 738;

How to retrieve these reverses became the chief problem for the radical leadership. Despite their setback, not one of the ultras was willing to give up the ultimate goal of universal suffrage; as Colfax announced, "The standard must not be lowered one inch."[2] The question was merely one of deciding how to proceed. With a presidential election in the offing, it was essential to nominate the right man for the office. And the right man had to be one who sympathized with radical goals as well as one who could win the election.

In settling on a candidate, the advanced Republicans were again plagued by disunity. The most popular figure at the time was undoubtedly General Grant. His political opinions were not entirely clear; before the war, he had only voted for one President —Buchanan—and had not been particularly interested in public issues.[3] But he had led the nation's armies to victory; he had finally brought the war to a successful conclusion. As so often in the past, the victorious general had become a national hero, and he was so well known that he was very much available. Nevertheless, although his principal sponsor, Elihu B. Washburne, was himself fairly radical, many of his ultra colleagues were not at all happy with the prospect of Grant's candidacy.

There were several reasons for the radicals' hesitation. For one thing, the general seemed too close to President Johnson, with whom he had maintained social intercourse as well as fairly intimate political relations. In 1866, he had accompanied the President on the swing-around-the-circle; despite criticism, in 1867, he went even further. When Johnson suspended Secretary of War Stanton, who had refused to resign after the breakup of

---

E. B. Warner–Washburne, November 12, 1867, Washburne Papers; Washington *Daily Morning Chronicle,* November 6, 1867.

[2] *Independent,* October 14, 1867. "The Republican party cannot abandon the negroes, under penalty of losing all its excuse for existing," wrote Georges Clemenceau (Clemenceau, *American Reconstruction,* p. 135).

[3] E. B. Long, ed., *Personal Memoirs of U. S. Grant* (New York, 1962), pp. 107–9

the Cabinet, he appointed Grant Secretary *ad interim,* and the general accepted. The radicals were dubious about his motives.[4]

Another difficulty was Butler's hostility. Ever since Grant had relieved the the ebullient radical from command, relations between the two generals had been strained, and Butler accused his superior of unnecessary bloodletting in the campaign against Richmond. Then Grant's report appeared, a document stigmatizing the position of Butler's army at Bermuda Hundred in 1864 "as if it had been in a bottle strongly corked." The outraged Massachusetts politician broke off social intercourse altogether, and, when the presidential contest began, was still preparing a manuscript of a hostile biography castigating his accuser.[5]

Grant's unwillingness to commit himself also troubled many radicals. "As quick as I'd talk politics, he'd talk horses, and he could talk for hours on that without getting tired," Wade was reported to have described an interview with the general. Chandler suggested that Grant be "smoked out" before any radical endorsement, while John R. Young of the New York *Tribune* tried desperately to groom Philip Sheridan as an alternative candidate. But the result of the elections had made it certain that Grant would have to be the nominee; not only had such rivals as Chase and Wade been eliminated because of their party's defeat in Ohio, but the radicals in general were now dependent on the strongest contender in order to overcome the setback.[6]

The difficulties of leading a divided party were also highlighted by the controversy about the increasingly frequent demands for the impeachment of Johnson. The situation created by the

[4] Welles, *Diary,* II, 477–8; M. D. Defrees–Washburne, August 23, 1866, Horace White–Washburne, September 14, 1866, Washburne Papers; *Independent,* August 29, 1867.

[5] Trefousse, *Butler,* pp. 174, 183, 193.

[6] *New York Times,* November 8, 1867; Chandler-Greeley, August 19, 1867, Greeley Papers; Hay, *Diaries,* p. 285; J. M. Read–Ward, October 11, 1867, Marcus Ward Papers; S. Purviance–Washburne, October 12, 1867, Galusha Grow–Washburne, October 13, 1867, Washburne Papers; Clemenceau, *American Reconstruction,* pp. 135–6.

President's hostility to his own party brought about further splits among the ultras; every time Congress stood ready to adjourn some radicals sought to induce their colleagues to stay in session in order to keep watch on the President. In 1866, Boutwell, Butler, and John A. Logan had been among those urging continuous sessions; Shelby Cullom had warned Trumbull not to allow Congress to go home, but even so radical a member as Julian had been dubious about so demanding a course. In 1867, Sumner and Howard were the chief protagonists of continued congressional vigilance. But, unable to convince even Timothy Howe, they had to content themselves with recesses lasting several months.[7] The situation called for drastic remedies, and some of the more advanced radicals thought they had the solution: the impeachment of the President.

But not all radicals were willing to take this ultimate step. Was it really possible to remove Johnson? Was it desirable to do so? And would the country and party benefit by the attempt? The answers to these questions were so problematic that not even all radicals, to say nothing of the moderates, were willing to risk the consequences.

Ben Butler and James M. Ashley were the chief advocates of impeachment. His initial fondness for the President having turned into bitter hatred, Ashley convinced himself that, somehow or other, Johnson had been implicated in Lincoln's assassination. Butler likewise sought to link the President to the crime. Advocating his removal during the fall of 1866, the general never failed to castigate the President in the most opprobrious terms. Other radicals—Stevens and Chandler, for example—were also investigating the possibility of deposing Johnson, but there was serious opposition. "I feel constrained to inform you of the great anxiety prevailing here, & daily increasing, in regard to the course of some of the seemingly prominent members, if not the apparent

---

[7] *Commonwealth,* July 21, 1866; Shelby Cullom–Trumbull, July 17, 1866, Trumbull Papers, LC; Julian–Mrs. Julian, July 13, 1866, Julian Papers; Blaine, *Twenty Years of Congress,* II, 294, 296; *Cong. Globe,* 40th Cong., 1st Sess., 755.

leaders of the Republican party in Congress. . . ," wrote George Loring to Sumner in January, 1867.

> I am, as you know, an earnest supporter of the measures of that party in its opposition to the President's policy . . . & my social intercourse . . . is mainly with those concurring with me in political opinion & action. And I assure you that I have not heard one person, whose opinions are of consideration, express any other than that of decided opposition to any attempt at impeachment.

Butler's friend J. W. Shaffer also cautioned him. The impeachment issue was unclear; failure might strengthen Johnson and bring disaster to the Republican party.[8] With the radicals themselves split, moderate support would be difficult to obtain.

Ashley, however, was undaunted. On January 7, 1867, he introduced resolutions charging the President with high crimes and misdemeanors and calling on the judiciary committee to conduct an investigation of Johnson's conduct. The committee, chaired by the radical James F. Wilson of Iowa, began hearings; Ashley sought to procure as much evidence as possible, and when, at the end of the session, it reported that it had not been able to complete its labors, the Ohio congressman saw to it that it was again charged with the problem in the new Congress. In spite of its extremist membership, however, the committee on June 10 informed Congress that although it was divided 5–4, it was not prepared to report, its chairman having seen no evidence to enable him to recommend impeachment. It turned out that such radicals as James F. Wilson and Chief Justice Chase opposed the proceedings against the President, while Sumner, Butler, Boutwell, and Stevens were among those calling for his deposition.

In December, 1867, the ultras tried once more. Since John C. Churchill of New York had changed his mind, the committee

[8] New York *Herald*, December 22, 1867; Butler–J. W. Shaffer, April 8, 1867, J. W. Shaffer–Butler, December 16, 1866, Butler Papers; Chicago *Tribune*, October 18, 1866; Boston *Daily Advertiser*, November 3, 1866, *New York Times*, November 25, 1866; Robert Schenck–Stevens, September 23, 1866, Stevens Papers; Chandler–J. A. J. Creswell, October 22, 1866, Chandler Papers, Detroit Public Library; George Loring–Sumner, January 31, 1867, Sumner Papers.

was able to bring in a report written by Boutwell which recommended impeachment. But the radicals were still disunited; the moderates were antagonistic to the attempt, and the House voted unfavorably upon the committee's recommendations. For the radicals, this action was particularly embarrassing because Chairman Wilson had continued his opposition to impeachment.[9]

Because of these divisions and the necessity to cooperate with the moderates, the radicals were much less successful after the Civil War than during the conflict and before. Without homesteads for the freedmen, it would be impossible to give the Negroes enough power to maintain their equality. "The real misfortune of the Negro race is in owning no land of its own," wrote Georges Clemenceau, then in the United States as a reporter. "There can be no real emancipation for men who do not possess at least a small portion of the soil." Thaddeus Stevens recognized this fact clearly; continually advocating land for the former slaves, he favored confiscation of Confederate property in order to achieve it. But he was able to garner little support for his scheme. A few radicals, particularly George W. Julian, a lifelong friend of agrarian reform, and Ben Wade as well as Sumner, occasionally lent their help. But neither the Senate nor the House of Representatives ever took action upon the proposal, so that Reconstruction was doomed before it even began. Had the President cooperated with them in achieving their minimum demands, the radicals might have been able to press forward to achieve agrarian reform; as it was, they were unable to accomplish more than the political innovations embodied in the Reconstruction amendments.[1]

[9] Milton Lomask, *Andrew Johnson: President on Trial* (New York, 1960), pp. 222–34; *Commonwealth,* January 12, July 27, December 11, 1867; DeWitt, *The Impeachment and Trial of Andrew Johnson,* pp. 152 ff., 209 ff., 298; *Cong. Globe,* 40th Cong., 1st Sess., 21, 565; Blaine, *Twenty Years of Congress,* II, 341–7; *Independent,* July 11, 1867; McPherson, *Reconstruction,* pp. 187–90, 264–5.

[1] Clemenceau, *American Reconstruction,* p. 40; *New York Times,* September 10, 1865; New York *Herald,* May 29, June 22, 1867; Washington *National Intelligencer,* June 13, 1867; Riddleberger, *Julian,* p. 242; Sumner, *Works,* XI, 124–36.

Thus it came about that at the very moment of their greatest triumph, the radical Republicans found themselves enmeshed in tremendous complications. Overcoming their rivalries and keeping together enough votes to enact a program, they succeeded in checking the President. They forced the Fourteenth Amendment through both Houses of Congress and put it on the way to ratification. They even imposed universal suffrage upon the South, at least for a time. But they were unable to carry their program to its logical conclusion and give land to the Negroes. Their failure was to have the most serious consequences.

XI

The Radicals Blunder

THE DIFFICULTIES which the radicals had encountered by the end of 1867 were to prove ominous. Ostensibly successful in checking the President, the advanced Republicans were nevertheless divided about future policy. And those who were perspicacious could detect signs of decline—portents that must have given many a politician pause. The radicals were not really as firmly in control as was generally assumed.

The first indication of the radicals' weakness was Thaddeus Stevens's failure in his bid for election as United States senator from Pennsylvania. Undoubtedly the best known extremist leader in the House of Representatives, the Commoner, as Stevens was called, became anxious to secure the position when Edgar Cowan's seat was about to fall vacant. In December, 1866, and January, 1867, he tried to garner voters in the state legislature; John W. Forney, the famous Republican editor, even publicly withdrew from the contest and recommended Stevens as Cowan's successor, but somehow or other, the campaign stalled.

The Commoner was old, and while he occupied a position of leadership in the House, in the Senate he would have no seniority. Moreover, Simon Cameron, eager to return to the Senate, was engaged in a titanic struggle with his ancient enemy, A. G. Curtin, who was also an aspirant for the office. With his superbly organized machine, Cameron finally carried off the prize. That he tended to vote with the radicals was true, but the lack of support for the Commoner was stunning. "The result surprises all," wrote Gideon Welles, "more in the fact that Stevens was so feebly supported than that Cameron succeeded. While I have no high estimate of Cameron in many respects, I think him greatly preferable to either of his competitors. No worse man than Stevens could be elected." The Secretary of the Navy's reaction was significant. Stevens's defeat was an ill omen for the future of radicalism.[1]

More serious than the Commoner's failure—serious both in its implications and direct results—was the defeat the Republicans suffered in the fall elections of 1867. That the hostile New York *Herald* called the outcome an "extraordinary counter-revolution" was to be expected, but that the sympathetic *Independent* came to a similar conclusion was disheartening. Conceding that the setback had ended the effort to impeach Johnson, frustrated all schemes of confiscation, and decidedly delayed the passage of an equal suffrage bill, the paper's Washington correspondent declared that the radicals would stick to principle. But he could hardly explain away the defeat of Negro suffrage in Ohio and Kansas, and although he quoted Ben Wade's assertion that the senator was glad the Republicans had raised the issue of equal rights, it could not be denied that the Ohio legislature would elect a Democrat to take the old radical's place. Not even the prospect

[1] R. J. Sypher–Stevens, December 31, 1866, Edward Reilly–Stevens, December 31, 1866, D. McConaughy–Stevens, January 4, 1867, L. Kaufman–Stevens, January 4, 1867, Stevens–Col. Stambach, January 6, 1867, Stevens–Members, Pennsylvania legislature, January 12, 1867, Stevens Papers; Cameron-Chase, January 7, 1867, Chase Papers, HSP; *Independent,* December 20, 1867; Bradley, *Cameron,* pp. 284–5; Welles, *Diary,* III, 16, 21.

of Grant's victory in the following year could make up for the loss.[2]

The third problem was the continued racial feeling in the North as well as in the South. "The prejudice against the Negro is not wholly overborne," Dr. C. H. Ray wrote to Trumbull in 1866. "Say what we may, you and I share it." Believing that thinking people could deal with this emotion because of a desire to be faithful to principle and a commitment to the "brotherhood of man," he was certain that the masses always gave way to prejudice uncontrolled. "To dislike, I will not say to hate a negro is just as natural as to distinguish black from white," he asserted, thus well expressing the attitude of the time. The result was that all efforts to elevate nonwhites tended to meet with serious opposition unless they were coupled with legislation to control the South. It was the general consensus that the losses sustained in 1867 were due principally to bigotry, so that it was not surprising when practical politicians sought to avoid the issue. As one of Washburne's Philadelphia correspondents wrote,

> In the last four years the Republican Party have done a great work for the Negro, and we should be satisfied *for the present* with what we *have* done, and protect him in the rights we have given him in those States where he was formerly a Slave and had no rights at all, but here we should stop for the present! If the Republican party in Congress intend to keep up this agitation of the Negro question and attempt to enforce it in the Northern, and Western States at this time, . . . even Genl. Grant's great popularity will not save us. The people will not stand any more of it just now!

That there was a growing weariness with the struggle about racial equality was a commonly heard complaint—a trend of public opinion which had serious implications for Reconstruction, the success of universal suffrage, and a group whose principal article of faith was the elevation of the Negro.[3]

[2] New York *Herald,* October 10, 1867; *Independent,* November 14, 1867.

[3] C. H. Ray–Trumbull, February 7, 1866, Trumbull Papers, LC; *New*

In addition, the radicals were still beset by disunity. Unable to agree on impeachment and divided even about new Reconstruction measures, they created an impression of factionalism which could encourage the opposition. They also disagreed about the best way to bring about Negro suffrage, Sumner advocating a mere congressional enactment, others favoring a constitutional amendment. And some of the most advanced radicals still argued that the freedmen must have land. Even in Russia the emancipated serfs had not been cast adrift without homesteads, Carl Schurz had pointed out in 1865. But there was no general consensus about the wisdom of land reform; nor could Republicans agree on the best method of achieving it. Although in January, 1868, there were some signs that they were trying to heal their rifts, their underlying differences had not been resolved.[4]

Finally, there was the problem of the Supreme Court. Although the Chief Justice was still considered a radical, at least until the spring of 1868, his refusal to hold court in Virginia as long as the state was occupied by the military complicated the arraignment of Jefferson Davis. In addition, the tribunal had greatly disappointed the ultras because of the *Milligan* and Test Oath cases. By holding that military commissions were unconstitutional when the civil courts were open and by striking down the test oaths required of Missouri ministers and Supreme Court lawyers, it had complicated Reconstruction, put further obstacles in the way of the trial of the Confederate President, and seemingly defied the dominant faction. The radical press was outraged—"The New Dred Scott," *Harper's Weekly* called the *Milligan* case—and con-

---

York Times, November 8, 1867; John Birney–Colfax, November 7, 1867, Fessenden Papers; H. D. Moore–Washburne, December 7, 1867, Samuel Purviance–Washburne, November 12, 1867, J. A. Putnam–Washburne, January 29, 1868, Washburne Papers.

[4] Cincinnati *Daily Gazette,* January 10, 18, 19, 21, 24, February 7, 1868; New York *Herald,* January 24, 1868; Sumner, *Works,* XI, 409–13; E. F. Bullard–Butler, November 4, 1867, Butler-Bullard, November 7, 1867, Butler Papers; *New York Times,* November 8, 1867; J. A. Butler–Richard Yates, December 8, 1867, Yates Papers, Illinois State Historical Library, Springfield; Bancroft, *Speeches, Correspondence and Political Papers of Carl Schurz,* I, 338; Stampp, *The Era of Reconstruction,* pp. 126–30.

gressional leaders made efforts to restrict the Court's power to declare laws unconstitutional. But again the radicals could not agree; some favored a bill requiring unanimity among the Justices in constitutional decisions, others, a measure providing for a two-thirds majority. And although the milder version passed the House, it never received the Senate's consent. Not until March, 1868, after a Vicksburg editor named William McCardle had endangered the entire Reconstruction program by appealing to the Supreme Court the denial of a writ of habeas corpus from the United States Circuit Court in Mississippi to prevent his trial for sedition by a military tribunal, did the radicals interfere successfully with the Judiciary. For once, the Republicans, radicals and moderates alike, acting with great unanimity, repealed the section of the law under which the appeal had been taken; the Court complied, and the Chief Justice, who had dissented in the *Milligan* and Test Oath decisions, approved of the procedure. But the attitude of the majority of the Justices was threatening; the tribunal had substantially increased its powers by striking down provisions of state constitutions, and, despite the *McCardle* case, the radicals were not able substantially to curtail its pretensions. Within half a year, in *ex parte Yerger,* a unanimous Court would reaffirm its right to grant a writ of habeas corpus to a Southerner held by a military commission.[5]

All these developments had greatly endangered the progress of Reconstruction. To be sure, during the winter of 1867–8, elections took place in Southern states in accordance with the Reconstruction Acts requiring Negro suffrage; conventions met and accepted new constitutions. But reports from the South were not encouraging. Evidence mounted that Unionists and their

[5] Warren, *The Supreme Court in United States History,* II, 421 ff., 465–88; *Harper's Weekly,* XI (January 19, 1867), 34; McPherson, *Reconstruction,* pp. 350–1; Harold M. Hyman, *Reconstruction and Political-Constitutional Institutions: The Popular Expression,* in Harold Hyman, ed., *New Frontiers of the American Reconstruction* (Urbana, Ill., 1966), p. 36; Stanley I. Kutler, "*Ex parte McCardle:* Judicial Impotency? The Supreme Court and Reconstruction Reconsidered," *American Historical Review,* LXXII (April, 1967), 835–51.

colored allies were in danger; it seemed that the only salvation was prompt action by Congress. "Indeed God only knows the hardships of a live Union man in this den of rebel lions," complained Judge J. C. Underwood in Virginia, who demanded federal help to "relieve us from the oppression of our rebel rulers." From Mississippi, where the conservatives eventually defeated the radical constitution submitted to the electors by the convention, comparable warnings reached Washington. New legislation was needed to secure the state, averred the mayor of Woodville, who thought that it was absolutely essential to prevent the ex-Confederates from voting. As he saw it, the conservatives entertained hope that the Supreme Court would set the Reconstruction Acts aside, an expectation which hindered the completion of a constitution.[6]

Similar conditions prevailed in Alabama, where a radical constitution had been framed with the aid of Northern members of Congress. The convention was safely Republican, but the usual difficulties troubled its members. The intense hostility of the conservatives, the fear of executive disfavor, and the intimidation of Negroes by their former masters boded ill for local radicals, whose appeal could hardly be overlooked. Already adversely affected by the Democratic victories in the fall of 1867, the Unionists panicked when the new constitution failed to receive a majority of the registered votes. "And now that the cabals are flushed with supposed victory, the boldest insolence and the grossest indignities are everywhere heaped upon Union men," a Republican wrote to Senator Yates.

> Violence and expulsion are threatened, and without this constitution is accepted and a friendly civil government put in operation with power in loyal hands and Union men sustained, and protected from prosecution, proscription and ruin, we shall all be compelled to leave here, and the republican party and reconstruction are for all time at an end in Alabama.

[6] J. C. Underwood–Greeley, November 27, 1867, Greeley Papers; W. H. Gibbs–Washburne, November 29, 1867, January 16, 1868, Washburne Papers; Dunning, *Reconstruction, Political and Economic*, pp. 112–19.

In another letter, the same correspondent, certain that Johnson's appointees had been decisive in the electoral setback, bluntly stated: "Is reconstruction to go down in Ala. now because fraud and villainy have cheated us out of our rights? We can only look to Congress to come to the rescue." His point of view was shared by others who admonished the lawmakers to stand firm and "keep a faithless executive from obstructing the work."[7]

The situation in Florida was little better. Although the state's population was smaller than that of any of its neighbors, factionalism among the Republicans was pronounced. A radical group led by Liberty Billings and Daniel Richards was opposed by a conservative faction headed by Harrison Reed, who was often able to secure the support of the Democrats. The result was that the radicals were in grave trouble. Clearly expressing their feelings, in January, 1868, Richards wrote to E. B. Washburne:

> We learn that the Supreme Court is about to decide the reconstruction acts unconstitutional and the President is determined to enforce the decision. . . . Congress has got to move rapidly in the matter or we shall be again turned over to the tender mercies of Johnson's rebel government with the military to compel obedience.

In February, a convention, with Richards in the chair, assembled, but the conservatives allied with Reed seceded and eventually took over. A warning not to admit the state under the constitution prepared by the successful Reed faction reached members of Congress; conditions were evidently most unsettled.[8]

In Georgia, Republican politicians were also worried. "Unless Congress affords the delegates to the Constitutional Convention

[7] D. H. Bingham–Stevens, October 23, 1867, Stevens Papers; D. H. Bingham–Sumner, October 23, 1867, Sumner Papers; F. W. Kellogg–Washburne, December 16, 1867, George Ely–Washburne, February 8, 1868, C. W. Buckley–Washburne, January 9, 1868, Washburne Papers; George Ely–Yates, February 12, 1868, Yates Papers.

[8] William Watson Davis, *The Civil War and Reconstruction in Florida* (New York, 1913), pp. 470–2, 500–12; D. Richards–Washburne, February 11, 1868, Washburne Papers; W. P. Dockray–Sumner, February 22, 1868, Sumner Papers.

immediate relief we shall all be compelled to leave the State," a radical wrote to Stevens. "The crisis is now upon Congress. They must take no step backwards or the cause is lost." What upset the ultras particularly was Johnson's order removing General Pope and replacing him with Meade. Bitterly complaining about the change, Foster Blodgett, a leading local radical, pointed out to John Sherman:

> The rebels are rejoicing over it and are now bragging that Reconstruction is a failure & that the Georgia Constitutional Convention will never re-assemble, that the Republican party is dead, etc. The fact is that Reconstruction is now on a pivot, if Congress will stand firm . . . all will be well. . . . While on the other hand if Congress shows any weakness and fails to support our friends and allows the President to do as he pleases, then our party is in fact dead in Georgia and the entire South.

Joshua Hill, a consistent Unionist, expressed doubts about the wisdom of the reconstruction of Georgia and the other states; the people were not worthy of the peace offering, he thought. And Sumner heard that all kinds of underhanded means were used to prevent the Negroes' voting. The federal government must help—this was the common voice of Georgia's radicals.[9]

Similar reports came from other Southern states. In December, 1867, Albion Tourgée, the carpetbagger and author, warned that premature amnesty would cause trouble in North Carolina; by February he emphasized the importance of passing another Reconstruction act if radicalism were to prevail. In South Carolina, federal employees protested that they were being persecuted by the President; in Louisiana, conservatives heartily cheered Jefferson Davis while Republicans were divided into antagonistic factions; and even in Tennessee there were signs of impending trouble. The outlook was so bleak that even those Northern Republicans who sometimes tended toward moderation were becoming uneasy. "I have participated to some extent in the rather

[9] T. H. Hopkins–Stevens, January 3, 1868, Stevens Papers; Foster Blodgett–John Sherman, December 30, 1867, Joshua Hill–John Sherman, January 10, 1868, Sherman Papers; J. Sumner Powell–Sumner, January 20, 1868, Sumner Papers.

gloomy feeling which you express concerning the present phase of reconstruction," wrote Horace White to E. B. Washburne. "My idea of the whole matter in brief is, that inasmuch as Johnson carries all his points, by sheer audacity and doggedness, it is necessary for Congress to meet him on the same ground and to be as audacious and obstinate as he is."[1]

But how were the Republicans to deal with presidential interference and to help their Southern supporters? Immersed in difficulties and obliged to cooperate with the moderates, during the second session of the Fortieth Congress the radicals were still disunited. Thaddeus Stevens moved the adoption of a bill which would have greatly strengthened the army in the process of Reconstruction, but Ben Butler offered a substitute making the state conventions legal governments. When his proposal was defeated by a vote of 53 to 112, such stalwart radicals as Thomas Williams and Samuel Shellabarger refusing to support it, Stevens's bill passed on January 21, 1868, only to die in the Senate. Not until March did Congress adopt a fourth Reconstruction act, a measure designed to break the deadlock in Alabama by providing that a majority of the actual voters was sufficient for the ratification of state constitutions. Moderates as well as radicals favored the bill, but it was manifestly much weaker than Stevens's original proposal.[2]

In the Senate, radical disunity became evident when Philip F. Thomas of Maryland presented his credentials. Considered totally unfit because of his pro-Southern sympathies during the

---

[1] Albion Tourgée–Sumner, December 23, 1867, February 13, 1868, T. A. Hamilton–Sumner, March 23, 1868, Sumner Papers; J. P. M. Epping–Washburne, February 22, 1868, W. C. Carroll–Washburne, March 6, 1868, Horace White–Washburne, January 16, 1868, Washburne Papers. Horace White, then editor-in-chief of the Chicago *Tribune,* was becoming increasingly moderate. Medill-Washburne, June 25, 1868, Washburne Papers. Although a few of these letters date from a period later than February 22, 1868, they are characteristic of conditions existing in the states prior to that time. On Tourgée, cf. Otto H. Olsen, *Carpetbagger's Crusade: The Life of Albion Winegar Tourgée* (Baltimore, 1965).

[2] McPherson, *Reconstruction,* pp. 336–7, 338–9.

war, Buchanan's Secretary of the Treasury had incurred additional censure because he had given his son $300 to enlist in the Confederate army. But although the senators voted to deny him his seat, so well known a radical as Timothy O. Howe defended him and cast his ballot in his favor. The most advanced Republicans were evidently unable to work together.[3]

Perhaps it was the uncertainty and the troubles facing the radicals which made them rush into impeachment with such abandon. It was almost as if they were being driven to it. After the defeat in December of Boutwell's majority report, some advanced Republicans still expressed relief that the perils of a trial had been avoided. As F. V. Balch put it in a letter to Charles Sumner,

> I do not know what to think of the impeachment matter. I have not seen the testimony. I most heartily wish a case could be made that would be clear beyond dispute & then I would have him impeached—expediency or no expediency. But as the case seems to stand, with difference in our ranks as to the law I am inclined to think we have escaped a danger in rejecting the scheme.

This was a fitting comment, but Johnson's behavior during the next few weeks so exasperated radicals and moderates alike that they were ready for any measure. First the President asked Congress for a vote of thanks for General W. S. Hancock, whom he had appointed as Sheridan's successor in Louisiana, and who had openly defied radical sentiment by backing local conservatives; then he suspended both Generals Pope and Edward O. C. Ord from their commands in Georgia and Mississippi. And in January, after having been rebuked by the Senate for the dismissal of Stanton, he ordered Grant not to carry out any orders emanating from the Secretary of War unless they had his specific endorsement. The ensuing acrimonious correspondence between him and the general was published; social relations between the two men ceased, and

---

[3] *Cong. Globe,* 40th Cong., 2d Sess., 325–30, 657–8, 1271; Sumner, Works, XII, 256–69; Howe-Rublee, January 7, 1868, Howe–Grace Howe, January 10, 1868, Howe Papers. George Williams also opposed the majority.

whatever Grant's shortcomings, the radicals could be certain that he would no longer cooperate with the President in any way.[4]

But the party was still divided. Stevens sought to use the evidence of the Johnson-Grant correspondence to obtain in the Reconstruction committee an immediate resolution for impeachment, only to find that Boutwell and Farnsworth alone were willing to support him. Furious about the result, he called the Republican party a party of cowards.[5]

It is against this background that the dramatic events of 1868 must be considered. Had there been no setbacks to the radical cause, had Southern affairs looked more promising, and had Stevens not lost his sense of proportion, it is conceivable that the embarrassment of the impeachment of Johnson might have been avoided. But 1868 was a presidential year; the radicals were hard pressed, and they must have felt that some sort of action was necessary. As all indications pointed to the probable nomination and election of General Grant, it seemed a fortuitous omen when the President broke with the general. Foolishly offending Grant by charging him with treachery because of his compliance with the Senate's refusal to concur in the suspension of Edwin M. Stanton as Secretary of War, Johnson became more isolated than ever before. When, on February 21, 1868, by suspending Stanton again and appointing Lorenzo B. Thomas Secretary of War *ad interim,* he committed the final act which led to his impeachment, he unwittingly led his opponents into their greatest blunder. But so tactless had his actions been that virtually the entire Republican membership of the House was ready to oust him.

The details of the dramatic scenes which followed—Stanton's refusal to give up his office, his receipt of Sumner's famous

[4] F. V. Balch–Sumner, December 10, 1867, Sumner Papers; McKitrick, *Andrew Johnson and Reconstruction,* pp. 499–503; Richardson, *Messages and Papers of the Presidents,* VI, Cincinnati *Daily Gazette,* December 30, 31, 1867; Bruce Catton, *U. S. Grant and the American Military Tradition* (New York, 1954), p. 152; Welles, *Diary,* III, 491.

[5] Clemenceau, *American Reconstruction,* pp. 148–9; Cincinnati *Daily Gazette,* February 13, 14, 1868.

one-word telegram, "Stick," the cooperation of General Grant, and the excited proceedings in the House of Representatives have often been described. In great haste, John Covode offered a resolution that "Andrew Johnson, President of the United States, be impeached of high crimes and misdemeanors," a proposal which was referred to Stevens's Reconstruction committee; the committee reported favorably, and the House, after listening to numerous speeches castigating the Chief Executive, adopted the resolution by a party vote, moderates joining with radicals in demanding the President's ouster. After Stevens proposed a committee of two to notify the Senate and one of seven to prepare articles of impeachment, Speaker Colfax appointed the "Commoner," John A. Bingham, George S. Boutwell, James F. Wilson, John A. Logan, George W. Julian, and Hamilton Ward, Stevens and Bingham serving on both. "Oh, these are grand times and the Lord God reigns over all," wrote the exultant George W. Julian. The ultras entertained high hopes of success.[6]

In spite of their exaltation, however, the radicals had committed a serious error. The whole proceeding was unwise from beginning to end. To be sure, Johnson had goaded his critics and his support of Southern conservatives had caused Unionists to plead for his removal, but as the ultras themselves well knew, the charges against the President were weak, and the real reason for the impeachment was his defiance of congressional policy. Never did the radicals' lack of experience in administration become so evident as in the unreasonable demand to remove the President. He had but one year to serve until a successor would take over; his strength had been curtailed, and impeachment was always doubtful. By undertaking it, the advanced Republicans ran the risk of losing, and the consequences of failure were disastrous.

[6] DeWitt, *The Impeachment and Trial of Andrew Johnson*, pp. 346 ff.; Lomask, *Andrew Johnson, President on Trial*, pp. 262–75; Milton, *The Age of Hate*, pp. 501 ff.; Clemenceau, *American Reconstruction*, pp. 151–5; Claude G. Bowers, *The Tragic Era* (2d ed., Boston, 1957), pp. 174–9; McPherson, *Reconstruction*, pp. 264–6; Julian–Mrs. Julian, February 24, 1868, Julian Papers; Blaine, *Twenty Years of Congress*, II, 352–61, esp. 357.

Perhaps much of the difficulty had to do with Thaddeus Stevens's ill health. So weak that he could hardly speak, he was carried in and out of the chamber in a chair borne by his servants; in fact, he was already mortally stricken. By February, 1868, he had become obsessed with the necessity of impeaching the President. Furious about his failure to obtain a favorable vote after the revelation of Johnson's correspondence with Grant, he seized upon the opportunity presented by the President's defiance of the Senate. Moving about from group to group, he constantly repeated:

> Didn't I tell you so? What good did your moderation do you? If you don't kill the beast, it will kill you.

The committee appointed to draw up a formal indictment prepared nine tedious articles detailing Johnson's effort to replace Stanton with Thomas and charging the President with the intent of violating the Command-of-the-Army Act as well; but Stevens, fearing that these specifications were not strong enough, now committed a tactical error. Only if the trial were conducted with dignity was there any hope of success, and the "Commoner" contributed to its failure by inviting General Butler to take a leading role in it.[7]

That the Massachusetts congressman was clever was beyond dispute. A skillful lawyer, he was genuinely interested in radical causes. But his legal successes had been won more by the audacious use of technicalities than by any profound knowledge of the law, and he was an inveterate brawler. Throughout his career, he had engaged in undignified quarrels with his opponents, whether political antagonists, military associates, or foreign consuls. It was clear that he would be singularly unfit to prosecute the President, and although he had played a prominent role in the original attempts at impeachment, his quarrel with Grant had made him less powerful in Congress. It was for this reason that he was not

[7] Clemenceau, *American Reconstruction,* pp. 138, 153; McPherson, *Reconstruction,* pp. 266–9; Cox, *Three Decades of Federal Legislation,* p. 585; Stevens-Butler, February 28, 1868, Butler Papers (new collection).

appointed to the committee drawing up charges against Johnson. Only Stevens now called him in. "As the Committee are likely to present no articles having any real vigor in them," the "Commoner" wrote,

> I submit to you if it is not worth our while to attempt to add at least two other articles (and as many others as you choose) in the House as amendments, and see whether they will adopt anything worth convicting on. Had I my usual strength, I would not ask you to undertake this movement, but I deem it so important that I send you copies which serve as hints for you to act upon.[8]

The general eagerly complied. Enthusiastically tackling the task, he drew up an article accusing the President of attempting to bring Congress into disrepute because of his provocative speeches. And once Butler was in the limelight, he not only succeeded in securing election to the Board of Managers selected to try the case, but, because of his energy and flamboyance, also emerged as one of the leaders in the proceedings. The House accepted his proposal as well as an additional catch-all article written by Stevens—they became articles ten and eleven—and it fell to Butler to deliver the opening address for the prosecution. Having made up his mind to conduct the trial "in the same manner as . . . a horse case," he totally misjudged the solemnity of the occasion. His tactics may well have contributed to the managers' ultimate failure.[9]

In view of the gravity of the step which Congress was undertaking, it is surprising how little discussion there was about the propriety of impeachment. John A. Bingham, James F. Wilson, James G. Blaine, and James A. Garfield, all formerly opposed to the attempted deposition of the President, now fell in line, and all

[8] Trefousse, *Butler*, pp. 24–7, 103–4, 153–4, 168–9, 125–7, 191–2, 194–5; *Harper's Weekly*, XII (May 2, 1868), 274; Robert W. Winston, *Andrew Johnson, Plebeian and Patriot* (New York, 1928), pp. 424 ff.; Stevens-Butler, February 28, 1868, Butler Papers (new collection).

[9] *Commonwealth*, March 7, 1868; *Butler's Book*, pp. 926–30; *Cong. Globe*, 40th Cong., 2d Sess., 1618–19, 1640 ff.; Ellis Paxson Oberholtzer, *A History of the United States Since the Civil War* (New York, 1922), II, 96 ff., 138; Rhodes, *History of the United States*, VI, 135.

Republicans present in the House voted for the Covode Resolution. Instead of considering the merits of the serious measure which they were proposing, the Republican speakers dealt mainly with the necessity of removing an obstreperous executive—the "great criminal," as William D. Kelley called him—whose defense was left to the Democrats alone. Success was generally believed to be certain, some predicting that Wade would be President within ten days. Even Lyman Trumbull, who would eventually vote against conviction, strongly advised Congressman Shelby Cullom to vote for impeachment. Johnson was an obstruction and should be removed, he advised.[1]

If Trumbull was in favor of deposing the President, statesmen of a more radical state of mind were delighted that the party had at last taken action against the man they hated. "Impeachment is up & I have seen no such excitement since the first battle of Bull Run," Julian wrote to his wife. "We shall impeach now, & all the hazards will sustain us, though Johnson's last act is far less recreant than many previous ones." Robert G. Ingersoll, the famous radical orator, was equally pleased. Glad that matters had at last reached a crisis, he expressed his satisfaction that it was finally going to be settled whether a President had any legislative powers and whether he could obstruct legislation except by his veto. Boutwell, Yates, Wilson, Howard, and John M. Thayer were among those strongly urging Stanton to hold out; on the day before the vote a group of radical and moderate senators and congressmen visited the secretary to assure him of their support; Governor Richard Oglesby of Illinois sent to Speaker Colfax a telegram demanding immediate impeachment, and various state legislatures passed commendatory resolutions. The only problem James Medill foresaw was one of time. "It will be some weeks before you extract the bad tooth in the White House," he wrote to Senator Sherman. That the outcome might be in doubt did not seem to bother him. Equally certain of success, Schuyler Colfax predicted,

[1] Cincinnati *Daily Gazette*, February 25, 1868; Blaine, *Twenty Years of Congress*, II, 356–60; New York *Herald*, February 24, 1868; Cullom, *Fifty Years of Public Service*, p. 154.

"I do not believe the Senate will fail to convict. The hour of our deliverance from this shameless apostate & high priest of discord draweth nigh." And in Columbus, former Postmaster General William Dennison, who was about to take a trip to Europe, assured Sherman: "Our friends here seem a unit for impeachment."[2]

It was no secret that there were some Republicans who were not so certain of victory. "The House of Representatives has met the occasion. No dissenting vote on the Republican side. Will the Senate come up to the action of the House? I fear not," wrote Samuel Hooper to Sumner. F. W. Bird was afraid the Supreme Court might intervene; John Bigelow thought the radicals would fail because of widespread dislike for Ben Wade, and former Governor J. D. Cox also expressed serious doubts about the party's course. When the independent New York *Herald,* as early as February 28, predicted acquittal, it based its forecast on facts which the party leadership should have realized. But the House of Representatives as well as the majority of the party was caught up in a general wave of excitement which obscured the perils ahead.[3]

The radical mood of the House was reflected in its choice of managers to try the impeachment. Thaddeus Stevens, John A. Logan, George S. Boutwell, Ben Butler, and Thomas Williams were all radicals, and James F. Wilson, though differing at times

[2] Julian–Mrs. Julian, February 21, 1868, Julian Papers; R. G. Ingersoll–Oglesby, February 26, 1868, E. C. Ingersoll–Oglesby, March 16, 1868, Richard J. Oglesby Papers, Illinois State Historical Library; Boutwell-Stanton, February 21, 1868, Yates-Stanton, February 21, 1868, Thayer-Stanton, February 21, 1868, Howard-Stanton, February 21, 1868, Henry Wilson–Stanton, February 21, 1868, Stanton Papers; *New York Times,* February 24, 1868; Cincinnati *Daily Gazette,* February 26, 1868; Colfax–K. G. Shryock, March 7, 1868, Colfax Papers, Chicago Historical Society; Medill–John Sherman, March 9, 1868, William Dennison–John Sherman, March 2, 1868, Sherman Papers. Ingersoll was dubious about the technicalities of the impeachment proceedings, however. Orvin Larson, *American Infidel: Robert G. Ingersoll* (New York, 1962), pp. 91–2.
[3] Samuel Hooper–Sumner, February 24, 1868, W. F. Bird–Sumner, February 24, 1868, Sumner Papers; Welles, *Diary,* III, 293; J. D. Cox–John Sherman, March 4, 1868, Sherman Papers; New York *Herald,* February 28, 1868; Schurz, *Reminiscences,* III, 252.

with the ultras, had often supported them. Only John A. Bingham was in 1866 generally considered a moderate. But although he had long been opposed to the attempt to depose the President, he was wholly won over when George Boutwell, refusing to accept the chairmanship offered to him by majority vote, nominated Bingham instead. The managers acted as a radical unit thereafter.[4]

Although the trial caused great excitement throughout the country, the vast crowds that poured into the Capitol to witness the proceedings must have been disappointed. To be sure, on March 4, there was drama when the managers presented the charges to the Senate; on the next day, suspense developed when the senators were sworn in by the Chief Justice because Wade's right to take the oath was challenged on the grounds that he could not be impartial, and on March 13, there was a moment of tension when the President was summoned to appear before the High Court of Impeachment. Well advised by his counsel, which included such eminent lawyers as former Supreme Court Justice Benjamin R. Curtis and future Secretary of State William M. Evarts, Johnson did not present himself in person. But something was lacking—some dramatic incident upon which the outcome would hinge. As it was, the facts were clear. Johnson had dismissed Stanton; the President had delivered his derogatory speeches, and no one denied it. The only question was whether these acts constituted "high crimes and misdemeanors" within the meaning of the Constitution. This was a matter of interpretation, especially since there was considerable doubt about the constitutionality of the Tenure-of-Office Act and some question whether it applied to Cabinet members at all. Consequently, when on March 30 the trial finally got under way, the managers brought out little that was new. The charges were technicalities; Johnson's opposition to the party's Reconstruction policy was the real issue.[5]

[4] Boutwell, *Reminiscences of Sixty Years,* II, 120–1.
[5] New York *Tribune,* March 5, 6, 7, 14, 1868; *Butler's Book,* p. 929; Clemenceau, *American Reconstruction,* pp. 164–78; Howe–Grace Howe, March 31, 1868, Howe Papers; R. G. Ingersoll–Oglesby, February 26, 1868, Oglesby Papers. For the record of the trial, cf. *Cong. Globe,* 40th

It was because of this fact that the trial became so important for the radicals. "Radicalism will not only be dead, but will rot if they fail," commented Gideon Welles, and his point of view was echoed by the ultras themselves. "Johnson's claim to derive his power directly from the Constitution, independent of, and in defiance of law, will justify him in arresting every member of Congress to-morrow, and nothing will prevent the sanctioning of that claim by the Supreme Court, but the certainty of impeachment by the Senate or another uprising of the people like that of 1861," F. W. Bird cautioned Sumner. "This is revolution, more desperate, more dangerous than the first. God help us if the Senate deal with this as Seward would have dealt with the first." Other Massachusetts observers were equally certain that if the Senate failed to convict Johnson, the Republican cause would receive its "death blow." And C. P. Markle, John Covode's radical henchman in Pennsylvania, fully agreed. As he wrote on February 27,

> Well I see you are in the midst of another crisis—all I can say [is] I hope and pray that Congress will succeed, to fail is ruin. Defeat will follow defeat until the country is caught in the hands of the rebels.

The radicals had staked their political future on impeachment.[6]

The spring elections of 1868 demonstrated the importance of the trial for the fortunes of the party. When New Hampshire gave the Republicans a decided majority, Mason M. Tappan, a local radical, was certain that the outcome had been favorably affected by the events in Washington. Writing to E. B. Washburne on March 12, he stated:

> There has never been anything in this State like the political campaign through which we have just passed. . . . No dodging of the issues. . . . *Reconstruction*—"taxes"—impeachment— these have been the great questions, and we have met them

Cong., 2d Sess., *Supplement Containing the Proceedings of the Senate Sitting for the Trial of Andrew Johnson, President of the United States* (Washington, 1868).

[6] Welles, *Diary*, III, 294; F. W. Bird–Sumner, February 24, 1868, Jason White–Sumner, March 5, 1868, Sumner Papers; C. P. Markle– John Covode, February 27, 1868, Covode Papers, LC.

squarely everywhere. . . . Impeachment instead of hurting us has given us at least 500 votes! Whenever you stand stiff at Washington we all straighten up at home, and I trust this will be maintained—especially by the Senate. If there is a faltering . . . in the matter of impeachment, not only our party, but the country is lost! *New Hampshire says put it through!*[7]

Confirmation of Tappan's analysis came shortly afterward from Connecticut. The Nutmeg State too held an election that spring, and unfortunately for the Republicans, the popular Democratic governor, James E. English, was running for a second term. As in New Hampshire, impeachment had an important impact on the race, and visiting statesmen implored radicals to be resolute. "Now, my dear Mr. Washburne," wrote Sickles to the Illinois congressman, "I wish to impress upon you and through you upon our friends in the Senate that we can carry Connecticut if they will stand up firmly to the House of Representatives & to the people on the issue made with Johnson. . . . If the verdict of guilty were now recorded, I would give my head as a hostage for Connecticut." Another worker in the campaign concurred. "All our hopes here are teeming on the course of the Senate," warned John Cochrane. "If they show a manifest disposition to try the 'cuss' with a reasonable dispatch and without cavil, or delay, the Union men here will spring to their guns and carry the State. If otherwise, I am afraid that we shall suffer." The election resulted in the Republicans' controlling the legislature, although English succeeded in his bid to retain office.[8]

If Northern Republicans believed the impeachment crucial for political contests, their Southern supporters considered the trial a matter of vital importance for their very survival. "I am very anxious about the result in the case of Impeachment of the President as his remaining in office will compel the loyal men of Tennessee to leave," wrote one of Sumner's correspondents, who expressed hope that the Senate would dispose of Johnson in the

[7] M. Tappan–Washburne, March 12, 1868, Washburne Papers.
[8] Sickles–Washburne, March 17, 1868, John Cochrane–Washburne, March 25, 1868, Washburne Papers; Welles, *Diary,* III, 329.

shortest possible time. A Mississippi Unionist who had long emphasized the need for the President's removal in order to make possible a Republican victory in 1868, a success he considered essential if any radical were to remain in the state, saw no reason to change his mind after the House had in fact taken action. "I will take the liberty of saying what I know to be the universal idea here among loyal men that if the President is not convicted & removed," he warned, "our efforts here will be defeated, and it will no longer be safe for a white man to advocate the principles of the Republican party in the State except under the immediate protection of federal bayonets."[9]

Alabama Republicans arrived at similar conclusions. Impeachment was absolutely essential because Johnson was the chief obstacle to the success of Reconstruction, a Mobile Unionist had written on New Year's Day, 1868, and when the House complied with his wishes, radicals took heart. "We Southern loyalists are in a state of suspense, much as during the war," F. G. Bromberg, a firm Unionist, stated. "The decisive contest upon which hangs our peace has at length been begun, in the way that should have been taken twelve months ago. We pray that such strength and wisdom may be given to the Court of Impeachment that the misdeeds of the President shall be stopped forever. Punishment for them is out of the question. . . . Security for the future, hitherto denied us on grounds of expediency, is all we ask at the hands of our Senators. The impeachment of the President will be the death blow to the rebellion, still strong with life." His opinions were shared by other Alabama Republicans who stated categorically that without impeachment, "the hopes of Unionists will be crushed." They rejoiced at what they hoped would be the impending removal of the President, "the root of all evil."[1]

[9] T. A. Hamilton–Sumner, March 23, 1868, Sumner Papers; W. H. Gibbs—Washburne, September 30, 1867, April 11, 1868, Washburne Papers.
[1] S. Horton–Henry Edwards, January 1, 1868, F. G. Bromberg–Sumner, March 5, 1868, G. Horton–Sumner, April 23, 1868, Sumner Papers; Louis Fritz and Francis Widmer–Washburne, March 11, 1868, Washburne Papers.

The situation was similar elsewhere. In North Carolina, Unionists deemed conviction essential. "The loyal people of these Southern States, with the fruits of an assured victory already in their grasp, are tremblingly looking for encouragement and support . . . ," a Wilmington Republican stated. "It will be hard for them and worse than it ever has been . . . to find their hopes blasted by the continuance in office of one who has so basely betrayed [them]." In his analysis, he did not differ much from the opinions of neighbors in Virginia, who informed Sumner that Union men could not live in the South if Andrew Johnson were acquitted. As the senator's correspondent put it, "The party who support him [Johnson] and his doctrines in this section have a strong hope of his acquittal and say that the Senate *dare* not remove him." The result of conviction, the writer thought, would be similar to the impression created by Lee's surrender at Appomattox. Florida radicals eagerly awaited conviction, and even in the border states, Unionists considered the President's removal vital. Maryland Republicans had been advocating strong measures against him for a long time, while their friends in Kentucky gained new confidence as the result of the action of the House. As General Brisbin wrote from Lexington,

> The rebels are very quiet here and a good deal alarmed about impeachment but, if that measure fails the Union men will have to leave the state. Here in the South we cannot calmly think of the failure of impeachment and the long train of evils that would follow in its wake.

For Southern radicals, the trial was of transcendent importance.[2]

As time went on, in spite of the Republicans' initial optimism, the successful conviction of the President no longer seemed so certain. For one thing, within a short period it appeared that the Chief Justice was opposed to impeachment. His antagonism was a serious blow, not merely because he was presiding

[2] J. T. Simpson–Sumner, April 15, 1868, D. D. Durboraw–Sumner, May 2, 1868, G. W. Z. Black–Sumner, January 16, 1868, Sumner Papers; Daniel Richards–Washburne, May 6, 1868, Washburne Papers; J. S. Brisbin–Stanton, March 20, 1868, Stanton Papers.

over the trial, but also because he had been one of the original radicals. Uniformly designed to stress the judicial rather than the political character of the proceedings, his rulings revealed the weakness of the managers' case and his influence lessened their chances for success, although he was generally overruled by a two-thirds majority. The *Independent,* which had favored his nomination for President, practically read him out of the party, and no matter how much he protested, he was never again able to enjoy the radicals' full confidence.[3]

It also soon became manifest that several Republican senators were not at all certain to vote for conviction. Because the twelve Democrats and conservatives would vote in Johnson's favor anyway, if seven Republicans defected, the President would be acquitted, nineteen senators constituting just one more than the managers could spare from the required two-thirds majority. That the seven would be found was the opinion of even so cautious an observer as former Secretary of the Treasury Thomas Ewing. By the middle of April, Speaker Colfax had despaired of three senators—Joseph S. Fowler of Tennessee, James W. Grimes of Iowa, and Edmund G. Ross of Kansas, while rumors about William P. Fessenden, Lyman Trumbull, Henry B. Anthony, John B. Henderson, and Peter G. Van Winkle were also circulating. When Grimes, who was known to dislike Ben Wade as heartily as he despised Johnson, let the administration know that he needed certain guarantees that the President would not do anything foolish, he received reassurances, Johnson having already wooed the moderates by nominating General Schofield as Stanton's successor.[4] The result was that, by the first week of May, even the radicals were doubtful about the outcome, Chandler hearing that the Presi-

[3] J. C. Kennedy–Johnson, February 22, 1868, Johnson Papers; *Independent,* April 30, 1868; Chase-Tilton, April 19, 1868, Chase Papers, HSP; Clemenceau, *American Reconstruction,* pp. 183–4; Chase-Greeley, May 25, 1868, Greeley Papers; Schuckers, *Chase,* pp. 581–2; Theodore Clarke Smith, *The Life and Letters of James Abram Garfield* (New Haven, 1925), I, 426; Belden and Belden, *So Fell the Angels,* pp. 186 ff., 200; Howe–Grace Howe, March 31, 1868, Howe Papers.

[4] Thomas Ewing–Hugh Ewing, April 3, 1868, Ewing Papers, LC; Colfax–J. R. Young, April 16, 1868, Young Papers, LC; New York

dent was assured of acquittal, Julian writing to his wife that there was a "fearful impression" that impeachment would fail, and J. R. Young of the New York *Tribune* confiding his worries to the Secretary of War. When newspapers began to publish lists of doubtful senators, the Cabinet became more confident of victory. Publicly Ben Butler still predicted that "Wade and prosperity" were "sure to come in with the apple blossoms"; privately, however, he admitted that his case was "in the greatest of danger." So desperate were the managers that on May 12 the Senate unexpectedly postponed the final vote. "Probable Acquittal of Johnson," read the headline in the radical Cincinnati *Gazette*.[5]

The radicals' apprehensions were heightened by their conviction that a verdict of "guilty" was essential for the success of Reconstruction. Nothing that had occurred had changed their opinion that the future of Republicanism depended on Johnson's removal. As B. Gratz Brown put it on April 21, "There is but one thought in all the loyal nation, and that is if the Republican Senate is not prepared to take charge of the government and visit punishment on gross violation of its laws, then the war is a failure and the peace a surrender." On April 30, an Ohio state senator expressed similar sentiments when he wrote,

> Upon the result of the impeachment trial depends our success as a party in Ohio and if the Senate fail to oust the usurper we have no hope in Ohio. Our ardent friends vow they will not vote the ticket any longer unless the Senate impeach Johnson. This I know is the sentiment in Ohio.

Chandler heard that failure in the trial would spell the end of the Republican party, and although the Philadelphia politician John

---

Tribune, May 1, 6, 12, 1868; G. B. Lincoln–Butler, May 1, 1868, Butler Papers; Cox, *Three Decades of Federal Legislation,* p. 593; *New York Times,* April 27, 1868; Thomas and Hyman, *Stanton,* p. 604 .

[5] John C. Hamilton–Chandler, May 6, 1868, Chandler Papers; Julian–Mrs. Julian, May 5, 1868, Julian Papers; J. R. Young–Stanton, May 6, 1868, Stanton Papers; New York *Tribune,* May 6, 12, 13, 1868; New York *Herald,* May 6, 1868; Welles, *Diary,* III, 342; Browning, *Diary,* II, 196; *New York Times,* May 6, 1868; Butler–Marcus Ward, May 12, 1868, Ward Papers; Cincinnati *Daily Gazette,* May 12, 13, 1868.

M. Read was less pessimistic, he too reported that there was alarm among Republicans about the issue of the trial, "some thinking that if the accused is not convicted it will be fatal to us." And on May 1, John Covode's confidant C. P. Markle wrote again that acquittal meant "ruin & eternal mischief . . . the overthrow of everything that has been fought for and won at the price of much blood and treasure." These warnings were difficult to overlook.[6]

At last, after almost three months, on May 16, the Senate prepared to vote. A tremendous crowd made its way to the Capitol; the galleries were packed; the Chief Justice entered, and after some technical proceedings, the High Court decided to take a ballot on the eleventh article first. It was the one most likely to obtain a two-thirds vote.

Breathlessly the spectators waited as the Chief Justice asked the clerk to call the roll. Senator Anthony, first to be called upon, rose. "Mr. Senator Anthony," asked Chase, "how say you; is the respondent, Andrew Johnson, President of the United States, guilty or not guilty of a high misdemeanor as charged in this article?" Anthony voted guilty; the role call proceeded; senator after senator rose, and as the doubtful Republicans deserted the party, excitement mounted. Fessenden, Fowler, Grimes, Henderson, Ross, Trumbull, Van Winkle—all voted not guilty, so that impeachment failed by one vote. In spite of the small hope for a reversal the court recessed until May 26, and although the managers put heavy pressure on the recusants—they charged bribery and began an investigation—two weeks later the vote on the second and third article was no different. Johnson won by the margin of one vote.[7]

The managers' defeat was so crushing a blow to radicalism that its causes require the closest examination. Why was it that

[6] B. Gratz Brown–Sumner, April 21, 1868, B. F. Potts–Sumner, April 30, 1868, Sumner Papers; J. C. Hamilton–Chandler, May 6, 1868, Chandler Papers; J. M. Read–Washburne, April 30, 1868, Washburne Papers; C. P. Markle–Covode, May 1, 1868, Covode Papers, LC.

[7] *Cong. Globe,* 40th Cong., 2d Sess., *Supplement,* pp. 410 ff.; 412–15; New York *Tribune,* May 18, 27, 1868.

the radicals, after achieving success upon success in carrying the party forward to enact one measure after another, were unable to muster enough strength to convict the President of the charges upon which he had been impeached? Why was it that party discipline, usually so strong, collapsed at the very time when it seemed most important to so many leading Republicans? Although the reasons for the failure were manifold, they could have been foreseen, so that the mistake of embarking upon so dangerous a venture could have been avoided.

In the first place, the case against the President was very weak. To accuse him of violation of the Tenure-of-Office Act because of the suspension of a Cabinet officer was a highly dubious procedure. At the time of passage of the act, Senator Howe's amendment specifically to include the Secretaries had been voted down, and although he was a radical, he was not at all happy about the basis for the impeachment. As he wrote to his niece on February 21:

> The newspapers tell you of events in Congress. To-day we were informed by the President that he had removed Mr. Stanton. Our friends were taken by surprise. I was not. I have only been surprised that he delayed it so long. The Republican press will deny his authority to remove Mr. Stanton. If so the Republican press will lie. I struggled for weeks in the Senate to secure an Amendment to the tenure of office bill which would protect the Secretary of War. . . . The House at first rejected the Amendment but finally agreed to it and insisted upon it, which led to a Committee of Conference. That Committee reported a clause to which both Houses agreed and now the dispute is as to whether it protects the Secretary or not. I know two things about it. 1st That by its terms it does *not* protect the Secretary—and 2nd That when it was reported to the Senate Mr. Sherman . . . stated that it did not and was not designed to protect the Secretary of War and no man contradicted his statement. I gave them to understand this afternoon they must do their own lying.

According to the language of the act, Cabinet members were to hold office "for and during the term of the President by whom they may have been appointed, and for one month thereafter." But Stanton had been appointed by Lincoln, and Johnson was the man who had dismissed him. As early as February 28, the New York *Herald* predicted senators like Fessenden, Anthony, Sprague, Tipton, Van Winkle, Willey, and Sherman would not find Johnson guilty. "Men of such strong judicial minds . . . see that there is really no charge on which to base a conviction," the editor wrote.[8]

Second, the tripartite system of government was at stake. That Americans would easily endorse a course which in effect would render one of the three branches of government paramount was not likely, and on April 29, the New York *Herald* explained:

> The impeachment of President Johnson, with his removal, will mark a new departure of the republican party. The extreme radicals, who have worked their way into the foreground, will rule in every department of the government.

The desire to maintain the separation of powers was an especially important consideration for Senator Grimes, whose vote was vitally affected by it.[9]

Another problem was the fact that Ben Wade was next in line as Johnson's successor. While the old ultra's antislavery credentials were excellent, his espousal of other social and economic reforms, to say nothing of his lack of tact, had offended many of his colleagues. A thoroughgoing radical, the senator favored votes for women, higher wages for the laboring man, and better relations between employers and employees as well as civil rights for Negroes. As he had explained to a reporter from the Cincinnati *Commercial,* he believed that a system of labor "which degrades the poor man and elevates the rich, which makes the rich richer and the poor poorer, which drags the very soul out of a poor man for a pitiful existence is wrong." No matter how strongly they were committed to the freedmen's welfare, the representatives of the dominant industrial order could hardly be expected to agree with these views.[1]

That Wade constituted an obstacle to impeachment had been

[8] T. O. Howe–Grace Howe, February 21, 1868, Howe Papers; Mc-Pherson, *Reconstruction,* p. 176; New York *Herald,* February 28, 1868.
[9] New York *Herald,* April 29, 1868; Salter, *Grimes,* pp. 366–7.
[1] Trefousse, "Ben Wade and the Failure of the Impeachment of Johnson," loc. cit.; *New York Times,* July 1, 1867.

evident for some time. In March, 1867, calling attention to a growing disinclination to proceed with impeachment, Thaddeus Stevens said, "It seems to be preferred that the present Executive should remain where he is to his being substituted by the present Presiding Officer of the Senate." In July, in an interview with the New York *Herald,* he repeated the accusation, and in September, speaking to a reporter from the Boston *Advertiser,* Ben Butler concurred. But, in spite of his enemies, Wade remained President of the Senate.

As soon as actual impeachment proceedings started, careful observers took Wade's influence upon the voting into account. Immediately after the action of the House, John Bigelow told Secretary Welles that the "large conservative force in the Senate, with the Chief Justice," looked "with horror to the accession of Wade and would prefer to continue the President." A few days later, the New York *Herald* predicted categorically that impeachment would fail, because of, among other factors, "Jealousy of Ben Wade and doubts as to his competency."[2]

Wade's economic views worried more conventional Republicans. To be sure, his protectionist stance was not unusual, although it was bound to alienate free traders, but on labor and finance, he was not safe at all. As Edward Atkinson, one of Sumner's economic advisers, wrote to him on February 25:

> You are aware that I distrust Senator Wade's discretion as a leader of a majority, having the greatest respect for him as one of a minority to defeat unjust measures by his vigor and pluck. It seems to me now probable that he may become President. The one irreparable injury which I think the Executive can do, and almost the only one, is to tamper with the currency and to commit the country to disguised repudiation. Upon this question Johnson has been right and Mr. Wade is suspected of being wrong.

Although Sumner tried to reassure his correspondent, Atkinson and his circle remained suspicious. Their attitude was not helpful to the radical cause.[3]

<hr/>

[2] *Cong. Globe,* 40th Cong., 1st Sess., 317; New York *Herald,* July 8, September 7, 1867, February 8, 1868; Welles, *Diary,* III, 293.

[3] *New York Times,* March 31, 1868; Cincinnati *Daily Gazette,*

In addition to the distrust Wade had engendered in the commercial community, he had gravely offended several of his fellow senators. Having often clashed with him about matters of policy as well as the proprieties, Grimes, Trumbull, and Fessenden were known to be personally hostile to him. Moreover, ever since the Chicago convention in 1860, the Chief Justice had disliked him. Convinced that Wade's candidacy had ruined his own chances for the presidency, Chase had no desire to assist in his rival's elevation. When so radical a newspaper as the Chicago *Tribune* suggested that Wade was unfit for the Presidency, some proposed that he step down as the presiding officer of the Senate. Nothing came of the scheme, however, and when Johnson was acquitted, hostility to his would-be replacement was widely held responsible. "Andrew Johnson is innocent because Ben Wade is guilty of being his successor," wrote the Detroit *Post.* In part, it was right.[4]

A final difficulty faced by the impeachers was that Johnson's term was almost up. Within less than a year, the election of 1868 would terminate his tenure of office. Worried about the constitutional implications of the trial, many senators saw no reason why they should displace Johnson, whose shortcomings they knew, with Wade, whose faults they did not fully know, for so short a period of time. That the Ohioan, whose mandate in the Senate was about to expire, would use the patronage of his new office to further his career was generally expected—his Cabinet had reputedly already been chosen. Some Republicans were not willing to take the risk.[5]

March 13, 1868; Washington *Daily National Intelligencer,* May 5, 1868; Atkinson-Sumner, February 25, 1868, March 4, 1868, Sumner Papers; Sumner-Atkinson, February 27, 1868, Edward Atkinson Papers, Massachusetts Historical Society.

[4] Trefousse, *Wade,* pp. 307–9; Washington *Daily National Intelligencer,* May 1, 9, 16, 1868; New York *Tribune,* May 19, 1868.

[5] John Bigelow, *Retrospections of an Active Life* (New York, 1909–13), III, 171; New York *World,* May 4, 1868; McClure, *Recollections of Half a Century,* pp. 65–6; McCulloch, *Men and Measures of Half a Century,* p. 400; John B. Henderson, "Emancipation and Impeachment," *The Century,* LXXXV (1912–13), 205.

Whatever the reasons for the failure of the impeachment, the results became manifest almost immediately. Hardly had the Senate adjourned after the vote on the eleventh article than the Republican convention met at Chicago to nominate a ticket for the forthcoming presidential campaign. No one was surprised when Grant was quickly chosen as his party's standard-bearer. The selection of a candidate for Vice President, however, was not so easy. Although Ben Wade had a plurality for several ballots, he failed to secure a majority, and finally, Schuyler Colfax became Grant's running mate.[6]

The substitution of Colfax for Wade was an indication of the changing nature of the Republican party. The Speaker of the House of Representatives had generally supported radical measures, but before the war he had not been as prominently identified with the antislavery struggle as his rival. In many ways, he was representative of the new brand of leaders who were rapidly transforming the party from a forward looking organization dedicated to reform to a group primarily concerned with the support of the existing economic order. Because of their close identification with the powerful industrial forces released by the favorable outcome of the Civil War, men like James G. Blaine, Roscoe Conkling, James A. Garfield, Rutherford B. Hayes, and Oliver P. Morton were taking the place of Charles Sumner, Ben Wade, Thaddeus Stevens, George W. Julian, Joshua Giddings, and Owen Lovejoy, and Colfax's nomination was symbolic of the change. Had Wade become President because of Johnson's conviction, he would probably have been able to secure second place on the ticket. But the party of Abraham Lincoln was becoming the party of Ulysses S. Grant.

The decline of fervor could also be seen in the voting plank adopted at Chicago. Instead of clearly endorsing universal suffrage as demanded by many radicals, the Republicans merely gave their blessing to congressional guarantees of equal voting rights in the

---

[6] *Proceedings of the National Union Republican Convention, Held at Chicago, May 20 and 21, 1868* (Chicago, 1868), pp. 98 ff., 103, 118; McClure, *Recollections of Half a Century* p. 69.

South. In the loyal states, according to the platform, the question belonged to the people of those states. Radicalism was clearly at a discount.[7]

Perhaps the most important result of the failure of impeachment was the demoralization of the Union forces in the South. While it is true that radical Reconstruction took place largely after the President's acquittal, the events in Washington may well have been a significant factor in bringing about its eventual failure. Southern Unionists were in dismay as soon as the outcome was known. "It is with sadness we learn that the greatest traitor of the century is acquitted," wrote Daniel Richards, the Florida carpetbagger.

> News of the failure to convict Johnson will be like Greek fire throughout the entire South. May God save our country from the consuming conflagration. The eyes of rebels sparkle like those of the firey [sic] serpent. They hope they have found their 'lost cause' and think they see it. I am not certain but they are right.[8]

From Alabama, George E. Spencer, the Register in Bankruptcy in Tuscaloosa, reported a similar decline in morale. "It is impossible to paint in true colors the woeful condition of the Union men in the South since the news of the failure of Impeachment," he wrote.

> Our best men both white & black are leaving us & making haste to place them in a condition to be allowed to remain in the country. But it is useless for me to tell you the state of affairs in this state. . . . I hope Congress will not now be foolish enough to admit Alabama & let her vote be cast for the Democratic candidate for President, in November. There is no possible chance for us to carry the State for General Grant. Everybody nearly is intimidated.

It turned out that for 1868 his prediction was wrong, but six

[7] *Independent,* July 16, 1868; Draft letter, Stevens–C. S. Spence, June 24, 1868, Stevens Papers; T. W. Conway–Chase, May 24, 1868, Chase Papers, LC; McPherson, *Reconstruction,* pp. 364–5.

[8] Daniel Richards–Washburne, May 18, 1868, Washburne Papers.

years later, the state deserted Grant and returned to the Democratic column.[9]

In South Carolina, too, Unionists complained. "The failure of Impeachment has hurt us. . . ," wrote D. F. Corbin to Justin S. Morrill. "The rebels are in great glee, and two nights since in a public meeting took such a stand against reconstruction as they would not have dared to take two weeks ago." Sumner heard even more disquieting news from the Palmetto State. Conditions were terrible, reported one of his confidants, who averred that Union men were in deadly danger because of the "procrastination" of the Senate. Unionists thought the murder of a Republican member-elect of the state legislature was "one of the results of the acquittal," a circumstance they hoped might "possibly lead such men as Mr. Ross & Co. at least thinking whether Andrew Johnson is guilty of high crimes and misdemeanors." The prospect did not look favorable for the success of Republican government in South Carolina.[1]

In Mississippi, the effects of the failure to convict the President were also felt immediately. As J. L. Alcorn, the state's most prominent scalawag, explained the situation to E. B. Washburne,

> Long before this reaches you, you will have seen that the constitution submitted by the convention to the people of this state has been rejected. This constitution was the most conservative of any that has been submitted to the Southern people, under the reconstruction acts. The causes which have led to this result, you doubtless well understand. The impeachment failure has revived the spirit of the rebellion, it comes with more than its original wrath, nothing but the presence of the bayonet saves the opponents of democracy, or I should say the friends of the government from being driven from the state. The proscriptions of 1861 were not as feared as those of the present day. . . . Can it be possible that the Northern people have made the negro free, but to be returned, the slave of society, to bear in such slavery the vindictive resentments that the satraps of Davis

[9] George E. Spencer–Washburne, May 23, 1868, Washburne Papers; Walter L. Fleming, *Civil War and Reconstruction in Alabama* (New York, 1905), pp. 747, 795.

[1] D. F. Corbin–Morrill, May 29, 1868, Justin S. Morrill Papers, LC; J. H. Feriter–Sumner, June 6, 1868, Sumner Papers.

maintain today towards the people of the north? Better a thousand times for the negro that the government should return him to the custody of his original owner, where he would have a master to look after his well being, than that his neck should be placed under the heel of a society, vindictive towards him because he is free.

The defeat of the constitution kept the state from regaining representation in Congress for almost two years more. When, in 1870, it was finally readmitted, it proved to be wholly unprepared for Republican rule. Murder and violence abounded, and by 1875, it was back in the hands of the "redeemers."[2]

If white Unionists deeply felt the effects of Johnson's acquittal, their Negro supporters were even more downcast. Sadly commenting about his failure to obtain a commission in the army although he had fought for the Union, a Georgia Negro Republican wrote to Charles Sumner:

> Our condition South since the acquittal of Andrew Johnson is a perilous one. Since the election in this State colored men have been thrown out of employment and driven from their homes and some reduced to beggary simply because their conscience and interest would not allow them to vote with old master. . . . I myself had to be guarded at night by colored men and finally had to leave the county on account of the threats made against my life, and unless more adequate protection is afforded us in the coming Presidential struggle we cannot canvass the State.

That his predictions were correct was borne out by the election results. The Democrats carried Georgia in November.[3]

Thus it was evident from the first that the radical cause had suffered a severe reversal. James Medill and others, who feared that the acquittal would damage Grant's prospects, missed

[2] J. L. Alcorn–Washburne, June 29, 1868, Washburne Papers; James Wilfred Garner, *Reconstruction in Mississippi* (New York, 1901), pp. 216, 269 ff., 338 ff., 382 ff.; Hodding Carter, *The Angry Scar, The Story of Reconstruction, 1865–1890* (Garden City, 1959), p. 219.

[3] Edwin Belcher–Sumner, June 23, 1868, Sumner Papers; Bowers, *The Tragic Era*, p. 235; Alan Conway, *The Reconstruction of Georgia* (Minneapolis, 1966), pp. 173–4.

the point. Not the party, but its most advanced members had been hurt. As the *Independent* pointed out, "the action of Fessenden and Trumbull was not at all for the President's sake, . . . but was chiefly to seize the helm of the Republican party from the Radicals, and steer the ship themselves."[4] Upon hearing the verdict, Stevens, brandishing his arms in the air, shouted, "The country is going to the devil!" a sentiment which expressed his assessment of the ultras' prospects. The old "Commoner," who had only a few more weeks to live, became exceedingly pessimistic. "My life has been a failure," he said. "With all this great struggle of years in Washington, and the fearful sacrifice of life and treasure, I see little hope for the Republic." James M. Ashley's biographer, writing many years later, considered the defeat of impeachment "the real death knell of radical republicanism as a controlling factor in Congress and in the country." And Charles Sumner, linked in the popular mind with Stevens as the principal spokesman for the radicals, summed up his dismay in his formal opinion which he submitted to the Senate:

> Alas for all the evil that must break upon the country, especially the suffering South, as it is confirmed that this bad man is confirmed in the prerogatives he has usurped! . . . Alas for that race so long oppressed, but at last redeemed from bondage, now plunged back into another hell of torment! . . . Alas for the Unionists, white and black alike, who have trusted to our flag. . . . May they find in themselves, and in the goodness of an overruling Providence, that refuge and protection which the Senate refuses to give![5]

His forecast was not far from wrong. When, in June, 1868, several of the reconstructed states were readmitted, the seeds of failure for the experiment had already been sown. As the Cin-

---

[4] Medill-Washburne, June 15, July 10, 1868, Washburne Papers; Hinsdale, *Correspondence Between James Abram Garfield and Burke Aaron Hinsdale,* pp. 136–7; James Scovel–Sumner, May 20, 1868, H. Snapp–Sumner, May 23, 1868, Sumner Papers; *Independent,* May 21, 1868.

[5] Margarit Spaulding Garry, ed., William H. Crook, *Through Five Administrations* (New York, 1910), p. 133; McClure, *Lincoln and the Men of War-Times,* pp. 263–4; Ashley, "Governor Ashley's Biography and Messages," loc. cit., p. 189; Sumner, *Works,* XII, 409.

cinnati *Gazette* remarked, Tennessee, the last commonwealth to come back into the Union, had given to the country President Johnson and Senator Fowler. The new ones were not even that good. "It must be confessed that neither the fruits of reconstruction already accomplished, nor the promises from the other states, are especially encouraging," was the editor's comment. The future was to confirm his judgment.[6]

Viewed in retrospect, therefore, the unsuccessful effort to impeach the President was a serious blunder. Goaded on by reverses in the North and difficulties in the South, the radicals sought to revitalize the party by removing the President. But by attempting to implement a policy for which they did not have sufficient support, they risked defeat. And their failure, coupled with their losses in 1867, suggested to their enemies that their strength was ebbing. Although they were still able to exert some influence during the Grant administration, in essence radical Reconstruction was a stillborn experiment.

[6] Cincinnati *Daily Gazette,* June 15, 1868.

XII

The Last Triumphs

IN SPITE of the setback which the radicals suffered because of the impeachment proceedings against Johnson, the years 1869 to 1872 were not entirely barren of achievement. True, the ultras' importance was declining, but they still managed to score a number of triumphs—their last successes perhaps, but significant for the future just the same. The ratification of the Fourteenth Amendment, the restoration of the Southern states with universal suffrage, the passage and ratification of the Fifteenth Amendment, and the framing and implementation of the Force Acts—all these constituted accomplishments for which the radicals deserved credit.

The most notable triumph during this period was the ratification of the Fourteenth Amendment. With the exception of emancipation, it was the radicals' single greatest contribution and so important did the measure appear, even at the time, that enemies of Reconstruction determined to use every means to defeat it. Not only did Johnson utilize his entire influence to prevent its ratification in the South—in the long run, his opposition could be overcome by the reorganization of the Southern states in accordance with the Reconstruction acts which required assent to the change —but as soon as the Democrats won control of individual Northern legislatures, they passed ordinances repealing previous ratification. Whether this procedure was constitutional was questionable; however, if the radicals wanted the amendment to be incorporated beyond any reasonable doubt into the basic law, they had to see to it that its acceptance did not depend on counting the ratifications of states that had sought to withdraw their previous assent.

These circumstances made essential the speedy restoration of as many Southern states as possible. By the summer of 1868, eight of these had framed constitutions, several had signified their assent to the amendment and had held elections ratifying their new basic laws. Loyal Leagues had seen to it that the freedmen were given political guidance, and with radical influence prevailing in most of these commonwealths, their readmission to the Union became feasible. The states in question sufficed to secure final ratification of the amendment.[1]

But there were difficulties in the way. Because of the continued disorders in the South, there were many Republicans in the disaffected section who would have preferred continued congressional control to premature completion of Reconstruction. Already demoralized because of Johnson's acquittal, they sought to delay readmission. In Florida especially, radical politicians were pessimistic. "Were we in the Union the whole Reed party would wheel into line with the rebels & carry the state against General Grant," warned Daniel Richards, the disappointed Florida carpetbagger, whose faction had been feuding with Governor Harrison Reed. Richards's colleague, Liberty Billings, who believed "Rebel Herods & Johnson office holding Copperhead Pilates" were combining to "crucify Radical Republicanism," shared his apprehensions. "The Republican party gain nothing by admitting Florida into the Union," he cautioned. And G. W. Atwood, one of Stevens's confidants, implored the Commoner not to admit the

---

[1] Sumner, *Works*, XII, 253–6; McPherson, *Reconstruction*, p. 353; Franklin, *Reconstruction After the Civil War*, p. 130; Cason, "The Loyal League in Georgia," loc. cit., p. 125.

state. Its present government would only defraud Congress and the Negro.[2]

In Georgia, too, conditions gave rise to pessimism. So worried was a colored Unionist that he confessed to Sumner he would have voted against the amendment had he not felt that no Negro should oppose a Republican measure. "For," he explained, "I would sooner remain out of the Union forever and be protected by the military (inadequate as that protection is) than go into the Union and be in the power of Rebels and traitors." The outlook was far from favorable, especially as disorders prevailed in other Southern states as well.[3]

The uncertainty of the amendment's fate, however, made any hesitation impossible, and the radicals took the lead in pressing for the restoration of the states. Not unmindful of their allies' fears, they sought to protect Southern Republicans by adding stringent conditions to the readmission bills, Senator Drake moving that Arkansas, the first state to be restored in 1868, should never be allowed to abridge the right of the elective franchise by reasons of race or color. His amendment was accepted by the Senate, although a committee of conference with the House changed the wording somewhat in the final version. A similar fundamental condition was included in the "Omnibus Bill" for the admission of North Carolina, South Carolina, Louisiana, Georgia, Alabama, and Florida, Charles Sumner taking the lead in pleading strongly for the proviso. After the President had vetoed both measures, on June 22 Arkansas and on June 25 the other states, were restored to full representation by Congress, which overrode his objections with little trouble.[4]

That the Fourteenth Amendment had much to do with the

[2] Daniel Richards–Washburne, June 6, 1868, Billings-Washburne, June 7, 1868, Washburne Papers; G. W. Atwood–Stevens, June 11, 1868, Stevens Papers.

[3] Edwin Belcher–Sumner, July 23, 1868, Sumner Papers; W. H. Gibbs–Washburne, July 14, 1868, B. F. Saffold–Washburne, July 9, 1868, Washburne Papers.

[4] *Cong. Globe,* 40th Cong., 2d Sess., 2600; McPherson, *Reconstruction,* p. 337.

radicals' determination to enact the readmission bills was evident at the time. In the debates leading to the passage of the measure restoring Arkansas, Charles Drake vowed not to vote for the admission of any state until the amendment was part of the Constitution. Oliver P. Morton, however, replied that it would be wise to bring in Arkansas in order to hasten the disappearance of Confederate influence there. Two days later, Henry Wilson, who was taking a leading part in the discussion about the Omnibus Bill, had a better rejoinder for his fellow radical: "If twenty-eight States are necessary to the adoption of that constitutional amendment," he said, "I implore the friends of that amendment to admit these seven States at once, and thus secure the twenty-eight States necessary to make the amendment part of the Constitution." Jacob Howard used the same argument, and the Arkansas act specifically cited the legislature's ratification of the amendment as a reason for her full restoration. In the case of the Omnibus Bill, favorable action upon the constitutional change was specifically required as a fundamental condition for readmission. The result was that on July 20, 1868, the Secretary of State was able to certify that the necessary number of states had adopted the measure. Even if the votes of New Jersey and Ohio, the states which had withdrawn their assent, were not counted, the Fourteenth Amendment had become part of the Constitution.[5]

The radicals' success was to have far-reaching consequences. The amendment not only incorporated in the Constitution the great shift of balance from the state to the federal governments, a change caused by the Civil War, but it also made possible the federal government's intervention in favor of civil rights in later years—a contingency which could have been foreseen by its sponsors despite the long period of disuse of national power. If the amendment was to be perverted for decades into an agency of economic oppression, its original purposes could always be reasserted. Had it not been for the radicals' efforts, the due process

[5] *Cong. Globe,* 40th Cong., 2d Sess., 2628 ff., 2691, 2967; McPherson, *Reconstruction,* pp. 337–8, 379–80.

clause of the Constitution might never have applied to the states.[6]

The importance of the ratification of the Fourteenth Amendment was only one of the reasons for the Republicans' advocacy of speedy restoration. Thaddeus Stevens hoped to obtain a better radical majority in the Senate, where the impeachment of Johnson was pending. The moderates, however, were opposed to so questionable a method of deposing the President, and it is significant that even after the states were readmitted, and the party commanded an undoubted two-thirds majority in the upper House, Stevens's renewed schemes to try the President came to naught. Hateful as Johnson appeared to most Republicans, he was permitted to serve out the remainder of his term.[7]

Other factors also militated against further delay in Reconstruction. Congress was committed to certain conditions; these conditions had been met, and it would have been difficult to keep the states out indefinitely. Many radicals felt bound by legislation enacted by themselves. As Samuel C. Pomeroy said in the Senate,

> I have thought the best and surest method of reconstruction would be to convince the South that on their return they are to be dealt with in the most liberal and cordial manner, not only in being welcomed back but in our subsequent treatment of and legislation in regard to those States. When we completed the legislation called the reconstruction acts that was a covenant between me and them, and I think it was a covenant between Congress and those States; but for my action it was certainly a covenant that if they complied substantially, in good faith and earnestly, with the conditions of reconstruction as placed in the law they should be received back into the Union.[8]

Some politicians may also have had the election of 1868 in mind; closely divided, the country might well fall to the Democrats except for the control of certain Southern states. Others were certain that readmission might actually give greater security to Unionists

[6] Cf. Ten Broek, *The Antislavery Origins of the Fourteenth Amendment,* esp. p. 219.

[7] *Cong. Globe,* 40th Cong., 2d Sess., 2464; Clemenceau, *American Reconstruction,* p. 183; *Independent,* July 30, 1868; New York *Herald,* July 28, 1868.

[8] *Cong. Globe,* 40th Cong., 2d Sess., 2900.

—some Southern Republicans expressed this idea, and others were anxious to hasten the process lest the Negroes become apathetic and surrender control to the Democrats.[9] But, whatever the radicals' motives, the most significant result of the passage of the bills readmitting the eight states was the ratification of the Fourteenth Amendment.

————

In the minds of some observers, the successful political campaign of 1868 also constituted a radical victory. While General Grant was not the ultras' original choice for President, his break with Johnson and his willingness to subscribe to Republican doctrines on Reconstruction contributed to the success of their policies. Whether they could have won with another candidate is doubtful, and they gave the general their wholehearted support. It was not yet clear that he was poorly qualified to carry out the functions of the presidency; in comparison with Johnson, he seemed a veritable savior of Republican ideals.[1]

For a short period of time, there appeared to be a chance that the opposition might also endorse the radical program. The Chief Justice, whose hopes for the Republican nomination had vanished, was flirting with the Democrats. Although he had broken with the radical leadership because of his disapproval of the impeachment, he had not forgotten his principles. Anxious as ever to secure the presidency, he lent himself to a movement to convert the Democratic party to radicalism. He had always sympathized with Jacksonian doctrines; twenty years earlier he had insisted on calling the Free-Soil party Free Democratic, and he believed that all that was necessary to effect harmony between himself and Grant's opponents was to induce the Democrats to accept Negro

[9] Dunning, *Reconstruction, Political and Economic,* p. 119; E. Merton Coulter, *The South During Reconstruction, 1865–1877* (Baton Rouge, 1947), p. 137; C. W. Buckley–Washburne, May 1, 1868, Washburne Papers; C. S. Evans–Stevens, May 30, 1868, Stevens Papers.

[1] Cincinnati *Daily Gazette,* February 24, 1868; C. A. Page–Washburne, October 12, 1867, Galusha Grow–Washburne, October 13, 1867, J. C. Cochrane–Washburne, October 17, 1867, Washburne Papers; J. M. Read–Marcus Ward, October 11, 1867, Ward Papers; W. Jayne–J. D. Strong, April 23, 1867, John D. Strong Papers, Illinois State Historical Library; *Independent,* April 2, July 16, 1868.

suffrage and the principles of racial equality. "Nothing would gratify me more than to see the Democratic Party advance its standards to the full height of a true expression of democratic ideas," he wrote to Hiram Barney, the former Collector of the Port of New York. "What a grand & noble organization it would then be!" Democratic ideas to him signified equal rights for black and white alike, whether the ultras cooperated with him or not.[2]

Most of his former associates considered Chase's course outrageous. Already incensed at him because of his opposition to the impeachment, they could only credit his actions to one motive: ambition. As they saw it, ambition had been his reason for failure to cooperate during the trial, and ambition seemed the only explanation for his bid for the Democratic nomination. When Theodore Tilton, the editor of the *Independent,* in an article entitled "The Folded Banner," castigated Chase severely for flirting with the opposition, the Justice wrote him an indignant denial. But though radical friends sent him alarming letters, he could not deny the charges, and soon his candidacy was out in the open. "I feel tempted to ask you whether you are coming round to my view of Chase, which I have held without variation since 1864 up to the present hour," Judge E. R. Hoar, a leading Massachusetts Republican, wrote to Sumner. The Judge was confident that Chase was wholly lost. But these observers were unjust. Ambitious as the Justice was, he refused to give up his insistence upon an equal-rights platform. "If things turn out as seems likely, it will be the Democratic party which will go over to Mr. Chase, and not Mr. Chase who will go over to the Democratic party," commented Georges Clemenceau.[3]

There were some old antislavery friends who understood Chase's aims. "You are about to become if you please the candi-

---

[2] Chase–Hiram Barney, May 29, 1868, Chase Papers, HSP; Schuckers, *Chase,* pp. 560 ff.

[3] Chase–Theodore Tilton, April 19, 1868, Chase Papers, HSP; *Independent,* April 30, 1868; T. W. Conway–Chase, May 24, 1868, Chase Papers, LC; Smith, *Garfield,* I, 426; E. R. Hoar–Sumner, July 27, 1868, Sumner Papers; Clemenceau, *American Reconstruction,* p. 197.

date of the democratic party for the office of President of the United States," William Cullen Bryant wrote to him.

> The older leaders of that party who have their prejudices against Negro suffrage to overcome, will be drawn into this measure by the younger men who are inclined to more generous views, and by such of the older leaders as care nothing for principles but everything for party supremacy. It is in your power . . . to dictate the platform of principles upon which you are to be nominated.

Joshua Leavitt, the veteran New York abolitionist, was equally enthusiastic. "Your own position appears to me to be perfectly sound and honorable," he commented, "and if the move should be successful, it would be the greatest blessing the country has received since the 'Rising of a Great Nation' in 1861." Gerrit Smith also endorsed Chase's candidacy, and A. N. Cole, a radical Brooklynite, summed up the situation by stating:

> The Democratic party, warring as it has for long years with you and I and others like us, on the question of the Rights of Man, gravely proposes to surrender, if you will only be their candidate. Well, their surrender settles the most momentous of all issues . . . and great good cannot but come of it.

For a moment, at least, it seemed possible that radicalism would be safe no matter who won the election.[4]

But Chase's candidacy was short-lived. Used largely as a stalking horse for financially conservative opponents of George H. Pendleton, whose inflationary notions frightened them, the Chief Justice was unable to persuade the party to abandon its opposition to racial equality. When the convention met in New York, Chase's backers were defeated; Horatio Seymour and Francis P. Blair became the party's standard-bearers; the platform severely condemned what it called the "Radical party" as well as "negro supremacy," and Blair wrote a lurid letter of acceptance in which he charged Grant with sanctioning a peace of "despotism

[4] J. C. Bryant–Chase, June 13, 1868, Gerrit Smith–Chase, June 20, 1868, Chase Papers, HSP; Joshua Leavitt–Chase, June 16, 1868, A. N. Cole–Chase, June 13, 1868, Chase Papers, LC.

and death." No radical could any longer question the importance of a Republican victory.[5]

Because of their conviction that Grant's success was essential for the cause, the radicals once again campaigned strenuously for the Republican party. Canvassing critical states, they helped candidates in closely divided areas. Because General Nathan Bedford Forrest had been honored at the Democratic convention, James G. Blaine prepared 100,000 copies of the Fort Pillow report; Horace Greeley wrote articles extolling the Victor of Appomattox; John A. J. Creswell stumped Maine; Charles Sumner delivered well-thought-out orations in which he castigated the Democrats as rebels; Zach Chandler campaigned without let-up in Michigan; John W. Forney marshaled the Republicans of Pennsylvania, and Ben Wade and Edwin M. Stanton lent their prestige to the party in Ohio. With the old spirit animating even those who were not pleased with the platform, the radicals' enthusiasm contributed materially to Republican success.[6]

The outcome of the election was no great surprise. To be sure, the Democrats had made inroads upon their opponents, but with the aid of the reconstructed states, the Republicans swept the country. Of the Northern constituencies, only New York, New Jersey, and Oregon failed to endorse the general, and Congress went Republican by heavy majorities. The party's future seemed assured.

Whether Grant's victory was in fact an unqualified success for the ultras is doubtful. Although Democrats tended to use the word "radical" for all Republicans, in October the New York

[5] Welles, *Diary*, III, 382–3, 397–401; Blaine, *Twenty Years of Congress*, II, 402–3; McPherson, *Reconstruction*, pp. 367–71. Chase himself became highly critical of the Democratic platform and ticket, even though a movement to have Seymour withdraw in his favor persisted. Chase–Hiram Barney, August 9, 1868, Alexander Long–Chase, September 10, November 2, 1868, Chase Papers, HSP; Chase–John Van Buren, September 2, 1868 (draft), Chase Papers, LC.

[6] Blaine-Washburne, July 11, 1868, Washburne Papers; *Independent*, August 13, 1868; Creswell-Chandler, September 7, 1868, Stanton-Chandler, October 1, 1868, Chandler Papers; Detroit *Post and Tribune, Chandler*, p. 298; Sumner, *Works*, XII, 510 ff.; Forney-Sumner, September 28, 1868, Sumner Papers; Ashtabula *Sentinel*, September 17, 1868; Wade–Mrs. Wade, October 21, 1868, Wade Papers.

Herald boasted that Republican majorities in the Northwest actually constituted a triumph for moderation. One month later, the newspaper asserted that Grant's election showed that people were tired of radicalism; they had voted for the general in order to have him secure the peace which he won on the battlefield. That there was some truth in these assertions could be seen by the fact that the Republicans lost their two-thirds majority in the House. As the historian of the election wrote many years later, the Democrats had forced their opponents to put aside their statesmen and nominate the military hero of the war because of widespread discontent with radical measures. The New York *Round Table* even predicted that "open war" would break out between Grant and the extremists.[7]

In the main, however, the advanced wing of the party had scored a triumph. Reconstruction would go on; such stalwarts as Boutwell, Butler, Covode, Kelley, Julian, Logan, Wilkinson, and E. C. Ingersoll were all returned to the House; and the violent claims of the Democratic platform had been decisively rejected. Many contemporary observers were certain that radicalism had prevailed. "The ideas that you have pursued, with your life in your hand, will be indelibly stamped upon the nation," John S. Cunningham, a Philadelphia ultra, wrote to Sumner on October 14. "The great elections of yesterday are *your* triumphs." Although he himself suffered defeat, James M. Ashley, rejoicing at the party's success, consoled himself with the hope that "a bright morning" would succeed the "long, dark and stormy political night." Benson Lossing, the chronicler of both the Revolution and the Civil War, agreed. He thought that the victory constituted the "harvest" of Sumner's "patient seed-time of effort in the field of National justice," while William Lloyd Garrison was certain that Grant would sustain Congress in its efforts at Reconstruction. The

---

[7] New York *Herald,* August 21, October 15, November 7, 1868; Clemenceau, *American Reconstruction,* p. 262; Charles Coleman, *The Election of 1868* (New York, 1933), pp. 375, 377; *The Round Table,* November 7, 1868. The loss of the two-thirds majority was only temporary; the admission of the remaining reconstructed states restored the dominant party's edge.

radical *Commonwealth* triumphantly announced that the hopes of the Founding Fathers had been realized, and on November 19, the *Independent* expressed many extremists' feelings when it contrasted the condition of affairs in July with the situation after the victory. In summer, impeachment had just failed, "rebel sympathizers abounded, and an ugly sentiment existed against the colored people. Prominent Democrats were sanguine of the defeat of 'Radicalism,' and were laying their plans for subjugation of the colored people of the South. . . . But now everything is changed. The infamous reactionists are beaten." In spite of some misgivings, on the whole the radicals were satisfied with the election results.[8]

That their assessment was at least partially justified became evident almost immediately. Although they had reluctantly acquiesced in the evasive suffrage program of their party, they had never given up their insistence upon an impartial franchise, the logical capstone of the reforms which they had advocated for so long. With both Houses of Congress safely Republican and a sympathetic President-elect, the road was clear for the passage of another amendment to the Constitution. Oddly enough, the party's failure to secure two thirds of the House may have hastened its consideration. Unless the amendment were enacted prior to March 4, the date upon which the Fortieth Congress expired, it would be difficult to induce the House to accept it.[9]

Immediately after the election, determined members of the party took steps to prepare the country for the speedy passage of a constitutional change. In November, Senator William M. Stewart of Nevada explained to General Grant the advantages of universal suffrage. If nonwhites in Northern states could vote, he said somewhat optimistically, they would hold the balance of power

[8] McPherson, *Reconstruction,* pp. 407, 507; J. S. Cunningham–Sumner, October 14, 1868, Ashley-Sumner, October 15, November 5, 1868, Benson Lossing–Sumner, November 9, 1868, Garrison-Sumner, January 20, 1869, Sumner Papers; *Commonwealth,* November 7, 1868; *Independent,* November 19, 1868.

[9] Clemenceau, *American Reconstruction,* pp. 279–80; *Commonwealth,* November 14, 1868. The Southern states which would restore the two-thirds majority were not readmitted until 1870.

in elections, so that there would always be a majority of citizens who would take an interest in protecting Negro rights. Early in the same month, the Philadelphia *Press,* in an article entitled "Forward," called for prompt action, and on the 18th, the *Independent* published a demand for "The Next Step." Conceding that Stevens and Sumner had advocated a legislative rather than constitutional guarantee, the radical organ nevertheless concluded that an amendment was preferable. As Grant himself was said to favor it, it was evident that the Republican majority would seek to enact the reform during the coming session of Congress.[1]

When the lawmakers met in December, a number of suffrage amendments were introduced in both Houses, the radicals playing a prominent role in framing them. J. M. Broomall, W. D. Kelley, and George W. Julian were among those offering varying versions in the House, and George Boutwell, the chairman of the House Judiciary Committee, took charge of the measure when it was reported in January. In the Senate, William M. Stewart, who was then acting with the radicals, performed a similar service. Henry Wilson not only took a prominent part in the debates but sought in newspaper articles to popularize the idea of Negro enfranchisement. Drake, Howard, Morton, and Williams in the Senate, as well as Shellabarger and Broomall in the House, attempted to strengthen the measure, and of all the ultras, only Sumner stood aloof. Still maintaining that the Constitution already guaranteed the right of universal suffrage, he delivered a speech advocating legislative sanctions. But not even Wendell Phillips agreed with him. The radicals as well as many former abolitionists were in the forefront of the struggle for the amendment.[2]

The parliamentary maneuvers leading to the final passage of the reform were complicated. On January 30, 1869, the House

---

[1] Stewart, *Reminiscences,* p. 232; Philadelphia *Free Press,* quoted in *Commonwealth,* November 14, 1868; *Independent,* November 19, 1868.

[2] *Cong. Globe,* 40th Cong., 3d Sess., 9, 368, 378, 1625, App., 102–3, 154; Julian, *Political Recollections,* p. 324; Wilson, *History,* III, 669–79; *Independent,* December 17, 1868; *Commonwealth,* January 9, 1869; Sumner, *Works,* XIII, 33–52; McPherson, *Reconstruction,* pp. 399–406; Boutwell, *Reminiscences of Sixty Years,* II, 44 ff.

accepted Boutwell's proposition of an amendment substantially like the one eventually enacted. Such earnest radicals as Samuel Shellabarger, correctly predicting its probable ineffectiveness in the face of Southern hostility, sought to make it stronger. The provision prohibiting states from abridging the right to vote "by reason of race, color, or previous condition" must be eliminated, the Ohio congressman argued, because the South would find ways to circumvent it. But his proposed substitute, which would have prevented the states from depriving citizens of sound mind of the right to vote for any reason other than rebellion did not pass. Fearful about the effect upon the country, even many radicals voted against it.[3]

The Senate, which had been debating a version of its own, took up the House measure four days later. Both William M. Stewart and Henry Wilson were instrumental in amending the proposition to include the right to hold office as well as the right to vote, the Massachusetts radical also adding a prohibition against discrimination on account of "nativity, property, education or religious belief." At the same time, Oliver P. Morton successfully sponsored a sixteenth amendment designed to take away the states' power to permit legislatures to choose presidential electors to circumvent voting laws. When the House refused to accept these changes, the Senate agreed to recede. Declining to adopt the House version, however, it proceeded to reconsider its own measure instead. This still contained the controversial office-holding clause, which in effect made it more radical than its counterpart in the lower chamber. When it was sent to the House, Bingham, for reasons not entirely clear, partially restored Wilson's amendment, a change to which the Senate would then no longer assent. Finally, on February 25 and 26, a conference committee reported the present version. "The right of citizens of the United States to vote shall not be denied or abridged by the United States or by any State on account of race, color, or previous condition of servitude," it read, the House having receded from Bingham's phraseol-

[3] *Cong. Globe,* 40th Cong., 3d Sess., 743, Ap., 638–9; Wilson, *History,* III, 666–72.

ogy, and the Senate having dropped its insistence upon office-holding. All the radicals except Sumner, who was absent, voted "yea."

Because of the fact that the ultras did not cooperate in voting on the various amendments offered during the debates about the constitutional change, their real achievement in securing the final passage of the amendment may easily be overlooked. But although in this reform as in others, they failed to act in a unified manner, Boutwell and Shellabarger, Ashley and Williams, Wilson and Drake, Sumner and Wade, all voting at cross purposes, every radical was in favor of some measure guaranteeing the franchise to the Negro. And it was for this aim that they finally won moderate support. Not counting the Johnsonians, Dixon, Doolittle, and Daniel S. Norton, only two Republicans in the Senate and three in the House voted against the final version of the amendment.[4]

No matter how much they had differed about its text, the radicals were delighted about the passage of the constitutional change. "Reconstruction is nearly concluded, and the great principle on which the party rests is that of equal suffrage. It is the last step taken, or to be taken," editorialized the *Independent*. George Wilkes, the extremist editor of *Wilkes's Spirit of the Times*, commented: "Fortunately, the great questions for which I labored are all safe. The rebellion is crushed, the black man is free, the fifteenth amendment will secure everybody civil rights, and . . . there is little left for me to do." Henry Wilson, addressing the thirty-sixth meeting of the American Anti-Slavery Society, called the reform the boon which the Negro required, and even Chase, unpopular though he was in radical circles, strongly endorsed it and urged its ratification.[5]

A special source of satisfaction for the radicals was the fact that

[4] McPherson, *Reconstruction*, pp. 399–406; William Gillette, *The Right to Vote: Politics and the Passage of the Fifteenth Amendment* (Baltimore, 1965), pp. 46–78.

[5] *Independent*, February 25, 1869; George Wilkes–Sumner, May 8, 1869, Sumner Papers; New York *World*, May 12, 1869; Chase–T. H. Yeatman, October 19, 1869, Chase Papers, HSP.

the amendment had been passed in the face of determined opposition. Accused at the time and since of mere political self-interest and insincerity about the Negroes' fate, they could take justified pride in their record. Writing fifteen years later, James G. Blaine still quoted Henry Wilson's rejoinder to Senator Garrett Davis, who had accused the Republicans of low political motives. "The Senator from Kentucky tells us that in proposing this amendment we are seeking to perpetuate our power," Wilson said.

> He knows and I know that this whole struggle in this country to give equal rights and privileges to all citizens of the United States has been an unpopular one. . . . I say to the Senator from Kentucky that the struggle of the last eight years to give freedom to four and a half millions of men who were held in slavery, to make them citizens of the United States, to clothe them with the right of suffrage . . . has cost the party with which I act a quarter of a million votes.

On another occasion, he recurred to this theme. "Senators accuse us of being actuated by partisanship," he averred,

> by the love of power, and the hope of retaining power; yet they never tire of reminding us that the people have in several States pronounced against equal suffrage and will do so again. I took occasion early in the debate to express the opinion that in the series of measures for the extirpation of slavery and the elevation and enfranchisement of the black race the Republican party had lost at least a quarter of a million votes. In every great battle of the last eight years the timid, the weak faltered, fell back or slunk away into the ranks of the enemy.

Many radicals still believed in the principles which they were advocating, whatever their other motives.[6]

To prove their commitment to the cause, a number of ultras also resisted efforts of Western representatives to exclude the Chinese from the newly enacted guarantees. This was a difficult

---

[6] Blaine, *Twenty Years of Congress,* II, 414; *Cong. Globe,* 40th Cong., 3d Sess., Ap., 154, 672. Cf. LaWanda and John H. Cox, "Negro Suffrage and Republican Politics: The Problem of Motivation in Radical Reconstruction History," *Journal of Southern History,* XXXIII (August, 1967), 303–30. Blaine's quotes vary slightly from this version as given in the *Cong. Globe.*

problem, and many radicals eventually gave way to prejudice, but before the year was out, Sumner, vindicating the Orientals' claims to equal justice, would move—without success—to strike the word "white" from the naturalization laws; Ashley, as governor of Montana, would recommend that the territorial legislature rescind its tax upon Orientals, and Wade, while in California, would publicly criticize anti-Chinese excesses. Although the New York *Herald* eventually accused the remaining radicals of seeking to capitalize upon the Chinese question, quite a few of the old antislavery vanguard had remained constant.[7]

The ultras also benefited from Grant's victory in another respect. Because the terms of office of a number of senators were about to expire, it was essential to secure control of the state legislatures which were going to choose their successors. The Republican successes in the fall of 1868 solved this problem, and sympathetic local lawmakers elected a number of prominent radicals.

The best known beneficiary of this development was Charles Sumner. Long before he was up for re-election, his friends had carefully prepared his campaign by inducing the Republican state convention to adopt a plank specifically endorsing him. To the delight of his old associates, in January he was re-elected to a fourth term. "I remember very well the time of your election in '51—your *first* —when the office sought you—and succeeded only after a long time in finding you because you belonged to an 'unhealthy organization'!" the temperance reformer Neal Dow wrote to him.

No man has had a larger share than yourself in the great work abolishing slavery in this country—perhaps not one has done so much in that direction as yourself—for your labors have been earnest and most influential from the beginning when your un-

7 New York *Herald*, July 4, 1870; McPherson, *Reconstruction*, pp. 402, 618–19; Ashley, "Governor Ashley's Biography and Messages," loc. cit., pp. 271–5; *New York Times*, July 3, 1869. Hamlin also remained consistent on the Chinese question, and Wilson, who did not, maintained he merely took his stand in order not to endanger passage of the bill. C. A. Stackpole–Hamlin, February 17, 1879, E. L. Pierce–Hamlin, February 15, 1879, Hamlin Papers; *Cong. Globe*, 41st Cong., 2d Sess., 5161.

wavering hostility to slavery drew down upon you the dislike—even the hate of the majority of our people. All that is changed —you have fought that battle through with indomitable perseverance and courage and have won, and the great body of your countrymen now recognize the infinite value of your services.

Garrison reacted in a similar vein, and Sumner returned to Washington with greater confidence than ever.[8]

A second contest resulting in the success of a prominent antislavery statesman took place in Maine. Because of the Republican victory in September, it was certain that Senator Lot Morrill's successor would not be a conservative, Morrill himself having been close to the advanced members of the party. But former Vice President Hannibal Hamlin was staging a comeback, and in a closely fought election he secured the prize. His return to Washington brought back into the Senate one of the prewar radical leaders, whose services to the cause had been substantial, and whose attitude toward the colored race had not changed. To the end of his life, he sought to make the promises of the Civil War amendments a reality.[9]

Zach Chandler was also a candidate for re-election. Although it was fairly certain that the Republicans would carry Michigan, the senator had to contend with a number of rivals, among them ex-Governor Austin Blair and Congressman Thomas W. Ferry. The Detroit *Advertiser & Tribune* turned against him, and opponents made the most of his alleged intemperance. But Chandler, relying heavily on his excellent political organization, fought back. After approaching his adversaries, he came to an understanding with Ferry, whom he promised to support in 1871. In answer to the *Advertiser,* he started the Detroit *Post* as a rival newspaper, and radical supporters like Stanton and Butler wrote letters vindicating Chandler's record and charges that the senator was intemperate. The result was that the Republican caucus re-

[8] Sumner, *Works,* XII, 518; Neal Dow–Sumner, January 21, 1869; Garrison–Sumner, January 20, 1869, Sumner Papers.

[9] Hamlin–Mrs. Hamlin, January 6, 1869, Hamlin–J. A. Peters, January 12, 1869; Neal Dow–Hamlin, January 20, 1869, C. M. Clay–Hamlin, February 5, 1869, Hamlin Papers; Welles, *Diary,* III, 505; Hamlin, *Hamlin,* pp. 528–9.

nominated him, so that, in January, he secured his re-election to the Senate. As one of the most extreme members of the upper House, Chandler was considered a leading ultra. His vindication in part offset his friend Wade's previous defeat in Ohio.[1]

Other senatorial campaigns also seemed to augur well for the cause. Ex-Governor Reuben Fenton replaced Edwin D. Morgan as senator from New York. Since Morgan, despite Sumner's and Wade's endorsement, had been accused of conservatism because he had not always supported the ultras in Congress, and Fenton, while governor, had openly snubbed his old rival, Seward, the change was not unwelcome. In Missouri, the radical legislature elected Carl Schurz, whose past record gave no indication of his imminent break with the extremists. Still believing that he would be "among the ablest men in the Senate," they hoped that the country would find in him, "under all circumstances, a faithful champion of radical principles." And when Wisconsin replaced James Doolittle with Matthew Carpenter, most Republicans rejoiced. The opposition characterized the new senator as a "thoroughgoing radical."[2]

As the fourth of March approached, speculation grew about the ultras' relations to the new administration. Was Grant friendly to their cause? How much influence would they have in the Cabinet? Would the general appoint leading extremists to important positions? While newspapers conjectured and individuals wondered, the general remained silent. Refusing to reveal his plans prior to his inauguration, he kept the radicals in suspense.[3]

[1] Harris, *Chandler,* pp. 103, 106–10; George, Chandler, pp. 219–26; Willis F. Dunbar, *Michigan Through the Centuries* (New York, 1955), II, 200; H. B. Maynard–Jacob Howard, January 9, 1869, Howard Papers; Stanton–N. W. Brooks, December 22, 1868, Chandler Papers; *Commonwealth,* December 26, 1868.

[2] *Independent,* January 21, 1869; Welles, *Diary,* III, 505, 508, 509; New York *Evening Post* (semiweekly), January 19, 1869; Roscoe C. E. Brown and Ray B. Smith, *Political and Governmental History of the State of New York* (Syracuse, 1922), III, 38, 97–101; New York *Herald,* January 24, 1869.

[3] Welles, *Diary,* III, 530–1; New York *World,* January 16, February

The ultras wasted no time in pressing their claims upon the President-elect. Pointing out that New England expected him to appoint Charles Sumner Secretary of State, Samuel Hooper emphasized that the offer would be viewed as an indication of the general's intention to look to the Republican party for guidance; Joseph Medill and Horace White urged the elevation of Ben Wade to become Postmaster General; newspapers speculated about Timothy O. Howe's prospects, and John Cochrane sought to impress upon the general's closest advisers the importance of a progressive policy. "Men are looking to him [Grant] for the formation of a new party . . . ," he wrote to E. B. Washburne,

> the growth and success of which they anticipate, will strengthen for many years, the elements of national growth. Radical principles is one of these elements—their equal application, another. Radicalism—the radicalism of the war for the Union—the radicalism of the reconstruction of the Union—the radicalism of Grantism is as appropriate, and, indeed, indispensable now, to the conservatism which looks to the national safety, as it has been at any foregone period.

But the President-elect kept silent. Continuing to take his own counsel, he remained totally unwilling to commit himself.[4]

When Grant finally did announce his Cabinet, the radicals were somewhat disappointed. With the exception of Postmaster General Creswell, not one well-recognizable extremist was included. Charles Sumner protested immediately against the appointment of Alexander T. Stewart as Secretary of the Treasury because the nominee, the owner of one of the largest department stores in the world, was actively engaged in trade, and according to the law, this made him ineligible for the post. Other radicals strongly supported the senator from Massachusetts. Within a short time,

20, 1869; New York *Evening Post* (semiweekly), February 2, 1869; *Independent,* February 25, 1869.

[4] Samuel Hooper–Sumner, November 16, 1868, Sumner Papers; Medill-Washburne, November 25, 26, 27, 1868, Horace White–Washburne, November 28, 1868, John Cochrane–Washburne, November 20, 1868, Washburne Papers; New York *Evening Post* (semiweekly), December 8, 1868, February 2, 1869.

Timothy O. Howe detected a decided letdown in morale. "I looked for the 4th of March to bring Grant and Peace and Rest," he confided to his niece. "Well, the 4th of March has come and passed six days since—and as yet I have seen nothing but Grant. Under the rose let me say I have had rather an excess of him. But Peace and Rest seem as far off as ever." Hannibal Hamlin was more guarded. Writing that there were different opinions about Grant's radicalism, he commented, "We must wait, and see 'what we shall see.' "[5]

In spite of the ultras' misgivings, the President seemed well disposed. In his inaugural address, he endorsed the Fifteenth Amendment, and when Stewart withdrew a few days later, he appointed George Boutwell as his successor. The new Secretary's radicalism was beyond question, so that the radicals obtained in the Cabinet the representation to which they believed themselves entitled. Moreover, despite serious opposition, Grant appointed James M. Ashley governor of Montana Territory, while Sumner's friend, the historian John Lothrop Motley, went to London as envoy to the Court of St. James. Samuel Shellabarger was offered a diplomatic mission also, and, most surprising of all, Grant composed his quarrel with Ben Butler.[6]

Of all the radicals, Butler had probably been most disappointed about Grant's nomination. Bitterly hostile to the general because of his references in his final report to the misfortunes of the Army of the James, the Massachusetts congressman sought to block his former superior's political advancement. When he failed in this endeavor, he found himself in an awkward situation. His hatred

[5] *Commonwealth,* March 13, 20, 1869; New York *Herald,* March 9, 1869; Welles, *Diary,* III, 543–4; L. U. Reavis–Sumner, March 5, 1869, Thomas Webster–Sumner, March [7], 1869, Thaddeus Hyatt–Sumner, March 10, 1869, Sumner Papers; Howe–Grace Howe, March 10, 1869, Howe Papers; Hamlin–Mrs. Hamlin, March 14, 1869, Hamlin Papers.
[6] Richardson, *Messages and Papers of the Presidents,* VII, 6–8; *Independent,* March 18, 1869; April 15, 1869; Adam Badeau, *Grant in Peace* (Hartford, 1887), pp. 197–8, 471; New York *Evening Post* (semiweekly), April 20, 1869.

for Grant was well known; yet he was a Republican candidate for re-election to Congress, and the general was his party's nominee for President. The radical editor George Wilkes sought to bring the two men together, an effort in which he succeeded up to a point, Butler expressing his willingness to cooperate if Grant apologized, and the general indicating that he held no further grudge. Then, when the newspapers announced prematurely that a reconciliation had been effected, Butler publicly endorsed the Republican ticket, although the accord was far from complete. Privately, he was still very dubious, especially since he disapproved of the Republicans' deflationary platform, and since the hard-money wing entered Richard H. Dana as a rival candidate in Butler's congressional district. But despite Grant's secret backing, Dana lost, and when Butler returned to Washington he left his card at the general's residence. Within a short time, the resumption of social relations and the performance of political services led not merely to a complete reconciliation but to an exceptionally close cooperation. And since Butler was a thoroughgoing radical, his influence was important for the cause.[7]

With the return to the White House of a regular Republican, the radicals attempted to revert to the policies which they had found so effective with Lincoln. Theirs was the task of leading the way; they hoped Grant would follow. Still well represented in Congress, influential in the Cabinet, and supported by important newspapers and periodicals, they sought to make their experiment of racial democracy a reality. Up to a point, they succeeded. But Grant was no Lincoln. Possessing neither insight into political problems nor a gift of leadership in civilian affairs, the general proved an ineffectual President. When he yielded to the radicals, he offended the conservatives, and when he engaged in personal favoritism, he alienated radicals as well. Unlike the wartime President, he was never able to balance the various factions within the party. But for a short time, it seemed as if the radicals might prevail once again.

[7] Trefousse, *Butler*, pp. 205–9.

At the time of Grant's election, the process of Reconstruction was not functioning at all smoothly. In spite of Republican successes at the polls, Southern conservatives sought by every means to regain power. Threats and violence against Unionists and freedmen were common occurrences; secret organizations like the Ku Klux Klan terrorized the countryside, and while Republican officials were browbeaten and murdered, the party was splitting, into factions. In Georgia, the legislature went so far as to expel its colored members. Their right to hold office was not guaranteed, it asserted, and the lawmakers assigned the vacated seats to the Negroes' defeated rivals. So offensive was the behavior of Southern conservatives that American prestige abroad was beginning to suffer. "I suppose the first thing now in hand is to stop outrages— wholesale murders, at the South . . . ," wrote Charles A. Page, the war correspondent who was serving as United States consul at Zurich, shortly after the election.

> It does seem to me that you leaders are not enough alive to the stinging shame of the state of things at the South. I assure you that abroad the best men—the Liberals—cannot see why the Republican Party does not, in the wealth of its power, cause these southern outrages upon its members, white & black, to cease. They ask—Do not your institutions admit of the exercise of some power, martial law or some [illegible] akin to it, whereby stern & severe punishment may follow upon any such crime and so to prevent its repetition?" . . . Is it not possible to put a little of Sheridan or a little of Butler into the administration of the South?

By the fall of 1868, even a former moderate like ex-Governor Hahn of Louisiana was in despair. As he wrote shortly before the election, "Murder and intimidation are the order of the day in this State. There is now more cruelty practiced toward Republicans than there was against Unionists during the rebellion." The radicals' task was far from finished.[8]

[8] W. R. Moore–Washburne, November 17, 1868, W. E. Chandler– Washburne, November 7, 1868, Charles A. Page–Washburne, November 17, 1868, Michael Hahn–Washburne, October 26, 1868, Washburne Papers; William Alexander–Sumner, December 10, 1868, Sumner

Grant's victory did not change this situation. To be sure, Unionists were encouraged, but the terror continued. The Democrats carried Louisiana and Georgia, and so widespread were the disorder and the voting frauds in the South that local radicals begged their Northern friends to do something. Because of the expulsion of the Negro legislators which had taken place in Georgia, Sumner in the Senate and Butler in the House introduced a bill to take action; an investigation took place, but prior to the general's inauguration, little had been accomplished. The House had actually passed a measure for the holding of elections in Virginia, one of the remaining unreconstructed states; during the remainder of session, however, the Senate had failed to vote on it.[9]

Once Grant was in the White House, the radicals began to make preparations for completing the process of Reconstruction. In view of the deplorable state of affairs in the South, they might have kept Virginia, Mississippi, and Texas under military rule somewhat longer, but the need for the ratification of the Fifteenth Amendment overrode these considerations. When the President published a message recommending speedy submission of the new constitutions of Virginia and Mississippi, Congress, adding Texas, complied, even though Grant favored separate action upon controversial clauses disfranchising former Confederates. To make certain of the triumph of universal suffrage, Oliver P. Morton, now one of the leading radicals in the Senate, saw to it that an amendment requiring ratification of the Fifteenth Amendment became part of the bill. It was adopted by a vote of 30–20, virtually all the radicals rallying to the cause. If they were unable to stop Southern depredations, the ultras were at least determined to

Papers; Cox, *Three Decades of Federal Legislation,* pp. 451 ff., 510–11; Du Bois, *Black Reconstruction,* pp. 501–3.

9 W. Goodloe–Sumner, n.d., 1868, J. H. Caldwell–Sumner, November 23, 1868, William Alexander–Sumner, December 10, 1868, J. C. Laizer–Sumner, December 15, 1868, Sumner Papers; J. L. Alcorn–Washburne, December 5, 1868, January 18, 1869, W. J. Colburne–Washburne, January 7, 1868, Washburne Papers; G. H. Penfield–Chandler February 5, 1869, Chandler Papers; *Cong. Globe,* 40th Cong., 3d Sess., 27, 74; *Harper's Weekly,* XIII (January 16, February 13, 1869), 34, 99; McPherson, *Reconstruction,* p. 410.

secure constitutional protection for the Negroes' right to vote. In this endeavor, they were to be successful.[1]

The campaign in Virginia proved to be a disaster. Combining with the conservatives, the moderate Republicans, headed by Gilbert C. Walker, encouraged by the belief that Grant would lend them support, overwhelmed the extremist wing led by H. H. Wells. With the hostile press gloating over "the downfall of the Southern Radicals," Forney thought the election was the worst blow the party had sustained since the failure of the impeachment. But the ultras were not disposed to give up. They decided that it was time to put pressure upon the administration.[2]

A few days after the results were known, the Cabinet met in Washington. Vigorously upholding the radical cause, Boutwell and Creswell deprecated the outcome in the Old Dominion. The Secretary of the Treasury delivered a long speech denouncing the administration's policy of giving aid to conservatives in Mississippi, Texas, and Virginia. Urging extreme caution, he counseled "rigid adherence to the well known principles of the party of which he and his associates had been selected as representatives." The Virginia fiasco must not be repeated.[3]

The radical Secretaries' presentation was effective. Influenced by their arguments, the President and Cabinet decided not to hold the elections in Mississippi and Texas until after the fall campaigns in the North and as close to the reassembling of Congress as possible. And this was not all. In Mississippi, where the conservative Republicans, hoping for executive aid, had nominated Grant's brother-in-law Lewis Dent to oppose James Lusk Alcorn, the radical candidate for governor, the President refused to assist his relative, to whom he wrote an open letter deprecating the extremists'

[1] Ibid., pp. 408–10, 417; *Cong. Globe,* 41st Cong., 1st Ses., 633, 699, 654. Edmunds and Fenton were the exceptions.
[2] New York *Herald,* July 8, 17, 21, 1869; New York *Evening Post* (semiweekly), July 9, 1869; Forney-Sumner, July 19, 1869, Sumner Papers; William Best Hesseltine, *Ulysses S. Grant, Politician* (New York, 1935), p. 182.
[3] New York *Tribune,* July 10, 14, 15, 1869; Allan Nevins, *Hamilton Fish, The Inner History of the Grant Administration* (New York, 1937), pp. 290–2.

opponents. A conservative delegation which sought Boutwell's aid received a decided rebuff, and when the elections were held, Alcorn easily beat his challenger. For the time being, at least, the radicals had prevailed.[4]

The final admission of the remaining states was delayed until 1870. Once more the ultras, mustering all their resources, achieved a victory by imposing conditions which Virginia, Mississippi, Texas, and Georgia had to meet. None of these states was ever to be permitted to amend its constitution in such a way as to deprive the newly enfranchised citizens of the right to vote, hold office, or receive an education. Although these terms met with vigorous moderate opposition, Bingham offering an amendment to delete them altogether, the radicals, led by Sumner, Drake, Butler, and George Edmunds of Vermont, insisted upon them. The notorious disorders in the South and the expulsion of Negro legislators in Georgia showed that guarantees were needed, and the ultras' eloquent pleas contributed to victory. In a legal sense at least, the rights of the freedmen seemed secure.[5]

In the case of Georgia, Reconstruction was greatly complicated by the domestic turmoil in the state. After the passage of a measure introduced by Ben Butler—a bill to remand the state to military rule because of its failure to comply with the conditions of the Omnibus Bill, moderates sought to restore normalcy as quickly as possible. But the radicals insisted that the legislature elected in 1868 be recalled and given another term of two years, a measure which eventually passed when in May, 1870, the state was readmitted. And in the case of Georgia as well as in that of all the other states restored that year, acceptance of the Fifteenth Amendment had been one of the fundamental conditions.[6]

---

[4] New York *Tribune,* July 15, 1869; Boutwell-Sumner, July 19, 1869, Sumner Papers; New York *Evening Post* (semiweekly), July 20, August 13, 1869; Cox, *Three Decades of Federal Legislation,* pp. 529–30.

[5] McPherson, *Reconstruction,* pp. 572–9; *Commonwealth,* January 22, February 19, 1870.

[6] *Cong. Globe,* 41st Cong., 2d Ses., 244 ff., 290 ff., 1701 ff., 1765 ff.; *Commonwealth,* December 25, 1869; *Independent,* March 24, 1870; C. Mildred Thompson, *Reconstruction in Georgia* (New York, 1915),

The ratification of the suffrage amendment was a matter of great importance for the radicals. Considering the granting of the right to vote as the culmination of their efforts on behalf of the colored race, they exerted themselves without stint to secure the assent of three quarters of the states. As they saw it, the amendment was right for its own sake; in addition, it might protect the Negro's rights in the South, and it might redress the balance of power in closely divided Northern states. They were convinced that the Negroes would not desert them.[7]

Because of these factors, the ultras made unceasing efforts to make certain of ratification. Almost to a man, they supported Morton's proposition to require assent to the amendment as one of the conditions for Reconstruction of the remaining states; John M. Thayer, the radical senator from Nebraska, and Charles Sumner put pressure upon the governor of the state to call an extra session of the legislature in order to hasten acceptance, and Chase also lent his prestige to the work. "I am now as always . . . for universal suffrage and universal amnesty," he wrote on October 19, 1869, to Thomas H. Yeatman, his former deacon, "and though I should have preferred to see the principles of the amendt. adopted by the States, in their State Constitutions, I have become convinced that the best thing for the South and the whole country is to make sure of their adoption by ratifying the amendment." His correspondent made good use of the letter to influence Ohio politicians; Grant's interest in the measure was a matter of public record, and on March 30, 1870, the Secretary of State was able to announce that the necessary number of states had taken affirmative action.[8]

---

pp. 255 ff.; *The Nation,* X (January 13, 1870), 17; E. Merton Coulter, *Georgia, A Short History* (Chapel Hill, 1960), p. 373.

[7] *Cong. Globe,* 40th Cong., 3d Ses., Ap., 154; *Independent,* May 12, 1870; Schurz, *Reminiscences,* III, 246, 248–9; William Claflin–Sumner, December 25, 1868, Sumner Papers; E. F. Bullard–Butler, November 4, 1867, Butler–Bullard, November 7, 1867, Butler Papers; Washington *Daily Morning Chronicle,* May 6, 1867; Gillette, *The Right to Vote,* p. 165.

[8] McPherson, *Reconstruction,* pp. 410, 417, 545–6; John M. Thayer–Sumner, October 13, 1869, David Butler–Sumner, October 30,

For the radicals, news of the amendment's success was most gratifying. "The Victory Complete," announced the *Independent,* which called the addition "the most precious part of the Constitution of the United States . . . the voice of the American people saying, 'A man is a man, whether he be black or white.' " Henry Wilson, writing a few years later, considered the success of the measure in the face of widespread anti-Negro prejudice so grand an achievement that he found it "hardly explicable on any other theory than that God willed it." Believing that its work had been done, the American Anti-Slavery Society held a last meeting at Apollo Hall in New York, where the members formally dissolved the organization in the presence of all the old stalwarts, including George W. Julian. "The Chinese Wall is broken, and, however minute the aperture, it can never be closed again," commented the *Commonwealth.* And Charles Sumner, who had opposed the constitutional change on the grounds that it was not needed, was serenaded by a group of citizens who had also called on the President and the Vice President. Responding to his well-wishers, the senator expressed his delight that the Declaration of Independence had at last become a reality. When President Grant, who had already expressed his satisfaction privately, took the unusual step of forwarding a special message to Congress to announce his pride in the amendment, it seemed that the radicals had secured a complete triumph. As Grant pointed out, a measure which made at once "four millions of people voters, who were heretofore declared by the highest tribunal in the land not citizens of the United States" and considered to possess no rights "which the white man was bound to respect," was indeed a measure of grand importance. At least it appeared so at the time.[9]

1869, Sumner Papers; Chase–H. W. Yeatman, October 19, 1869, T. H. Yeatman–Chase, January 22, 1870, Chase Papers, HSP; Gillette, *The Right to Vote,* pp. 146, 159. Senator Edmunds was an exception.

[9] *Independent,* February 24, 1870; Wilson, *History,* III, 682; *Commonwealth,* April 9, 16, 1870; Julian MS Diary, April 11, 1870, Julian Papers; Sumner, *Works,* XIII, 350–2; Grant-Washburne, January 28, 1870, Grant Papers, Illinois State Historical Library; Richardson, *Messages and Papers of the Presidents,* VII, 55–6.

Shortly before the Secretary of State's announcement, the radicals were able to celebrate what seemed to them still another major victory. In Mississippi, the state legislature had returned a Negro, Hiram R. Revels, to the United States Senate for the short term. Born in North Carolina, Revels had lived and attended college in the North, where he became a Methodist minister. After coming South during the war, when he was serving as chaplain with the troops, he remained in politics, and although he was by no means an extremist, his election to the Senate signified the beginning of a new era. Admitted after three days of debate, he was assigned the seat vacated in 1861 by Jefferson Davis. Poetic justice seemed to have been well served. To the annoyance of opposition newspapers, radical senators made every effort to pay him their respects. Seated on a lounge, he recieved the personal attention of Sumner, Thayer, Chandler, Howard, Cameron, Howe, Drake, and others, while the Massachusetts senator delivered a speech welcoming him. "Senator Revels, the black Senator from Mississippi, has been admitted & occupies the old seat of Jefferson Davis," Julian recorded in his diary. "What a beautiful . . . retribution!"[1]

But despite all seeming success, the South was still in turmoil. Neither the election of Grant nor the inauguration of local radical government had changed the attitude of the majority of Southern whites. Determined never to admit the freedmen to an equal share in society, they persisted in employing ever more violent tactics. Attacks on life and property continued; murders and intimidation were more common than ever before, and the power of the Ku Klux Klan was unbroken. In 1869, the conservatives in Tennessee recaptured the legislature, and within a few months, radical politicians wrote to Sumner asking that the state be remanded to military rule. In Virginia, conservatives made life miserable for the freedmen, whom they threatened with loss of livelihood should they attempt to vote. And economic conditions

[1] New York *Herald*, February 3, 1870; *Independent*, March 3, 1870, March 2, 1871; Sumner, *Works*, XIII, 335–8; Du Bois, *Black Reconstruction*, p. 442; Julian MS Diary, February 20, 1870, Julian Papers.

were such that these threats were effective. Merely to enfranchise the Negro poor was not sufficient. Something more would have to be done. And since the amendments contained clauses giving Congress the right to take all necessary measures for their enforcement, the remedy seemed obvious. Appropriate legislation would have to be passed.[2]

This was the background of the famous Enforcement Acts, measures which sought to protect Negroes and other Republicans at the polls. Among the last triumphs of the radicals, these acts were passed at a time when there was still some hope that the completion of Reconstruction might also result in the peaceful integration of the Negroes into Southern society. The first of these laws was the act of May 30, 1870, which forbade discrimination among voters because of race or color, sought to make threats of force illegal, and attempted to outlaw economic pressure upon the voters. Such radicals as Morton, Chandler, Edmunds, and Williams played leading roles in steering it through Congress, but its results were not what its authors expected. Consequently, they proceeded to strengthen it. John C. Churchill of New York, who had long acted with the radicals, in 1871 sponsored a second Force Bill; Sumner presented memorials in its favor, and even the moderates took an effective part in its passage on February 28, 1871.[3]

The Ku Klux Klan, however, still gave no sign of abandoning its lawlessness. Because of unusually disturbing reports of violence in North Carolina, in December, 1870, Congress asked Grant for specific information about the atrocities. In compliance with the request, the President transmitted evidence strong enough to

[2] New York *Herald,* August 5, 1869; *Independent,* August 12, September 9, 23, November 25, 1869; T. H. Pearne–Sumner, March 4, 1870, G. H. Seldon–Sumner, April 23, 1870, Sumner Papers.

[3] Everette Swinney, "Enforcing the Fifteenth Amendment, 1870–1877," *Journal of Southern History,* XXXVIII (May, 1962), 202–18; *Cong. Globe,* 41st Cong., 2d Sess., 2808, 3479 ff., 3489, 3491, 3507 ff., 3558 ff.; McPherson, *Reconstruction,* pp. 546–57; Chandler-Howard, May 21, 1870, Howard Papers; *Cong. Globe,* 41st Cong., 3d Ses., 1190, 1285, 1655; New York *Evening Post* (semiweekly), February 19, 21, 1871; *Independent,* March 2, 1871; *New York Times,* February 16, 1871.

cause the Senate, under Morton's lead, to set up a committee to investigate. In part, these hearings facilitated the passage of the second Enforcement Act, but many radicals felt that additional legislation to curb the Klan was needed. Accordingly, when the new session began, Ben Butler sought to secure Republican consent to a new measure. At first, it seemed as if the moderates would sidetrack his efforts by ordering a new investigation instead, a tactic which infuriated the Massachusetts congressman. Nevertheless, he and other radicals kept up the debate, and when the President, who had been asked to send troops to South Carolina in order to suppress outrages, sent Congress a message asking for appropriate legislation, the prospects for an effective act improved. George Edmunds in the Senate and Samuel Shellabarger in the House finally succeeded in pushing through Congress a third Enforcement Act, often called the Ku Klux Act, a measure which became law on April 20. Designed to put teeth into previous legislation, it gave the Executive power to intervene in troubled states without waiting for an application by local authorities, as well as the authority to suspend the writ of habeas corpus in counties where disturbances occurred. Without the constant prodding of radicals in both Houses, it could not have been passed.[4]

The Ku Klux Act possibly marked the radicals' last substantial victory. Using the extraordinary powers it granted to him, Grant suspended the writ of habeas corpus several times; the Ku Klux committee produced damaging evidence, and, although it had many successors, the original terrorist organization disappeared. For years, Charles Sumner continued to plead for a new Civil

[4] Oberholtzer, *History of the United States*, II, 376–83; Stanley F. Horn, *Invisible Empire: the Story of the Ku Klux Klan, 1866–1871* (Boston, 1939), pp. 295 ff.; *Cong. Globe*, 42d Cong., 1st Ses., 338 ff., 440–51, 173, 493, 792–3, 18–19, 116 ff., 487 ff., Ap., 247–51, 254–57: New York *Tribune*, December 17, 1870, March 7, April 21, 1871; Foulke, *Morton*, II, 196; Hoar, *Autobiography of Seventy Years*, I, 201–5; *Commonwealth*, April 1, 15, 1871; Walter L. Fleming, *Documentary History of Reconstruction* (Cleveland, 1906–7), II, 123–8; Selig Adler, *The Senatorial Career of George Franklin Edmunds, 1866–1891, An Abstract of A Thesis Submitted for the Degree of Doctor in Philosophy* (Urbana, 1934), p. 5.

Rights Act guaranteeing equal accommodations in inns, public conveyances, and schools, and after his death, Ben Butler in the House and George Edmunds in the Senate were still able to induce Congress to pass it. But the school desegregation provisions had already been deleted; the law was virtually unenforceable, and within a few years, the Supreme Court declared it unconstitutional.[5] Times were changing; the old radical spirit was on the decline, and before long the leading radicals themselves would pass from the scene. But in the meantime, they had been able to add permanent changes to the Constitution, amendments which eventually made possible great progress. If their attempts to enforce racial equality failed at the time, these efforts were nevertheless remarkable.

[5] Carter, *The Angry Scar,* p. 218; New York *Herald,* October 18, 1871; *Joint Select Committee on Conditions of Affairs in the Late Insurrectionary States, Report,* 42d Cong., 2d Sess. (Washington, 1872); Pierce, *Sumner,* IV, 499–503, 580–2; Springfield *Republican,* February 6, 11, 1875; James M. McPherson, "Abolitionists and the Civil Rights Act of 1875," *Journal of American History,* LII (December, 1965), 493–510.

XIII

The Decline
of the Radicals

ON AUGUST 11, 1868, Thaddeus Stevens died. A few days before the end, stubbornly struggling to the last, he told his doctor, "Well, this is a square fight."[1] His death marked the passing of an era.

It was evident that the "Commoner's" passing would have far-reaching consequences. "It was his marvelous obstinacy," the hostile New York *Herald* pointed out,

> his Hannibal-like animosity against the South, which postponed the settlement of our national differences. His death, however much it may be lamented by his immediate personal friends and by his party, sounds the death knell of the extravagant hopes of the radicals. It was he alone whose firm will held together the most refractory among his partisans. Now that the control of his influence no longer exists, what is to hinder the disintegration of the party to which Mr. Stevens more than any other Republican leader had given concentration and force?[2]

While this assessment was exaggerated, the newspaper article proved prophetic. Already in a state of decline, within a few years

---

[1] Brodie, *Stevens,* p. 365.
[2] New York *Herald,* August 13, 1868.

the radical movement would cease to exist. The word "radical" itself would lose its antislavery meaning.

The downfall of radicalism began at the very time of its greatest success. Thaddeus Stevens's failure to win election to the Senate, the Republican losses in the fall of 1867, the persistence of racial intolerance in the North as well as in the South, the unfavorable decisions of the Supreme Court, the endemic factionalism of the Republican party, and the unsuccessful effort to convict Johnson were all straws in the wind. As early as March, 1867, when the supplementary Reconstruction Act was under consideration, John T. Harris, a former Virginia congressman, astutely wrote to John Sherman: "The people in the South do not, as I think, understand the true relation which Stevens & Sumner bear to their party. They are regarded as the *leaders,* hence all they say is taken for *law.* . . ."[3] He himself knew better, and was delighted to hear from Sherman that there would soon be an end to extremism. But the radicals, adept at marshaling popular opinion, generally kept their moderate colleagues in line as long as Johnson remained in the White House. Considering the President an apostate, most Republicans were not ready to relax their vigilance.

When Johnson's term drew to a close, however, the moderates began to reassert themselves. Even before the President's trial had ended in a defeat for the ultras, the Republican campaign of 1868 furnished new evidence of the radicals' weakness. As early as January, 1868, Friedrich Hassaurek, the Ohio German newspaper editor who had long played a prominent part in the Republican organization, wrote to John Sherman:

> We cannot be blind to the fact that a reaction has set in. The desire for a change which always arises when a party has been in power for some time, hard times which are always charged upon the ruling party, the negro prejudice, the greenback scheme, our financial embarrassments, the exemption of the bonds from taxation and other inevitable disadvantages under which we labor, can only contribute to swell the reactionary tide. . . . If the brakes are not put on in time, not even Gen.

[3] J. T. Harris–John Sherman, March 13, 1867, Sherman Papers.

Grant's great popularity will be able to save us next October and November.

Marcus Ward warned Washburne not to allow William D. Kelley to campaign in New York; as he put it, "Mr. Kelley . . . is Tariff, radical and enthusiastic, whereas the solid men of New York are the reverse." The adoption of an evasive suffrage platform and the nomination for Vice President of Schuyler Colfax instead of Benjamin F. Wade were generally interpreted as concessions to the antiradical feeling, a trend which became even more evident when, in the midst of the campaign, Congress consented to the gradual abolition of the Freedmen's Bureau. That John Broomall, Thomas Williams, and Thomas D. Eliot did not even seek renomination contributed to the weakening of radicalism in the House, and when the returns were in, it was found that James M. Ashley, the author of the original impeachment resolution, as well as Ignatius Donnelly, the outspoken Minnesota reformer, had been defeated. Since Ben Wade, rejected by the Ohio legislature in the previous year, would have to retire on March 4, 1869, the new Congress would lack some of the most active ultras.[4]

To some degree, Grant's readiness to appoint radicals to office obscured their declining influence. Creswell's and Boutwell's Cabinet posts had augured well for the future, and during the eight years which followed, George H. Williams and Zachariah Chandler joined the Cabinet as Attorney General and Secretary of the Interior; Edwin M. Stanton was selected for the Supreme Court; James M. Ashley became governor of the Territory of Montana; Ben Wade served as commissioner to Santo Domingo; Henry Wilson was nominated and elected Vice President; and scores of

[4] Friedrich Hassaurek–John Sherman, January 27, 1868, Sherman Papers; Marcus Ward–Washburne, January 27, 1868, Samuel Galloway–Washburne, May 25, 1868, Washburne Papers; Stevens–C. S. Spence, June 24, 1868, Stevens Papers; George R. Bentley, *A History of the Freedmen's Bureau* (Philadelphia, 1955), pp. 201–2; *Biographical Directory of the American Congress, 1774–1961* (Washington, 1961), pp. 604, 852; Konkle, *Williams*, II, 731; New York *Herald*, October 15, 1868, Martin Ridge, *Ignatius Donnelly: The Portrait of a Politician* (Chicago, 1962), p. 122.

lesser radicals received lucrative posts. But many of these appointments were made at a time when radicalism was already becoming an academic concept, and the President's own lack of commitment was indicative of the faction's diminishing importance.

That the advance guard was losing influence was noticed at the time. "How is it that the Republican press is so lukewarm to support the Radicals? . . .," wrote the abolitionist Lydia Maria Child on August 19, 1869. "The Radicals are the *soul* of the Republican party. The ideas which they represent brought that party into existence; and it was the vitality thence derived which brought it out alive through . . . the Rebellion." Commenting that of the original leaders who had guided and built up the Republican party almost everyone had fallen into discredit, the New York *World* cited the estrangement or lack of position of such present or former radicals as Seward, Chase, Hale, Wade, and Greeley, while the New York *Herald* published lengthy editorials on the decline of radical power. The impact of Grant's appointments could not hide the evident truth that the party's vanguard was dwindling.[5]

The elections of 1870 were another indication that radicalism was becoming less consequential. Although the Republicans won, the Democrats made such sizable gains that they prevented their opponents from obtaining a two-thirds majority in the House. And this time there would be no newly reconstructed states to offset the loss, as had happened after 1868. Moreover, again some of the best-known radicals disappeared from Capitol Hill. George W. Julian, George H. Williams, and John Covode were among those who would not return to the 42d Congress.[6]

Julian's defeat was symptomatic of the trends of the time. As

[5] *Independent,* August 19, 1869; New York *World,* March 31, August 30, 1869; New York *Herald,* February 23, 24, 1869, November 18, 1870, January 6, 1871.

[6] Blaine, *Twenty Years of Congress,* II, 508; Robert Selph Henry, *The Story of Reconstruction* (Indianapolis, 1938), pp. 320–1. Julian lost his bid for renomination, and Covode did not run again.

radical as ever and totally unwilling to compromise on such issues as Negro rights, land reform, or hostility to protectionists, inflationists, and monopolies, the Indiana congressman had long been the target of opponents within his party. Because his district had been gerrymandered by the state legislature, he had already experienced difficulty in 1868 in securing re-election. Then he fell ill; absent from home, he was unable to prevent his antagonists from denying him renomination. So bitter that he would eventually turn against the Republican party itself, he nevertheless remained true to his principles. For the radicals, his absence was a sore loss.[7]

George H. Williams was also a victim of the resurgence of the opposition. Long a prominent member of the Senate who prided himself on the authorship of the first Reconstruction Act, the Oregon radical was ousted after the Democrats won a majority of the state legislature. After serving as one of the commissioners to negotiate the Treaty of Washington with Great Britain, Grant appointed him Attorney General and afterwards attempted to elevate him to the Supreme Court. Although this suggestion raised a furor because of doubts about Williams's probity, his exit from the Senate had been a clear mark of waning radical strength.[8]

John Covode's experiences were similar. Re-elected in 1868, his seat was disputed by his Democratic opponent. Congress found in his favor, and he served for most of his term; in 1870, however, he declined to seek re-election. A Democrat took his place, and, early in 1871, the Pennsylvania radical died.[9]

The ultras' worst defeat took place in Missouri. Long a scene

[7] Julian–Mrs. Julian, April 21, 1868, Mrs. Julian–Brother, March 17, 1870, Julian MS Diary, January 15, February 20, April 25, 1870, Julian Papers; Julian, *Political Recollections,* pp. 303, 320–1; *Independent,* February 3, 1870; *National Standard,* February 11, 1871.

[8] Sidney Teiser, "Life of George H. Williams: Almost Chief Justice," *Oregon Historical Quarterly,* XLVII (1946), 255–80, 416–40, esp. 271–4, 279; Portland *Oregon Journal,* April 9, 1910; William Fenton, "Political History of Oregon From 1865–1876," *The Quarterly of the Oregon Historical Society,* II (December, 1901), 321–35.

[9] *New York Times,* January 12, 1871.

of contention between radicals and their moderate, or, as they were now styling themselves, "liberal" opponents, the state had become something of a testing ground of the rival factions' respective strength. The point at issue was the end of disenfranchisement of secessionists, a program which, in the long run, was bound to redound to the liberals' advantage. Under the leadership of Carl Schurz and B. Gratz Brown, both of whom had broken with the radicals, the liberals, aided by the Democrats, completely routed their opponents and elected Brown governor. When Congress met in December, 1870, Schurz delivered a speech in which he denounced the radicals and attacked the President without reserve. His colleague, Charles Drake, sought to reply by castigating his antagonists a few days later; having been appointed to the Court of Claims, however, he then resigned his Senate seat. Francis P. Blair, Jr., was his successor, a change which illustrated not merely the end of radical rule in Missouri, but the antiradical trend in Congress as well.[1]

The ultras' lessening influence was soon to be reflected in the press. As time went on, the word "radical" would virtually disappear from the news columns. To be sure, Democratic organs continued to use it, but for them, it had merely become an epithet of opprobrium to castigate the Republican party in general, much in the same way that, in an earlier era, their opponents had referred to all Democrats as Loco-Focos. Some liberals characterized the Grant ticket in 1872 as radical; in February, 1871, the *Independent* still referred to Boutwell as the "radical" Cabinet member; radical clubs continued to exist in various cities, and in the late 1870's and 1880's, the stalwarts, Senator Conkling's faction of friends of Grant, were sometimes called by the old name. But in general, the concept itself disappeared. Writing in his paper, the *Golden Age,* the old antislavery advocate Theodore Tilton, on September 9, 1871, summed up the situation:

[1] William E. Parrish, *Missouri Under Radical Rule, 1865–1870* (Columbia, Mo., 1965), pp. 268–326; Blaine, *Twenty Years of Congress,* II, 507, 517; Bancroft, *Speeches, Correspondence, and Political Papers of Carl Schurz,* II, 25; *The Nation,* XI (December 22, 1870), 413; *Independent,* December 22, 1870.

The outlook, as it appears to our eyes, reveals the coming necessity for a new party in American politics—a Radical Party. Our newspaper neighbor *The World* casts its flings at Republicans as Radicals. But Republicans are not Radicals. The Republican party, whose issues . . . fired men's blood, has lost the manly mettle of its early youth. Its soul is languid. Ceasing to battle for ideas, it now sits down to count figures. It does not sow new seed—it is only garnering its former harvest. It needs the thorn of the doctrinaire in its side.[2]

What caused the loss of radical influence, if not the end of radicalism itself? How was it that a faction which had seemed all-powerful in 1866 was hardly in existence five years later? The evident collapse of the movement has attracted the attention of many historians who have shed much light on the subject. W. R. Brock has written that the difficulty of imposing upon a traditionalist nineteenth-century laissez-faire society the necessity of increased federal action helped the decline; Kenneth Stampp has shown that loss of enthusiasm as well as a lack of rapport between successful Northern business men and depressed Southern Negroes hastened a development facilitated by the appearance of new Republican strongholds in the Northwest; C. Vann Woodward has pointed out that the persistence of racial animosities in the North as well as in the South contributed to the debacle, which was made final by a community of economic interests of former Southern Whigs with conservative Northern Republicans, and Harold Hyman has stated that the decline in the interest in the Negro as well as the weakening of the reformist core of the Republican party had much to do with the problem. Among other factors, growing disillusionment with the Southern Republican regimes has been emphasized by David Donald and E. Merton Coulter; class conflict by David Montgomery; and the disappearance of Northern radical leadership by John Hope Franklin. All are in agreement that the movement was dying during Grant's ad-

[2] New York *World,* April 1, September 10, 1869; New York *Herald,* April 16, May 18, 1870, November 3, 1872; R. W. Topp–Trumbull, September 2, 1872, Trumbull Papers, ISHL; *Independent,* February 9, 1871; Koerner, *Memoirs,* II, 615, 619, 638; Myers, *The Republican Party,* p. 216; *Golden Age,* January 6, 1872, September 9, 1871.

ministration.[3] Why the end came so quickly remains a vital question.

As many commentators have recognized, it was probably impossible to maintain the Republican party at the high pitch of excitement to which its advanced wing for many years had tried to commit it. Generally ingrained racial antipathies were too great, and the immediate rewards of racial equality too small to permit the question of civil rights for nonwhites to play a permanent role in politics. What is surprising is not that the radicals were unable to prevail in the 1870's, but that they managed to sustain enthusiasm for their program for as long as they did. Forced to compromise on the suffrage in the Republican platform of 1868, less than one year later they nevertheless succeeded in passing the Fifteenth Amendment. But when this constitutional change was ratified, an adverse reaction set in. Had not the party completed its mission?

The belief that the successful passage and ratification of the Fifteenth Amendment had rendered Republicanism superfluous was widespread. As early as June 12, 1868, Georges Clemenceau observed that the question of racial equality, for eight years "the ground upon which the parties" had "met in their sharpest struggles," was now practically settled, and when the amendment was passed, his comments were echoed by others. Julian thought that the constitutional guarantee of universal suffrage had fulfilled the party's aims; George Wilkes was certain that his work was finished; Horace White entertained similar notions, and Vice President Colfax considered "the removal of the strong cohesive power of the Rcn. issues" one of the problems complicating the

[3] Brock, *An American Crisis,* pp. 274–304; Stampp, *The Era of Reconstruction,* pp. 204–5; C. Vann Woodward, "Seeds of Failure in Radical Race Policy," *Proceedings, American Philosophical Society,* CX (February, 1966), 1–9; C. Vann Woodward, *Reunion and Reaction: The Compromise of 1877 and the End of Reconstruction* (Garden City, 1956), pp. 3, 36–7; Harold M. Hyman, ed., *The Radical Republicans and Reconstruction, 1861–1870* (Indianapolis, 1967), pp. 521–3; J. G. Randall and David Donald, *The Civil War and Reconstruction* (Boston, 1961), pp. 679 ff.; Coulter, *The South During Reconstruction,* pp. 344 ff.; Montgomery, *Beyond Equality,* X; Franklin, *Reconstruction After the Civil War,* pp. 197–8.

1870 campaign. President Grant did not believe that the party's usefulness was at an end, but he, too, thought that a milestone had been reached. "You will see by the papers that the ratification of the Fifteenth Amendment is assured," he wrote to Washburne. "With this question out of politics, and reconstruction completed, I hope to see such good feeling in Congress as to secure rapid legislation and an early adjournment." His assessment of the importance of ratification was correct; his estimate of the results could not have been more mistaken.[4]

The private comments of Republican leaders were reflected in the newspapers. "Republicanism was brought together from chaos by the question of slavery," asserted the New York *World* in January, 1869. "Its leaders were carried into power by using the negro as their hobby horse. Now that he can carry them no longer, their differences of opinion are more clearly shown." Half a year later, the New York *Evening Post* observed that, slavery having been abolished and the war having ceased, a number of Republicans were beginning to ask, "What next?" In February, 1870, the dissensions in the Republican party led the New York *Herald* to highlight the problem. "A revolution in the Northern public mind against negro slavery . . . brought the republican party into power," it stated.

> Its strength was next increased and established on the grand idea of the war for the Union . . ., and with the collapse of the rebellion, involving the abolition of slavery, the republicans found a new bond of cohesion in reconstructing the Southern States, the constitution and the Union on the grand idea of equal rights, civil and political, regardless of race and color. The stupendous work of revolution thus embodied in that initiative republican idea, the extinction of slavery, is now completed.

Did not the party need a new issue to hold it together? This was an opinion Ben Butler was soon to express in a Lyceum lecture, and the *Nation,* no longer radical, observed that with the passage

---

[4] Clemenceau, *American Reconstruction,* pp. 196–7; Julian, *Political Recollections,* p. 326; George Wilkes–Sumner, May 8, 1869, Horace White–Sumner, April 13, 1872, Sumner Papers; Colfax-Anthony, August 7, 1870, Colfax Papers, LC; Grant-Washburne, January 28, 1870, Grant Papers, ISHL.

of the Fifteenth Amendment a great many persons who had formerly acted with the Republican organization would feel that its part had been played and would withdraw from it.[5]

Because of the evident fact that this analysis was not correct, some radical leaders sought vainly to counteract it. Never ceasing to protest that the radicals' work was far from finished, Charles Sumner, in April, 1870, warned the abolitionists who had assembled at the last meeting of the American Anti-Slavery Society that he did not think the work final so long as the word "white" was permitted to play any part in legislation. Recurring to this theme in October, at the ratification meeting of Massachusetts Republicans at Faneuil Hall, he said:

> I would add one further word in reply to those who insist that the Republican party has done its work, and therefore may die. Nothing is more absurd. It has done a great and memorable work; but much remains to be done. . . . The whole work of Reconstruction and the establishment of Equal Rights is still disputed and assailed by the Democratic party.

And at the beginning of the new year, he contributed to the *Independent* an article expressing similar sentiments.[6]

Oliver P. Morton also sought to remind voters of the fact that great tasks continued to challenge advocates of equal rights. As he said in July, 1870, at Terre Haute, "The Republican party has not performed its mission—not until the work of reconstruction is completed." This aim, he asserted, could only be achieved when the hostility toward Unionists and Negroes in the South had been eradicated. Wendell Phillips, who professed no great love for the party, nevertheless asserted that it could not be abandoned until the position of the Negro was secure, and Frederick Douglass likewise warned that the Republicans' purposes had not yet been achieved, an analysis substantiated by the famous orientalist Tayler Lewis in a scholarly article in the *Independent*. The general public,

[5] New York *World*, January 26, 1869; New York *Evening Post* (semiweekly), June 25, 1869; New York *Herald*, February 11, 1870; *Commonwealth*, November 26, 1870; *The Nation*, X (February 24, 1870), 114.

[6] Sumner, *Works*, XIII, 375 ff.; XIV, 1–5, 132–8.

however, connected the party, and especially its radical wing, with emancipation and the Reconstruction amendments. Because these had been accepted, at least in theory, there seemed to be no further need for vigilance.[7]

Closely related to the erroneous impression that the Republicans' mission was complete was the idea that it was time for a thorough realignment of political organizations. Even a radical like George W. Julian, outraged by the growth of monopoly and passionately devoted to land reform, was interested in this possibility. "A reorganization of parties is inevitable," he wrote in his diary on August 29, 1869, "and the issues tendered by the working men cannot be ignored." In June, 1870, he again commented on what he considered the complete demoralization of the Republican party; in the next year, he expressed his belief in a regrouping of forces according to what he called "the living issues," reforms in land tenure, labor relations, civil service, and the status of women. "The country greatly needs a thorough pacification, which it can't have while the business of saving the Union allows wholesale thieving to go on under color of Radicalism," he commented. In view of the ever more noticeable cooperation of the party with the essentially conservative property interests of the gilded age, his reaction was not surprising, and as serious scandals undermined the Grant administration, he became more and more certain that his analysis had been correct.[8]

Other observers arrived at similar conclusions. Convinced that widespread corruption had completely sapped the moral fiber of the Republican party, James W. Grimes avowed that he would no longer support it. Theodore Tilton, who would soon state that old parties were dead, in September, 1871, called for an entirely new grouping. In 1872, the New York *Herald* cited the emergence of

[7] Hon. O. P. Morton's Terre Haute Speech, Delivered July 18, 1870, at Terre Haute, Indiana (Washington, 1870); Phillips-Sumner, August 4, 1872; Douglass-Sumner, August 11, 1872, Sumner Papers; Independent, August 1, 1872.

[8] Julian MS Diary, August 29, 1869, June 26, 1870, May 28, 1871, November 24, 1872, March 4, 1873, June 7, 1874, August 27, 1876, Julian Papers.

Liberal Republicanism as a symptom of the breakup of political organizations; William S. Robinson, the long-time contributor to the Springfield *Republican,* pointed out to Sumner that existing parties had outlived their usefulness; and in the following year, Gerrit Smith confided to Julian that if he were twenty years younger he might work for the birth of another party far better than either of the existing ones. He had lost much of his hope for the Republican organization. "I fear it is past becoming a Reform party," he wrote, emphasizing a feeling which was becoming more and more widespread. In May of 1873, *Harper's Weekly,* in a detailed article, expressed its satisfaction about the "decay of parties."[9]

The gradual change in popular interests also contributed to the decline of radicalism. The economic forces unleashed by the industrial revolution and accentuated by Northern success in the Civil War were becoming increasingly identified with the party in power, which was developing more and more into an organization dedicated to the maintenance of the status quo. That such a group, representing as it did the leaders of Northern industry, would find it easy in the long run to make common cause with the poorest segment of Southern society was not to be expected, and the result was a perceptible lessening of radical enthusiasm.[1]

Another factor hastening the disappearance of radicalism was the disorder which continued to afflict the Southern states. The very fact that life and property were not secure in the former Confederacy might have been expected to strengthen demands for extreme measures. Up to a point, this was the case. Southern contumacy led to the passing of the Enforcement Acts; the Ku Klux Klan disappeared although violence continued, and individual Republicans were still able to win elections by appealing

[9] Grimes-Trumbull, July 11, 1870, Trumbull Papers, LC; *Golden Age,* September 9, 1870; New York *Herald,* May 25, 1872; Robinson-Sumner, July 11, 1872, Sumner Papers; Gerrit Smith–Julian, September 23, 1873, Julian-Giddings Papers; *Harper's Weekly,* XVII (May 17, 1873), 410.

[1] Cf. Woodward, *Reunion and Reaction,* pp. 36–7.

to wartime emotions. But as time went on, Northern voters became tired of the Southern problem. Reporters emphasized the corruption so common in the reconstructed states without reminding their readers that venality existed elsewhere also; judicial decisions narrowed the scope of the Fourteenth Amendment, and eventually the federal government became more and more reluctant to intervene. "With the exception of a few extreme radicals who are anxious to perpetuate the power of the Republican party in the South," commented the New York *Herald* in January, 1871, "there is no disposition to meddle with affairs in that section. Anything like a fresh attempt at reconstruction would, it is thought, react upon the administration and make it obnoxious before the people." The result was that one state after another reverted to conservative rule.[2]

The conservative victories in Virginia and Tennessee were merely the beginning. In spite of warnings from radical politicians not to rush matters, Congress admitted the remaining states in 1870. In November, Georgia and North Carolina; in January, 1873, Texas; and in November, 1874, Arkansas and Alabama rejected Republican rule. In Louisiana, where several radical factions vied for control, only General Grant's interference enabled Governor William P. Kellogg to perpetuate his contested administration. Arkansas radicals also asked for help from Washington after strife had broken out between Elisha Brooks and Joseph Baxter, rival claimants for the governorship; the President refused, however, and enabled the conservatives to return to power. Where Republican regimes lasted a little longer, the end could also be foreseen in the not too distant future. With the granting of amnesty to former Confederates, the Southern power base of radicalism was being eroded.[3]

[2] Franklin, *Reconstruction After the Civil War,* pp. 165 ff.; 198 ff., 206–9; Paul H. Buck, *The Road to Reunion, 1865–1900* (Boston, 1937), pp. 74 ff.; New York *Herald,* January 15, 1871.

[3] William Alexander–Sumner, December 2, 1869, T. M. Brown–Sumner, December 11, 1869, S. F. Maddox–Sumner, December 12, 1869, Sumner Papers; Rembert E. Patrick, *The Reconstruction of the Nation* (New York, 1967), pp. 142 ff., 254; Henry Clay Warmoth, *War, Politics and Reconstruction: Stormy Days in Louisiana* (New York,

In addition to these problems, the important controversies of the 1870's often found the remaining radicals on opposite sides. Having never agreed on anything except the need to elevate the Negro, they could not be expected to close ranks on a variety of questions agitating the nation during the Grant era. Because these issues were assuming ever increasing importance, however, they also tended to become more and more divisive. The result was that whatever radical strength remained was fast being dissipated.

Perhaps the most difficult political problem of the time was the issue of inflation. Whether the national debt should be paid in greenbacks or in gold, whether paper money should be retired and specie payments resumed, or whether the nonmetallic currency should be expanded were problems of tremendous emotional impact. And the radicals were no more in agreement on these questions than they had been in previous years.

The most prominent radical influencing financial policies was the Secretary of the Treasury, George S. Boutwell. But because he was fanatically devoted to reducing the national debt and establishing a hard currency, he tended to appeal to those elements of the population whose monetary views were usually labeled conservative. And he was not alone. Sumner, Creswell, Julian, Chandler, to mention but a few, supported him wholeheartedly, and so powerful was the deflationists' influence that they induced President Grant to veto the inflation bill of 1874.[4]

Other influential radicals, however, were desperately opposed to hard money. Ben Butler especially became the spokesman for inflationary elements, and so strident was his bid for paper money that he threatened to tear the party apart, particularly in his home

1930), pp. 51–4, 161 ff., 200 ff.; Powell Clayton, *The Aftermath of the Civil War in Arkansas* (New York, 1915), pp. 346–9; Thomas S. Staples, *Reconstruction in Arkansas, 1862–1874* (New York, 1923), pp. 389 ff., 408 ff.; Hesseltine, *Grant,* pp. 341–3, 347.

[4] Boutwell, *Reminiscences of Sixty Years,* II, 140; Nevins, *Fish,* pp. 288, 711–12; Sumner, *Works,* XIII, 234–98; Julian MS Diary, February 22, June 7, 28, December 13, 1874, Julian Papers; S. D. Elwood–Chandler, January 24, 1874, S. Trowbridge–Chandler, January 28, 1874, Chandler Papers; Sharkey, *Money, Class and Party,* pp. 279–82.

state of Massachusetts. Again and again he urged the defeat of the advocates of hard money; over and over again he accused them of callous conservatism. Like Thaddeus Stevens, whose place as radical leader and chairman of the House Committee on Reconstruction he was trying to take, Butler was always intrigued by financial unorthodoxy. And Morton, Medill, and Kelley, among others, sympathized with his views.[5]

The problem of the tariff also divided the radicals—in the seventies as well as in earlier years. Opponents of protection like Julian, Sumner, and James F. Wilson clashed with protectionists like "Pig Iron" Kelley, Chandler, and Butler. What was radical and what was conservative in relation to the tariff was anybody's guess; members of Congress tended to line up with their section, and it was no mere accident that Pennsylvanians like Kelley and Ulysses Mercur generally voted for higher and higher duties. Thaddeus Stevens had shown them the way, and the differences of opinion among the old antislavery vanguard could not be hidden.[6]

An equally challenging question concerned the rights of labor. By and large, the radicals were sympathetic toward the eight-hour day and a better deal for workingmen. Julian, Covode, Henry Wilson, Kelley, Butler, and, earlier, Wade, enjoyed labor's confidence. But many labor leaders distrusted Sumner, and the third-party candidates they nominated had little in common with those radicals who endorsed the major organizations. The activities of the Paris Commune, which was then frightening conservatives everywhere, revealed a further split in radical ranks. While extremists like Ben Butler strongly supported it, others, represented

[5] Ibid.; Trefousse, *Butler*, pp. 193–4, 218–19; Butler–Mrs. Butler, April 24, 1874, Butler Papers; Springfield *Republican*, April 24, 1874; Brock, *An American Crisis*, p. 223.

[6] Julian, *Political Recollections*, pp. 326 ff.; *National Standard*, February 11, 1871; New York *Herald*, December 9, 1871; Sumner, *Works*, XI, 91–7, XV, 61; *Independent*, June 25, 1868; Edward Winslow Martin, *Behind the Scenes in Washington* (Washington, 1873), pp. 211–12; Harris, *Chandler*, p. 111; *Cong. Globe*, 42d Cong., 2d. Ses., 3518; Edward McPherson, *A Handbook of Politics for 1872* (Washington, 1872), pp. 90, 95, 96.

by the *Independent,* roundly condemned his stand. They considered the Communards' revolutionary theories anathema.[7]

Questions of diplomacy proved even more divisive. Most radicals had long combined militancy in domestic affairs with chauvinism abroad. Ever since the 1840's, Chase had advocated territorial aggrandizement; Chandler's violent antipathy toward Great Britain was well known, and Giddings had preached hatred of the rulers of Canada even while consul in Montreal. Hale had been inalterably opposed to the surrender of Mason and Slidell; Henry Winter Davis had agitated against imperial Mexico as well as against the British in North America, and most other radicals strongly sympathized with these views. But the one extremist whose influence in American diplomacy was most marked was Charles Sumner, the chairman of the Senate Committee on Foreign Relations, and in spite of some aggressive speeches, in his approach to other powers he had always been more moderate than his colleagues. As a lifelong pacifist, he deplored foreign wars.[8]

During the postwar years, the radicals' differences about foreign policy constituted a serious obstacle to Republican unity. The problems of Mexico, where the French had taken advantage of the disturbed conditions in North America to set up a puppet empire, might have caused a serious rift because of Winter Davis's and other extremists' insistence on strong measures had not Seward's skillful diplomacy contributed to Napoleon III's withdrawal from the Western Hemisphere. This left the Mexican liberals under Benito Juarez free to overthrow the Emperor

[7] Montgomery, *Beyond Equality,* pp. 123 ff.; Montgomery, Labor and the Radical Republicans, pp. 209, 309, 540–4, 590–600; Julian, *Political Recollections,* pp. 274–5; Julian MS Diary, August 23, 1870, Julian Papers; J. C. Whaley–Covode, March 27, 1867, Covode Papers, WPHS; New York *World,* June 10, 1869; Trefousse, *Butler,* p. 219; Cincinnati *Daily Gazette,* July 2, 1867; L. U. Reavis–Sumner, October 28, 1868, Sumner Papers; New York *Herald,* July 30, 1871; *Independent,* July 13, 1871.

[8] Chase, *Diary and Correspondence,* p. 173; Schuckers, *Chase,* p. 392; George, *Chandler,* pp. 160 ff., 229; Giddings-Sumner, April 5, 1864, Sumner Papers; Giddings-Seward, April 15, 1863, Giddings Papers; Sumner, *Works,* VI, 156, 161; XIV, 10–85, XV, 80–7; Dixon-Greeley, May 27, 1864, Greeley Papers; Steiner, *Davis,* p. 261.

Maximilian, so that further involvement in the republic's affairs became unnecessary. With Great Britain, however, relations became more and more strained. Widely held responsible for prolonging the Civil War because of aid to the Confederates, the British government became a public whipping boy in the United States, especially since both parties were anxious to woo Irish voters incensed about Britain's treatment of their homeland. Almost unanimously, the Senate rejected a treaty to settle the wartime claims against the offending nation negotiated by Reverdy Johnson with Foreign Secretary Lord George Clarendon; and radical orators, particularly Chandler and Butler, delivered bellicose, intemperate speeches. But Charles Sumner again stood his ground. No matter how strongly he denounced the Johnson-Clarenden Convention, no matter how succinctly he expressed his eagerness for the annexation of Canada, he made it clear that he considered war between modern nations unthinkable. It was a stand which greatly impressed such veteran antislavery workers as Gerrit Smith.[9]

The outstanding problems with Great Britain were finally settled by the Treaty of Washington, which undercut the more belligerent extremists. By agreeing to submit its differences with the United States to an international tribunal at Geneva, the London government made possible a peaceful solution. In spite of misgivings, the Senate accepted the settlement, and although Charles Sumner had again attempted to make any agreement dependent upon the cession of Canada, he was vindicated in his insistence upon avoidance of hostilities.[1]

But the Massachusetts senator was already encountering new difficulties. Anxious to annex Santo Domingo, President Grant had sent emissaries to the tropical republic to negotiate a treaty.

[9] Patrick, *The Reconstruction of the Nation,* pp. 194–5, 197–99; New York *Herald,* April 23, May 29, 1870; New York *Evening Post* (semiweekly), April 20, 1869; *Commonwealth,* November 26, 1870; Worcester *Evening Gazette,* December 7, 1870, clipping in Butler Papers; Sumner, *Works,* XIII, 53–93, XIV, 10–85; XV, 80–2; Sumner-Howe, August 28, 1870, Howe Papers; *Independent,* July 8, 1869.

[1] Nevins, *Fish,* pp. 486–93; Rhodes, *History of the United States,* VI, 468–87.

At first he sought to win Sumner over; then it became evident that the chairman of the Senate's Committee on Foreign Relations was opposed to the scheme. The result was a complete break between the two men. When the treaty of annexation failed, the President ordered the recall of Sumner's friend John Lothrop Motley from his post as minister to the Court of St. James, an act of spite which did not improve relations between the two antagonists. The President's attempt to reopen the issue in December was the signal for a violent philippic against the administration. "Naboth's Vinyard," Sumner called his speech, in which he mercilessly condemned Grant, the annexationist project, the American emissaries, and the president of Santo Domingo. So violent were his charges that Morton and Chandler felt called upon to reply, and the public spectacle of distinguished radicals openly upbraiding each other in the Senate did not contribute to the success of their cause in the South. The immediate result was the appointment of a commission to investigate conditions in the disputed island, a body to which Grant appointed Benjamin F. Wade, Samuel Gridley Howe, and the distinguished educator Andrew D. White.[2]

Administration leaders now committed a major blunder. Furious at Sumner's charges—he referred to the resolution to appoint the commission as a "dance of blood"—they decided to remove him from his position as chairman of the Senate Committee on Foreign Relations. Consequently, when the new Congress met in March, 1871, a Republican caucus determined to place Cameron at the head of Sumner's old committee and to transfer him to the Committee on Privileges and Elections. The outraged senator refused to serve, and the situation was not made any less painful by the fact that radicals like Morton, Chandler, Hamlin, and Howe had played a leading role in the deposition.[3]

[2] Pierce, *Sumner,* IV, 429–61; Howe-Sumner, August 25, 1870, Sumner-Howe, August 28, 1870, Howe Papers; Sumner, *Works,* XIV, 89–131; Foulke, *Morton,* II, 151–68; Andrew Dickinson White, *Autobiography of Andrew Dickinson White* (New York, 1905), I, 283.

[3] Sumner, *Works,* XIV, 94, 253; Blaine, *Twenty Years of Congress,* II, 503–6; New York *Herald,* March 10, 1871; Hamlin, *Hamlin,* p. 531;

Many of Sumner's old friends rallied to his cause. Considering his removal uncalled for, Garrison, Forney, Ashley, Julian, and Chase were among those expressing their sympathies; the abolitionist *National Standard,* Tilton's *Golden Age,* and even the *Independent,* which considered Sumner's opposition to the annexation of Santo Domingo wrong, condemned the Republican caucus. *Harper's Weekly* characterized the senator's deposition as "a grave political blunder," and the New York *Herald* printed lengthy accounts of what it called "The Radical Fight Against the President."[4] But its nomenclature was inexact. Hamlin, Chandler, Howe, Morton, Butler, and others all continued to support Grant; Ben Wade not only accepted his appointment to serve as one of the commissioners to the island republic, but urged strongly that the commission's final report include a firm recommendation favoring annexation, while Frederick Douglass, sad at the necessity of differing with his old friend Sumner, consented to serve as secretary of the commission. Rarely if ever had the radicals been so much at odds with one another.[5]

If these factors had been weakening the radicals' position, the rift in the Republican party caused by the rise of the liberal movement in 1872 sapped their strength even further. In their effort to repeat on a national scale what they had accomplished in 1870 in Missouri, the so-called Liberal Republicans succeeded in winning over a number of old reformers, although the bulk of the radicals remained loyal to Grant and the Republican organization. Carl Schurz was possibly the most enthusiastic sup-

Foulke, *Morton,* II, 170–4; *Golden Age,* April 1, 1871; Howe–Grace Howe, March 21, April 4, 1871, Howe Papers.

[4] Garrison-Sumner, March 4, 1871, Forney-Sumner, March 9, 1871, Ashley-Sumner, March 12, 1871, Chase-Sumner, March 12, 1871, Sumner Papers; Julian MS Diary, March 12, 1871, Julian Papers; *National Standard,* March 18, 1871; *Golden Age,* March 18, 1871; *Independent,* March 16, 23, 1871; *Harper's Weekly,* XV (March 25, 1871), 258; New York *Herald,* March 15, 1871.

[5] Hamlin–Mrs. Hamlin, December 21, 28, 1870, Hamlin Papers; *National Standard,* March 18, 1871; Trefousse, *Butler,* pp. 210–11; White, *Autobiography,* I, 506; Douglass-Sumner, January 6, 1871, Sumner Papers; Douglass, *Life and Times,* p. 453.

porter of the effort to forge a new coalition appealing to advocates of revenue revision and a civil service law as well as to other opponents of the administration. But although he professed never to have changed his ideas about the need for equal rights in the South, his attempts to conciliate the Democrats soon led him to assume strange positions. In December, 1870, in a widely circulated speech attacking the Grant regime, he argued that the parties were due for reorganization. Had not the Republicans achieved their goals? And had not the Democrats been forced to change their outlook? Instead of opposing liberals in Missouri, to restore peace, the President should have supported them. The iron-clad oath led to abuses; vindictive measures should be dropped, and only by economy, regard for states' rights, and hostility to monopolies could the Republican party regenerate itself. Charles Drake, his radical colleague and antagonist, delivered an incisive reply, but Schurz continued on his course, finally going so far as to oppose the Ku Klux Act.[6]

Other radicals shared the Missouri senator's ideas. Theodore Tilton was certain that Clement L. Vallandigham's "New Departure," a call for Democratic acceptance of wartime changes, offered a good opportunity for reform. Advocating the nomination of any candidate other than Grant in 1872, he became the special pleader for the candidacy of Horace Greeley, then disappointed by the President's failure to accept his suggestion of universal amnesty. Salmon P. Chase, seeing in the "New Departure" another opportunity for the party reorganization he had advocated in 1868, also favored it, and George W. Julian, estranged from the administration by his defeat and the influence of his old antagonist, Oliver P. Morton, enthusiastically welcomed the marshaling of forces against it. George Wilkes and James M. Ashley also became converts, and as time went on, Trumbull, Greeley, and Schurz became the leading advocates of the policy of uniting dissident Republicans with the Democrats. But was the movement

[6] Bancroft, *Speeches, Correspondence, and Political Papers of Carl Schurz,* I, 521–2; II, 2–70, 252–4, 257–306; *Independent,* December 22, 1870.

radical? Could it really combine reform and cooperation with the Democrats with justice to the Negroes in the South? This question was crucial, and the liberals' ultimate fate might well depend on the answer.[7]

Schurz tried his best to prove that Liberal Republicanism was compatible with radicalism. In a speech delivered at Nashville, Tennessee, in August, 1871, he sought to set forth his philosophy. Let Southerners accept the conditions brought about by the postwar amendments so that they would win Negro votes, he urged. The time for reconciliation had come, and the "New Departure" was the way to effect it. In a note to Sumner, he expressed himself even more succinctly in opposing the spoilsmen surrounding Grant. "You tell me in your letter that the Republican party must be saved," he wrote. "I am convinced that it can be done only by making it the party of reforms and by suppressing the bad influences governing it." Continuing to emphasize his satisfaction about Southerners' rallying about the flag "as the symbol of universal freedom," he sought to keep Democratic influences in the background and preached amnesty as a way to end Ku Klux outrages. He even suggested that Sumner place himself at the head of the movement.[8]

Cassius Clay was equally convinced that radicalism and the "New Departure" could be fused. Seeking to enlist Henry Wilson in the cause, he insisted that it was necessary to displace President Grant or Republicanism would be lost. "Is it too late to save the fruits of the war by a generous course—and an honest capable man at the head of affairs?" he asked. The answer seemed simple to him, and such prominent radicals supported the movement that

---

[7] *Golden Age,* June 3, 1871; James M. McPherson, "Grant or Greeley? The Abolitionist Dilemma in the Election of 1872," *American Historical Review,* LXXI (October, 1965), 43–61, esp. 49; New York *Herald,* June 26, December 9, 1871; Julian MS Diary, p. 95, pp. 112–13, October 12, 1871, Julian Papers; George Wilkes–Sumner, November 17, 1871, Sumner Papers; Ashley, "Governor Ashley's Biography and Messages," loc. cit., pp. 196 ff.; Earle Dudley Ross, *The Liberal Republican Movement* (New York, 1919), p. 12.

[8] Bancroft, *Speeches, Correspondence, and Political Papers of Carl Schurz,* II, 257–306, 256–7, 311–13, 307–8.

some historians have interpreted their action as an effort to lodge a protest against the abandonment of the Negro, an attempt to revive the reforming spirit of the increasingly conservative Republican party.[9]

In the long run, however, the organization of the Liberal Republican movement spelled disaster rather than revival for radicalism. Unwilling to make common cause with many of their former antagonists, three quarters of the old abolitionists and radicals remained loyal to Grant, and although in May, 1872, the bolters agreed upon a platform pledging civil rights and equality to all, not even the nomination of Horace Greeley and B. Gratz Brown at Cincinnati could hide the fact that the dissidents' success would bring antiradicals of all types back to power. As W. C. Flagg, a member of the Illinois legislature, wrote to Trumbull,

> The great difficulty in the way of reforming the present state of things is the persistence of the Democratic party in not dying. If it had the ability like the old Whig party to go into liquidation . . . there would be a much better chance than I now see for a new organization. Such an one must rely upon the Democratic party, as such, to an extent that must greatly color its opinions and affect its standing.[1]

One of the factors making the Liberal movement suspect was the type of leadership which propagated it. Lyman Trumbull's prominence was not reassuring; the Illinois Republican had long drifted into ever more conservative circles. If most radicals found it difficult to forgive him for his vote against the conviction of Johnson, they were more than ever convinced of their former colleague's apostasy when he consistently opposed the Ku Klux Act. Carl Schurz, too, had not merely fought the radical organization in Missouri, but opposed the Enforcement Acts as well. That

[9] C. M. Clay–Wilson, March 17, 1871, Wilson Papers; George Seldon Henry, Jr., "Radical Republican Policy Toward the Negro During Reconstruction, 1862–72," doctoral dissertation, Yale University, 1963, p. 331.
[1] McPherson, "Grant or Greeley? The Abolitionist Dilemma in the Election of 1872," loc. cit., p. 43; Fleming, *Documentary History of Reconstruction,* II, 98; Hale, *Greeley,* pp. 334 ff.; W. C. Flagg–Trumbull, July 15, 1872, Trumbull Papers, LC.

Charles Francis Adams was frequently mentioned as a possible Liberal presidential candidate did not make matters easier; radical Republicans had distrusted the former Free-Soiler ever since his espousal of compromise in January, 1861. B. Gratz Brown, another Liberal hopeful, had been one of the most effective leaders of the antiradical faction in Missouri, and David Davis, who was also prominently identified with the movement, had always been known for his moderate if not conservative attitude. From the radical point of view, with the exception of Horace Greeley, the principal Liberals had little to offer.[2]

If the leaders of the new faction were largely conservative or moderate, their supporters reflected their attitude. On January 12, 1872, Joseph Brown, the president of the Missouri Pacific Railroad, urging Trumbull to run for the presidency, wrote: "You could command, if put in nomination by the conservative republicans, the entire vote of the Democratic party, to which of course would be added all the outs of the republican party." Coalition against the "radical" organization, as he called the regulars, was his prescription. In Iowa, the Liberals rejoiced at their success in defeating the radical senator, James Harlan; in Kansas, Edmund Ross, who had not only voted against conviction in the impeachment trial, but had generally followed a moderate line since, was one of the party's organizers; and in Wisconsin, James R. Doolittle, who had never disavowed his support for Johnson, was an enthusiastic backer of the movement. As a Massachusetts Liberal wrote to Trumbull, "A change of Administration is sincerely wished for by Conservative men of all parties. . . ," a sentiment which was echoed elsewhere. Perhaps the prevailing idea was best expressed by a Delaware politician who warned that nominations should be made in such a way that Democrats could endorse the candidates chosen:

> The first important step is to select as the presiding officer a person well known throughout the country but who, if possible,

[2] Ross, *The Liberal Republican Movement*, p. 12; L. U. Reavis–Sumner, November 15, 1870, W. S. Robinson–Sumner, March 18, 1872, Sumner Papers; Browning, *Diary*, II, 295; B. C. Cook–Trumbull, March 21, 1872, Trumbull Papers, LC; Duberman, *Adams*, pp. 250, 358 ff.

has not been conspicuous in party affairs of late—a Republican, of course, but not one with such pronounced views upon the questions connected with emancipation (including re-construction) as Mr. Sumner.[3]

The most telling indictment against the Liberal Republicans was their Southern policy. Demanding in their platform "local self-government," they avowed that it would guard the rights of all citizens more securely than "any centralized power." In a condemnation of the Enforcement Acts, they asserted that the public welfare required the supremacy of the civil over the military authority, "and freedom of person under the protection of the habeas corpus." Their attacks against the administration combined demands for local autonomy, civil service reform, and rigid economy with an insistence upon universal amnesty and an end of abuses in the South. Although this stance was qualified by a full acceptance of the Reconstruction amendments and equal justice to all, it naturally appealed to Southern conservatives. As early as 1870, a dissatisfied faction in South Carolina, seeking to cut loose from radical connections, had approached Chase about the advisability of forming a new party; Georgia conservatives had sought Trumbull's help against the radical governor, Rufus Bullock, and in 1871, Arkansas dissidents had attempted to make use of the "New Departure" to enlist Chase as their candidate for the presidency. It was hardly surprising that in 1872, conservatives in other Southern states showed eagerness to join the movement. The support of J. S. Fowler in Tennessee and the conservative politician Benjamin Hill in Georgia was indicative of the trend of events, and when a Southern correspondent in Arkansas wrote to Trumbull that the Southern people were delighted with the party, he unwittingly pointed out why most ultras remained aloof.[4]

[3] B. G. Brown–Trumbull, January 12, 1872, James W. McDill–Trumbull, January 19, 1872, E. G. Ross–Trumbull, February 21, 1872, J. R. Doolittle–Trumbull, March 20, 1872, S. W. Kendal–Trumbull, April 24, 1872, J. P. Comegys–Trumbull, April 15, 1872, Trumbull Papers, LC.

[4] Kirk H. Porter and Donald Bruce Johnson, *National Party Platforms, 1840–1964* (Urbana, 1966), pp. 44–5; A. G. McGrath–Chase,

Because of these circumstances, many radicals who disliked Grant were faced with a dilemma. Pointedly expressing their quandary, on September 25, 1871, Sumner wrote to Schurz:

> I tremble for my country, when I contemplate the possibility of this man [Grant] being fastened upon us for another four years. ... I also tremble when I think of reconstruction, with Liberty and Equality, committed for four years to the tender mercies of the Democrats. Which way is daylight?

Schurz sought to reassure him, but despite the Massachusetts senator's increasingly hostile attitude toward the administration, he hesitated.[5]

Because Sumner was the most prominent antislavery senator, his actions tended to overshadow those of his colleagues. In the long run, it was not so much his interest in Liberal Republicanism as his detestation of the President which swayed him. The key to his thinking was his determination to defeat the renomination of Grant and at the same time to protect Negro rights. "I think I understand Sumner's position now," D. A. Wells, the liberal economist, had written to Trumbull prior to the Liberal Republican convention.

> He is for the negro first & last. He means to make Cincinnati come out for equality irrespective of caste or color before the law, & then force [the Republicans at] Philadelphia to bid higher.

To some degree, this was Sumner's idea, but it was not surprising. Having devoted a lifetime to the ideal of racial justice, the radicals could not be expected to forsake their aims. Concern for the freedmen and a realization of the Liberals' weakness in regard to Southern policy made Sumner's position delicate.[6]

July 4, 1870, J. B. Hussey–Chase, August 30, 1871, Chase Papers, LC; J. R. Sneed–Trumbull, July 22, 1870, J. S. Fowler–Trumbull, February 1, 1872, D. H. Moore–Trumbull, April 17, 1872, Trumbull Papers, LC; Coulter, *The South During Reconstruction*, p. 345.

[5] Bancroft, *Speeches, Correspondence and Political Papers of Carl Schurz*, II, 309, 311–13; Whitelaw Reid–Sumner, March 28, 1872, Sumner Papers.

[6] D. A. Wells–Trumbull, April 22, 1872, Trumbull Papers, LC; Pierce, *Sumner*, IV, 519; New York *Herald*, April 19, 1872; *Independent*, June 6, 1872.

Greeley's nomination at Cincinnati did not solve the senator's dilemma. As John W. Forney pointed out, there was no question about the merits of Sumner's quarrel with Grant, but he had received alarming news from the South, where Negroes were being abused and even Republican judges backed by the military powerless to protect them. "Now how can we cooperate with a party, or support a candidate pledged to surrender the entire South into the hands of the slave tyrants?" he asked. Sumner's Negro correspondents also warned him. "Do you not believe that if they [the Bourbons] should come in power with Mr. Greeley . . . that they would repeal the enforcement acts of Congress. . . ," wrote G. M. Arnold from North Carolina. "The Ku Klux Klan are only sleeping—if Mr. Greeley or any other man other than the nominee of the Philadelphia Convention should be the next President of the United States I fear it is the beginning of new Slavery. . . ." Gerrit Smith also expressed his doubts. Much as he liked and honored Greeley, he stated, he could not get himself to lift a finger toward bringing the Democrats to power. It would ruin the Negro. And Garrison, warning Sumner that Greeley's nomination was merely reviving the old slavery struggle, expressed his satisfaction that the senator had not taken part in the convention. Sumner was certainly aware of the dangers of a Democratic revival.[7]

The senator's hatred of Grant, however, made him oblivious of these warnings. On May 31, 1872, stung to the quick by the attacks of his enemies, he delivered a violent diatribe against the President. "Republicanism v. Grantism," he called his Senate speech. Castigating Grant as an incapable military despot, he pronounced himself not merely a Republican but "one of the straitest of the sect." But he charged that the party was being debauched by Grantism, that its tone of moral uplift was disappearing, and that nepotism was sapping its strength. The unmeasured tone of Sumner's attack made it easy for other radicals, Chandler, Morton, Conkling, and Carpenter, to come to the President's de-

[7] Forney-Sumner, May 13, 1872, G. M. Arnold–Sumner, May 20, 1872, Gerrit Smith–Sumner, May 25, 1872, Garrison-Sumner, May 27, 1872, Sumner Papers.

fense. Even Garrison expressed his consternation. Carried away by his own frustrations, the senator was moving closer to the Greeley camp.[8]

When in June Grant was renominated at Philadelphia with Henry Wilson as a running mate, old associates again sought to warn Sumner not to endorse the Liberals. Wendell Phillips, George Boutwell, Frederick Douglass, and Lydia Maria Child were among those trying to persuade him, but their entreaties were in vain. In spite of the Democrats' endorsement of the Liberal ticket, on July 29 in a public letter addressed to colored citizens, the senator came out for Greeley and urged freedmen to follow suit. Old friends wrote to him in dismay; old antagonists like James Dixon were delighted, and Sumner himself decided to take a long trip to Europe. The country watched in astonishment as the outstanding crusader for Negro rights was separated from the organization many still called the radical party.[9]

As the campaign wore on, it became more and more obvious that only with a decided Republican victory could radical principles survive, although Sumner, Julian, and Ashley tried to delude themselves. The Massachusetts senator's long hesitation was in itself partial proof of this fact. If so bitter an opponent of the administration could not make up his mind until late, something had to be wrong. And something was wrong. As a Louisiana Negro observed, when he went into the hotel where Greeley posters were displayed, he was thrown out before he had a chance to say anything. Could anyone blame him for remaining true to Grant and his friends rather than supporting his enemies? A Tennessee freedman agreed. "We'll teach you Niggers to say Sir, & Master, when Mr. Greeley takes his seat," a local planter had said to his hired

[8] Sumner, *Works,* XV, 83–171; *Independent,* June 6, 1872; New York *Herald,* June 7, 1872; Garrison-Sumner, June 1, 1872, Sumner Papers.
[9] Wendell Phillips–Sumner, July 19, August 4, 1872, Boutwell-Sumner, June 19, 1872, Douglass-Sumner, July 5, August 11, 1872, Lydia Maria Child–Sumner, June 21, 1872, Forney-Sumner, August 12, 1872, Samuel Hooper–Sumner, October 6, 1872, James Dixon–Sumner, August 2, 1872, Sumner Papers; Sumner, *Works,* XV, 173–95; New York *Herald,* July 31, August 3, 1872; *Independent,* August 8, 1872; Pierce, *Sumner,* IV, 531 ff.

hand, and it was taken for granted that all those who were perpetrating terrorist outrages were going to vote for Grant's opponent. Consequently, in November, after Greeley had been decisively defeated, the *Independent* concluded that "The American people decrees that the right of the enfranchised negroes must and shall be preserved." But the radical Republicans had again been weakened by the rift.[1]

The successful party was soon to be in trouble again. Gradually, the scandals that were to plague the Grant administration for the next four years were coming to light. First came the revelations concerning the Crédit Mobilier, the construction company organized by an inside ring of the Union Pacific Railroad, whose manipulations reached into Congress. In order to keep them from interfering with the scheme, any number of members had received stocks at favorable prices, and when the affair was investigated, it appeared that such well-known radicals as William D. Kelley, Henry Wilson, and James Harlan did not escape without taint, while Vice President Colfax was so thoroughly implicated that he was never able to clear himself afterward. Nor was the Crédit Mobilier the only instance of corruption in politics. In 1873, when a state legislator rose in the Kansas senate to show the astonished members $7,000 which had been given to him to vote for Samuel Pomeroy's return to Washington, it became evident that the Kansas radical was deeply involved in bribery. In the same year, Congress, under the leadership of Ben Butler, voted itself a raise in salary including back pay for two years; and in 1874 it uncovered large-scale irregularities in the collection of back taxes in the Boston area. This affair again undermined confidence in Ben Butler, at whose insistence the dubious collector, John D. Sanborn, had originally been appointed. The atmosphere of moral fervor in which radicalism had flourished was rapidly being dissipated.[2]

[1] Sambo Estelle–Sumner, August 5, 1872, J. Braden–Sumner, August 6, 1872, Sumner Papers; *Independent,* November 7, 1872.
[2] Martin, *Behind the Scenes in Washington,* pp. 248–301, 151, 163–6, 173–84; Buffalo *Courier,* August 28, 1873, copy in Sumner

In 1873, the Republicans encountered an even more serious difficulty. The failure of Jay Cooke's banking house ushered in a major depression which had world-wide ramifications. Because the widespread suffering naturally tended to react against the party in power, Republican control of Congress was endangered. And without Republican ascendancy the radicals would be powerless. When, in the following year, the mid-term elections took place, the Republicans not only lost the House, but any number of radical constituencies as well. Ben Butler was defeated in Massachusetts; Richard C. Parsons in Ohio, and Horace Maynard in Tennessee, and before another Congress assembled, Chandler failed of re-election to the Senate, while the Tennessee legislature replaced William G. Brownlow with none other than former President Andrew Johnson. The man whom the ultras had tried so desperately to remove from the White House had returned to the Capitol—a living symbol of radicalism's lessening importance.[3]

Last but not least, the decline of radicalism was accentuated by the departure or death of many of the leading ultras. For over twenty years, the band of determined men who had led the Republican party forward in the struggle against slavery and prejudice had constituted an easily identifiable core. Chase, Sumner, Stevens, Julian, Wade, Chandler, Wilson, Hale and others were known throughout the country; now one after the other of these stalwarts disappeared from public life. The defeats of Wade, Julian, Ashley, Harlan and others thinned the ranks in Congress, and these setbacks assumed greater significance because of the deaths of many radical leaders: in August, 1868, Thaddeus Stevens; in December, 1869, after having been appointed Associate Justice of the Supreme Court, former Secretary of War Stanton; in January, 1871, John Covode; in May, 1873, Chief

Papers; William S. Robinson, *The Salary Grab* (Boston, 1873); Springfield *Republican,* February 24–March 7, 1873; Trefousse, *Butler,* pp. 228–9; W. P. Phillips–Wilson, February 21, 1873, Wilson Papers.

[3] Julian MS Diary, November 16, 1873, Julian Papers; *New York Times,* October 14, November 4, 5, 6, 1874; Springfield *Republican,* November 4, 9, 1874; Marcus Ward–W. L. Ransom, November 18, 1874, Ward Papers; Blaine, *Twenty Years of Congress,* II, 551, 552.

Justice Chase; in December, 1873, after a disagreeable involvement in irregularities as minister to Spain, John P. Hale; in March, 1874, Charles Sumner; and in November, 1875, Henry Wilson. When, in 1878, Ben Wade also died, followed the next year by his friend Zachariah Chandler, for all practical purposes radical Republicanism had become a matter of the past. Hamlin, Julian, Boutwell, and Butler survived, but by and large, the generation which had given rise to the movement was no more.

The results of this gradual weakening of radicalism were far-reaching. In the main, the Republican party, founded as a reformist organization dedicated to the restriction of slavery and pushed forward to ever more advanced positions by the radicals, became increasingly the party of respectability and the status quo. If Grant's principal advisers, men like Morton, Carpenter, Cameron, and Conkling still paid lip service to Negro rights, they were nevertheless identified much more closely with business and industry than with any campaigns for civil liberties. Ben Butler retained his revolutionary fervor; to the end of his life he championed various extreme causes, and as governor of Massachusetts he appointed the first Negro to judicial office in the commonwealth. But his reputation had suffered severely because of his involvement in various scandals, and in 1878 he left the Republican party. Chandler also remained one of the principal figures of Grant's entourage; his interest in Negro advancement did not flag, but he too became more closely connected with the needs of commerce and industry than with the demands of reformers. By and large, after 1870, progressives devoted to radical causes were to be found outside of the Republican party. And they would pay scant attention to racial problems.[4]

These developments made the task of the remaining radicals more and more difficult, as Charles Sumner's fruitless effort to induce Congress to pass a civil rights bill clearly showed. Pro-

[4] Trefousse, *Butler,* pp. 240 ff., 247, 250, 254; Detroit *Post and Tribune, Chandler,* pp. xii, 298–9; George, Chandler, p. 219; Howard, *Civil War Echoes,* p. 53. Cf. Stampp, *The Era of Reconstruction,* p. 190; Montgomery, Labor and the Radical Republicans, p. 565.

viding for a prohibition of segregation in inns, public places of amusement, juries, schools, churches, and cemeteries, the measure was first introduced by the senator in May, 1870, only to die when Trumbull reported it unfavorably from his Committee on the Judiciary. When, in December, 1870, Congress met again, Sumner reintroduced the bill, but it was killed in committee once more. In March, 1871, introducing it a third time, he demanded that it be acted upon without reference to the committee. Failing to have the subject considered during the short session, he revived it in December, finally moving it as an amendment to an amnesty bill passed by the House. In reply to objections that this procedure would require a two-thirds vote for passage, he asserted that, in order to make reconciliation complete, everyone voting for the amnesty bill ought to vote for justice to the colored race as well. But in spite of his efforts, the legislation failed, although it was revived in May, 1872, when a new House bill providing for amnesty was under debate. This time, after Senator Matthew H. Carpenter had struck out all references to schools, churches, cemeteries, and juries, during Sumner's temporary absence the amendment carried. Outraged at the emasculation of his measure, the Massachusetts senator finally voted against the amnesty bill, which passed by an overwhelming vote. But since the House refused to concur in the modified amendment, only the amnesty measure was enacted into law.

Late in 1872 and in 1873–4, Sumner tried again, but without success. Consequently, it was not until after his death, and after the disastrous elections of 1874 that the members of the House, many of them already defeated, bestirred themselves to enact a measure similar to the one so long advocated by the radical Bostonian. The bill passed Congress in the last days of the short session, but only after the most controversial provisions, especially those providing for integrated schools, had been withdrawn. Moreover, an accompanying force bill which would have given the President renewed power to suspend the habeas corpus in the South was held up too long in the House to be acted upon in the Senate. "The conservative reaction against radical Reconstruction was well under way by the time the bill was passed," commented Edward McPherson, a circumstance which rendered it "virtually unenforceable." If the remaining radicals, Butler, Edmunds, and others, still fought actively for the reform, the party as a whole had proved most reluctant, Butler clashing violently with Speaker James G. Blaine, whose rulings had delayed passage of the Force Bill until it was too late to carry it through the Senate.[5]

With the Republican party no longer in a progressive frame of mind, the remaining Southern states gradually succumbed to Bourbon "redeemers." In 1875, after a campaign marked by violence and the eventual impeachment of Governor Adelbert Ames, the conservatives recaptured Mississippi. In Louisiana, Florida, and South Carolina, Republican regimes lasted until 1876–7, but the forces which had weakened the party in other states were at work there as well. Radicalism was dying, and without a radical spirit in Washington, without the will to protect the gains of the Reconstruction amendments, it was impossible to retain the radical governments in the South. That these regimes had furthered education, streamlined the tax structure, and established long overdue eleemosynary institutions did not matter. Conservatives made use of white prejudice against Negroes, Democratic resentment of Republicans, and smoldering Southern antagonism toward Northerners to sap confidence in the new order. Violence and lessening Northern interest did the rest, especially since renewed scandals further diminished the administration's hold on the public. Revelations that persons close to the President had been defrauding the government of whisky taxes, that the American minister to Great Britain was involved in a swindle concerning a mining venture in Colorado, that the envoy to Brazil was dishonest, and the Secretary of War had accepted

---

[5] Sumner, *Works,* XIV, 357–66, 369–413, 416–71, 472–73; XV, 266–9, 286–90, 301–14; Wirt Armistead Cate, *Lucius Q. C. Lamar* (Chapel Hill, 1935), pp. 184–91; Springfield *Republican,* February 4, 11, 25, 26, 27, March 1, 27, 1875; Edward McPherson, *A Handbook of Politics for 1875* (Washington, 1875), p. 510.

bribes did not contribute to public confidence in the Republican party.[6]

The final collapse of Reconstruction and the end of the radical movement was confirmed by the elections of 1876. Because of the troubles besetting the government, the outlook was bleak. Deliberately avoiding any identification with the administration, the Republicans nominated Rutherford B. Hayes for President. But Hayes, the reformist governor of Ohio, was a moderate, and although the ultras still campaigned for him—Zachariah Chandler served as chairman of the Republican National Committee— the candidate had little sympathy for their point of view. And so nebulous a concept had radicalism become that an old antislavery leader like Julian actually endorsed the democratic nominee, Samuel J. Tilden.

The aftermath of the election brought the country no respite. Because of the disorders in the South, two sets of returns from the remaining Republican states reached Washington, so that it was not at all clear whether Hayes or Tilden had been elected. If Florida, Louisiana, and South Carolina were to be counted for Hayes, he would secure a majority of the electoral college; if only one elector in any of these went for Tilden, the Democrats would return to power. Faced with this problem, visiting statesmen, including radicals like Howe and Chandler on the Republican side, and Julian on the Democratic, descended upon the disputed states in order to influence the returning boards. In the end, the interested parties arrived at a series of compromises. Congress established an electoral commission; Southern conservatives received promises of economic support and the withdrawal of federal troops, and on March 4, 1876, Hayes took the oath as President of the United States. He promptly abandoned the Republican regimes in the South.[7]

[6] Cf. Franklin, *Reconstruction After the Civil War*, pp. 197 ff., 139 ff.; Patrick, *The Reconstruction of the Nation*, pp. 184–91; Nevins, *Fish*, pp. 642 ff.

[7] Blaine, *Twenty Years of Congress*, II, 567–87; Julian MS Diary, August 27, December 10, 1876, January 21, 1877, Julian Papers; Howe—

The new President's policy horrified the ultras. A Republican who permitted the Democrats to seize control of Reconstruction governments and who appointed a former Confederate officer, David M. Key of Tennessee, Postmaster General, was too much for them, especially since he also made Carl Schurz Secretary of the Interior. Within little more than a month of the inauguration, Ben Wade, living in retirement at his Ohio home, bitterly denounced the administration. "You know with what untiring zeal I labored for the emancipation of the slaves of the South and to procure justice for them before and during the time I was in Congress, and I supposed Governor Hayes was in full accord with me on this subject," he wrote to Uriah Painter of the *New York Times.*

> But I have been deceived, betrayed, and even humiliated by the course he has taken to a degree that I have not language to express. . . . I feel that to have emancipated those people and then to leave them unprotected would be a crime as infamous as to have reduced them to slavery when they were free.

T. O. Howe found it difficult to hide his disgust when he was required to vote for the confirmation of Carl Schurz, although he sought to retain some sort of friendly relationship with the President in order to salvage party interests, and Zachariah Chandler, too, was greatly disappointed at the results of his efforts in Hayes's behalf. When he was returned to the Senate once more in 1879, he sought to revive radical policies, but died soon afterward. At any rate, new issues were holding popular attention, a more prosaic group of men was in control of both parties, and the problems of racial readjustment were no longer considered paramount. "All is changed and the caliber & moral character of the members [of Congress] are fearfully below the level of the House during the war," Julian wrote to his wife after a visit to the Capitol in 1877. "There is no moral tone in either party and the spectacle is sicken-

Grace Howe, December 9, 1876, January 4, 8, February 10, 1877, Howe Papers; Chandler–E. C. Wade, December 1, 1876, Chandler Papers; Woodward, *Reunion and Reaction,* esp. pp. 201–20. One of the electoral votes of Oregon was also in dispute.

ing." It was evident that the crusade against slavery and its aftermath was over.[8]

So the radicals passed from the scene, the very term
gradually losing its meaning. For almost a generation, they had
been in the forefront of the political struggle for human rights,
and their accomplishments were astonishing. The liberation of the
slaves, the enlargement of national power, and the constitutional
guarantee of the Negroes' right to vote were achievements of no
mean import. That they could never have secured these reforms
by themselves does not alter the fact that they were the propelling
force within the party. Without them, Lincoln might not have
succeeded in crushing the rebellion and at the same time destroy-
ing slavery, and Johnson might have prevented the completion
of the wartime revolution by defeating the Fourteenth Amendment. If at the time they were unable fully to protect Negro rights,
if in the nineteenth century they failed to accomplish their vision
of the equality of all citizens, they nevertheless laid the foundation
for the achievement of their goals in the twentieth. This was their
last contribution. They deserve to be remembered for it.

[8] *New York Times,* April 23, 1877; Howe–Grace Howe, March 10,
15, April 4, October 15, 17, November 3, 16, 1877, Howe Papers;
Detroit *Post and Tribune, Chandler,* pp. 358, 374–6, 390; Julian–Mrs.
Julian, December 7, 1877, Julian Papers.

Bibliography

MANUSCRIPT COLLECTIONS

Adams Family Papers, Massachusetts Historical Society, Boston.

Andrew, John Albion: Papers, Massachusetts Historical Society.

Atkinson, Edward: Papers, Massachusetts Historical Society.

Blair, Austin: Papers, Burton Collection, Detroit Public Library.

Blakeslee, Joel: Papers, Western Reserve Historical Society, Cleveland.

Butler, Benjamin F.: Papers, Library of Congress.

Cass, Lewis: Papers, William L. Clements Library, University of Michigan, Ann Arbor.

Catlin, G. B.: MS Biography of Zachariah Chandler, Burton Collection, Detroit Public Library.

Chandler, Zachariah: Papers, Burton Collection, Detroit Public Library.

———: Papers, Library of Congress.

Chase, Salmon P.: Papers, Library of Congress.

———: Papers, Historical Society of Pennsylvania, Philadelphia.

Colfax, Schuyler: Papers, Library of Congress.

———: Papers, Chicago Historical Society.

———: Items, Illinois State Historical Library, Springfield.

Corwin, Thomas: Papers, Library of Congress.

Covode, John: Papers, Library of Congress.

———: Papers, Historical Society of Western Pennsylvania, Pittsburgh.

Creswell, John A. J.: Papers, Library of Congress.

Dana, Charles A.: Papers, Library of Congress.

Davis, David: Papers, Chicago Historical Society.

Day, Timothy C.: Papers, Ohio Philosophical and Historical Society, Cincinnati.

Deady, Matthew P.: Papers, Oregon Historical Society, Portland.

Donnelly, Ignatius: Papers, Minnesota Historical Society, St. Paul.

Doolittle, James R.: Papers, New York Public Library.

————: Papers, Wisconsin Historical Society, Madison.

Drake, Charles D.: Autobiography, Missouri State Historical Society, Columbia.

DuPont, Samuel F.: Papers, Winthertur Collection, Eleutherian Mills Library, Greenville, Delaware.

Ewing, Thomas: Papers, Library of Congress.

Fish, Hamilton: Papers, Library of Congress.

Frémont, John C.: Papers, Bancroft Library, University of California, Berkeley.

French, Benjamin B.: Papers, New York Historical Society, New York.

Giddings, Joshua Reed: Papers, Ohio State Historical Society, Columbus.

————: Giddings-Julian Papers, Library of Congress. See Julian-Giddings Papers.

Grant, U. S.: Papers, Illinois State Historical Library.

Greeley, Horace: Papers, New York Public Library.

Hale, John P.: Papers, New Hampshire Historical Society, Concord.

Hamlin, Hannibal: Papers, Maine Historical Society, Portland, and microfilm collection, Columbia University.

Heintzelman, Samuel P.: Diaries, Library of Congress.

Howard, Jacob M.: Papers, Burton Collection, Detroit Public Library.

Howe, Timothy O.: Papers, Wisconsin Historical Society.

Johnson, Andrew: Papers, Library of Congress.

Jones, Stiles P.: Papers, Minnesota Historical Society.

Joy, James F.: Papers, Burton Collection, Detroit Public Library.

Julian, George W.: Papers, Indiana State Library, Indianapolis.

Julian-Giddings Collection: Library of Congress.

Lincoln, Robert Todd: Papers, Library of Congress.

Lovejoy, Owen: Papers, William L. Clements Library, University of Michigan.

McPherson, Edward: Papers, Library of Congress.

Morrill, Justin S.: Papers, Library of Congress.

Nicolay, John G.: Papers, Library of Congress.

Norton, Charles Elliot: Papers, Houghton Library, Harvard University, Cambridge, Massachusetts.

Oglesby, Richard J.: Papers, Illinois State Historical Library.

Pike, James S.: Papers, Calais Free Library, Calais, Maine. Microfilm, Alderman Library, University of Virginia.

Ramsay, Alexander: Papers, Minnesota Historical Society.

Raymond, Henry J.: Papers, New York Public Library.

Riddle, Albert G.: Papers, Western Reserve Historical Society.
Schleiden, Rudolf: Papers, Berichte des Minister-Residenten **Dr.** Schleiden, Staatsarchiv, Bremen, Microfilm, Library of Congress.
Schouler, William: Papers, Massachusetts Historical Society.
Seward, William H.: Papers, University of Rochester.
Sherman, John: Papers, Library of Congress.
Stanton, Edwin M.: Papers, Library of Congress.
Stevens, Thaddeus: Papers, Library of Congress.
Strong, John D.: Papers, Illinois State Historical Library.
Sumner, Charles: Papers, Houghton Library, Harvard University.
Swift, Henry A.: Papers, Minnesota Historical Society.
Trumbull, Lyman: Papers, Library of Congress.
————: Papers, Illinois State Historical Library.
Wade, Benjamin F.: Papers, Library of Congress.
————: Miscellaneous, Western Reserve Historical Society.
Ward, Marcus L.: Papers, New Jersey Historical Society, Newark.
Washburne, Elihu B.: Papers, Library of Congress.
Weld, Theodore, Angelina Grimke: Weld-Grimke Collection, William L. Clements Library, University of Michigan.
Whittlesey, Elisha: Papers, Western Reserve Historical Society.
Wilson, Henry: Papers, Library of Congress.
Yates, Richard: Papers, Illinois State Historical Library.
Young, James Russell: Papers, Library of Congress.
Zug, R. M.: Papers, Burton Collection, Detroit Public Library.

NEWSPAPERS

Albany *Evening Journal*
Boston *Advertiser*
Boston *Commonwealth*
Boston *Evening Transcript*
Boston *Journal*
Chicago *Tribune*
Cincinnati *Daily Gazette*
Columbus, Ohio, *Crisis*
Columbus, Ohio, *Statesman*
Detroit *Free Press*
Harper's Weekly
Jefferson, Ohio, *Ashtabula Sentinel*
The Nation
New York *Evening Post*
New York *Golden Age*
New York *Herald*
New York *Independent*
New York *National Standard*
New York *Round Table*

New York *Sun*
New York *Times*
New York *Tribune*
New York *World*
Philadelphia *Public Ledger*
Portland, Oregon, *Journal*
Springfield *Republican*
Washington *Daily Morning Chronicle*
Washington *Daily National Intelligencer*
Washington *National Era*

OTHER PUBLICATIONS

Adams, Henry: *The Great Secession Winter of 1860–61.* Edited by George Hochfield. New York: Sagamore Press; 1958.

Adler, Selig: *The Senatorial Career of George Franklin Edmunds, 1866–1891.* Thesis abstract. Urbana, Illinois: University of Illinois Press; 1934.

Alexander, De Alva Stanwood: *A Political History of the State of New York.* New York: Henry Holt & Co.; 1909. 4 vols.

Ambler, Charles Henry: *Waitman Thomas Willey.* Huntington, West Virginia: Standard Print & Publication Co.; 1954.

————: *West Virginia, the Mountain State.* New York: Prentice-Hall; 1940.

Ambrose, Stephen E.: *Halleck: Lincoln's Chief of Staff.* Baton Rouge: Louisiana State University Press; 1962.

The American Annual Cyclopaedia and Register of Important Events of the Year. New York: Appleton & Co.; printed annually.

Armstrong, William A.: *E. L. Godkin and American Foreign Policy 1865–1900.* New York: Bookman Associates; 1957.

Arnold, Isaac N.: *The History of Abraham Lincoln and the Overthrow of Slavery.* Chicago: Clarke & Co.; 1866.

Ashley, Charles S.: "Governor Ashley's Biography and Messages," *Contributions to the Historical Society of Montana,* VI (1907), 143–289.

Ashley, James M.: *Reminiscences of the Great Rebellion, Calhoun, Seward, Lincoln, Address of Hon. J. M. Ashley, at Memorial Hall, Toledo, Ohio, June 2, 1890.*

Ashley, Margaret (Paddock): "An Ohio Congressman in Reconstruction." Master's Essay, Columbia University; 1916.

Badeau, Adam: *Grant in Peace, A Personal Memoir.* Hartford: S. S. Scranton & Co.; 1887.

Baker, George (ed.): *The Works of William H. Seward.* See Seward, William H.

Baker, John J.: "A Few Recollections of Governor Ashley by John J.

Baker, President of the Toledo Savings Bank," *Historical Society of Montana*, VI (1907), 221–3.

Baldensperger, Fernand (ed.): *Georges Clemenceau, American Reconstruction.* See Clemenceau, Georges.

Ballard, Colin A.: *The Military Genius of Abraham Lincoln.* Cleveland: World Publishing Co.; 1952.

Bancroft, Frederick: *The Life of William H. Seward.* New York: Harper & Bros., 1900. 2 vols.

————: *Speeches, Correspondence and Political Papers of Carl Schurz.* New York: G. P. Putnam's Sons; 1913. 6 vols.

Bartlett, Irving H.: *Wendell Phillips, Brahmin Radical.* Boston: Beacon Press; 1961.

Basler, Roy P. (ed.): *The Collected Works of Abraham Lincoln.* New Brunswick: Rutgers University Press; 1953. 9 vols.

Bates, Edward: *The Diary of Edward Bates, 1859–1866.* Edited by Howard K. Beale. Annual Report of the American Historical Association for 1930. Vol. IV. Washington: Government Printing Office; 1933.

Beale, Howard K.: *The Critical Years: A Study of Andrew Johnson and Reconstruction.* New York: Frederick Ungar; 1958.

———— (ed.): *The Diary of Edward Bates.* See Bates, Edward.

———— (ed.): *Diary of Gideon Welles.* See Welles, Gideon.

Belden, Thomas Graham, and Marva Robins Belden: *So Fell the Angels.* Boston: Little, Brown and Co.; 1956.

Bellows, Henry W.: *Historical Sketch of the Union League Club of New York, Its Origin, Organization, and Work, 1863–1879.* New York: Union League Club House; 1879.

Bentley, George R.: *A History of the Freedman's Bureau.* Philadelphia: University of Pennsylvania Press; 1955.

Bigelow, John: *Retrospections of an Active Life.* New York: The Baker & Taylor Co.; 1909–17. 5 vols.

Bigelow, Martha: "The Political Services of William Alanson Howard," *Michigan History*, XLII (1958), 1–23.

Blaine, James G.: *Twenty Years of Congress.* Norwich, Conn.: The Henry Bill Publishing Co.; 1884.

Blair, Montgomery: *Speech of the Hon. Montgomery Blair (Postmaster General), on the Revolutionary Schemes of the Ultra Abolitionists, and in Defense of the Policy of the President, Delivered at the Unconditional Union Meeting Held at Rockville, Montgomery Co., Maryland, on Saturday, October 3, 1863.* New York; 1863.

Bogue, Allen G.: "Bloc and Party in the United States Senate; 1861–1863," *Civil War History*, XIII (1967), 221–41.

Boutwell, George S.: *Reminiscences of Sixty Years in Public Affairs.* New York: McClure, Phillips & Co.; 1902. 2 vols.

Bradford, Gamaliel: *Union Portraits.* Boston: Houghton Mifflin Co.; 1916.

Bradley, Erwin Stanley: *Simon Cameron, Lincoln's Secretary of War.* Philadelphia: University of Pennsylvania Press; 1966.

Brigham, Johnson: *James Harlan.* Iowa City: The State Historical Society of Iowa; 1913.

Brock, W. R.: *An American Crisis: Congress and Reconstruction, 1865–1867.* London: Macmillan; 1963.

Brockett, L. P.: *Men of Our Day.* Philadelphia: Zeisler, McCurdy & Co.; 1868.

Brodie, Fawn: *Thaddeus Stevens: Scourge of the South.* New York: W. W. Norton & Co.; 1959.

Brooks, Noah: *Washington in Lincoln's Time.* Edited by Herbert Mitgang. New York: Rinehart & Co.; 1958.

Brown, Roscoe C. E., and Ray B. Smith: *Political and Governmental History of the State of New York.* Syracuse: The Syracuse Press; 1922. 6 vols.

Browning, Orville Hickman: *The Diary of Orville Hickman Browning.* Edited by Theodore C. Pease and J. G. Randall. Collections of the Illinois State Historical Library, XX and XXII. Springfield; 1933. 2 vols.

Buck, Paul H.: *The Road to Reunion, 1865–1900.* Boston: Little, Brown; 1937.

Buel, Clarence, and Robert Johnson, eds.: *Battles and Leaders of the Civil War.* New York: Thomas Yoseloff; 1956. 4 vols.

Buell, Walter: "Zachariah Chandler," *Magazine of Western History,* IV (1886), 271–8, 338–52, 432–3.

Butler, Benjamin F.: *Private and Official Correspondence of Gen. Benjamin F. Butler During the Period of the Civil War.* Compiled by Jessie Ames Marshall. 5 vols. Norwood, Mass.: Plimpton Press; 1917.

Carman, Harry J., and Reinhard H. Luthin: *Lincoln and the Patronage.* New York: Columbia University Press; 1943.

Carpenter, F. B.: *Six Months at the White House with Abraham Lincoln: The Story of a Picture.* New York: Hurd & Houghton; 1867.

Carter, Hodding: *The Angry Scar: The Story of Reconstruction.* Garden City, N.Y.: Doubleday; 1959.

Caskey, Willie Malvin: *Secession and Restoration in Louisiana.* Baton Rouge: Louisiana University Press; 1938.

Cason, Roberta F.: "The Loyal League in Georgia," *The Georgia Historical Quarterly,* XX (1936), 125–53.

Chandler, Zachariah: An Outline Sketch of His Life and Public Services. Detroit; 1880. See Detroit *Post and Tribune.*

Channing, Edward: *A History of the United States.* New York: Macmillan; 1925. 6 vols.

Chapman, Ervin: *Latest Light on Abraham Lincoln and War-time Memories.* . . . New York: Fleming H. Revell Co.; 1917. 2 vols.

Chase, Salmon P.: *Diary and Correspondence of Salmon P. Chase.* Annual Report of the American Historical Association, 1902. Washington: Government Printing Office; 1903.

————: *Inside Lincoln's Cabinet: The Civil War Diaries of Salmon P. Chase.* Edited by David Donald. New York: Longmans Green; 1954.

Chittenden, L. E.: *Recollections of President Lincoln and His Administration.* New York: Harper & Bros.; 1891.

————: *A Report of the Debates and Proceedings in the Secret Sessions of the Conference Convention for Proposing Amendments to the Constitution of the United States, Held at Washington, D. C., in February, A.D. 1861.* New York: Appleton & Co.; 1864.

Church, Charles A.: *History of the Republican Party in Illinois, 1854–1912.* Rockford, Ill.: Wilson Bros. Co.; 1912.

Clayton, Powell: *The Aftermath of the Civil War, in Arkansas.* New York: The Neale Publishing Co.; 1915.

Cleaves, Freeman: *Meade of Gettysburg.* Norman: University of Oklahoma Press; 1960.

Coben, Stanley: "Northeastern Business and Radical Reconstruction: A Re-examination," *Mississippi Valley Historical Review,* XLVI (1959), 67–90.

Cochrane, John: *The War for the Union: Memoir of General John Cochrane.* New York: n.p.; 1875.

Coffin, Charles C.: *Abraham Lincoln.* New York: Harper & Bros.; 1893.

Cole, Arthur Charles: *The Era of the Civil War, 1848–1870.* Vol. III, *The Centennial History of Illinois.* Springfield: Illinois Centennial Commission; 1919.

————: "President Lincoln and the Illinois Radical Republicans," *Mississippi Valley Historical Review,* IV (1918), 417–36.

Coleman, Charles H.: *The Election of 1868: The Democratic Effort to Regain Control.* New York: Columbia University Press; 1933.

Conway, Alan: *The Reconstruction of Georgia.* Minneapolis: University of Minnesota Press; 1966.

Conway, Moncure Daniel: *Autobiography: Memoirs and Experiences of Moncure Daniel Conway.* Boston: Houghton Mifflin; 1904. 2 vols.

Cornish, Dudley Taylor: *The Sable Arm: Negro Troops in the Union Army, 1861–1865.* New York: Longmans, Green & Co.; 1956.

Corwin, E. S.: "The Dred Scott Decision in the Light of Contemporary Legal Doctrine," *American Historical Review,* XVII (1911), 52–69.

Coulter, Ellis Merton: *The Civil War and Readjustment in Kentucky.* Chapel Hill: University of North Carolina Press; 1926.

————: *Georgia, A Short History.* Chapel Hill: University of North Carolina Press; 1960.

————: *The South During Reconstruction, 1865–1877.* Baton Rouge: Louisiana State University Press; 1947.

Cox, John H., and LaWanda Cox: "Andrew Johnson and His Ghost Writers," *Mississippi Valley Historical Review,* XLVIII (1961), 460–79.

————: "Negro Suffrage and Republican Politics: The Problem of Motivation in Reconstruction History," *Journal of Southern History,* XXXIII (1967), 303–30.

Cox, LaWanda: "The Promise of Land for the Freedmen," *Mississippi: Valley Historical Review*, XLV (1958), 413–40.

Cox, LaWanda, and John H. Cox: *Politics, Principle, & Prejudice, 1865–1866, Dilemma of Reconstruction America.* New York: Macmillan; 1963.

Cox, Samuel S.: *Union—Disunion—Reunion, Three Decades of Federal Legislation.* Providence, R.I.: J. A. & R. A. Reid; 1885.

Crandall, Andrew Wallace: *The Early History of the Republican Party.* Boston: Richard G. Badger; 1930.

Craven, Avery.: *The Coming of the Civil War.* New York: Charles Scribner's Sons; 1942.

Croffut, W. A., ed.: *Fifty Years in Camp and Field.* See Hitchcock, Ethan Allen.

Crook, William H.: *Through Five Administrations, Reminiscences of Colonel William H. Crook, Body-Guard to President Lincoln.* Edited by Margarit Spalding Garry. New York: Harper & Bros.; 1910.

Cullom, Shelby M.: *Fifty Years of Public Service. Personal Recollections of Shelby M. Cullom, Senior United States Senator from Illinois.* Chicago: A. C. McClurg & Co.; 1911.

Current, Richard N.: *Old Thad Stevens: A Story of Ambition.* Madison: University of Wisconsin Press; 1942.

————: *The Lincoln Nobody Knows.* New York: McGraw-Hill; 1958.

Curry, Richard Orr: *A House Divided: Statehood Politics and the Copperhead Movement in West Virginia.* University of Pittsburgh Press; 1961.

Curti, Merle: *The American Peace Crusade, 1815–1860.* Durham, N.C.: Duke University Press; 1929.

Curtis, Francis: *The Republican Party: A History of Its Fifty Years' Existence and a Record of its Measures and Leaders.* New York: G. P. Putnam's Sons; 1904. 2 vols.

Dana, Charles A.: *Recollections of the Civil War: With the Leaders at Washington and in the Field in the Sixties.* New York: D. Appleton & Co.; 1898.

Davis, Henry Winter: *Speeches and Addresses Delivered in the Congress of the United States and on Several Public Occasions.* New York: Harper & Bros.; 1867.

Davis, Stanton Ling: *Pennsylvania Politics, 1860–1863.* Cleveland: Western Reserve University; 1935.

Davis, William Watson: *The Civil War and Reconstruction in Florida.* New York: Columbia University Press; 1913.

Dennet, Tyler, ed.: *Lincoln and the Civil War in the Diaries and Letters of John Hay.* New York: Dodd, Mead & Co.; 1939.

Detroit *Post and Tribune: Zachariah Chandler.* See Chandler, Zachariah.

DeWitt, David Miller: *The Impeachment and Trial of Andrew*

Johnson, Seventeenth President of the United States. New York: Macmillan, 1903.

Dilla, Harriette M: *The Politics of Michigan.* New York: Columbia University Press; 1912.

Dillon, Merton L.: *Elijah P. Lovejoy: Abolitionist Editor.* Urbana: University of Illinois Press; 1961.

Dix, Morgan: *Memoirs of John Adams Dix, Compiled by his Son.* New York: Harper & Bros.; 1883. 2 vols.

Dixon, Mrs. Archibald: *The True History of the Missouri Compromise and Its Repeal.* Cincinnati: The Robert Clarke Co.; 1899.

Donald, David: *Charles Sumner and the Coming of the Civil War,* New York: Alfred A. Knopf; 1960.

————: *Devils Facing Zionwards.* See McWhiney, Grady.

————: *Inside Lincoln's Cabinet.* See Chase, Salmon P.

————: *Lincoln Reconsidered.* 2d ed. New York: Vintage; 1956.

————: *The Politics of Reconstruction.* Baton Rouge: Louisiana State University Press; 1965.

Dorris, Jonathan T.: *Pardon and Amnesty under Lincoln and Johnson.* Chapel Hill: University of North Carolina Press; 1953.

Douglass, Frederick: *Life and Times of Frederick Douglass.* Hartford: Park Publishing Co.; 1881.

Duberman, Martin B., ed.: *The Antislavery Vanguard: New Essays on the Abolitionists.* Princeton: Princeton University Press; 1965.

————: *Charles Francis Adams, 1807–1886.* Boston: Houghton Mifflin Co.; 1961.

DuBois, James T., and Gertrude S. Mathews: *Galusha A. Grow: Father of the Homestead Law.* Boston: Houghton Mifflin Co.; 1917.

Du Bois, W. E. Burghardt: *Black Reconstruction.* New York: S. A. Russell Co.; 1935.

Dumond, Dwight L.: *Antislavery. The Crusade for Freedom in America.* New York: W. W. Norton; 1966.

————: *The Secession Movement, 1860–1861.* New York: Macmillan; 1931.

Dunbar, Willis F.: *Michigan Through the Centuries.* New York: Lewis Historical Publication Co.; 1955. 4 vols.

Dunning, William A.: *Reconstruction, Political and Economic, 1865–1877.* New York: Harper & Bros.; 1907.

Durden, Robert F.: *Ambiguities in the Antislavery Crusade of the Republican Party.* See Duberman, Martin B., ed.: *The Antislavery Vanguard.*

Dusinberre, Walter: *Civil War Issues in Philadelphia, 1856–1868.* Philadelphia: University of Pennsylvania Press; 1965.

Eckloff, Christian F.: *Memoirs of a Senate Page (1855–1859).* Edited by Percival G. Melbourne. New York: Broadway Publishing Co.; 1909.

Eisenschiml, Otto: *The Celebrated Case of FitzJohn Porter: An American Dreyfus Affair.* Indianapolis: Bobbs-Merrill; 1950.

Fenton, William D.: "Political History of Oregon from 1865 to 1876," *The Quarterly of the Oregon Historical Society,* II (1901); 321–65.

Fessenden, Francis: *Life and Public Services of William Pitt* Fessenden. . . . Boston: Houghton Mifflin Co.; 1907. 2 vols.

Filler, Louis: *The Crusade Against Slavery. 1830–1860.* New York: Harper & Bros.; 1960.

Fischer, LeRoy H.: *Lincoln's Gadfly, Adam Gurowski.* Norman, Okla.: University of Oklahoma Press; 1964.

Fleming, Walter Lynwood: *Civil War and Reconstruction in Alabama.* New York: Columbia University Press; 1905.

————: *Documentary History of Reconstruction.* . . . Cleveland: A. H. Clark Co.; 1906–07. 2 vols.

————: *The Sequel to Appomattox.* New Haven: Yale University Press; 1919.

Flexner, Eleanor: *Century of Struggle: The Woman's Rights Movement in the United States.* Cambridge, Mass.: Harvard University Press; 1959.

Flower, Frank A.: *Edwin McMasters Stanton.* Akron, Ohio: The Saalfeld Publishing Co.; 1905.

————: *Life of Matthew Hale Carpenter.* Madison, Wis.: David Atwood & Co.; 1883.

Foote, Henry S.: *Casket of Reminiscences.* Washington: Chronicle Publishing Co.; 1874.

Forbes, John Murray: *Letters and Recollections of John Murray Forbes.* Edited by Sarah Forbes Huges. Boston: Houghton Mifflin; 1899. 2 vols.

Foulke, William Dudley: *Life of Oliver P. Morton.* Indianapolis; The Bowen-Merrill Co.; 1899. 2 vols.

Franklin, John Hope: *The Emancipation Proclamation.* Garden City, N.Y.: Doubleday; 1963.

————: *Reconstruction After the Civil War.* University of Chicago Press; 1961.

Freidel, Frank: *Francis Lieber: Nineteenth Century Liberal.* Baton Rouge: Louisiana State University Press; 1947.

Gambrill, Edward: "Who Were the Senate Radicals?" *Civil War History,* XI (1965), 237–44.

Garfield, James Abram: Garfield-Hinsdale Letters. Edited by Mary L. Hinsdale. Ann Arbor: University of Michigan Press; 1949.

Garner, James Wilford: *Reconstruction in Mississippi.* New York: Macmillan; 1901.

George, Sister Mary Karl: "Zachariah Chandler: Radical Republican." Unpublished doctoral dissertation, St. Louis University; 1965.

Gibson, Guy James; "Lincoln's League: The Union League Movement during the Civil War." Unpublished doctoral dissertation, University of Illinois; 1951.

Giddings, Joshua Reed: *History of the Rebellion; Its Authors and Causes.* New York: Follet, Foster & Co.; 1864.

Gillette, William: *The Right to Vote: Politics and the Passage of the Fifteenth Amendment.* Baltimore: Johns Hopkins University Press; 1965.

Gilmore, James R.: *Personal Recollections of Abraham Lincoln and the Civil War.* Boston: L. C. Page & Co.; 1898.

Going, Charles Buxton: *David Wilmot, Free Soiler.* New York: D. Appleton & Co.; 1924.

Grant, U. S.: *Personal Memoirs of U. S. Grant.* Edited by E. B. Long. New York: Grosset & Dunlap; 1952.

Gray, John Chipman, and John Codman Ropes: *War Letters of John Chipman Gray and John Codman Ropes.* Edited by Worthington C. Ford. Boston: Houghton Mifflin Co.; 1927.

Greeley, Horace: *The American Conflict: A History of the Great Rebellion in the United States of America, 1860–'65.* Hartford: O. D. Case & Co.; 1866. 2 vols.

Greenwood, Grace: "An American Salon," *Cosmopolitan,* VIII (1890), 437–47.

Gurowski, Adam: *Diary.* Vol. I, Boston: Lee & Shepard; 1862; Vol. II, New York: Carleton; 1864; Vol. III, Washington: W. H. & O. H. Morrison; 1866.

Hacker, Louis M.: *The Triumph of American Capitalism.* New York: Columbia University Press; 1946.

Hale, William Harlan: *Horace Greeley: Voice of the People.* New York: Harper & Bros.; 1950.

Halstead, Murat: *Caucuses of 1860.* . . . Columbus: Follet, Foster & Co.; 1860.

Hamilton, James A.: *Reminiscences of James A. Hamilton or Men and Events, At Home and Abroad During Three Quarters of a Century.* New York: Charles Scribner's Sons; 1869.

Hamilton, J. G. de Roulhac: *Reconstruction in North Carolina.* New York: Columbia University Press; 1914.

Hamlin, Charles Eugene: *The Life and Times of Hannibal Hamlin.* Cambridge, Mass.: Riverside Press; 1899.

Harlow, Ralph Volney: *Gerrit Smith: Philanthropist and Reformer.* New York: Henry Holt; 1939.

Harrington, Fred Harvey: *Fighting Politician: Major General N. P. Banks.* Philadelphia: University of Pennsylvania Press; 1948.

Harris, Wilmer C.: *Public Life of Zachariah Chandler, 1851–1875.* Doctoral dissertation, University of Chicago, 1917.

Hart, Albert Bushnell: *Slavery and Abolition, 1831–1841.* New York: Harper & Bros.; 1907.

Haugland, John C.: "Alexander Ramsey and the Republican Party, 1855–1875: A Study in Personal Politics." Unpublished doctoral dissertation, University of Minnesota; 1961.

Hay, John: *Diaries.* See Dennet, Tyler.

Henderson, John B.: "Emancipation and Impeachment," *Century,* LXXXV (1912–13), 205.

Hendrick, Burton J.: *Lincoln's War Cabinet.* Boston: Little, Brown & Co., 1946.

Henry, George Selden: "Radical Republican Policy Toward the Negro During Reconstruction, 1862–1872." Unpublished doctoral dissertation, Yale University; 1963.

Henry, Robert Selph: *The Story of Reconstruction.* Indianapolis: Bobbs-Merrill; 1938.

Hensel, W. U.: "Thaddeus Stevens As a Country Lawyer," *Historical Papers and Addresses of the Lancaster County Historical Society,* X (1905–06); 217–90.

Hesseltine, William Best: *Lincoln and the War Governors.* New York: Alfred A. Knopf; 1955.

————: *Lincoln's Plan of Reconstruction.* Tuscaloosa, Ala.: Confederate Publishing Co.; 1960.

————: *Ulysses S. Grant, Politician.* New York: Dodd, Mead & Co.; 1935.

Hinsdale, Mary L., ed.: *Garfield-Hinsdale Letters.* See Garfield, James Abram.

Hitchcock, Ethan Allen: *Fifty Years in Camp and Field. Diary of Major-General Ethan Allen Hitchcock.* Edited by W. A. Croffut. New York: G. P. Putnam's Sons; 1909.

Hoar, George F.: *Autobiography of Seventy Years.* New York: Charles Scribner's Sons; 1903. 2 vols.

Hollister, O. J.: *Life of Schuyler Colfax.* New York: Funk & Wagnalls; 1886.

Horn, Stanley: *Invisible Empire: The Story of the Ku Klux Klan, 1866–1871.* Boston: Houghton Mifflin Co.; 1939.

Howard, Hamilton Gay: *Civil-War Echoes: Character Sketches and States Secrets.* Washington: Howard Publishing Co.; 1907.

Howells, William Dean: *Years of My Youth.* New York: Harper & Bros.; 1916.

Hughes, Sarah, ed.: *Letters and Recollections of John Murray Forbes.* See Forbes, John Murray.

Hurlburt, William Henry: *General McClellan and the Conduct of the War.* New York: Sheldon & Co.; 1864.

Hyman, Harold M.: "Lincoln and Equal Rights For Negroes: The Irrelevancy of the 'Wadsworth Letter,' " *Civil War History,* XII (1966), 258–66.

————, ed.: *New Frontiers of the American Reconstruction.* Urbana, Ill.: University of Illinois Press; 1966.

————, ed.: *The Radical Republicans and Reconstruction, 1861–1870.* Indianapolis: Bobbs-Merrill Co.; 1967.

Jaffa, Harry V.: *Crisis of the House Divided: An Interpretation of the Issues in the Lincoln-Douglas Debates.* Garden City, N.Y.: Doubleday; 1959.

James, Joseph B. *The Framing of the Fourteenth Amendment.* Urbana: University of Illinois Press; 1956.

Jellison, Charles A.: *Fessenden of Maine: Civil War Senator,* Syracuse University Press; 1962.

Johnson, Ludwell E.: "Lincoln and Equal Rights, The Authenticity of the Wadsworth Letter," *Journal of Southern History,* XXXII (1966), 83–7.

Julian, George W.: "The First Republican National Convention," *American Historical Review,* IV (1899), 313–22.

————: *The Life of Joshua R. Giddings.* Chicago: A. C. McClurg & Co.; 1892.

————: *Political Recollections, 1840–1872.* Chicago: Jansen, McClurg & Co.; 1884.

Keckly, Elizabeth: *Behind the Scenes, or Thirty Years a Slave, and Four Years in the White House.* New York: G. W. Carleton & Co.; 1868.

Kelley, William Darrah: *Addresses of the Honorable W. D. Kelley, Miss Anna E. Dickinson, and Mr. Frederick Douglass, at a Mass Meeting, Held At National Hall, Philadelphia, July 6, 1863, For the Promotion of Colored Enlistments.* N.d., n.p.

————: *Lincoln and Stanton: A Study of the War Administration of 1861 and 1862, With Special Consideration of Some Recent Statements of Gen. Geo. B. McClellan.* New York: G. P. Putnam's Sons; 1885.

Kendrick, Benjamin F.: *The Journal of the Joint Committee of Fifteen on Reconstruction, 39th Congress, 1865–1867.* New York: Columbia University Press; 1914.

Kleeberg, Gordon S. P.: *The Formation of the Republican Party as a National Political Organization.* New York: 1911.

Klement, Frank L.: *The Copperheads in the Middle West.* University of Chicago Press; 1960.

Koerner, Gustave: *Memoirs of Gustave Koerner, 1809–1896.* Edited by Thomas J. McCormack. Cedar Rapids, Ia.: The Torch Press; 1909. 2 vols.

Konkle, Burton Alva: *The Life and Speeches of Thomas Williams, Orator, Stateman and Jurist, 1806–1872.* Philadelphia: Campion & Co.; 1905. 2 vols.

Krenkel, John H., ed.: See Yates, Richard.

Krug, Mark M.: *Lyman Trumbull: Conservative Radical.* New York: A. S. Barnes & Co.; 1965.

Kutler, Stanley: "*Ex parte McCardle:* Judicial Impotency? The Supreme Court and Reconstruction Reconsidered," *American Historical Review,* LXXII (1967), 835–51.

Lader, Lawrence: *The Bold Brahmins: New England's War Against Slavery.* New York: E. P. Dutton; 1961.

Larson, Orvin: *American Infidel: Robert G. Ingersoll.* New York: The Citadel Press; 1962.

Levy, Leonard, and Harlan B. Phillips: "The *Roberts* Case: Source of the 'Separate but Equal' Doctrine," *American Historical Review*, LVI (1951), 510–18.

Lincoln, Abraham: *The Collected Works of Abraham Lincoln*. Edited by Roy P. Basler. New Brunswick, N. J.: Rutgers University Press; 1953. 9 vols.

Linden, Glenn Marston: "Congressmen, 'Radicalism' and Economic Issues 1861 to 1873." Unpublished doctoral dissertation, University of Washington; 1963.

————: "Radical and Economic Policies: The Senate, 1861–1873," *Journal of Southern History*, XXXII (1966), 189–99.

————: "Radicals and Economic Policies: The House of Representatives, 1861–1873," *Civil War History*, XIII (1967), 51–65.

Livingstone, William: *Livingstone's History of the Republican Party*. . . . Detroit, Mich.: W. Livingstone; 1900. 2 vols.

Lomask, Milton: *Andrew Johnson: President on Trial*. New York: Farrar, Straus & Cudahy; 1960.

Lonn, Ella: *Reconstruction in Louisiana After 1868*. New York: G. P. Putnam's Sons, 1918.

Luthin, Reinhard H.: *The Real Abraham Lincoln*. Englewood Cliffs, N. J.: Prentice-Hall; 1960.

McCarthy, Charles H.: *Lincoln's Plan of Reconstruction*. New York: McClure, Phillips & Co.; 1901.

McClellan, George B.: *McClellan's Own Story: The War for the Union*. . . . New York: C. L. Webster & Co.; 1887.

McClure, A. K.: *Abraham Lincoln and Men of War-Times*. Philadelphia: The Times Publishing Co.; 1892.

————: *Old Time Notes of Pennsylvania*. Philadelphia: The John C. Winston Co., 1905. 2 vols.

————: *Recollections of Half A Century*. Salem, Mass.: The Salem Press Co.; 1902.

McCormack, Thomas J.: See Koerner, Gustave.

McCulloch, Hugh: *Men and Measures of Half A Century: Sketches and Comments*. New York: Charles Scribner's Sons; 1888.

McCutcheon, O. E.: "Recollections of Zachariah Chandler," *Michigan History Magazine*, V (1921), 140–1.

McKee, T. H., ed.: *The National Conventions and Platforms of All Political Parties, 1789–1905*. Baltimore: The Friedenwald Co.; 1906.

McKitrick, Eric L.: *Andrew Johnson and Reconstruction*. University of Chicago Press; 1960.

McPherson, Edward. *A Handbook of Politics For 1872*. . . . Washington: Philp & Solomons; 1872.

————: *A Handbook of Politics for 1874*. . . . Washington: Solomons & Chapman; 1874.

————: *The Political History of the United States of America During the Great Rebellion*. 2d ed. Washington: Philp & Solomons; 1865.

————: *The Political History of the United States of America Dur-*

ing the Period of Reconstruction, From April 15, 1865, to July 15, 1870. 3d ed. Washington, James J. Chapman; 1880.

McPherson, James M.: "Abolitionists and the Civil Rights Act of 1875," *Journal of American History,* LII (1965), 493–510.

———: "Grant or Greeley? The Abolionist Dilemma in the Election of 1872," *American Historical Review,* LXXI (1965), 41–61.

———: *The Struggle for Equality: Abolitionists and the Negro in the Civil War and Reconstruction.* Princeton, N. J.: Princeton University Press, 1964.

McWhiney, Grady, ed.: *Grant, Lee, Lincoln and the Radicals: Essays on the Civil War.* Evanston, Ill.: Northwestern University Press; 1964.

Magdol, Edward: *Owen Lovejoy: Abolitionist in Congress.* New Brunswick, N. J.: Rutgers University Press; 1967.

Mallam, William D. "Lincoln and the Conservatives," *Journal of Southern History,* XXVIII (1962); 31–45.

Mann, Mary Peabody. *Life of Horace Mann.* Centennial Edition. Washington: National Educational Association of the United States; 1937.

Martin, Edward Winslow: *Behind the Scenes in Washington.* New York: Continental Publishing Co.; 1873.

———: *The Life and Public Services of Schuyler Colfax.* New York: U. S. Publishing Co.; 1868.

Meade, George G.: *The Life and Letters of George Gordon Meade.* Edited by G. G. Meade. New York: Charles Scribner's Sons; 1913. 2 vols.

Meigs, M. C.: "General M. C. Meigs on the Conduct of the Civil War," *American Historical Review,* XXVI (1921), 285–303.

Miller, Alphonse: *Thaddeus Stevens.* New York: Harper & Bros.; 1939.

Milton, George Fort: *The Age of Hate: Andrew Johnson and the Radicals.* New York: Coward McCann; 1931.

———: *Abraham Lincoln and the Fifth Column.* New York: Colliers, 1962.

———: *The Eve of Conflict: Stephen A. Douglas and the Needless War.* Boston: Houghton Mifflin Co.; 1934.

Mitgang, Herbert: See Brooks, Noah.

Montgomery, David: *Beyond Equality. Labor and the Radical Republicans, 1862–1872.* New York: Alfred A. Knopf; 1967.

———: "Labor and the Radical Republicans: A Study of the Revival of the American Labor Movement, 1865–1874." Unpublished doctoral dissertation, University of Minnesota; 1962.

Moos, Malcolm: *The Republicans: A History of Their Party.* New York: Random House; 1956.

Mordell, Albert: See Welles, Gideon.

Myers, William Starr: *The Republican Party: A History.* 2d ed. New York: The Century Co.; 1931.

Nevins, Allan: *The Emergence of Lincoln.* New York: Charles Scribner's Sons; 1950. 2 vols.

————: *Frémont, Pathfinder of the West.* New York: D. Appleton; 1939.

————: *Hamilton Fish, The Inner History of the Grant Administration.* New York: Dodd, Mead & Co.; 1937.

————: *Ordeal of the Union.* New York: Charles Scribner's Sons; 1947. 2 vols.

————: *The War for the Union.* New York: Charles Scribner's Sons, 1959, 1960. 2 vols.

————: and Milton Halsey Thomas, eds.: See Strong, George Templeton.

Nichols, Roy F.: *The Disruption of American Democracy.* New York: Macmillan; 1948.

————: "The Kansas-Nebraska Act: A Century of Historiography," *Mississippi Valley Historical Review,* XLIII (September, 1956); 187–212.

Nicolay, Helen: *Lincoln's Secretary: A Biography of John G. Nicolay.* New York: Longmans, Green; 1949.

Niven, John: *Connecticut for the Union. The Role of the State in the Civil War.* New Haven: Yale University Press; 1965.

Oberholzer, Ellis Paxson: *A History of the United States Since the Civil War.* New York: Macmillan; 1917–37. 5 vols.

Olsen, Otto H.: *Carpetbagger's Crusade: The Life of Albion Winegar Tourgée.* Baltimore: The Johns Hopkins Press; 1965.

Overmeyer, Philip Henry: "Attorney-General Williams and the Chief Justiceship," *Pacific Northwest Quarterly,* XXVIII (1937), 251–2.

Owen, Robert Dale: "Political Results from the Varioloid," *Atlantic Monthly,* XXXV (1875), 660–70.

Paddock, Margaret Ashley: See Ashley, Margaret.

Palmer, Friend: *Early Days in Detroit.* Detroit: Hunt & June, 1906.

Palmer, John M.: *Personal Recollections of John M. Palmer: The Story of an Earnest Life.* Cincinnati: The R. Clarke Co.; 1901.

Paris, Comte de.: *History of the Civil War in America.* Philadelphia: Jos. H. Coates & Co.; 1876. 4 vols.

Parrish, William E.: *Missouri Under Radical Rule, 1865–1870.* Columbia: University of Missouri Press; 1965.

————: *Turbulent Partnership: Missouri and the Union, 1861–1865.* Columbia: University of Missouri Press; 1963.

Patrick, Rembert W.: *The Reconstruction of the Nation.* New York: Oxford University Press; 1967.

Perkins, Howard Cecil: *Northern Editorials on Secession.* New York: D. Appleton Century; 1942. 2 vols.

Peterson, Norma: *Freedom and Franchise: The Political Career of B. Gratz Brown.* Columbia, Mo.: University of Missouri Press; 1965.

Pierce, Edward L.: *Memoir and Letters of Charles Sumner.* Boston: Roberts Bros.; 1877–93. 4 vols.

Pierson, Henry Greenleaf: *James S. Wadsworth of Geneseo.* New York: Charles Scribner's Sons; 1913.

Pike, James S.: *First Blows of the Civil War.* New York: The American News Company; 1879.

Poore, Ben Perley: *Perley's Reminiscences of Sixty Years in the National Metropolis,* Philadelphia: Hubbard Bros.; 1886.

Porter, George H.: *Ohio Politics During the Civil War Period.* New York: Columbia University Press; 1911.

Porter, Kirk H., and Donald Bruce Johnson. *National Party Platforms, 1840–1964.* Urbana: University of Illinois Press; 1966.

Proceedings of the First Three Republican National Conventions, 1856, 1860 and 1864 ... As Reported by Horace Greeley. Minneapolis: Charles W. Johnson; 1893.

Randall, J. G.: *Lincoln the Liberal Statesman.* New York: Dodd, Mead & Co.; 1947.

————: *Lincoln the President.* Volume IV co-authored by Richard N. Current. New York: Dodd, Mead & Co.; 1945–55. 4 vols.

————: "Some Legal Aspects of the Confiscation Acts of the Civil War," *American Historical Review,* VIII (1912), 79–96.

————, ed.: See Browning, Orville Hickman.

Raymond, Henry J.: *The Life and Public Services of Abraham Lincoln.* ... New York: Derby & Miller; 1865.

Rice, Allen Thorndike, ed.: *Reminiscences of Abraham Lincoln By Distinguished Men of His Time.* New York: North American Publishing Co.; 1886.

Richardson, James D.: *A Compilation of the Messages and Papers of the Presidents, 1789–1897.* Washington: Government Printing Office; 1896–99.

Riddle, Albert Gallatin: *The Life of Benjamin F. Wade.* Cleveland: W. W. Williams, 1887.

————: *Recollections of War Times: Reminiscences of Men and Events in Washington, 1860–1865.* New York: G. P. Putnam's Sons; 1895.

Riddleberger, Patrick. "The Break in the Radical Ranks: Liberals v. Stalwarts in the Election of 1872," *Journal of Negro History,* XLIV (1959), 136–57.

————: *George Washington Julian, Radical Republican: A Study in 19th Century Politics and Reform.* Indianapolis: Indiana Historical Bureau; 1966.

————: "The Making of a Political Abolitionist: George W. Julian and the Free Soilers, 1848," *Indiana Magazine of History,* LI (1955), 221–36.

————: "The Radicals' Abandonment of the Negro During Reconstruction," *Journal of Negro History,* XLV (1960), 88–102.

Ridge, Martin. *Ignatius Donnelly: The Portrait of a Politician,* University of Chicago Press; 1962.

Robinson, W. S.: *The Salary Grab.* Boston: Lee & Shepard, 1873.

Rose, Willie Lee: *Rehearsal for Reconstruction: The Port Royal Experiment.* Indianapolis: Bobbs-Merrill; 1964.

Roseboom, Eugene H.: "Salmon P. Chase and the Know Nothings," *Mississippi Valley Historical Review,* XXV (1938), 335–50.

Ross, Earle Dudley: *The Liberal Republican Movement.* New York: Henry Holt & Co., 1919.

Ross, Milton. *Memoirs of a Reformer, 1832–1890.* Toronto: Hunter, Rose & Co.; 1893.

Russell, William H.: "Timothy O. Howe, Stalwart Republican," *Wisconsin Magazine of History,* XXXV (1951), 90–9.

Salter, William: *The Life of James W. Grimes, Governor of Iowa, 1854–1858, A Senator of the United States, 1859–1869.* New York: D. Appleton & Co.; 1876.

Schafer, Joseph, ed.: *Intimate Letters of Carl Schurz, 1841–1869.* Madison: State Historical Society of Wisconsin; 1928.

Scharf, J. Thomas, and Thompson Westcott: *History of Philadelphia, 1609–1884.* Philadelphia: J. H. Evarts & Co., 1884. 3 vols.

Schofield, John M.: *Forty-Six Years in the Army.* New York: The Century Co.; 1897.

Schuckers, J. W.: *The Life and Public Services of Salmon Portland Chase.* New York: D. Appleton & Co.; 1874.

Schurz, Carl: *The Reminiscences of Carl Schurz.* New York: The McClure Co.; 1907–8. 3 vols.

———: *Speeches, Correspondence and Political Papers of Carl Schurz.* Edited by Frederick Bancroft. New York: G. P. Putnam's Sons; 1913. 6 vols.

Scroggs, Jack B. "Southern Reconstruction: A Radical View," *Journal of Southern History,* XXIV (1958), 407–29.

Sewall, Richard H.: *John P. Hale and the Politics of Abolition.* Cambridge: Harvard University Press; 1965.

Seward, Frederick W.: *Seward at Washington As Senator and Secretary of State....* New York: Derby and Miller; 1891. 3 vols.

Seward, William Henry: *The Works of William H. Seward.* Edited by George Baker. Boston: Houghton Mifflin & Co.; 1889. 5 vols.

Sharkey, Robert P.: *Money, Class, and Party: An Economic Study of Civil War and Reconstruction.* Baltimore: Johns Hopkins University Press; 1959.

Sheridan, P. H.: *Personal Memoirs of P. H. Sheridan, General, U.S. Army.* New York: Charles L. Webster & Co.; 1886. 2 vols.

Sherman, John: *John Sherman's Recollections of Forty Years in the House, Senate and Cabinet.* Chicago: The Werner Co.; 1895. 2 vols.

Sherman, William T.: *Memoirs of General William T. Sherman.* New York: D. Appleton; 1886. 2 vols.

———: *The Sherman Letters, Correspondence Between General*

and Senator Sherman from 1837 to 1891. Edited by Rachel Sherman Thorndike. New York: Charles Scribner's Sons; 1894.

Sherwin, Oscar: *Prophet of Liberty: The Life and Times of Wendell Phillips.* New York: Twayne Publishers; 1958.

Sherwood, Isaac R.: *Memories of the War.* Toledo, Ohio: H. J. Chittenden; 1923.

Shortreed, Margaret: "The Anti-Slavery Radicals, 1840–1868," *Past and Present,* XVI (1959), 63–85.

Shover, Kenneth B.: "Maverick at Bay: Ben Wade's Senate Reelection Campaign, 1862–1863," *Civil War History,* XII (1966), 23–42.

Shugg, Roger W.: *Origins of Class Struggle in Louisiana: A Social History of White Farmers and Laborers During Slavery and After, 1840–1875.* Baton Rouge: Louisiana State University Press; 1939.

Simkins, Francis Butler, and Robert Hilliard Woody: *South Carolina During Reconstruction.* Chapel Hill: University of North Carolina Press; 1932.

Siviter, Anna Pierpont: *Recollections of War and Peace, 1861–1868.* Edited by Charles Henry Ambler. New York: G. P. Putnam's Sons; 1938.

Smiley, David L.: *Lion of Whitehall: The Life of Cassius M. Clay.* Madison: University of Wisconsin Press; 1962.

Smith, Theodore Clarke. *The Liberty and Free Soil Parties of the Northwest.* New York: Longmans, Green; 1897.

———: *The Life and Letters of James Abram Garfield.* New Haven: Yale University Press; 1925. 2 vols.

———: *Parties and Slavery, 1850–1859.* New York: Harper & Bros.; 1906.

Smith, Willard H.: *Schuyler Colfax: The Changing Fortunes of a Political Idol.* Indianapolis: Indiana Historical Bureau; 1952.

Smith, William Ernest: *The Francis Preston Blair Family in Politics.* New York: Macmillan; 1933. 2 vols.

Solberg, Richard W.: "Joshua Giddings: Politician and Idealist." Unpublished doctoral dissertation, University of Chicago; 1952.

Sproat, John G.: "Blueprint for Radical Reconstruction," *Journal of Southern History,* XXIII (1957), 25–44.

Stampp, Kenneth M.: *The Era of Reconstruction, 1865–1877.* New York: Alfred A. Knopf; 1965.

———: *Indiana Politics During the Civil War.* Indianapolis: Indiana Historical Bureau; 1949.

Stanton, Henry B.: *Random Recollections.* New York: Harper & Bros.; 1887.

Staples, Thomas S.: *Reconstruction in Arkansas, 1862–1874.* New York: Columbia University Press; 1923.

Steiner, Bernard: *Life of Henry Winter Davis.* Baltimore: John Murphy Co.; 1916.

Sterling, Ida, ed.: *A Belle of the Fifties: Memoirs of Mrs. Clay, of Alabama. . . .* New York: Doubleday; 1904.

Stewart, William M.: *Reminiscences of Senator William M. Stewart of Nevada.* Edited by George Rothwell Brown. New York: The Neale Publishing Co.; 1908.

Stiles, Edward H.: *Recollections and Sketches of Notable Lawyers and Public Men of Early Iowa.* Des Moines: The Homestead Publishing Co.; 1916.

Strode, Hudson: *Jefferson Davis.* New York: Harcourt, Brace & World; 1955–64. 3 vols.

Strong, George Templeton: *The Diary of George Templeton Strong.* Edited by Allan Nevins and Milton Halsey Thomas. New York: Macmillan; 1952. 4 vols.

Stryker, Lloyd Paul: *Andrew Johnson: Profile in Courage.* New York: Macmillan; 1929.

Sumner, Charles: *The Works of Charles Sumner.* Boston: Lee & Shepard; 1870–83. 15 vols.

Swanberg, W. A.: *Sickles the Incredible.* New York: Charles Scribner's Sons; 1956.

Swinney, Everette: "Enforcing the Fifth Amendment, 1870–1877," *Journal of Southern History,* XXXVIII (1962), 202–18.

Teiser, Sidney: "Life of George H. Williams: Almost Chief-Justice," *Oregon Historical Quarterly,* XLVII (1946), 255–80, 416–40.

Ten Broek, Jacobus: *The Antislavery Origins of the Fourteenth Amendment.* Berkeley: University of California Press; 1951.

Thomas, Benjamin P.: *Abraham Lincoln.* New York: Alfred A. Knopf; 1952.

————, and Harold M. Hyman: *Stanton: The Life and Times of Lincoln's Secretary of War.* New York: Alfred Knopf; 1962.

Thompson, A. Mildred: *Reconstruction in Georgia.* New York: Columbia University Press; 1915.

Thompson, Richard W.: *Recollections of Sixteen Presidents From Washington to Lincoln.* Indianapolis: Bowen-Merrill; 1894, 2 vols.

Trefousse, Hans Louis: *Ben Butler: The South Called Him Beast.* New York: Twayne Publishers; 1957.

————: *Benjamin Franklin Wade: Radical Republican From Ohio.* New York: Twayne Publishers; 1963.

————: "Ben Wade and the Failure of the Impeachment of Johnson," *Historical and Philosophical Society of Ohio, Bulletin,* XVIII (1960), 241–52.

————: "Ben Wade and the Negro," *The Ohio Historical Quarterly,* LXVIII (1959), 161–76.

————: "The Joint Committee on the Conduct of the War: A Reassessment," *Civil War History,* X (1964), 5–19.

————: "The Motivation of a Radical Republican: Benjamin F. Wade," *Ohio History,* LXXIII (1964), 63–74.

Trelease, Allen W.: "Who Were the Scalawags?" *Journal of Southern History,* IXXX (1963), 445–68.

Unger, Irwin: *The Greenback Era: A Social and Political History of*

American Finance, 1865–1879. Princeton, N.J.: Princeton University Press; 1965.

United States Government Documents:

Congressional Globe.

36th Congress, 2d Session, House of Representatives Document No. 31. *Journal of the Committee of Thirty-three.* Washington: Government Printing Office; 1861.

36th Congress, 2d Session, Senate Report No. 288. *Report of the Committee of Thirteen.* Washington: Government Printing Office; 1861.

37th Congress, 3d Session, Report No. 108. *Report of the Joint Committee on the Conduct of the War.* Washington: Government Printing Office; 1863. 3 vols.

38th Congress, 1st Session, House of Representatives Report No. 65. *Fort Pillow Massacre.* Contains also *Returned Prisoners.* Washington: Government Printing Office; 1864.

38th Congress, 2d Session, Senate Report No. 142. *Report of the Joint Committee on the Conduct of the War.* Washington: Government Printing Office; 1865. 3 vols.

42d Congress, 2d Session. *Report of the Joint Select Committee on the Condition of Affairs in the Late Insurrectionary States.* Washington: Government Printing Office; 1872. 13 vols.

Van Deusen, Glyndon G.: *William Henry Seward.* New York: Oxford University Press; 1967.

Wade, Benjamin F.: *Facts for the People: Ben Wade and McClellan.* ... Cincinnati: C. Clark; 1864.

Wagandt, Charles: *The Mighty Revolution: Negro Equality in Maryland, 1862–1864.* Baltimore: The Johns Hopkins University Press; 1964.

The War of the Rebellion: ... Official Records of the Union and Confederate Armies. Washington: Government Printing Office; 1880–1901. 128 vols.

Warden, Robert B.: *An Account of the Private Life and Public Services of Salmon Portland Chase.* Cincinnati: Wilstack, Baldwin & Co.; 1874.

Ware, Edith Ellen: *Political Opinion in Massachusetts During Civil War and Reconstruction.* New York: Columbia University Press; 1916.

Warmoth, Henry Clay: *War, Politics and Reconstruction: Stormy Days in Louisiana.* New York: Macmillan; 1930.

Welles, Gideon: *Civil War and Reconstruction.* Compiled by Albert Mordell. New York: Twayne Publishers; 1960.

———: *Diary of Gideon Welles.* Edited by Howard K. Beale. New York: W. W. Norton & Co.; 1960. 3 vols.

———: *Lincoln's Administration.* Compiled by Albert Mordell. New York: Twayne Publishers; 1959.

White, Andrew Dickinson: *Autobiography of Andrew Dickinson White.* New York: Century Co.; 1905. 2 vols.

White, Horace: *The Life of Lyman Trumbull.* Boston: Houghton Mifflin Company; 1913.

Whitney, Henry C.: *Life on the Circuit with Lincoln.* Boston: Estes & Lauriat; 1892.

Whitridge, Arnold: *No Compromise: The Story of the Fanatics Who Paved the Way to the Civil War.* New York: Farrar, Straus & Cudahy; 1960.

Williams, E. I. F.: *Horace Mann: Educational Statesman.* New York: Macmillan; 1937.

Williams, George H.: "Political History of Oregon from 1853 to 1865," *Oregon Historical Society Quarterly,* II (1900), 1–35.

Williams, T. Harry: "Benjamin F. Wade and the Atrocity Propaganda of the Civil War," *Ohio State Archaelogical and Historical Quarterly,* XLVIII (1939), 33–43.

————: *Lincoln and His Generals.* New York: Grosset & Dunlap; 1952.

————: *Lincoln and the Radicals.* Madison: U. of Wisconsin Press, 1941.

————: *Lincoln and the Radicals: An Essay in Civil War History and Historiography.* See McWhinney, Grady.

Williams, W. Wiliams: *History of Ashtabula County, Ohio.* . . . Philadelphia: Williams Bros.; 1878.

Williamson, Harold Francis: *Edward Atkinson: The Biography of on American Liberal, 1827–1905.* Boston: Old Corner Book Store; 1934.

Wilson, Henry: *History of the Rise and Fall of the Slave Power in America.* Boston: James R. Osgood & Co.; 1876. 3d edition. 3 vols.

Wilson, Henry: "Jeremiah Black and Edwin M. Stanton," *Atlantic Monthly,* XXVI (1870), 743–4.

Winston, Robert Watson: *Andrew Johnson: Plebeian and Patriot:* New York: Henry Holt; 1926.

Winthrop, Theodore: *Life in the Open Air and Other Papers.* New York: Henry Holt; 1876.

Woodburn, James Albert: *The Life of Thaddeus Stevens.* Indianapolis: Bobbs-Merrill; 1913.

Woodward, C. Vann: *Reunion and Reaction: The Compromise of 1877 and the End of Reconstruction.* Garden City: Doubleday Anchor Books; 1956.

————: "Seeds of Failure in Radical Race Policy," *American Philosophical Society Proceedings,* CX (1966), 1–9.

Yates, Richard, and Catherine Yates Pickering: *Richard Yates: Civil War Governor.* Edited by John H. Krenkel. Danville, Ill.: Interstate Printers and Publishers; 1966.

Zornow, William Frank: " 'Bluff Ben' Wade in Lawrence, Kansas: The Issue of Class Conflict," *Ohio Historical Quarterly,* LXV (1956), 44–52.

————: *Lincoln and the Party Divided.* Norman, Okla.: University of Oklahoma Press; 1954.

Index